The Visitation Of Shropshire, Part 1: Taken In The Year 1623, By Robert Tresswell, Somerset Herald, And Augustine Vincent

George Grazebrook

The
Visitation of Shropshire,

TAKEN IN THE YEAR 1623,

BY ROBERT TRESSWELL, SOMERSET HERALD, AND AUGUSTINE
VINCENT, ROUGE CROIX PURSUIVANT OF ARMS;

Marshals and Deputies to William Camden,
Clarenceux King of Arms.

WITH ADDITIONS FROM THE PEDIGREES OF SHROPSHIRE
GENTRY TAKEN BY THE HERALDS IN THE YEARS
1569 AND 1584, AND OTHER SOURCES.

EDITED BY

GEORGE GRAZEBROOK, F.S.A.,

AND

JOHN PAUL RYLANDS, F.S.A.,

OF THE MIDDLE TEMPLE, BARRISTER-AT-LAW.

PART I.

LONDON:
1889.

Introduction.

———+———

THE several Visitations of Shropshire, usually so called, were taken in the years 1569, 1584, 1623, and 1664.

The first of these is MS. G 9 in the College of Arms, and is called "The booke of the gatherings of Churches halls and howses." It relates to the counties of Gloucester and Hereford, as well as to Salop, and does not look like a Visitation.* No Herald's name is given in the MS., but it is said to be the work of Robert Cooke, Clarenceux King of Arms. Alexander Evesham had a copy of this manuscript made, which is now Harl. MS. 615, and is included in the following pedigrees. It is thus described in the printed Catalogue of the Harleian Manuscripts :

"615.
A book in fol. fairly written, in the first Leaf whereof are the following words,
Genealogyes of Gentlemen of Hereford, Wooster, Gloster & Shropshire, taken by Robert Cooke Clarenticux King of Heralds, at his Visitation of the same Sheres, 1569. And copyed out of their several Pedgrees subscrybed by everye gentleman of the Same Sheres ; At the chardge of me Alexander Evesham."

The second of the manuscripts (MSS. G 15 and D 10 in the College of Arms) is called "Pedigrees of Shropshire Gentry," and does not appear to have been a Visitation proper, though so called in the Heralds' College list. This so-called Visitation is also embodied in the following pages from Harl. MS. 1241, which is thus described in the printed Catalogue of the Harleian Manuscripts :

"1241.
An Heraldical Book in fol., thus entituled,
A copie of the Visitation of Shropshire, taken & made by Richard Lee, alias Richmond Herauld, & Marshall to Robert Cooke (William Hervey) alias Clarenceux Kinge of Armes ; taken in the yeare of our Lord God 1564 [1584]. Augmented by many Notes and Gatherings of Lewis Dunne and others, by me Jacob Chaloner of London Gentleman, untill the yeare 1620. Copied by me Thomas Hanford of Wigmore, Anno 1661.

* The Editors desire to thank GEORGE WILLIAM MARSHALL, Esq., LL.D., F.S.A., Rouge Croix Pursuivant of Arms, for this and other information relating to the Shropshire Visitations.

I am apt to believe that the Date of the Visitation last mentioned may be mistaken, and that it should be 1584. For Mr Weever ('Fun. Mon.,' p. 673) sheweth that Mr Robert Cooke was made Clarenceux A.D. 1566, nor was Richard Lee, from Portcullis, created Richmond Herald until the year 1584. Besides Mr Withie's Book in this Library 81 B 12 and other good Copies, ascribe this Visitation to Richard Lee, Portcullis, and affirm that he took the same A.D. 1584.

And as the date of 1564, seems not to be right; so I suspect that Mr Hanford may not have been the most accurate Copyist in some other places; not but that the Book being a Painter's Book only (wherein the Seals and other Proofs of Descents are almost intirely omitted) may upon divers occasions prove of good use."

The third of the so-called Visitations of Shropshire contains 160 pedigrees, and is MS. C 20 in the College of Arms. It was taken in the year 1623 "by Robt Treswell Esqr Somerset & Aug. Vincent Rouge Croix," who were Marshals and Deputies to William Camden, Clarenceux King of Arms. This Visitation forms the basis of the following pages, and Harl. MS. 1396 has been transcribed for that purpose. The printed Catalogue describes this MS. as follows:

"1396.

A book in fo. for the most part written and tricked by the hand of Mr John Withie and by him entitled

1. The Visitation of Shropsheire made & taken by Robert Tresswell Somersett & Augustine Vincent, Rouge Croix, officers of Armes Marshalls & Deputies to William Camden Esq. Clerenceux, King of Armes, Anno 1623. Together with the Visitation made by Richard Lee, Portcullis, Marshall & Deputie to Robert Cooke Clarenceux, King of Armes, Anno Domini 1584 with other Collections (or additions) made by me John Withie.

Here it may be noted that these two Visitation Books are not to be understood as if the one was kept distinct from the other; but rather that the fresh Descents taken A.D. 1623 do supply the former Visitation of A.D. 1584.

That this being transcribed from the original book Mr Withie has imitated the hands of those gentlemen who gave the Information in Anno 1623. That the above mentioned officers being men of Learning & Judgement: here are copies & Extracts of the private Evidences of divers antient Shropshire families: the Seals whereof as also the Arms, all along, are well tricked by Mr Withie. That divers of the Descents are not of Mr Withie's hand, but are done by Jacob Chaloner, & others employed by him.

Moreover, in this book, I observe

2. The original Paper, containing the hands of those, who during this Visitation of A.D. 1623 did disclaim the Titles of Esquire and Gentlemen, at Oswaldestre: by subscribing to a Preamble written by Mr Withie, who rode Painter at the same Visitation.

At the beginning

3. Arms of some of the Shropshire Gentlemen putt down by way of Alphabet.

fo. 2.

4. Tricks of the Seales of the Towne of Brugenorth. fo. 18.

5. Labour'd Pedegree of Bromleigh or Bromley, as the same was attested by Robert Cooke Clarenceux & Robert Glover Somerset A.D. 1583. fo. 36.

6. Some very modern Continuations, made perhaps by Mr Robert Dale, now Suffolk Herald & others before the Book came hither. ff. 41, 43, 251, 432.

7. Some late Continuations have been made by Mr John Withie himself: as at fo. 160ᵇ after fo. 190ᵇ. fo. 439.

By my Lord's Command Mr James Greene Blewmantel Poursuivant at Arms, did enter a Pedegree of Corbet &c. into this Book beginning at fo. 53ᵇ, and also put the Persons Names in the Index.

8. Part of Descent of Harnage, by the hand of Mr Richard Mundy, is placed betw. ff. 165ᵇ & 166.

9. Descent, Funeral Certificate & Arms of David Lloyd of Shrewsbury: taken ... & Stafford.
 inter ff. 259 & 260.

10. Trick of the Seale of the Towne of Bishops Castle. 52ᵇ.

11. An old Painting of the Arms of Pytt. inter ff. 313ᵇ & 314.

12. Copie of the Proclamation of Richard Lee, Portcullis dated the 12ᵗʰ of Sept. 1584, whereby he disclaimed many residing within the Towne & Liberties of Salop, the Hundred of Oswestry, Chirbury, Condover, Pimhill, Clunne, Foord & Bradford, as Usurpers of the Appellations of Esquire & Gentlemen.

13. Alphabetical Table of the Surnames of those Families whose Descents are to be found in this Book. At the end."

There is another copy of the Visitation of 1623 in the School Library at Shrewsbury, and by the kindness of the School Committee we have been able to incorporate a collation of this interesting MS. in the present volume, which therefore consists of Harl. MS. 1396, with additions from Harl. MSS. 615 and 1241, and from the Shrewsbury MS., and comprises the Visitations of 1569, 1584, and 1623. To distinguish these various MSS., Harl. MS. 1396 is printed in ordinary Roman type, the additions from Harl. MS. 1241 are printed in italics, the additions from Harl. MS. 615 are printed in italics within parentheses, and the additions and variations taken from the Shrewsbury MS. are printed in italics within square brackets. Other variations are explained in the footnotes, and additions by the Editors are printed in ordinary Roman type within square brackets.

The copy of the Visitation of 1623, which is preserved in the Shrewsbury School Library, is a large folio manuscript, written on very thick paper. At the beginning of the volume there are eight leaves of trickings of the arms of various local families. After these come 308 leaves of pedigrees which, in most cases, are written on both sides of the leaves, with the arms neatly tricked, and where representations of seals are given they are more carefully executed than the arms. After the pedigrees there follows a large quantity of blank leaves, on one or two of which appears a fragment of a list of arms, evidently such as occur in the Salop district; this seems to have been copied from another list, for the arms are roughly arranged in alphabetical order, and only the first three or four letters have been entered. At the very end of the book is the Proclamation and List of Disclaimers, dated 20th September 1623, appended to which is a pencil note, signed "Isaac Heard, Lancaster Herald, 1 July 1766," declaring these four leaves to be in the writing of R. (*sic*) Warburton, Somerset Herald. John Warburton was Somerset Herald from the year 1720 until his death in 1759.

This manuscript is stated to have come from the library of John Warburton, Somerset, and to have been bought by Richard Hill Waring, Esq., Recorder of Oswestry from 1764 to 1798, who sold it to Jonathan Scott, of Shrewsbury, Esq., and he presented it to the School Library in the year 1766. Pencil notes, signed "Is. Heard, Lancaster Herald," occur in the Acton pedigree at fo. 16, where, in July 1764, he declares certain additions to the pedigree to be in the handwriting of R. Warburton, Somerset Herald; and again, at fo. 45, where the Bromley pedigree is stated to be in the handwriting of John Philipot, Somerset Herald, who obtained that office in 1624. We have, therefore, these several clear dates: John Philipot 1624, John Warburton died 1759, the pencil memoranda ranging from July 1764 to July 1766, when the volume would be in the possession of either Waring or Scott, and the presentation of the manuscript to the School in the last-mentioned year. It is to be noticed that the pedigrees of Albaney, Blunden, Bauldwyn, and Barnfield are all signed in the Shrewsbury MS., whilst those of Albaney, Bauldwyn, and Barnfield are not signed in the Harleian MSS. It is remarkable also that these signed pedigrees occur very early in the volume. Copyists became very expert in imitating the various signatures; the three Bauldwyn signatures for instance, at folios 25ᵇ and 26, are so different and ingenuous that it is hard to think they are not originals, and perhaps Sir Isaac Heard may have been in this way deceived when he declared parts of the manuscript to be in the handwriting of Philipot.

Another copy of the Visitation of 1623, with additions and continuations by Morris, may be seen in the Shrewsbury Free Library. Morris says, on his title-page, "Two other copies I have seen differ: one, now penes Sir Henry Edwards Barᵗ was made by Isaac Richardson painter & deputy to the King of Arms 1705; but that from which I transcribed these pedigrees & drew the arms is in the Shrewsbury Free School Library, to which it was presented by Jonathan Scott of Shrewsbury, Esq., in 1766, he having bought it for £5 5s. from Richard Hill Waring, Esq., who bought it at a sale for a similar sum. It came from the Library of John Warburton, Esq., Somerset Herald."

Another copy of the same Visitation, in the possession of R. Jasper More, Esq., and preserved at Shipton in Coverdale, Salop, is thus described by Mr. H. Maxwell Lyte in the Report of the Historical Manuscripts Commission: "Transcript of a book formerly in the possession of Lord Newport at Eyton, co. Salop, containing the Visitation of the County made by Rob' Tresswell, Somerset, and Augustin Vincent, Rouge Croix, in 1623, that made by Richard Lee, Portcullis, 1584, and certain other genealogies." (Salop Archæological Society, vol. x.)

It is almost needless to discuss the date of the Visitation of 1623, as it appears plainly in the dating of the various pedigrees; but, since in at least two works it is erroneously stated to have been taken in 1624, it may be well to give the funeral certificate of the learned Camden, by whose Marshals and Deputies the Visitation was taken, from the Book of Funeral Certificates in the College of Arms, I 22, p. 90:

"Wm Camden Esquier al's Clarenceux King of Armes of the East West and South parts &c. &c. being a batchelor departed this mortall life at Chislhurst in Kent the ixth daye of November 1623 being Sundaye in the morning about 4 or 5 of the clock. Testified by Doctor Heather."

Our Visitation therefore was Camden's last work; and Gough ('Topog.,' ii., p. 276) informs us that Robert Tresswell, Somerset, surrendered his office in 1624, and was succeeded by John Philipot.*

The last Visitation of Shropshire was taken in the year 1664 (MS. C 35 in the College of Arms), and does not come within the scope of the present volume.

To account for the great number of gentry in Shropshire and the bold and independent character which has gained for them the popular name of "proud Salopians," it is necessary that we give a hurried description of social arrangements in early times, from which no doubt these characteristics of the Shropshire gentry are derived. Situate on the disturbed borders of Wales, and holding in fee a large part of the Marches, the Barons were placed there with a very peculiar tenure; each had his castle subject to constant attack from the Welsh, and his estates extended to so much land as he could hold or capture from them; many of the charters by which they held their lands are so worded (Lansdowne MS. 216). Of necessity the men who accepted such a position and trust must have been, and their descendants must have grown up for generations, bold and self-reliant, in the constant expectation of war. The Lords of Manors were mostly Barons, and sat in Parliament, and in the Red Book

* The exact date was 8 July 1624.

of the Exchequer we find them called "Marchiones Walliæ" (Duke's 'Antiquities of Shropshire,' p. xii). Shropshire is the seat of Judicature for all North Wales, and all suits were tried at Shrewsbury.

Old Fuller (p. 254) tells us that out of 186 castles in all England,[*] thirty-two were in Shropshire; every manor-house must in fact have been like a castle, moated, and able to withstand sudden attack.

This constant state of unrest continued from the Norman Conquest till the death of Owen Glendwr in 1415. But the ferocity which necessarily grew out of such a state of society hung on in the district long after the Welsh were reduced to quietness, until two very remarkable men became Lords President of the Marches. These were Rowland Lee, Bishop of Lichfield and Coventry, and Sir Henry Sidney. The former was appointed in 1535, and by his governance the Marches were at length cleared of bands of robbers. Before his time it was not a very uncommon[†] thing for one of the gentry to collect a band, and capture and hold to ransom any neighbouring gentleman who it was supposed could pay for his delivery. By his influence and constant personal inspection for eight years Bishop Lee raised the moral tone of the whole district under his command. He died 24 January 1543, and was buried at Shrewsbury, leaving the Marches in a state of tranquillity and security, very different from that in which he had found them.

Six Lords President followed, colourless men who have left behind them no marks of labours bestowed during their short tenures of office, and it is a singular testimony to the discreet government of Bishop Lee that the Marches did not in this interval relapse again into barbarism. In 1559, however, the ever celebrated Sir Henry Sidney succeeded as Lord President, and to his admirable government of twenty-seven years, for he died 5 May 1586, Wales and the border districts owe even more than to that of Rowland Lee. He in fact completed the difficult task so admirably begun by his predecessor. But something even more powerful than good govern-

---

[*] The date at which Fuller wrote (1662) must be taken into account, for we have it on record that Henry II., at the beginning of his reign, ordered 1100 petty castles to be destroyed (Wright's 'History of Ludlow,' p. 50); these would not be on the Welsh or Scotch Marches, where protection against constant raids was required. Fuller's figures were taken from Speed, whose 'Historie' was published in 1611.

There is a paper by the late Rev. R. W. Eyton on the Castles of Shropshire in 'Collect. Genealogica,' 1861, reprinted in Salop Archæological Society, vol. x.

Also in Cotton MS. Vespasian A. xviii., fo. 139, is given a list of the most important castles of Salop in early Henry III.'s time.

A paper on the Castles of England, by Mr. Geo. T. Clarke ('Archæological Journal,' vol. xxxix., p. 156), of course includes Shropshire, but only notices the most important ones.

[†] See Wright's 'History of Ludlow,' pp. 267-269 et seq., who obtains his information from the Rolls of Parliament.

ment was needed to tranquillize this district, which had continued in a constant ferment for ages, and that was the general prosperity of trade. In 1331 Edward III. introduced seventy families of clothworkers from Flanders (John Kempe and others) to teach the English weaving. From all ages British wool had been considered the best in Europe, and it had been largely exported for the foreign looms; but this trade of weaving, then introduced into England, had so enormously increased by the end of the fifteenth century that large areas of arable land were converted into pastures to supply the insatiable demand for wool.* Profitable farming lulled the angry passions which were hereditary in the Marches; the produce of Wales, brought on the backs of Welsh ponies (merlins as they were called), poured into Shrewsbury and Oswestry, and very great wealth was accumulated by the merchants who there dealt with such wool. This seems to have begun to be extensive about the middle of the fifteenth century, and so by the end of that century we find a great accretion of wealth in Shropshire.

Now let us glance for a moment at the general state of politics in England at this time. The Wars of the Roses were now ended, and had left many of the ancient feudal landholders in great embarrassment; their estates, encumbered by wars and pretentious extravagance, had to be broken up; and we find in Shropshire persons engaged in trade were ready to come forward and purchase. Many of these fortunate traders were cadets of ancient stems; others again were new names in Shropshire, introduced from Wales and the neighbouring counties. A List of the Gentry of Salop in 1433, given by Fuller in his 'Worthies,' p. 265, comprises only forty-five names.† In this present Work we find 375 families returning their pedigrees to the Heralds, while 95 were disclaimed, having the reputation of gentlemen, but not having attended to shew their right thereto; in all 470 families. We see how large a number of these successful "Merchants of the Staple" must have come forward to purchase and settle upon estates throughout the county. They were all necessarily com-brothers of the guilds established in the large towns, Shrewsbury, Ludlow, Oswestry, Newport, and Bridgnorth, and these were imbued with feelings of sturdy independence, and some of their leading

---

* The woolsack on which the Lord Chancellor sits was first introduced on the passing of an act of Queen Elizabeth forbidding the export of wool. To keep ever in mind this source of our national wealth, woolsacks were placed in the House of Lords whereon the Judges sat.

This is thus referred to in 'A Discourse concerning the motives for the enlargement and freedom of Trade,' London, 1645: "The principal reason why in time of Parliament our Judges do sit in the House of Peers upon woolsacks is to put them in mind of preserving and advancing the trade and manufactory of wool."

† The inq. p. mort. of Richard, Earl of Arundel, 21 Ric. II (1397-8), supplies a good number of names and holdings of the early Shropshire subtenants. To those who are curious about them, it is abstracted in the Record Commission volume.

members belonged to the Council of the Marches, a very honourable distinction.

On the decay and dismemberment of the ancient feudal nobility, and the dispersion portion by portion of their estates, these self-reliant and influential burghers, already connected more or less with the old landed proprietors, were ready at once to purchase and step into their estates, and their descendants became the now numerous body of proud Salopian gentry.

Before leaving this subject, it may be well to speak of the guilds, which, as a sort of trading parliaments, certainly helped to form a tone of intelligent independence. The principal one was " the Guild of Mercers, Ironmongers, and Goldsmiths of Shrewsbury;" its earliest books begin 3 Henry VI. (1424-5), and it had an elaborate " Composition " granted to it 20 Edward I. (1480-1). It admitted on to its rolls those of other trades ; " poticaries " and "makers of cakes and junkets" are found in the lists, all seeking the protection of a great guild, as well as anxious from their membership to attain, after a certain interval, the rights of free burgesses. None could trade in the town or liberties without being a com-brother of one of these guilds. Very strict regulations were administered on all matters affected, the customs of the trades were declared and upheld, and, of course, the entry into a guild was by apprenticeship and a money fine. In 1576 it was enacted :

" No master to take any apprentice that is of French, Flemish, wild Irish, Dutch, Scot or any other nation, but only English born, on pain of 100ˢ."

The council of this guild enjoyed very large influence, and many of the gentry of the county became members, paying a heavy extra fine, and undertaking not to trade. This no doubt was as a protection to them in those troublous times, but other reasons are shadowed forth in the following entry from the records :

" 1529-30 Foulke Colle Gent made request forasmoche as his Uncle Robert Colle was one of the fellowship that he might be accepted and taken in as a Combrother onely to have the p'yr of the p'est and pore people and to goo yearly in p'cession on Corpus Xi day and not to trade. Paid 16ˢ 8ᵈ."

The simple state of society in the sixteenth and seventeenth centuries did not draw lines of demarcation at retail trades ; great foreign merchants, such as we now have, had not yet been developed. War as a profession for younger sons had ceased ; also the custom of attaching them to the suites of the greater nobility, and the consequence was they could only enter the learned professions, or be apprenticed to some ordinary retail trade and so become members of one of these guilds ; thus we find that the younger sons of extensive estates became tradesmen in the neighbouring towns, and did not thereby cease to be members of the county gentry.

One instance of this, drawn from the records of the Mercers' Guild, will be sufficient (see Visitation, p. 290): Katherine, daughter and coheir of Robert Knight of Basticouta and Shrewsbury, by his wife Elizabeth, daughter and coheir of Rowland Jaye of Jay, married, for her first husband, David Ireland (p. 270); all these belonged to the old gentry, and shewed shields with many quarterings. She afterwards married Robert Dudley, Esq., a half-brother of the Baron Dudley, who represented Shrewsbury in Parliament in 1530; but she did not cease to follow her first husband's trade of a dealer in iron, and we find in the Bailiff's Accounts for 1543: "Payd to Maysters Dudley for di C. of Irenn &c. ij^u iiij^s ij^d." It was not a matter of need; at his death Robert Dudley must have been a wealthy man, for we find, by his will, proved 28 May 1539, that he left a sum of money to the Mercers' Company on condition that they find "an honest priest" to sing mass daily at the altar of St. Michael in St. Chad's Church; and of this bequest £33 6s. 8d. was applied by the Company 1540-1. (Salop Archæological Society, viii., p. 400; William Salt Society, ix., p. 80.) This was a very large sum at that date, even supposing it to have absorbed the whole of the bequest. We can draw no other conclusion but this, that it was considered no detriment in those days for younger branches of the ancient gentry to occupy themselves with a retail trade, and to sell a half-hundredweight of iron to the Shrewsbury Corporation. Nice social distinctions are but of recent growth, and when we find a family putting forth the boast that they never had any connection with trade it only shews that they have not full records for the sixteenth, seventeenth, and eighteenth centuries; unless indeed, as sometimes happens, a family continued for several generations with very few sons.

Shropshire has always been largely agricultural. At the time of which we speak there was no manufacturing. The iron trade, which has since grown to large proportions, was confined to a few charcoal forges, and indeed to this day it must be considered mainly a pastoral county; such a district as would expand under the great demand for wool in the fifteenth century, and continue unchanged during the later developments of manufacturing which have in other counties led to extensive transfers of landed estates.

Referring with this inquiry to Mr. Shirley's valuable work on 'The Noble and Gentle Men of England,' we find in many counties only two or three families recorded. Staffordshire has but fifteen, Cheshire twenty, Devonshire twenty-one, Yorkshire with its large area only twenty-six, while Shropshire shews the largest total of any county, viz., twenty-eight families which have held their estates in the male line since the sixteenth century.

To recapitulate what we have now arrived at: forty-five feudal gentry of Shropshire in the list returned in 1433, the dismemberment of their great estates at the end of that century and during the first half of the sixteenth century, the great accumulation of wealth by trade from the middle of the fifteenth century, the investment of this wealth in estates, and we are quite prepared for the large number of gentry returned in our Visitation, viz., 470 summoned as bearing the reputation of gentlemen. If we compare this with the neighbouring county of Stafford, which was considered to have a very strong body of gentry, we find at the two Visitations of 1614 and 1633-4, as embodied by the William Salt Society (vol. v.), 244 pedigrees were returned and 169 disclaimed, making a total of 413 reputed gentry.

In comparing Visitations it must be borne in mind that in those of later dates numbers of new families, with only two or three generations, shewed an eagerness to record their names in the Heralds' books, and thus the totals became largely increased. It is well to remark that the Shropshire Visitation now before us does not give so accurately as we could desire the exact list of the Heralds' Visitation; some of the pedigrees have been unquestionably added from other sources, but it is also probable that some are wanting.

In Owen and Blakeway's 'History of Shrewsbury' (i., p. 380) is given a list of those families, numbering four, who returned themselves as residing "in Shrewsbury" at the 1569 Visitation; also at that of 1584, ten names; at page 404 thirty-four names are so given as residing "in" Shrewsbury at our Visitation 1623; and at page 484 twenty-seven families who are so returned at that of 1663. This suggests the impression that a great increase of the gentry resident within the town had at one time taken place, and requires some explanation. Shrewsbury proper is confined within the river and its own town walls; it is within 300 yards of being entirely an island! The important parish churches have a small extent of town proper, but the parishes attached to them extend for miles into the country. The area of the "City and Liberties" of Shrewsbury is estimated (Philips's 'History of Shrewsbury, 1779,' p. 152) at 10,000 to 12,000 acres. In Domesday Book Sciropesberie Hundred contained, as it does now, the town and liberties of Shrewsbury. An old Nomina Villarum et Villatorum et Hamblettorum intra libertates Villæ Salop' occurs in a Ledger Book in the Exchequer marked A. P. (post 11 Henry VII.), and gives the list as follows:

Eton juxta Pitchford, Betton Straunge, Altemere, Sutton, Meole Bracy, Pullyley, Newbolde, Welbache, Whytley, Hanwood Magna, Hanwood Parva, Horton, Woodcote, Aldemere, Newton, Preston Gubbald, Lee, Herdwyk, Burghton, Yorton Allerton, Clyve, Sandsawe, Grylleshill, Acton Reynald, Hadnall, Edgbald, Meole

Monachorum, Schelton, Onnyslowe, Bykton, Rossal Parva, Calcote, Preston, Dynthyll, Leton, Wolascote, Berwych Lebron, Berwich Parva, Smethcote Haston, Adbright Husseye, Adbright Monachorum, Halescote, Astley, Adbrightleye, Battlefield, Pymley, Longnore, Derbald, and Hencote.

The gentry on this large extent of outlying estates would all return their pedigrees as within the "liberties of Shrewsbury"—an extensive tract of country 21 miles long by 14½ miles wide at its greatest dimensions. Sansaw in St. Mary's parish is 6½ miles N., Whitley in St. Chad's parish 4 miles S., Eton 6 miles S.W., Longnore 8 miles S., Lee 6 miles N., Grylleshill 7 miles N. of the city proper. New-made money, then as now, purchased a few hundred acres, a mere tithe in extent of the ancient holdings, and placed upon it a mansion, and hence the "city and liberties" were quickly covered with fine houses inhabited by a large number of gentry. Some of the more distant county families had town residences actually within the walls, and many fine old houses remain with the name of "mansion" or "place," coupled with that of the family which formerly occupied them.

We now proceed to shew whether the character thus ingrained by centuries of self-reliance in the Shropshire gentry may be traced in the competition of life.

Soldiers we cannot particularize; at one time all were soldiers, and it is the profession in which it is most difficult to say that one proficient excels another. We would only mention John, Lord Talbot, slain 17 July 1453. Fuller ('Worthies,' p. 260) describes him as "that terrible Talbot, so famous for his sword, a sword with bad Latin upon it, but good steel within it."

But we can gather up from our Visitation those mentioned as having attained legal eminence. Sir Robert Burnell, Lord Chancellor 21 Sept. 1274, of Acton Burnell. He continued in this high office for eighteen years, and has left his mark for ever by the enlightened reforms which under his auspices were introduced into the laws of England. The Parliament of 1283, held at Shrewsb... ... l to Acton Burnel, where the celebrated statute "De Mercatoribus" was passed. During his tenure of office were also added to our laws, the Statute of Gloucester, 1278; the Statute of Mortmain, 1279; the Statute of Westminster, 1285; the Statute of Winchester, 1285; the Statute Circumspecte Agatis, 1285; the Statute quo Warranto, 1290; the Statute Quia Emptores, 1290; and the Ordinatio pro Statu Hiberniæ, 17 Edward I. Nine remarkable ordinances which have marked him out to all after ages as beyond doubt the most able man that ever held the office of Lord Chancellor.

Richard Burnell of the Irish branch of this family was Chancellor of Ireland, and died 1554.

Sir Thomas Bromley created Chief Justice of England 4 Oct. 1553; died 1555.

Sir Edward Bromley, Baron of the Exchequer 1609; died 1626.

Sir Thomas Bromley created Lord Chancellor 26 April 1579; died 12 April 1587.

Sir Robert Brooke created Chief Justice of Common Pleas 28 Oct. 1554; died 1558.

Hugo Burgh,* Grand Treasurer of England, mentioned at pp. 104, 135.

Reginald Corbett de Stoke, Justice of King's Bench in 1559; died 1566.

Sir Thomas Egerton created Lord Chancellor 6 May 1596; died 1617.

Sir Richard Fowler, Chancellor of the Duchy of Lancaster temp. Edward IV.

Sir Christopher Hatton created Lord Chancellor 29 April 1517; died 20 Nov. 1591.

Sir William Lacon, Justice of King's Bench 1466; died 6 Oct. 1475.

Christopherus Lacon, " unus Stipendariorum R'næ Eliz.," mentioned p. 307, a title which is not quite clear.

Sir John Needham, Justice of King's Bench 1472.

Thomas Owen created Justice of Common Pleas 1593; died 1598.

Sir Roger Townshend made Justice of Common Pleas 29 Jan. 1484-5.

Sir Robert Townshend, his second son, Justice of Wales.

Sir Henry Townshend, third son of Sir Robert, Justice of Chester.

Sir George Vernon made Baron of Exchequer 13 Nov. 1627; died 16 Dec. 1639, buried in the Temple Church.

Sir Henry Wallop, one of the Lords Justices and Vice-Treasurer of Ireland 1582.

Edmund Walter, Chief Justice of South Wales; and his son,

Sir John Walter, born at Ludlow 1563, created Chief Baron of the Exchequer 12 May 1625, died 18 Nov. 1630, and was buried under a splendid monument at Wolverscote, near Oxford.

All these Salopians are mentioned in our Visitation as having attained to the highest legal positions, and among them we find three in the Bromley and three in the Townshend family.

---

* Philips's ' History of Shrewsbury,' 4to, 1779, p. 146, relates that Hugo or Hubert de Burgh, a Chief Justice of England, made Vaughan's Place in Shrewsbury his town house, and that this portion of his estate came to the Mytton family (see the descent at p. 104), but we have failed clearly to trace who this Hugo or Hubert was. In ' Byegones relating to Wales and the Border Counties,' Oct. 1878, p. 119, a Hugh Burgh is mentioned as Sheriff of Salop in 1430, who was appointed by Henry V. Treasurer of Ireland, and founder of a great family there, but that does not seem to agree with our pedigree at p. 104.

We notice the occurrence of three Speakers of the House of Commons chosen from the Onslow family, viz.,

Richard Onslow, born 1528, Speaker 8 Eliz. (1563), died 1571, buried in St. Chad's.

Sir Richard Onslow, Bart., Speaker 8 Anne (1708), afterwards Lord Onslow.

Arthur Onslow, better known as "Speaker Onslow." He was elected 1727, and continued Speaker of the House for thirty-three years. This oversteps the boundaries of our Visitation, but seemed too remarkable to be omitted, and especially as it is unique in English family history.

We have six Bishops mentioned, viz.,

Robert Burnell, Bishop of Bath and Wells, and Lord Chancellor, died 1292.

William Grey, Bishop of London 1426, after of Lincoln 1431.

George Day, Bishop of Chichester, died 1556.

William Day, Bishop of Winchester, died 1596.

Edmund Fox, Bishop of Hereford, died 1535.

Richard Talbot, Archbishop of Dublin, died 1449.

One Confessor, Thomas Gataker, who died 1593, and his learned son Thomas Gataker. (Fuller's 'Worthies,' p. 256.)

Five Heralds more or less connected with the county, viz.,

Henry Chitting, Chester Herald (p. 310).

Robert Owen,* deputy to Clarenceux at this Visitation, buried 8 Nov. 1632 (p. 390).

John Raven, Richmond Herald (p. 176).

Francis Sandford, Lancaster Herald, died 1693 (p. 432).

John Yonge, Somerset Herald, died 1510 (p. 425).

But perhaps the best comparison between this and other counties may be drawn from trade. The younger sons we now refer to went out into the world to fight their way; their connection with old landed families had no direct influence on their success, that was entirely the result of individual character. We find the following Shropshire Lord Mayors of London :

Sir Roger Acherley, 1511.

Sir Rowland Hill, 1549.

Sir Thomas Lee, 1558.

Sir Thomas Lodge, 1562 (Kenrick Pedigree, p. 284).

Sir Rowland Heyward, 1570.

---

* There is a volume in the Free School Library, Shrewsbury, entitled "Armorial Bearings of the several Bailiffs and Mayors of Shrewsbury from 46 Edw. III. emblasoned, with MS notes, by Robert Owen Gent a deputy herald." See also page vii

Sir Humphrey Weld, 1595 (not in the Visitation).

Sir Stephen Slaney, 1595.

Sir Robert Lee, 1602.

Sir Henry Billingsley, 1606.

John Swinnerton, 1612. He was son of Thomas Swinnerton of Oswestry (not in the Visitation).

Sir Francis Jones, 1620.

Peter Probey, 1622 (not in the Visitation).

Allen Cotton, 1625.

Sir George Whitmore, 1631.

Thomas Adams, 1646.

Fuller (p. 264) says "twelve in all: see here a jury of Lords Mayors born in this (which I believe will hardly be parallel'd in a greater) county, all (no doubt) honest men and true." We find in the above list fifteen Lord Mayors in 135 years. Surely a very large proportion for one county.

Before leaving this division of our subject we give the inscription on a brass representing the figures of a woman between two husbands which was formerly in St Alkmund's Church: "*Hic jacent Joh'es Hercey et Joh'es Humfreston burgenses ville Salopiæ et Margeria uxor cor' et p'dict Joh'es Hercey obiit a° d'ni 1470, et p'dict Joh'es Humfreston obiit ultimo die me's Marcii a° d'ni 1491, ac etiam Margeria uxor p'dictor' obiit . . . . die mensis . . . . a° d'ni 1500 quor' animabus p'piciet' de' ame'.*" It will be noticed that the date is not 1497 as given on p. 263. The startling abruptness with which she is described as *uxor eorum* or *prædictorum* is characteristic of the downright simplicity of those times.

A remarkable instance of a lady having married two Richard Owens occurs in this Visitation. At p. 364, Katherine, daughter of Thomas Montgomery, p. 391, married first Richard Owen, Bailiff in 1559 [Arms: Sable, three nags' heads erased argent]. At p. 397, Hugo Philips of Kaersous married Elizabeth, daughter of Richard Owen and Katherine his wife, "fil. Ric' (*sic*) Montgomery." This Richard Owen was the son of Owen ap Gruff of Llanllo by Gwen, daughter of Thomas Ireland [Arms: Argent, a lion rampant sable]. Katherine, his widow, administered to this second Richard Owen's will, which was proved in the P.C.C. 2 January 1576.

Many ancient gravestones found in St. Alkmund's, St. Chad's, and St. Julian's were removed when those churches were rebuilt, and were placed in country churches near to which the descendants of the persons commemorated had purchased estates. As a contrast to the above crude inscription we quote an unusually beautiful epitaph on the tomb of John Gardiner of Sansaw, dated 1628, in St. Mary's Church (see p. 196):

" Gratia Sancta Dei, tibi fulsit, chare Johannes!
Ex re nomen habes : hoc tibi vita probat.
Horti Cultor eras : tibi Cura, soloque poloque
Plantas egregias addere summa fuit.
Resurgentis lætitia,
Hinc surgo : properat Mediator in aëre Christus
Obvius huic rapior : semper eroque comes."

Thus skilfully rendered :

" John is the ' grace of God,' to thee it came ;
Thy character depicted in thy name,
A Gardner too : 'twas thine with anxious care,
For earth and heaven new scions to prepare.
The deceased speaks,
I rise : my Saviour meets me through the sky :
To dwell with Him, I mount, no more to die ! "

But no translation could convey the subtle beauties evolved from the Latin.

It seems necessary now to consider the various circumstances and forms attending a Visitation, and the inquiry will no doubt throw light on many points which will be touched upon in succession, and the result cannot fail to be a more exact appreciation of the difficulties, expenses, shortcomings, and at the same time the extreme value, even with all their imperfections, of such Visitation Records. It is probable also we may thus more clearly understand the long lists of Disclaimers proclaimed after every Visitation.

The original proclamation by King Henry V., which was the first step towards Heraldic Visitations, was dated 2 June 1417 (printed in Mr. Grazebrook's ' Heraldry of Worcestershire,' p. xiv), and was to the effect that no man of what estate, degree, or condition soever should assume arms unless he held them by right of inheritance, or by donation of some person who had the power to give them, and that all persons should make it appear to officers to be appointed, by whose gift they enjoyed such arms, excepting those who had borne arms with the King at the battle of Agincourt. The College of Arms was not established until 1483.

At irregular intervals, when the Visitation of a county was determined upon, Clarenceux or Norroy King of Arms, armed with special powers by the Sovereign and the Lords of the Privy Council, issued his summonses to the Bailiffs of each Hundred or to the Mayors or other chief officers, commanding them to notify to each of the gentry, included in an accompanying list of names, that they should appear before his deputies at a certain place and on a certain day, in order that their pedigrees might be duly recorded, and their right to the arms and to the consequent title of "gentleman" be certified, and any irregularities corrected. Perhaps the fullest particulars we can have of this stage of the proceedings are printed in the 'Visitation of Staffordshire, 1583' (Wm. Salt Society, vol. v.), where copies of the warrants and directions are set forth. It will be noticed there that the deputies are only directed to inquire of "all such are called or wrytten Knights, Esquires, and Gentlemen;" the fact being that the Peerage was reserved to the care of Garter King of Arms, and to Norroy or Clarenceux was committed all of lesser rank, Clarenceux's Kingdom being South of the Trent, and that of Norroy to the North of that river. It is suggested as a complaint that these lists of reputed gentry were drawn up from the Sheriffs' or Under-Sheriffs' books, and therefore that they are nothing more than the names of such as were liable to serve on Juries and paid a certain taxation; and it is advanced by those who seek to depreciate the Heralds that they did not take sufficient account whether those individuals whom they summoned had been claiming the rank of gentlemen or had been using arms. After inquiring into this point, I have to say that the lists of those summoned, so far as we are able to examine them, were carefully and judiciously drawn up and out of a full knowledge of the districts; the names were supplied by the Heralds to the chief officers of the hundred or place, and were not left to them to fill up, although possibly their official knowledge would be made use of when drawing up these lists. The early Heralds had a much more accurate knowledge of such matters than would be possible in our days, when the assumption to belong to the rank of "gentry" is universal; those who then started such a claim became at once conspicuous. In the 'Visitation of London, 1633,' p. 190, occurs this note: "These arms made by Mr John Taylor of Fleet Street since Michaelmas last;" and I find instances are not infrequent in which such an intimate and exact acquaintance with details is disclosed. These accusations therefore do not seem to have any foundation in visible facts, but have arisen from the disappointment of some who, not finding their families recorded as they would desire, and unwilling to blame the neglect of their own ancestors, have sought to vent their spite on the Heralds, and have put forward suggestions which do not, on examination, seem to be true. This is a point we shall carefully examine presently.

The Heralds appointed as deputies, accompanied by their staff of registrar, scribes, and draughtsmen, proceeded in due time to sit, as announced, in the most convenient towns, to receive and record, as brought in to them by the neighbouring gentry, their descents, and to acknowledge, or respite, or refuse altogether the arms which might be put forward, according as the proofs submitted to them were satisfactory or not.

'Visitation of Staffordshire, 1583,' William Salt Society, vol. v., p. 3 : "And these that may not commodiously bring wth them such their evidences, auncient writinges, and monuments (sic) as would serve to prove the antiquitie of theire race and familye, but shalbe desirous to have me home to their houses : upon the signification of such theire desires for the furtherance of Her Maties service, I will make my repaire unto them soe soone as conveniently I maye." Every facility was therefore offered on the part of the Heralds to make their work complete.

The first question that naturally arises is, What fees were required? Randle Holme, in his 'Academy of Armory,' 1688, book i., chap. i., sec. 25, gives us the following information, and he was well acquainted with the customs of the College of Heralds :

"But the Kings of Arms their principal Fees are those of the Visitations of their Provinces : that is once in 20 or 30 years at the most they ride through their part of the Kingdom assigned to them : where (in certain places most convenient) they summon in all the Gentry, as Baronets, Knights, Esquires, Gentlemen, and Freeholders (or any whom he pleaseth to call before him) there to give an account unto them of their Family, Matches, Issues, Coats of Arms belonging to them, and their Title as Esquire, Knight, etc., all which is registered or recorded in a Book called the Visitation-Book for such and such a c.... taken at such a time. For which regestring, travelling Expences and entertaining all his Visiters, the Kings of Arms, and his Marshall, demands from every Gentleman 25^s, an Esquire 35^s, a Knight or Baronet 55^s. All which being summed up through the Kingdom, will amount to such a value as may sustain them, with good husbandry, till the next Visitation : but that is seldom twice in one King at Arms's life-time."

These fees do not seem to have been exactly adhered to in every county ; on the fly-leaf of a MS. by Christopher Barker, Garter, relating to Norfolk and Suffolk, 1661, is this memorandum :

"For ye entring of every descent :

	£	s.	d.
Every Gent	£1	7	6
An Esquire	1	17	6
A Knight	2	7	6
A Baronett	2	17	6 "

But the trifling difference only gives us confidence in the statement of Randle Holme. As a result of the Visitations, many new families would apply for and receive grants of arms, and " then a Fee accordingly of £10 or £20 is payable for Confirmation and granting such Coats of Arms and regestring them among the gentry of that shire." (Randle Holme, sec. 24, book i., chap. i.)

The following from Brit. Mus. Add. MS. 14,294, fo. 110, is so curious that we add it to our notes on this subject of Heralds' remuneration :

"The number of Arms & Creasts granted by Sir Gilbert Dethick Garter,   Are about
 Singly, from yᵉ 5ᵗʰ yeare of Edward yᵉ VIᵗʰ An'o 1551 unto yᵉ 10ᵗʰ
 yeare of Eliz. An'o 1568   57

Armes & Creastes graunted by him yᵉ yeare 1568 unto yᵉ yeare 1572,
 joyntly with yᵉ provinciall Kings of Armes   40

And in that tyme, being little above foure yeares, he besides granted
 singly about   5

And from yᵉ 14ᵗʰ to yᵉ 26ᵗʰ of Queene Eliz. An'o 1584 he again
 graunted singly about   80

Robert Cooke, Clarencieux, delivered Patents of Armes synce yᵉ tyme
 that George Earle of Shrewsbury was Earle Mareschall of England
 An'o 1573 unto yᵉ yeare 1580 yᵉ 26ᵗʰ of Queene Eliz. singly unto
 diuers of them of very good condition and quality to yᵉ number of   40

The announcement of the approaching Visitation we know caused
excitement, and in many cases alarm. The Heralds were armed with great
authority, and it depended entirely on the character of the individual
deputy whether this was used in an arbitrary manner, even to the extent
of breaking down family monuments and destroying other heraldic
devices, a power which Dugdale put into force in 1667. This extensive
authority was declared 1528 ('Heraldry of Worcestershire,' p. xix), but
we do not notice that it was exercised in the earlier Visitations. We
know from the letter of Robert Greisbrooke of Shenstone, 23 March
1662 (preserved among Dugdale's papers at the College of Heralds, and
printed William Salt Society, vol. v., p. 156), how he hastened to get a
drawing of his arms prepared, the picture of them being at present with
his sister Chamberlayne in Oxfordshire, although his arms had been more
than once acknowledged by the Heralds, and Sir William Dugdale's sister
had married Mr. Richard Seawall of Coventry, whose mother was a
daughter of Alverey Greysbrooke of Stoke Hall. Sir William therefore
would be well acquainted with the family bearings.

"Letters written to Dugdale shew that he possessed a sway equal to
or almost superior to the authority of the secular sovereign." (Chetham
Society, vol. lxxxiv., p. xii.) We can readily understand therefore how
the old gentry, whose position was known and assured in their own
district, might hesitate to submit their degree to the judgment of a
stranger, who was himself judge and jury, and there was no appeal. It was
not in human nature, at least not in the character of most men, to be
thus exalted as the representatives of the Earl Marshal, and through him
of the Crown itself, and sent down into a country district, without having
a due sense of the great dignity with which they had been clothed; and
so we find the Heralds particularly sensitive to any neglect or want of
respect. There seems to be something in the profession of a Herald

which makes him combative. It is impossible to read of Vincent and Brooke, Dugdale and Holme, or the remarks in Le Neve's works and numberless other quarrels, without coming to this conclusion. But the inquiry before us is—How, in all the senses of that word, were the Visitations conducted ? and the character of individual Heralds seems subsidiary. It must be clearly borne in mind that their interests lay in recording the largest possible number of the gentry of a county; but the limits within which they must work were distinctly marked out for them, and every instinct of the dignity of their position, loyalty to their order, and fear of the consequences of any fault, constrained them to carry out their instructions fearlessly, which they certainly did. These jealousies and bickerings, which we know abounded between themselves, are a guarantee to us that rivals at the time were not able to substantiate any damaging accusations. Still the fact remains, and must be allowed for, that Heralds are apt to be irritable and quarrelsome ; perhaps it is a tendency which comes with the accurate study of any exact science. In those who acknowledge only facts which have been proved, the introduction of one gritty grain of what is inexact immediately produces friction and consequent heat. But from whatever causes, and no doubt they came from both sides, we find in some counties, and more especially in the northern counties, where the correspondence is more fully known, that much angry feeling was aroused, the Heralds' authority was slighted, and their summons to appear greatly neglected. It is probable that in the earlier Visitations this was not the case. We can understand how families who had already once registered their descent, and had their arms duly a [....] not care to pay again thirty years or so afterwards ; and some of these may have regarded the Heralds' Visitations as only a means of extorting money, overlooking the fact that they were the official registration of their legitimate descent, and consequent right to bear arms.

Much information on this point may be obtained from Mr. Rylands's ' Disclaimers at the Heralds' Visitations.'* It is advanced, as if it were a known fact, that in many cases persons of substance on the list for the hundred were summoned who had never assumed to use arms. Thus (Gloucestershire Disclaimers 1682) Richard Tyler of St. Briavels says, " I know of no coat of arms belonging to me;" and William Davies, Clerk de Abenall, declares, " I know of no coat of arms belonging to me at present." Both were disclaimed. In the Visitation of Hereford, 1634,

* ' A List of Persons who were Disclaimed as Gentlemen of Coat-armour by the Heralds at the Visitations of the various counties of England, with an Introduction by John Paul Rylands, F S A. Guildford: printed by Billing and Sons, 1888.' 8vo. Of this work only one hundred copies were printed for subscribers.

James Lane, draper, who disclaimed for himself, " saith that Jonathan Wellington is a dark [*i.e.* blind] sickly man and no gentleman of coat armour." Both were disclaimed. In the Visitation of Worcester, 1634, " Thomas Simonds of White Lady Aston : I know none of right, and further saith that his father and grandfather were yeomen, and so writ themselves." Now this may mean that as a yeoman he ought not to have been summoned, or it may imply that he had used arms himself although he knew of no " right." He was disclaimed.

But in considering these complaints we must remember we have not heard and cannot arrive at the defendants' answers. It seems very hard if persons not making any pretensions to arms were summoned only because their wealth gave them a certain position as taxpayers, and were then proclaimed in the most public manner as *ignobiles, i.e.* not gentlemen of coat armour, in the neighbouring towns. But, after a careful examination, this seems to greatly overstate the case. Accidents of this kind must sometimes have been made, but we know that in those days, as now, it was looked upon too much as a venial offence to defraud the Government.

We find the List of Disclaimed at the Staffordshire Visitation, 1583 (William Salt Society, vol. iii., p. 14), thus headed : " The names of those that in the time of this Visitacyon of Staffordshire have made noe proofe of their Gentry, bearing noe armes, and yet, before tyme, *had called and written themselves Gentlemen,* and were therefore disclaymed in the chiefe places of the Hundreds wherein they dwell." Nothing could be more distinct. They had pretended and put themselves forward as gentlemen ; that is, had borne and used arms before time. They could not, when called upon, shew any lawful right, and therefore they were disclaimed.

We know that the shields pulled down and defaced by the Heralds were set up again the moment their backs were turned. Dugdale notes pulling down a second time Cheshire arms which he had already destroyed (' Dugdale's Life,' Chetham Society, vol. lxxxviii., pp. 30-1) ;* and Mr. H. S. Grazebrook, in the Preface to the Staffordshire Visitation of 1663 (William Salt Society, vol. v., p. xi), says that " many, I may almost say most, of those who made no proof continued the use of the arms they claimed and displayed them without scruple on seals, furniture, etc."

In vol. v. of the William Salt Society, p. xii (footnote), are given the arms of several families on the county map in Plott's ' Natural History of Staffordshire, 1686,' which had been unproved or disclaimed at the

* At Chester, " where I pulled down those atchievements wᶜʰ Holmes the paynter had set up again in Sᵗ John's Church for Alderman Walley wᶜʰ I took down in Aᵒ 1644 ;" and again, pulled down and defaced those atchievements at Budworth " which Holme the paynter of Chester had hung up again for Mʳ Marbury wᶜʰ I puld down once before." (' Life of Sir William Dugdale,' by William Hamper, 4to, 1827.)

Visitations, and which were therefore still improperly put forward by these families, who persisted that they were gentry.

The fairest way to view the position of these complainants seems to be, if they made no claim to be gentlemen of coat armour, it was then but a very mitigated thing to complain of if their names should be published at the Market Cross as not belonging to the order of Heraldic Gentry, to which, as they declared to the Heralds, they did not aspire. They could readily attain that rank by applying for a grant; the sting of such publicity would lie in their having sailed about in stolen or usurped plumage, and then been exposed before their neighbours. The Heralds' position seems to be this: you are forbidden to use arms without due and proper right to them; we enter up and register the descents of all who apply, but we publicly notify those who have no right to coat armour; and thus it is that we find many genealogies entered in Visitations without any arms attached, and the names occur among the List of Disclaimers.

The privilege of bearing coat armour emanated only from the King by his appointed officers, and any person usurping such a privilege was guilty of fraud, and if he used the armorial bearings the property of any other family to which such appertained he was guilty of stealing. A coat of arms is an incorporeal hereditament vested in the descendants of the first acknowledged owner, and descending only to those who could prove their legitimate descent from him. There are instances, chiefly in the fifteenth and sixteenth centuries, of the rightful and acknowledged owner granting his coat of arms to some other individual, but they are so curious and rare that we notice one by note hereafter as the one exception to this law.* The heritable right in a coat of arms cannot be sold. With the above-noticed rare exceptions there is no title but of legitimate inheritance; this is plainly declared in the wording of all grants. Richmond alias Clarenceux, 9 Henry VII., grants "to William Greene and to his posteritie he and they to have, occupie & inioye the same and therein to be revested at ther pleasures." (Harl. MS. 1115, fo. 3ᵇ.) Also in the same MS., fo. 6, Gueyenne, King of Arms, grants " to have, use & hold unto the said William Swayne and to the yssue &

* The following abstract from the College of Arms Register of Nobles and Gentles, vol. viii., p 170ᵇ, is an interesting and late example of such a grant, and its acknowledgment by the College of Heralds.

"Anstis, Garter, and Ward Clarenceux, 15 Aug. 1733, exemplified to Lord Anne Hamilton, Whereas Francis Edwards of Welham, co. Leicester, was entitled to bear, Per bend sinister ermine and ermines, a lion rampant or, and for crest a lion's head couped and parted per bend sinister of the same, and upon his death the said arms descended to his only daughter and heiress Mary Edwards, who hath, by an Instrument dated 2 July 1733 under her hand and seal, assigned to Lord Anne Hamilton, 3ʳᵈ son of James, Duke of Hamilton and Brandon, now of Kensington, co. Middlesex, the said arms and crest to be borne by him and the heirs of his body," etc. etc.

d

procreation of his body lawfully begotten in all worship & gentleness everlasting."

Precisely the same line of law will now punish an individual who infringes a patent, or who makes use of the name of some well-known firm in order to get an advantage in business. The only difference is that in these instances the gain is in money, while in the Visitation times heraldic distinctions and the rank of gentleman which they brought were a social gain and in great estimation.

We have many instances of consideration and forbearance on the part of the Heralds. There are cases in which the scion of an ancient stock attended the Heralds and recorded his descent and arms, and was excused the fees on *account of poverty;* that is, more regard was paid to *blood than position.* In the Visitation of Hereford, 1634, we have " Charles Whitney of Norton to be spared for his name "; " Philips of Ashton to be spared from disgrace "; " Jno. Abrahall of Stoke Edith to be spared from disclaiming for his name's sake." In the Visitation of Worcestershire, 1634, " Thomas Wild to be spared from the Post "; " I have no interest in Arms, Edmᵈ Boothby." He, one would suppose, should not have been summoned, but the Herald at the time had other facts before him and was not satisfied, for, he adds, " to be spared from disclaiming in regard of his being a souldier and of deserts."

The above quotations shew that the itinerant Heralds would in some cases have willingly shielded individuals, but the terms of their commission were inexorable; the rank of *nobilis* must be distinctly upheld; the mandate of the Earl Marshal's Court had gone forth—prove your lawful right to the arms which you have been using, or be disclaimed. And so we find all of those mentioned, Whitney, Philips, Abrahall, Wild, and Boothby, among Mr. Rylands's List of the Disclaimed. Any idea therefore that the Heralds could shield their own friends is quite inadmissible; the dignity of their commission surmounted all personal considerations, and its terms were strictly carried out.

In the Visitation of Worcestershire, 1682, " I, Joseph Ruthorn of Evesham, doe promise to forbeare using any Coat of Arms untill I can make out what coat doth belong to me "—surely this implies that he had beforetime done so? Disclaimed 1682. Gloucester, 1623, " Richᵈ Warren of Stainton falsely usurped Arms which were defaced & he disclaymed "; " Edwᵈ Hill Customer of Gloucester, neither gent. of Bloud Ancestry nor Arms." Edward Hopkins disclaimed at Boston, co. Lincoln, 1634, " an Usurper of Armes." Walter Cary of Wicomb (Visitation of Bucks, 1634), " no gent. nor hath any (right) to bear arms which he usurpeth "; and again (Visitation of Derby, 1634), " Robᵗ

Wilmott of Chadderton disclaimed for usurping the Title of Gent. not-withstanding having been disclaimed in the Visitation made 1611."

Every allowance was made for those who had difficulty in proving their right to the arms. The pedigree was entered and the arms respited for proof.* Mr. H. S. Grazebrook mentions (William Salt Society, vol. v., p. xi) the case of Amphlett, whose family had used arms which the Heralds said belonged of right to the name of Hastings. This was respited for proof, and, after suitable delay, proof to the satisfaction of the Heralds had not been shewn. This name, however, does not appear among the disclaimed, but the arms were not allowed.

Arms so respited were not publicly disclaimed at the Staffordshire Visitations of 1614 and 1663, although in many instances a note is made that nothing further had been done; and we notice that Dugdale at his Yorkshire Visitation of 1665 allowed two years to elapse before he proceeded to publish the lists of Disclaimed. In the Visitation of Hereford, 1634, occurs this memorandum: "John Philips of Ledbury to be disclaimed at our next 'sizes because he was not disclaimed at our being in the country, being respyted for proofe, but cannot make any proofe."

Again, in the Lancashire Visitation, 1613 (Chetham Soc., vol. lxxxii., p. x), Winckley produced charters from a remote date proving his pedigree, "but because the legend on an ancient seal was partly defaced the arms were not allowed." Now this is a most unfair way of putting it. The deed in question (p. 38) to which this seal was attached was dated 50 Edward III.: "Adam filius Johannis de Winkley dedit et concessit Johanni filio Johannis de Bayly," etc. The seal shewed an eagle displayed, with the legend "Sigillum Johannis," and the rest is broken away. It certainly was not Adam's seal, it *might* have been his father's; but to those who know how often borrowed seals were used in charters it is quite plain that the Herald could never acknowledge a single occurrence of these arms and allow them to Winckley.

Taking the above view of the vested property of the rightful owners in heraldic bearings, we have many cases where similar want of sufficient proof caused their rejection. Page viii of the same volume: Travers brought evidences and muniments, but the two seals shewn led to a question which was the proper bearing, and it could not be decided.

At page x of the same Visitation Robert Holt of Stubley had married "an olde woman" and would not enter. The Heralds declared in 1613 that this family had no coat, although it was allowed by Flower in 1567.

* In our List of Disclaimed, 1623, three names are included, viz., Jobber of Heton, Moor of Moore, and Ockley of Ockley, pedigrees for these names, and with the arms, occur on pp. 37?, 36?, and 37?, and there is nothing to show that the arms were a later addition to our MSS.

In this case there can be no doubt the legitimate descent from that member in 1567 was not clearly shewn to the Heralds, otherwise they had no power to refuse. The onus of proof lay with the claimant. It seems strange that Robert Holt should refuse to enter, and that a complaint against the Heralds should in after times be based thereupon. Again, Hindley produced evidences for three hundred years, but was not "allowed" arms. There are many instances of families who can shew much longer pedigrees and own considerable estates, but who cannot prove that they ever lawfully used arms. "Allow" has two meanings. The heraldic is "acknowledge," and this the Heralds could not do without satisfactory proof; the other sense is "permit," a sense excluded from all heraldic matters, which only deal with facts. We are obliged to expose the insinuation involved in that term. The only liberty left to the Heralds was that of judgment whether or not the facts adduced were sufficient to prove the claims. They had no choice of "allowing" in the charitable sense to "permit."

This naturally leads to the question, What proof was required by the Heralds before they would allow the arms? Of course a grant or proof that the Heralds had already allowed such to a direct legitimate ancestor, or as "their ancestral arms" to collaterals in a certain degree, was sufficient; or the grant by one who had the right thus to delegate his arms to another; there are such instances, as already noticed. Prescription with use by his ancestors was readily conceded when the arms were not those belonging to some other family. In the William Salt Society (vol. v., pp. x and 145) the Gaywoods of Bishops Offley in Staffordshire, who had been disclaimed in 1583, were allowed in 1614 a coat which was represented in an old window in Eccleshall Church, although the same King makes a note at the time in the Visitation Book: "*Care* as to the coat of Gaywood, for, if they have right to bear three pheons, it must be by the interposition of a chevron argent, for so does the coat stand in the window of Eccleshall Church. Without a chevron it is the coat of Malpas." Woodhouse of Woodhouse (p. 327): "These arms were in an old glasse window of the church at Wombourne neere to the seat of this family in the same church, and likewise depicted on that seat." Stonyer of Biddulph (p. 282): "For proof he vouches yᵉ picture of his great grandfather made in Qu. Eliz. time, on which these arms are."

The remarks of Sir Samuel Egerton Brydges on this matter of usage are very interesting (Collins's 'Peerage,' edit. Brydges, vol. i., p. 382, and they are quoted in a paper on "Proofs of Arms Required by Heralds," in the 'Herald and Genealogist,' vol. ii., p. 154):

"There is much more in the *use* of arms than light or interested critics in genealogy admit. When carried up to such a period as to be beyond memory it operates in the nature of prescription, and is of a directly opposite nature from a late assumption, where the want of authority is fatal to the right."

The following copy of a letter from Sir William Dugdale to Mr. William Horsley, 15 June 1668, will shew this clearly, and what was considered prescriptive right. The original is preserved in the Lansdowne MS. No. 870, and it is printed in the 'Retrospective Review' for 1827, p. 145:

"Therefore it will be requisite that he do look over his own evidences for some seals of arms, for perhaps it appears in them, *and if so, and that they have used it from the beginning of Q. Elizabeth's reign, or about that time, I shall allowe thereof, for our directions are limiting us so to do, and not a shorter prescription of usage.*"

This was the spirit in which the Heralds approached the consideration of evidences laid before them; but the unwarranted assumption of arms was promptly met with all the weapons at their command, and properly so, for they had a duty to perform, viz., to protect the order of gentry, and to uphold the terms of their own commission under the great seal. Dallaway ('Heraldic Enquiries,' p. 308), says:

"It will strike an examiner of pedigrees to which no arms are attached that the families so degraded were not unfrequently of high ancestry and of extensive property in those counties where they are registered; and that the escocheon disclaimed in a former was allowed and confirmed in a subsequent Visitation. This circumstance depended entirely upon the individual representative, who in some instances treated the Earl Marshal's summons with contempt, or at least with neglect. Their descendants are therefore excluded from armorial claims unless," etc., etc.

The Heralds underwent privations and labours, travelling through their district on horseback, and stopping in country inns in those centres which seemed most convenient and where the neighbouring gentry could most readily wait upon them. The established scale of fees in their court was not excessive, and during the later Visitations, when expenses must presumably have increased, these must have been little more than sufficient to repay the labours and outlay of the Herald and his staff. Randle Holme, book i., chap. i., sec. 21, informs us that "the yearly Pention allowed them was Garter £40 per annum: Clarencieux and Norroy £20 each: six heraulds at £13 6s. 8d. apiece: four Pursevants having amongst them all £93 6s. 8d.:—anything beyond this arose from fees." We quote Randle Holme because he wrote in 1688, very near the time we are discussing, and he was well acquainted with all the facts. They came clothed with an authority so high, that it entitled them officially to every reasonable deference and respect. It is true their punishment for contempt was not prompt imprisonment and a fine, as with the Law Judges; but it reached forward for generations! If no member of a family would take the trouble, or let us say had the civility, to answer their summons and satisfy the representatives of the Earl Marshal, and indirectly of the reigning Sovereign, as to their right to use armorial distinctions and the title of gentry, which it was only in the power of the Earl Marshal, delegated to him by the Sovereign, to grant, or ratify and acknowledge; the verdict of the Earl Marshal's Court, the sole heraldic authority, could only take this form: "Such a one having been summoned before one of our principal officers and invited to explain by what right he is using certain ancient heraldry, and being unable to prove his descent and right thereto, and probably unwilling to expose his want of that right, is by us proclaimed *ignobilis.*"*

To shew that this verdict could be reversed by properly and decently satisfying the constituted authorities and proving to them that the using was rightful, we print a curious Certificate by St. George, Norroy, extracted from Harl. MS. 1470 by Mr. H. S. Grazebrook in his Staffordshire Visitation of 1583, so frequently quoted (Wm. Salt Society, iii., p. 16, note):

"The King's most excellent Matie being desirous that ye Gentry of his Kingdom might be preserved in every degree, estate, etc., and to that end hath given full power and authority under the Greate Seale of England unto mee Richard St George, Norroy King of Armes, not only to summon all the Gentlemen w'thin my Province, but also to distinguish and make infamous by Proclamation all such as shall usurpe or take upon them the name of Esquire or Gentleman without just authority. And whereas Stephen Longsdon of Longsdon in co. Derby appeared before me in my Visitacion and disclaimed the title of a gentleman under his hand, as not knowing how he might justifie the same, I proceeded against him according to my Com'ission. Since wch tyme, he, making further enquiry, and finding that his Auncestors have been of long time reputed Gentlemen and borne Armes, w^ch (as I am informed by some of good sort in the Contrey) he is able to prove by evidence and other good record, he hath desired me to affirm his right and publish the same. Wherefore these are to make knowne unto all manner of p'sons whatsoever that the said Stephen Langsdon may lawfully use and bear such armes and Creasts as his Auncestors have done before him, and as he may lawfully justifie; And also that it shall be lawfull for him to beare the name title and dignity of a Gentleman in such manner and forme as any of his predecessors have done or as he may lawfully justifie. In witness whereof I the said Norroy King of Armes have sett to my hand and seale

---

* In Coke upon Lyttelton, ii., 667, the law is clearly laid down: "As in ancient [Roman] times statues or images of their ancestors were proofs of their nobility"—he quotes Juvenal, Sat. 8. and Cicero—"*Nobiles sunt qui imagines generis sui proferre possunt,* so in later times Coat armes came in lieu of those statues or images, and are the most certaine proofes and evidence of nobility and gentry, so as in these daies the rule is, *Nobiles sunt qui insignia gentilicia generis sui proferre possunt.*" It thus follows that a man might be an Esquire, or a Knight, or even bear a title, and yet be *ignobilis.* Wharton (Law Lexicon, article *Nobilis*): "The gentry are those who are able to produce armorial bearings derived by descent from their own ancestors."

of my office. Dated the xxth day of November in the ixth yeare of o'r Sovereigne Lord James by the grace of God King of Great Brittaign, France and Ireland.

RICH : St GEORGE, Norroy King of Armes."

We are accustomed nowadays to hear hard words against the Heralds of the sixteenth and seventeenth centuries. Students, regretful that vastly more has not come down to us in their Visitations, and descendants of some of the families, smarting under the results of the carelessness or insolence of the then representative of their family whose contempt of the duly constituted authority has robbed them of what they now feel would be of exceeding value, and further has cast a deep shadow of doubt over their heraldic rights. In several instances we know that this has so irritated the honest straightforwardness of this generation (we mention it with admiration and respect) that the present representatives have taken out new grants of arms rather than feel every time the carriage drove up to the door that they were shewing about the county heraldic pretensions to which they had no heraldic right.

The position of the Heralds in the sixteenth and seventeenth centuries is unassailable and perfectly clear; legally and heraldically they could have taken up no other ground. The value of their acknowledging and passing certain arms is in exact ratio to their known heraldic strictness. Descendants of the Disclaimed forget that if the Visitations had been conducted in a careless slipshod way, supposing for a moment such to have been possible with authorities so solemnly constituted, in that case the records they covet would not bear the sterling value placed upon those weighty records which we now possess. It is more just and dispassionate to acknowledge that the Heralds did all in their power, and, being human, they encourged the gentry to come in with their fees and to shew such satisfactory heraldic proof as would confirm to them their proper social distinctions. To enable them to do this the Heralds warned them of their approach a month or so beforehand, and came down with books and attendants to their very doors. In order further to induce their attendance they had to proclaim that this inquiry was made to check the unlawful assumption of arms, and that such cases would be dealt with either by granting such honours to those who were worthy, or by publicly disgracing, and if necessary further proceedings in the Earl Marshal's Court against such impostors as had pretended falsely to heraldic rank. Would not the natural and honest course have been to assist the Heralds in the purging out of su' ' ' ' ' ' ' ' ' ' ' ' enables them to purchase heraldic rights, and they enter among the ancient gentry and keep up the decaying numbers of a most important power in the state. It was a public benefit to expose and disgrace impostors so mean that they could flaunt in the absence of the Heralds heraldic pretensions, and sneak away when the approaching Visitation reminded them that they had for all these years been impudent cheats; they must now either honestly pay for and acquire the rights they had been dishonestly using, if the Heralds could see their way to make such grants, or else they must be put down into their real rank. It is no injustice to declare a man's real rank, nor does it cause any irritation unless his self-estimation exceeds his intrinsic value. In Heraldry there is no room for supposition; either a man is a gentleman of coat armour or he is not; he may be an equally respected and respectable yeoman; all the Heralds sought to establish was the truth.

Let us now try to discover by evidence what sort of reception and deference the Heralds received, and how they were seconded and assisted in this laudable work; and when putting it in this way we do not for a moment seek to conceal their desire to make it pay; they had heavy expenses to incur, their actual salaries were absurdly small, and of course a Visitation brought in fees both for registrations and grants; but the Earl Marshal's Court fixed when such were needful to keep together our heraldic annals, and the heraldic trust that was committed to its care. It gave the licence, but the expenses and financial results accrued to the individual Herald.

It is better for various reasons that we quote our facts in order of date, the advantage of which will appear when we come to consider further details. We must remember that the Heralds were few, and only occasionally do they express the indignation they felt at the neglect of their mission on the part of some of the gentry, or as they put it contempt of their office and position as representing the Earl Marshal, and through him their sovereign, the head of all heraldic distinctions. We know more of these matters as to Lancashire than the other counties; all the Visitations for that county having been ably edited for the Chetham Society, and we are thus able to give the following quotations from the 1533 Visitation; these shew that the Heralds were willing to accord every facility when they were civilly treated, and we would ask in common fairness, What could they do with such men as he who "wold not be spoken withall"?

Page 35 : "John Talbott of Salesberry .... a verrey gentle Esquir & worthy to bee taken payne for."

Page 43 : "Sr John Townley of Townley Knight had to his firste wief one who he beareth the goats. I wote not what her name is nor I made no greate inquisition for he would have no noate taken of hym saying that ther was no more Gentilmen in Lancashire But my Lord of Derbye & Mountegle. I soght hym all day

Rydinge in the wyld conntrey & his reward was ij* w^h the guyde had the most p'te and I had as evill a jorney as ev' I hadd."

Page 47 : " Robert Holt of Stubbley maried an olde woman by whom he hadd no yssue & therfore he wold not have her name entered."

Page 48 : " Sr Ric. Houghton Knight did mary Alice doughter and one of the heyres to Sr Thoms. of Asheton Knight and they have yssue Katherine who is maried to Sr Thoms. Gerard Knight. The said Sr Ric. hath putt away his lady and wife and kepeth a concobyne in his house by whom he hath divers children and by the lady he hath Ley Hall w^h armes he beareth quartered with his in the first q^r he says that Mr Garter licensed him so to doe and he gave Mr Garter an angle noble but he gave me nothing nor made me no good chere but gave me proude woords."

Page 182 : " Gerrard of the Brynne wold not be spoken withall."

Page 231 : " Sir William Poole Knight lieth at the Abbay of Vale Royall and he wolde have not taken " (*sic*).

In the Lancashire Visitation, 1613, we find (Chetham Society, vol. lxxxii., p. viii) Bradshaw of Bradshaw " produced two ancient letters, but the members referred to could not be placed in the pedigree." The Heralds therefore could only take the evidence before them.

Dugdale's Visitation, 1664-5, occurred at an unfortunate juncture. The feelings of rival parties ran high. Chetham Society, vol. lxxxiv., p. xiii : " The Puritans refused, the tribunal was considered by them expensive, arbitrary, and incompetent, Norroy himself being both judge and jury." He was a strong Royalist, and likely to regard critically those of the other side who in some cases perhaps had obtained grants during the Commonwealth times, and all of these had been declared only four years before to be null and void, and as if they had never been made. There was therefore sufficient material for friction on both sides. Dugdale had a duty to perform, those gentry whose position from any cause was doubtful contemned his authority, and a large portion of the county supported them in their attitude of heraldic rebellion; and this in a county where a strong feeling of the distinctions of rank was supposed to be and really did exist.

In Dugdale's Visitation of Yorkshire, 1665 (Surtees Society, 1859), we find the pedigrees of 472 families entered, and a long list of 257 disclaimers. At page xii we read : " It is evident the pride of family was wanting in Yorkshire, nearly one-third of the old gentry summoned treated the summons with neglect "; and at page xiv: " Mr. Robert Stafford of Thwing Dickering slighted the summons."

Certain accidents partly contributed to this neglect, for Mr. Charles Fairfax thus writes to Sir William Dugdale in June 1666 :

" Some gentlemen will attend you at the next assizes to whom I gave notice : but many (not sensible of the honour of their families) I find remiss, yet hope (upon their better thought) they will do right to posterity and give their attendance. Your too short stay in your several circuits (and their coincident appearances upon summonses before the Deputy Lieutenants) they alledge for excuse they could not wait on you." (Hamper's 'Life of Dugdale,' p. 364.)

We may add as confirming the moderate tone of the Heralds and their anxiety to make as complete as possible their lists of gentry, that the resulting List of Disclaimed in Yorkshire was delayed for two years before it was proclaimed, in order to gather up any further gentry that might be persuaded to come in.

We would further refer to the Proclamation of Norroy, 2 February 17 Charles II., addressed to the Balive of the Hundred of Salford (quoted in the 'Herald and Genealogist,' vol. ii., p. 151, from the appendix to Mr. Ormerod's paper, "A Fragment Illustrative of Sir William Dugdale's Visitation of Lancashire"). Certain persons, "whose names were given in a schedule, had not made their appearance, and they were *once more* required and expected at the sign of the King's Head in Salford upon Saturday the 11th day of March following," etc. The schedule contained seventy-three names, and the result was that many obeyed this second request and entered their pedigrees.

"In the Heralds' College are some interesting letters addressed to Sir William Dugdale by gentlemen in Lancashire on the subject of this Royal Commission. Some, whose ancestors had long borne arms, disclaimed their right altogether: others stated that they were not entitled to any such distinction, not being 'Gentlemen;' and the friends of some courteously assigned reasons for the summons not having been obeyed, *e.g.*, 'Mr Beswyke of Manchester is in Ireland,' 'Mr Alexr Butterworth of Belfield is a young man on his travels, but will enter on his return home.' The Nonconformist families generally appear to have disdained the noble science, 'feeling assured' (as Macaulay in the 'Edinburgh Review' observes of the old Puritan) 'that if his name was not found in the Registers of Heralds it was recorded in the Book of Life, and hence originated his contempt for all terrestrial distinctions, accomplishments, and dignities.' It may, however, be easily inferred from his rough MS. notes, now in the College of Arms, that Dugdale's high notions, not only of the Royal prerogative, but also of his own office, led him in numerous instances to offend the prejudices of those whose views on both subjects were not exactly in accordance with his own. Of these the following is a specimen:

'July 23 1666 Hundesffield — Mr James Halliwell of Pyke-house, his estate 200li per ann. 3 or 4 Sons brought upp at University & some at Inns of Court, yett disclaymed under his hand rather than be at the charge. He is ritch and misserable & a Puritan withall.'"

(Printed in the Chetham Miscellanies for 1851, being vol. xxiv. of the Chetham Society's Publications.)

Modern critics must acknowledge that the Heralds on their part did all they could to record full lists of gentry, and must feel that the default

entirely rests upon those who refused to attend. In the 'Herald and
Genealogist,' vol. ii., pp. 149-154, it is stated that "Some objected to the
charges, and others had a total indifference to armorial distinctions. On
one occasion few gentlemen appeared because there was a horse race at
Brackley.* Such as came he (Sir Edward Bysshe, Clarenceux) entered if
they pleased. If they did not enter, he was indifferent. So the Visitation
was a trite thing, many looked on it as a trick to get money." Now as
we read these facts the Herald and his staff attended at great personal
labour, and he ran the risk of the fees ingathered not being sufficient to
cover the expenses, which were relatively much heavier at these latest
Visitations. Under such circumstances he could not be "indifferent."
But the gentry did not realize their opportunity and the duty incumbent
upon them to assist in upholding their social rank. Some names are
returned as "extra com" or "hors du pays."

Mr. H. S. Grazebrook (Visitation of Staffordshire, 1583; William
Salt Society, vol. iii., p. xiii) says: "Some men, no doubt, were too proud
to have their ancient standing brought at all into question or to allow
that it required recognition. Others were altogether careless and indifferent, and their tastes were for very different objects. Others would
be absent from home at the time of the Heralds' circuit, or if summoned
to attend them at a neighbouring town were possibly prevented by illness
or indisposed by domestic sorrow and trouble;" and he refers to 'Herald
and Gen.,' vol. vii., p. 47.

From whatever cause the following well-known names are among the
defaulters in Staffordshire: Congreve, Wolseley, Sneyd, Fowke, Lane,
Kynnersley, Draycott, Chetwynd, Stanley, Skeffington, Swynfen, etc.

In Lancashire Ormerod remarks that Hulton of Hulton is only entered
at the first and last Visitations, and Gerard of Bryn never appears.

Such names shew that although it is very pleasant to a family to find
their descents duly recorded, still the absence of their name altogether
from the list is no proof whatever that their social position and heraldic
rights were not all the time perfectly well assured.

---

* Brackley is in Northamptonshire. We are not told at which Visitation this occurred. All
Bysshe's Visitations were between the years 1662 and 1668, so late a date that even the character
of such a man as Sir William Dugdale was unavailing. The constant devotion of the gentry to
sports is advanced as a probable reason for their carelessly neglecting the summonses of Heralds;
but we can only allow of this with serious reservations, because the Visitations were purposely
fixed at those seasons when travelling across country roads would be practicable, viz. March to
September, and this was not the time for sports. Except fishing and racing, in any, all sports
were suspended during the spring and summer, which nature has set apart for the increase of
the animal creation and the growth of its young; shooting and hunting therefore must
always have ceased at the times of the Heralds' Visitations; and even hawking, for merlins
get sick with moulting from March to August. Otters were sometimes hunted during the summer
in order to exterminate them and their young.

We have left till now the scathing remarks of Blackstone ('Commentaries,' vol. iii., p. 105), because they refer to a time much later than the Visitations, when the Heralds and their science had sunk in public estimation (Blackstone wrote in 1765), and the rank of "gentleman" had then ceased to be an exact term.   He says:

"The marshalling of coat armour, which was formerly the pride and study of all the best families in the kingdom, is now greatly disregarded, and has fallen into the hands of certain officers and attendants upon this Court, called Heralds, who consider it only as a matter of lucre and not of justice, whereby such falsity and confusion have crept into their records (which ought to be the standing evidence of families, descents, and coat armour) that though formerly some credit has been paid to their testimony, now even their common seal will not be received as evidence in any court of justice in the kingdom."

To us this is so evidently a contrasting of the " now," that is 1765, with the former condition of the Heralds' College, that it seems to have no reference to our subject; but since it has been introduced into the able paper in the 'Herald and Genealogist,' vol. ii., pp. 149-154, entitled "The Proofs of Arms required by the Heralds at their Visitations," we feel constrained to point out that this has no reference to the Heralds' Visitations, which are the ostensible subject-matter of that paper.

The quotation therefore which is put forward to depreciate the Heralds in Visitations tells quite the other way, for Sir William Blackstone* holds them up to reverence, and regrets the laxity which had brought about so striking a change in his own times.   The writer of a more able paper in the 'Herald and Genealogist,' vol. vii., p. 46, had no difficulty in reading Blackstone's remarks as complimentary to the earlier Heralds.

We must make a further reference to this learned paper in the 'Herald and Genealogist,' vol. ii., p. 151, which says: "In 1661 Holme writes to Dugdale in behalf of a young gentlewoman, illegitimate, 'linked in affections' to a near relation of his own, 'not to a have a Batune crosse the coat,' but the colours in the arms to be changed; the fee offered is five pounds, though Holme suggests that the favour might be granted gratuitously" (Dugdale, 'Diary,' etc., p. 358); and a footnote: "The P.S. is amusing: 'There is an alderman's sone in Chester whose great-grandfather was base borne, whom I have bine treating with sev'all tymes about the alteration of his coat, telling him for £10, and not under, it may be accomplished; five he is willing to give, but not above; if yⁿ please to accept of that sume yⁿ may writt me a line or two.' "

Why seek to twist these round into an accusation against the Heralds, when the meaning is quite obvious; these persons were to apply for new

---

* See also Cruise on 'Dignities and Titles of Honour,' 1810, chap. vi., sec. 62, where it is laid down that the official Records of the Heralds' College are accepted as evidence.

grants of arms, and they were anxious only that under the circumstances such might be obtained, and on the most favourable terms.

In very early times bastardy was thought little detriment. Public opinion progressed, and both heraldry and the law continued throughout to draw their marked distinction against it. Now we see in 1661 the baton sinister had become too palpable. They sought for some less conspicuous brand, and would sooner have a new coat altogether than continue the ancient arms with a stain upon them. Better to appear as a *novus homo* than bear the ancient arms with a blot which public opinion understood and noticed. See the grant to Hariot Eliot, 16 July 1726, printed in the 'Miscellanea Genealogica et Heraldica, 1868, vol. ii., p. 43. Her maiden name is not given; she was the natural daughter of the Right Hon. James Craggs, Secretary of State. She would not impale with her husband's coat armour that which was branded, and so she applied for and received a new coat altogether.

We now come to consider the frequent errors observed in Visitation pedigrees. We quite endorse what is said in the Chetham Society's vol. lxxxviii., p. 40: "The pedigrees ought most assuredly to be received with great caution, and few of them to be regarded as indisputably correct unless tested by documentary evidence." This is simply the result of unskilful or careless genealogists who, when preparing their papers in anticipation of the Heralds' Visitations, had not the necessary documentary evidences supplied to them. The wills and other sources of information, now so accessible, enable us to supplement and correct statements which they drew up in all honesty, from such materials as they had at their command. What is a matter of much astonishment in many Visitations is the strange omissions to be found in pedigrees which are signed as correct by the heads of the families; the maiden names of their wives or mothers are frequently wanting. Mr. H. S. Grazebrook (in the William Salt Society, vol. iii., p. xiii; also vol. v., p. xii) points to some remarkable instances which the Heralds could easily have filled in at the time by verbal inquiry, and goes on to remark that the Heralds who were enjoined in their Commissions not only to peruse and take knowledge of all manner of arms, but also to note the descents, pedigrees, and marriages of the *nobiles* in their provinces, paid far more attention to the heraldry than to the genealogical part of their duties. The editor of the Lancashire Visitation, 1613 (Chetham Society, vol. lxxxii.), advances a most extraordinary statement (p. vi), that *viva voce* evidence was the general practice at Visitations —we give the exact quotation, "which was the general mode of taking information at the Visitation;" and again at p. viii, "parole evidence," etc., etc., and thus seeks to account for many deficiencies and mistakes;

but we cannot accept this. The Visitation which follows his Preface contains many long pedigrees which alone would refute his suggestion, and a glance at our Shropshire MS. of 1623 shews many long pedigrees most carefully drawn up and including all the branches of ancient and widely extended families. We would also refer to page 125 of our Visitation; two accounts of the ancient descent of the Cole family were submitted: there were no evidences to shew which was the correct one, and so the Heralds entered both and joined on at foot the more modern portion of which they were assured.* The fact is that some knowledge of Heraldry, and as a consequence the rudiments of descent, was considered at the time of which we write a part of every gentleman's education; no man could be Peacham's Complete Gentleman without knowing of all manner of sports, etc., also the blazoning of arms, etc. In almost every old country house a pedigree, drawn in many cases in Elizabeth's time, is to be found, and only occasionally are they signed by a Herald. The interest felt in such social rank produced men in every district who made it their business to draw pedigrees, and no doubt the announcement of an approaching Visitation set them busily to work. We know from Robert Greisbrook's letter, 1662 (Wm. Salt Society, vol. v., p. 156), that he at once wrote to Mr. Kirke, an arms painter in Lichfield. These pedigrees contain sometimes the emblazonments. One "John Cainet of Oswestry," who flourished at the time of our 1623 Visitation, skilfully illuminated the Heraldry, and there were many such working Heralds while Visitations lasted. Dugdale would have spoken of them as "Paynters," and their work was regarded with suspicion by the College of Heralds as trenching upon their privileges; but the requirements of the gentry called them into existence and supported them, and it is hard to see how the Heralds' Visitations could have been carried out without the collective labours of such men. The progress of a Herald on Visitation was necessarily hurried; he had a great space to cover and many families to enter up, and had to fulfil his duties with critical care, as his decisions would govern the College ever after. We find that Dugdale and his staff took and entered thirty-two pedigrees on one day at Lichfield on 30 March 1663 (Wm. Salt Society, vol. v., p. xii, note), the first day of his Visitation; no wonder that

* How the Hall Pedigree at pp. 205-7 passed the Heralds must ever remain a matter for astonishment and regret. Since our work was in the press, an article has appeared on this subject in ' Northern Notes and Queries ' for December 1888 (vol. iii., p. 89).

† He was a poet and genealogist; see references in ' Byegones relating to Wales and the .. ..unties ' for 1882, pp. 1, 3, 6, 8, 12.

In the ' Visitation of London, 1633,' i., p. 248, the pedigree of Edwards of Oswestry appears with this note: " The descent set forth by John Caine of Oswalestre 1629." Many such descents were drawn by him about this time.

omissions might escape notice which it would have involved great labour afterwards to supply. There is remarkably little cause to complain of such omissions in our present Visitation, for, except in the fragmentary pedigrees which occur here and there, the great bulk are very fully given.

The names of places are as usual difficult. This arises from three causes: firstly, they spelled phonetically, and any oral information collected either by heralds or painters was thus liable to strange aberrations; secondly, the modern spellings have settled down into different forms, such as "Bechfield," now "Bettisfield," etc.; thirdly, errors in transcribing from writing, which was very likely indistinct to begin with, and bad writing of that date may often be read several ways, and especially as the Heralds were not likely to know the small hamlets in Shropshire. It is noticeable that there are in our county many places bearing the same name. The most remarkable instance is Eyton; under its various spellings of "Eyton," "Eaton," and "Eton," there are eight hamlets of this name in Shropshire, while in the neighbouring counties, which might easily occur in our Visitation, there are two in Herefordshire and four in Cheshire. Five separate Shropshire families of the name bear different coat armour for Eyton. This name is also vulgarly spoken of as "Yatton," "Yeaton," and "Yetton." As an example of these difficulties, how could one unacquainted with the facts recognise Kenilworth when spelled "Killingworth," or "Up-a-tree," as given in the Visitation of Devonshire, for Up-Ottery.

By carefully searching out the earliest notices, and in some cases finding the original grants, we have striven to arrive at the correct blazons and names of quarterings. The custom of families in Wales and the border lands is to retain the arms of their distinctive or favourite ancestor, no matter what changes the surname may have undergone, and it was hardly possible to give in shields of quarterings the exact surname under which these happened to be brought in; the original bearer has in these cases been given. With Papworth's valuable book at hand nothing would be easier, but we have refrained from naming any quartering unless, by tracing out the exact connection or finding satisfactory authority elsewhere, we could ensure accuracy. Mistakes in the tinctures frequently creep in from careless painting or re-painting over faded colours. The long list of arms formerly painted up in Ludlow Castle, and printed from the MS. *penes* John Mytton of Halston in 'Documents connected with the History of Ludlow, collected by the Hon. R. H. Clive' (Van Voorst, 1841), is most incorrect on this account. Monuments in churches for the same reasons frequently undergo startling changes.

White becomes yellow with age and is re-painted or; blue turns black, or in some instances fades altogether; while in some cases red, from atmospheric causes, will shew as a distinct green or black until the careful scratching off of a small portion shews the red below; green again turns to black. But it is hard to say what changes differently compounded oil-paints would assume if exposed, as the Bold memorials at Farnworth Church, Lancashire, to all the chemical fumes of Widnes. Of all the heraldic evidences left to us painted monuments are, for these reasons, the most unreliable. Emblazonments in water colours, on the other hand, never fade into contradictory tinctures, nor does stained glass change colour, although the order of the marshalling is frequently found to have been altered. In the tricking of coats of arms some Heralds have hastily written " gules " in such a way that it is often hard to say whether "Gu." or "Sa." is intended, and a careless reading would be sure to select the wrong tincture.

In conclusion, let us give the exact words of quaint old Fuller (1648, 'Profane State,' cap. xiv., ed. 1840, p. 332) from the end of his description of the " Degenerous Gentleman " : " Within two generations his name is quite forgotten that ever any such was in the place, except some Herald in his Visitation pass by and chance to spell his broken arms in a church window. And then how weak a thing is Gentry, than which IF IT WANTS VIRTUE, brittle glass is the more lasting monument."

G. G.

Oak Hill Park, near Liverpool.
13 June 1889.

The Visitation of Shropshire, 1628.

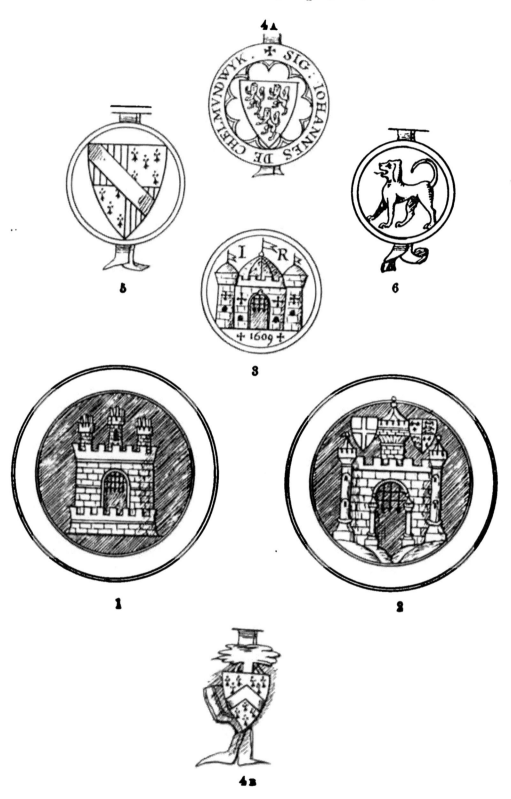

PLATE I.

1. HALL.
2. AUBEMOND.

3. MORTIMER.
4. ANTINGHAM.

7

8

9

12

10

11

PLATE II.

The Visitation of Shropshire, 1623.

13

16

17

14

18

19

15

PLATE III.

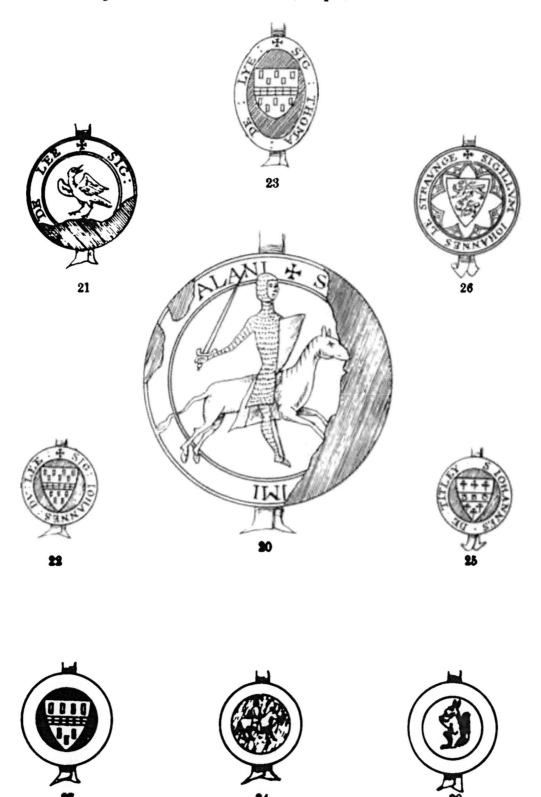

23

21

26

20

22

25

27

24

28

References to the Plates.

PLATE I.

PLATE II.

PLATE III.

* In Harl. MS. 1396 the drawings of these two Seals are identical.

PLATE IV.

The

Visitation of Shropshire, 1623.

The Visitation of Shropshire

TAKEN IN THE YEAR 1623;

WITH ADDITIONS.

———◆———

Disclaimers 1585.

THE NAMES OF THOSE WHOE WERE DISCLAYMED FOR GENTLEMEN BY THE HERALD 1585.

[Harl. 1396, fo. 335.]

Salop.

WHEREAS it hath pleased the Queenes Matie of her Royall and absolute power for a due to be kept and observed in all thinges touching and concerning the office and duties app'teyning to Armes, and that every person and persons may bee the better knowne in his and theire estate, degree, and mistery, without confusion or disorder, Her Matie hath therefore directed her highnes Comission vnder the greate seale of England bearing date at Westm^r the xxiiijth day of March in the xth yeere of her Ma^{tes} Raigne vnto Robert Cooke Esqr al's Clarencieulx Kinge at Armes of the East, West, and South p'tes of this Realme of England from the River of Trent southwardes, to make a gen'all survey and visitac'on throughout all the province, p'tes, and members thereof, acording to such order of survey as is p'scribed and sett furth in the office, chardge, and oath taken by the said Clarencieulx Kinge of Armes at his creation and coronation. And forasmuch as this Countie of Salop is within the province of the said Clarencieulx, and I Richard Lee al's Portcullis, his marshall and deputie for the whole viewe and visitac'on of the said Shire, Having fownde divers and sundry p'sons within the Towne and Lib'ties of Salop, the hundred of Oswestry, the Towne and Lib'ties of Oswestry, Chirbury, Condover, Pimhill, Clunne, ffoord, and Bradford, p'cell of the said Shire, most p'sumptuously to vsurpe the name, title, and Dignitie of Esquiers and Gentlemen contrary to all right and the laudable vsage of the Lawes of Armes, and most contemptuouslie, vpon som'ons geven, have denyed theire orderly app'aunce. Wherefore those are straightly to chardge and in the Queenes Ma^{tes} name to command all those p'sons whose names are herevnder written that they nor any of them doe from henceforth by any wayes or meanes vse or take vpon him or them the names of Esquier or Gentleman vnles they bee therevnto authorised acording to such order as is p'scribed and sett furth by the Lawes of Armes. And further-

B

more the said Richard Lee al's Portcullis doth by the aucthoritie aforesaid straightlie chardge and in the Queenes Ma^tes name comaund all Sherriffes, Com'issioners, Archdeacons, Officialls, Scriveno^rs, Clarkes, writers, or others whatsoeu' [not] to call, name, or write in any Assize, Sessions, Court, or other open place or places, any one of these persons by the addition of Esquier or Gentleman, whoe at this p'sent by this proclamac'on are reprooved, controwled, and made infamous of that name and diguitie, as they or any of them will answer to the contrary at theire p'ills before the Right Ho^ble George Earle of Shrewsbury, Earle Marshall of England. Yeoven vnder my hand and seale of office the xij^th of Septemb^r in the xxvi^th yeere of the Raigne of our Sou'aigne Lady Elizabeth, by the grace of God Queene of England, ffraunce, and Ireland, Defender of the faith, etc., 1584.

RICHARD LEE, Portcullis,
Marshall to Clarencieulx.

Salop cum Lib'tatib.

ROGER LUTER.
WILLIAM PEERS.
WILLIAM TENCH.
RICHARD POWELL.
ROGER HARRIES.
THOM'S LEWIS.
WILLIAM LOWE.
DAVID LLOYD.
JOHN HOSYER.
THOM'S ROCK.
JOHN PERCH.
THOM'S STURY.
WILLIAM PROWD.
THOM'S WOLLASCOT.
THOM'S BURNELL.
RICHARD MEDLICOT.
JOHN COLE.
JOHN BYSTON.
RICHARD MOUNTGOM'Y.
RICHARD LANGLEY.
ROBERT HUSSEY.
JOHN DAWES.
RICHARD BETTON.

Oswestry cum Lib'tatib.

JAMES EATON of Dudleston.
RICHARD AP JEN'N AP HOWELL.
JOHN TREVOR of Daywell.
HUGHE LLOYD of St Martins.
ROGER LLOYD of Lle'llin.
RANDLE HANMER of Bryn.

JOHN EDWARDES.
ROGER AP JEN'N.
THOM'S GETHIN.
JOHN DAVIES of Mideleton.
MORRICE AP ROBERT.
RICHARD LLOYD of Swinney.
DAVID HANMER of Porkinton.
MORRIS KEFFIN.
JOHN LLOYD of Reyton.
WILL'M AP JH'N AP LLEWELLIN.
ROB'T MORRIS AP TUDOR.
TIMOTHIE EDWARDES.
ROBERT STANNEY.
HUGHE AP DAVID HOWELL.
DAVID MORRIS of Bryn.
TUDOR AP JOHN GOUGHE.

Villa de Oswestry.

JOHN STANNEY.
RICHARD WILLIAMS.
THOM'S EVANS.
DAVID EDWARDS.
JOHN WYNNE AP DAVID.
RICHARD JOHN AP MEREDITH.
JOHN EDWARDS.
HUGHE YALE.
ROBERT AP REES.
ROGER STANNEY.
RICHARD GITTINS.

Chirbury.

EDMUND MIDDLETON.
JOHN RIDGE.

DAVID LLOYD of Wooderton.
HUGH MIDDLETON.
THOM'S CHARLETON.
RICHARD GWIN.

Condover.

RICHARD JONES.

Pimhill.

JOHN VAUGHAN.
RICHARD TREVOR.
EDWARD HANMER of Cockshut.
WILL'M ETON.
FFRANCIS MEREDITH.

Clun.

JOHN AP MATHEW.
THOM'S HARRIS.
THOM'S PREES.
JOHN D'D GOUGHE.
OWEN AP MATHEWE.
RICHARD AP JAMES.
JOHN AP HOWELL AP REES.
CHRISTOPHER JONESON.

Bradford.

RICHARD CONSTANTINE.
THOM'S WOODCOCK.
ROBERT DYCHER.
THOM'S DYCHER.
WILL'M BENTLEY.
WILL'M WOLLASTON.
GEORGE WOLLASTON.
WILL'M CHIDLOWE.
WILL'M HOSSALL.
WILL'M SANDBROOKE.
THOM'S CROMPTON.
RIC'US BARNEFEILD.
ROB'TUS BARNEFEILD.

Ford.

ROWLAND COWPER.
JOHN LINGEN.
JOHN GOUGHE.
HUGHE HIGGONS.
THOM'S LINGHAM.
HUGHE PORTER.
THOM'S LAKE.

Disclaimers 1623.

[Shrewsbury MS.]

The Kings Most Excellent Majesty being desirous that nobility and gentrie of this his Realm should be preserved in every degree as well in Honour as in Worship, and that every Person and Persons, bodies politique, Corporate, and others should be known in their Estates and mysteries without confusion and disorder: hath authorised us Robert Treswell, Esq., Somerset Herald, and Augustine Vincent, Rouge Croix, Officers of Arms, as Marshalles and Deputies to Clarenceux King of Arms of the South parts of this Realm of England, not only to visit all this county of Salop, to peruse and take knowledge, survey, and view of all manner of Arms, Cognizances, Crests, and other like devices, with the notes of the Descents, Pedigrees, and Marriages of all the Nobility and Gentry therein throughout contained, but also to reprove, controll, and make infamous by proclemation all such as unlawfully and without just Authority, vocation, or due calling do, or have done, or shall usurpe or take upon him or them any name or Title of Honour or Dignity as Esquire or Gentleman or other: as by his Highness gracious Commission under the great seal of England more plainly may appear. Know ye therefore that we the said Somerset and Rouge Croix, for the accomplishment of his Majesties desire and further of his Highness Service that way, at this present making Survey within the said County, have found these Persons whose names are under written presumptuously without any good ground or Authority to have usurped the name and Title of Gentlemen contrary to all right and to the Ancient Custome of this Land and the Usage of the Law of Arms, which name and Title they are from hencefourth no more to use or take upon them upon such further paine and perill as by the Right Honble the Earl Marshal of England shall be inflicted and laid upon them. Whereof also we thought good hereby to advertise all others his Majesties good and Loving Subjects that as they tender his Highnesses Pleasure and desire in this behalf they from Henceforth shun and avoid the like and forbear to use in any writing or otherwise the addition of an Esquire or Gentleman unless they be able to stand unto and Justifye the same by the Law of Arms and the Law of the Realme. Given at Brugenorth the 20th Day of Septemb^r A° D^l 1623 in the 21st year of the Reign of our most gracious Sovereign Lord James, by the Grace of God King of England, France, Ireland, defender of the faith, etc. . . . . [blotted] and of Scotland the go'.

RICHARD MILWARD of Shrewsbu' no gentleman.

WILLIAM AMIAS of Alderton no gent.

GEORGE COTTON of Haston no gent.

FRANCIS WICHERLEY of Yorton no gent.

JOSEPH WICHERLEY of Broughton no gent.

DANIELL WICHERLEY of Shrewsbury no gent.

RICH^d KILFORD of Preston no gent.

RICHARD BOYERS of Fencote no gent.

RICHARD WATFORD of Smethcot no gent.

THOMAS GRINSELL of Ashley no gent.

ROBERT MADOX of Ashley no gent.

RICHARD FELTON of Shrewsbury no gent.

JOHN BOWDLER of Wosaston no gent.

ROWLAND BARLEY of Wilderley no gent.

EDWARD FARMER of Brome no gent.

JOHN FARMER of Eaton Mascott no gent.

ROGER FARMER of do. no gent.

WILLIAM CHURCH of Berington no gent.

RICHARD BROWN of Cund no gent.

JOHN HARRIS of Westbury no gent.

HUGH TUDOR of Bitton no gent.

RICHARD OULD of Brosbury no gent.

THOMAS HASHOULD of Detton no gent.

ROGER MENLOVE of Acton Renold no gent.

EDWARD PEERS of Creasage no gent.

EDWARD WYER of Woodhouse no gent.

THOMAS BUTCHER of Westwood gent. [sic].

WILLIAM CHERS of Astley no gent.

THOMAS GROVE of Alveley no gent.

WILLIAM FEWTERELL of Wrickton no gent.

THOMAS SELMAN of Harrington no gent. 258^b.

HENRY SELMAN of the same no gent. 258^b.

HUMPHREY SELMAN of the same no gent. 258^b.

JOHN CLARKE of Albrighton no gent.

STEPHEN ELLIOT of Ludston no gent.

RICHARD JOBBER of Heton no gent. 159^a.

JOHN BARRET of Oldington no gent.

JOHN YALE of Rowton no gentleman.

EDWARD FARMER of Chicknell no gent.

RICHARD YATE of Ludston no gent.

WILLIAM HENCKES of Sutton no gent.

. . . . SKYRME of Ludlow no gent.

WILLIAM COOKE of Fearne no gent.

JOHN THOMPSON of Sherehouse no gent.

JAMES BICK of Bellerley no gent.

THOMAS DYKE of Nash no gent.

JAMES BAILY of Whitton no gent.

JOHN PARDO of Cleaton no gent.

THOMAS LANE of Nash no gent.

JAMES B . . . . [sic].

RICHARD KERRY of Whitton no gent.

JOHN ROBERTS of Rorington no gent.

EDMUND LLOYD of Stockton no gent.

JOHN LLOYD of Stockton no gent.

JOHN AP HOWELL AP REES of Brompton no gent.

THOMAS MATHEWES of the same no gent.

WILLIAM BRAY of Marton no gent.

GEORGE LLOYD of Marton no gent.

FRANCIS WHATELEY of Winsbury no gent.

RERID THOMAS of Brompton no gent.

JOHN AP RICHARD of Middleton no gent.

THOMAS GITTINS of Liddom no gent.

EDWARD MODLECOT of Modlecot no gent.

CHARLES MOOR of Moore no gent. 210ᵇ.

ROBERT OCKLEY of Ockley no gent. 226ᵃ.

EDWARD SHEPPARD of Abcot no gent.

FRANCIS MORRIS of the same no gent.

FRANCIS JONES of Alston no gent.

JOHN HEATH of Bedston no gent.

CHARLES MOOR of Brockton no gent.

RICHARD COLBACH of Colbach no gent.

PHILIP JONES of the same [no gent.].

JOHN EVANS of Down no gent.

THO. HICKS of Hardwick no gent.

WILLIAM MARRET of Bucknal no gent.

THOMAS MARSON of the same no gentleman.

FRANCIS PHILIPS of Westanstow no gent.

JOHN PRICE of Trebrodder no gentleman.

EVAN DAVIES of Trebert no gent.

PHILIP DAVIES of the same no gent.

JOHN PRICE of Rylby no gent.

WILLIAM JONES of the same no gent.

OWEN AP EVAN of Skyborren no gent.

MORRICE AP WILLIAM of Hobendred no gent.

JOHN AP LEWIS of the same no gent.

MATHEW AP HARRY of Spode no gent.

ROBERT FRANCES of Whitcot no gent.

HOPKIN AP OWEN de Edicliffe no gent.

ROBERT JAMES of Finanvaure no gent.

HUGH MATHEWS of Stannayer no gent.

OLIVER AP HOWELL of Mainston no gent.

STEPHEN PRICE of Skyboren no gent.

The above is [in] the handwriting of R. [*sic*] Warburton, Somerset Herald.

IS. HEARD, *Lancaster*,
July 1, 1766.

[This list of Disclaimers occurs at the end of the Shrewsbury School MS., and has appended to it the above note signed by Sir Isaac Heard.]

The Town of Bishop's Castle.

Harl. 1396, fo. 52ᵇ.

[Drawing of the Town Seal, Plate I., Fig. 3.]

This is the Common Seale of the Towne of Bishops-Castell in the County of Salop, incorporated by the name of Baileiff and Burgeses of Bishops-Castell, and inabled with diuers and sundry large preveleiges, as that the Bayleife for his yeare and one yeare after is a Justice of Peace and quorum, Clerke of the Market, Coroner, and Escheater within the said Towne and liberties; that they shall haue a Common Seale an may alter it at their pleasures, etc., of which the said Towne at the time of this Visitat'on, viz' 24 Septembris Aᵒ 1623, Maurice Tanner, gent., was Bayleiff, Edward Mason, gent., the last Bayleiffe, are both now Justices of Peace; Edward Bowen, Richard Colbach, Edward Thomas, Edward Okeley, Rowland Says, William Joanes, Walter Wollaston, Henry Boole, Ambrose Kinge, Owen Bowen, Esay Thomas, John Tanner, and Hugh Richards are Burgesses; Sʳ James Whitlock, Knight, cheife Justice of Chester, is Recorder; and Edward Thomas, gent., is Towne Clarke; and for the yeare next coming Ambrose King is Baileiff elect.

(Signed) {
     MORRYS TANNER, Bayleve.
     AMBROSE KINGE.
     EDWARD THOMAS, town clerck.
     WALTER WOLLASTON.
}

The Town of Bridgnorth.

Harl. 1396, fo. 18.

The Seales of the Towne of Brugenorth in com. Salop; Arms they haue none.
[Drawings of the Obverse and Reverse of the Town Seal, Plate I., Figs. 1 and 2.]

These are the Seales now vsed by the Towne of Bruges in the County of Salop, auntiently soe called, but of latter times corruptly nominated Brugenorth or Bruggenorth, when indeede that Attribute of North ought to be Morfe, as standing vpon the side of the Forrest of Morfe in the said County; it hath beene of many ages since endowed with many large priuileiges, which at this daye they not onely enioye, but also by the succeeding Kinges and Princes of this Kingdome the same haue beene confirmed and much enlarged, as by their Seuerall Charters vnder the greate Seale of England more plainly appeareth; of which Towne, John Smith of Morvile, Esqʳ, Justice of the Peace, and Richard Singe, gent., were chosen Bayliffs the very daye that wee in our Visitation went from thence to Ludlowe, viz.,   die September Aᵒ 1623; Rowland Preene and Will'm Pears were Chamberlaines; and Sʳ Edw. Bromley, Knight, one of his Maᵗᵉˢ Barons of the Exchequer, Recorder.

JOHN SMITH, } bailieffs.
RICHᵈ SYNGE, }
ROWLAND PREENE, } Chamberlaynes.
WILLIAM PEARS, }

Acherley of Stanwardine.

S., fo. 65ᵃ.

ARMS: Shrewsbury MS.—*Gules, on a fesse engrailed argent between three griffins'
heads erased or three crosses patée fitchée sable.*

[*Thomas Acheley of Stanwardine.*🬀 . . . .

Sir Roger Acheley Knt. Lord Major of London.]

Acton of Acton Scot.

Harl. 1396, fo. 17.   Harl. 1241, fo. 14.   Harl. 615, fo. 250ᵇ.   S., ff. 16½ and 17.

ARMS: Harl. 1241.—*Quarterly of six :* 1, *Quarterly per fesse indented argent and
gules, in the first quarter a martlet sable ;* 2, *Or, a fesse gules within a bordure
sable* [HENALT]; 3, *Azure, three chevrons or* [COLLINS, misdrawn ?];
4, *Quarterly per fesse indented ermine and gules, a label of five points* . . . .
[FITZWARINE]; 5, *Azure, on a bend cottised or three lions passant gules*
[WYNNESBURY]; 6, *Per pale argent and gules, a lion rampant counterchanged*
[ROBERTS].

ARMS: Harl. 615.—*Quarterly :* 1, *Quarterly per fesse indented* . . . . *in the first quarter
a bird* . . . .; 2, *Azure, three bugle-horns unstringed or* [EYTON]; 3, *Quarterly
per fesse indented ermine and gules, a label of three points of the second*
[FITZWARINE]; 4, *Per pale argent and gules, a lion rampant sable* [ROBERTS].

ARMS: Shrewsbury MS.—*Quarterly of ten :* 1, ACTON ; 2, *Gules, a cross tau portate
throughout or,* HAD; 3, *Or, two bars azure,* COLLINS ; 4, HENALD; 5, *Or, a
fesse between three water-bougets sable,* ROSSELL ; 6, *Azure, three bugles
stringed or,* EIGHTON; 7, FITZWARINE ; 8, *Barry of six argent and vert,*
MARSHE ; 9, WINSBURY ; 10, ROBERTS.

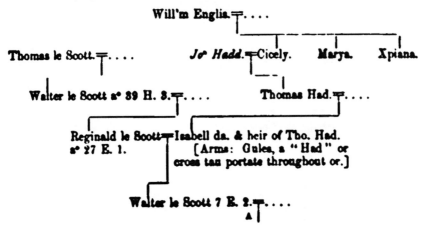

A

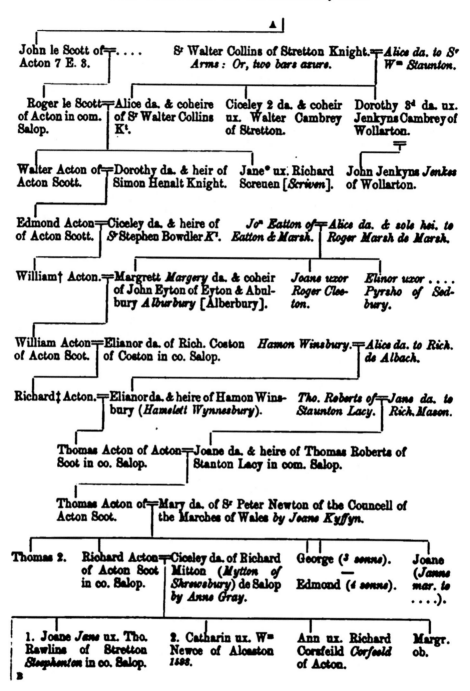

John le Scott of Acton 7 E. 3. = ...

Sr Walter Collins of Stretton Knight. *Arms: Or, two bars azure.* = *Alice da. to Sr Wm Staunton.*

Roger le Scott of Acton in com. Salop. = Alice da. & coheire of Sr Walter Collins K^t.

Ciceley 2 da. & coheir ux. Walter Cambrey of Stretton.

Dorothy 3^d da. ux. Jenkyns Cambrey of Wollarton. =

Walter Acton of Acton Scott. = Dorothy da. & heir of Simon Henalt Knight.

Jane* ux. Richard Screuen [*Scriven*].

John Jenkyns *Jenkes* of Wollarton.

Edmond Acton of Acton Scott. = Ciceley da. & heire of Sr Stephen Bowdler K^t.

Jo^n Eatton of Eatton & Marsh. = *Alice da. & sole hei. to Roger Marsh de Marsh.*

William† Acton. = Margrett *Margery* da. & coheir of John Eyton of Eyton & Abulbury *Alburbury* [Alberbury].

Joane uxor Roger Cleeton.

Elinor uxor . . . . Pyrsho of Sedbury.

William Acton of Acton Scot. = Elianor da. of Rich. Coston of Coston in co. Salop.

Hamon Winsbury. = *Alice da. to Rich. de Albach.*

Richard‡ Acton. = Elianor da. & heire of Hamon Winsbury (*Hamelett Wynnesbury*).

Tho. Roberts of Staunton Lacy. = *Jane da. to Rich. Mason.*

Thomas Acton of Acton Scot in co. Salop. = Joane da. & heire of Thomas Roberts of Stanton Lacy in com. Salop.

Thomas Acton of Acton Scot. = Mary da. of Sr Peter Newton of the Councell of the Marches of Wales *by Joane Kyffyn.*

Thomas 2.

Richard Acton of Acton Scot in co. Salop. = Ciceley da. of Richard Mitton (*Mytton of Shrewsbury*) de Salop *by Anne Gray.*

George (*3 sonne*).

Edmond (*4 sonne*).

Joane (*Janne mar. to . . . .*).

1. Joane *Jane* ux. Tho. Rawlins of Stretton *Sleephenton* in co. Salop.

2. Catharin ux. Wm Newce of Alcaston *1598.*

Ann ux. Richard Corsfeild *Corfeeld* of Acton.

Margr. ob.

B

* Harl. 1241 makes her a da. of Sir Walter Collins.

† Harl. 615 makes him son of Wm Acton and father of Richard.

‡ Harl. 1241 makes this Richard the brother of William.

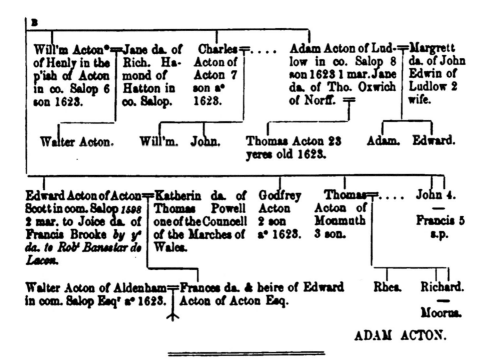

B

Will'm Acton* of Henly in the p'ish of Acton in co. Salop 6 son 1623. = Jane da. of Rich. Hamond of Hatton in co. Salop.

Charles Acton of Acton 7 son a° 1623. = ...

Adam Acton of Ludlow in co. Salop 8 son 1623 1 mar. Jane da. of Tho. Oxwich of Norff. = Margrett da. of John Edwin of Ludlow 2 wife.

Walter Acton.   Will'm.   John.   Thomas Acton 23 yeres old 1623.   Adam.   Edward.

Edward Acton of Acton Scott in com. Salop 1598 2 mar. to Joice da. of Francis Brooke by y° da. to Rob' Banester de Lacon. = Katherin da. of Thomas Powell one of the Councell of the Marches of Wales.

Godfrey Acton 2 son a° 1623.

Thomas Acton of Monmuth 3 son. = ...

John 4.
—
Francis 5 s.p.

Walter Acton of Aldenham in com. Salop Esq' a° 1623. = Frances da. & heire of Edward Acton of Acton Esq.

Rhea.   Richard.
—
Moorna.

ADAM ACTON.

Acton of Aldenham.

Harl. 1396, fo. 16.   Harl. 615, fo. 258.   S., fo. 16.

ARMS: Shrewsbury MS.—*Quarterly of eight* : 1, *Gules, two lions passant in pale argent armed and langued azure between nine cross-crosslets* [fitchée or], ACTON; 2, *Argent, three mascles in fesse sable, ...*; 3, *Gules, two lions passant in pale argent, a label of five points or,* STRANGE OF KNOCKING; 4, *Per fesse gules and vert, a fesse and in chief a chevron argent,* SPRINGROSE; 5, *Azure, a lion rampant within an orle of cross-crosslets or,* BREWER; 6, *Argent, semée of cross-crosslets azure, two organ-pipes gules,* DOWNTON; 7, *Barry of six or and gules,* ST. OWEN; 8, *Azure, a lion rampant argent within a bordure or,* TIRELL.

CREST.—*In a circular wreath gules and argent a leg in armour, couped at the thigh proper, spurred, etc.* [or].

Will'm of Acton Burnell a° 14 E. 3. = ...

Fulke le Strange of Betton Strange in com. Salop frater Hamonis le Strange. = ...

John de Acton.

Edw. Acton of Aldenham in the p'ish of Morvile [Morville] in com. Salop a° 10 R. 2 [Sheriff 1383]. = Elianor da. and one of the heires of S' Fulke le Strange K' a° 10 R. 2.

Jane da. and coheir ux. John Carles of Albrighton in co. Salop.

Walter Acton of Longnor in com. Salop Esq. = ... da. of .... Stepleton.

* Harl. 1241 calls him 5 son, and says he married Sara da. to W'm Waters.

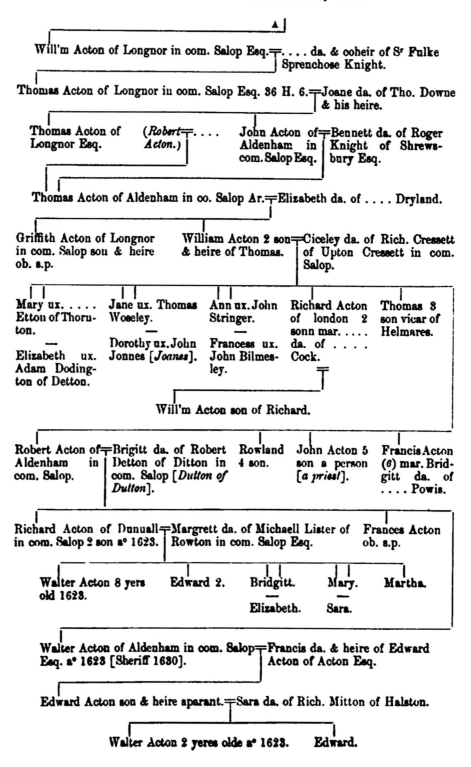

▲

Will'm Acton of Longnor in com. Salop Esq.=.... da. & coheir of Sr Fulke Sprenchose Knight.

Thomas Acton of Longnor in com. Salop Esq. 36 H. 6.=Joane da. of Tho. Downe & his heire.

Thomas Acton of Longnor Esq.　　(Robert=.... Acton.)　　John Acton of=Bennett da. of Roger Aldenham in com. Salop Esq.　Knight of Shrews-bury Esq.

Thomas Acton of Aldenham in co. Salop Ar.=Elizabeth da. of .... Dryland.

Griffith Acton of Longnor in com. Salop son & heire ob. s.p.　　William Acton 2 son=Ciceley da. of Rich. Cressett & heire of Thomas.　of Upton Cressett in com. Salop.

Mary ux. .... Etton of Thorn-ton.

—

Elizabeth ux. Adam Dodington of Detton.

Jane ux. Thomas Woseley.

—

Dorothy ux. John Jonnes [Joanes].

Ann ux. John Stringer.

—

Francess ux. John Bilmes-ley.

Richard Acton of london 2 sonn mar. .... da. of .... Cock.

Thomas 8 son vicar of Helmares.

Will'm Acton son of Richard.

Robert Acton of=Brigitt da. of Robert Aldenham in com. Salop.　Detton of Ditton in com. Salop [Dutton of Dutton].　Rowland 4 son.　John Acton 5 son a person [a priest].　Francis Acton (6) mar. Brid-gitt da. of .... Powis.

Richard Acton of Dunuall in com. Salop 2 son a° 1623.=Margrett da. of Michaell Lister of Rowton in com. Salop Esq.　Frances Acton ob. s.p.

Walter Acton 8 yers old 1623.　Edward 2.　Bridgitt.

—

Elizabeth.　Mary.

—

Sara.　Martha.

Walter Acton of Aldenham in com. Salop=Francis da. & heire of Edward Esq. a° 1623 [Sheriff 1630].　Acton of Acton Esq.

Edward Acton son & heire aparant.=Sara da. of Rich. Mitton of Halston.

Walter Acton 2 yeres olde a° 1623.　Edward.

Adams of Cleeton.

Harl. 1396, fo. 11. Harl. 1241, fo. 19[b]. Harl. 615, fo. 264. S., fo. 18.

ARMS: Harl. 1396.—*Ermine, a chevron vairy or and azure between three roses gules* [seeded or].

CREST.—*A gryphon's head erased ermine, beaked gules, charged on the neck with a chevron vairy or and azure.*

ARMS: Shrewsbury MS.—*Per pale argent and gules, a chevron between three leaves counterchanged; per Camden Clar' quer'.*

ARMS:[*] Shrewsbury MS.—*Quarterly: 1, Argent, a martlet sable; 2, Quarterly argent and sable, on a cross gules five mullets or; 3, Per pale azure and sable, three fleurs-de-lys or; 4, Azure, a chevron between three lions' heads erased or.*

Will'm Adams of Cleeton in com. Salop.=. . . .

Thomas Adams 3 sonne.=. . . .   William Adams of Cleeton 4th sonne.=. . . .

Thomas Adams.   Isabell da. of Tho. Hopton of Butterley *Bitterley* (*Botterley*).=William Adams of Cleeton.=Anne da. of . . . . Windsore *Winford*.

Edward (*Edmonde*).   John Adams.=. . . . da. of . . . . Holt.   Mary. (*Jone mar. to . . . . Holte.*)

Richard (*2 sonne*).
John† (*3 sonne*).   William Adams of Cleeton.=Vrsula da. of W[m] Goore of Ridmarle [? Gower of Ridmarley].   Alice.   Ann ux. . . . . Blashfeild [*Blathfield*].

William Adams son & heir.   John 2 son.   Elizabeth.

Richard Adams 2 son.   John Adams of Cleeton son & heire.=Alice da. of . . . . Byrey of Kynton in co. Wigornj.

Richard 1 son.   John Adams of Cleeton in co. Salop 2 sonne.=Joyce da. of . . . . Whitton of Whitton in co. Salop.   Thomas Adams 3 son.   William Adams 4 sonne.

Thomas Adams of Cleeton 2 son s° 1584.=Margrett da. of . . . . Harley [*Harley*] of Brampton *Brampton* Brian.   Alice‡ ux. Phillip ap Richard.   Margrett‡ ux. . . . . Seyney of Coventrey.   Mary‡ ux. Thomas ap Harrey in com. Heref.

Thomas.   John 2 sonne.   Isabell.   Ann.

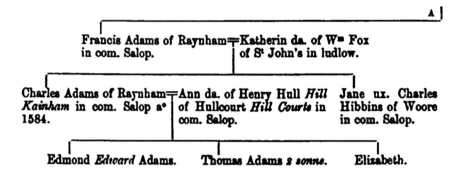

Francis Adams of Raynham=Katherin da. of Wm Fox
in com. Salop.   of St John's in ludlow.

Charles Adams of Raynham=Ann da. of Henry Hull *Hill*   Jane ux. Charles
Kainham in com. Salop a° of Hullcourt *Hill Courts* in   Hibbins of Woore
1584.   com. Salop.   in com. Salop.

Edmond *Edward* Adams.   Thomas Adams *2 sonne.*   Elizabeth.

Adams of Longdon and Adams alias Tasker.

Harl. 1396, fo. 9^b.   Harl. 1241, fo. 42.   Harl. 615, fo. 259^b.   S., fo. 12.

ARMS: Harl. 1396: ADAMS.—*Quarterly : 1 and 4, Ermine, three cats a mountain
in pale tails coward proper ;*° 2, Per pale argent and gules, a chevron between
three bees counterchanged,†* MASCOTT ; *3, Argent, guttée de poix, a fesse sable,*
HIGGINS.
CREST.—*A greyhound's head erased ermine.*
ARMS: Harl. 1396: ADAMS ALIAS TASKER.—*Quarterly : 1,* ADAMS, *as above ;
2, Argent, three bars azure, in chief three lozenges of the second,* MASCOT [sic] ;
3, Or, a fesse between three lions rampant sable,* TASKER ; *4, Azure, a chevron
argent between three trefoils slipped or,* BEARD ; *over all a crescent for
difference.*

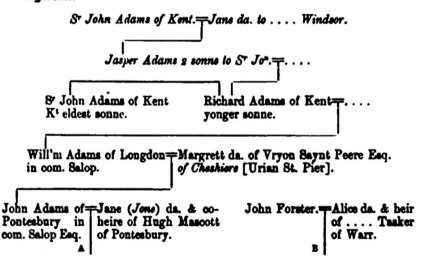

Sr John Adams of Kent.=*Jane da. to . . . . Windsor.*

Jasper Adams 2 sonns to S^r Jo^n.=. . . .

Sr John Adams of Kent   Richard Adams of Kent=. . . .
K^t eldest sonne.   yonger sonne.

Will'm Adams of Longdon=Margrett da. of Vryon Saynt Peere Esq.
in com. Salop.   *of Cheshiere* [Urian St. Pier].

John Adams of=Jane (*Jone*) da. & co-   John Forster.=Alice da. & heir
Pontesbury   in | heire of Hugh Mascott   of . . . . Tasker
com. Salop Esq. | of Pontesbury.   of Warr.
▲   B

° *Azure* in Shrewsbury MS., fo. 12.
   Given elsewhere in Visitation as, " Argent, a chevron between three bees volant gules."

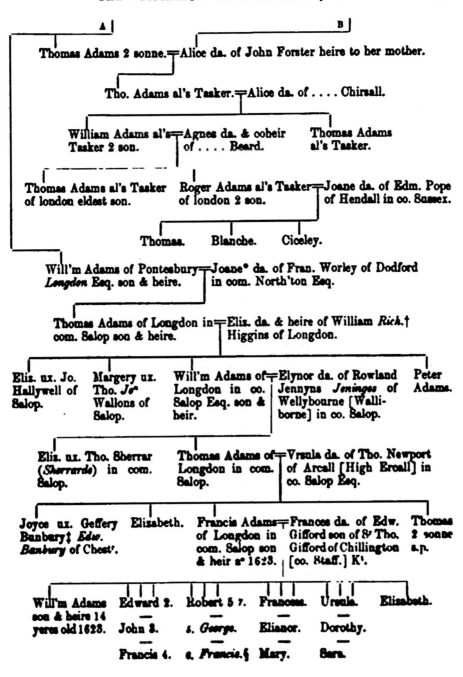

A | B |

Thomas Adams 2 sonne.=Alice da. of John Forster heire to her mother.

Tho. Adams al's Tasker.=Alice da. of .... Chirsall.

William Adams al's=Agnes da. & coheir   Thomas Adams
Tasker 2 son.   of .... Beard.   al's Tasker.

Thomas Adams al's Tasker   Roger Adams al's Tasker=Joane da. of Edm. Pope
of london eldest son.   of london 2 son.   of Hendall in co. Sussex.

Thomas.   Blanche.   Ciceley.

Will'm Adams of Pontesbury=Joane* da. of Fran. Worley of Dodford
Longdon Esq. son & heire.   in com. North'ton Esq.

Thomas Adams of Longdon in=Eliz. da. & heire of William *Rich.†*
com. Salop son & heire.   Higgins of Longdon.

Eliz. ux. Jo.   Margery ux.   Will'm Adams of=Elynor da. of Rowland   Peter
Hallywell of   Tho. *Jo*   Longdon in co. Jennyns *Jeninges* of   Adams.
Salop.   Wallons of   Salop Esq. son & Wellybourne [Walli-
        Salop.   heir.   borne] in co. Salop.

Eliz. ux. Tho. Sherrar   Thomas Adams of=Vrsula da. of Tho. Newport
(*Sherrarde*) in com.   Longdon in com. of Arcall [High Ercall] in
Salop.   Salop.   co. Salop Esq.

Joyce ux. Geffery Elizabeth.   Francis Adams=Frances da. of Edw.   Thomas
Banbury‡ *Edw.*   of Longdon in   Gifford son of S'r Tho. 2 sonne
Banbury of Chest'.   com. Salop son Gifford of Chillington s.p.
                & heir a° 1623. [co. Staff.] K't.

Will'm Adams Edward 2. Robert 5 7. Frances. Ursula. Elizabeth.
son & heire 14 —   —   —   —
yeres old 1623. John 3. *s. George.* Elianor. Dorothy.
             —   —   —   —
            Francis 4. *e. Francis.§* Mary. Sara.

* *Elinor* in Harl. 1241 and Harl. 615.   † *William* in Shrewsbury MS., fo. 12.
‡ *Jeffrey Banbury* in Shrewsbury MS., fo. 12.
‡ Harl. 1241 gives two sons named Francis.

Adams.

Harl. 1396, fo. 12. S., fo. 13.

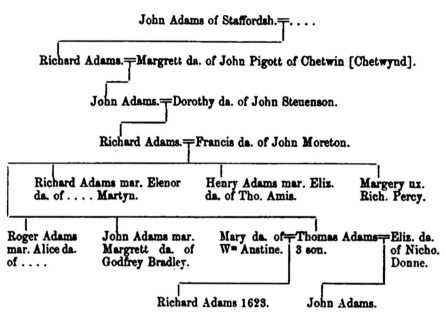

John Adams of Staffordsh.=....

Richard Adams.=Margrett da. of John Pigott of Chetwin [Chetwynd].

John Adams.=Dorothy da. of John Steuenson.

Richard Adams.=Francis da. of John Moreton.

Richard Adams mar. Elenor da. of .... Martyn. — Henry Adams mar. Eliz. da. of Tho. Amis. — Margery ux. Rich. Percy.

Roger Adams mar. Alice da. of .... — John Adams mar. Margrett da. of Godfrey Bradley. — Mary da. of Wm Austine.=Thomas Adams 3 son.=Eliz. da. of Nicho. Donne.

Richard Adams 1623. — John Adams.

Albany of Whittington.

Harl. 1396, fo. 13. Harl. 1241, fo. 59ᵇ. S., fo. 13ᵇ.

ARMS : Harl. 1396.—*Quarterly*: 1, *Argent,** on a fesse between three cinquefoils gules a greyhound courant or* ; 2, *Sable—gules* in Harl. 1241—*a chevron between three combs† argent* [BUTLER] ; 3, *Argent, on a chief gules an eagle displayed or* [CAMPION] ; 4, *Azure, fretty argent—ermine* in Harl. 1241—*on a canton or a fleur-de-lis of the first* [CAMPION].
CREST.—*Out of a ducal coronet gules a demi-dolphin haurient or.*

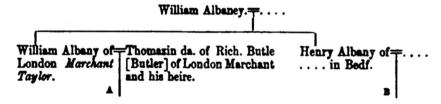

William Albaney.=....

William Albany of London *Marchant Taylor*.=Thomazin da. of Rich. Butle [Butler] of London Marchant and his heire.

▲

Henry Albany of .... in Bedf.=....

B

* ' Vis. London, 1568 ' (Harl. Soc.), says Francis son of William Albany bore the field *ermine.*
† Wine-piercers or large gimblets.

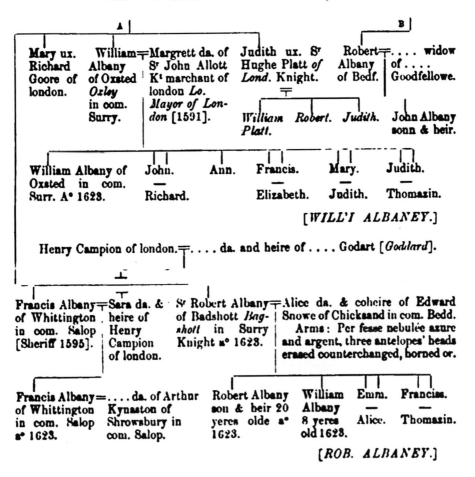

A   B

Mary ux. Richard Goore of london. | William Albany of Oxsted *Oxley* in com. Surry. ⊤ Margrett da. of Sᵣ John Allott Kᵗ marchant of london *Lo. Mayor of London* [1591]. | Judith ux. Sᵣ Hughe Platt *of Lond.* Knight. | Robert ⊤ .... widow Albany of .... of Bedf. | Goodfellowe.

⊤

William Robert. Judith.   John Albany
Platt.   sonn & heir.

William Albany of Oxsted in com. Surr. Aᵒ 1623. | John. — Richard. | Ann. | Francis. — Elizabeth. | Mary. — Judith. | Judith. — Thomazin.

[*WILL'I ALBANEY.*]

Henry Campion of london. ⊤ .... da. and heire of .... Godart [*Goddard*].

⊥

Francis Albany ⊤ Sara da. & of Whittington | heire of in com. Salop | Henry [Sheriff 1595]. | Campion | of london. | Sᵣ Robert Albany ⊤ Alice da. & coheire of Edward of Badshott *Bag-* | Snowe of Chicksand in com. Bedd. *shott* in Surry | Arms: Per fesse nebulée azure Knight aᵒ 1623. | and argent, three antelopes' heads | erased counterchanged, horned or.

Francis Albany = ... da. of Arthur of Whittington | Kynaston of in com. Salop | Shrowsbury in aᵒ 1623. | com. Salop. | Robert Albany son & heir 20 yeres olde aᵒ 1623. | William Albany 8 yeres old 1623. | Emm. — Alice. | Franciss. — Thomazin.

[*ROB. ALBANEY.*]

Alkington of Alkington and Oswestry.

Harl. 1396, fo. 14ᵇ.   Harl. 1241, fo. 61.   S., fo. 20.

ARMS: Harl. 1396.—*Quarterly or and gules, an eagle displayed counterchanged.*

William Alkington of Alkington ⊤ Eme *Emlyne* da. [to] .... Cheshire in co. Salop. | of Whitchurch in co. Salop.

Roger Alkington of Alkington marᵈ Eliz. da. of Jo. Wright of Bickley in com. Cheshire. ⊤ | George *3 sonne.* — John *4 sonne.* | Griffith *5 sonne.* | Thomas ⊤ Jane *Jeane* da. Alkington | & coheir to 2 sonne. | Rich. Wootton | of Shropsh. | Alice. — Margery. — Elinor.

A   B

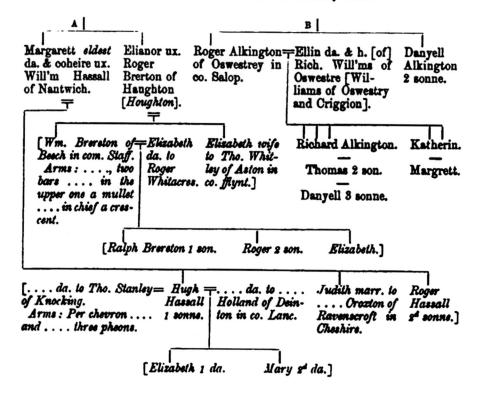

A

Margarett *eldest* da. & coheire ux. Will'm Hassall of Nantwich.

Elianor ux. Roger Brerton of Haughton [*Houghton*].

[*Wm. Brereton of Beech in com. Staff. Arms: . . . ., two bars . . . . in the upper one a mullet . . . . in chief a crescent.*] = *Elizabeth da. to Roger Whitacres.*

Elizabeth wife to Tho. Whitley of Aston in co. ffynt.]

[*Ralph Brereton 1 son.* *Roger 2 son.* *Elizabeth.*]

[*. . . . da. to Tho. Stanley of Knocking. Arms: Per chevron . . . . and . . . . three pheons.*] = *Hugh Hassall 1 sonne.* = *. . . . da. to . . . . Holland of Deinton in co. Lanc.*

Judith marr. to . . . . Croxton of Ravenscroft in Cheshire.

Roger Hassall 2d sonne.]

[*Elizabeth 1 da.* *Mary 2d da.*]

B

Roger Alkington of Oswestrey in co. Salop. = Ellin da. & h. [of] Rich. Will'ms of Oswestre [Williams of Oswestry and Criggion].

Danyell Alkington 2 sonne.

Richard Alkington. — Thomas 2 son. — Danyell 3 sonne.

Katherin. — Margrett.

Allen of Llandyssilio.

Harl. 1396, fo. 15. Harl. 1241, fo. 132.

Humfry Allen of Woluerhampton in co. Staff. = ...

John Allen. = ...

Humfry Lloyd. = Gwenllin wynn da. of Thomas ap Rees *of Newtowne.*

Thomas Allyn of Llandysulio [Llandyssilio, co. Denbigh ?]. = Margrett da. of Humfrey lloyd Esq.

Richard Allen of Treualdwyn. = Ciceley da. of George Price of Tralloge.

Arneway.

S., fo. 20ᵇ.

[ARMS.—*Ermine, three escallops sable.*]

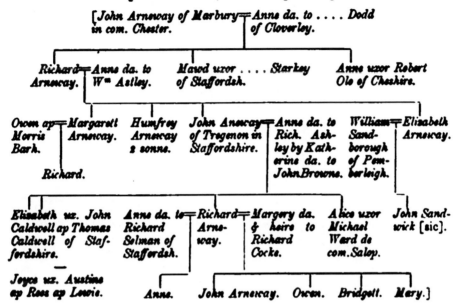

[*John Arneway of Marbury*⹀*Anne da. to . . . . Dodd*
in com. Chester. *of Cloverley.*

Richard⹀*Anne da. to* *Mawd uxor . . . . Starkey* *Anne uxor Robert*
Arneway. *Wᵐ Astley.* *of Staffordsh.* *Ole of Cheshire.*

Owen ap⹀*Margarett* *Humfrey* *John Arneway*⹀*Anne da. to* *William*⹀*Elisabeth*
Morris *Arneway.* *Arneway* *of Tregenon in* *Rich. Ash-* *Sand-* *Arneway.*
Bark. *2 sonne.* *Staffordshire.* *ley by Kath-* *borough*
   erine da. to *of Pem-*
Richard. *John Browne.* *berleigh.*

Elisabeth ux. John *Anne da. to*⹀*Richard*⹀*Margery da.* *Alice uxor* *John Sand-*
Caldwell ap Thomas *Richard* *Arne-* *& heire to* *Michael* *wick* [sic].
Caldwell of Staf- *Selman of* *way.* *Richard* *Ward de*
fordsh. *Staffordsh.* *Cocks.* *com. Salop.*

Joyce ux. Austine
ap Rees ap Lewis. Anne. John Arneway. Owen. Bridgett. Mary.]

Aron of Drayton.

Harl. 1396, fo. 14ᵇ.   Harl. 1241, fo. 136ᵇ.

[ARMS.—. . . . *on a bend three martlets.*]

Richard Aron.⹀Ciceley da. [of] Richard Okeley.

John Aron.⹀Catherin da. [of] John Foulke.

Christofer Aron.⹀Ann da. [of] Robert Morton.

Thomas Aron of Drayton⹀Ann da. of Tho. Kynardsly
in co. Salop. [Kynnersley] of Badger.

Ambrose Anthony⹀Ann da. of wᵐ Margrett ux. Geo. Vaughan l'ychan
Aron. Aron. weike *Wickes.* of Shinhall in com. Salop.

Phillip. James *Jacob Aron.* Susan. Sara.

D

Astley of Pateshull and Aston.

Harl. 1396, fo. 13ᵇ.   Harl. 1241, fo. 145.   S., ff. 14, 15.

ARMS: Harl. 1396.—*Quarterly*: 1, *Azure, a cinquefoil ermine*; 2, *Gules, two bars or* [HARCOURT]; 3, *Argent, a fesse wavy gules within a bordure sable bezantée* [WOLVEY?]; 4, *Gules, a lion rampant within a bordure engrailed or, a crescent for difference* [TALBOTT]; *over all the quarterings a crescent for difference.*

CREST.—*Out of a ducal coronet argent* [? or] *a plume of five ostrich-feathers gules surmounted by another plume or.*

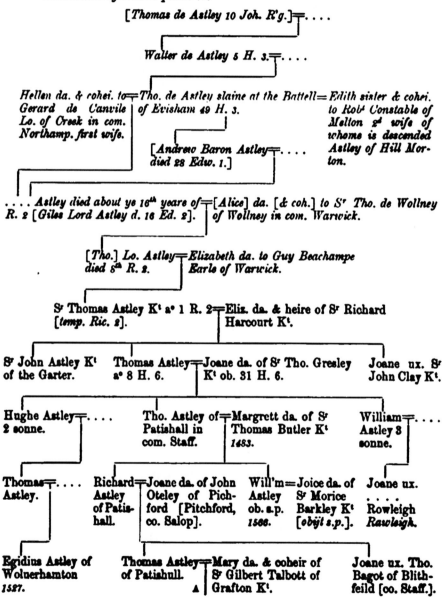

[*Thomas de Astley 10 Joh. R'g.*]=....

Walter de Astley 5 H. 3.=....

Hellen da. & cohei. to=*Tho. de Astley slaine at the Battell*=*Edith sister & cohei.*
Gerard de Canvile | *of Evisham 49 H. 3.* | *to Rob* Constable of*
Lo. of Creek in com. | | *Melton 2ᵈ wife of*
Northamp. first wife. | | *whome is descended*
| [*Andrew Baron Astley*=.... | *Astley of Hill Mor-*
| *died 28 Edw. 1.*] | *ton.*

.... *Astley died about ye 16ᵗʰ yeare of*=[*Alice*] *da.* [*& coh.*] *to Sʳ Tho. de Wollney*
R. 2 [*Giles Lord Astley d. 16 Ed. 2*]. | *of Wollney in com. Warwick.*

[*Tho.*] *Lo. Astley*=*Elizabeth da. to Guy Beachampe*
died 5ᵗʰ R. 2. | *Earle of Warwick.*

Sʳ *Thomas Astley Kᵗ aᵒ 1 R. 2*=*Eliz. da. & heire of Sʳ Richard*
[*temp. Ric. 2*]. | *Harcourt Kᵗ.*

Sʳ John Astley Kᵗ of the Garter.	Thomas Astley=Joane da. of Sʳ Tho. Gresley aᵒ 8 H. 6. Kᵗ ob. 31 H. 6.		Joane ux. Sʳ John Clay Kᵗ.

Hughe Astley=....   Tho. Astley of=Margrett da. of Sʳ   William=....
2 sonne.   Patishall in   Thomas Butler Kᵗ   Astley 3
                 com. Staff.   1483.   sonne.

Thomas=....   Richard=Joane da. of John   Will'm=Joice da. of   Joane ux.
Astley.   Astley Oteley of Pich-   Astley Sʳ Morice   ....
              of Pati- ford [Pitchford,   ob. s.p. Barkley Kᵗ   Rowleigh
              shall.   co. Salop].   1566.   [obijt s.p.]. Rawleigh.

Egidius Astley of   Thomas Astley=Mary da. & coheir of   Joane ux. Tho.
Wolverhamton   of Patishull. Sʳ Gilbert Talbott of   Bagot of Blith-
1527.   ▲   Grafton Kᵗ.   feild [co. Staff.].

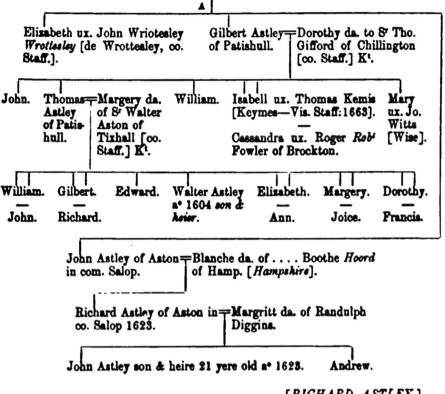

▲ |

Elizabeth ux. John Wriotesley *Wrottesley* [de Wrottesley, co. Staff.].

Gilbert Astley⊤Dorothy da. to Sʳ Tho. of Patishull. | Gifford of Chillington [co. Staff.] Kᵗ.

John.

Thomas⊤Margery da. Astley of Sʳ Walter of Patis- Aston of hull. Tixhall [co. Staff.] Kᵗ.

William.

Isabell ux. Thomas Kemis [Keymes—Vis. Staff: 1663]. — Cassandra ux. Roger *Robᵗ* Fowler of Brockton.

Mary ux. Jo. Witts [Wise].

William. — John.

Gilbert. — Richard.

Edward.

Walter Astley a° 1604 *son & heier*.

Elizabeth. — Ann.

Margery. — Joice.

Dorothy. — Francis.

John Astley of Aston⊤Blanche da. of . . . . Boothe *Hoord* in com. Salop. | of Hamp. [*Hampshire*].

Richard Astley of Aston in⊤Margritt da. of Randulph co. Salop 1623. | Diggins.

John Astley son & heire 21 yere old a° 1623.

Andrew.

[*RICHARD ASTLEY.*]

Attwood of Broughton.

Harl. 1396, fo. 15. Harl. 1241, fo. 152ᵇ. S., fo. 21.

ARMS: Harl. 1396.—*Gules, a lion rampant queue fourchée argent* [armed and langued azure].

John Attwood of Attwood Parke in com. [Worcester].⊤Anna.

Anthony Attwood.⊤Vrsula da. & h. of wᵐ Porter of worsterah.

Henry Attwood 2 sonne.

Anthony Attwood⊤Jane da.* of Rich. son & heire. | Sheldon of Beeley [Beoley, co. Warwick].

Susan ux. Edw. Adams.

Mary.

▲ |

* *Us.* in Harl. 1396.

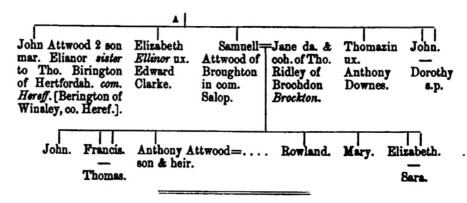

| John Attwood 2 son mar. Elianor *sister* to Tho. Birington of Hertfordsh. *com. Hereff.* [Berington of Winsley, co. Heref.]. | Elizabeth *Ellinor* ux. Edward Clarke. | Samuell Attwood of Broughton in com. Salop. | Jane da. & coh. of Tho. Ridley of Brochdon *Brockton.* | Thomazin ux. Anthony Downes. | John. Dorothy s.p. |

| John. | Francis. — Thomas. | Anthony Attwood= .... son & heir. | Rowland. | Mary. | Elizabeth. — Sara. |

Bagshawe.

S., fo. 98ᵇ.

ARMS: Shrewsbury MS.—[Argent], *a hunting-horn* [sable] *stringed* [vert] *between three roses* [gules].

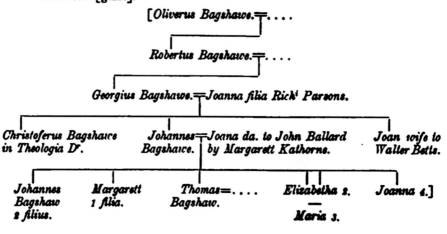

[*Oliverus Bagshawe.*=....

Robertus Bagshawe.=....

Georgius Bagshawe.=*Joanna filia Richᵈ Parsons.*

| *Christoferus Bagshawe in Theologia Dʳ.* | *Johannes Bagshawe.*=*Joana da. to John Ballard by Margarett Kathorne.* | *Joan wife to Walter Betts.* |

| *Johannes Bagshaw 2 filius.* | *Margarett 1 filia.* | *Thomas*=.... *Bagshaw.* | *Elizabetha 2.* — *Maria 3.* | *Joanna 4.*] |

Bagshawe.

S., fo. 99.

[ARMS: Visit. Staff. 1583.—*Or, a bugle-horn sable stringed vert between three roses gules.*]

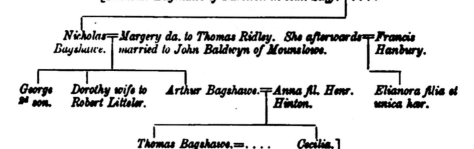

[*Nicholas Bagshawe of Farewell in com. Staff.*=....

Nicholas Bagshawe.=*Margery da. to Thomas Ridley. She afterwards*=*Francis married to John Baldwyn of Mounslowe. Hanbury.*

| *George 2ᵈ son.* | *Dorothy wife to Robert Littster.* | *Arthur Bagshawe.*=*Anna fil. Henr. Hinton.* | *Elianora filia et unica hær.* |

Thomas Bagshawe.=....   *Cecilia.*]

Baker of Hanwood.

Harl. 1396, fo. 50.　Harl. 1241, fo. 139ᵇ.

[A GRANT OF ARMS by SEGAR to JOHN BAKER of Shrewsbury ('Guillim,' 1724 ed.,
　p. 266).—*Sable, a griffin segreant ermine ducally gorged or, beaked and
　membered gules.*
CREST.—*Out of a ducal coronet or a dexter arm embowed vested or, gauntlet or,
　holding a broken tilting-spear in bend or, without the burr or vamplate, enfiled
　with a garland proper.*]

Thomas Baker.⹀Jana fil. . . . . . Corbet de Aston.

Thomas⹀Maria fil. et sola hæres Joh's Bromley
Baker.　de Hanwide [Hanwood].

Johannes⹀Eliz. fil. Ed'r'i
Jenkyns.　Leighton.

Johannes⹀Johanni *Jane* fil. Ric'i Pigot
Baker.　de Chetwin in co. Salop.

Thomas⹀. . . .
Stokyn.

Edward⹀Elizabetha
Marston.

Johannes Baker⹀Johanna *Jane* fil. Rogeri
de Hawede.　Hugons *Huggons.*

Willi'mus⹀Margeria fil. Edw.
Stokyn.　Marston.

Rogerus⹀Elizab. fil. Will'i Weale° *Webb*
Baker 2.　renupta Jacobi Barker.

Thomas Baker de⹀Maria fil. Willi'm'
Hawede [Hanwood].　Stokyn.

Abrahamus
Baker.

Daniell 2.
—
Johanna.

Sara nupta Will.
Ireland ap Tho.
Ireland.

Johannes⹀Anna filia
Baker　francisci
1586.　Charleton.

Johanna ux.
Tho. Taylor ap
Rob. Taylor.

Baldwin of Diddlebury.

Harl. 1396, fo. 21ᵇ.　Harl. 1241, fo. 58.　S., ff. 25ᵇ, 26.

ARMS: Harl. 1396.—*Quarterly: 1 and 4, Argent, a saltire sable; 2, Barry of six
　azure and argent, a chief ermine* [WIGLEY]; *3, Gules, a chevron ermine between
　three birds* [? *eaglets*] *close argent* [CHILDE].
CREST.—*On a mount vert a cockatrice with wings endorsed argent, beaked, combed,
　ducally gorged, and lined or.*

John Bawdwyn of Didlebury⹀Ann da. & heir to
in com. Salop.　Richard L'enfant.

Tho. Bawdewyn of Didlebury in com. Salop.⹀. . . .

° Wm. Weale was Bailiff of Shrewsbury 1573; John Webbe was Bailiff 1554.

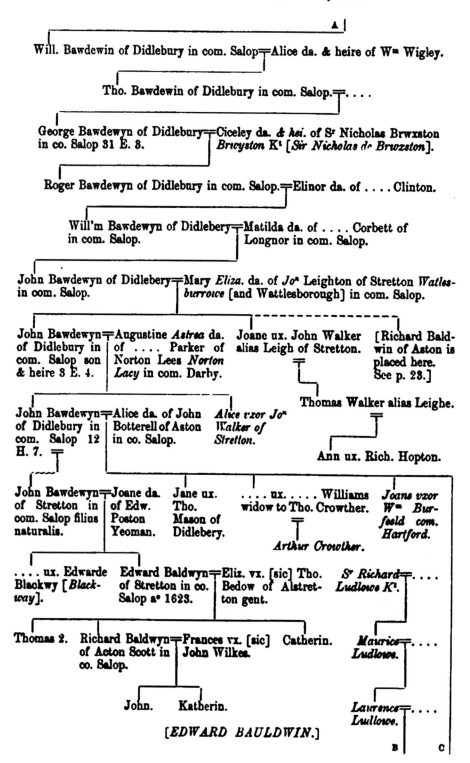

▲ |

Will. Bawdewin of Didlebury in com. Salop.=Alice da. & heire of Wᵐ Wigley.

Tho. Bawdewin of Didlebury in com. Salop.=....

George Bawdewyn of Didlebury=Ciceley da. & hei. of Sʳ Nicholas Brwxston
in co. Salop 31 E. 3.   *Brwyston* Kᵗ [*Sir Nicholas de Brwxston*].

Roger Bawdewyn of Didlebury in com. Salop.=Elinor da. of .... Clinton.

Will'm Bawdewyn of Didlebery=Matilda da. of .... Corbett of
in com. Salop.   Longnor in com. Salop.

John Bawdewyn of Didlebery=Mary *Eliza.* da. of *Joⁿ* Leighton of Stretton *Watles-*
in com. Salop.   *burrowe* [and Wattlesborough] in com. Salop.

John Bawdewyn=Augustine *Astrea* da.	Joane ux. John Walker	[Richard Bald-
of Didlebury in	of .... Parker of	alias Leigh of Stretton.	win of Aston is
com. Salop son	Norton Lees *Norton*		placed here.
& heire 3 E. 4.	*Lacy* in com. Darby.	♒	See p. 23.]

Thomas Walker alias Leighe.

John Bawdewyn=Alice da. of John   *Alice vxor Joⁿ*
of Didlebury in | Botterell of Aston   *Walker of*
com. Salop 12 | in co. Salop.   *Stretton.*
H. 7. ♒

Ann ux. Rich. Hopton.

John Bawdewyn=Joane da.	Jane ux.	.... ux. .... Williams	*Joane vxor*
of Stretton in	of Edw.	Tho.	widow to Tho. Crowther.	*Wᵐ Bur-*
com. Salop filius	Poston	Mason of		*feeld com.*
naturalis.	Yeoman.	Didlebery.	♒	*Hartford.*

Arthur Crowther.

.... ux. Edwarde	Edward Baldwyn=Eliz. vx. [sic] Tho.	*Sʳ Richard=....*
Blackwy [*Black-*	of Stretton in co.	Bedow of Alstret-	*Ludlowe Kᵗ.*
way].	Salop aº 1623.	ton gent.	

Thomas 2.	Richard Baldwyn=Frances vx. [sic]	Catherin.	*Maurice=....*
	of Acton Scott in	John Wilkes.		*Ludlowe.*
	co. Salop.		

John.   Katherin.

Laurence=....
Ludlowe.

[*EDWARD BAULDWIN.*]

B | C

B | C

John Bawdewyn 3 son mar. A . . . da. of Edw. Marston of Ascott [Afcote] in co. Salop.

Rich. Bawdewyn of Didlebery in com. Salop son & heire 1584. = Margery *Margarett* da. of Laurence Ludlow de la Morehouse in com. Salop.

Francis a parson of Wistanslow & William s.p.

John Baldwin of Pontfract in co. York.

Rich. s.p.

Henry Baldwyn of Didlebery 3 sonne.

Thomas Baldewyn of Didlebery in com. Salop. = Gertrude da. & cobeire of Robt Corbett of Stanwarden in com. Salop.

John 2.
—
Richard 3.

Edw. Baldwin of Didlebery in com. Salop a° 1623. = Mary ux. [sic] of Edward Lutwich *of Luttwich.*

Dorothy.
—
Susann.

[*EDWARD BAWDEWING.*]

Will'm Baldwyn of Elsich [*Elsick*] in co. Salop 2 son. = Barbary da. of Rich. Brooke of Whitchurch in com. South't.

Elizabeth ux. Richard Higgons *Huggons* [*Higgins*].

Dorothe ux. Walter Beck.

Mary ux. Gregorye *Geo.* Mason.

Charles Baldwyn of Elsich in co. Salop. 1623. = Mary da. of Fran. Holland of Burwarton in co. Salop.

A son not baptised.

Samuell Baldwyn 5 yeres old a° 1623.

Benjamyn 3 son.

Timotheus 2 sonne.

[*C. BALDWYN.*]

Baldwin of Aston near Munslow.

Harl. 1396, fo. 21^b. Harl. 1241, fo. 58. 8., fo. 26.

ARMS.—1, *Per pale argent and sable, a lion rampant counterchanged; 2, Barry of six ermine and azure* [WIGLEY ?]; *3, Gules, a chevron ermine between three birds close argent* [CHILDE].

CREST.—*On a mount vert a cockatrice with wings endorsed argent, beaked, combed, ducally gorged, and lined or.*

[The Quarterings and Crest are from Harl. 1241.]

[John Bawdewyn of Didlebury. = ... da. of . . . . Leighton See p. 22.   of Stretton.]

Richard Baldwyn had 22 childre' *by his two wiues.* = ... da. of . . . . Portoman.

A

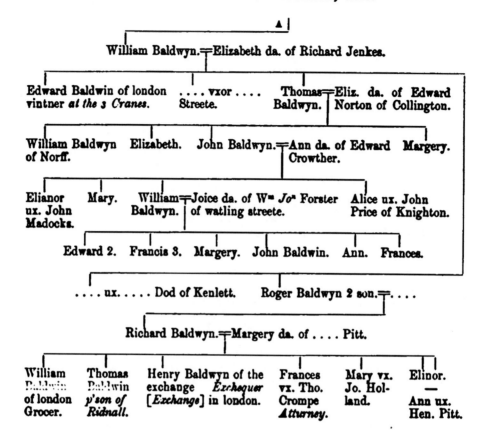

William Baldwyn.=Elizabeth da. of Richard Jenkes.

Edward Baldwin of london vintner *at the 3 Cranes.*

.... vxor .... Streete.

Thomas=Eliz. da. of Edward Baldwyn. | Norton of Collington.

William Baldwyn of Norff.

Elizabeth.

John Baldwyn.=Ann da. of Edward Crowther.

Margery.

Elianor ux. John Madocks.

Mary.

William=Joice da. of Wᵐ *Joⁿ* Forster Baldwyn. | of watling streete.

Alice ux. John Price of Knighton.

Edward 2.   Francis 3.   Margery.   John Baldwin.   Ann.   Frances.

.... ux. .... Dod of Kenlett.   Roger Baldwyn 2 son.=....

Richard Baldwyn.=Margery da. of .... Pitt.

William Baldwin of london Grocer.

Thomas Baldwin *y'son of Ridnall.*

Henry Baldwyn of the exchange *Exchequer* [*Exchange*] in london.

Frances vx. Tho. Crompe *Atturney.*

Mary vx. Jo. Holland.

Elinor. — Ann ux. Hen. Pitt.

Banaster or Banester of Hadnal.

Harl. 1241, fo. 35.   Harl. 615, fo. 261ᵇ.   S., fo. 56ᵃ.

ARMS: Harl. 1241.—*Argent, on a cross fleurée sable a plate.*
CREST.—*A peacock close proper.*
MOTTO.—AGERE ET PATI FORSSIA.

Thomas Banastar of=Eliza da. to Sʳ Robʹt Corbett Hadnoll 8 H. 6. | of Morton.

Humphrey Banastar.=....

1. Richard Banastar.=....

Phillipp Banastar.=....

Peter Banaster of Hadnoll.

Phillipp Banaster.

Banester of Lacon.

Harl. 1241, fo. 35.   Harl. 615, fo. 261ᵇ.   S., fo. 55ᵇ.

Raph Banaster (of Laken).=*.... da. to .... Eaton of Eaton.*

John Banaster.=*....*

Randolpe (Robart) Banaster=*Eliner da. to [Edward]* of Hadnoll [Hodnell].   Burton.*

Rob't (Edwards) Banaster=*Mary da. to Rich. Hussey of of Lacon.   Batsfeeld [Battlefield].*   [*Thomas Banester of London.*]

Edward Banaster.†=*Ellen da. to Edw. Brereton.*

Katherine da. to=*Edward Banaster*=*Ellen (Elynor) da.*   *Robert Banaster Thomas Ireland   of Hadnoll [Hod-   to Rich. Lacon of   2 sonne to Ed- 2 wife.   nell].   Willey [Wildey].   ward.*

John (Jone)   Rouland Banaster=*Mary da. to Tho.   Anne.   Susanna.   Andrew Banaster.   of Lacon.   Flasgett of London.   2 sonne.*

Richard 2 sonne.   Rouland Banaster of Lacon 1593.   1. Susanna.   Rebecka.

Banaster, or Banester, of Wem.

Harl. 1241, fo. 34ᵇ.   S., fo. 55.

[ARMS.—*Argent, a cross formée sable.*]

Nicholas Banaster.=*Anne da. to .... Preston.*

Lawrence Banaster=*Elizabeth da. & sole hei. to Rob't*=*Wᵐ Charlton 2 husband.   Allen wid. to Wᵐ Charlton.   1 husband.*

Sʳ Robert Banaster   William &   Sʳ Richard=*Winifred da. to   Elizabeth w⁰ Kᵗ Mʳ of yᵉ houshold   Margarett   Banaster of   Edward Norris of   Edw. Brulg- to K. James.   ob. [s.p.].   Wem.   Speak co. Lanc.   man.*

* In Shrewsbury MS., fo. 55ᵇ, the christian name was "Edward" and was afterwards altered to "John." There is a note to the effect that "Edward" is correct.
† This generation is omitted in Harl. MS. 615.

E

Bardsey, or Barzey, of Shrewsbury.

Harl. 1896, fo. 30ᵇ.   S., fo. 35ᵇ.

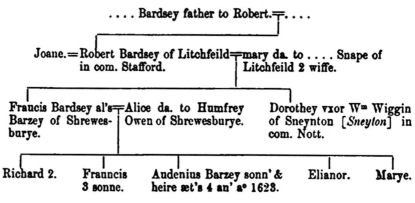

.... Bardsey father to Robert.⊤....

Joane.═Robert Bardsey of Litchfeild⊤mary da. to .... Snape of
         in com. Stafford. | Litchfeild 2 wiffe.

Francis Bardsey al's═Alice da. to Humfrey   Dorothey vxor Wᵐ Wiggin
Barzey of Shrewes- | Owen of Shrewesburye.   of Sneynton [Sneyton] in
burye.   com. Nott.

Richard 2.   Frauncis   Audenius Barzey sonn' &   Elianor.   Marye.
          3 sonne.   heire æt's 4 an' a° 1623.

FRA. BARDSEY.

Barker of Wollerton, Coulshurst, and Haughmond.

Harl. 1396, fo. 19ᵇ.   Harl. 1241, ff. 12, 93ᵇ.   Harl. 615, fo. 253ᵇ.   S., ff. 23, 24.

ARMS.—*Gules, a fesse checky or and azure between six annulets of the second.*
CREST.—*A falcon reguardant argent, wings endorsed or, beaked and belled of the
second, jesses gules.*

A patent granted to James Barker of Haghmond in com. Salop, Esq., by Will'm
Harvy, Clarenceux King of Armes, 1562, a° 4 Queene Elizabeth.

[These armes were confirmed by Cooke 17 Dec. 1582 to Rowland Barker of
Wollerton, Salop, son of Edward, son of John (Ashmol MS. of Grants, No. 844).
'Guillim,' 1724, page 248.]

In Harl. 1241, fo. 12, the above coat is given, quartering : *Azure, two bars
argent, a canton sable thereon upon a chevron between three pheons of the second as
many mullets* of the third* [Sir Rowland Hill, Lord Mayor of London—Vis. Lond.
1633, page 48].

ARMS : Harl. 1396.—*Quarterly: 1 and 4, Azure, five escallops in cross or,* for BARKER ;†
         2, *Gules, on a fesse between three saltires argent an annulet sable,* for GOULSTON;
         3, *Argent, on a fesse between six cross-crosslets fitchée sable three escallops or,*
         for TITLEY.

---

* Shrewsbury MS., fo. 23, has a wolf's head between two mullets on the chevron.
† Leigh of Stoneleigh quarters Barker *alias* Coverall of Camo, co. Salop: Azure, two bars
and in chief a griffin's head between two mullets argent (Vis. Warwickshire, p. 81); and the same
arms appear in Vis. of London, 1568, for Barker *alias* Gery of Wollerton, co. Salop.

ARMS.—*Azure, five escallops in cross or.*[*]
CREST.—*On a rock argent a falcon close or.*

Randulfe de Couerall⹀Margerett da. to Petter Pigott of
A° 12 E. 2. | Willaston in com. Salop.

William Barker ali's Couerall de Couerall⹀Margarett da. & heire to ....
[Coverall or Corverall]. | Goulston of goulston.

John Barker⹀.... | William Barker of Aston in Charely⹀.... da. & heire to
ali's Couerall | [Claverley] home juxta Brugs al's .... Colccloughe.
of Coulshurst. | bridge north.

Barker of Woluerton.
.... John Barker al's Couerall⹀Elizabeth da. to Thomas Hill (*of Hodnet & one of*
of Woluerton (Wollerton) in | *the coheirs*) sister & heire to Sr Rowland Hill K^t
com. Salop. | maior of London [1549, who purchased Haghmond].

Barker of Haughmond.
James Barker⹀Dorothy da. to Rich. Cliue | Edward Barker⹀Katharen da. to
of Haghmond | of Stuche in com. Salop | of Woluerton. | Raphe Egerton
in com. Salop. | *Cliffe of Stych.* | | of Wrinhill.

.... ⹀ Elizabeth da. to | Rowland Burker Margaret | Anne wiffe to
Barker | Edward *Edmond*[†] | of Woluerton | Raphe Rode
3 sonne. | Weale widow to | [conf. arms 1582]. | de Rode in
.... Baker of Salop. | | com. Chester.

John Barker of⹀Anne da. to Thomas | [*Anne m^d* | James Barker Captayne
London March- | Westrowe of London | *to Thomas* | of Douer castell son &
ant 1623 2 son | Alderman. | *Westrowe* | heire [now Liuing a°
[Living a° 1650]. | | *Alderman.*] | 1650].

[Nathaniell æt. 26 a° 1649 ob. s.p. a° 1650.]

Richard Barker⹀Dorothey da. & heire | John Barker | Mary wiff to Nicholas
2 sonne. | to William Poyner. | 4 sonne. | Chambers. ⹀

James Barker. | Dorothey. | Elizabeth. | *Michaell.* | *Judith.*

Andrew. | Mary 2. | *Andrewe.* | *Mary.*

Margarett wiff to Andrew | Rowland Barker of Hagh-⹀Ciccley da. to Andrew
Charleton of Appeleye in | monde in com. Salop (*sonne* | Charleton of Appeleye
com. Salop. | *& heire*) [Sheriff 1585]. | [Apley Castle].

A | | B

* There is a note in Harl. 1241, "this Coate left ymp'foct in y° originall," and the falcon is there represented reguardant with wings elevated.
† *Edward* in Shrewsbury MS., fo. 24.

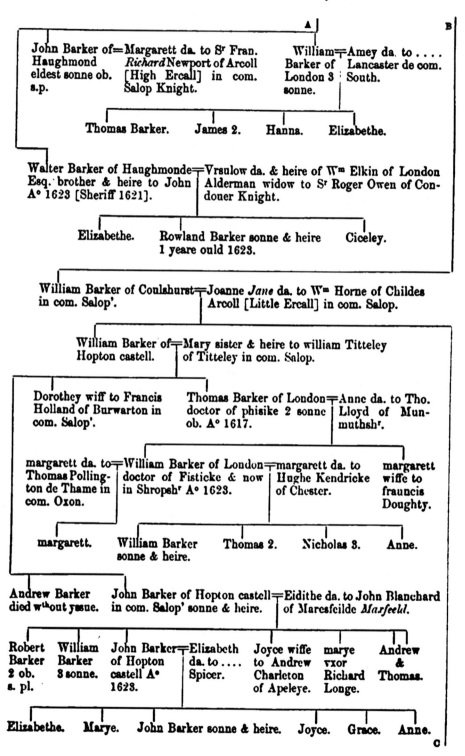

A   B

John Barker of = Margarett da. to Sr Fran. *Richard* Newport of Arcoll [High Ercall] in com. Salop Knight.
Haughmond eldest sonne ob. s.p.

William = Amey da. to . . . . Barker of Lancaster de com. London 3 South. sonne.

Thomas Barker. James 2. Hanna. Elizabethe.

Walter Barker of Haughmonde = Vrsulow da. & heire of Wm Elkin of London Alderman widow to Sr Roger Owen of Condoner Knight.
Esq. brother & heire to John Aº 1623 [Sheriff 1621].

Elizabethe. Rowland Barker sonne & heire 1 yeare ould 1623. Ciceley.

William Barker of Coulshurst = Joanne *Jane* da. to Wm Horne of Childes Arcoll [Little Ercall] in com. Salop.
in com. Salop'.

William Barker of = Mary sister & heire to william Titteley of Titteley in com. Salop.
Hopton castell.

Dorothey wiff to Francis Holland of Burwarton in com. Salop'.

Thomas Barker of London = Anne da. to Tho. Lloyd of Munmuthshr.
doctor of phisike 2 sonne ob. Aº 1617.

margarett da. to Thomas Pollington de Thame in com. Oxon. = William Barker of London doctor of Fisticke & now in Shropshr Aº 1623. = margarett da. to Hughe Kendricke of Chester.

margarett wiffe to frauncis Doughty.

margarett. William Barker sonne & heire. Thomas 2. Nicholas 3. Anne.

Andrew Barker died wthout yssue.

John Barker of Hopton castell in com. Salop' sonne & heire. = Eidithe da. to John Blanchard of Maresfeilde *Marsfeeld*.

Robert Barker 2 ob. s. pl. William Barker 3 sonne. John Barker of Hopton castell Aº 1623. = Elizabeth da. to . . . . Spicer. Joyce wiffe to Andrew Charleton of Apeleye. marye vxor Richard Longe. Andrew & Thomas.

Elizabethe. Marye. John Barker sonne & heire. Joyce. Grace. Anne.

C

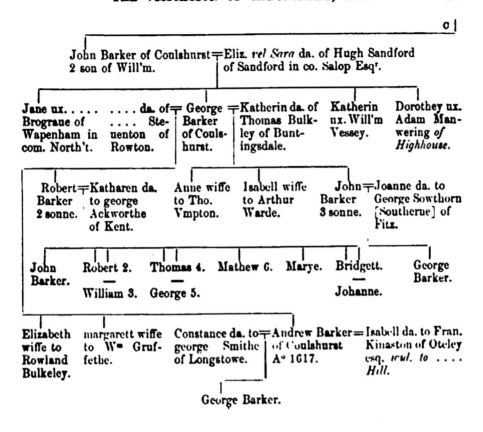

o |

John Barker of Coulshurst ⊤ Eliz. *vel Sara* da. of Hugh Sandford
2 son of Will'm. — of Sandford in co. Salop Esq'.

Jane ux. .... — .... da. of ⊤ George ⊤ Katherin da. of — Katherin — Dorothey ux.
Brograne of — .... Ste- | Barker | Thomas Bulk- ux. Will'm Adam Man-
Wapenham in — uenton of | of Couls- | ley of Bunt- Vessey. wering *of*
com. North't. — Rowton. | hurst. | ingsdale. — *Highhouse.*

Robert ⊤ Katharen da. — Anne wiffe — Isabell wiffe — John ⊤ Joanne da. to
Barker | to george — to Tho. — to Arthur — Barker | George Sowthorn
2 sonne. | Ackworthe — Vmpton. — Warde. — 3 sonne. | [Southerne] of
 | of Kent. — Fitz.

John — Robert 2. — Thomas 4. — Mathew 6. — Marye. — Bridgett. — George
Barker. — — — — Barker.
 William 3. — George 5. — — — Johanne.

Elizabeth — margarett wiffe — Constance da. to ⊤ Andrew Barker = Isabell da. to Fran.
wiffe to — to Wᵐ Gruf- — george Smithe | of Coulshurst — Kinaston of Otcley
Rowland — fethe. — of Longstowe. | A° 1617. — esq. *vxd. to ....*
Bulkeley. — — — *Hill.*

George Barker.

Barkley of Planches, Bradley, Cwdness, Clungunford, Lea Hall, and Stoke.

Harl. 1396, fo. 47.   Harl. 1241, fo. 28.   Harl. 615, fo. 248.   S, ff. 51ᵇ, 52.

ARMS: Harl. 1396.—*Gules, on a chevron between ten crosses pattée, six above and four below, argent an estoile sable*—Harl. 615 makes it *a cinquefoil.*
CREST.—*A mitre gules charged with a chevron between ten crosses*, etc., *as in the arms.*

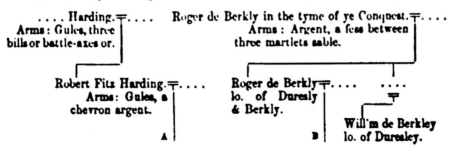

.... Harding. ⊤ .... — Roger de Berkly in the tyme of ye Conquest. ⊤ ....
Arms: Gules, three — Arms: Argent, a fess between
bills or battle-axes or. — three martlets sable.

Robert Fitz Harding. ⊤ .... — Roger de Berkly ⊤ .... — .... ⊤
Arms: Gules, a — lo. of Duresly —
chevron argent. — & Berkly. — Will'm de Berkley
 — lo. of Duresley.

▲ | B |

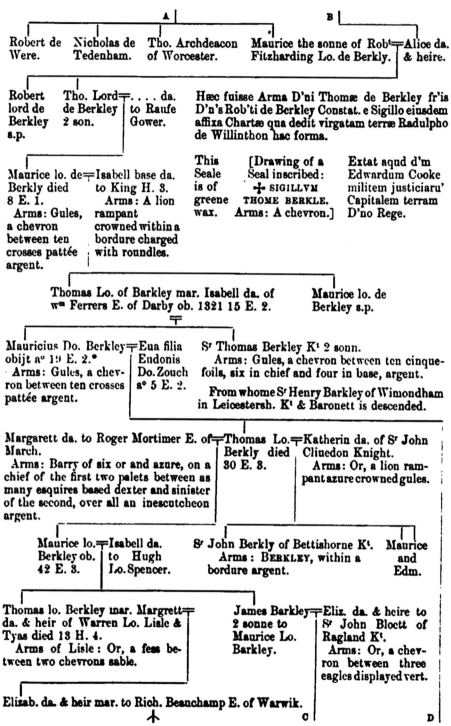

A   B

| Robert de | Nicholas de | Tho. Archdeacon | Maurice the sonne of Robᵗ⹀Alice da. |
| Were. | Tedenham. | of Worcester. | Fitzharding Lo. de Berkly. & heire. |

Robert   Tho. Lord⹀.... da.
lord de   de Berkley│to Raufe
Berkly   2 son.   Gower.
s.p.

Hæc fuisse Arma D'ni Thomæ de Berkley fr'is
D'n's Rob'ti de Berkley Constat. e Sigillo eiusdem
affixa Chartæ qua dedit virgatam terræ Radulpho
de Willinthon hac forma.

Maurice lo. de⹀Isabell base da.
Berkly died   to King H. 3.
8 E. 1.   Arms: A lion
  Arms: Gules, rampant
a chevron   crowned within a
between ten   bordure charged
crosses pattée with roundles.
argent.

This   [Drawing of a   Extat aqud d'm
Seale Seal inscribed: Edwardum Cooke
is of   ✠ SIGILLVM militem justiciaru'
greene THOME BERKLE. Capitalem terram
wax.   Arms: A chevron.] D'no Rege.

Thomas Lo. of Barkley mar. Isabell da. of   Maurice lo. de
wᵐ Ferrers E. of Darby ob. 1321 15 E. 2.   Berkley s.p.

Mauricius Do. Berkley⹀Eua filia   Sʳ Thomas Berkley Kᵗ 2 sonn.
obijt aᵒ 19 E. 2.*   Eudonis   Arms: Gules, a chevron between ten cinque-
 Arms: Gules, a chev- Do. Zouch foils, six in chief and four in base, argent.
ron between ten crosses aᵒ 5 E. 2.
pattée argent.   From whome Sʳ Henry Barkley of Wimondham
                  in Leicestersh. Kᵗ & Baronett is descended.

Margarett da. to Roger Mortimer E. of⹀Thomas Lo.⹀Katherin da. of Sʳ John
March.   Berkly died Clinedon Knight.
 Arms: Barry of six or and azure, on a 30 E. 3.   Arms: Or, a lion ram-
chief of the first two palets between as   pant azure crowned gules.
many esquires based dexter and sinister
of the second, over all an inescutcheon
argent.

Maurice lo.⹀Isabell da.   Sʳ John Berkly of Bettishorne Kᵗ. Maurice
Berkley ob.│to Hugh   Arms: BERKLEY, within a and
42 E. 3.   Lo. Spencer. bordure argent.   Edm.

Thomas lo. Berkley mar. Margrett⹀   James Barkley⹀Eliz. da. & heire to
da. & heir of Warren Lo. Lisle &   2 sonne to │Sʳ John Bloctt of
Tyas died 13 H. 4.   Maurice Lo. Ragland Kᵗ.
 Arms of Lisle: Or, a fess be- Barkley.   Arms: Or, a chev-
tween two chevrons sable.   ron between three
                          eagles displayed vert.

Elizab. da. & heir mar. to Rich. Beauchamp E. of Warwik.

A   C   D

* The pedigree in Shrewsbury MS., fo. 51ᵇ, begins here, and does not give the descendants
of Thomas, Lord Barkeley.

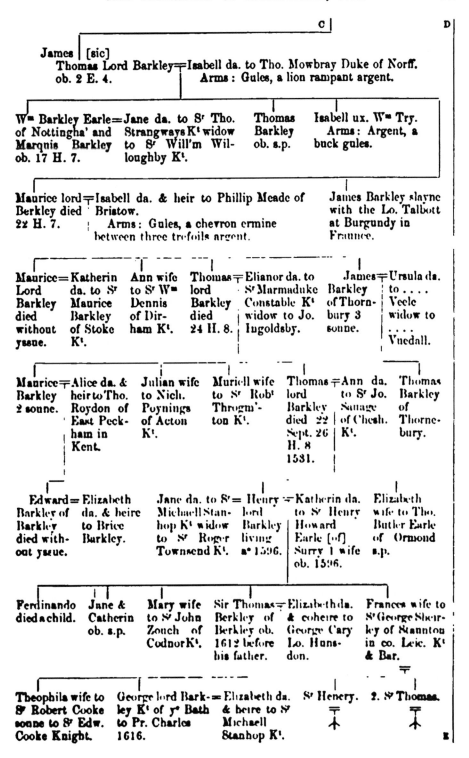

C | D |

James | [sic]

Thomas Lord Barkley══Isabell da. to Tho. Mowbray Duke of Norff.
ob. 2 E. 4.   Arms: Gules, a lion rampant argent.

Wm Barkley Earle══Jane da. to Sr Tho.   Thomas   Isabell ux. Wm Try.
of Nottingha' and   Strangways K^t widow   Barkley   Arms: Argent, a
Marqnis Barkley   to Sr Will'm Wil-   ob. s.p.   buck gules.
ob. 17 H. 7.   loughby K^t.

Maurice lord══Isabell da. & heir to Phillip Meade of   James Barkley slayne
Berkley died   Bristow.   with the Lo. Talbott
22 H. 7.   Arms: Gules, a chevron ermine   at Burgundy in
        between three trefoils argent.   Fraunce.

| Maurice Lord Barkley died without yssue. | Katherin da. to Sr Maurice Barkley of Stoke K^t. | Ann wife to Sr Wm Dennis of Dirham K^t. | Thomas lord Barkley died 24 H. 8. | Elianor da. to Sr Marmaduke Constable K^t widow to Jo. Ingoldsby. | James Barkley of Thornbury 3 sonne. | Ursula da. to .... Veele widow to .... Vnedall. |

| Maurice Barkley 2 sonne. | Alice da. & heir to Tho. Roydon of East Peckham in Kent. | Julian wife to Nich. Poynings of Acton K^t. | Muriell wife to Sr Robt Throgm'ton K^t. | Thomas lord Barkley died 22 Sept. 26 H. 8 1531. | Ann da. to S^r Jo. Sauage of Chesh. K^t. | Thomas Barkley of Thornebury. |

| Edward Barkley of Barkley died without yssue. | Elizabeth da. & heire to Brice Barkley. | Jane da. to Sr Michaell Stanhop K^t widow to Sr Roger Townsend K^t. | Henry lord Barkley living a^o 1596. | Katherin da. to Sr Henry Howard Earle [of] Surry 1 wife ob. 1596. | Elizabeth wife to Tho. Butler Earle of Ormond s.p. |

| Ferdinando died a child. | Jane & Catherin ob. s.p. | Mary wife to Sr John Zouch of Codnor K^t. | Sir Thomas Berkley of Berkley ob. 1612 before his father. | Elizabeth da. & coheire to George Cary Lo. Hunsdon. | Frances wife to Sr George Shearley of Stannton in co. Leic. K^t & Bar. |

| Theophila wife to Sr Robert Cooke sonne to Sr Edw. Cooke Knight. | George lord Barkley K^t of y^e Bath to Pr. Charles 1616. | Elizabeth da. & heire to Sr Michaell Stanhop K^t. | Sr Henery. | 2. Sr Thomas. |

E |

E

Joh'es Berkeley cui pater=.... | Maurice de Berkley.   Peter.
eius dedit Planches.   Arms: Gules, a chevron ermine between   —
  Arms: Gules, a chevron   ten crosses pattée argent.   Iuo.
between three crosses
pattée argent.   The Barkleys of Stoke Gifford in Glouc.
                            & of Bruitam [Bruton] in co. Som'sett
                            are descended from this Maurice.

Edmundus Berkley.=....

Joh's Berkley de Planches.=....

Ed'r'us *Edmund* Berkley de Planches aº 14 E. 4.=....

Joh'es Berkley=.... filia et hæres Joh'es Knight   quæ attulit marito medietatem
de Planches.   de Fekenham in com. Wigorn.   manerij de Bradley et Stoke in
                                                    com. Wigorn.

Ed'r'us *Edmond* Berkley de Bradley=.... filia Tho. Poyner de
Stoke et Planches.   Beslow in com. Salop.

John Barkley de Bradley Stoke=*Sibill da. to John Mampas*
(of Cressage).   *(Maupas).*

Elizabetha fil.=Willimus=Katherina   Edwardus Berkley   *Margarett*   *Elinor vxor*
Ric'i Day de   Berkley fil.Willimi   fil. et hæres s.p. *vxor Jo*   *Edw. ap*
Hattone   2 fil. & Chambers   —   *Gardner.*   *Rice.*
[*Hawne*] in   hæres   de com.   Alicia nupta Hen.   —   —
Parochia de   vendidit Stafford   Stanley de Lea-   *Anne vxor* *Joane vxor*
Warfeild   Planches Ar. vx. j.   Hall in com.   *Henry*   *Rich. Hor-*
[*Worfield*]   (*of Cres-*   Radnor.   *Stanley.*   *den.*
relicta Will'i *sage co.*
Felton.   *Salop*).   WILLIAM BARKLEY.

Willimus Berkley de Clunganford [Clungunford]=Francisca filia George
in co. Salop *Mr of Arts p'son of Glyngunford* Detton de Detton in
3 fil. 1623.   co. Salop Ar.

Samuell   Willimus 3.   Maria.   Susanna.   Edwardus.   Francisca.
Berkley   —   —   —   —   —
ætatis 23   Edwardus 4.   Elizabetha. Hester.   Alicia.   Josephus
an' 1623.   —   —   —   s.p.
—   Anna.   Jana.   Elizabetha.
George 2.   —
                          Francisca.

F

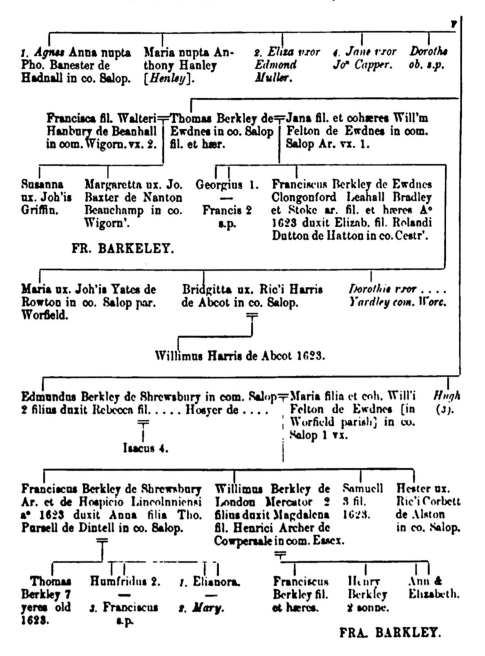

1. Agnes Anna nupta Pho. Banester de Hadnall in co. Salop.   Maria nupta Anthony Hanley [*Henley*].   *2. Eliza vxor Edmond Muller.*   *4. Jane vxor Jo^n Capper.*   *Dorothe ob. s.p.*

Francisca fil. Walteri Hanbury de Beanhall in com. Wigorn. vx. 2. = Thomas Berkley de Ewdnes in co. Salop fil. et hær. = Jana fil. et cohæres Will'm Felton de Ewdnes in com. Salop Ar. vx. 1.

Susanna ux. Joh'is Griffin.   Margaretta ux. Jo. Baxter de Nanton Beauchamp in co. Wigorn'.

FR. BARKELEY.

Georgius 1. — Francis 2 s.p.   Franciscus Berkley de Ewdnes Clongonford Leahall Bradley et Stoke ar. fil. et hæres A° 1623 duxit Elizab. fil. Rolandi Dutton de Hatton in co. Cestr'.

Maria ux. Joh'is Yates de Rowton in co. Salop par. Worfield.   Bridgitta ux. Ric'i Harris de Abcot in co. Salop.   *Dorothie vxor . . . . Yardley com. Worc.*

Willimus Harris de Abcot 1623.

Edmundus Berkley de Shrewsbury in com. Salop = Maria filia et coh. Will'i Felton de Ewdnes [in Worfield parish] in co. Salop 1 vx.   *Hugh (5).*
2 filius duxit Rebecca fil. . . . . Hosyer de . . . .

Isacus 4.

Franciscus Berkley de Shrewsbury Ar. et de Hospicio Lincolnniensi a° 1623 duxit Anna filia Tho. Pursell de Dintell in co. Salop.   Willimus Berkley de London Mercator 2 filius duxit Magdalena fil. Henrici Archer de Cowpersale in com. Essex.   Samuell 3 fil. 1623.   Hester ux. Ric'i Corbett de Alston in co. Salop.

Thomas Berkley 7 yeres old 1623.   Humfridus 2. — 3. Franciscus s.p.   *1. Elianora.* — *2. Mary.*   Franciscus Berkley fil. et hæres.   Henry Berkley 2 sonne.   Ann & Elizabeth.

FRA. BARKLEY.

Barnfeld of Edgmond and Newport.

Harl. 1396, fo. 23.   Harl. 1241, fo. 105.   S., fo. 27.

ARMS : Harl. 1396.—*Or, on a bend gules three mullets argent, an annulet for difference, sable.*

CREST.—*A lion's head erased sable, ducally crowned gules.*

[These arms and crest were confirmed, 18 May 1604, to Robert Bamfield, or Barnfield, of Edgmond, co. Salop, a kinsman of Sir Amyas Barnfeld of Poultemore, co. Devon.—'Guillim,' 1724, p. 102.]

Walter Barnfeld.=Grace da. of Sr Raufe Pudsey Kt.

Walter Barnfeild of Poulmore in com. Deuon.=Ellen da. of Nicho. Eyton of Wigmore Knight *Sr Nicholas Etton of Wildemore by the Earle of Salop's da.* [Eyton super Wildmores].

Thomas Barnfeild.=Ann Warde.

William Barnfeild of Newport 2 sonne.=. . . .

John Barnfeild of Newport.=Alice da. of Francis Palmer of Arrold *Arcoll.*

| Robert s.p. — Richard s.p. | John s.p. — Joane *Jane* s.p. | Will'm Barn-feld of New-port Aᵒ 1623.= | Eliz. da. of Nicholas Pare *Nicholas Pope Clerke of yᵉ Kitchen.* | Frances vx. . . . . Caldecot *Collcott.* — Isabell vx. Foulk Roberts. | Elizabeth vx. Tho. Nowell. |

Robert Barnfeld.=Ellynor Taylor.

Richard Barnfeild of Edgmond *Edgcombe.*=Mary *yongest* da. of Jo. Skrymshire of Newbery *Norbury* in com. Staff.

| Richard Barnfeild [the Poet] son & heir 1604 [born 1574 at Norbury, died 1627]. | Robert [*Roger*] Barn-feld of Edgmond *Edg-combe* 2 sonne *1604.*=*Milburghe* da. of John Brooke of Madley Esq. | John Barn-feld 3 son. |

Ann.   Mary.

Robert Barnfeld 2 sonne *1604.*=Ellen da. of Thurstan Woodcock.

▲

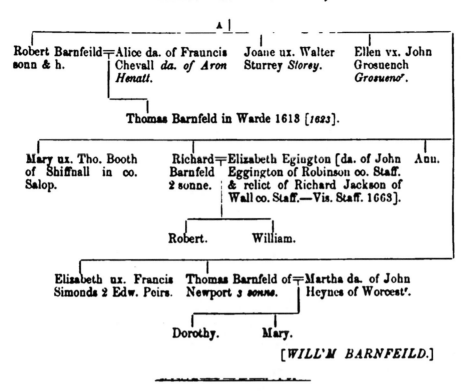

A |

Robert Barnfeild=Alice da. of Frauncis   Joane ux. Walter   Ellen vx. John
sonn & h.   Chevall *da. of Aron*   Sturrey *Storey.*   Grosuench
   Henatt.   *Grosueno*.

Thomas Barnfeld in Warde 1618 [*1623*].

Mary ux. Tho. Booth   Richard=Elizabeth Egiugton [da. of John   Ann.
of Shiffnall in co.   Barnfeld   Eggington of Robinson co. Staff.
Salop.   2 sonne.   & relict of Richard Jackson of
   Wall co. Staff.—Vis. Staff. 1663].

Robert.   William.

Elizabeth ux. Francis   Thomas Barnfeld of=Martha da. of John
Simonds 2 Edw. Peirs.   Newport *3 sonne.*   Heynes of Worcest.

Dorothy.   Mary.

[*WILL'M BARNFEILD.*]

𝕭arton of 𝕯idleston.

S., fo. 33b.

[ARMS.—*Argent, a bend between two double-colises sable.*

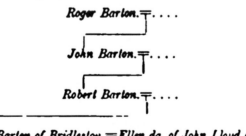

Roger Barton.=. . . .

John Barton.=. . . .

Robert Barton.=. . . .

Edw[d] Lloyd Barton of Bridleston.=*Ellen da. of John Lloyd of Halghton.*

Robert 2[d] son.   *Jane uxor John*   *Lowry ux.*   *Alice.*   *Thomas*=*Jone da.*
—   *Edwards of S[t]*   *Rob[t] ap*   *Ball of*   *to Edward*
John 3.   *Matthew's.*   *John ap*   *Malpas.*   *Jones.*
—   *Howell of*
Roger 4.   *Norton.*

Katherine.   *Ellen.*   *Ermyn.*   *Owen Barton of Didleston*=*Jenne da. & heirs to*
                [*Duddleston*].   *Tho. Ball of Malpas.*]

Baugh of Aldon Court.

Harl. 1396, fo. 28^b. S., fo. 31.

ARMS.—*Gules, a fesse vair between three mullets argent.*
CREST.—*Out of a ducal coronet or a talbot sejant sable.*

[These arms and crest were confirmed by Robt Cooke, Clarenceux, 11 Nov. 1579, to Rowland Baugh of Twyniage (Twyning), co. Glouc. (Harl. MS. 1441).

They were confirmed to the Aldon Court Family 1588, who were thus apparently descended (see Visit. Glouc.).]

John Baugh of Aldencourte=Joanne da. to John Dale of
in com. Salope.   Langtoll in com. Salope.

- William Baughe of Alden 2 son'.
- Thomas Baugh of Aldencourte sonn & heire.=Dorothey da. to George Parkes of Bromfeild in com. Salope.
- Richard Baughe of Norton in com. Radnor 3 sonne.
- Thomas Baughe of Sapy in com. Worster 4 sonne.

- William 2 sonne ob. a p'le.
- Henrey Baughe of Aldencourte son' & h. 1623.=Alice da. to Francis Holland of Boreatton [*Borealton*] [Burwarton] in com. Salope [died 1662, M.I. Stokesay Church].
- Thomas Baughe de Aldencourt 3 sonne living 1623.

- John 2 sonne.
- Rowland 3 sonne.
- Thomas Baughe son' & heire æt'is 21 1623.
- Marye.
- Margarett.

HENRY BAUGHE.

Bayley.

S., fo. 307^a.

ARMS.—[Argent, a chevron between three martlets sable.]
CREST.—*A griffin segreant gules guttée de larmes.*

[*Thomas Bailey of .... in com. Salop.*=*Alice da. to .... Rey of the Hawtt.*

William Bayley.=*Jane da. to Nich. Naunton by Dowce Doulog.*

- *Thomas Bayley a Captaine ob. s.p.*
- *Elizabeth. — Dionysia. — Alice.*
- *William Bayley Captaine.*=*Anne da. to John Bower.*
- *Frances. — Mary.*
- *Anne. — Margery.*
- *George Bayly a Lieutenant.*

William Bayley sonne & heire.]

Bayllie, or Bayley, of Shrewsbury.

Harl. 1396, fo. 43ᵇ. Harl. 1241, fo. 115. S., fo. 306ᵇ.

ARMS: Harl. 1396.—*Quarterly: 1 and 4, Vert, a chevron or between three unicorns' heads erased argent, armed of the second*—BAYLY in Shrewsbury MS.; *2 and 3, Gules, a fesse or between three birds close—argent*, PONTESBURY in Shrewsbury MS.

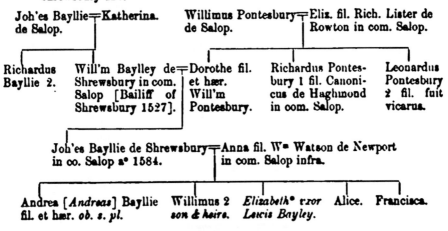

Joh'es Bayllie de Salop.=Katherina.

Willimus Pontesbury de Salop.=Eliz. fil. Rich. Lister de Rowton in com. Salop.

Richardus Bayllie 2.

Will'm Baylley de Shrewsbury in com. Salop [Bailiff of Shrewsbury 1527].=Dorothe fil. et hær. Will'm Pontesbury.

Richardus Pontesbury 1 fil. Canonicus de Haghmond in com. Salop.

Leonardus Pontesbury 2 fil. fuit vicarus.

Joh'es Bayllie de Shrewsbury in co. Salop aº 1584.=Anna fil. Wᵐ Watson de Newport in com. Salop infra.

Andrea [*Andreas*] Bayllie fil. et hær. ob. s. pl.

Willimus 2 *son & heire*.

Elizabeth[*] *uxor Lewis Bayley*.

Alice.

Francisca.

Bechfield, now Bettisfield, of Woden.

S., fo. 21ᵇ.

[*Humfrey Bechfield*.=. . . .

John Bechfield.=. . . .

John Bechfield.=*Margarett da. to John Badi of Worden parish*.

Howell Bechfield of Worden aº 1598.=*Anne da. to Thomas Browne of Westbury*.

Jane ux. Thomas ap Owen.

George 1 s.p. — *Thomas 2 s.p.*

Edward 3 s.p.

Richard Bechfield Mʳ of Arts.

Ralph Bechfield 4 son.=*Margery da. to Hugh Wilcocks.*

Joane ux. John Draper.

Edward Owen.

Alice.

Edward 3 sonne. — *Richard 3 sonne.*

William Bechfield.

George 1. — *Thomas 2.* — *Richard 3.*

William 4. — *Henry 5.* — *John 6.*

Francis Draper 1.]

[*] She does not appear in Shrewsbury MS, fo. 306.

Beeston of Shrewsbury.

Harl. 1396, fo. 49[b].   Harl. 1241, fo. 128[b].

ARMS: Harl. 1396.—*Argent, on a bend between six bees volant sable a mullet—or,* Harl. 1241—*for difference.*

Rand'us Beeston a familia les Beestons in co. Cestr' oriundus.=. . . .

Ric'us Beeston de Shrewsbury=Elianora fil. Georgij Harborow=Richardus Mitton
in com. Salop.   [Harborne ?].   2 vir.

Randulphus=. . . . fil.   Johannes=Sibillia fil. Joh'is   Adam   Isabella   Jana ux.
Beeston de | Johannis   Beeston.   Knight *by y[e] da.*   Mitton.   ux. Tho.   Edwardi
Shrewsbury | Leighton.   *of Kynaston.*   Oteley.   Ireland.
1602.

Thomas Beeston.   Richardus s.p.

Beist of Atcham.

S., fo. 307[b].

[ARMS.—*Gules, three bundles of three arrows, 2 and 1, or, headed and feathered argent, tied with ribbons of the third.*
CREST.—*A cubit arm holding a bow.*

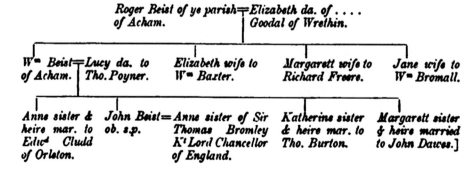

Roger Beist of ye parish=Elizabeth da. of . . . .
of Acham.   Goodal of Wrethin.

W[m] Beist=Lucy da. to   Elizabeth wife to   Margarett wife to   Jane wife to
of Acham. | Tho. Poyner.   W[m] Baxter.   Richard Freere.   W[m] Bromall.

Anne sister &   John Beist=Anne sister of Sir   Katherine sister   Margarett sister
heire mar. to | ob. s.p.   Thomas Bromley   & heire mar. to   & heire married
Edw[d] Cluud   K[t] Lord Chancellor   Tho. Burton.   to John Dawes.]
of Orleton.   of England.

Benbowe* of Newport and Bolas.

Harl. 1396, fo. 34ᵇ.   Harl. 1241, fo. 120.   S., ff. 40ᵇ, 41.

ARMS: Harl. 1396.—*Sable, two bows endorsed in pale or, garnished gules, stringed argent, between two bundles of arrows (three in each) of the second, barbed and feathered of the fourth, banded of the third.*

CREST.—*A harpy close or, face proper, her head wreathed with a chaplet of roses gules.*
[*Per Camden Clarenc.*]†

ARMS: PERYNS: Shrewsbury MS.—[Argent], *on a chevron* [sable] *between three pine-cones* [vert] *three leopards' faces* [of the field].

Peryns of Brockton.

Petter Peryns of=Dorothey da. to John Chardwicke in com. Derbye. | Parker of north Ice [*Norhill*] in co. Derbye.

Roger Benbowe=.... of Newport in com. Salope.

John Peryns of=Ciceley da. & heire Brockton in com. Salope. | to Wᵐ Brampton of Chesterfeilde.

Thomas Benbowe=Margarett da. to of newport in com. salope. | Anthoney Bayley de com. Stafford.

Roger Peryns of=Elizabeth da. to Brockton in com. Salope. | .... Stoakes.

Thomas Benbowe of=Elizabeth da. to Roger Peryns Newport in com. salope. | of Brockton in com. salope.

Gilbert Peryns of Brockton in com. Salope.

| Thomas s.p. — Gilbert s.p. | Robert s.p. — William ob. s. pl. | Issabell uxor John Bowes of newport. | Elizabethe vxor Tho. grosvenor of nantwiche in com. Chester. | Joanne uxor John Robson of newport. | John & William ob. s. pl. | Alice uxor John Melhuishe [*Mellinigh*] of London. |

Anne vxor Robert Dymbleton de London.

Dorothey da. to=John Benbowe [*of Newport co.*=Katharen da. John Prowde of *Salop now*] of London clarke of | & heire to Sutton in com. | the Crowne 1623 mar. Elizabeth | Robert Sparke salop 1 wiffe. | da. to Will'm Hodges of *Ilchester* | 2 wiffe. Somersetsh. he died 1625.

Saraha [*Sarah*] & Marye *Sara & Marg'* ob. s. p'le.

William Benbowe borne 25 Marche Aᵒ 1621.

Robert & Anne obijt s. p'le ob. infans.

JO. BENBOWE. A

* In the sixteenth century this name was spelt *Bendbow.*
† This refers to a grant of these arms and crest, by William Camden, Clarenceux, to John Benbow, Deputy Clerk of the Crown in Chancery, who died 7 October 1625 and was buried at St. Martin's in the Fields.

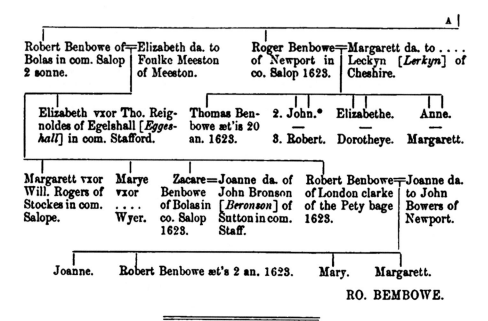

Robert Benbowe of=Elizabeth da. to   Roger Benbowe=Margarett da. to . . . .
Bolas in com. Salop | Foulke Meeston   of Newport in | Leckyn [Lerkyn] of
2 sonne. | of Meeston.   co. Salop 1623. | Cheshire.

Elizabeth vxor Tho. Reig-   Thomas Ben-   2. John.*   Elizabethe.   Anne.
noldes of Egelshall [Egges- bowe æt'is 20   —   ———   ———
hall] in com. Stafford.   an. 1623.   3. Robert. Dorotheye.   Margarett.

Margarett vxor   Marye   Zacare=Joanne da. of   Robert Benbowe=Joanne da.
Will. Rogers of vxor   Benbowe | John Bronson   of London clarke | to John
Stockes in com. . . . . of Bolas in | [Beronson] of   of the Pety bage | Bowers of
Salope.   Wyer.   co. Salop Sutton in com. 1623. | Newport.
                         1623.   Staff.

Joanne.   Robert Benbowe æt's 2 an. 1623.   Mary.   Margarett.

RO. BEMBOWE.

Bentall of Bentall.

Harl. 1396, fo. 47ᵇ.   Harl. 1241, fo. 57ᵇ.   S., ff. 52ᵇ, 53.

ARMS : Harl. 1396.—*Quarterly: 1 and 4, Or, a lion rampant queuée furchée azure crowned gules*—BENTALL in Shrewsbury MS. ; *2, Azure, a chevron ermine between three swans with wings expanded argent*—WOLRICH in Shrewsbury MS.; *3, Argent, a cross moline sable [azure ?] within a bordure engrailed azure [sable ?], in dexter chief a bird reguardant gules*—DUDMASTON in Shrewsbury MS.
CREST.—*On a ducal coronet or a leopard statant argent, spotted sable.*

Rogerus Bentall de Bentall in co. Salop.=. . . .

Robertus Bentall de Bentall in com. Salop.=. . . .

Humfridus Bentall de Bentall in com. Salop.=. . . .

Henricus Bentall de Bentall in com. Salop.=. . . .

Hamond Bentall de Bentall in com. Salop.=. . . .

* This John Benbow served first in the army of the Parliament and afterwards in the King's forces. He fought at the battle of Worcester, was afterwards taken prisoner, condemned by court-martial at Chester, together with the Earl of Derby and Sir Thomas Featherstonhough, was shot in the cabbage garden under Shrewsbury Castle 15 October 1651, and buried at St. Chad's Church.

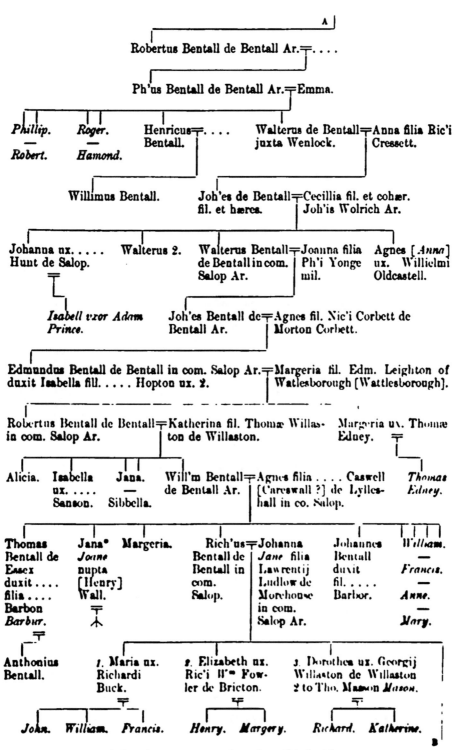

A |

Robertus Bentall de Bentall Ar.⊤.....

Ph'us Bentall de Bentall Ar.⊤Emma.

Phillip. — *Robert.*   *Roger.* — *Hamond.*   Henricus⊤.....
Bentall.   Walterus de Bentall⊤Anna filia Ric'i
juxta Wenlock.   Cressett.

Willimus Bentall.   Joh'es de Bentall⊤Cecillia fil. et cohær.
fil. et hæres.   Joh'is Wolrich Ar.

Johanna ux.....   Walterus 2.   Walterus Bentall⊤Joanna filia   Agnes [*Anna*]
Hunt de Salop.   de Bentall in com.   Ph'i Yonge   ux. Willielmi
⊤   Salop Ar.   mil.   Oldcastell.

Isabell vxor Adam Prince.   Joh'es Bentall de⊤Agnes fil. Nic'i Corbett de
Bentall Ar.   Morton Corbett.

Edmundus Bentall de Bentall in com. Salop Ar.⊤Margeria fil. Edm. Leighton of
duxit Isabella fil..... Hopton ux. 2.   Watlesborough [Wattlesborough].

Robertus Bentall de Bentall⊤Katherina fil. Thomæ Willas-   Margeria ux. Thomæ
in com. Salop Ar.   ton de Willaston.   Edney. ⊤

Alicia.   Isabella   Jana.   Will'm Bentall⊤Agnes filia.... Caswell   *Thomas*
ux.....   —   de Bentall Ar.   [Careswall?] de Lylles-   *Edney.*
Sanson.   Sibbella.   hall in co. Salop.

Thomas   Jana*   Margeria.   Rich'us⊤Johanna   Johannes   *William.*
Bentall de   *Joane*   Bentall de   *Jane* filia   Bentall   —
Essex   nupta   Bentall in   Lawrentij   duxit   *Francis.*
duxit....   [Henry]   com.   Ludlow de   fil.....   —
filia....   Wall.   Salop.   Morehouse   Barbor.   *Anne.*
Barbon   ⊤   in com.   —
Barbur.   ⊼   Salop Ar.   *Mary.*
⊤

Anthonius   *1*. Maria ux.   *2*. Elizabeth ux.   *3*. Dorothea ux. Georgij
Bentall.   Richardi   Ric'i W'm Fow-   Willaston de Willaston
Buck.   ler de Bricton.   2 to Tho. Mason *Mason.*
⊤   ⊤   ⊤

John. *William.* *Francis.*   *Henry.* *Margery.*   *Richard.* *Katherine.*

B

* *Jane* does not occur in Shrewsbury MS., fo. 52ᵇ.

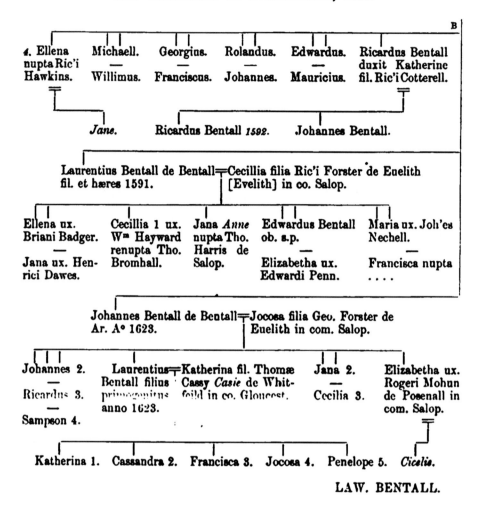

LAW. BENTALL.

Berington of Shrewsbury and Moat Hall.

Harl. 1396, fo. 45ᵇ.   Harl. 1241, fo. 97.   S., ff. 50ᵇ, 51.

ARMS: Harl. 1396.—*Quarterly:* 1 *and* 4, *Sable, three greyhounds courant in pale argent collared or, within a bordure gules*—Harl. 1241 omits the *bordure;* 2 *and* 3, *Argent, two bars sable, over all a bend gules* [LINDE].

Edward Longshankes Kinge of England⊤. . . . da. to the Earle of
by the name of Ed. 1.   ⎰ Kildare in Ireland.

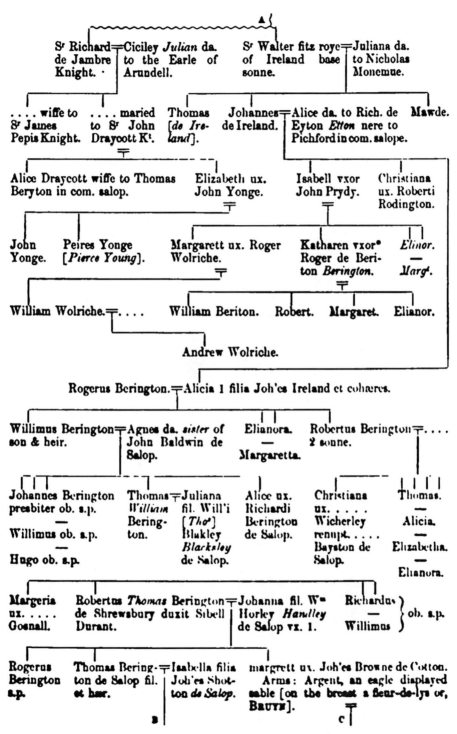

Sʳ Richard = Ciciley *Julian* da.
de Jambre   to the Earle of
Knight. ·   Arundell.

Sʳ Walter fitz royc = Juliana da.
of Ireland base   to Nicholas
sonne.   Monemue.

.... wiffe to
Sʳ James
Pepis Knight.

.... maried
to Sʳ John
Draycott Kᵗ.

Thomas
[*de Ire-
land*].

Johannes = Alice da. to Rich. de
de Ireland. Eyton *Etton* nere to
            Pichford in com. salope.

Mawde.

Alice Draycott wiffe to Thomas
Beryton in com. salop.

Elizabeth ux.
John Yonge.

Isabell vxor
John Prydy.

Christiana
ux. Roberti
Rodington.

John
Yonge.

Peires Yonge
[*Pierce Young*].

Margarett ux. Roger
Wolriche.

Katharen vxor*
Roger de Beri-
ton *Berington*.

Elinor.

Margᵗ.

William Wolriche. = ...

William Beriton.   Robert.   Margaret.   Elianor.

Andrew Wolriche.

Rogerus Berington. = Alicia 1 filia Joh'es Ireland et cohæres.

Willimus Berington = Agnes da. *sister* of
son & heir.   John Baldwin de
                     Salop.

Elianora.
—
Margaretta.

Robertus Berington = ...
2 sonne.

Johannes Berington
presbiter ob. s.p.
—
Willimus ob. s.p.
—
Hugo ob. s.p.

Thomas = Juliana
William fil. Will'i
Bering- [*Thᵒ*]
ton.   Blukley
         Blacksley
         de Salop.

Alice ux.
Richardi
Berington
de Salop.

Christiana
ux. ....
Wicherley
renupt. ....
Bayston de
Salop.

Thomas.
—
Alicia.
—
Elizabetha.
—
Elianora.

Margeria
ux. ....
Gosnall.

Robertus *Thomas* Berington = Johanna fil. Wᵐ
de Shrewsbury duxit Sibell | Horky *Handley*
Durant. | de Salop vx. 1.

Richardus ⎫
—   ⎬ ob. s.p.
Willimus ⎭

Rogerus
Berington
s.p.

Thomas Bering- = Isabella filia
ton de Salop fil. | Joh'es Shot-
et hær. | ton *de Salop.*

margrett ux. Joh'es Browne de Cotton.
Arms: Argent, an eagle displayed
sable [on the breast a fleur-de-lys or,
BAUYN].

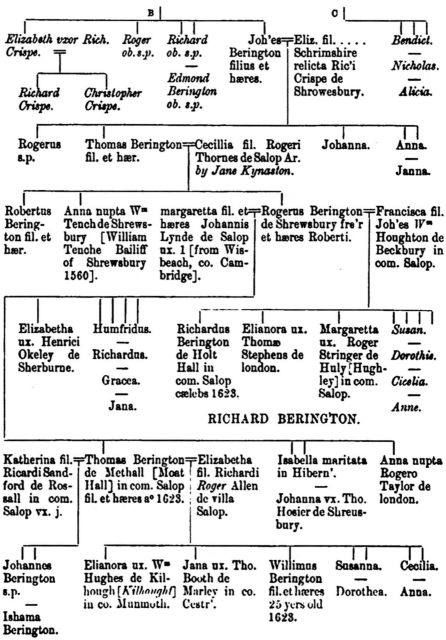

RICHARD BERINGTON.

THOMAS BERINGTON.

Berry of Ludlow.

Harl. 1396, fo. 29. S., fo. 34.

ARMS: Harl. 1396.—*Ermine, on a bend azure three fleurs-de-lis or, a crescent for difference.*

John Berry of the County of Deuon.=....

Robert Berry of Ludlowe=winifred da. to Robᵗ Hall of wotton in com. salope. | vndʳ Edge in com. wigor.

Robert 2 sonne ob. s. p'le. — Thomas Berrye of Ludlowe=margarett da. to george Esqʳ Sup'visor of Herefordsh. | Catfeilde [*Calfield*] de & Shropsh. 1623. | com. Oxon Esqʳ. — mary vxor Edw. wright of Sutton in com. Leicester.

Robert Berrye 5 years ould Aᵒ 1623.   Mary Berry.

THO. BERRY.

Betton of Great Berwick.

Harl. 1396, fo. 31. S., fo. 36.

ARMS: Harl. 1396.—*Argent, two pallets sable each charged with three cross-crosslets fitchée or.*

Thomas Betton of Berwicke in com. Salope.=....

Richard Betton of Berwicke son & heire.=....

Robert Betton of Shrewesbury [bailiff 1604?]. — Richard Betton of=.... shrewesbury. — John. — Samuell. — Thomas.

2. James. — 4. Josephe.
3. Samuell. — 5. Daniell.

Richard Betton of=Elianor da. to Berwicke in com. | Edward Purcell salope sonne & | of Oneslowe in heire Aᵒ 1623. | com. Salope. — Elianor maried to Edward Purcell of Oneslowe in com. Salope.

Edward 2.   Richard Betton sonne & heire æt's 7 ann. Aᵒ 1623.   Anne 1.   Margarett.   Lucrecia.

RICHARD BETTON.

Billingsley.

Harl. 1396, fo. 23ᵇ.   Harl. 1241, fo. 115.   S., ff. 27ᵇ, 28.

ARMS: Harl. 1396.—*Quarterly*: 1 *and* 4, *Gules, a fleur-de-lis or, a canton of the second* [BILLINGSLEY]; 2 *and* 3, *Argent, a cross sable voided of the field, five estoiles in cross between four lions rampant all of the second* [BILLINGSLEY].
CREST.—*On a mount vert a leopard couchant or, spotted sable.*

[Sir Henry Billingsley, Lord Mayor of London, bore: *Argent, within a cross voided between four lions rampant five estoiles sable; and in the 1st quarter: Gules, a fleur-de-lis and canton or.*—Visitations of London, 1568 and 1633.]

Shrewsbury MS., fo. 27, gives another coat: *Gules, a fleur-de-lis and a canton or* [BILLINGSLEY of Astley].

In Shrewsbury MS., fo. 28, the Arms are: *Argent, five lions rampant to the sinister in cross sable.* Crest: *On a mount vert a leopard couchant argent, spotted sable.*

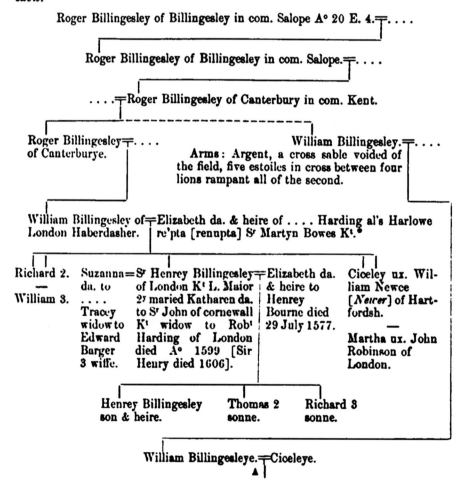

* Shrewsbury MS., fo. 27, does not name Sir Martin Bowes.

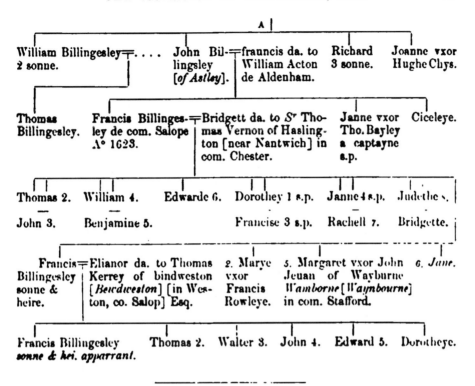

A |

William Billingesley=....   John Bil-=frauncis da. to   Richard   Joanne vxor
2 sonne.   lingsley   William Acton   3 sonne.   Hughe Chys.
                    [of Astley].   de Aldenham.

Thomas   Francis Billinges-=Bridgett da. to Sr Tho-   Janne vxor   Ciceleye.
Billingesley.   ley de com. Salope   mas Vernon of Hasling-   Tho. Bayley
            Aº 1623.   ton [near Nantwich] in   a captayne
                    com. Chester.   s.p.

Thomas 2.   William 4.   Edwarde 6.   Dorothey 1 s.p.   Janne 4 s.p.   Judethe s.

John 3.   Benjamine 5.   Francise 3 s.p.   Rachell 7.   Bridgette.

     Francis=Elianor da. to Thomas   2. Marye   5. Margaret vxor John   6. Jane.
Billingesley   Kerrey of bindweston   vxor   Jeuan of Wayburne
sonne &   [Beicdweston] [in Wes-   Francis   Wamborne [Waynbourne]
heire.   ton, co. Salop] Esq.   Rowleye.   in com. Stafford.

Francis Billingesley   Thomas 2.   Walter 3.   John 4.   Edward 5.   Dorotheye.
sonne & hei. apparrant.

Birche of Ludlow.

Harl. 1396, fo. 29ᵇ.   Harl. 1241, fo. 119ᵇ.   S., fo. 34ᵇ.

ARMS: Harl. 1396.—*Argent, a chevron between three mullets sable.*
CREST.—*A bird's head between two wings expanded sable.*

Henry Birche of Birche hall=Anne da. to Petter Hewde of Hewdshall
in com. Lancast'.   in com. Lanc. *Hedod of Howdall.*

Richard Birche of birchehall=margarett da. to .... Denneis
in com. Lancast'.   *Dennis [Denneys].*

Richard Birche of medow-=Elizabeth da. to John Loman *Lomaxe*   John Birche
crofte in com. Lanc.   by Elianor da. to petter Ingole *Yngoll.*   2 sonne.

Abdy Birche mᵣ   Josephe   Abell Birche of=Sara da. to   Anne vxor John   Alice.
of the artes 2   3 sonne.   Ludlowe in   Richard   Colyns *Collyn* of
sonne.   com. Salope.   Hopkinsons.   Cambridgeh.

Birche of Milson.

Harl. 1396, fo. 30. S., fo. 35.

[ARMS.—Argent, three fleurs-de-lis azure.]

John Birch of Pillaton hall in com. Stafford.⊤. . . .

Thomas Birche of Pillaton hall⊤Katharen da. to . . . .
in com. stafford.⊥ffletcher.

| 1. Edward.
—
2. William.
—
3. Thomas. | Isabell vxor
RichardCox
of Albridge
[Aldridge]
in com.
staff. | John Birche⊤
of milson in
com. salope
4 sonne
1623. | Elizabeth da.
to Edward
Littelton of
Pillaton hall. | Elizabeth
vxor Wᵐ
Turner of
Pencrich
in com.
Staff. | Anne vxor
Edward
Tunckes of
Pencriohe
[Penkridge]
in com. Staf-
ford. |

John Birche of milson⊤Alice da. to John Sheparde of Hill vponcote
in com. Salope 1623.⊥[Hill Luppencotc] in com. Salope.

James Birche sonne & heire.   Elizabeth.

JOHN BIRCHE, SEN.

Blonden, or Blunden, of Bishops Castle.

Harl. 1396, fo. 21.   Harl. 1241, fo. 45ᵇ.   Harl. 615, fo. 250ᵇ.   S., fo. 25.

ARMS : Harl. 1396.—*Quarterly : 1 and 4, Argent, a lion passant-guardant sable*
[azure] [BLUNDEN] ;* *2, Vert, a gryphon segreant or* [COLLINS] ; *3, Argent,*
three cocks gules combed and legged or [FORDE].
CREST.—*A demi-gryphon segreant or collared ermine.*

ARMS : Harl. 1241.—*Quarterly : 1 and 4, Argent, a lion passant-guardant sable ;*
2 and 3, Vert, a gryphon segreant or ; impaling, PLOWDEN, *Azure, a fesse*
dancettée or, in chief two fleurs-de-lis of the second.

ARMS : Harl. 615.—*Quarterly : 1 and 4, Argent, a lion passant sable ; 2 and 3, Vert,*
a gryphon segreant or.

Sʳ peter Collins Kᵗ *Collings* [of Corley ?].⊤. . . .

Adam Collins.⊤. . . .

Geffry Collins.⊤. . . . da. of . . . . Bowdler de hope Bowdler.
▲

* Shrewsbury MS., fo. 25, makes the Blunden lion *azure*, and says " p' Camden Clarenc'."

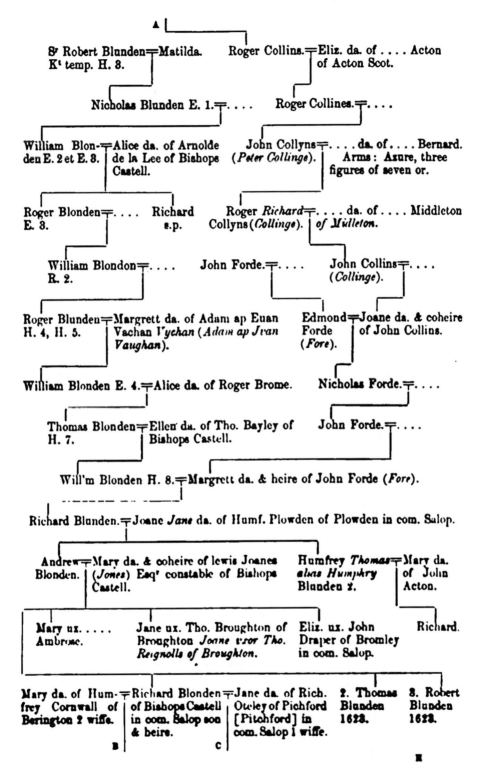

A

Sᵣ Robert Blunden=Matilda.   Roger Collins.=Eliz. da. of .... Acton
Kᵗ temp. H. 8.   of Acton Scot.

Nicholas Blunden E. 1.=....   Roger Collines.=....

William Blon-=Alice da. of Arnolde   John Collyns=.... da. of .... Bernard.
den E. 2 et E. 3. | de la Lee of Bishops   (*Peter Collinge*).   Arms: Azure, three
               | Castell.   figures of seven or.

Roger Blonden=....   Richard   Roger *Richard*=.... da. of .... Middleton
E. 3.   s.p.   Collyns(*Collinge*). | of *Midleton*.

William Blondon=....   John Forde.=....   John Collins=....
R. 2.   (*Collinge*).

Roger Blunden=Margrett da. of Adam ap Euan   Edmond=Joane da. & coheire
H. 4, H. 5. | Vachan *Vychan* (*Adam ap Jvan*   Forde | of John Collins.
           | *Vaughan*).   (*Fore*).

William Blonden E. 4.=Alice da. of Roger Brome.   Nicholas Forde.=....

Thomas Blonden=Ellen da. of Tho. Bayley of   John Forde.=....
H. 7. | Bishops Castell.

Will'm Blonden H. 8.=Margrett da. & heire of John Forde (*Fore*).

Richard Blunden.=Joane *Jane* da. of Humf. Plowden of Plowden in com. Salop.

Andrew=Mary da. & coheire of lewis Joanes   Humfrey *Thomas*=Mary da.
Blonden. | (*Jones*) Esqʳ constable of Bishops   *alias* Humphry | of John
        | Castell.   Blunden 2. | Acton.

Mary ux. ....   Jane ux. Tho. Broughton of   Eliz. ux. John   Richard.
Ambrose.   Broughton *Joane vxor Tho.*   Draper of Bromley
                 Reignolls of Broughton.   in com. Salop.

Mary da. of Hum-=Richard Blonden=Jane da. of Rich.   2. Thomas   3. Robert
frey Cornwall of | of Bishops Castell | Owley of Pichford   Blunden   Blunden
Berington 2 wiffe. | in com. Salop son | [Pitchford] in   1623.   1623.
                 | & heire. | com. Salop 1 wiffe.

B   C   E

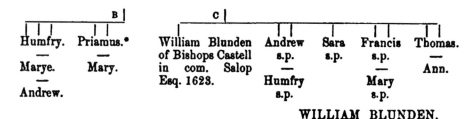

	B		C				
Humfry.	Priamus.*		William Blunden	Andrew	Sara	Francis	Thomas.
—	—		of Bishops Castell	s.p.	s.p.	s.p.	—
Marye.	Mary.		in com. Salop	—		—	Ann.
—			Esq. 1623.	Humfry		Mary	
Andrew.				s.p.		s.p.	

WILLIAM BLUNDEN.

Blount.

Harl. 1396, fo. 41ᵇ.　Harl. 1241, fo. 39.　Harl. 615, fo. 252ᵇ.
S., ff. 46ᵇ—49ᵇ.

ARMS: Harl. 1396: BLUNT DE KINLET.—*Quarterly of twenty-nine:* 1, *Barry nebulée of six or and sable,* BLOUNT ; 2, *Argent, three leopards' heads jessant de lis sable,* SODINGTON ; 3, *Or, a fret gules,* VERDON ; 4, *Or, a fesse gules,* LACY ; 5, *Per pale or and vert, a lion rampant gules,* MARSHALL ; 6, *Gules, a bend lozengy or,* MARSHALL ; 7, *Or, six lions rampant, three and three, sable,* STRONGBOWE ; 8, *Sable, three garbs argent,* MACMURGH ; 9, *Or, three chevrons gules,* CLARE ; 10, *Gules, three rests or clarions or,* CONSULL ; 11, *Azure, a lion rampant-guardant or,* FITZHAMON ; 12, *Ermine, a lion rampant gules crowned or, within a bordure engrailed sable bezantée,* CORNWALL ; 13, *Or, two lions passant gules,* BRAMPTON ; 14, *Or, two lions passant-guardant gules,* ST. VALEREY ; 15, *Barry of six vair and gules,* BREWES ; 16, *Gules, two bendlets, the upper one or, the other argent,* MILO ; 17, *Gules, five fusils in fesse or,* NEWMARCH ; 18, *Azure, three round buckles or,* REMEUILE ; 19, *Or, two ravens in pale sable,* CORBETT ; 20, *Or, on a chief indented azure three annulets of the field,* HEREFORD ; 21, *Argent, a cross the ends fleury sable, on a canton gules a lion's head erased of the first crowned or,* PESHALL ; 22, *Azure, a chevron between three mullets or,* CHETWIN ; 23, *Azure, fretty argent, a fesse gules,* CARESWELL ; 24, *Quarterly ermine and paly of six or and gules, within a bordure azure,* KNIGHTLEY ; 25, *Gules, two bars ermine,* PANTOLPH ; 26, *Argent, a cross formée fleury sable,* SWINERTON ; 27, *Gules, a cross ermine,* BEEK ; 28, *Azure, a chief gules, over all a lion rampant or,* HASTANGE ; 29, *Argent, a fret gules, the joints bezantée,* TRUSSELL.

CREST.—*On a chapeau . . . . turned up ermine, a lion statant gules, crowned or.*

ARMS: Harl. 1396: BLOUNT OF MAPLEDURHAM.—*Quarterly of eight:* 1 and 8, *Barry nebulée of six or and sable,* BLOUNT ; 2, *Vair,* BEAUCHAMP ; 3, *Sable, a fesse argent between three escallops or,* BROLT [BRITT ?] ; 4, [*Argent,*] *two wolves passant* [*sable*] *within a bordure or, charged with ten sallires gules,* AYLELA [AYALA] ; 5, *Or, a tower* [*triple towered*] *azure,* SANCHET ; 6, *Argent, a pale sable,* DELAFORD ; 7, *Azure, a chevron between three pheons or,* MOORE.

CREST.—*A wolf passant sable, between two cornets or, issuing out of a ducal coronet of the same.*

ANOTHER CREST.—*A sun or, charged with an eye.*

* Shrewsbury MS., fo. 25, gives *Priamus, Mary,* and then a second *Mary.*

ARMS: Harl. 1396: BLOUNT DE HEREFORD.—*Quarterly*: 1 and 4, *Barry nebulée of six or and sable, in chief three pellets ; 2 and 3, Argent, on a cross sable a leopard's face or, in dexter chief a trefoil of the second* [BRUGES].

ARMS: Harl. 1396: BLOUNT DE OSBALDESTON.—*Quarterly*: 1 and 4, *Barry nebulée of six or and sable, within a bordure gobony of the first and azure*, BLOUNT ; 2, *Or, a lion rampant queuée furchée vert, charged with a mullet*, SUTTON ; 3, *Azure, a chevron between three martlets or*, WICHARD.

ARMS: Harl. 1396: BLUNT OF STRETTON.—*Quarterly*: 1 and 4, *Barry nebulée of six or and sable ; 2, Ermine, a lion rampant gules crowned or, within a bordure engrailed sable bezantée* [CORNWALL] ; 3, *Argent, a fesse gules between three peacocks close sable* [YEE of YEO].

CREST.—*A sun or, charged with a gauntlet argent—gauntlet sable* in Harl. 1241.

[Cottonian MS. Cleopatra C.V.: Among the Banners of those who entered France 16 June 1513 occurs, "Shrop. Banerett, Sir Thomas Blont bayryth sylver a Lyon passant goulls, the tayle reversed, wyth a crown apon his hed gold, and sapits in the sonne, Made Banerett at thys tyme : and Edward Blount his sonne his Pety Captayn."

In the same MS. there occurs, "Shrop.—John Blount bayryth sylver a Lyon passant goulls, the tayll reversed, with a crown apon his hed gold, and a Crescent apon his shulder for a difference : and Ric. Laycon his Pety Captayn."]

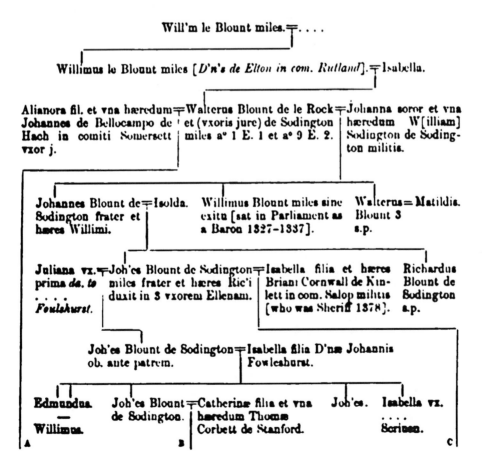

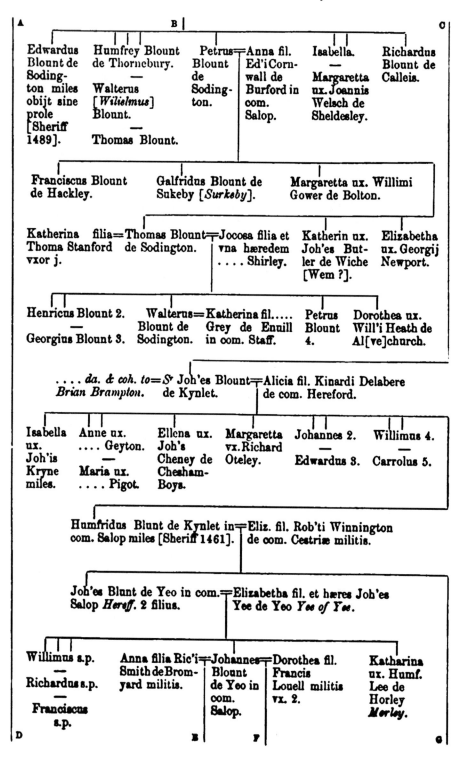

A

B

C

Edwardus Blount de Sodington miles obijt sine prole [Sheriff 1489].

Humfrey Blount de Thornebury.
—
Walterus [Wilielmus] Blount.
—
Thomas Blount.

Petrus Blount de Sodington.

=Anna fil. Ed'i Cornwall de Burford in com. Salop.

Isabella.
—
Margaretta ux. Joannis Welsch de Sheldesley.

Richardus Blount de Calleis.

Franciscus Blount de Hackley.

Galfridus Blount de Sukeby [Surkeby].

Margaretta ux. Willimi Gower de Bolton.

Katherina filia Thoma Stanford vxor j.

=Thomas Blount de Sodington.

=Jocosa filia et vna hæredem .... Shirley.

Katherin ux. Joh'es Butler de Wiche [Wem ?].

Elizabetha ux. Georgij Newport.

Henricus Blount 2.
—
Georgius Blount 3.

Walterus Blount de Sodington.

=Katherina fil..... Grey de Enuill in com. Staff.

Petrus Blount 4.

Dorothea ux. Will'i Heath de Al[ve]church.

.... da. & coh. to Brian Brampton.

=Sr Joh'es Blount de Kynlet.

=Alicia fil. Kinardi Delabere de com. Hereford.

Isabella ux. Joh'is Kryne miles.

Anne ux. .... Geyton.
—
Maria ux. .... Pigot.

Ellena ux. Joh's Cheney de Chesham-Boys.

Margaretta vx. Richard Oteley.

Johannes 2.
—
Edwardus 3.

Willimus 4.
—
Carrolus 5.

Humfridus Blunt de Kynlet in com. Salop miles [Sheriff 1461].

=Eliz. fil. Rob'ti Winnington de com. Cestriæ militis.

Joh'es Blunt de Yeo in com. Salop Hereff. 2 filius.

=Elizabetha fil. et hæres Joh'es Yee de Yeo Yee of Yee.

Willimus s.p.
—
Richardus s.p.
—
Franciscus s.p.

Anna filia Ric'i Smith de Bromyard militis.

=Johannes Blount de Yeo in com. Salop.

=Dorothea fil. Francis Louell militis vx. 2.

Katharina ux. Humf. Lee de Horley Morley.

D   E   F   G

D   E   F   G

| Eliz. ux. W⁼ Berington (*Beryton*) s.p. | Georgius Blount 2 fil. duxit .... filiam Walteri Blount de Astley et postea duxit Dorothea fil. Thomæ Hill. | Johannis Blount de Yeo. | =Katherina fil. Ricardi Warncombe. | Henricus Blount de Church Stretton in com. Salop 3 fil. aᵒ 1623. | =Eliz. fil. Hen. Lisle de Moxhall [Moxhull] in co. Warr. 1623. |

| Richardus Blount 2. | Johannes Blount de Yeo in co. Salop. | =Eliz. fil. .... Price de Monaltie *Monnaughty* in co. Radnor. | Eliz. ux. .... Darington *Birrington* [*Barington*] de Winesley. |

| Thomas 2. — Franciscus 3. | Walterus Blount de Stretton in com. Salop filius et hæres 1623. | =Mariæ filia D'ni Brabason de Hibernia. | Edwardus 4. — Herbertus 5. |

| Richardus. | Johannes ætatis 13 An'or' aᵒ 1623. | Carolus. | Susanna. |

| Thomas Blount de Kynlet in com. Salop miles h'uit 20 liberos [Sheriff 1480]. | =Anna filia Ric'i Croftes militis. | Edmundus Blount 2. | Walterus Blount 3.=.... Carolus. |

| Walterus Blunt 2. | =Margretta fil. et hær. W⁼ Acton. | Ann vx. Humfry Massy. | Elianora vx. Thomas Scriuen de Frodesley. — Arthur. | Rob'tus Blount anteambulo* 3 com. Salop ob. 1580. | =Eliz. fil. .... Columbell de Darley in co. Derby. |

| Francisca ux. .... Tye renupta Tho. Smith. | Ann ux. Nicholai Towers. | Eliz. ux. Nicholai Browne. | Mari ux. Jo. Longe. | Goditho [*Godithn*] ux. Tho. Statham. |

| Georgius Blunt de Eckington in com. Derby aᵒ 1591. | =Rosamond fil. Petrie Frecheulle de Staley relicta Eliæ Markha'. | Godfridus 2 son. |

Charles Blunt filius naturalis.

| Edwardus Blount duxit .... filia et hæres Joh's Garneis [*Garneys*]. | Margaretta vx. Joh'es Corbet de leigh. | Jocosa ux. Tho. Thornes de com. Wigorn' relicta Francisci Gower *Tho. Thorney of co. Worc. by a da. to Fra. Gower.* |

E   I

* Anteambulo means *Serjeant-at-mace*, and is sometimes used for *Gentleman-usher*.

H   I

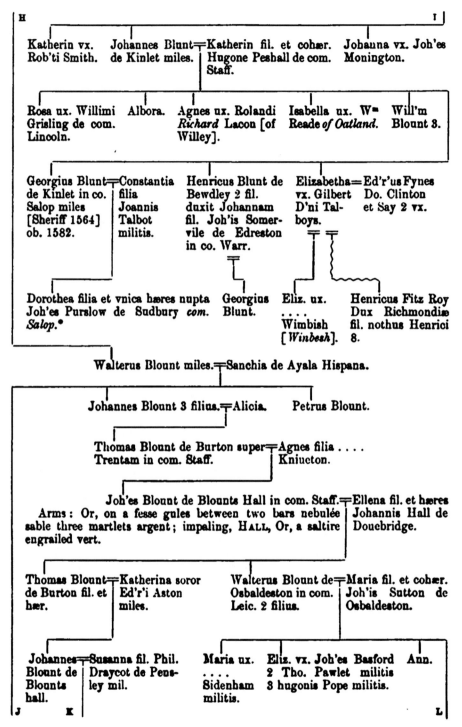

Katherin vx. Rob'ti Smith.

Johannes Blunt de Kinlet miles.=Katherin fil. et cohær. Hugone Peshall de com. Staff.

Johanna vx. Joh'es Monington.

Rosa ux. Willimi Grisling de com. Lincoln.

Albora.

Agnes ux. Rolandi *Richard* Lacon [of Willey].

Isabella ux. W= Reade *of Oatland*.

Will'm Blount 3.

Georgius Blunt=Constantia de Kinlet in co. filia Salop miles Joannis [Sheriff 1564] Talbot ob. 1582. militis.

Henricus Blunt de Bewdley 2 fil. duxit Johannam fil. Joh'is Somervile de Edreston in co. Warr.

Elizabetha=Ed'r'us Fynes vx. Gilbert Do. Clinton D'ni Tal- et Say 2 vx. boys.

Dorothea filia et vnica hæres nupta Joh'es Purslow de Sudbury *com. Salop.**

Georgius Blunt.

Eliz. ux. . . . . Wimbish [*Winbesh*].

Henricus Fitz Roy Dux Richmondiæ fil. nothus Henrici 8.

Walterus Blount miles.=Sanchia de Ayala Hispana.

Johannes Blount 3 filius.=Alicia.

Petrus Blount.

Thomas Blount de Burton super=Agnes filia . . . . Trentam in com. Staff. Kniucton.

Joh'es Blount de Blounts Hall in com. Staff.=Ellena fil. et hæres
Arms : Or, on a fesse gules between two bars nebulée | Johannis Hall de
sable three martlets argent ; impaling, HALL, Or, a saltire | Douebridge.
engrailed vert.

Thomas Blount=Katherina soror de Burton fil. et Ed'r'i Aston hær. miles.

Walterus Blount de=Maria fil. et cohær. Osbaldeston in com. Joh'is Sutton de Leic. 2 filius. Osbaldeston.

Johannes=Susanna fil. Phil. Blount de Draycot de Pens- Blounts ley mil. hall.

Maria ux. . . . . Sidenham militis.

Eliz. vx. Joh'es Basford 2 Tho. Pawlet militis 3 hugonis Pope militis.

Ann.

J   K   L

* She married secondly Edward Bullock of Bradley (*Blakeway's ' Sheriffs '*).

J | K | L |

Anthonius Blount 2 fil. | Edwardus Blount de Alleston in com. Derb. mar. Katherina fil. Henrici D'n's Audley Comes Castell-Hauen. | Thomas Pope Blount de Osbaldeston in com. Leic. miles a° 1602 mar. Francisca fil. . . . . Pigot de Doderahull in com. Bucks. ᵀ | Georgius Blount 2 fil. mar. Martha fil. Ric'i Turuile de Thurlston in in com. Leic. | Walterus.

Sʳ Harry Blount of Titenbanger in Hertf. Knight.* ᵀ . . . .

. . . . vx. Tho. Tirrell Barᵗ de Thornton in co. Bucks. | Sʳ Tho. Pope ᵀ . . . . da. Blount Baronet of Sʳ . . . . of Titenbanger. Cæsar. | Charles ᵀ . . . . Blount. | Vlisses ᵀ . . . . Blount.

Ann ux. . . . . Griffith de Wichenor in com. Staff. | Jacobus Blount ᵀ . . . . filia Jacobi Parker 2 filius. de Lellinghall.

Rogerus Blount. ᵀ Elizabetha fil. Rob'ti Whitney militis.

Thomas Blount. ᵀ . . . . filia et hæres Ricardi a Brugis.

Walterus Blount de Grindon. ᵀ Perin filia Tho. a Barton de Webley.

Thomas Blount de Heref. ᵀ Maria.

Edm. Blount de Pembrigg in co. Hereff. mar. Katherina fil. Hen. Bracey de Noke [co. Hereford]. | Rogerus Blount 2 fil. mar. Maria filia wᵐ Berington of Winstowe [*Winslowe*] [Wimbersley, co. Chester]. ᵀ

Richard. | Thomas. | Elizabeth.

Thomas Blount miles ᵀ Margaretta fil. Thomæ fil. et hær. Greseley. | Constantia ux. Johannis Sutton Baro' Dudley.

Margaretta fil. Gervasij Clifton de Clifton in com. Nott. vx. 2. | Thoma Blount 2 filius et frater d'ni Montioy. | Anna filia et vna hæredum Joh'ia Hally militis vx. j. | Elizabetha ux. Rad'i Shirley. | Sanchia ux. . . . . Langford. | Anna ux. . . . . Worseley.

M | N | O |

* These last two descents are in another hand.

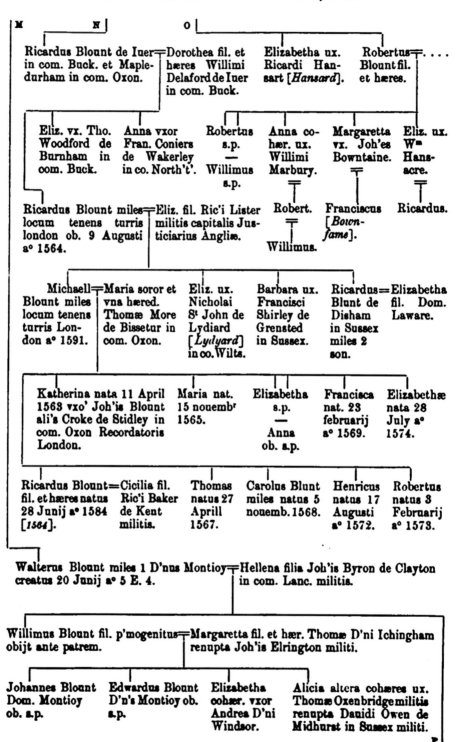

M   N | O |

Ricardus Blount de Iuer=Dorothea fil. et   Elizabetha ux.   Robertus=. . . .
in com. Buck. et Maple-   hæres Willimi   Ricardi Han-   Blount fil.
durham in com. Oxon.   Delaford de Iuer   sart [Hansard].   et hæres.
                          in com. Buck.

Eliz. vx. Tho.   Anna vxor   Robertus   Anna co-   Margaretta   Eliz. ux.
Woodford de   Fran. Coniers   s.p.   hær. ux.   vx. Joh'es   Wᵐ
Burnham in   de Wakerley   —   Willimi   Bowntaine.   Hans-
com. Buck.   in co. North't'.   Willimus   Marbury.   acre.
                              s.p.

Ricardus Blount miles=Eliz. fil. Ric'i Lister   Robert.   Franciscus   Ricardus.
locum   tenens   turris   militis capitalis Jus-   =   [Bown-
london ob. 9 Augusti   ticiarius Angliæ.   fame].
aº 1564.   Willimus.

Michaell=Maria soror et   Eliz. ux.   Barbara ux.   Ricardus=Elizabetha
Blount miles   vna hæred.   Nicholai   Francisci   Blunt de   fil.   Dom.
locum tenens   Thomæ More   Sᵗ John de   Shirley de   Disham   Laware.
turris Lon-   de Bissetur in   Lydiard   Grensted   in Sussex
don aº 1591.   com. Oxon.   [Lydyard]   in Sussex.   miles 2
                          in co. Wilts.   son.

Katherina nata 11 April   Maria nat.   Elizabetha   Francisca   Elizabethæ
1563 vxo' Joh'is Blount   15 nouembʳ   s.p.   nat. 23   nata 28
ali's Croke de Stidley in   1565.   —   februarij   July aº
com. Oxon Recordatoris   Anna   aº 1569.   1574.
London.   ob. a.p.

Ricardus Blount=Cicilia fil.   Thomas   Carolus Blunt   Henricus   Robertus
fil. et hæres natus   Ric'i Baker   natus 27   miles natus 5   natus 17   natus 3
28 Junij aº 1584   de Kent   Aprill   nouemb. 1568.   Augusti   Februarij
[1564].   militis.   1567.   aº 1572.   aº 1573.

Walterus Blount miles 1 D'nus Montioy=Hellena filia Joh'is Byron de Clayton
creatus 20 Junij aº 5 E. 4.   in com. Lanc. militis.

Willimus Blount fil. p'mogenitus=Margaretta fil. et hær. Thomæ D'ni Ichingham
obijt ante patrem.   renupta Joh'is Elrington militi.

Johannes Blount   Edwardus Blount   Elizabetha   Alicia altera cohæres ux.
Dom. Montioy   D'n's Montioy ob.   cohær. vxor   Thomæ Oxenbridge militis
ob. a.p.   a.p.   Andrea D'ni   renupta Dauidi Owen de
                  Windsor.   Midhurst in Sussex militi.

P |

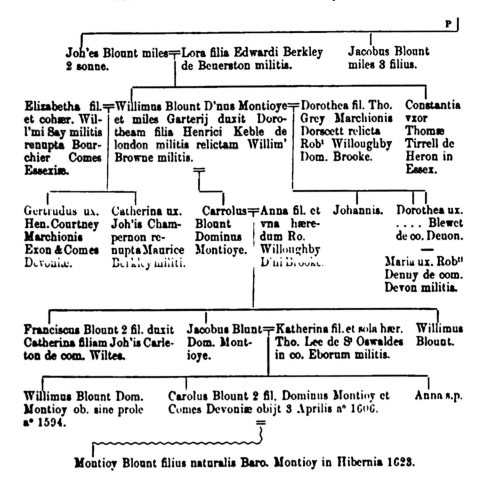

P |

Joh'es Blount miles ᴛ Lora filia Edwardi Berkley
2 sonne. | de Beuerston militis.

Jacobus Blount
miles 3 filius.

Elizabetha fil. ᴛ Willimus Blount D'nus Montioye ᴛ Dorothea fil. Tho.　Constantia
et cohær. Wil- | et miles Garterij duxit Doro- | Grey Marchionis　vxor
l'mi Say militis | theam filia Henrici Keble de | Dorscett relicta　Thomæ
renupta Bour- | london militis relictam Willim' | Rob' Willoughby　Tirrell de
chier Comes | Browne militis.　Dom. Brooke.　Heron in
Essexiæ.　ᴛ　Essex.

Gertrudus ux.　Catherina ux.　Carrolus ᴛ Anna fil. et　Johannis.　Dorothea ux.
Hen. Courtney　Joh'is Cham-　Blount | vna hære-　.... Blewet
Marchionis　pernon re-　Dominus | dum Ro.　de co. Deuon.
Exon & Comes　nupta Maurice　Montioye. | Willoughby
Devoniæ.　Berkley militi.　D'ni Brooke.　Maria ux. Rob'
　Denuy de com.
　Devon militis.

Franciscus Blount 2 fil. duxit　Jacobus Blunt ᴛ Katherina fil. et sola hær.　Willimus
Catherina filiam Joh'is Carle-　Dom. Mont- | Tho. Lee de S' Oswaldes　Blount.
ton de com. Wiltes.　ioye. | in co. Eborum militis.

Willimus Blount Dom.　Carolus Blount 2 fil. Dominus Montioy et　Anna s.p.
Montioy ob. sine prole　Comes Devoniæ obijt 3 Aprilis n° 1606.
a° 1594.　=

Montioy Blount filius naturalis Baro. Montioy in Hibernia 1623.

Blyke, Filylode, and Astley, all of Astley, near Bridgnorth.

Harl. 1396, fo. 14.　S., fo. 19.

John Astley lord of Astley in co. Salop. ᴛ ....
Arms: Azure, a cinquefoil pierced ermine within
a bordure engrailed of the second.

John Astley son & heire. ᴛ ....

John Astley son & heire. ᴛ ....　Roger Astley 2 sonne. ᴛ ....
▲ |　B |

1

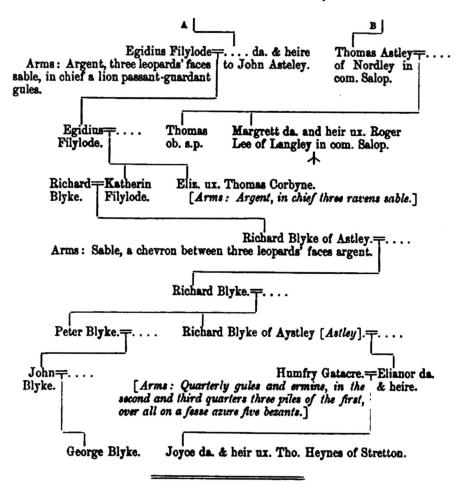

A | Egidius Filylode=.... da. & heire to John Asteley.
Arms: Argent, three leopards' faces sable, in chief a lion passant-guardant gules.

B | Thomas Astley=.... of Nordley in com. Salop.

Egidius=.... Filylode.   Thomas ob. s.p.   Margrett da. and heir ux. Roger Lee of Langley in com. Salop.

Richard=Katherin Blyke.   Filylode.   Eliz. ux. Thomas Corbyne. [Arms: Argent, in chief three ravens sable.]

Richard Blyke of Astley.=....
Arms: Sable, a chevron between three leopards' faces argent.

Richard Blyke.=....

Peter Blyke.=....   Richard Blyke of Aystley [Astley].=....

John=.... Blyke.   Humfry Gatacre.=Elianor da. & heire.
[Arms: Quarterly gules and ermine, in the second and third quarters three piles of the first, over all on a fesse azure five bezants.]

George Blyke.   Joyce da. & heir ux. Tho. Heynes of Stretton.

Booth of Ludlow.

Harl. 1396, fo. 44ᵇ.   Harl. 1241, fo. 12ᵇ.   Harl. 615, fo. 252.

ARMS: Harl. 1396.—*Argent, three boars' heads erect and erased sable, in chief a rose gules.*

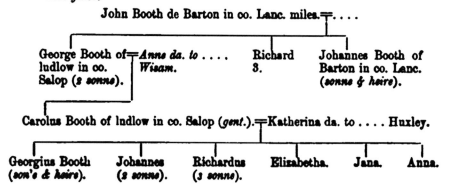

John Booth de Barton in co. Lanc. miles.=....

George Booth of=Anne da. to .... ludlow in co.   Wisam. Salop (2 sonne).   Richard 3.   Johannes Booth of Barton in co. Lanc. (sonne & heire).

Carolus Booth of ludlow in co. Salop (gent.).=Katherina da. to .... Huxley.

Georgius Booth (son's & heire).   Johannes (2 sonne).   Richardus (3 sonne).   Elizabetha.   Jana.   Anna.

Booth of Shiffnal.

Harl. 1396, fo. 44ᵇ. S., fo. 50.

ARMS : Harl. 1396.—*Argent, three boars' heads erect and erased sable, in chief a rose gules.*

Oliverus Boothe de com. Derby a familia les⹀Elizabetha fil. . . . . Hatfeild de
Boothes de Barton in co. Lancastr' oriund'. | Whitfeild in co. Derb.

Nicholaus Booth de co. Derb' 1 fil.	Carolus Booth de Nor-folc 2 fil. ⹀ . . . . fil. . . . . Boult de Trunche [co. Nor-folk].	Thomas 4 fil. s.p.	Oliuett [*Oliverus*] Boothe de com. Derbij 5 fil.	Joh'es Boothe⹀ . . . . de Hansworth Woodhouse in c . . . . Ebor. 3 fil.

1. Anna nupta Tho. Stary de Baneyfeild in co. Eborum.

2. Elizab. 1 uxor Wᵐ Castelford de Wosper in co. Ebor. 2 Jervitio Hanson de co. Eborum.

3. Katherina ux. Joh'es Hodder de Hansworth Woodhouse in com. Eborum.

Tho. Booth de Shiffnall in co. Salop a° 1623. ⹀ Maria fil. Rob. Baumpfeild [Barnefield] de Newport in com. Salop.	Johannes 1 s.p. — X'poferus 2 s.p.	Anna nupta Jo. Stocking de Poswick in co. Norf.

Carolus Booth fil. et hær. 9 yer old a° 1623.	Gabriell ob. Infans.	Baumfeild 3 fil.	Sylas 4.

Borough of Dinas Mowthwy.

[ARMS.—Azure, three fleurs-de-lis argent.]

Hugo Borough miles Dom. de Borough super Sanes⹀ . . . . fil. . . . .
[Burgh upon Sands, Cumberland]. | Dom. Mowbray.
Arms : Azure, three fleurs-de-lis.

Guido Burghe qui vendidit Baroniam de Burgh Domino Darcy.	Will'us⹀ . . . . Borough Do. de Midle-ton miles.	Willimus 4 filius Griff. ap Gwynwin ap Owen Keueliok D'm' de Powis H. 2. Arms : Or, a lion rampant gules within a bordure indented en-grailed sable.	⹀Margaretta fil. et hær. Tho. ap Lluellin ap Owen ap Mer'dd ap Owen ap Gruff. ap Rees ap Gruff. ap Rees ap Tudor principis Sowth Wallis.
▲		B	

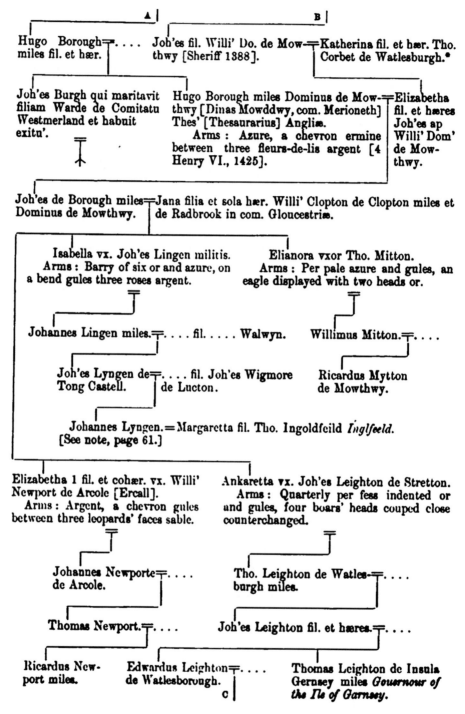

Hugo Borough⚯. . . .
miles fil. et hær.

Joh'es fil. Willi' Do. de Mow-⚯Katherina fil. et hær. Tho.
thwy [Sheriff 1388].　Corbet de Watlesburgh.*

Joh'es Burgh qui maritavit
filiam Warde de Comitatu
Westmerland et habuit
exitu'.

Hugo Borough miles Dominus de Mow-⚯Elizabetha
thwy [Dinas Mowddwy, com. Merioneth]　fil. et hæres
Thes' [Thesaurarius] Angliæ.　Joh'es ap
　Arms : Azure, a chevron ermine　Willi' Dom'
between three fleurs-de-lis argent [4　de Mow-
Henry VI., 1425].　thwy.

Joh'es de Borough miles⚯Jana filia et sola hær. Willi' Clopton de Clopton miles et
Dominus de Mowthwy.　de Radbrook in com. Gloucestriæ.

Isabella vx. Joh'es Lingen militis.
　Arms : Barry of six or and azure, on
a bend gules three roses argent.

Elianora vxor Tho. Mitton.
　Arms : Per pale azure and gules, an
eagle displayed with two heads or.

Johannes Lingen miles.⚯. . . . fil. . . . . Walwyn.

Willimus Mitton.⚯. . . .

Joh'es Lyngen de⚯. . . . fil. Joh'es Wigmore
Tong Castell.　de Lucton.

Ricardus Mytton
de Mowthwy.

Johannes Lyngen.=Margaretta fil. Tho. Ingoldfeild *Inglfeild*.
[See note, page 61.]

Elizabetha 1 fil. et cohær. vx. Willi'
Newport de Arcole [Ercall].
　Arms : Argent, a chevron gules
between three leopards' faces sable.

Ankaretta vx. Joh'es Leighton de Stretton.
　Arms : Quarterly per fess indented or
and gules, four boars' heads couped close
counterchanged.

Johannes Newporte⚯. . . .
de Arcole.

Tho. Leighton de Watles-⚯. . . .
burgh miles.

Thomas Newport.⚯. . . .

Joh'es Leighton fil. et hæres.⚯. . . .

Ricardus New-
port miles.

Edwardus Leighton⚯. . . .
de Watlesborough.
　　　c

Thomas Leighton de Insula
Gernsey miles *Gouvernour of
the Ile of Garnsey*.

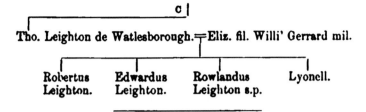

Harl. 1241, fo. 88.

Linghen and Wallwyn : Barry of six or and azure, on a bend gules three roses argent;
impaling, Sable, a fesse between three leopards' faces argent.
Walter Linghen, m'ied y[e] da. to Jo[n] Wigmor de Lucton. Linghen, as above; impaling,
Sable [argent], three greyhounds courant in pale [sable], collared gules, or or.[*]
Jo[n] Lingen, m'ied y[e] da. to S[r] Tho. Inglefeeld K[t]. Lingen, as above; impaling, Barry
of six [gules and argent], on a chief [or] a lion passant [azure].
Barton of Rosse, m'ied Jane da. to Linghen. .... a cockatrice displayed; .... impal-
ing Linghen.

Bostock of Morton Say.

S., fo. 149.

[ARMS.—*Quarterly : 1 and 4, Sable, a fesse humettée and in chief a martlet argent;*
2 and 3, Or, a lion rampant sable.
CREST.—*A martlet.*

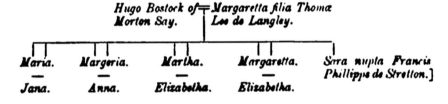

Boterell of Aston Boterell.

Harl. 1396, fo. 45.   Harl. 1241, fo. 67.   Harl. 615, fo. 244.

ARMS : Harl. 1396.—*Argent, a chief gules, over all a lion rampant sable, armed and*
langued or.

[Sir Wm. de Boterell temp. Edw. I.: *Checky or and gules, a chevron azure*
(Military Summons).]

(*Arms of*   *Richard sonne & heire to John Botrell the 8th*
Botrell.   *yere of Ric. 2.*
Arms of   *Robart Botrell Lorde of Aston Botrell in the*
Botrell.   *County Salopie vicesimo secundo of H. 7.*
            Sir Thomas Botrell sans date.
            Phillipe Botrell sans date.

* A family of the same name in Herefordshire bore : Sable, three greyhounds courant in pale
argent, collared or.

Richard Botrell sans date.

John Botrell did confirme to Thomas Botrell   Arms of
   my sons & Margarett his wiff Tricessimo   Botrell.
   nono of E. 3.

John Botrell & Isolda his wiff Decimo of H. 4.

John Botrell Lorde of Aston in the Countie
   of Salopie Tercio of E. 4.

John Botrell Lorde of Aston Botrell did con-
   firme to Johan's sonne to Roger of Aston
   Botrell quarto decimo of E. 3.)

(*Sir*) Thomas Boterell de Aston Boterell in co. Salop miles.=....

Johannes Boterell.   Phillippus Boterell.=....   Willimus Boterell.

Joh'es Boterell aº 3 E. 2.=....   Matilda ux. Ric'i Lacon de Lacon in co. Salop.

Thomas Boterell aº 39 E. 3.=Margaretta fil. Ricardi Eyton *Eton.*

Richardus Boterell=....   Henricus Boterell cæsus
ob. ante p'rem.   in Francia s.p.

Joh'es Boterell aº 45 E. 3.=Margretta fil. Roberti Corbett.

Richardus Boterell aº 9 R. 2.=Jana Bruen.

Johannes Boterell aº 10 H. 4.=Isolda.   Thomas 2 sonne.   Henricus s.p.

Joh'es Boterell de Aston Boterell nº 3 E. 4 *1479* [monumental=Maria fil..... Cor-
effigy in Aston Boterel Church, together with Mary his wife].   bett de Longnor.

....*da.*=Rob'tus Boterell de=Elizabetha   Richardus.   Elizabetha   Alicia vx.
to ....   Aston Boterell in co. fil. ....   —   vx. Ed'r'i   Johannis
1 wife.   Salop 22 H. 7.   Cotton 2   Thomas.   Hopton.   Baldwin
                              wife.   *Bawdewin.*

Thomas Boterell de Boterells=Jooosa fil. Tho. Cressett de Vpton
Aston in co. Salop.*   Cresset in co. Salop.

Robt Boterell   Ann vx.   Eliz. vx. Johannis   Leonardus Boterell 4 fil.
fil. et hær. s.p.   Johannis   Perton de Wor-   (5 sons) duxit Margarettam
             Puralow.   cester.   filliam .... Deene.

A   B

* Harl. 1241 omits this generation.

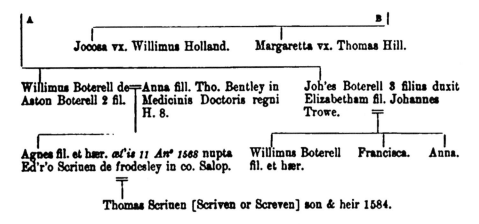

A | B |

Jocosa vx. Willimus Holland.   Margaretta vx. Thomas Hill.

Willimus Boterell de⹀Anna fill. Tho. Bentley in   Joh'es Boterell 8 filius duxit
Aston Boterell 2 fil. | Medicinis Doctoris regni   Elizabetham fil. Johannes
 | H. 8.   Trowe.

Agnes fil. et hær. æt'is 11 An° 1568 nupta   Willimus Boterell   Francisca.   Anna.
Ed'r'o Scriuen de frodesley in co. Salop.   fil. et hær.

Thomas Scriuen [Scriven or Screven] son & heir 1584.

Bowdler of Bromton.

Harl. 1396, fo. 31ᵇ.   S., fo. 86ᵇ.

[ARMS.—Argent, two Cornish choughs in pale proper—other copies of the 1623
 Visitation.]

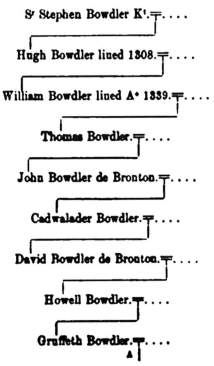

Sʳ Stephen Bowdler Kᵗ.⹀. . . .

Hugh Bowdler lived 1308.⹀. . . .

William Bowdler lived A° 1339.⹀. . . .

Thomas Bowdler.⹀. . . .

John Bowdler de Bronton.⹀. . . .

Cadwalader Bowdler.⹀. . . .

David Rowdler de Bronton.⹀. . . .

Howell Bowdler.⹀. . . .

Gruffeth Bowdler.⹀. . . .
A |

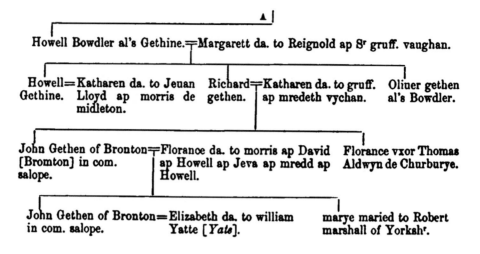

Howell Bowdler al's Gethine.══Margarett da. to Reignold ap Sr gruff. vaughan.

Howell══Katharen da. to Jeuan   Richard══Katharen da. to gruff.   Oliuer gethen
Gethine.   Lloyd ap morris de   gethen.   ap mredeth vychan.   al's Bowdler.
            midleton.

John Gethen of Bronton══Florance da. to morris ap David   Florance vxor Thomas
[Bromton] in com.   ap Howell ap Jeva ap mredd ap   Aldwyn de Churburye.
salope.   Howell.

John Gethen of Bronton══Elizabeth da. to william   marye maried to Robert
in com. salope.   Yatte [Yate].   marshall of Yorksh.

𝕭𝖔𝖜𝖉𝖑𝖊𝖗 𝖔𝖋 𝕳𝖔𝖕𝖊 𝕭𝖔𝖜𝖉𝖑𝖊𝖗.

Harl. 1396, fo. 32.   S., fo. 37.

ARMS: Harl. 1396.—[Argent,] *two Cornish choughs* [in pale proper].

John Bowdler of Hope Bowdler in com. salope.══. . . .

John Bowdler of Hope Bowdler.══. . . .

Stephen Bowdler.══. . . .

Sr Will'm Bowdler of Hope══Anne da. to Sr Phillipe
Bowdler Knight.   grant Knight.

Sr Stephen Bowdler of Hope══Joanne da. & h. to Sr Nicholas
Bowdler Kt.   Brinsbon Knight.

Ciceley vxor Edward Acton   Alice maried to John Jenkes
of Acton Scotte.   of Wolverton.

Bowdler of Ludlow.

Harl. 1396, fo. 32.   S., fo. 37ᵇ.

ARMS : Harl. 1396.—*Argent, two Cornish choughs* [in pale] *proper.*

Richard Bowdler of Ludlowe═margery da. to Thomas Lane
in com. Salope esqʳ.   of Ludlowe.

Joanne &
Margerey.

Richard Bowdler of Ludlowe in com. Salope 3 sonne
maried Suzanna da. to . . . .

da.   da.

John Bowdler of Ludlowe
2 sonne [*mar.*] Elianor da.
to John Couper of Ludlowe
ob. s. p'le.

Thomas
Bowdler.

William Bowdler of═Isabell da. to Tam-
Ludlowe in co. Salop   berlaine gwill'm of
sonne & heire Aº   Wellington (*Willing-*
1623.   *ton*) in com. Salop.

Tamberlaine Bowdler son & h. æt's 4 ann' Aº 1623.   Anne.

W. BOWDLER.

Bowdler of Harlescott and Shrewsbury.

Harl. 1396, fo. 32ᵇ.   S., ff. 38ᵃ, 39.

ARMS : Harl. 1396.—*Argent, two Cornish choughs* [in pale] *proper.*

Hughe Bowdler of Hope Bowdler.═. . . .

William Bowdler of Worceston [sic].═Anne da. to Raphe Thinne of Stretton.

Thomas Bowdler.═. . . .

John Bowdler.═. . . .

William Bowdler.═. . . .

William Bowdler Aº 1623.

▲

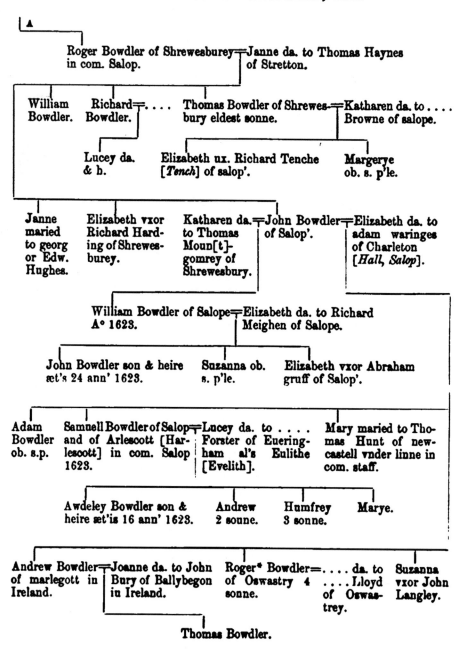

Roger Bowdler of Shrewesburey═Janne da. to Thomas Haynes
in com. Salop.   of Stretton.

William   Richard═. . . .   Thomas Bowdler of Shrewes-═Katharen da. to . . . .
Bowdler.   Bowdler.   bury eldest sonne.   Browne of salope.

                Lucey da.   Elizabeth ux. Richard Tenche   Margerye
                & h.   [*Tench*] of salop'.   ob. s. p'le.

Janne   Elizabeth vxor   Katharen da.═John Bowdler═Elizabeth da. to
maried   Richard Hard-   to Thomas   of Salop'.   adam waringes
to georg   ing of Shrewes-   Moun[t]-   of Charleton
or Edw.   burey.   gomrey of   [*Hall, Salop*].
Hughes.   Shrewesbury.

William Bowdler of Salope═Elizabeth da. to Richard
A° 1623.   Meighen of Salope.

John Bowdler son & heire   Suzanna ob.   Elizabeth vxor Abraham
æt's 24 ann' 1623.   s. p'le.   gruff of Salop'.

Adam   Samuell Bowdler of Salop═Lucey da. to . . . .   Mary maried to Tho-
Bowdler   and of Arlescott [Har-   Forster of Euering-   mas Hunt of new-
ob. s.p.   lescott] in com. Salop   ham al's   Eulithe   castell vnder linne in
            1623.   [Evelith].   com. staff.

            Awdeley Bowdler son &   Andrew   Humfrey   Marye.
            heire æt'is 16 ann' 1623. 2 sonne.   3 sonne.

Andrew Bowdler═Joanne da. to John   Roger* Bowdler═. . . . da. to   Suzanna
of marlegott in│Bury of Ballybegon   of Oswastry 4 . . . . Lloyd   vxor John
Ireland.   │in Ireland.   sonne.   of Oswas-   Langley.
                                                    trey.

                Thomas Bowdler.

                                SAMUEL BOWDLER.

---

* In Shrewsbury MS., fo. 39, Roger appears as the fourth son of John, as above; but Samuel,
Mary, and Andrew appear as Roger's children.

Brereton of Bursham or Burras.

Harl. 1396, fo. 49.   Harl. 1241, fo. 129.

ARMS: Harl. 1396.—*Quarterly of six*: 1, *Argent, two bars sable, in chief a crescent gules*; 2, *Argent, a chevron between three crescents gules* [IPSTONES]; 3, *Or, a raven sable* [CORBETT]; 4, *Argent, a cross formée fleurée sable* [azure, MALPAS?]; 5, *Argent, a chevron sable, on a chief of the second three martlets of the first* [WILDE]; 6, *Ermine, a lion rampant azure* [EYTON].

Randolphus Brereton de = [Alice da. to Sir Wᵐ | Thomas Wilde de Burs = T. . . .
Malpas in co. Cestr' [2ᵈ | Ipstons of Ipstons | ham in co. Denby *Den-*
son of Sir Wᵐ Brereton | co. Staff.—Vis. Che- | *bigh.*
of Brereton—Vis. Che- | shire] [æt. 8 in 1399 | Arms: Argent, a chevron
shire, p. 43]. | —Wm. Salt Soc., i., | sable, on a chief of the
 | p. 300.] | second three martlets of
 | | the first.

Randulphus | Willimus Brereton de Bursham = Katherina fil. | Elizabetha vx. Hen-
Brereton de | [Burres—Vis. Cheshire 1580] | et hæres. | rici Diue *of Bed-*
Malpas. | in com. Denby. | | *fordsh.*

Dorothea fil. Thomæ = Edwardus Brereton = Elizabetha fil. Joh'is Roydon de Burs-
Hanmer militis vx. 2. | de Bursham. | ham [Bursham or Burras, co. Den-
 | | bigh] vx. 1.

Randolphus Brere- = Margaretta fil. | Johannes Brereton = Margarett fil. et hær.
ton di'us [dictus] | et hær. Ellys | de Burras [co. Den- | Ric'i ap Jem vichan
Rufus fil. 1. | ap Ellis Eyton. | bigh] 2 filius. | ap Jem ap D'd ap
 | | | Howell vichan.

Jana fil. et hær. vx. Rob' fil. | Owenus Brereton = Elizabetha filia Joh'is
Ed'r'i Pulleston de Ecludsham. | de Burras. | Salisbury.

Edwardus Brereton de Burras. = Anna soror Jenan Lloyd de Yale miles.

Owen Brereton de Burras.

Tho. Brereton rector de Llandinio | Eliz. vx. | Johanna vx. | Katherina vx.
et Gresford in co. Denbigh duxit | Jacobi | Kendrick ap | Lancelotti
Margaretta fil. Ithell ap Griffith ap | Eyton de | Richard de | Lloyd de
Belyn vx. Kendrick ap Euan. | Eyton. | Pinachblock. | Allington.

Petrus Brereton in artib' Mʳ | Hugo s.p. | Randulphus | Dorothea | Maria.
et Vicarius de Llanvyhangell | — | Brereton. | vx. Willim'
1597 duxit Jana fil. Owen ap | Johannes. | | Lewis de
John ap Howell vichan. | — | | Wrexham.
 | Bad'm. |

Bridgeman.

S., fo. 46.

[ARMS.—*Azure, ten bezants, 4, 3, 2, and 1, on a chief argent a lion passant sable.*

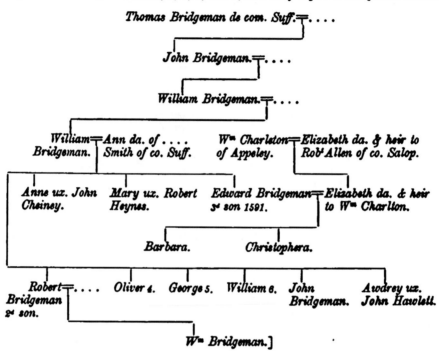

Barbara.   Christophera.

W*^m* Bridgeman.]

Briggs of Ernestree and Haughton.

Harl. 1396, fo. 43.   Harl. 1241, fo. 22^b.   Harl. 615, fo. 263^b.   S., fo. 306^a.

ARMS: Harl. 1396.—*Quarterly: 1 and 4, Gules, three bars-gemelles or, on a canton sable a crescent of the second,* BRIGGES ; *2, Or, a boar passant sable,* GYLPIN ; *3, Argent, a chevron gules between three square buckles sable,* MORTON.

CREST.—*On a stump of a tree couped and eradicated or a pelican of the same vulning herself proper.*

Exemplified by Wm Dethick Garter King of Armes a° 1584.

These Armes were borne by Oliuer Brigges & entred in the old Visitation.

ARMS.—*Argent, a fleur-de-lis sable between three escutcheons gules, each charged with a bend of the first.*

CREST.—*An arm embowed habited in leaves vert, holding in the hand proper a bow gules, stringed sable, and an arrow argent.*

S., fo. 306^a, adds "*p' Camden Clarenc.*"

Joh'es Briggs D'n's de Hall [Sall].⹀. . . .

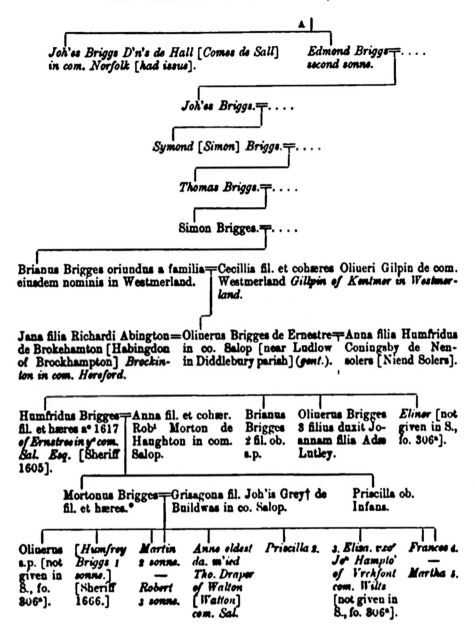

▲

Joh'es Briggs D'n's de Hall [Comes de Sall] in com. Norfolk [had issue].　　　*Edmond Briggs=.... second sonne.*

Joh'es Briggs.=....

Symond [Simon] Briggs.=....

Thomas Briggs.=....

Simon Brigges.=....

Brianus Brigges oriundus a familia=Cecillia fil. et cohæres Oliueri Gilpin de com. eiusdem nominis in Westmerland.　Westmerland *Gilpin of Kentmer in Westmerland.*

Jana filia Richardi Abington=Oliuerus Brigges de Erneatre=Anna filia Humfridus de Brokehamton [Habingdon　in co. Salop [near Ludlow　Coningsby de Nen- of Brockhampton] *Brockin-*　in Diddlebury parish] (*gent.*).　solers [Niend Solers]. *ton in com. Hereford.*

| Humfridus Brigges=Anna fil. et cohær. fil. et hæres aº 1617 Rob¹ Morton de *of Ernstree in yᵉ com.* Haughton in com. *Sal. Esq.* [Sheriff Salop. 1605]. | Brianus Brigges 2 fil. ob. s.p. | Oliuerus Brigges 3 filius duxit Jo- annam filia Adæ Lutley. | *Elinor* [not given in S., fo. 306ª]. |

| Mortonus Brigges=Grisagona fil. Joh'is Greyt de fil. et hæres.* Buildwas in co. Salop. | Priscilla ob. Infans. |

| Oliuerus s.p. [not given in S., fo. 306ª]. | [*Humfrey Briggs 1 sonne.*] [Sheriff 1666.] | *Martin 2 sonne.* — *Robert 3 sonne.* | *Anne eldest da. m'ied Tho. Draper of Walton* [*Watton*] *com. Sal.* | *Priscilla 2.* | 3. *Eliza. vxoᵣ Joᵇ Hamplo' of Vrchfont com. Wilts* [not given in S., fo. 306ª]. | *Frances 4.* — *Martha 5.* |

___

* Called *Edward* in Harl. 1241 and in Shrewsbury MS., fo. 306ª. Edward Grey was of Buildwas in 1601, and Crysogon, his daughter, died at the age of 97.
† Harl. 1396, fo. 43, has, in a later hand, "or. Baronet 12 Aug. 1641," and his son "& Humphrey Briggs of Haughton com. Salop Baronet in vita (patris) 1679."

Brome of Brome.

Harl. 1396, fo. 48ᵇ.   Harl. 1241, fo. 61ᵇ.

ARMS: Harl. 1396.—*Azure, a dexter hand couped and erect argent.*

[Arms confirmed by Segar 12 July 1602 to George Brome, Sub-protonotary and Secondary of King's Bench ('Guillim,' 1724, p. 254).
The same coat confirmed by Segar May 1627 to .... Brome of Broome, co. Salop (MS. Le Neve, Norroy).]

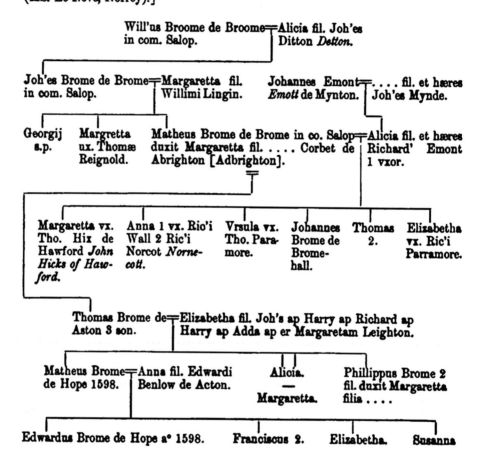

Will'us Broome de Broome=Alicia fil. Joh'es in com. Salop. | Ditton *Detton.*

Joh'es Brome de Brome=Margaretta fil. in com. Salop. | Willimi Lingin.   Johannes Emont=.... fil. et hæres *Emott* de Mynton. | Joh'es Mynde.

Georgij s.p.   Margretta ux. Thomæ Reignold.   Matheus Brome de Brome in co. Salop=Alicia fil. et hæres duxit Margaretta fil. .... Corbet de | Richard' Emont Abrighton [Adbrighton]. | 1 vxor.

Margaretta vx. Tho. Hix de Hawford *John Hicks of Hawford.*   Anna 1 vx. Ric'i Wall 2 Ric'i Norcot *Nornecott.*   Vrsula vx. Tho. Paramore.   Johannes Brome de Bromehall.   Thomas 2.   Elizabetha vx. Ric'i Parramore.

Thomas Brome de=Elizabetha fil. Joh's ap Harry ap Richard ap Aston 3 son. | Harry ap Adda ap er Margaretam Leighton.

Matheus Brome=Anna fil. Edwardi de Hope 1598. | Benlow de Acton.   Alicia. — Margaretta.   Phillippus Brome 2 fil. duxit Margaretta filia ....

Edwardus Brome de Hope aº 1598.   Franciscus 2.   Elizabetha.   Susanna

Bromley.

Harl. 1396, fo. 36. S., ff. 41ᵇ—45.

ARMS: Harl. 1396: BROMLEY OF DARFOLD.—*Quarterly of seven*: 1, *Quarterly per fesse indented gules and or, a bordure gobonée* [argent] *and* [azure], *over all an escutcheon argent charged with a gryphon segreant vert*, BROMLEIGH;[*] 2, *Argent, on a chevron gules five bezants within a bordure engrailed of the second*, CHETILTON; 3, [Argent,] *on a fesse between six fleurs-de-lis* [gules] *three cross-crosslets* [or], OLIFTON;[†] 4, *Gules, a scythe and three fleurs-de-lis argent*, PRAERS; 5, *Vert, a cross engrailed ermine*, WHETENHALL [WETENHALL]; 6, *Sable, on a chevron between three bulls' heads cabossed argent as many mullets gules*, BULKELEGH; 7, *Argent, a chevron sable between three bucks' heads cabossed gules*, PARKER.

CREST.—*A demi-lion rampant argent issuing out of ducal coronet or, holding a standard gules charged with a lion passant-guardant or, the staff proper.*

ARMS: Harl. 1396.—*Quarterly*: 1 and 4, *Quarterly per fesse indented gules and or.* 2, *Argent, on a chevron gules five bezants, a bordure engrailed of the second* [CHETELTON]; 3, *Argent, on a fesse sable between six fleurs-de-lis gules three cross-crosslets or* [CLAYTON or CLIFTON].

CREST.—*A pheasant sitting proper combed gules.*

ANOTHER CREST.—*A lion's gamb erect argent.*

STEMMATA ET PROPAGATIONES ANTIQUÆ FAMILIÆ ET NOMINÆ DE BROMLEIGH VEL BROMLEY COMITATU' SALOPIÆ.

Warinus de Burwardeslegh domi'us manerij de⊤.... Esseleghe in com. Staffordiæ temp' Regis Joh'is.

Rogerus de Burwardes-legh de Esseleghe ob. s. p'le.

.... soror 2ᵈ Rogeri de Burwardeslegh nupta Johannis de Ipstones.

Margeria (*Margareta*) de Burwardeslegh tercia sororum ob. sine p'le.

Johannes de Ipston's qui obijt sine p'le A° 21 E. 1. Arms: Argent, a chevron between three crescents gules.

Walterus de Bromleghe miles do'nus de Bromlegh.⊤Alicia soror ætate maxima et vna Arms: Quarterly per fess indented gules and or. | hered' Rogeri de Burwardeslegh.

Galfridus de Bromleghe ob. A° 1 E. 1.⊤....

Robertus‡ de Bromlegh de Asheley in com. Stafford miles ob. A° 1 E. 2.⊤.... A | B

* The crest and the inescutcheon were given as an honourable augmentation to Sir John Bromley of Bartomley for his valiant recovery of the standard at the battle of Corbia, which preceded the passage of the Soame and the battle of Agincourt.

† This quartering is named Clayton in the Nedeham and Newport pedigrees infra and in the Visit. of Stafford 1583, in each case as a quartering of Bromley; apparently Clayton is a mis-reading of Clifton. Le Neve's ' Knights ' gives the same bearing for Clifton.

‡ Robertus de Bromlegh subscriptus filius & heires Galfridi de Bromlegh fuit consanguinius & heires Johannis de Ipstones, Qui Galfridus et Johannes fuerunt heredes Margeriæ de Burwardesley tertiæ sororum et heredum Rogeri de Burwardesley de Essheleghe in com. Staff. M. R. 21 E. 1 rot. 2.

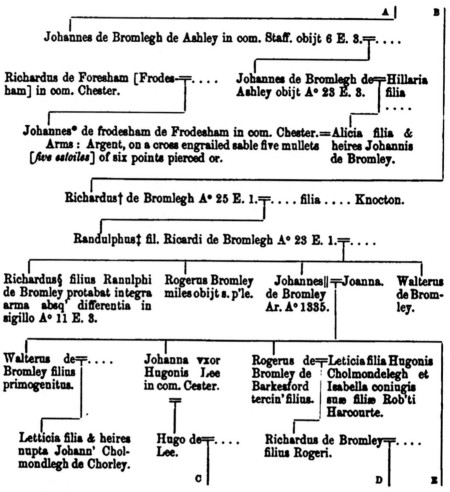

A | B

Johannes de Bromlegh de Ashley in com. Staff. obijt 6 E. 3.⊤....

Richardus de Foresham [Frodes-⊤....   Johannes de Bromlegh de⊤Hillaria
ham] in com. Chester.   Ashley obijt A° 23 E. 3. | filia
                                                                     ....

Johannes* de frodesham de Frodesham in com. Chester.=Alicia filia &
Arms : Argent, on a cross engrailed sable five mullets heires Johannis
[*five estoiles*] of six points pierced or.   de Bromley.

Richardus† de Bromlegh A° 25 E. 1.⊤.... filia .... Knocton.

Randulphus‡ fil. Ricardi de Bromlegh A° 23 E. 1.⊤....

Richardus§ filius Ranulphi   Rogerus Bromley   Johannes‖=Joanna.   Walterus
de Bromley protabat integra   miles obijt s. p'le. de Bromley   de Brom-
arma absq' differentia in   Ar. A° 1335.   ley.
sigillo A° 11 E. 3.

Walterus de=....   Johanna vxor   Rogerus de=Leticia filia Hugonis
Bromley filius | Hugonis Lee   Bromley de Cholmondelegh et
primogenitus. | in com. Cester.   Barkesford Isabella coniugis
              | tercin' filius. suæ filiæ Rob'ti
              | =   Harcourte.
              |
Letticia filia & heires   Hugo de=....   Richardus de Bromley=....
nupta Johann' Chol-   Lee. | filius Rogeri. |
mondlegh de Chorley. | |
                                  C   D   E

* John frodesham espousa Alles fille & heire a John de Bromley q' enfeffer Thomas person
de frankton enfee de la manoir de Winnington q'il person seo dono a John fitz Richard de
Frodesham a terme de sa vie, le remainder a Thomas fitz Robert de Bromley et Margareta sa
femme en le tayle, le remaynder .... droictes heires Ales Bromley ladys femme a John ffrodesham,
et le dit Thomas Bromley et Margaret avoit yssue William qui avoit yssue John et Margarett et
morut sans issue Margarett espousa William Hextall qui avoit issue Jonne qui espousa Johen'em
Bromley militem qui auoit issue Mo'sr .... Margaret & Isabell. [Harl. 1396.]

† Sciant p'ntes & futuri q'd ego Ricardus de Bromley dedi Petro de Arderne duas placeas
prati in Cnocton etc. hijs testibs dom. Will'mo de Merc, dom. Rob'to de Stawndon dom. Rogero
de Swinerton militibus etc. Dat. apud Cnocton die mer'lis in festo S' gregorij confessoris A° 25 E. 1.
[Harl. 1396.]

‡ Sciant p'ntes & futuri q'd ego Radulphus filius Ricardi de Bromlegh dedi Eliæ de Knocton
duas placeas t'ræ de vasto meo in Knocton. Dat. in vigelia beat's Lawrencij A° 1294 23 E. 1.
[Harl. 1396.]

§ Vniuersis X'pi fidelibus etc. Ricardus filius Ranulphi de Bromley & noueritri me relaxasse
Joh'nis de le Delues tertiam p'tem de Burlemore infra feodum de Knocton etc. Dat. A° 11 E. 3.
[Seal, Plate II., Fig. 10.] [Harl. 1396.]

‖ Johannes de Bromley dat. Thomas filio Roberti de Sonde terram juxta terras Thomæ filij
Ricardi de Sonde et terram quam habuitt ex dimissione Walteri Bromley fratris sui quæ
Will'mus ffowleshurst sibi relaxauit post mortem Margaretæ filiæ Henrici Cholmondelegh et
terram quam habuit ex concessione Ricardi de Bromlegh fratris sui etc. Testibs Ada le Parker
Johannes de Wrenburye Thomas de Harcourt et Thomas filio Will'mi de Sonde. Dat. A° 1335.
In custodia Ed'r'i Leighe de Rushall .... miles. [Harl. 1396.]

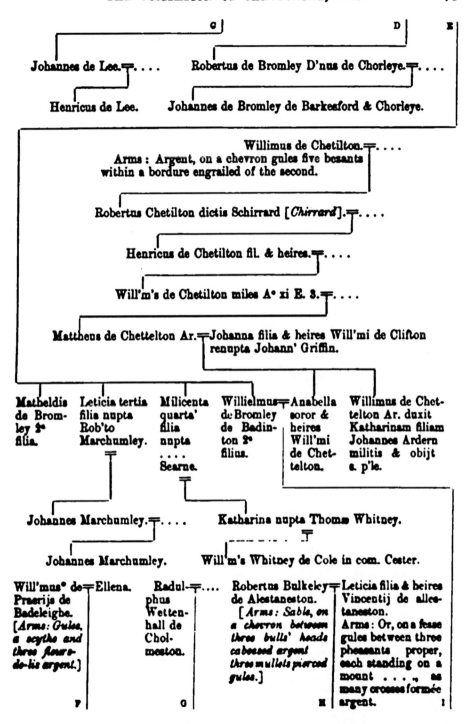

C | D | E

Johannes de Lee.=....   Robertus de Bromley D'nus de Chorleye.=....

Henricus de Lee.   Johannes de Bromley de Barkesford & Chorleye.

Willimus de Chetilton.=....
Arms : Argent, on a chevron gules five besants
within a bordure engrailed of the second.

Robertus Chetilton dictis Schirrard [*Chirrard*].=....

Henricus de Chetilton fil. & heires.=....

Will'm's de Chetilton miles A° xi E. 3.=....

Mattheus de Chettelton Ar.=Johanna filia & heires Will'mi de Clifton
renupta Johann' Griffin.

| Matheldis de Bromley 2° filia. | Leticia tertia filia nupta Rob'to Marchumley. | Milicenta quarta' filia nupta .... Searne. | Willielmus de Bromley de Badinton 2° filius. | Anabella soror & heires Will'mi de Chettelton. | Willimus de Chettelton Ar. duxit Katharinam filiam Johannes Ardern militis & obijt s. p'le. |

Johannes Marchumley.=....   Katharina nupta Thomas Whitney.

Johannes Marchumley.   Will'm's Whitney de Cole in com. Cester.

| Will'mus* de=Ellena. Praerijs de Badeleigbe. [*Arms: Gules, a scythe and three fleur-de-lis argent.*] | Radul-=.... phus Wettenhall de Cholmeston. | Robertus Bulkeley=Leticia filia & heires de Alestaneston. [*Arms: Sable, on a chevron between three bulls' heads caboosed argent three mullets pierced gules.*] | Vincentij de allestaneston. Arms: Or, on a fesse gules between three pheasants proper, each standing on a mount ...., as many crosses formée argent. |

F | G | H | I

* Will'mus de Praers de Badeleigh et Helena vxor eius & Thomas Praers filius dictorum
Will'mi & Helena citantur in Carta data n° 22 E. 3.

L

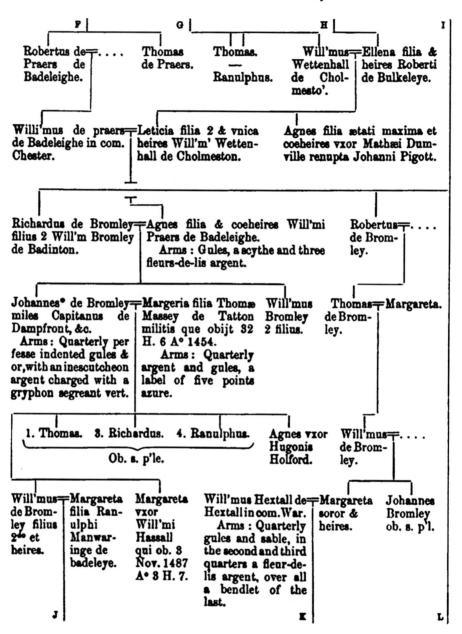

F

Robertus de=.... Praers de Badeleighe.

G

Thomas de Praers.

Thomas.
—
Ranulphus.

H

Will'mus=Ellena filia & Wettenhall de Cholmesto'.

heires Roberti de Bulkeleye.

I

Willi'mus de praers=Leticia filia 2 & vnica de Badeleighe in com. Chester.

heires Will'm' Wettenhall de Cholmeston.

Agnes filia ætati maxima et coeheires vxor Mathæi Dumville renupta Johanni Pigott.

Richardus de Bromley=Agnes filia & coeheires Will'mi filius 2 Will'm Bromley de Badinton.

Praers de Badeleighe.
Arms : Gules, a scythe and three fleurs-de-lis argent.

Robertus=.... de Bromley.

Johannes* de Bromley=Margeria filia Thomæ miles Capitanus de Dampfront, &c.
Arms : Quarterly per fesse indented gules & or, with an inescutcheon argent charged with a gryphon segreant vert.

Massey de Tatton militis que obijt 32 H. 6 A° 1454.
Arms : Quarterly argent and gules, a label of five points azure.

Will'mus Bromley 2 filius.

Thomas=Margareta. de Bromley.

1. Thomas.   3. Richardus.   4. Ranulphus.

Ob. s. p'le.

Agnes vxor Hugonis Holford.

Will'mus=.... de Bromley.

Will'mus=Margareta de Bromley filius 2do et heires.

filia Ranulphi Manwaringe de badeleye.

Margareta vxor Will'mi Hassall qui ob. 8 Nov. 1487 A° 3 H. 7.

Will'mus Hextall de=Margareta Hextall in com. War.
Arms : Quarterly gules and sable, in the second and third quarters a fleur-de-lis argent, over all a bendlet of the last.

soror & heires.

Johannes Bromley ob. s. p'l.

J

K

L

* Joh'es iste de Bromley miles Capitaneus generalis de Dampfront Senescallus et Magnus Constabularius de Bosseville le Rose et marchiarum ib'm dedit dilecto consanguineo suo Waltero de Audeley pro bono et fideli servitio suo, sibi tam infra Regnum Angliæ quam extra, et præcipue contra francos præstito annualem reddetum xxᴹ percipiend' ex mannerio suo de Bromley et omnibus alijs terris suis et ten'tis infra Regum Angliæ durante vita naturali d'c'i Walteri, cum clausula districc'onis pro defectu soluconis. Et id quidem per l'ras suas patentes datas apod Dampfront 12 die Augusti A° 6 H. 5 et sigillatus cum sigillo Armorum dicti Joh'is Bromley Quod in scuto maiori quarteriato et ex transuerso indentato præ se ferebat minorem scutem gryphone rapaci conspicuum super galliam demediati Leonis pars anterior e corona emergebat, vexillum Ducatus Guiennæ siue Aquitanniæ ambobus sustentantem tibiis. [Harl. 1396.]

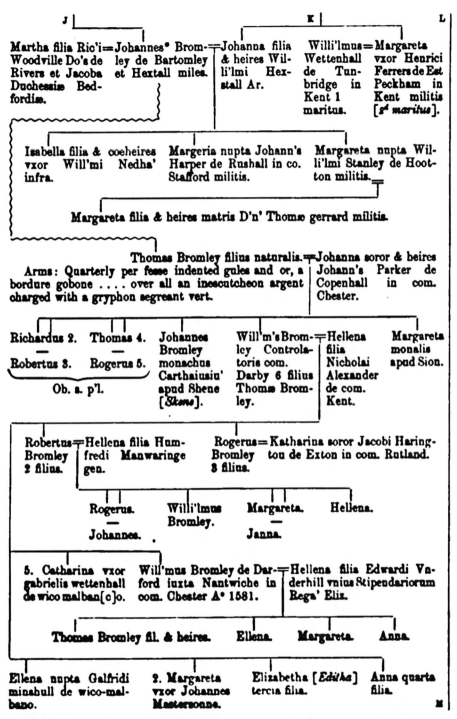

J

Martha filia Ric'i=Johannes* Brom-=Johanna filia
Woodville Do's de ley de Bartomley & heires Wil-
Rivers et Jacoba et Hextall miles. li'lmi Hex-
Duchessiæ Bed-   stall Ar.
fordiæ.

K

Willi'lmus=Margareta
Wettenhall vxor Henrici
de Tun- Ferrers de Est
bridge in Peckham in
Kent 1 Kent militis
maritus. [s⁴ maritus].

L

Isabella filia & coeheires   Margeria nupta Johann's   Margareta nupta Wil-
vxor   Will'mi   Nedha'   Harper de Rushall in co.   li'lmi Stanley de Hoot-
infra.   Stafford militis.   ton militis.

Margareta filia & heires matris D'n' Thomæ gerrard militis.

Thomas Bromley filius naturalis.=Johanna soror & heires
Arms: Quarterly per fesse indented gules and or, a   Johann's Parker de
bordure gobone .... over all an inescutcheon argent Copenhall   in   com.
charged with a gryphon segreant vert.   Chester.

Richardus 2.   Thomas 4.   Johannes   Will'm's Brom-=Hellena   Margareta
—   —   Bromley   ley Controla- filia   monalis
Robertus 3.   Rogerus 5.   monachus   toris com.   Nicholai   apud Sion.
                             Carthaiusin' Darby 6 filius Alexander
        Ob. a. p'l.   apud Shene   Thomæ Brom- de com.
                             [Stone].   ley.   Kent.

Robertus=Hellena filia Hum-   Rogerus=Katharina soror Jacobi Haring-
Bromley fredi Manwaringe   Bromley ton de Exton in com. Rutland.
2 filius. gen.   3 filius.

Rogerus.   Willi'lmus   Margareta.   Hellena.
—   Bromley.   —
Johannes.   Janna.

5. Catharina vxor   Will'mus Bromley de Dar-=Hellena filia Edwardi Va-
gabrielis wettenhall ford iuxta Nantwiche in   derhill vnius Stipendariorum
de wico malban[c]o.   com. Chester A° 1581.   Rega' Eliz.

Thomas Bromley fil. & heires.   Ellena.   Margareta.   Anna.

Ellena nupta Galfridi   2. Margareta   Elizabetha [Edith]   Anna quarta
minshull de wico-mal-   vxor Johannes   tercia filia.   filia.
bano.   Mastersoone.

M

* Rgo Johannes de Bromley miles dedi dilecto filio meo Thomæ Bromley filio & hæredi
apparenti mei præfati Joh'is de Bromley militis annualem redditum viginti marcarum & datum
apud Wicum Malbaam 4° April 18 E. 4.   [Harl. 1396.]

M |

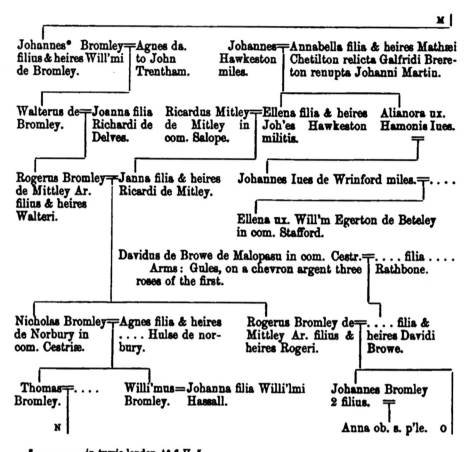

Johannes* Bromley=Agnes da. to John Trentham.
filius & heires Will'mi de Bromley.

Johannes=Annabella filia & heires Mathæi
Hawkeston Chetilton relicta Galfridi Brere-
miles. ton renupta Johanni Martin.

Walterus de=Joanna filia Ricardus Mitley=Ellena filia & heires Alianora ux.
Bromley. Richardi de de Mitley in Joh'es Hawkeston Hamonis Iues.
Delves. com. Salope. militia.

Rogerus Bromley=Janna filia & heires Johannes Iues de Wrinford miles.=. . . .
de Mittley Ar. Ricardi de Mitley.
filius & heires Walteri.

Ellena ux. Will'm Egerton de Beteley
in com. Stafford.

Davidus de Browe de Malopasu in com. Cestr.=. . . . filia . . . .
Arms: Gules, on a chevron argent three Rathbone.
roses of the first.

Nicholas Bromley=Agnes filia & heires Rogerus Bromley de=. . . . filia &
de Norbury in . . . . Hulse de nor- Mittley Ar. filius & heires Davidi
com. Cestriæ. bury. heires Rogeri. Browe.

Thomas=. . . . Willi'mus=Johanna filia Willi'lmi Johannes Bromley
Bromley. Bromley. Hassall. 2 filius. =

N | Anna ob. s. p'le. O |

* . . . . in turris london A° 6 H. 5.

. . . . omnibus ad quos p'ntes l'ra peruenerit salutem. Sciatis quod de gra' n'ra speciali et pro bono seruitio quod dilectus seruiens noster Joh'es Bromley nobis nuper dit in futurum dedimus et concessimus ei hospicium de Molay Bacon' infra comitatum n'rum de Baieux ac omnia t'ras ten'ta redditus hæreditates et possessiones infra Ducatam n'rum Normanniæ quæ futurunt Alani de Beaumont nobis rebellis vt dicitur. Habend' et tenend' præfato Joh'is et hæredibus suis masculis de corpore suo procreatis etc. ad valorem quadraginta librarum sterlingorum per annum tantum de nobis et hæred' n'ris per homagium etc. ac reddendo nobis et eisdem hæredibus n'ris apud Castellum n'rum de Baieux vna' sonam pro lorica ad festum S'c'i Joh'es Baptistæ singulis annis etc. Teste me ipso apud d'cam ciuitatem n'ram de Baieux 18 die Aprillis An° Regni n'ri sexto Per ipsum Regem. [Harl. 1396.]

* Hoc præsens scriptum testatur quod nos Hugo de Stafford D'nus de Bourghchier concessimus et per p'ntes confirmauimus prædilecto consanguineo n'ro Joh'i Bromley de Bromley Armigero, pro suo magno auxilio nobis impenso in oppugnatione contra Franc' prope le Corbye et præcipue pro suo laudabili seruitio in recuperatione et supportatione vexilli D'ni Regis de Guienne sub nostra conductione, vnam annuetatem siue annualem redditum quadraginta librarum legalis monetæ annuatim percipiend' durante tota vita naturali præd'c'i Joh'is de Bromley de et in omnibus mannerijs terris et tenementis nostris cum pertinentia in co. Stafford et Warrwic' ad festa Pentecostis et S'c'i Martini in yeme equis portionibus etc. Et si contingat etc. et ut hac nostra concessio et scripti huius confirmatio durante tota vita prædic' Joh's de Bromley vt præfectur rata et stabilis permaneat, hoc scriptum impressione sigilli Armorum meorum roboraui. Hijs testibus Johanne de Hollande, Ricardo de Greuill, Ricardo de Harewood, Thoma lo Forestar et alijs dat. aped Madeley decimo die mensis Martij An° Regni Regis Hen. Quinti post conquestum Quarto.

Supra scripta omnia ex chartarum, euidentiarum, monumentorum aliarumq' rerum venerandæ antiquitatis et indubitatæ fidei (è quibus plærunq' veritas ipsa elici solet) diligenti in spectione et curiosa in dagatione, fideliter esse de sumpta testantur qui hic in calce subscripserunt a° 1583.

ROBERT COOKE, Clarenceux. ROBERT GLOVER, Somersett. [Harl. 1396.]

N

O

Thomas Bromley de Hampton.⚌Elizabetha filia .... Wilbraham.

Willimus Bromley.⚌Elizabetha filia .... Huntington.

Alicia filia & heires⚌Hugo Bromley de⚌Elizabetha filia .... Dimocke
[Thomas] Egerton   Hampton in com.   de Willington in com. Denbighe
de Hampton.   Cestriæ.   vx. 2ᵃ.

Hugo Bromley de Norbury in⚌Anna filia Davidis massey de
com. Cestriæ Aᵒ 1597.   Broxton in com. Cestriæ.

Thomas Bromley fil. & heires.   Dorothia.   Alicia.

Rogerus Bromley⚌Janna filia Thomæ   Humfridus Bromley quartus filius
3 filius.   Jenninges.   obijt sine prole legitima.

Willimus Bromley de Stoke⚌Margareta filia Francisci Yonge
fil's primogen's.   de Kenton in com. Salop.

Willimus Bromley ob. s. p'le.   Thomas Bromley ob. s. p'le.

Elizab. fil.⚌Thomas Bromley⚌Elizabetha filia   Rogerus Bromley⚌Janna filia
Ric. Lister miles 2 filius Capit' Joh'n' Dodd de   de Broughton 3 Pettri New-
de Rowton. Justi's Angliæ. Chorley.   filius s. p̃. ton militis.

Margareta filia & heires vxor Ric'i Newport militis infra.

Franciscus Newport de Arcall in com. Salop miles.

8ʳ Richard Newport of Arcall in co. Salop Knight sᵒ 1623.

Will'm Bromley of Mitley⚌Beatrix da. of Humfry Hill of
Esq' son and heire.   Blore and Buntingsdale.

P

P

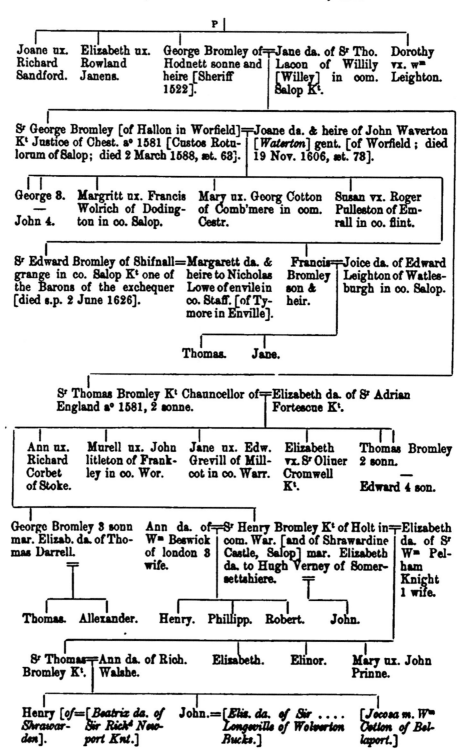

Joane ux. Richard Sandford.

Elizabeth ux. Rowland Janens.

George Bromley of Hodnett sonne and heire [Sheriff 1522].=Jane da. of Sʳ Tho. Lacon of Willily [Willey] in oom. Salop Kᵗ.

Dorothy vx. wᵐ Leighton.

Sʳ George Bromley [of Hallon in Worfield] Kᵗ Justice of Chest. aº 1581 [Custos Rotulorum of Salop; died 2 March 1588, æt. 63].=Joane da. & heire of John Waverton [Waterton] gent. [of Worfield; died 19 Nov. 1606, æt. 78].

George 8.
—
John 4.

Margritt ux. Francis Wolrich of Dodington in co. Salop.

Mary ux. Georg Cotton of Comb'mere in com. Cestr.

Susan vx. Roger Pulleston of Emrall in co. flint.

Sʳ Edward Bromley of Shifnall grange in co. Salop Kᵗ one of the Barons of the exchequer [died s.p. 2 June 1626].=Margarett da. & heire to Nicholas Lowe of envile in co. Staff. [of Tymore in Enville].

Francis Bromley son & heir.=Joice da. of Edward Leighton of Watlesburgh in co. Salop.

Thomas.   Jane.

Sʳ Thomas Bromley Kᵗ Chauncellor of England aº 1581, 2 sonne.=Elizabeth da. of Sʳ Adrian Fortescue Kᵗ.

Ann ux. Richard Corbet of Stoke.

Murell ux. John litleton of Frankley in co. Wor.

Jane ux. Edw. Grevill of Millcot in co. Warr.

Elizabeth vx. Sʳ Oliuer Cromwell Kᵗ.

Thomas Bromley 2 sonn.
—
Edward 4 son.

George Bromley 3 sonn mar. Elizab. da. of Thomas Darrell.

Ann da. of Wᵐ Beswick of london 3 wife.=Sʳ Henry Bromley Kᵗ of Holt in com. War. [and of Shrawardine Castle, Salop] mar. Elizabeth da. to Hugh Verney of Somersettshiere.=Elizabeth da. of Sʳ Wᵐ Pelham Knight 1 wife.

Thomas.   Allexander.

Henry.   Phillipp.   Robert.   John.

Sʳ Thomas Bromley Kᵗ.=Ann da. of Rich. Walshe.

Elisabeth.

Elinor.

Mary ux. John Prinne.

Henry [of Shrawarden].=[Beatrix da. of Sir Rickᵈ Newport Knt.]

John.=[Elis. da. of Sir . . . . Longeville of Wolverton Bucks.]

[Jocosa m. Wᵐ Cotton of Bellaport.]

Brooke of Madeley, Claverley, Church Stretton, etc.

Harl. 1396, fo. 51ᵇ. Harl. 1241, fo. 64. S., ff. 53ᵇ, 54.

ARMS: Harl. 1396.—*Quarterly*: 1 *and* 4, *Checky argent and sable* [BROOKE];
2, *Argent, a cross patonce sable* [BANASTRE]; 3, *Gules, a fesse componée
or and azure between seven—eight in* Harl. 1241—*billets argent* [LEE];
over all a crescent for difference.

CREST.—*On a mount vert a brock proper charged with a crescent for difference.*

Harl. 1241 gives as the fourth quartering: *Gules* in Shrewsbury MS.—*on a fesse
engrailed or between three bucks' heads cabossed argent, attired gold, as many
crescents* [bugle-horns] *sable* [WARING].

ANOTHER COAT: Shrewsbury MS.—*Checky argent and sable, on a chief or a brock
proper.*

CREST.—*A stork or.*

Per Cooke Clarenc, 1587.—S. fo. 53ᵇ.

Richardus Brooke de = ... filia .... Banester de Hadon-
Cloreby *Cloreley*. | hall *Hadnoll* [Hadnall].

Thomas Brooke. = ... fil. ... Hill de Beckington.

Richardus Brooke. = Emma fil. et hæ. Ric'i Morffe de Bridgnorth *Morffe of Morffe.*

Richardus Brooke. = Margeria fil. et hær. Joh'es Lee de Stanton et Langley.

Thomas Brooke. = Margaretta fil. Ric'i Spicer de Charley *Clareley* [Claverley].

Joh'es Brooke de Bouenton = ... filia .... Butler de Bewsey
Berenton in com. Staff. | in com. Lancastriæ.

Radulphi Brooke 1. | Griffinus 3. | Margaretta VI. | .... nupta ....
— | — | .... Whitwick. | Brooke de Rowton
Johannes 2. | Michaell 4. | | in com. Salop.

Franciscus Brooke de Blakeland = Elizab. fil. Roberti Banester de
in co. Staff. 5 filius. | lacon in com. Salop.

Robertus | Ed'r'us Brooke de = Francisca fil. Ric'i | Joonsa VI. Ed-
Brooke 2. | Church Stretton | Leighton de le Cotes | wardi Acton de
| in com. Salop fil. | in p'och' de Bashbery | Acton Scott in
| et hær. | in co. Salop. | com. Salop.

A B

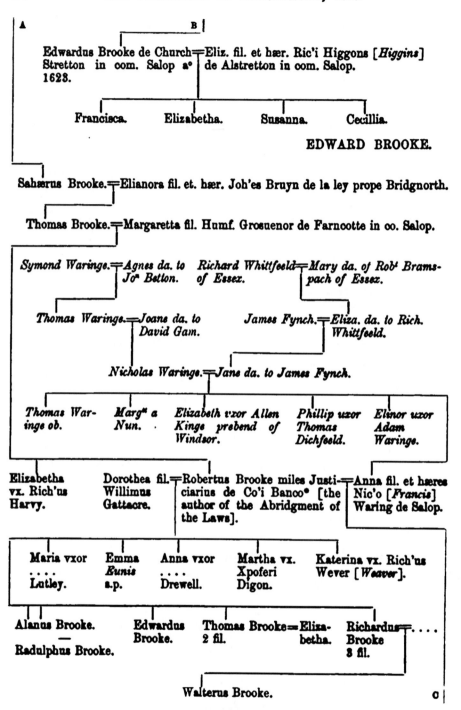

A

B

Edwardus Brooke de Church=Eliz. fil. et hær. Ric'i Higgons [*Higgins*]
Stretton in com. Salop a° | de Alstretton in com. Salop.
1623.

Francisca.   Elizabetha.   Susanna.   Cecillia.

EDWARD BROOKE.

Sahærus Brooke.=Elianora fil. et. hær. Joh'es Bruyn de la ley prope Bridgnorth.

Thomas Brooke.=Margaretta fil. Humf. Grosuenor de Farncotte in co. Salop.

Symond Waringe.=*Agnes da. to*   *Richard Whittfeeld*=*Mary da. of Rob¹ Brams-*
                 Jo⁰ Betton.   *of Essex.*   *pach of Essex.*

        Thomas Waringe.=*Joane da. to*   *James Fynch.*=*Eliza. da. to Rich.*
                          David Gam.   *Whittfeeld.*

        Nicholas Waringe.=*Jane da. to James Fynch.*

Thomas War-   *Marg^t a*   *Elizabeth vxor Allen*   *Phillip uxor*   *Elinor uxor*
inge ob.   *Nun.*   *Kinge prebend of*   *Thomas*   *Adam*
                              Windsor.   *Dichfeeld.*   *Waringe.*

Elizabetha   Dorothea fil.=Robertus Brooke miles Justi-=Anna fil. et hæres
vx. Rich'us   Willimus   ciarius de Co'i Banco* [the   Nic'o [*Francis*]
Harvy.   Gattacre.   author of the Abridgment of   Waring de Salop.
                              the Laws].

    Maria vxor   Emma   Anna vxor   Martha vx.   Katerina vx. Rich'us
    ....   *Eunis* ....   Xpoferi   Wever [*Weaver*].
    Lutley.   s.p.   Drewell.   Digon.

Alanus Brooke.   Edwardus   Thomas Brooke=Eliza-   Richardus=....
    —   Brooke.   2 fil.   betha.   Brooke
Radulphus Brooke.   3 fil.

                Walterus Brooke.   C

* M.P. for London ; Speaker 1552 ; Chief Justice of Common Pleas 8 October 1552 ;
knighted 27 January 1555 ; died 6 September 1558 ; buried at Claverley ; purchased Madeley
in 1544, for £946 3s. 8d.

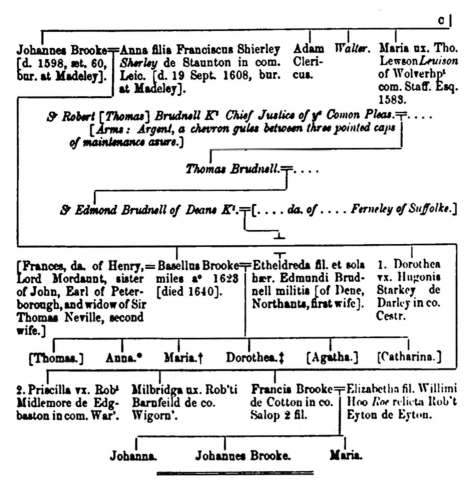

Johannes Brooke=Anna filia Franciscus Shierley   Adam   *Walter.*   Maria ux. Tho.
[d. 1598, æt. 60, *Sherley* de Staunton in com.   Cleri-   Lewson*Leuison*
bur. at Madeley].   Leic. [d. 19 Sept. 1608, bur.   cus.   of Wolverhp[t]
                    at Madeley].   com. Staff. Esq.
                                                                       1583.

& Robert [Thomas] Brudnell K[t] Chief Justice of y[e] Comon Pleas.=. . . .
        [Arms: Argent, a chevron gules between three pointed caps
of maintenance azure.]

Thomas Brudnell.=. . . .

& Edmond Brudnell of Deane K[t].=[. . . . da. of . . . . Ferneley of Suffolke.]

[Frances, da. of Henry, = Basellus Brooke=Etheldreda fil. et sola   1. Dorothea
Lord Mordaunt, sister   miles a° 1623   hær. Edmundi Brud-   vx. Hugonis
of John, Earl of Peter- [died 1640].   nell militis [of Dene,   Starkey de
borough, and widow of Sir   Northants, first wife].   Darley in co.
Thomas Neville, second   Cestr.
wife.]

[Thomas.]   Anna.*   Maria.†   Dorothea.‡   [Agatha.]   [Catharina.]

2. Priscilla vx. Rob[t]   Milbridga ux. Rob'ti   Francis Brooke=Elizabetha fil. Willimi
Midlemore de Edg-   Barnfeild de co.   de Cotton in co. Hoo *Roe* relicta Rob't
baston in com. War'.   Wigorn'.   Salop 2 fil.   Eyton de Eyton.

            Johanna.   Johannes Brooke.   Maria.

Broughton of Broughton and Henley.

Harl. 1396, fo. 24[b].   Harl. 1241, fo. 58[b].   Harl. 615, fo. 243.   S., ff. 32[b], 33.

ARMS: Harl. 1396.—*Quarterly of seven: 1, Argent, two bars gules, on a canton of
the second a saltire§ of the first; 2, Gules, a bend ermine between two mullets
argent* [HODNETT]; *3, Azure, three boars' heads couped [or ?] between nine
cross-crosslets fitchée or [? argent,* HEVIN]; *4, Argent in* Harl. 615—*crusily
—azure in* Harl. 615—*and two trumpets pilewaye—gules in* Harl. 615
[DOWNTON]; *5, Barry of six gules and or—gules and argent in* Shrewsbury MS.
—gules, two bars or in Harl. 615—[argent, ST. OWEN']; *6, Azure, a lion
rampant argent within a bordure engrailed or* [argent, TIRRELL]; *7, Vert,
a gryphon segreant or within a bordure‖ of the second* [COLLINS].
CREST.—*A talbot statant gules.*

    * Anne was the wife of William Fitzherbert, Esq., great-grandson (pronepos) of Sir Anthony
Fitzherbert, Chief Justice of the Common Pleas. (M.I. Madeley Church.)
    † Mary was the wife of Thomas More, Esq., great-great-grandson (abnepos) of Sir Thomas
More, Lord Chancellor. (M.I. Madeley Church.)
    ‡ According to Foster's 'Lancashire Pedigrees,' Dorothy was married in 1622 to Joseph
Glassbrooke of Madeley, gent.
    § A cross is given, instead of a saltire, in Harl. 1241 and Harl. 615.
    ‖ The bordure omitted in Harl. 1241.

M

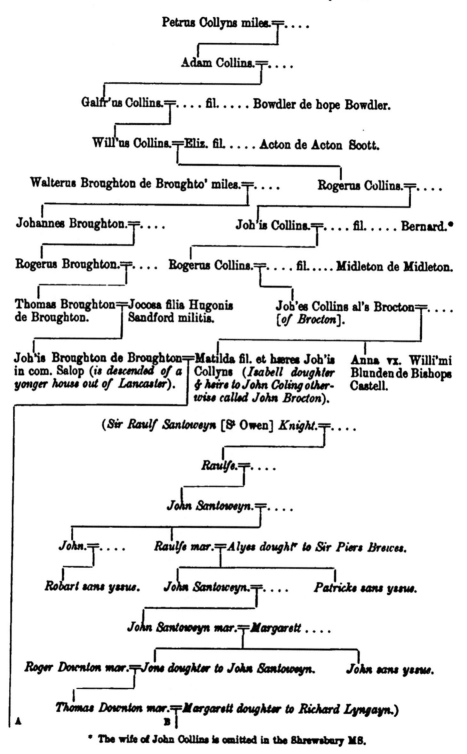

Petrus Collyns miles.=....

Adam Collins.=....

Galfr'us Collins.=.... fil. .... Bowdler de hope Bowdler.

Will'us Collins.=Eliz. fil. .... Acton de Acton Scott.

Walterus Broughton de Broughto' miles.=....   Rogerus Collins.=....

Johannes Broughton.=....   Joh'is Collins.=.... fil. .... Bernard.*

Rogerus Broughton.=....   Rogerus Collins.=.... fil.... Midleton de Midleton.

Thomas Broughton=Jocosa filia Hugonis   Joh'es Collins al's Brocton=....
de Broughton.   Sandford militis.   [of Brocton].

Joh'is Broughton de Broughton=Matilda fil. et hæres Joh'is   Anna vx. Willi'mi
in com. Salop (is descended of a   Collyns (Isabell doughter   Blunden de Bishops
yonger house out of Lancaster).   & heire to John Coling other-   Castell.
                                          wise called John Brocton).

(Sir Raulf Santoweyn [S' Owen] Knight.=....

Raulfe.=....

John Santoweyn.=....

John.=....   Raulfe mar.=Alyes dought' to Sir Piers Brewes.

Robart sans yssue.   John Santoweyn.=....   Patricke sans yssue.

John Santoweyn mar.=Margarett ....

Roger Downton mar.=Jone doughter to John Santoweyn.   John sans yssue.

Thomas Downton mar.=Margarett doughter to Richard Lyngayn.)

A   B

* The wife of John Collins is omitted in the Shrewsbury MS.

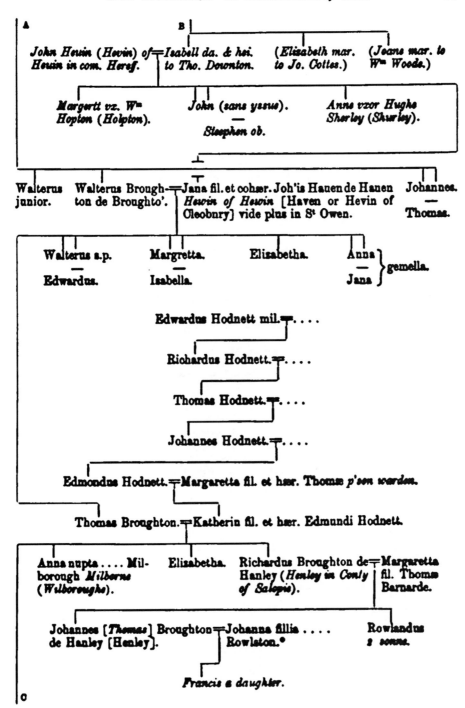

* Harl. 1241 and Harl. 615 say "Soana da. to Lawrence Rowiston or Roiston de Rowiston in com. Stafford."

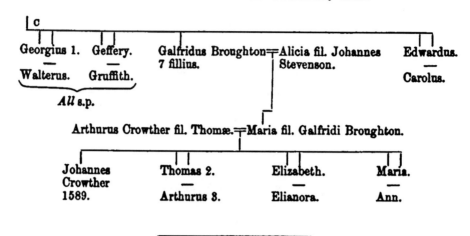

Georgius 1.   Geffery.   Galfridus Broughton=Alicia fil. Johannes   Edwardus.
—   —   7 fillius.   Stevenson.   —
Walterus.   Gruffith.   Carolus.

All s.p.

Arthurus Crowther fil. Thomæ.=Maria fil. Galfridi Broughton.

Johannes   Thomas 2.   Elizabeth.   Maria.
Crowther   —   —   —
1589.   Arthurus 3.   Elianora.   Ann.

Broughton of Broughton, near Bishops Castle; Lloyd of Marrington, etc.

Harl. 1396, fo. 27.   S., fo. 33.

ARMS: Harl. 1396.—*Quarterly:* 1, *Sable, three horses' heads argent erased gules* [LLOYD OF MARRINGTON]; 2, *Gules, a gryphon segreant or* [LLOWDDEN]; 3, *Sable, three owls argent* [BROUGHTON]; 4, *Gules, three serpents interlaced argent* [EDNOWEN AP BRADWEN].

ARMS: Harl. 1396: LLOYD OF MARRINGTON.—*Quarterly of eight:* 1, *Sable, three horses' heads erased argent;* 2, *Gules, a gryphon segreant or* [LLOWDEN and VAUGHAN]; 3, *Sable, a chevron between three owls argent* [BROUGHTON or HAFORD OF EVETT]; 4, *Gules, three serpents interlaced argent* [EDNOWEN AP BRADWEN]; 5, *Argent, on a bend vert three wolves' heads erased of the first* [MIDDLETON]; 6, *Vert, a chevron between three wolves' heads erased argent* [RIRID VLAIDD]; 7, *Gules, on a bend or three lions passant sable* [WYNNESBURY]; 8, *Argent, two Cornish choughs in pale sable, beaked and legged gules* [BOWDLER].

CREST.—*A horse's head erased argent.*

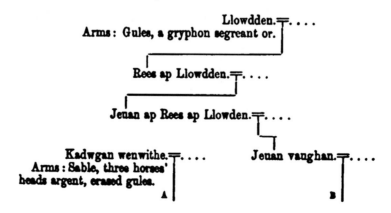

Llowdden.=. . . .
Arms: Gules, a gryphon segreant or.

Rees ap Llowdden.=. . . .

Jeuan ap Rees ap Llowden.=. . . .

Kadwgan wenwithe.=. . . .   Jeuan vaughan.=. . . .
Arms: Sable, three horses'
heads argent, erased gules.

A   B

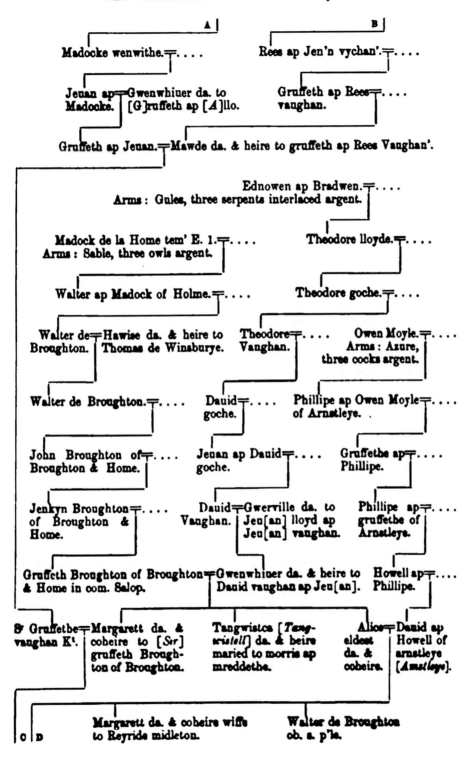

A |

Madocke wenwithe.=....

B |

Rees ap Jen'n vychan'.=....

Jenan ap=Gwenwhiuer da. to
Madocke. | [G]ruffeth ap [A]llo.

Gruffeth ap Rees=....
vaughan.

Gruffeth ap Jenan.=Mawde da. & heire to gruffeth ap Rees Vaughan'.

Ednowen ap Bradwen.=....
Arms: Gules, three serpents interlaced argent. |

Madock de la Home tem' E. 1.=....
Arms: Sable, three owls argent.

Theodore lloyde.=....

Walter ap Madock of Holme.=....

Theodore goche.=....

Walter de=Hawise da. & heire to
Broughton. | Thomas de Winsburye.

Theodore=....
Vaughan.

Owen Moyle.=....
Arms: Azure,
three cocks argent.

Walter de Broughton.=....

Dauid=....
goche.

Phillipe ap Owen Moyle=....
of Arnstleye.

John Broughton of=....
Broughton & Home. |

Jenan ap Dauid=....
goche.

Gruffethe ap=....
Phillipe.

Jenkyn Broughton=....
of Broughton &
Home.

Dauid=Gwerville da. to
Vaughan. | Jeu[an] lloyd ap
Jeu[an] vaughan.

Phillipe ap=....
gruffethe of
Arnstleye.

Gruffeth Broughton of Broughton=Gwenwhiuer da. & heire to
& Home in com. Salop. | Dauid vaughan ap Jeu[an].

Howell ap=....
Phillipe.

Sr Gruffethe=Margarett da. &
vaughan Kt. | coheire to [Sir]
gruffeth Brough-
ton of Broughton.

Tangwistca [Tang-
wistoll] da. & heire
maried to morris ap
mreddethe.

Alice=Dauid ap
eldest | Howell of
da. & | arnstleye
coheire. | [Amstleye].

O | D

Margarett da. & coheire wiffe
to Reyride midleton.

Walter de Broughton
ob. a p'le.

O | D

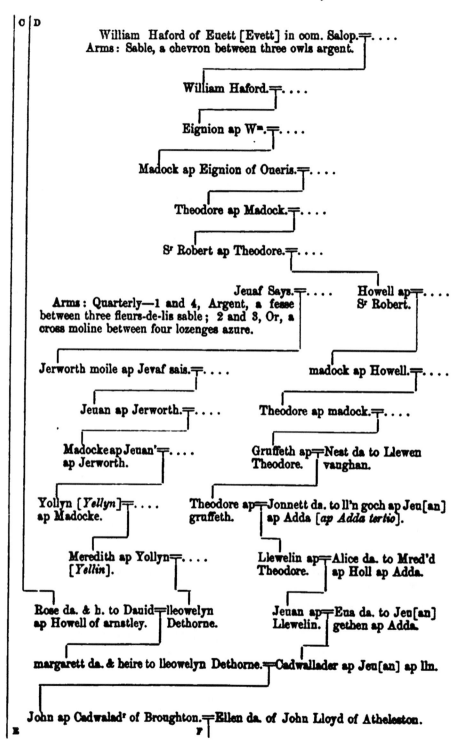

William Haford of Euett [Evett] in com. Salop.=....
Arms: Sable, a chevron between three owls argent.

William Haford.=....

Eignion ap W^m.=....

Madock ap Eignion of Oneris.=....

Theodore ap Madock.=....

Sr Robert ap Theodore.=....

Jenaf Says.=....   Howell ap=....
                                    Sr Robert.

Arms: Quarterly—1 and 4, Argent, a fesse
between three fleurs-de-lis sable; 2 and 3, Or, a
cross moline between four lozenges azure.

Jerworth moile ap Jevaf sais.=....   madock ap Howell.=....

Jenan ap Jerworth.=....   Theodore ap madock.=....

Madocke ap Jenan'=....   Gruffeth ap=Neat da to Llewen
ap Jerworth.   Theodore. | vaughan.

Yollyn [Yollyn]=....   Theodore ap=Jonnett da. to ll'n goch ap Jen[an]
ap Madocke.   gruffeth. | ap Adda [ap Adda tertio].

Meredith ap Yollyn=....   Llewelin ap=Alice da. to Mred'd
[Yellin].   Theodore. | ap Holl ap Adda.

Rose da. & h. to Dauid=lleowelyn   Jenan ap=Ena da. to Jen[an]
ap Howell of arnstley. | Dethorne. Llewelin. | gethen ap Adda.

margarett da. & heire to lleowelyn Dethorne.=Cadwallader ap Jen[an] ap lln.

John ap Cadwalad^r of Broughton.=Ellen da. of John Lloyd of Atheleston.

E   F

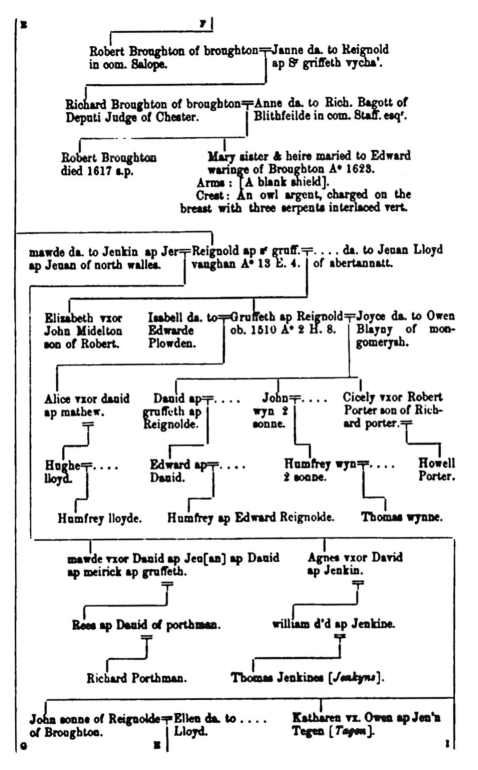

E   F

Robert Broughton of broughton╤Janne da. to Reignold
in com. Salope.   ap & griffeth vycha'.

Richard Broughton of broughton╤Anne da. to Rich. Bagott of
Deputi Judge of Chester.   Blithfeilde in com. Staff. esq'.

Robert Broughton   Mary sister & heire maried to Edward
died 1617 s.p.   waringe of Broughton A° 1623.
               Arms : [A blank shield].
               Crest : An owl argent, charged on the
               breast with three serpents interlaced vert.

mawde da. to Jenkin ap Jer╤Reignold ap s' gruff.╤.... da. to Jenan Lloyd
ap Jenan of north walles.   vanghan A° 13 E. 4.   of abertannatt.

Elizabeth vxor   Isabell da. to╤Gruffeth ap Reignold╤Joyce da. to Owen
John Midelton   Edwarde   ob. 1510 A° 2 H. 8.   Blayny of mon-
son of Robert.   Plowden.   gomeryrh.

Alice vxor danid   Danid ap╤....   John╤....   Cicely vxor Robert
ap mathew.   gruffeth ap   wyn 2   Porter son of Rich-
╤   Reignolde.   sonne.   ard porter.╤

Hughe╤....   Edward ap╤....   Humfrey wyn╤....   Howell
lloyd.   Danid.   2 sonne.   Porter.

Humfrey lloyde.   Humfrey ap Edward Reignolde.   Thomas wynne.

mawde vxor Danid ap Jen[an] ap Danid   Agnes vxor David
ap meirick ap gruffeth.   ap Jenkin.
╤   ╤

Rees ap Danid of porthman.   william d'd ap Jenkine.
╤   ╤

Richard Porthman.   Thomas Jenkines [*Jenkyns*].

John sonne of Reignolde╤Ellen da. to ....   Katharen vx. Owen ap Jen'n
of Broughton.   Lloyd.   Tegen [*Tegen*].

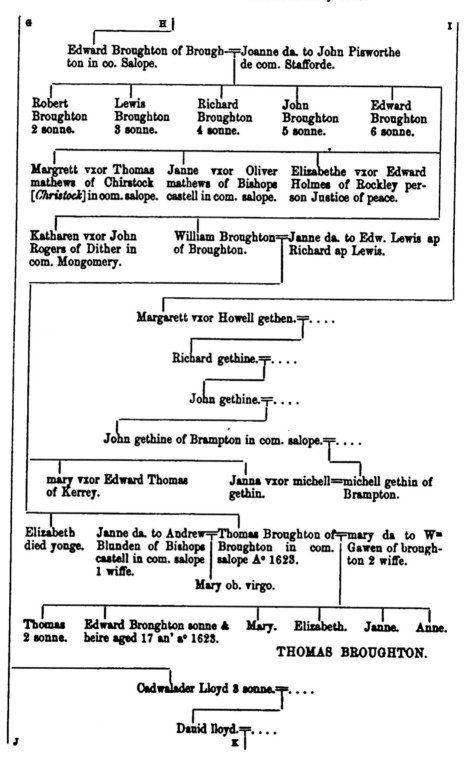

G | H | I

Edward Broughton of Brough-=Joanne da. to John Pisworthe
ton in co. Salope. | de com. Stafforde.

Robert Broughton 2 sonne. | Lewis Broughton 3 sonne. | Richard Broughton 4 sonne. | John Broughton 5 sonne. | Edward Broughton 6 sonne.

Margrett vxor Thomas mathews of Chirstock [*Christock*] in com. salope. | Janne vxor Oliver mathews of Bishops castell in com. salope. | Elizabethe vxor Edward Holmes of Rockley person Justice of peace.

Katharen vxor John Rogers of Dither in com. Mongomery. | William Broughton=Janne da. to Edw. Lewis ap of Broughton. | Richard ap Lewis.

Margarett vxor Howell gethen.=. . . .

Richard gethine.=. . . .

John gethine.=. . . .

John gethine of Brampton in com. salope.=. . . .

mary vxor Edward Thomas of Kerrey. | Janna vxor michell=michell gethin of gethin. | Brampton.

Elizabeth died yonge. | Janne da. to Andrew=Thomas Broughton of=mary da to Wm Blunden of Bishops castell in com. salope 1 wiffe. | Broughton in com. salope Aº 1623. | Gawen of broughton 2 wiffe.

Mary ob. virgo.

Thomas 2 sonne. | Edward Bronghton sonne & heire aged 17 an' aº 1623. | Mary. | Elizabeth. | Janne. | Anne.

THOMAS BROUGHTON.

Cadwalader Lloyd 3 sonne.=. . . .

Dauid lloyd.=. . . .

J | K

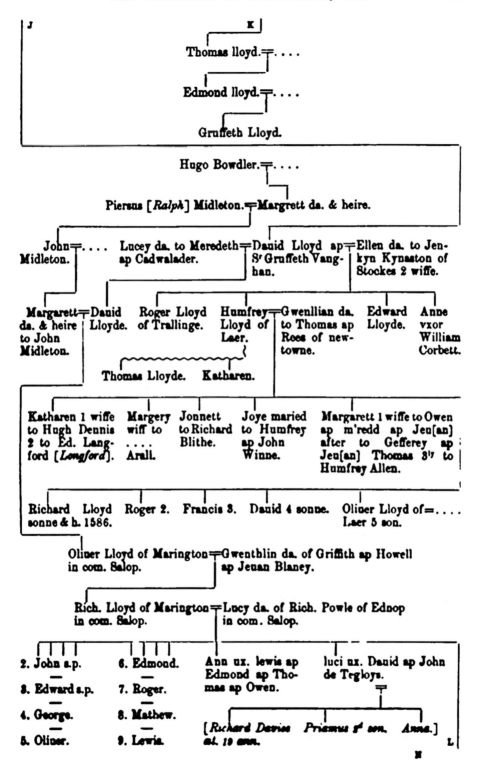

J   K

Thomas lloyd.=....

Edmond lloyd.=....

Gruffeth Lloyd.

Hugo Bowdler.=....

Piersus [*Ralph*] Midleton.=Margrett da. & heire.

John= ....   Lucey da. to Meredeth=Dauid Lloyd ap=Ellen da. to Jen-
Midleton.   ap Cadwalader.   Sᵗ Gruffeth Vang-   kyn Kynaston of
                      han.   Stockes 2 wiffe.

Margarett=Dauid   Roger Lloyd   Humfrey=Gwenllian da.   Edward   Anne
da. & heire | Lloyde.   of Trallinge.   Lloyd of | to Thomas ap   Lloyde.   vxor
to John   Laer. | Rees of new-   William
Midleton.   towne.   Corbett.

Thomas Lloyde.   Katharen.

Katharen 1 wiffe   Margery   Jonnett   Joye maried   Margarett 1 wiffe to Owen
to Hugh Dennis   wiff to   to Richard   to Humfrey   ap m'redd ap Jeu(an)
2 to Ed. Lang-   ....   Blithe.   ap John   after to Gefferey ap
ford [*Longford*].   Arall.   Winne.   Jeu(an) Thomas 3ˡʸ to
                                   Humfrey Allen.

Richard Lloyd   Roger 2.   Francis 3.   Dauid 4 sonne.   Oliuer Lloyd of=....
sonne & h. 1586.   Laer 5 son.

Oliuer Lloyd of Marington=Gwentblin da. of Griffith ap Howell
in com. Salop.   ap Jeuan Blaney.

Rich. Lloyd of Marington=Lucy da. of Rich. Powle of Ednop
in com. Salop.   in com. Salop.

2. John s.p.   6. Edmond.   Ann ux. lewis ap   luci ux. Dauid ap John
—   —   Edmond ap Tho-   de Tegloys.
3. Edward s.p.   7. Roger.   mas ap Owen.
—   —
4. George.   8. Mathew.
—   —
5. Oliuer.   9. Lewis.   [*Richard Dauies Priamus sᵗ son. Anna.*]
                            at. 19 ann.

L

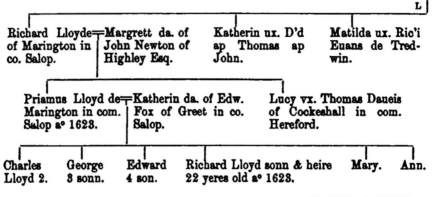

L|

Richard Lloyde══Margrett da. of John Newton of Highley Esq.   Katherin ux. D'd ap Thomas ap John.   Matilda ux. Ric'i Euans de Tredwin.

Priamus Lloyd de══Katherin da. of Edw. Fox of Greet in co. Salop.   Lucy vx. Thomas Daueis of Cockeshall in com. Hereford.

Charles Lloyd 2.   George 3 sonn.   Edward 4 son.   Richard Lloyd sonn & heire 22 yeres old a° 1623.   Mary.   Ann.

PRIAMᵇ LLOYD.

Browne of Morfe.

S., fo. 32.

[ARMS.—*Argent, a chevron between three mullets sable.*

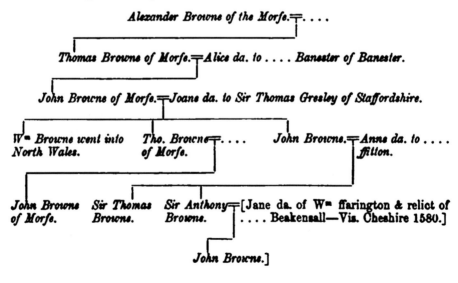

Alexander Browne of the Morfe.══ . . . .

Thomas Browne of Morfe.══Alice da. to . . . . Banester of Banester.

John Browne of Morfe.══Joane da. to Sir Thomas Gresley of Staffordshire.

Wᵐ Browne went into North Wales.   Tho. Browne══ . . . . of Morfe.   John Browne.══Anne da. to . . . . ffitton.

John Browne of Morfe.   Sir Thomas Browne.   Sir Anthony══[Jane da. of Wᵐ ffarington & relict of Browne.   . . . . Beakensall—Vis. Cheshire 1580.]

John Browne.]

Bullock of Sidnell.

S., fo. 38ᵃ.

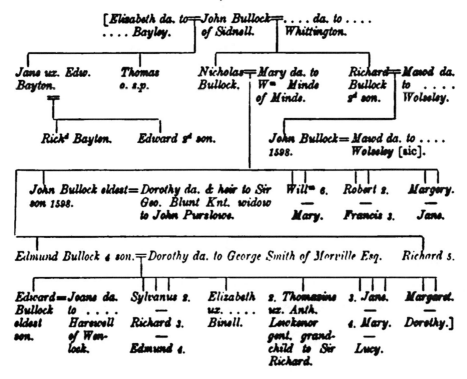

Edmund Bullock 4 son.＝Dorothy da. to George Smith of Morville Esq.   Richard 5.

Edward＝Joane da.	Sylvanus 2.	Elizabeth	2. Thomasine	3. Jane.	Margaret.
Bullock to	—	ux.	ux. Anth.	—	—
oldest Harewell	Richard 3.	Binell.	Leckenor	4. Mary.	Dorothy.]
son. of Wen-	—		gent. grand-		
lock.	Edmund 4.		child to Sir	Lucy.	
			Richard.		

═══════════

Burnell of Acton Burnell.

Harl. 1396, fo. 33ᵇ.   Harl. 1241, fo. 148ᵇ.   S., fo. 39ᵇ.

& Nicholas Burnell of acton Burnell in com. Salope Knight.＝....

Henry Burnell of Acton＝....	Edward Burnell of acton Burnell＝....
Burnell 2 sonne.	son & heire.

Edward *Edmond* Burnell of＝....	Joane da. & heire vxor Roger
Acton Burnell.	Lee of Langleye.

Thomas Burnell of frodesley＝.... da. to .... walker of pichford
in com. Salope.   in com. Salop.

▲

▲

Humfreye Burnell of Betton in com. Salop 1 sonne.	Foulke Burnell of Baschurche=.... in com. Salop 2 sonne.

Tho. Burnell of=Eleanor da. to Edw. Oweslowe Shrewesbury in [Onslow] of Owenslowe in com. Salope 1584. com. salope.	Anne maried to William Clarke of Hussington *Crussington* in com. Mungumrey.

𝔅urnell.

Harl. 1896, fo. 34.   S., fo., 40.

ARMS: Harl. 1896.—*Argent, a lion rampant sable crowned or within a bordure azure.*[*]

Ex libro Abbathiæ de Beldewas [Buildwas] in com. Salope.	Sr Robert Burnell Knight came in[to] England=.... with Will'm Conquerour died A° 1087 & buried at Buldewas.

Sr John Burnell Knight died A° 1107 & buried at Buldewas.=Petronell Corbett.

Sr Roger Burnell Knight died 1145 & buried at Buldewas.=....

Sr Hughe Burnell Knight died 1169=.... & buried at Buldewas.	Hellena Burnell died A° 1147.

Sr Richard Burnell Knight died A° 1189.=....

Sr William Burnell Knight died in the holy land=Isabell de Longespe. & buried at Buldewas [*1212*].

Sr Hugh Burnell Knight died 1242.=Petronell Cheynie.

Will'm Burnell submersus apud Neruin [*Nerum*] 1282.	Sr Robert Burnell Knight=.... sonn & heire died A° 1269.	Sr Phillipe Burnell Knight 1282.

▲

[*] Sir Edward Burnell, temp. Edw. I., bore: Argent, a lion rampant sable crowned or (Milit. Summonses). On 20 October 1395 a plea of arms for this coat was prosecuted by Sir John Lovel, as heir-general of the Burnells, against Sir Thomas Morley (Blomfield's 'Hist. of Norfolk,' vol. i., pp. 6 and 675). The evidence shews that Sir Philip de Burnell bore these arms and had issue Sir Edward Burnell, Knt., who died without issue, leaving Maude his sister and sole heir; she married Sir John, Lord Lovel, and had a son, Sir John Lovel, the plaintiff.

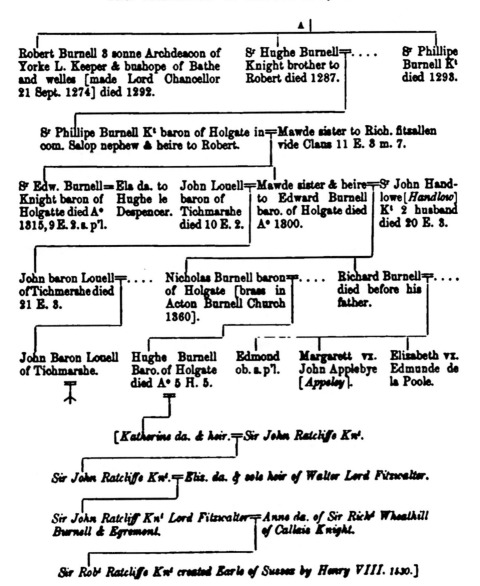

Robert Burnell 3 sonne Archdeacon of Yorke L. Keeper & bushope of Bathe and welles [made Lord Chancellor 21 Sept. 1274] died 1292.

Sr Hughe Burnell Knight brother to Robert died 1287.=....

Sr Phillipe Burnell Kt died 1293.

Sr Phillipe Burnell Kt baron of Holgate in com. Salop nephew & heire to Robert.=Mawde sister to Rich. fitzallen vide Claus 11 E. 3 m. 7.

Sr Edw. Burnell Knight baron of Holgatte died Aº 1315, 9 E. 2. s. p'l.=Ela da. to Hughe le Despencer.

John Louell baron of Tichmarahe died 10 E. 2.=Mawde sister & beire to Edward Burnell baro. of Holgate died Aº 1300.=Sr John Handlowe [Handlow] Kt 2 husband died 20 E. 3.

John baron Louell of Tichmerahe died 21 E. 3.=....

Nicholas Burnell baron of Holgate [brass in Acton Burnell Church 1360].=....

Richard Burnell died before his father.=....

John Baron Louell of Tichmarahe.

Hughe Burnell Baro. of Holgate died Aº 5 H. 5.

Edmond ob. s. p'l.

Margarett vx. John Applebye [Appeley].

Elizabeth vx. Edmunde de la Poole.

[Katherine da. & heir.=Sir John Ratcliffe Knt.

Sir John Ratcliffe Knt.=Eliz. da. & sole heir of Walter Lord Fitzwalter.

Sir John Ratcliff Knt Lord Fitzwalter Burnell & Egremont.=Anne da. of Sir Richd Wheathill of Callais Knight.

Sir Robt Ratcliffe Knt created Earle of Sussex by Henry VIII. 1530.]

Burnell.

S., fo. 94.

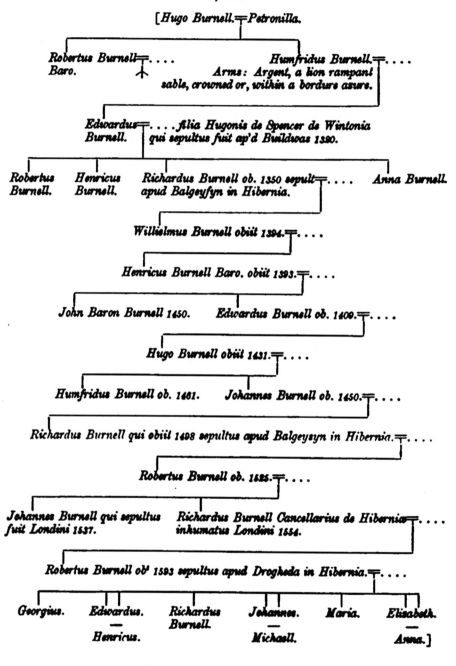

[*Hugo Burnell.*⚌*Petronilla.*

Robertus Burnell⚌....   *Humfridus Burnell.*⚌....
Baro.   Arms: *Argent, a lion rampant*
sable, crowned or, within a bordure azure.

Edwardus⚌....*filia Hugonis de Spencer de Wintonia*
Burnell.   *qui sepultus fuit ap'd Buildwas 1390.*

Robertus   *Henricus*   *Richardus Burnell ob. 1350 sepult*⚌....   *Anna Burnell.*
Burnell.   *Burnell.*   *apud Balgeyfyn in Hibernia.*

Willielmus Burnell obiit 1394.⚌....

Henricus Burnell Baro. obiit 1393.⚌....

John Baron Burnell 1450.   *Edwardus Burnell ob. 1409.*⚌....

Hugo Burnell obiit 1431.⚌....

Humfridus Burnell ob. 1461.   *Johannes Burnell ob. 1450.*⚌....

Richardus Burnell qui obiit 1498 sepultus apud Balgeysyn in Hibernia.⚌....

Robertus Burnell ob. 1525.⚌....

Johannes Burnell qui sepultus   *Richardus Burnell Cancellarius de Hibernia*⚌....
fuit Londini 1537.   *inhumatus Londini 1554.*

Robertus Burnell ob^t 1593 sepultus apud Drogheda in Hibernia.⚌....

Georgius.   *Edwardus.*   *Richardus*   *Johannes.*   *Maria.*   *Elisabeth.*
        —   *Burnell*   —   —
      Henricus.   *Michaell.*   *Anna.*]

Burton of Longnor, in the parish of St. Chad, Shrewsbury.

Harl. 1396, fo. 44.   Harl. 615, fo. 263.

ARMS: Harl. 1396—*Quarterly purpure and azure—azure and purpure* in Harl. 615—*a cross engrailed or between four roses argent—seeded gold* in Harl. 615 —*a crescent for difference; impaling* [BYST or BEIST], *Gules, three sheaves of as many arrows, points downwards, or, headed and flighted argent, banded of the last.*

CREST.—*A gauntlet erect proper.*

Edwardus Burton Grome of the Stoole to H. 7=Jocosa fil. Tho. Cressett de Upton
(*Knight of the Rodes who came out of Yorkshire*[*])   [Cressett of Upton Cressett] in
[made a Knight Bannerett 1460].   com. Salop.

Joh'es Burton de longnor=Elizabetha fil. Tho. Poynar [Poyner]
in co. Salop.   de Beslowe in com. Salop.

Jane ux. . . . . Corbett de longnor.	Ellena ux. . . . . Banester de lacon.	. . . . ux. . . . . Bostock de morton Say.	. . . . nupta . . . . Barker de Bridgnorth.

. . . . ux. . . . . Wright de london.	. . . . vx. . . . . Pasqo de london.	Ankaretta monialis iuxta Shrewsbury.

Edwardus Burton de longnor=Anna fil. et hær. Nich'i Madocks
in co. Salop fil. et hær.   de Wem & Cotton.

Edwardus 2. — Humfr'us 3. — Timotheus 4.	Dorothea vx. Joh'es Mitton de Wiston.	Thomas Burton de Longnor fil. et hær.	=Katherina fil. W'm Byst de A[t]cham Ar. et soror et cohær. Joh'is Byst.	Maria vx Ric'i Lloyd de Royton [or Ropton].	Katherina vx Georgij Corbett de Hope in com. Salop.

Willimus 2. — Johannes 3.	Sarah 1.	Edwardus Burton fil. et hær.	Margaretta 2. — Anna 3.	Elizabetha.

---

[*] Johan Wrythe, Norroy, granted at York, 22 May 1478, to Robert Burton of the County of York: Per pale azure and purpure, a cross engrailed or between four roses argent, seeded gold, barbed vert (Add. MS., Brit. Mus., 14,333). In an emblazoned pedigree at Longnor the field is per pale azure and gules.

Butler, Baron of Wem.

S., fo. 72ª.

[ARMS.—*Per fesse sable and gules, a fesse checky argent and sable between six crosses formée fitchée argent.*

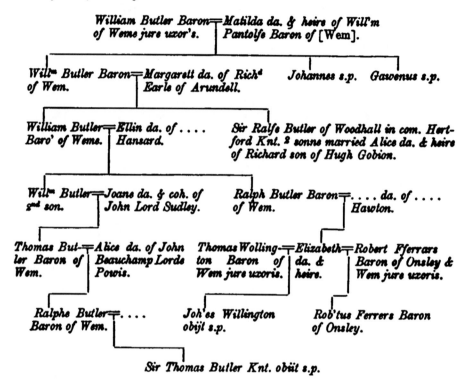

Calcott of Preston Mountford.

Harl. 1896, fo. 77ᵇ.   S., fo. 64.

[CALCOTT of Calcott, co. Chester, bore : *Argent, a fesse azure, frettée or, between three cinquefoils pierced gules.*—Visit. Cheshire.]

Thomas Calcott de Preston Mountfort in co. Salop a=.... filia .... Orton [Over-
familia Calcottorum de Calcott in co. Cestr' oriund'. | ton] de Malpas in com. Cestr'.

Henricus Calcott de Preston=Alicia fil. .... Lee de Langley
Mountford in com. Salop. | in com. Salop.

▲

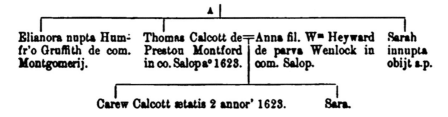

Elianora nupta Humfr'o Gruffith de com. Montgomerij.	Thomas Calcott de Preston Montford in co. Salopa° 1623.=Anna fil. Wᵐ Heyward de parva Wenlock in com. Salop.	Sarah innupta obijt s.p.

Carew Calcott ætatis 2 annor' 1623.   Sara.

THOMAS CALLCOTT.

Chambers or Chambre of Petton.

Harl. 1396, fo. 80ᵇ.   Harl. 1241, fo. 76ᵇ.   S., ff. 67ᵃ—68ᵃ.

ARMS: Harl. 1396.—*Quarterly: 1 and 4, Azure, an arm in armour fesseways emboiced* [proper]—*or* in Shrewsbury MS.—*the hand* [or]—*proper* in Shrewsbury MS.—*holding a rose gules, slipped* [vert]—*sable* in Shrewsbury MS.* [CHAMBERS]; 2, *Argent, a fesse componée—countercomponée* in Shrewsbury MS.—*or and azure between three lions' heads erased sable, within a bordure gules charged with eight escallops of the first—argent* in Shrewsbury MS. [CHAMBERS]; 3, *Ermine, three lozenges conjoined in fesse sable, within a bordure engrailed of the second* [PIGOTT].

CREST.—*A greyhound's head erased argent, collared with a garter azure, edged and buckled or.*

ANOTHER CREST.—*A camel's* [?] *head quarterly argent and or, eared gules, and charged with a fesse between three annulets, one above and two below, of the last.*

Ex chartis Arthuri Chambre de . . . . in co. Salop Ar. 29 Septembr' a° 1623.

Henricus de Lacy Comes Lincoln' Constabularius Castrum Do. de Roos et Rewenick' concessit Joh'es de la Chambre Camerario pro homage et scrutio suo duas carucatas terræ cum pertinentijs in Lewenny. [Harl. 1396; S., fo. 67ᵃ.]

Heere lyeth buried in the Mercy of Jesus Christ the Body of Arthur Chambers gent. true Patron of this parish church of Midle, and Margᵗ his wife, by her he had Issue one Sonn & one Daughter wᵗʰ Arthur deceased the 19ᵗʰ Day of August 1564, whose body & soule God graunt a Joyfull Resurrection Amen. [Harl. 1241.]

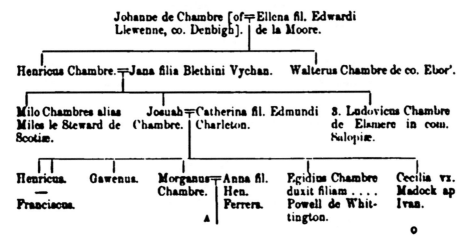

Johanne de Chambre [of=Ellena fil. Edwardi Llewenne, co. Denbigh]. | de la Moore.

Henricus Chambre.=Jana filia Blethini Vychan.   Walterus Chambre de co. Ebor'.

Milo Chambres alias Miles le Steward de Scotia.   Josuah=Catherina fil. Edmundi Chambre. | Charleton.   3. Ludovicus Chambre de Elsmere in com. Salopiæ.

Henricus. — Franciscus.   Gawenus.   Morganus=Anna fil. Chambre. | Hen. | Perrers.   Egidius Chambre duxit filiam . . . . Powell de Whittington.   Cecilia vx. Madock ap Ivan.

o

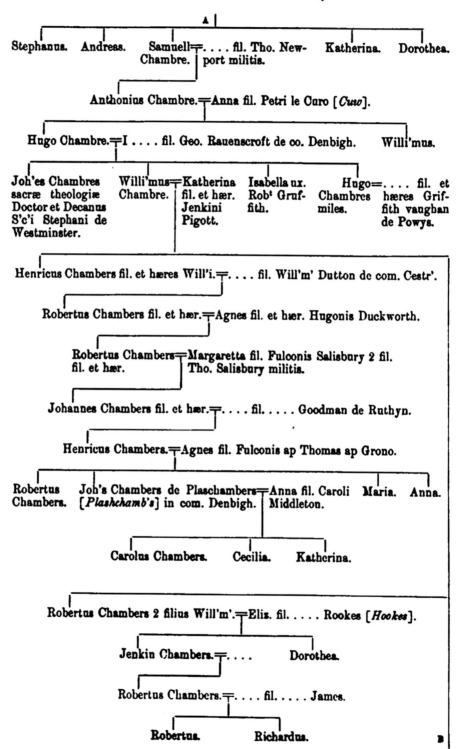

Stephanus.   Andreas.   Samuell=.... fil. Tho. New-   Katherina.   Dorothea.
Chambre.   port militis.

Anthonius Chambre.=Anna fil. Petri le Curo [*Curo*].

Hugo Chambre.=I .... fil. Geo. Rauenscroft de co. Denbigh.   Willi'mus.

Joh'es Chambres   Willi'mus=Katherina   Isabella ux.   Hugo=.... fil. et
sacræ theologiæ   Chambre.   fil. et hær.   Robt Gruf-   Chambres   hæres Grif-
Doctor et Decanus   Jenkini   fith.   miles.   fith vaughan
S'c'i Stephani de   Pigott.   de Powys.
Westminster.

Henricus Chambers fil. et hæres Will'i.=.... fil. Will'm' Dutton de com. Cestr'.

Robertus Chambers fil. et hær.=Agnes fil. et hær. Hugonis Duckworth.

Robertus Chambers=Margaretta fil. Fulconis Salisbury 2 fil.
fil. et hær.   Tho. Salisbury militis.

Johannes Chambers fil. et hær.=.... fil. .... Goodman de Ruthyn.

Henricus Chambers.=Agnes fil. Fulconis ap Thomas ap Grono.

Robertus   Joh's Chambers de Plaschambers=Anna fil. Caroli   Maria.   Anna.
Chambers.   [*Plashchamb's*] in com. Denbigh.   Middleton.

Carolus Chambers.   Cecilia.   Katherina.

Robertus Chambers 2 filius Will'm'.=Eliz. fil. .... Rookes [*Hookes*].

Jenkin Chambers.=....   Dorothea.

Robertus Chambers.=.... fil. .... James.

Robertus.   Richardus.

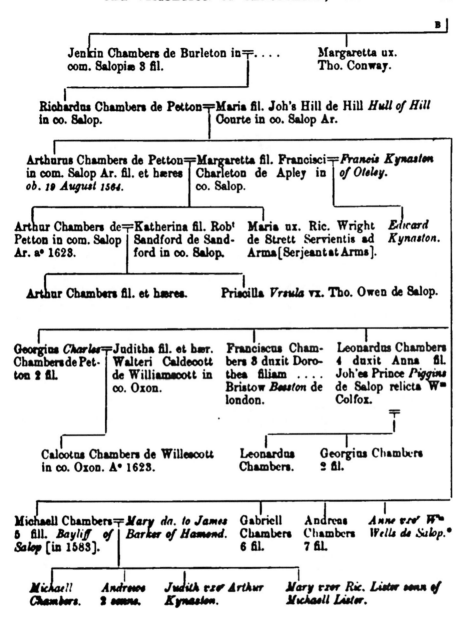

B

Jenkin Chambers de Burleton in⊤....   Margaretta ux.
com. Salopiæ 3 fil.   Tho. Conway.

Richardus Chambers de Petton⊤Maria fil. Joh's Hill de Hill *Hull of Hill*
in co. Salop.   Courte in co. Salop Ar.

Arthurus Chambers de Petton⊤Margaretta fil. Francisci⊤*Francis Kynaston*
in com. Salop Ar. fil. et hæres   Charleton de Apley in   *of Oteley.*
ob. 19 August 1564.   co. Salop.

Arthur Chambers de⊤Katherina fil. Robt   Maria ux. Ric. Wright   *Edward*
Petton in com. Salop   Sandford de Sand-   de Strett Servientis ad   *Kynaston.*
Ar. aº 1623.   ford in co. Salop.   Arma [Serjeant at Arms].

Arthur Chambers fil. et hæres.   Priscilla *Vrsula* vx. Tho. Owen de Salop.

Georgius *Charles*⊤Juditha fil. et hær.   Franciscus Cham-   Leonardus Chambers
Chambers de Pet-   Walteri Caldecott   bers 3 duxit Doro-   4 duxit Anna fil.
ton 2 fil.   de Williamscott in   thea filiam ....   Joh'es Prince *Piggins*
   co. Oxon.   Bristow *Beeston* de   de Salop relicta W^m
    london.   Colfox.

Calcotus Chambers de Willescott   Leonardus   Georgius Chambers
in co. Oxon. Aº 1623.   Chambers.   2 fil.

Michaell Chambers⊤*Mary da. to James*   Gabriell   Andreas   *Anne vx' W^m*
5 fill. *Bayliff of* | *Barker of Hamond.*   Chambers   Chambers   *Wells de Salop.**
Salop [in 1583].   6 fil.   7 fil.

Michaell   *Andrewe*   *Judith vx' Arthur*   *Mary vxor Ric. Lister sonn of*
Chambers.   *2 sonns.*   *Kynaston.*   *Michaell Lister.*

* Omitted in Shrewsbury MS. fo. 69º.

Charleton of Apley Castle and Withiford.

Harl. 1396, fo. 64.

Ex Euidencijs Francisci Charleton de Apeley in com. Salop Ar. a° 1623.

Sciant p'ntes & futuri quod ego Hugo fili' Aeris D'nus de magna Witeford dedi concessi & hac p'nti Carta mea confirmaui Joh'i filio meo vnam placeam terre & bosci que vocat Engeware de feodo meo p'd'c'æ Ville de Witiford &c. Et si contigerit quod p'd'cus Joh'es obierit sine herede de Corpore suo legitime p'creato omnia p'd'cta terre & ten'ta cum redditib' & reuersionib' &c. integre reuertantur Margerie filie mee primogenite sorori p'd'c'i Joh'es &c. Tenendum &c. Sans date.

Hugo filius Aeris D'nus de magna Withiford dedi concessi & hac Carta mea confirmavi Henrico filio meo vnam placeam de vasto meo p'd'c'æ villæ ad sup' edificandum &c. Sans date.

Sigillu' vt supra depingitur.*

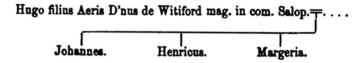

Hugo filius Aeris D'nus de Witiford mag. in com. Salop.=. . . .
    Johannes.   Henricus.   Margeria.

Ceste indentur' faite entre Aleyn filz Mouns' Aleyn de Charleton d'un parte & Henri filz Ayer de Autre parte testmoigne qe come le dist Henri soit tenuz & obliges p' estatute de merchaunt au dit Aleyn le filz Mouns' Aleyn in 100 marc' a paier a lui a Aston' Ayer le iour de la feste S¹ Michael proschien auenir voalt & groute le dit Aleyn le filz qe si mesmes oelq' Aleyn & Margerie sa femme & leur heires ne soient impleides chalenges ne entangle p' le dit Henri nep' ses heirs pour les terres &c. ne pour parcell' de eux quelx le dit Aleyn le filz Mouns' Aleyn & Margerie sa compaigne ount p'chases del dist Henri en la maior de Graunt Witiford come plus plenement piert par un Chart &c. Dat. Lundi prochein apres le feste de S¹ Kenelm lan du raigne le Roi Edward terce apres le Conquest 20ᵐᵉ.

[Cottonian MS. Cleopatra C. v., among the banners of those who entered France 16 June 1513 occurs, "Shrop. William Chorlton bayryth a Lyon's hed, the face holle goulls, iij labells gold upon the same under the mouth ; and William Chorlton hys Pety Captayn."]

Harl. 1396, fo. 65.   Harl. 1241, fo. 5.

Alanus de Charleton de Apeley in com. Salop miles ob. a° 35 E. 3.=. . . .

Alanus de Charleton=Margeria filia & vna heredum Hugonis   Thomas   Johannes
de Apeley ob. ante   filij Ayeris siue filz Aer de magna   2.   3.
Patrem a° 23 E. 3.   Witiford in com. Salop 20 E. 3.

Thomas Charleton de Apeley frater=. . . .   Johannes Charleton miles obijt sine
et heres Joh'is obijt a° 11 R. 2.   prole anno 4 R. 2.

Will'us Knyghtley=Anna Charle-   Thomas Charleton   Hellena vn'a sororum et
[from Fawsley,   ton soror &   de Apeley filius &   heredum Tho. Chaulton
co. Northants].   hær. Tho.   heres ob. 22 R. 2   et ætatis 12 Annorum ad
          Charleton.   s.p.   mortem fr'is a° 22 R. 2
                                     obijt sine prole a° 1 H. 4.

▲

* This seal is not given in any of the MSS.

A

Thomas Charleton *Thomas Knightley al's Charleton* ╤ Eliz. filia et coheres Adæ
ætatis 4 annor' ad morte' Hellenæ Charl' amitæ │ Franceis militis filij Ade
eius cuius heres ipse fuit ob. 38 Henr' 6. │ Francis de London.

Rob'tus Charleton de Apeley ╤ Maria filia Rob'ti Corbet
ob. 10 E. 4 [Sheriff 1472]. │ de Morton Ar.

Ricardus Charleton de Apeley ╤ Anna filia Will'i Manwaring
ob. 13 H. 8. │ in co. Salop.

Will'us Charleton de Apeley ╤ Alicia filia Tho. Horde de Bridgnorth
ob. 23 H. 8. │ in com. Salop.

| Joh'es Charleton de Willing-╤Anna relicta Will'i | Ricardus Charleton de Hay |
| ton in comit' Salop 3 filius. │ Alen de Willington. | 2 filius. |

Jocosa filia Ric'i Jenkens ╤ Thom. Charleton de ╤ Lucia filia Tho. Ireland
de Hay. │ Shrewsbury. │ de Shrewsbury.

| Robert son & heire. | Eliz. vxor Rog° Pope de | Thomas Charleton 2 filius. |
| | Lincolns Inne. | |

Rob'tus╤Anna fil. Piersi	Will'us Charle-	Alicia vx.	Cicilia vx.	Elizabetha
Charleton Stanley in Ew-	ton de Wom-	Rob'ti	Ric'i Mor-	vxor Thomæ
obijt ante low *Eulowe* in	bridg obijt a°	Cresset de	ton de	Eyton de Ey-
Patrem. com. Flint.	9 Eliz. s.p.	Upton	Houghton	ton in co.
		Cresset in	in com.	Salop.
		co. Salop.	Salop.	

| Franciscus Charleton de╤Cicilia filia Joh'is Fitton de Gos- | Johannes Charleton |
| Apeley ob. a° 4 Eliz. │ worth in com. Cestr' militis. | de Lylesham ob. s.p. |

2. Ursula vx.	3. Maria vx. Fran-	4. Elizabeth	5. Cecilia vx.	6. Anna nupta
Richardi	ciaci Rodes de co.	vxor Joh'is	Rob'ti Barker	Joh'i Baker
Grosvenor de	Dereby de Woode-	Mannors	de Hugh-	de Mordi in
Brond in	thop Justic de	Comitis	mond in com.	com. Mont-
com. Salop.	Banco communis.	Rutlandiæ.	Salop.°	gomery.

Willi'mus╤Elizabetha filia & heres	Andreas╤Margareta filia	1. Margareta vx.
Charlton de Rob'ti Alen de com.	Charl- │ Jacobi Barker	Artheri Cham-
Apeley fil. Salop renupta Lau-	ton de │ de Haghmond	bers de [Petton]
& her. ob. rencio Banester de	Apeley │ in com. Salop.	renupta Francis-
a° 1566. Wem.	in com. │	co Kynaston de
	Salop. │	Otteley.

B C

* Harl. 1341 calls her "Nibull wife of Roland Barker of Hamon."

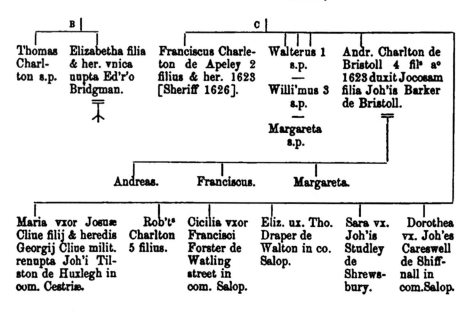

Charleton, Lord Powys.

Harl. 1396, fo. 66ᵇ. S., ff. 108ᵇ—110ᵇ.

ARMS OF CHARLETON : Harl. 1396.—*Quarterly : 1 and 4, Or, a lion rampant gules* [OWEN AP GRIFFITH]; *2 and 3, Gules—argent in Shrewsbury MS.—a human leg couped at the thigh argent—sable in Shrewsbury MS.*

CREST.—*Two lions' gambs embowed gules the outer edges fringed with demi-fleurs-de-lis or.*

ARMS : Shrewsbury MS.—*Quarterly : 1 and 4, Or, a lion rampant gules ; 2 and 3, Argent, a man's leg erect couped at the thigh sable.*

ARMS OF GREY : Shrewsbury MS.—*Gules, a lion rampant within a bordure engrailed argent.*

CREST.—*A ram's head.*

Resus filius Theodori magni⊤.... princeps South Wall. aᵒ 1077 occisus aᵒ 1091.
    Arms : Gules, a lion rampant within a bordure indented or.[*]

A

Grufinus ap Conan princeps⊤Angharad filia Nordwalliæ.
    Arms : Quarterly gules and or, four lions passant-guardant counterchanged.

Owini ap Edwin Regis Tegengle.

B

* These arms are not given in Shrewsbury MS., fo. 110ᵇ.

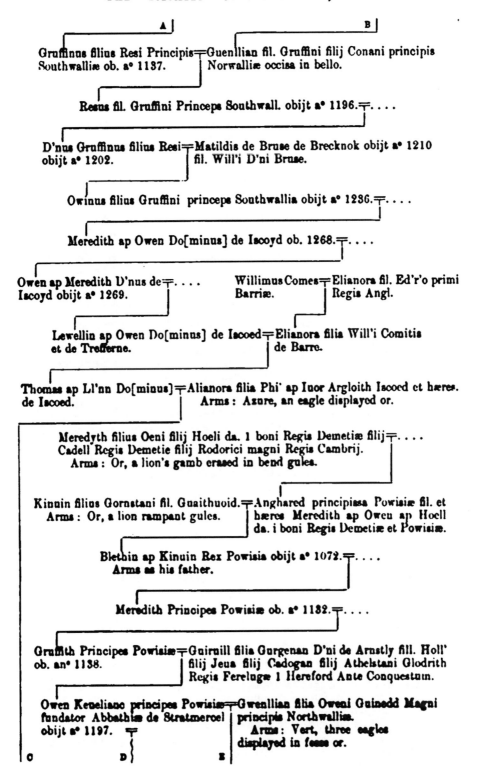

A | B |

Gruffinus filius Resi Principis⊤Guenllian fil. Gruffini filij Conani principis
Southwalliæ ob. aº 1137. | Norwalliæ occisa in bello.

Resus fil. Gruffini Princeps Southwall. obijt aº 1196.⊤. . . .

D'nus Gruffinus filius Resi⊤Matildis de Bruse de Brecknok obijt aº 1210
obijt aº 1202. | fil. Will'i D'ni Bruse.

Owinus filius Gruffini princeps Southwallia obijt aº 1236.⊤. . . .

Meredith ap Owen Do[minus] de Iscoyd ob. 1268.⊤. . . .

Owen ap Meredith D'nus de⊤. . . .   Willimus Comes⊤Elianora fil. Ed'r'o primi
Iscoyd obijt aº 1269.   Barriæ. | Regis Angl.

Lewellin ap Owen Do[minus] de Iscoed⊤Elianora filia Will'i Comitis
et de Trefferne.   de Barre.

Thomas ap Ll'nn Do[minus]⊤Alianora filia Phi' ap Iuor Argloith Iscoed et hæres.
de Iscoed. | Arms : Azure, an eagle displayed or.

Meredyth filius Oeni filij Hoeli da. 1 boni Regis Demetiæ filij⊤. . . .
Cadell Regis Demetie filij Rodorici magni Regis Cambrij.
Arms : Or, a lion's gamb erased in bend gules.

Kinuin filius Gornstani fil. Guaithuoid.⊤Anghared principissa Powisiæ fil. et
Arms : Or, a lion rampant gules. | hæres Meredith ap Owen ap Hoell
                                        | da. i boni Regis Demetiæ et Powisiæ.

Blethin ap Kinuin Rex Powisia obijt aº 1072.⊤. . . .
Arms as his father.

Meredith Principes Powisiæ ob. aº 1132.⊤. . . .

Gruffith Principes Powisiæ⊤Guirnill filia Gurgenan D'ni de Arnstly fill. Holl'
ob. anº 1138. | filij Jeua filij Cadogan filij Athelstani Glodrith
                          | Regis Fereluga 1 Hereford Ante Conquestum.

Owen Keueliauo principes Powisiæ⊤Gwenllian filia Oweni Guinedd Magni
fundator Abbathiæ de Stratmeroel | principis Northwalliæ.
obijt aº 1197.   ⊤ | Arms : Vert, three eagles
                 { | displayed in fesse or.

O   D }   E |

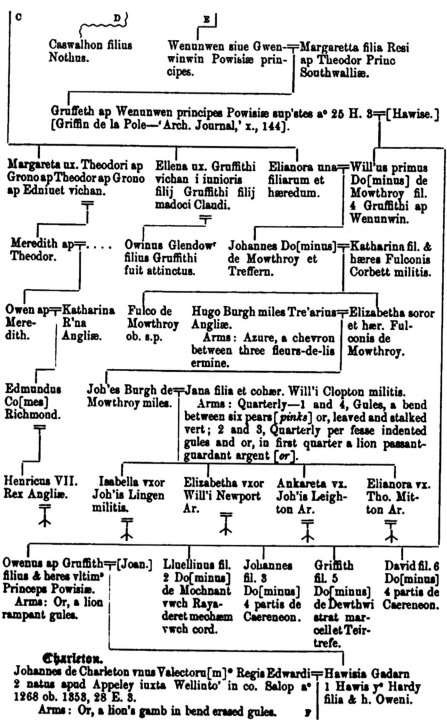

C

D

E

Caswalhon filius Nothus.

Wenunwen siue Gwen-=Margaretta filia Resi
winwin Powisiæ prin- ap Theodor Princ
cipes. Southwalliæ.

Gruffeth ap Wenunwen principes Powisiæ sup'stes aᵒ 25 H. 3=[Hawise.]
[Griffin de la Pole—'Arch. Journal,' x., 144].

Margareta ux. Theodori ap
Grono ap Theodor ap Grono
ap Edniuet vichan.

Ellena ux. Gruffithi
vichan i iunioris
filij Gruffithi filij
madoci Claudi.

Elianora una=Will'us primus
filiarum et Do[minus] de
hæredum. Mowthroy fil.
4 Gruffithi ap
Wenunwin.

Meredith ap=. . . .
Theodor.

Owinus Glendowᵉ
filius Gruffithi
fuit attinctus.

Johannes Do[minus]=Katharina fil. &
de Mowthroy et hæres Fulconis
Treffern. Corbett militis.

Owen ap=Katharina
Mere- R'na
dith. Angliæ.

Fulco de
Mowthroy
ob. s.p.

Hugo Burgh miles Tre'arius=Elizabetha soror
Angliæ. et hær. Ful-
  Arms: Azure, a chevron conis de
between three fleurs-de-lis Mowthroy.
ermine.

Edmundus
Co[mes]
Richmond.

Joh'es Burgh de=Jana filia et cohær. Will'i Clopton militis.
Mowthroy miles. Arms: Quarterly—1 and 4, Gules, a bend
between six pears [pinks] or, leaved and stalked
vert; 2 and 3, Quarterly per fesse indented
gules and or, in first quarter a lion passant-
guardant argent [or].

Henricus VII.
Rex Angliæ.

Isabella vxor
Joh'is Lingen
militis.

Elizabetha vxor
Will'i Newport
Ar.

Ankareta vx.
Joh'is Leigh-
ton Ar.

Elianora vx.
Tho. Mit-
ton Ar.

Owenus ap Gruffith=[Joan.]
filius & heres vltimᵒ
Princeps Powisiæ.
  Arms: Or, a lion
rampant gules.

Lluellinus fil.
2 Do[minus]
de Mochnant
vwch Raya-
deret mechæm
vwch cord.

Johannes
fil. 3
Do[minus]
4 partis de
Caereneon.

Griffith
fil. 5
Do[minus]
de Dewthwi
strat mar-
cell et Teir-
trefe.

David fil. 6
Do[minus]
4 partis de
Caereneon.

Charleton.
Johannes de Charleton vnus Valectoru[m]* Regis Edwardi=Hawisia Gadarn
2 natus apud Appeley iuxta Wellinto' in co. Salop aᵒ | 1 Hawis yᵉ Hardy
1268 ob. 1358, 28 E. 3. | filia & h. Oweni.
  Arms: Or, a lion's gamb in bend erased gules. F

* *Valector:* Gentleman of the Privy Chamber. He acquired the barony of Pole (Welshpool)
in right of his wife, which barony was held *in capite*, and was summoned to Parliament as Lord
Cherlton de Powys, 26 July 1818. His wife, Hawys Gadarn, was aged nineteen in 4 Edward II.

Y

Johannes de Charleton Dominus Powisiæ=Johanna filia Rad'i Stafford
ob. a° 1360 A° 35 E. 3. Comitis Staffordiæ.
[*Arms: Or, a lion rampant gules.*]

Johannes de Charleton Dominus=Matildis filia Rogeri Mortimer
Powisiæ ob. a° 1374 a° 50 E. 3. Comitis Marchie.

Johannes Charleton Do. Powis fil. et hær. obijt 1401 a° 2 H. 4 s.p.=Alicia fil.
Arms—Quarterly: 1 and 4, Or, a lion rampant gules; Ric'i Comit.
2 and 3, Gules [*argent*], a human leg couped at the thigh Aru'dell.
argent [*sable*].

Elizab. filia Joh'is=Edward Charleton Do. Powisiæ⊤Elianora soror⊤Rogerus
Berckley militis frater & heres Joh'is Dom. et una here- Mortimer
*renupta Baroni Powisiæ ob. a° 1420, 7 H. 5. dum Edmundi Co. Marchiæ
Dudley.† Arms: Quarterly, as his brother. Holland Com- 1 maritus.
 itis Kancij.

Johannes Grey de Berwicke miles.⊤. . . .
 Anna Comitissa Cantabrigiæ.
 ⊤
Thomas Grey cum=Catherina filia Joh'is Mowbray Richardus Dux Eborum.
torto pede miles. Ducis Norff.

Johannes Grey miles⊤Johanna filia ætate Jocosa° fil. 2 & coheres nupta
Dominus Powys vxoris maxima et coheres Joh'i Do[minus] Tiptoft de
iure Inq. 9 H. 5 Ed'r'i Domi' Powys Langer renupta Will'mo Stan-
[fought at Agincourt]. [died 1425]. ley de Holt.‡ ⊤
 ✠

Henricus Grey Dom. de Powys et Tylle Comes⊤Antigona filia notha Humfridi
de Tancarville et Camerarius Normanniæ Ducis Glouc. *dn. to Humphrey
created Earle of Tankervile by H. 5. *Duke of Buckingham & son to
 H. IV.*

Richardus Grey⊤Margareta filia Jacobi de Humfridus. Elizabetha vx.
miles de Powisiæ Audeley renupta Do[minus] Rogeri Kinas-
Inq. 6 E. 4. Berkley et 3° Henricus ton de Hordley
 Dom. Roos. militis.

Johannes Grey⊤Anna filia Will'i do[minus] de Elizabetha§ nupta Joh'is
D'nus de Powisiæ. Herbert Co. Pembrochiæ. Ludlow miles.
 ⊤
G **H** **I**

* Omitted in Shrewsbury MS.
† This was John de Sutton, Baron Dudley, K.G., who died 30 September 1487.
‡ She died 21 September 1446, and was buried at Enfield, Middlesex (Gough, 'Sepulchral
Monuments,' vol. ii., plate 2, p. 136).
§ The existence of this lady is doubted; see the Ludlow Pedigree, *postea.*

P

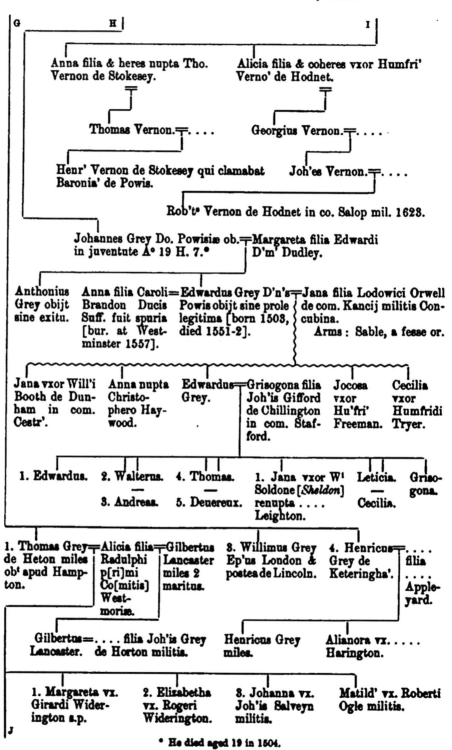

G   H   I

Anna filia & heres nupta Tho. Vernon de Stokesey.

Alicia filia & ooheres vxor Humfri' Verno' de Hodnet.

Thomas Vernon.⊤. . . .

Georgius Vernon.⊤. . . .

Henr' Vernon de Stokesey qui clamabat Baronia' de Powis.

Joh'es Vernon.⊤. . . .

Rob't⁂ Vernon de Hodnet in co. Salop mil. 1628.

Johannes Grey Do. Powisiæ ob.⊤Margareta filia Edwardi
in juventute A° 19 H. 7.*   D'm' Dudley.

| Anthonius Grey obijt sine exitu. | Anna filia Caroli Brandon Ducis Suff. fuit spuria [bur. at Westminster 1557]. | Edwardus Grey D'n's Powis obijt sine prole legitima [born 1503, died 1551-2]. | Jana filia Lodowici Orwell de com. Kancij militis Concubina. Arms : Sable, a fesse or. |

| Jana vxor Will'i Booth de Dunham in com. Cestr'. | Anna nupta Christophero Haywood. | Edwardus Grey. | Grisogona filia Joh'is Gifford de Chillington in com. Stafford. | Jocosa vxor Hu'fri' Freeman. | Cecilia vxor Humfridi Tryer. |

1. Edwardus.   2. Walterus.   4. Thomas.   1. Jana vxor Wⁱ   Leticia.   Grisogona.
                —   —   Soldone [*Sheldon*]   —
                3. Andreas.   5. Deuereux. renupta . . . .   Cecilia.
                                              Leighton.

| 1. Thomas Grey de Heton miles ob' apud Hampton. | Alicia filia Radulphi p[ri]mi Co[mitis] Westmoriæ. | Gilbertus Lancaster miles 2 maritus. | 8. Willimus Grey Ep'us London & postea de Lincoln. | 4. Henricus Grey de Keteringha'. | . . . . filia . . . . Appleyard. |

Gilbertus= . . . . filia Joh'is Grey
Lancaster.   de Horton militis.

Henricus Grey miles.

Alianora vx. . . . . .
Harington.

1. Margareta vx. Girardi Widerington s.p.

2. Elizabetha vx. Rogeri Widerington.

8. Johanna vx. Joh'is Salveyn militis.

Matild' vx. Roberti Ogle militis.

J

* He died aged 19 in 1504.

J

1. Tho. Grey primogenit* obijt sine exitu.

2. Johannes Grey miles sepultus apud Stokes s.p. = Comitissa de Essex vxor ejus soror Ducis Ebor'.

3. Radulph* Grey M[iles] Do[minus] de Werke obijt in Francia Inq. 21 H. 6. = Elizab. filia Henrici D'ni Fitzhugh renupta Simoni Montfort.

4. Will* Grey Episcopus Eliensis.

Radulph. Grey miles balneatus = ... & possessor de Greys Inne in villa de Novo Castro decapitatus apud Doncaster Anno 4 E. 4.

Thomas Grey miles duxit Aliciam fil. Edwardi Neuill D'ni de Albergauenny dux' etiam Katherinam Sampton sed sine liberis obijt.

Henricus. — Rob't*.

Thomas Grey æt. 40 Annorum a° 5 E. 4. = Margeria filia Rad'i Baronis de Greystoke.

Edwardus Grey de Chillingham miles. = Anna filia . . . . Gower de Stanley in com. Eborum.

Elizabetha.   Anna.

Rad'us Grey de Chillington [sic] miles. = Isabella filia & vna heredu' Thome Grey de Horton militis.

Thomas Grey 2 filius s.p.

1. Thomas Grey de Chillingham miles 1575.

2. Rad'us.

3. Edwardus. — 4. Henricus.

5. Rogerus. — 6. Arthur*.

Dorothea vxor Rob'ti Delavale de Seton Delavale in com. Northumbriæ.

Isabella. — Anna.

Charleton of Apley Castle.

Harl. 1241, fo. 51.

ARMS: Harl. 1241.—*Quarterly: 1 and 4, Or, a lion rampant gules* [OWEN AP GRIFFITH]; *2, Gules, ten besants, four, three, two, and one* [ZOUCHE]; *3, Argent, a chevron between three eagles displayed sable.*

[The third quartering is cancelled, as wrong, in Harl. 1396, fo. 79, but Sir John de Cherleton, temp. Edw. I., bore these arms: the chevron vert, the eagles or (Military Summonses).]

John Charleton of Apley in the right of his wife Lord of Powys. = *Hauis da. & heir to Owen son of Gruff. Gwinwinwin Lord of Powys.* [Arms: Or, a lion rampant gules.]

Sr Charleton Lord Powys 1360. = *Maud da. of Roger Mortymer Earle of March.*

▲

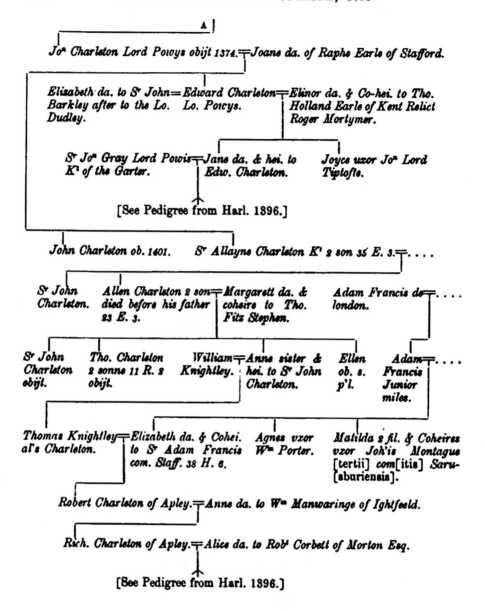

Jo[n] Charleton Lord Powys obijt 1374.=*Joane da. of Raphe Earle of Stafford.*

Elizabeth da. to S[r] John=*Edward Charleton*=*Elinor da. & Co-hei. to Tho.*
Barkley after to the Lo.   Lo. Powys.   *Holland Earle of Kent Relict*
Dudley.   *Roger Mortymer.*

S[r] Jo[n] Gray Lord Powis=*Jane da. & hei. to*   *Joyce uxor Jo[n] Lord*
K[t] of the Garter.   *Edw. Charleton.*   *Tiptofte.*

[See Pedigree from Harl. 1896.]

John Charleton ob. 1401.   *S[r] Allayne Charleton K[t] 2 son 35 E. 3.*=*. . . .*

S[r] John   *Allen Charleton 2 son*=*Margarett da. &*   *Adam Francis de*=*. . . .*
Charleton.   *died before his father*   *coheire to Tho.*   *london.*
                   23 E. 3.   *Fitz Stephen.*

S[r] John   *Tho. Charleton*   *William*=*Anne sister &*   *Ellen*   *Adam*=*. . . .*
Charleton   *2 sonne 11 R. 2*   *Knightley.* *hei. to S[r] John*   *ob. s.*   *Francis*
obijt.   *obijt.*   *Charleton.*   *p'l.*   *Junior*
                                                                                     miles.

Thomas Knightley=*Elizabeth da. & Cohei.*   *Agnes uxor*   *Matilda 2 fil. & Coheires*
al's Charleton.   *to S[r] Adam Francis*   *W[m] Porter.*   *uxor Joh'is Montague*
                    com. Staff. 38 H. 6.   *[tertii] com[itis] Saru-*
                                                                 [sburiensis].

Robert Charleton of Apley.=*Anne da. to W[m] Manwaringe of Ightfeeld.*

Rich. Charleton of Apley.=*Alice da. to Rob[t] Corbett of Morton Esq.*

[See Pedigree from Harl. 1896.]

Charleton of Tern.

Harl. 1396, fo. 79ᵇ, ink fo. 82ᵇ. Harl. 1241, fo. 104. S., ff. 66ᵇ, 67.

ARMS: Harl. 1396.—*Quarterly:* 1 *and* 4, *Or, a lion rampant gules*; 2, *Gules, ten bezants, four, three, two, and one*—ZOUCHE in Shrewsbury MS.; 3, *Argent, a chevron between three eagles displayed gules* [CHERLTON ?]; *over all four a crescent for difference.*

[The third quartering seems to be an old Cherlton coat. Sir John de Cherleton, temp. Edw. I., bore : Argent, a chevron vert between three eagles displayed or (Military Summons).]

CREST.—*A leopard's face gules, charged with a crescent for difference.*

[The third quartering is cancelled in Harl. 1396, and the following substituted, with these words, "this in the 3 quarter," viz. : Azure, on a mount vert a lion statant guardant or, which is the coat of FITZ AER of Withyford and Aston Aer, co. Salop.]

ARMS OF CHARLTON OF WELLINGTON : Harl. 1241.—*Or, a lion rampant gules, debruised by a bendlet of the same, thereon a mullet of the first.*

Wᵐ Charleton de Apeley=Alicia fil. Tho. Hoorde de
in co. Salop. | Bridgnorth in com. Salop.

Alicia ux. .... Cressett | John Charleton* of Wellington=Ann widow to Wᵐ
de Upton Cressett. | in com. Salop 3 sonne. | Alleyne of Wellington.

Joyce da. of Rich. Jenks of=Tho. Charleton=Lucy da. to Tho. Ireland
the Bay *Jenkins of Hay* in | of Shrewsbury. | of Salop Esq. 2 wife.
com. Salop.

Robert Charleton | Elizab. ux. Roger Pope | Thomas Charleton

Rob't Charleton de Apley | Elizabetha | Richardus Charleton =.... fil. ....
in co. Salop fil. et hær. | vx. Thomæ | of the Hay [in Made- | .... vxor
| Eyton. | ley parish ; Bailiff of | Eyton de ....
| | Wenlock 1538] 2 fill. | Eyton. Morton.

Robertus Charleton de Terne in co. Salop.=Dorothea fil. .... Brane de Withyford.

Robertus Charleton de Terne=Alicia filia Ric. Tyler [*Taylor*] de
in co. Salop 1623. | Hardwick in com. Salop.

Robertus Charleton de London | Stephanus Charleton | Thomas apprenticing
Mercator [and after of Whitton | jam in Francia 1623. | London.
in the parish of Burford].

A

* This John and his descendants are not given in Shrewsbury MS., fo. 67.

| A |

Andreas Charleton=Juditha fil. Ed'r'i Clud   Franciscæ vxor   Margaretta vx.
fil. et hæres ætatis   [Cludde] de Orleton   Ed'r'i Daneis de   Walteri Milling-
40 annor' 1623.   in co. Salop.   la Marches.   ton de Halles.

Rich'us.   Steph'us.   Robertus Charleton   Maria.   Elizabetha.
                      ætatis 5 annorum.

ROBARTE CHARLTON.

Chelmick of Chelmick and Ragdon.

Harl. 1396, fo. 63.   S., ff. 59ᵇ, 60.

ARMS.—*Vert, three lions rampant-guardant or.*
CREST.—*A lion sejant guardant or resting the dexter paw on a shield vert.*

A confirmac'on of the Armes & guift of the Creast to Will'm Chelmick of Ragdon in the county of Salop gent. by Rob't Cooke Clarenceux vndęr his hand & seale jᵒ June 1582, 25 Eliz.

Ex chartis Thomæ Chelmick de Chelmick in com. Salop Ar. 10 September aᵒ 1623.
Sciant p'ntes et futuri quod ego Stephanus D'nus de Hop' dedi et concessi et p'nte carta mea confirmavi Willi'mo filio Will'i de Chelmundewiks pro homagio et servitio suo illud assartum quod fuit Ricardi de la lude etc. Hijs testibus Waltero le Scot de Acton Rogero filio Sweini Phillippo de Wiboldeston. Ric'o de Chelmundewyks Ric'o filio Yarnard et multis alijs.
Sciant p'ntes et futuri quod ego Joh'es filius Ricardi de Chelmundwyk dedi Reginaldo filio Alani de Chelmundwyk vnam placeam t'ræ jacentem in la Lee infeodo de Hatton inter metas campi de Chelmundwyk, et t'ram D'ni de Hatton etc. Hijs testibus Johanne filio Ric'i de Hatton Ric'o fratre suo Joh'e Kete, Reginaldo filio Thomæ de Hatton, Ric'o filio Rogeri de eadem et multija. Dat. apud Chelmundwyk die Sab't' prox' post festum S'c'i Andreæ ap'li aᵒ 18 E. 2.

[Drawing of a Seal, Plate I., Fig. 4A.]

Sciant p'ntes et futuri quod ego Will'us filius Will'i de Chelmundewyke pro salute animæ meæ dedi simul cum corpore meo deo et b'tæ Mariæ de Buldewas dimid' virgatam t'ræ in villa de Hope etc. illam Scilicet quam Baldwinus filius Will'i de Mungomerie tenuet. Sans dat.
Relaxatio Matildis quondam vxoris Steph'i de Hope, primo vxoris Will'o filij Will'i de Chelmundewike de dicti t'res etc.
Charta Stephani D'ni de Hope in qua concessit Ricardo filio Herberti de Chelmundwike virgatam t'ræ in villa de Chelmundewike etc.
Emma relicta Roberti Coterell dedit Alano filio Ric'i filij Nicholaj de Chelmundewyke j mess. et dem virg. t'ræ in villa et campis de Chelmundwyke.
Rogerus de Chelmedwik rector eccl'iæ de Hope Bowdler' dedit Will'o filio Will'i Chelmedwik et Margeria vxori eius t'ræ et ten'ta in villa et campis de Chelmedwyke. Dat. Aᵒ 35 E. 3.
Ricardus filius Alani de Chelmdewyke dedit Agneti filiæ suæ duas acras t'ræ in campo de Hope in loco vocato le More: pro defectu talis exitus remanere Johannæ soror dictæ Agnetis. Dat. Aᵒ 7 Ric'i 2.
Thomas filius Reginaldi de Chelmewike et Alicia vxor eius Aᵒ 10 H. 4.

Will'us Chelmick de Chelmick=Sibbilla filia et hær. Ricardi
et Ragdon in com. Salop.   Wilkockes de Stretton.

Thomas   Joh'es Chelmick de=Johanna filia Will'   Fulco Chelmick de london
Chelmick   Chelmick in paro-   Thinne de Botevile   3 filius.
s.p.   chia de Bowdler in   in com. Salop.
        co. Salop.   A

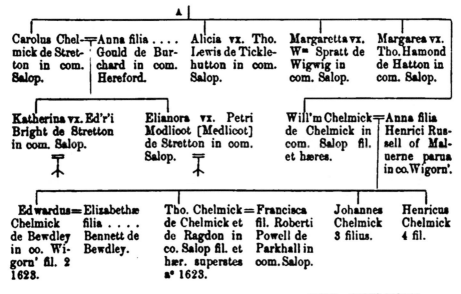

▲

Carolus Chelmick de Stretton in com. Salop.=Anna filia .... Gould de Burchard in com. Hereford.	Alicia vx. Tho. Lewis de Ticklehutton in com. Salop.	Margaretta vx. Wm Spratt de Wigwig in com. Salop.	Margarea vx. Tho. Hamond de Hatton in com. Salop.

Katherina vx. Ed'r'i Bright de Stretton in com. Salop.

Elianora vx. Petri Modlicot [Medlicot] de Stretton in com. Salop.

Will'm Chelmick de Chelmick in com. Salop fil. et hæres.=Anna filia Henrici Russell of Maluerne parua in co. Wigorn'.

Edwardus Chelmick de Bewdley in co. Wigorn' fil. 2 1623.=Elizabethæ filia .... Bennett de Bewdley.

Tho. Chelmick de Chelmick et de Ragdon in co. Salop fil. et hær. superstes a° 1623.=Francisca fil. Roberti Powell de Parkhall in com. Salop.

Johannes Chelmick 3 filius.

Henricus Chelmick 4 fil.

THO. CHELMICK.
THOMAS THYNNE.

Harl. 1396, fo. 63ᵇ.

Willimus de Chelmundwyk in com. Salop.=....

Nicholaus filius Willielmi de Chelmundewik.

Will'us fil. Will'i de Chelmundewik sepultus apud Bildwas.=Matildis.=Stephanus de Hope 2 maritus.

Richardus filius Nicholai D'ne de Chelmundwyk.

Herbertus nepos Nicholai=.... de Chelmundewyk.

Alanus pater Richardi de Chelmundewyk.

Richardus filius Herberti=.... de Chelmundewyk.

Richardus de Chelmundewyk.

Joh'es filius Ricardi de Chelmundewyk a° 18 E. 2.=.... Arms : Three lions rampant-guardant.

Agnes 7 R. 2.   Johanna a° 7 R. 2.

Willimus de Chelmedwyk.=....

Willimus de Chelmedwyk.=Margeria. 25 E. 3.

Alanus de Chelmundwyk=.... ob. ante p'r'm.

▲

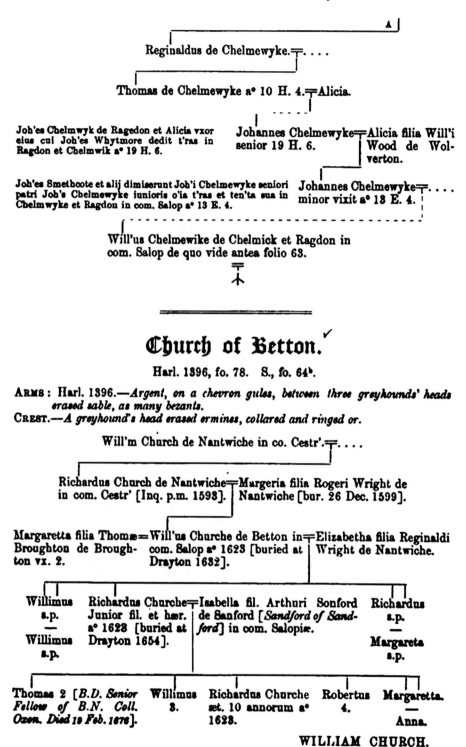

Reginaldus de Chelmewyke.=. . . .

Thomas de Chelmewyke aᵒ 10 H. 4.=Alicia.

Joh'es Chelmwyk de Ragedon et Alicia vxor eius cui Joh'es Whytmore dedit t'ras in Ragdon et Chelmwik aᵒ 19 H. 6.

Johannes Chelmewyke=Alicia filia Will'i senior 19 H. 6. | Wood de Wol- | verton.

Joh'es Smethcote et alij dimiserunt Job'i Chelmewyke seniori patri Job's Chelmewyke iunioris o'ia t'ras et ten'ta sua in Chelmwyke et Ragdon in com. Salop aᵒ 13 E. 4.

Johannes Chelmewyke=. . . . minor vixit aᵒ 13 E. 4.

Will'us Chelmewike de Chelmick et Ragdon in com. Salop de quo vide antea folio 63.

Church of Betton.

Harl. 1396, fo. 78.　S., fo. 64ᵇ.

ARMS : Harl. 1396.—*Argent, on a chevron gules, between three greyhounds' heads erased sable, as many bezants.*
CREST.—*A greyhound's head erased ermines, collared and ringed or.*

Will'm Church de Nantwiche in co. Cestr'.=. . . .

Richardus Church de Nantwiche=Margeria filia Rogeri Wright de in com. Cestr' [Inq. p.m. 1593]. | Nantwiche [bur. 26 Dec. 1599].

Margaretta filia Thomæ=Will'us Churche de Betton in=Elizabetha filia Reginaldi Broughton de Brough- | com. Salop aᵒ 1623 [buried at | Wright de Nantwiche. ton vx. 2. | Drayton 1632].

Willimus s.p. — Willimus s.p.

Richardus Churche=Isabella fil. Arthuri Sonford Junior fil. et hær. | de Sanford [*Sandford of Sand-* aᵒ 1623 [buried at | *ford*] in com. Salopiæ. Drayton 1654].

Richardus s.p. — Margareta s.p.

Thomas 2 [*B.D. Senior Fellow of B.N. Coll. Oxon. Died 19 Feb. 1676*].

Willimus 3.

Richardus Churche æt. 10 annorum aᵒ 1623.

Robertus 4.

Margaretta. — Anna.

WILLIAM CHURCH.

Clare of Crome D'Abitot, co. Worcester.

Harl. 1896, fo. 74.   Harl. 615, fo. 268ᵇ.

ARMS: Harl. 1896.—*Quarterly : 1 and 4, Or, three chevronels ermines ; 2, Argent, on a chevron between three spears' heads gules as many plates,* on a chief azure three birds or* [RYCE]; 3, Or, two lions passant-guardant in pale, the one in chief gules, the other azure* [D'ABITOT].
CREST: Harl. 615.—*A buck's head cabossed.*
ANOTHER COAT.—*Or, three chevronels gules, within a bordure engrailed azure.*

A patent granted to Simon Clare of Crome-Dabitot in co. Wigorn' who is lyneally descended of Gilbert Clare of the said county, by Wᵐ Herny Clar. King of Armes aᵒ 1562.

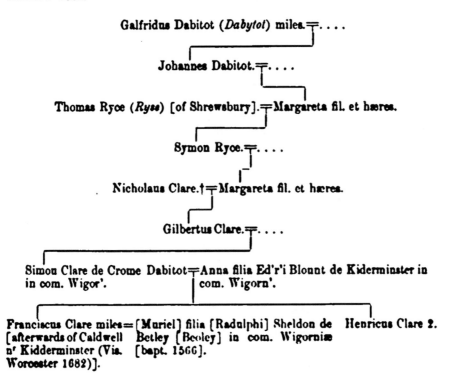

Galfridus Dabitot (*Dabytot*) miles.🟰....

Johannes Dabitot.🟰....

Thomas Ryce (*Ryse*) [of Shrewsbury].🟰Margareta fil. et hæres.

Symon Ryce.🟰....

Nicholaus Clare.†🟰Margareta fil. et hæres.

Gilbertus Clare.🟰....

Simon Clare de Crome Dabitot🟰Anna filia Ed'r'i Blount de Kiderminster in in com. Wigor'.   com. Wigorn'.

Franciscus Clare miles=[Muriel] filia [Radulphi] Sheldon de   Henricus Clare 2.
[afterwards of Caldwell   Betley [Beoley] in com. Wigorniæ
n' Kidderminster (Vis.   [bapt. 1566].
Worcester 1682)].

* In the Worcestershire Visitation the three plates are omitted.
† The Clare pedigree is given in Harl. Mss. 1566 and 1423, and Coll. of Arms K 4, fo. 24.

Clarke of Shrewsbury.

Harl. 1396, fo. 89ᵇ. S., 75ᵇ.

ARMS: Harl. 1396.—*Azure, three escallops in pale or between two flaunches ermine, on a chief argent three lions rampant-guardant of the first.*

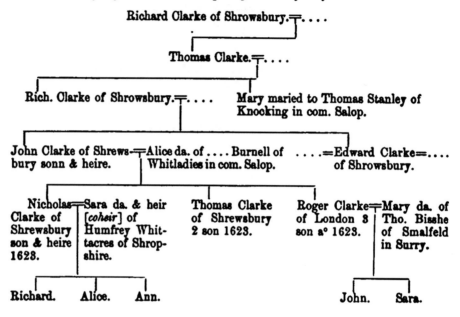

Richard Clarke of Shrowsbury.=....

Thomas Clarke.=....

Rich. Clarke of Shrowsbury.=....   Mary maried to Thomas Stanley of Knocking in com. Salop.

John Clarke of Shrews-=Alice da. of .... Burnell of   ....=Edward Clarke=....
bury sonn & heire.   Whitladies in com. Salop.   of Shrowsbury.

Nicholas=Sara da. & heir   Thomas Clarke   Roger Clarke=Mary da. of
Clarke of [*coheir*] of   of Shrewsbury   of London 3 Tho. Bisshe
Shrewsbury Humfrey Whit-   2 son 1623.   son aᵒ 1623. of Smalfeld
son & heire tacres of Shrop-   in Surry.
1623. shire.

Richard.   Alice.   Ann.   John.   Sara.

Clay of the Fells.

Harl. 1396, fo. 81ᵇ. S., 68ᵇ.

ARMS: Harl. 1396.—*Per pale vert and sable, a lion rampant ermine between three escallops argent.*
CREST.—*A lion's head couped per pale vert and sable, charged with an escallop argent.*

Robertus Clay de le Falls [*Fells*] [called also=....
Falls Green] in parochiâ de Prees in com. Salop.

Humfr'us Clay de le Fells in=Elizabetha fil. et hæres Joh'nis
com. Salop fil. et hæres.   Browne de Marchamley.

Richardus Clay de le Fells in=Margeryæ filia Will'i   Will'm s.p.
co. Salop fil. et hær.   Newens de Newton.

▲

▲

| Thomas ob. s.p. | Margaretta vx. Joh'es Puce de Hodnett in com. Salop. | Dorothea vx. Tho. Back-house in com. Cestr'. | Eliz. vx. Edw. Sandford. |

Katherina fil. Joh'is Dod de co. Cestr' vx. 1. = Georgius Clay filius et hæres a° 1623. = Jana fil. Ric. Lastley vx. 2.

| Andreas Clay fil. et hær. ætat. 30 1623. | Thomas Clay. — Richardus, s.p. | Richardus Clay de london aurifaber. | George. — Franciscus. — Johannes. | Margaretta. — Maria. — Dorothea. | Jana. — Katherina. |

GEORGE CLAY.

Clench or Clynch of Bridgnorth.

Harl. 1396, fo. 70. Harl. 1241, fo. 108b.

ARMS: Harl. 1396.—*Quarterly : 1 and 4, Gules, a saltire or, in chief an annulet of the second ; 2 and 3, Gules, three bars wavy or* [DE LA MERE].

Clench de Newcastell in com. Dublin in Hibernia. = ... filia et una hæredu' . . . . Delamere.

Will'us Clench de Newcastell in co. Dublin. = ... filia . . . . Lutterell de Lutterellston in co. Dublin.

. . . . filia . . . . Hackett *Hackluit* de Sutton in com. Dublin vx. 2. = Joh'es Clench de Tybergragan in com. Dublin 2 filius. = Elianora filia Jacobi Nutt de Gariston in com. Dublin.

Nicholaus Clench de Dublin in com. Dublia gen. = Thomasina filia Mathei Bath *Nath. Baylie* de Beshelston in com. Dublin Ar.
Arms : Gules, a cross inter four lions rampant argent.

| Jacobus Clench filius et hæres of Dublyn. | Will'us Clench de Brugenorth in com. Salop gen. 2 filius a° 1584. | Francisca fil. Ric'i Cresset de Upton Cresset in com. Salop. | Rogerus Smith 1 maritus. Joh'es Hopton 2 maritus. Francis. Hoord 3 maritus. |

Clough of Minsterley and Hockstowe.

Harl. 1396, fo. 69.   Harl. 1241, fo. 68.   S., ff. 60ᵇ, 61ᵃ, 61ᵇ.

ARMS: Harl. 1396.—*Gules, three pine-apples slipped argent, a martlet for difference.*

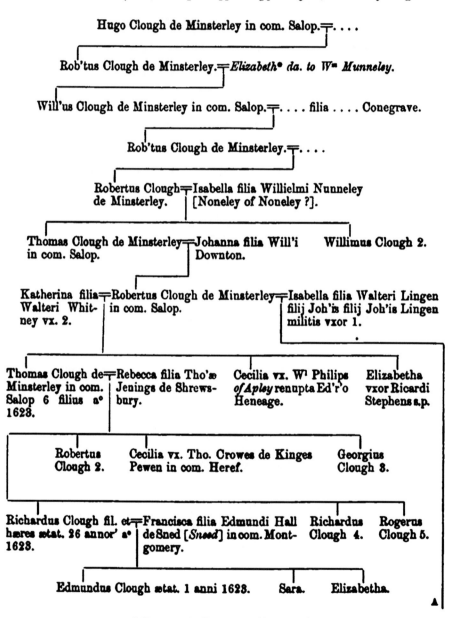

Hugo Clough de Minsterley in com. Salop.=. . . .

Rob'tus Clough de Minsterley.=*Elizabeth* da. to Wᵐ Munneley.

Will'us Clough de Minsterley in com. Salop.=. . . . filia . . . . Conegrave.

Rob'tus Clough de Minsterley.=. . . .

Robertus Clough de Minsterley.=Isabella filia Willielmi Nunneley [Noneley of Noneley ?].

Thomas Clough de Minsterley in com. Salop.=Johanna filia Will'i Downton.   Willimus Clough 2.

Katherina filia Walteri Whitney vx. 2.=Robertus Clough de Minsterley in com. Salop.=Isabella filia Walteri Lingen filij Joh'is filij Joh'is Lingen militis vxor 1.

Thomas Clough de Minsterley in com. Salop 6 filius aᵒ 1623.=Rebecca filia Tho'æ Jenings de Shrewsbury.   Cecilia vx. Wᵗ Philips *of Apley* renupta Ed'r'o Heneage.   Elizabetha vxor Ricardi Stephens s.p.

Robertus Clough 2.   Cecilia vx. Tho. Crowes de Kinges Pewen in com. Heref.   Georgius Clough 3.

Richardus Clough fil. et=Francisca filia Edmundi Hall hæres ætat. 26 annor' aᵒ 1623.=de Sned [*Sneed*] in com. Montgomery.   Richardus Clough 4.   Rogerus Clough 5.

Edmundus Clough ætat. 1 anni 1623.   Sara.   Elizabetha.

▲

* Not given in Shrewsbury MS., fo. 60ᵇ.

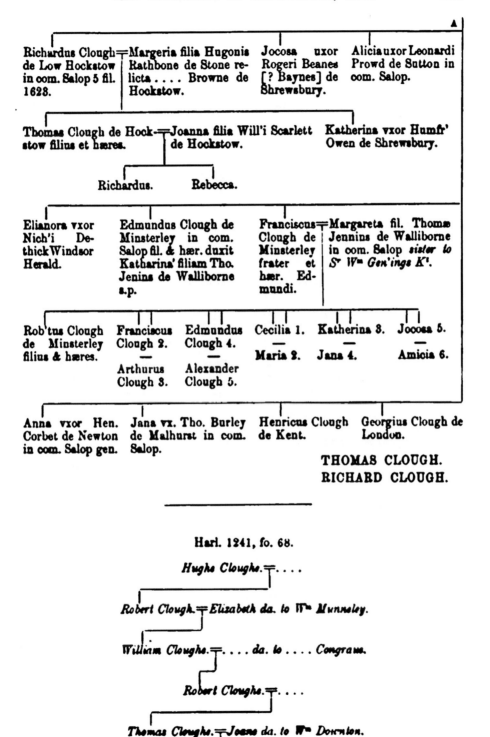

▲

Richardus Clough⹀Margeria filia Hugonis   Jocosa   uxor   Alicia uxor Leonardi
de Low Hockstow Rathbone de Stone re-   Rogeri Beanes   Prowd de Sutton in
in com. Salop 5 fil. licta .... Browne de   [? Baynes] de   com. Salop.
1623.   Hockstow.   Shrewsbury.

Thomas Clough de Hock-⹀Joanna filia Will'i Scarlett   Katherina vxor Humfr'
stow filius et hæres.   de Hockstow.   Owen de Shrewsbury.

            Richardus.   Rebecca.

Elianora vxor   Edmundus Clough de   Franciscus⹀Margareta fil. Thomæ
Nich'i   De-   Minsterley in com.   Clough de Jennins de Walliborne
thick Windsor   Salop fil. & hær. duxit   Minsterley in com. Salop sister to
Herald.   Katharinæ filiam Tho.   frater   et Sr Wm Gen'ings Kt.
                 Jenins de Walliborne   hær.   Ed-
                 s.p.   mundi.

Rob'tus Clough   Franciscus   Edmundus   Cecilia 1.   Katherina 3.   Jocosa 5.
de Minsterley   Clough 2.   Clough 4.   —   —   —
filius & hæres. —   —   Maria 2.   Jana 4.   Amicia 6.
                 Arthurus   Alexander
                 Clough 3.   Clough 5.

Anna vxor Hen.   Jana vx. Tho. Burley   Henricus Clough   Georgius Clough de
Corbet de Newton   de Malhurst in com.   de Kent.   London.
in com. Salop gen. Salop.

                                                THOMAS CLOUGH.
                                                RICHARD CLOUGH.

Harl. 1241, fo. 68.

Hughe Cloughe.⹀....

Robert Clough.⹀Elizabeth da. to Wm Munneley.

William Cloughe.⹀.... da. to .... Congrave.

Robert Cloughe.⹀....

Thomas Cloughe.⹀Joane da. to Wm Downton.
            ▲

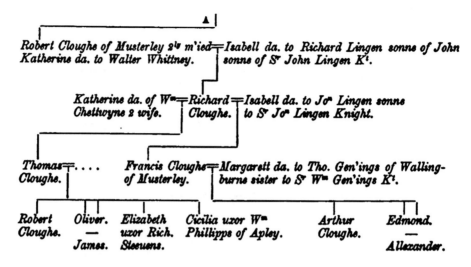

Robert Cloughe of Musterley 2ly m'ied=*Isabell da. to Richard Lingen sonne of John*
Katherine da. to Walter Whittney.   *sonne of Sr John Lingen Kt.*

Katherine da. of Wm=*Richard*=*Isabell da. to Jon Lingen sonne*
Chettwyne 2 wife.   *Cloughe.*   *to Sr Jon Lingen Knight.*

Thomas=*. . . .*   *Francis Cloughe*=*Margarett da. to Tho. Gen'ings of Walling-*
Cloughe.   *of Musterley.*   *burne sister to Sr Wm Gen'ings Kt.*

Robert   *Oliver.*   *Elizabeth*   *Cicilia uxor Wm*   *Arthur*   *Edmond.*
Cloughe.   *—*   *uxor Rich.*   *Phillipps of Apley.*   *Cloughe.*   *—*
        James.   *Steevens.*   *Allexander.*

Cludd of Clotley and Orleton.

Harl. 1396, fo. 70b.   Harl. 1241, fo. 43.   Harl. 615, fo. 268b.

ARMS: Harl. 1396.—*Quarterly of six: 1 and 6, Ermine, a fret sable, CLUDD; 2, Argent, a bend between two double cottises sable, ORLETON; 3, Argent, on a bend sable three martlets gules [argent], ANNE [HINTON ?]; 4, Per fesse indented sable and argent, six fleurs-de-lis counterchanged, HINTON; 5, Gules, nine arrows, three, three, and three, each parcel, two in saltire and one in pale, argent, banded . . . ., BIEST.**

CREST.—*An eagle with wings expanded preying on a coney, all proper.*

ARMS: Harl. 615.—*Argent, a bend between two double cottises sable, a martlet for difference.*

CREST, as above.

    Legitur quod Will'us filius Ricardi Cludd portabat in sigillo suo unam Antelopam passantem regardentem tempore E. 3.
    Notandum est quod Johannes filius Rogeri Cludd dedit Will'o Cludd vnum messuag' in Cotly [Clottley] cum boscis in Aston prope le wrekin aᵒ 5 H. 6.

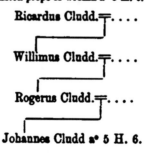

Ricardus Cludd.=. . . .

Willimus Cludd.=. . . .

Rogerus Cludd.=. . . .

Johannes Cludd aᵒ 5 H. 6.

Richardus Cludd de Cotley [Clottley].=. . . . filia . . . . Brereton de Brereton.

* Cooke, Clarenceux, confirmed these arms to John Biest of Atcham, co. Salop, with the arrows or, banded argent, with tassels to the ribbons or (Ashmole MS. 834, p. 59).

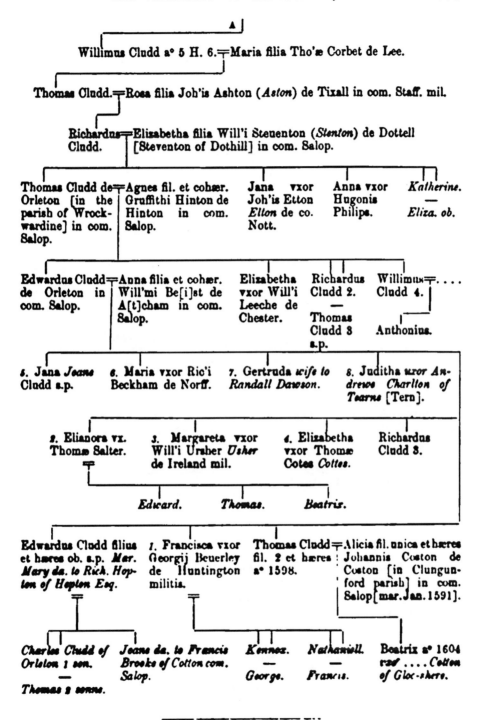

▲

Willimus Cludd a° 5 H. 6.⊤Maria filia Tho'æ Corbet de Lee.

Thomas Cludd.⊤Rosa filia Joh'is Ashton (*Aston*) de Tixall in com. Staff. mil.

Richardus⊤Elizabetha filia Will'i Steuenton (*Stenton*) de Dottell
Cludd. | [Steventon of Dothill] in com. Salop.

Thomas Cludd de⊤Agnes fil. et cohær.	Jana vxor	Anna vxor	*Katherine.*
Orleton [in the	Gruffithi Hinton de	Joh'is Etton	Hugonis	—
parish of Wrock-	Hinton in com.	*Elton* de co.	Philips.	*Eliza. ob.*
wardine] in com.	Salop.	Nott.		
Salop.				

Edwardus Cludd⊤Anna filia et cohær.	Elizabetha	Richardus	Willimus⊤....
de Orleton in	Will'mi Be[i]st de	vxor Will'i	Cludd 2.	Cludd 4.
com. Salop.	A[t]cham in com.	Leeche de	—	
	Salop.	Chester.	Thomas	
			Cludd 3	Anthonius.
			s.p.	

5. Jana *Joane*	6. Maria vxor Ric'i	7. Gertruda *wife to*	8. Juditha *vxor An-*
Cludd s.p.	Beckham de Norff.	*Randall Dawson.*	*drewe Charlton of*
			Tearne [Tern].

2. Elianora vx.	3. Margareta vxor	4. Elizabetha	Richardus
Thomæ Salter.	Will'i Ursher *Usher*	vxor Thomæ	Cludd 3.
⊤	de Ireland mil.	Cotes *Cottes*.	

| Edward. | Thomas. | Beatris. |

Edwardus Cludd filius	1. Francisca vxor	Thomas Cludd⊤Alicia fil. unica et hæres
et hæres ob. s.p. *Mar.*	Georgij Beuerley	fil. 2 et hæres	Johannis Coston de
Mary da. to Rich. Hop-	de Huntington	a° 1598.	Coston [in Clungun-
ton of Hopton Esq.	militis.		ford parish] in com.
			Salop[mar.Jan.1591].

Charles Cludd of	*Joane da. to Francis*	*Kennex.*	*Nathaniell.*	Beatrix a° 1604
Orleton 1 son.	*Brooke of Cotton com.*	—	—	*ræ* .... *Cotton*
—	*Salop.*	*George.*	*Francis.*	*of Gloc-shere.*
Thomas 2 sonne.				

Clun of Clun.

Harl. 1396, fo. 89.　Harl. 1241, fo. 164ᵇ.　S., ff. 74ᵇ, 75.

Rogerus Do[minus] de=Sibella fil. Wᵐ Burley fil. Joh'is
Edgeton [*Edgerton*].　Burley mil.

Tho.=Alicia fil.　Anna fil. et hær. vx. Simonis de Winbury a quo
Philley.　et hæres.　Sandford [*genus duxit*].

Johannes Clun Constabularius de Clun.=Eliza. fil. et hæres Tho. Philley.

Johannis Clun de Clun.=Margeria fil. Rob'ti Poole.

Howell 2.　　Matheus 4.　　Elizabeth 4.　　Margret 6.　　7. Dorothea vx. Rees ap
—　　　　　　　　　　　　　　　　—　　　　　　　　　　Edward ap John de
Willimus 3.　　　　　　　　　　Anna 5.　　　　　　　　Drogynon [*Drodgynon*].

1. Florencia　　2. Jana nupta Hugo Dyer　　Tho. Clun=Ellena fil. Jenan Gwyn ap
vx. Ric'i Col-　de london 2 Joh'es Walter　de Clun　James ap Rees Elystan
wich.　　　　　[*Walker*].　　　　　　　　de Salop.　*Glodred*.

Hugo Clun rector=....　　Jacobus Clun de=.... soror Petri　Margareta vx.
de Dodington in　　　　Orsett in Essex　Buck de Kanci　Tho. Powell
co. Glouc. 4.　　　　　2 fil.　　　　　[*Nancy*] militis.　de Shedwell.

Thomas　　....filia　　Thomas Clun de　　2. Edward.　　Elizabeth vx. Daniell
s.p.　　　nupta.　　Orsett in Essex.　　　　　　　　Holswik de Orsett.

Lodovicus　　Johannes　　Edwardus=....　　Edwardus Clun de
s.p.　　　　s.p.　　　Clun 5.　　　　　London 6 fil.

Mauritius Clun.　　John s.p.　　Elinor.　　Jane.

Mauricus Clun de Clun in com. Salop=Jonnetta* filia Gruff. Lloyd
Attornatus in March' Wall'.　　　　ap Richard Lloyd.

[.... *filia*　Tho. Clun de Clun=Maria fil. Ed'r'i Powell　Edwardus　Margareta
nupta....]　in com. Salop 1623.　de Shedwell.　　　de Scocia.　s.p.

Mauritius Clun fil. et hær.　Edwardus.　Katherin.　Margrett.　Rebecka.
aᵒ 1623 8 yers old.

* In Harl. 1241 she is called " Jane da. to Gruffith Vaughan of Coregedall " [Cors-y-gedol],
and her arms are : Or, a griffin segreant gules.

Clyve of Walford and Styche, co. Salop; and Huxley, co. Chester.

Harl. 1396, fo. 74ᵇ.

Ex antiquis chartis in custodia Edwardi Clyve de Walford in com. Salop. armigeri 29ᵉ die Septemb. aᵒ d'ni 1623.

Omnibus p'ntibus et futuri etc. quod ego Tho. fil. Ricardi de Stokes impignoravi et nomine pignoris dimisi Joh'i filio Madoci de Kynaston pro quinque marcis argenti quas mihi dedit præ-manibus in necessitate mea omnes t'ras et ten'ta mea in le Stokes infra hundr' de Elesmer' quæ mihi descendebant iure hæreditario post decessum præd'c'i Ricardi patris mei. Habend' a festo o'ium S'corum aᵒ Regni R' Ed'r'i tertij post conquestum 44ᵗⁱ usq' ad finem centum annor'. Testibus Edmundo de Burhton et alijs.

Madocus de Kynaston.⊤....

Johannes de Kynaston.

Omnibus Christi fidelibus ad quos p'ntes l'ræ peruenerint Joh'es Kynaston salutem. Noueritis me dedisse concessisse et hac p'nti carta confirmasse Joh'i Kynaston filio meo et Gaufrido fratri eius vnum annualem redditum 40 solidorum annuatim percipiend', ad festa Paschæ et S'c'i Michaelis etc. de omnibus illis terris et ten'tis quæ fuerunt Owen ap Griffith in villa de Pendeley infra d'nium de Mayllersayseneck* et quæ nuper ad quæ siui de D'no principe in feodo. Habend' et tenend' prædict' Joh'i et Gaufrido filijs meis hæred' et assignat' suis imp'petuum. Dat' apud Ellesmere Anno regni R' Henrici quarti post conquestam vndecimo.

[Drawing of a Seal, Plate I., Fig. 4B.]

Sciant præsentes et futuri quo ego Nicholaus persona ecclesiæ de Pecton [Purton] et Nicholaus persona Ecclesiæ de Hynstock dedimus concessimus et hac præsenti carta n'ra confirmauimus Rogero Hord de Walleford et Margaretæ vxori suæ maneria nostra de Walleford Stanwardyn in le Wood et tres partes manerij de Woderton etc. vna cum omnibus terris et ten'tis redditibus et servicijs ac reversionibus cum omnibus suis pertinentijs in Redinghurst et Chelmerdewyk. Habend' et tenend' etc. ad totam vitam vtriusq' eorum et hæred' ipsius Rogeri imp'petuum. Dat' apud Stanwardyn in le Wood die iouis proximo post festum beati Barnabæ apostoli aᵒ regni regis Ed'r'i tertij post conquest' quinquagesimo.

Omnibus Christi fidelibus etc. Griffinus Kynaston de Walford salutem in d'no cum Marga-reta filia Rogeri Hurd de Walford nuper vxor mea obijt seisita de Manerio de Walford cum pertinentijs in com. Salop. et de manerio de Stanwardyn cum pertin' in eodem com. ac de tribus p'tibus de Woderton vna cum alijs terris et ten'tis reddit' et servic' in d'co com. in d'nico suo ut de feodo quæ post mortem d'cæ Margaretæ habeo et teneo per saticiam anglicanam ad terminum vitæ meæ et quæ post decessum meum Philippo Kynaston filio et hæredi meo et ipsius Margaretæ integre remanerent etc. Noueritis me præd'c'um Griffinum Kynaston concessisse et sursum reddidisse præfato Philippo filio meo et ipsius Margaretæ totum ius etc. Dat' apud Walford 20 die Januarij anno 21 H. 6.

Hæc indentura testatur quod Rogerus Kynaston filius et hæres Philippi Kynaston d'nus de Walford et Onleley in com. Salop gentilman et Alicia Kynaston mater eiusdem Rogeri in sua pura et legitima viduitate tradiderunt concesserunt et ad feodi firma' demiserunt Will'o Lyte de Salop merchaunt vnam parcellum t'ræ vocat' Onleley. Dat' apud Ordeley præd'c'o in festo Puri-ficationis b'tæ Mariæ Virginis. Anno 18 E. 4.

Omnibus X'pi fidelibus etc. Rogerus Kynaston fil. et hær. Philippi Kynaston de Walford in com. Salop defuncti salutem. Noueritis me præfatum Rogerum concessisse et confirmasse Aliciæ matri meæ nuper vxori p'd'c'i Philippi quandam annuitatem sexaginta solidorum etc. Dat' apud Walford die lunæ prox. post festum S'c'i Petri aᵒ 21 E. 4.

Harl. 1396, fo. 76ᵇ. Harl. 1241, fo. 25. 8., ff. 62—63ᵇ.

ARMS: Harl. 1396: CLYVE OF WALFORD.—*Quarterly of fifteen: 1 and 15, Argent, on a fesse between three wolves' heads erased sable as many mullets or, CLYVE; 2, Ermine, on a bend coticed gules three crescents or, HUXLEGH; 3, Sable, three garbs or, STUCHE; 4, Sable, a lion rampant or, crowned argent, between three crosses formée fitchée of the last, WLONKESLOW; 5, Quarterly*

* Penley, although belonging to the Shropshire parish of Ellesmere, is in the hundred of Maelor, co. Flint, called in Welsh "Maelor Saesneg."

R

argent and sable, four cocks counterchanged, BROUGHTON ; 6, *Argent, a lion rampant sable*, KYNASTON ; 7, *Argent, a chevron engrailed between three mullets pierced sable*, KYNASTON ; 8, *Gules, on a chevron or three mullets sable*, FRANKTON ; 9, *Argent, on a chief or a raven sable*, HORD ; 10, *Argent, a fesse between six sparrowhawks sable*, ONSLOW [ONSLOW OF BOREATTON] ; 11, *Vert, a chevron ermine between three wolves' heads erased argent*, LLOYD ; 12, *Or, a lion rampant gules* [BLEDDYN AP CYNFYN] ; 13, *Argent, a chevron between three boars' heads couped close gules* [IDDON AP RHYS SAYS] ; 14, *Vert, two boars passant argent* [POWIS].

CREST.—*A wolf's head erased quarterly per pale indented argent and sable, a mullet for difference.*

ARMS : Harl. 1396 : CLYVE OF HUXLEY.—*Quarterly of six : 1, Argent, on a fesse sable three mullets or*, CLYVE ; 2, *Ermine, on a bend cotised gules three crescents or*, HUXLEY ; 3, *Azure, a chevron between three taus argent—Or, on a chevron azure three taus argent*, in Harl. 1241—TEW ; 4 *Sable, three garbs or*, STUCHE ; 5, *Sable, a lion rampant or, crowned of the same, between three crosses formée fitchée argent*,* WLONKESLOW ; 6, *Quarterly argent and sable, four cocks counterchanged—Quarterly or and argent, four cocks gules*, in Harl. 1241 [BROUGHTON].

CREST.—*On a mount vert a gryphon passant argent, ducally gorged gules.*

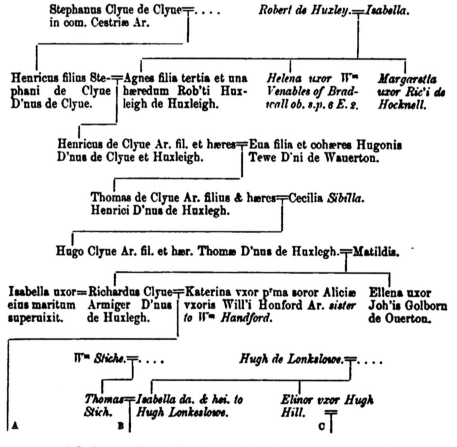

* In the quarterings of Clyve of Walford the lion is " crowned argent."

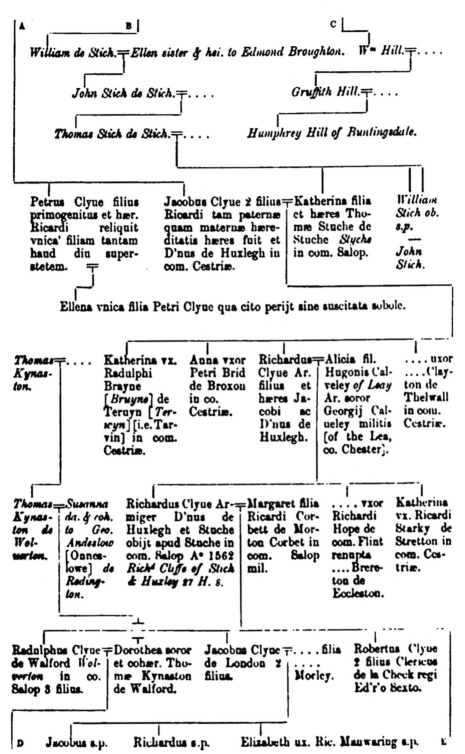

A   B   C

William de Stich.⊤*Ellen sister & hei. to Edmond Broughton.*   Wm *Hill.*⊤*....*

John Stick de Stich.⊤*....*   *Gruffith Hill.*⊤*....*

Thomas Stick de Stich.⊤*....*   *Humphrey Hill of Runtingsdale.*

| Petrus Clyue filius primogenitus et hær. Ricardi reliquit vnica' filiam tantam haud diu superstetem. ⊤ | Jacobus Clyue 2 filius Ricardi tam paternæ quam maternæ hæreditatis hæres fuit et D'nus de Huxlegh in com. Cestriæ. | Katherina filia et hæres Thomæ Stuche de Stuche *Styche* in com. Salop. | *William Stich ob. s.p.* — *John Slich.* |

Ellena vnica filia Petri Clyue qua cito perijt sine suscitata subole.

| Thomas Kynaston. ⊤.... | Katherina vx. Radulphi Brayne [*Bruyne*] de Teruyn [*Terxcyn*] [i.e. Tarvin] in com. Cestriæ. | Anna vxor Petri Brid de Broxon in co. Cestriæ. | Richardus Clyue Ar. filius et hæres Jacobi ac D'nus de Huxlegh. | Alicia fil. Hugonis Calveley *of Leay* Ar. soror Georgij Calueley militis [of the Lea, co. Chester]. | ....uxor ....Clayton de Thelwall in com. Cestriæ. |

| Thomas Kynaston de Wolxerton. | Susanna da. & coh. to Geo. Andeslow [Onneslowe] de Redington. | Richardus Clyue Armiger D'nus de Huxlegh et Stuche obijt apud Stuche in com. Salop A° 1562 *Richd Clife of Stich & Huxley* 27 H. s. | Margaret filia Ricardi Corbett de Morton Corbet in com. Salop mil. | ....vxor Richardi Hope de com. Flint renupta ....Brereton de Eccleston. | Katherina vx. Ricardi Starky de Stretton in com. Cestriæ. |

| Radulphus Clyue de Walford *Wolverton* in co. Salop 3 filius. | Dorothea soror et cohær. Thomæ Kynaston de Walford. | Jacobus Clyue de London 2 filius. | ....filia .... Morley. | Robertus Clyue 2 filius Clericus de la Check regi Ed'r'o Sexto. |

D   Jacobus s.p.   Richardus s.p.   Elizabeth ux. Ric. Mauwaring s.p.   E

D
E

Franciscus Clive de Shrewsbury 2 fil. 1623.

Robertus 3. — Johannes 4. — Mariæ s.p. — Sara s.p.

Margaretta vx. Georgij Monington of leightonshop in co. Heref.

Susanna vxor Anthonij Hanmer de Bechfeld in co. Flint.

Mariæ vx. Tho. Tompikes de Eyton in com. Salop.

Winifridæ ux. Wm Hanmer de Bechfeld in co. Flint.

Richardus Clyne 5 filius aº 1623.

Juditha fil. Roger Hanmer de Marton in co. Salop vx. 2. = Edwardus Clyne de Walford *Woluerton* in com. Salop fil. et hær. aº 1623. = Blanchea fil. et unica hær. Tho. Lloyd de Cayhowell [*Cakewell*] *Cowhall and* [derived from] *Rired Vlaydd* in com. Salop.

Juditha s.p.

Richardus 2 s.p. — Franciscus 7 s.p.

Robertus Clyne 3.

Stephanus 4. — Josuah 5. — Georgius 6.

Margaretta ux. Simonis Merick de Masbrooke [*Wasbrooke*] in co. Salop.

Tho. Clyne de Walford *Cliffe of Huxley 1608* = Maria fil. et hær. Geo. Onslow de Boreatton in co. Salop. fil. primogenitus æt. 34 annorum Aº 1623.

Thomas Clyne ætatis 12 Anor' Aº 1623.*   Katherinæ.

Dorothea fil. 2 vxor Jacobi Barker Ar. de Haghmond in com. Salop.

Alicia fil. 3 vxor Ric'i Lee de Lee *Lea de Lea* in parochia de Wibunbury in com. Cestriæ.

Jana filia 4 vxor Joh'is Creswell de com. Staff.

Elizabetha filia ætate maxima Ric'i s.p.

Richardus Clyue† Ar. D'n's de Stuche in com. Salop. et de Huxlegh. = Jana filia Will'i Brereton de Brereton in com. Cestriæ militis.

Rachell 1 fil. vx. Georgij Trenchard de Litchet in com. Dorcett.

Sara 2 s.p. — Rebecca 3 s.p. — Juditha 4.

Georgius Clyne de Huxlegh in co. Cestr' et Stuche in com. Salop miles obt 1 Septembris Aº 82 Eliz. = Susanna filia Henry Copinger de Deuington in co. Kent Ar. *and after to John Poole.*

Hester 5 filia vxor Joannis Starkey renupt..... Starkey de Huntrope [*Huntroyde*] in com. Lanc.

Susanna Clyne obijt virgo.

Ambrosius Clyne de Stuch in com. Salop 2 filius et hæres aº 1623. = Alicia fil. Tho. Towneshend de Brakenash [*Brakenagh*] in com. Norff. Ar.

Isaac Clyne 3 filius.

Stephanus Clyne 4 fil. cœlebs 1623.

Rebecca vxor Henrici Legh de Baguley in com. Cestr' Ar.

F

* " Æt. 10 in 1613 " in Harl. 1241.   † Spelled *Cliff* in his epitaph.

F|

Josuah Clyue de Huxley⹀Maria filia Andrea Charlton
Ar. fil. et hæres.　　　de Apley in co. Salop.

Georgius obijt aº　　Rachell uxor Tho. Wilbraham de　　Rebecca
ætatis suæ 12 s.p.　 Nantwiche in co. Cestr' Ar.　　　　s.p.

ED. CLYUE.　　　　STEUEN CLYUE.
ROBERT CLYUE.　　AMBROSE CLIUE.

Cole of Shrewsbury.

Harl. 1396, fo. 84ᵇ.　Harl. 1241.　S., ff. 72ᵇ, 73.

ARMS: Harl. 1396.—*Quarterly of eight : 1, Argent, a chevron gules between three scorpions sable; 2, Gules, an eagle displayed with two heads or* [MYTTON or EYTON ?]; *3, Argent, a fesse sable—gules* in Shrewsbury MS.—*between six Cornish choughs proper* [ONSLOW]; *4, Argent, a chevron between three talbots passant sable ; 5, Azure, three bars argent, in chief as many gryphons' heads erased or ;* 6, Gules, three birds each standing on a stump of a tree couped and eradicated argent; 7, Gules, a fleur-de-lis or* [FOULKES or GERBRAND OF TREFNANT ?]; *8, Argent, a fesse azure between a bull's head erased sable, armed or, in chief, and in base a gryphon passant of the third, winged of the last* [PIPE alias WALKER]; *over the whole of the quarterings a bendlet sinister.*

Will'us Cole fil. et hær. Joh'is Cole Ar. dedit Joh'i Oteley et Sibilla vx' eius fil. d'ci Will'i et hæredibus de corporibus suis inter eos legitime procreat' pastur' voc' Cole-forlonge Scituat' pone Castr' villa per Indenturam dat. 5 die Februarij aº 5 H. 7.

Inter Plet'a apud Westm. coram Joh'e Baldwyn mil. et socijs suis tunc Justic' H. 8 term. Sanctæ Trinitatis aº 30, rot. 119.

Quidam Rob'tus Cole fil. et hæres aparens cuiusdam Ed'r'i Cole venit Coram Joh'i Baldwyn mil. et Socijs suis Justic' D'ni R' de Banco et adtunc et ibid'm imposuit coram prefat' Justic' d'ni R's clameum sumus ad maner de Wigmore ac 20 mesuag' 16 cotag' 70 acr' t're 40 acr' prati mille acr' pastur' cc acr' bosci et 40s. redd' in Wigmore Erkall Hinkintar Monkfornat Oxton Salop bhotton Fortun et Montfort in com. pred'c'o etc.

Inter P'lacita irrot' apud Westm. coram Rob'to Brooke mil. et Socijs eius Termi Pasch' aº regnor Phi' et Mariæ 3 et 4, rotul. 433.

Quidam Hugo P'hillipe Thomæ Aston super montem Joh'es Lyne et Will'm's Hill clericus fuerunt seiseti de maner redd' terr' et ten' pred'c'u' cum pertin' in forma specificat' etc. Concess' pred'c'u' etc. Rich'o Churchyard et alijs pred'c'o etc. ad opus et vsum Edmundi Cole Armig' pro term' vitæ etc. et post eius decessum ad opus et vsum Rob'to Cole fil. et hær. apparens pred'c'o Edm. et hærod. de corpore ip'ius Rob'ti legitima procreatus etc.

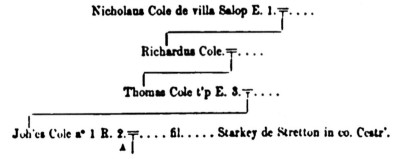

Nicholaus Cole de villa Salop E. 1.⹀....

Richardus Cole.⹀....

Thomas Cole t'p E. 3.⹀....

Joh'es Cole aº 1 R. 2.⹀.... fil. .... Starkey de Stretton in co. Cestr'.
▲|

* The fifth quartering closely resembles the arms of Barker *alias* Coverall of Camo, co. Salop, as given in the 'Visit. of Warwick, 1619,' p. 80, and Barker *alias* Gery, as given in the 'Visit. of London, 1568,' p. 11.

▲

Rogerus Cole fil. Johannes.⊤.... fil. .... Ludlow.

Johannes Cole t'p H. 6.⊤Eliz. fil. et hær. Thomæ Onslow.

Will'm Cole t'p E. 4.⊤Eliz. fil. et hær. Nich'i Eyton de Eyton.

Johan'es Otley a° 5 H. 7.⊤Sibbilla soror et   Edmundus Cole t'p H. 7.⊤
    hær. Edmundi.

Thomas⊤Johanna fil. et sola hær.=[Thomas   Robertus Cole⊤Maria fil. Euan
Oteley. | Hugonis Pipe al's Wal- | Berrington   filius naturalis | Lloyd vychan de
    ker [will 1560].   2 husb.]   a° 5 H. 8.   Abertannet Ar.

Maria fil. et cohær. nupta   Eleanora vx.   Elizabetha   Joh'es Cole de⊤Alicia fil.
Ric'o Owen de Cundon   Ric'i Hussy   vx. Humfri'   Shrowsbury. | Rich'i
[Condover] [marr. sett.   de Battles-   Kinaston. | Sandford.
dat. 1531]. ⊤   feld.

Thomas Owen miles vnus   Simon   Thomas Cole senior de⊤Margaretta
Justiciariorum de Banco   3 fil.   leighton in co. Salop | relicta ....
Regis.   ⚜   fil. et hær. a° 1623.   Wicherley.

Elizabetha* fil. et hæres nupta Ed'r'o Cholmeley de com. Staff.

Nicholaus Cole.⊤....

Hugo Cole.⊤....

Thomas Cole Burgens' Salop'.⊤....

Hugo Cole 33 E. 3.⊤....

Thomas Cole.⊤....

Thomas Cole a° 15 H. 6.⊤....

Johan'es Cole a° 15 H. 6.⊤Agnes.
    B   C

* Omitted in Shrewsbury MS., fo. 72ᵇ.

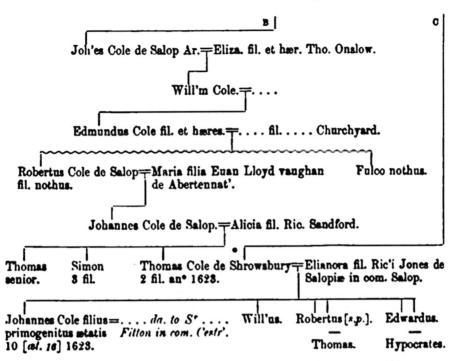

B |

C

Joh'es Cole de Salop Ar.=Eliza. fil. et hær. Tho. Onslow.

Will'm Cole.=. . . .

Edmundus Cole fil. et hæres.=. . . . fil. . . . . Churchyard.

Robertus Cole de Salop=Maria filia Euan Lloyd vaughan   Fulco nothus.
fil. nothus.   de Abertennat'.

Johannes Cole de Salop.=Alicia fil. Ric. Sandford.

Thomas   Simon   Thomas Cole de Shrowsbury=Elianora fil. Ric'i Jones de
senior.   3 fil.   2 fil. an° 1623.   Salopiæ in com. Salop.

Johannes Cole filius=. . . . *da.* to Sr . . . .   Will'us.   Robertus [*s.p.*].   Edwardus.
primogenitus ætatis *Fitton in com. Cestr'.*   —   —
10 [*al. 16*] 1623.   Thomas.   Hypocrates.

Signed by Tho. Cole of Shrowsbury.
THOMAS COLE.

Collins of Upton, and of Woodhyde, co. Hereford.

Harl. 1396, fo. 78b. 8, ff. 65b, 66.

ARMS: Harl. 1396.—*Quarterly: 1 and 4, Vert, a gryphon segreant or; 2 and 3, Or, a chevron ermine between three pheons reversed gules* [KADWGAN AP RIRID].
CREST.—*A demi-gryphon segreant or, collared ermine.*

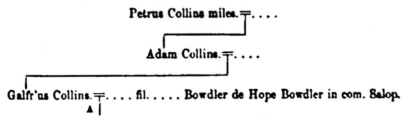

Petrus Collins miles.=. . . .

Adam Collins.=. . . .

Galfr'us Collins.=. . . . fil. . . . . Bowdler de Hope Bowdler in com. Salop.

▲ |

* The two pedigrees are not joined here, either in Harl. 1396, or in Shrewsbury MS, fo. 73b, although these children are given in both MSS. as the offspring of Thomas and Elianor.

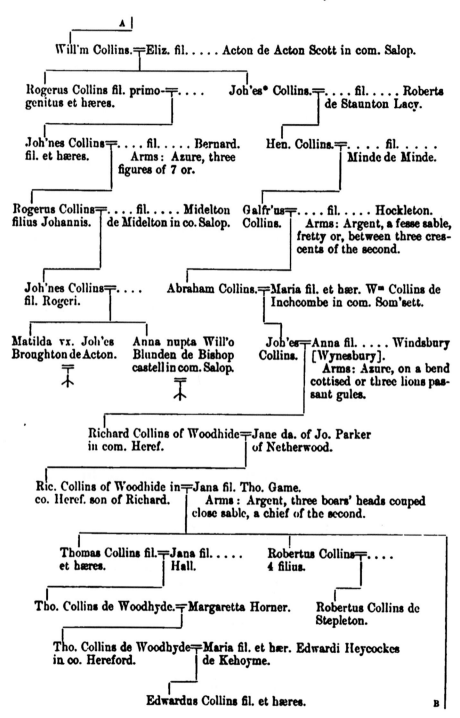

A |

Will'm Collins.=Eliz. fil. .... Acton de Acton Scott in com. Salop.

Rogerus Collins fil. primo-=. ....   Joh'es* Collins.=. ... fil. .... Roberts
genitus et hæres.   de Staunton Lacy.

Joh'nes Collins=. ... fil. .... Bernard.   Hen. Collins.=. ... fil. ....
fil. et hæres.   Arms: Azure, three   Minde de Minde.
                        figures of 7 or.

Rogerus Collins=. ... fil. .... Midelton   Galfr'us=. ... fil. .... Hockleton.
filius Johannis.│de Midelton in co. Salop.   Collins.   Arms: Argent, a fesse sable,
                                                           fretty or, between three cres-
                                                           cents of the second.

Joh'nes Collins=. ...   Abraham Collins.=Maria fil. et hær. W= Collins de
fil. Rogeri.   Inchcombe in com. Som'sett.

Matilda vx. Joh'es   Anna nupta Will'o   Joh'es=Anna fil. .... Windsbury
Broughton de Acton.   Blunden de Bishop   Collins.│[Wynesbury].
       ⚔   castellin com. Salop.   Arms: Azure, on a bend
                              ⚔   cottised or three lions pas-
                                                       sant gules.

                Richard Collins of Woodhide=Jane da. of Jo. Parker
                in com. Heref.   of Netherwood.

        Ric. Collins of Woodhide in=Jana fil. Tho. Game.
        co. Heref. son of Richard.   Arms : Argent, three boars' heads couped
                                            close sable, a chief of the second.

        Thomas Collins fil.=Jana fil. ....   Robertus Collins=. ...
        et hæres.   │Hall.   4 filius.

        Tho. Collins de Woodhyde.=Margaretta Horner.   Robertus Collins de
                                                         Stepleton.

        Tho. Collins de Woodhyde=Maria fil. et hær. Edwardi Heycockes
        in co. Hereford.   │de Kehoyme.

                Edwardus Collins fil. et hæres.   B

* Shrewsbury MS.; fo. 66, makes this John the *brother* of William, not his *son*.

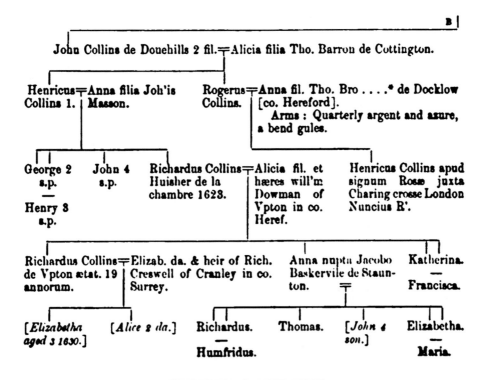

B |

John Collins de Douehills 2 fil.⹋Alicia filia Tho. Barron de Cottington.

Henricus⹋Anna filia Joh'is   Rogerus⹋Anna fil. Tho. Bro . . . .* de Docklow
Collins 1. | Masson.   Collins. | [co. Hereford].
       Arms : Quarterly argent and azure,
       a bend gules.

George 2   John 4   Richardus Collins⹋Alicia fil. et   Henricus Collins apud
s.p.   s.p.   Huisher de la | hæres will'm   signum Rosæ juxta
—   chambre 1623. | Dowman of   Charing crosse London
Henry 3   Vpton in co.   Nuncius R'.
s.p.   Heref.

Richardus Collins⹋Elizab. da. & heir of Rich.   Anna nupta Jacobo   Katherina.
de Vpton ætat. 19 | Creswell of Cranley in co.   Baskervile de Staun-   —
annorum.   Surrey.   ton.   Francisca.
                                           ⹋

[Elizabetha   [Alice 2 da.]   Richardus.   Thomas.   [John ♦   Elizabetha.
aged 3 1630.]   —   son.]   —
                          Humfridus.   Maria.

Coningsby of Nend Solers, Salop, and Morton Bagot, co. Staff.

Harl. 1396, fo. 87ᵇ.   Harl. 1241, fo. 101.   S., ff. 57ᵇ, 58.

ARMS: Harl. 1396.—*Quarterly of ten : 1, Gules, three conies couchant—sejant* in
Shrewsbury MS.—*argent; 2, Vert, a pelican in her nest feeding her young or*,
SOLERS in Shrewsbury MS.: 3, *Argent, two cheveronels azure*, BAGOTT in
Shrewsbury MS.; 4, *Or, a lion rampant gules within a bordure engrailed
sable*, FRENE in Shrewsbury MS. [of Nene Solers]; 5, *Per fesse azure and
or, a pale counterchanged and three lions rampant of the second*, WHETHILL
in Shrewsbury MS.; 6, *Or, a raven sable*, CORBETT in Shrewsbury MS.;
7, *Argent, a lion sejant gules within a bordure engrailed sable*, FARNWELL in
Shrewsbury MS.; 8, *Sable, three fishes naiant in pale argent*, LOCHARD in
Shrewsbury MS.; 9, *Argent, a saltire engrailed azure within a bordure
engrailed or—sable*, GREETE in Shrewsbury MS.; 10, *Argent, a fesse counter-
embattled sable, fretty or, between three lions passant of the second—gules* in
Harl. 1241, COTHERINGTON in Shrewsbury MS.

Johannes Coningsby.⹋Maria fil. Joh'is Salkers [Solers].

▲ |

---

* This word is the same in the copy of the Visitation in the College of Arms (Mr. H. Farnham
Burke, Somerset Herald). Arms such as are here described were borne by families named Bray,
Barkley, Hellers, and Blundeville. Mr. Heygate of Oaklands states that a family of *Bray* lived
until twenty years ago, in reduced circumstances, at Docklow Their last freehold farm was sold
about 1850, and they had been there for three or four generations, perhaps earlier.

S

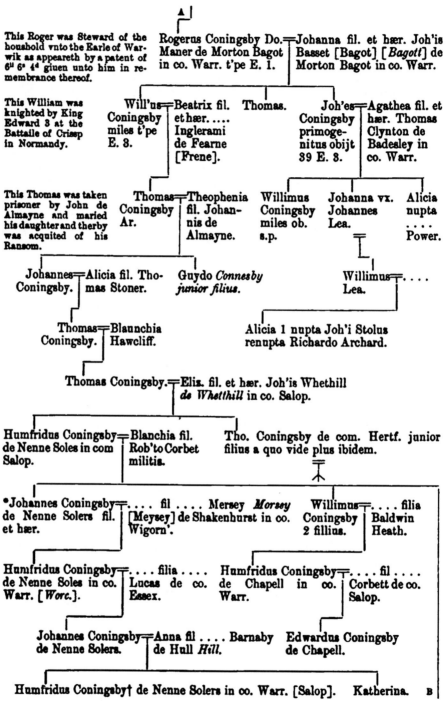

This Roger was Steward of the housbold vnto the Earle of Warwik as appeareth by a patent of 6ᵘ 6ˢ 4ᵈ giuen unto him in remembrance thereof.

Rogerus Coningsby Do.⹀Johanna fil. et hær. Joh'is Maner de Morton Bagot in co. Warr. t'pe E. 1. Basset [Bagot] [Bagott] de Morton Bagot in co. Warr.

This William was knighted by King Edward 3 at the Battaile of Crissp in Normandy.

Will'us⹀Beatrix fil.   Thomas.   Joh'es⹀Agathea fil. et Coningsby et hær. .....   Coningsby hær. Thomas miles t'pe Inglerami   primoge-   Clynton de E. 3.   de Fearne   nitus obijt Badesley in [Frene].   39 E. 3.   co. Warr.

This Thomas was taken prisoner by John de Almayne and maried his daughter and therby was acquited of his Ransom.

Thomas⹀Theophenia   Willimus   Johanna vx. Alicia Coningsby fil. Johan- Coningsby Johannes   nupta Ar.   nis de   miles ob. Lea.   .... Almayne.   s.p.   Power.

Johannes⹀Alicia fil. Tho-   Guydo Connesby   Willimus⹀.... Coningsby. mas Stoner.   junior filius.   Lea.

Thomas⹀Blaunchia   Alicia 1 nupta Joh'i Stolus Coningsby. Hawcliff.   renupta Richardo Archard.

Thomas Coningsby.⹀Eliz. fil. et hær. Joh'is Whethill de Whetthill in co. Salop.

Humfridus Coningsby⹀Blanchia fil.   Tho. Coningsby de com. Hertf. junior de Nenne Soles in com Rob'to Corbet   filius a quo vide plus ibidem. Salop.   militis.

*Johannes Coningsby⹀.... fil .... Mersey Morsey   Willimus⹀.... filia de Nenne Solers fil. [Meysey] de Shakenhurst in co. Coningsby Baldwin et hær.   Wigorn'.   2 fillius. Heath.

Humfridus Coningsby⹀.... filia ....   Humfridus Coningsby⹀.... fil .... de Nenne Soles in co. Lucas de co.   de Chapell in co. Corbett de co. Warr. [Worc.].   Essex.   Warr.   Salop.

Johannes Coningsby⹀Anna fil .... Barnaby   Edwardus Coningsby de Nenne Solers.   de Hull Hill.   de Chapell.

Humfridus Coningsby† de Nenne Solers in co. Warr. [Salop].   Katherina.   B

* Harl. 1241 makes this generation the brothers, and not the sons, of Humphrey; but apparently incorrectly.

† Apparently this was the great scholar and traveller.

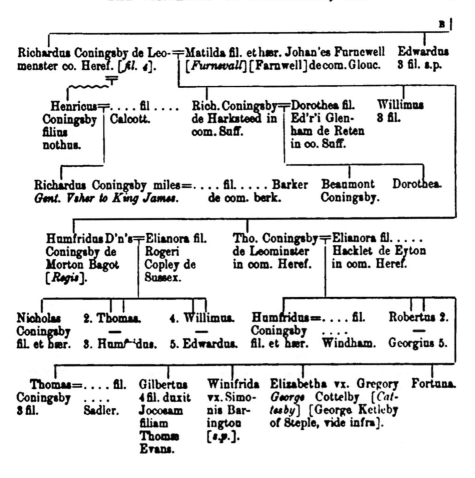

B |

Richardus Coningsby de Leo-=Matilda fil. et hær. Johan'es Furnewell　Edwardus
menster co. Heref. [*fil. 4*].　[*Furnevall*] [Farnwell] de com. Glouc.　3 fil. s.p.

Henricus=.... fil ....　　Rich. Coningsby=Dorothea fil.　　Willimus
Coningsby | Calcott.　　de Harksteed in | Ed'r'i Glen-　3 fil.
filius　　　　　　　　com. Suff.　　ham de Reten
nothus.　　　　　　　　　　　　in co. Suff.

Richardus Coningsby miles=.... fil. .... Barker　Beaumont　Dorothea.
Gent. Vsher to King James.　　de com. berk.　　Coningsby.

Humfridus D'n's=Elianora fil.　　Tho. Coningsby=Elianora fil. ....
Coningsby de | Rogeri　　　de Leominster | Hacklet de Eyton
Morton Bagot | Copley de　　in com. Heref.　in com. Heref.
[*Regis*].　　　Sussex.

Nicholas　　2. Thomas.　　4. Willimus.　　Humfridus=.... fil.　　Robertus 2.
Coningsby　　—　　　　—　　　　Coningsby | ....　　　—
fil. et hær.　3. Humf'dus.　5. Edwardus.　fil. et hær. | Windham.　Georgius 5.

Thomas=.... fil.　Gilbertus　Winifrida　Elizabetha vx. Gregory　Fortuna.
Coningsby | ....　4 fil. duxit　vx. Simo-　*George* Cottelby [*Cat-*
3 fil.　　Sadler.　Jocosam　nis Bar-　*tesby*] [George Ketleby
　　　　　　filiam　　ington　　of Steple, vide infra].
　　　　　　Thome　　[*s.p.*].
　　　　　　Evans.

Constantine of Dodington.

S., ff. 69b, 70.

[ARMS.—*Or, six flours-de-lis, three, two, and one, sable.*
p' Cooke Clarenc⁵ 18 July 1575.

Thomas Constantine of Dodington al's Dodington=....
in co. Salop neere Whitchurch.

John Constantine oldest son.=....　*William Constantine of Whitchurch 2ᵈ son.*=....

W⁵ *Constantine.*=....　*John Constantine oldest son.*

A |　　B |　　C |

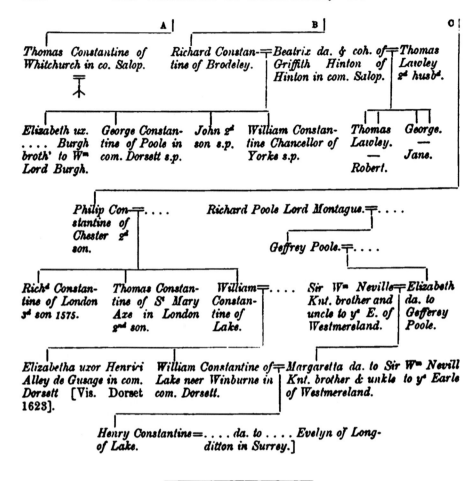

Corbet.

Harl. 1396, fo. 96.   Harl. 615, ff. 255ᵇ, 262ᵇ.   8., ff. 76ᵇ—85ᵇ.

ARMS OF Sʳ ANDREW CORBET OF MORETON, Kᵗ: Harl. 1396.—*Quarterly of twenty-two:* 1, *Or, a raven sable,* CORBETT ; 2, *Or, an escarbuncle sable,* TURET ; 3, *Azure, two lions passant or,* ERDINGTON ; 4, *Gules, crusily fitchée* [*semée of cross-crosslets fitchée*] *and a lion rampant or,* HOPTON ; 5, *Azure, a mermaid argent,* GUROS ; 6, *Vairé argent and sable, a canton gules,* STANTON ; 7, *Azure, six lions rampant, three, two, and one, argent, within a bordure engrailed or,* LEYBOURNE ; 8, *Gules, two lions passant argent, within a bordure engrailed or,* STRANGE ; 9, *Gules, a bend between two crescents or,* LANGBERGH ; 10, *Or, three bars and in chief two pallets sable, over all an inescutcheon ermine charged with three bars gules,* BURLEY ; 11, *Barry of six or and azure, a bend gules,* PENBRUGE ; 12, *Or, three roses gules,* YOUNGE ; 13, *Or, an eagle displayed vert, debruised by a bendlet gobonée argent and gules,* SYBTON ; 14, *Barry nebulée of six or and vert,* HAWBERKE ; 15, *Gules, crusily and three lucies hauriant or,* LUCY ; 16, *Argent, three chevronels*

sable, ARCHDEACON; 17, *Gules, three roaches naiant in pale argent*, ROCHE;
18, *Argent, three bendlets sable*, HACCOMBE; 19, *Gules, a lion rampant or
debruised by a bendlet azure, all within a bordure engrailed of the second*,
TALBOTT [OF RICHARDS CASTLE]; 20, *Barry of six or and vert, eighteen
fleurs-de-lis counterchanged*, MORTIMER [OF RICHARDS CASTLE]; 21, *Gules,
two bars vair*, SAYE; 22, *Gules, ten bezants, four, three, two, and one, a
label of three points azure*, ZOUCHE.

1 CREST.—*An elephant argent, on his back a castle triple-towered or, trappings of
the last and sable.*
2 CREST.—*A squirrel sejant or, cracking a nut.*

ARMS: Harl. 1396.—CORBET OF STANWARDIN quarters these four coates more:
1, *Argent, a chevron engrailed between three mullets sable* [KYNASTON];
2, *Argent, on a chief or a bird sable* [HORDE]; 3, *Ermine, a chevron gules*
[KYNASTON—the AUDLEY COAT]; 4, *Argent, a fesse between six martlets
gules* [Cornish choughs proper, ONSLOW].

ARMS: Harl. 1396: CORBET OF ALBRIGHTON AND LONGNOR.—*Quarterly: 1, Or,
two ravens sable, within a bordure engrailed gules bezantée; 2, Gules, two
lions passant argent, a label of five points azure*, STRANGE in Shrewsbury
MS.; 3, *Per fesse gules and vert, in chief a chevron of the
last*, SPRENCHEAUX in Shrewsbury MS.; 4, *Sable, two lions passant within
an orle of cross-crosslets argent*, SPRINGESLOW in Shrewsbury MS. [SPRING-
SEAUX].

CREST.—*A raven sable, holding in the beak a sprig of holly vert, fructed gules.*

ARMS: Harl. 1396: CORBET OF PONTESBURY.—*Quarterly: 1 and 4, Or, two ravens
sable; 2 and 3, Argent, a falcon close proper, belled or, perching on a staf
lying fesseways ragule vert* [EDGE alias HAWKINS].

This descent of Corbet entred by Peter Moss servant to M[r] Augustine Vincent.

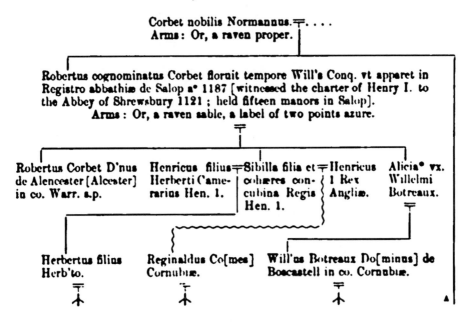

* Omitted in Shrewsbury MS.

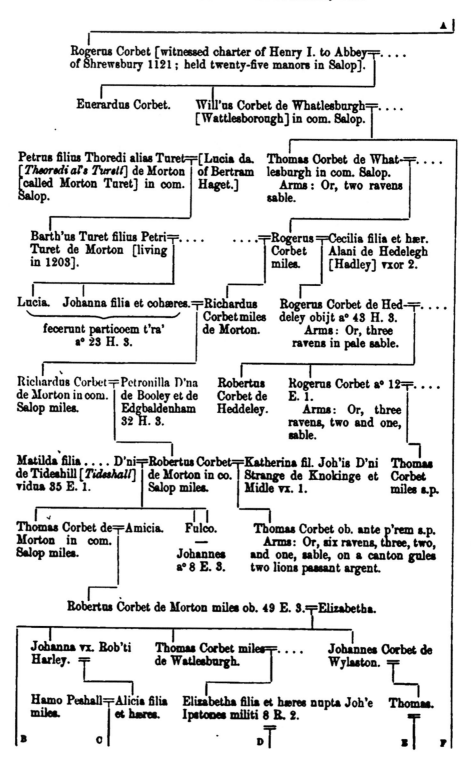

▲

Rogerus Corbet [witnessed charter of Henry I. to Abbey=....
of Shrewsbury 1121 ; held twenty-five manors in Salop].

Euerardus Corbet.   Will'us Corbet de Whatlesburgh=....
                      [Wattlesborough] in com. Salop.

Petrus filius Thoredi alias Turet=[Lucia da.   Thomas Corbet de What-=....
[Theoredi al's Turett] de Morton of Bertram   lesburgh in com. Salop.
[called Morton Turet] in com.   Haget.]   Arms: Or, two ravens
Salop.   sable.

Barth'us Turet filius Petri=....   ....=Rogerus=Cecilia filia et hær.
Turet de Morton [living   Corbet Alani de Hedelegh
in 1203].   miles. [Hadley] vxor 2.

Lucia.   Johanna filia et cohæres.=Richardus   Rogerus Corbet de Hed-=....
                                   Corbet miles deley obijt aº 43 H. 3.
   fecerunt particoem t'ra'   de Morton.   Arms: Or, three
     aº 23 H. 3.   ravens in pale sable.

Richardus Corbet=Petronilla D'na   Robertus   Rogerus Corbet aº 12=....
de Morton in com. de Booley et de   Corbet de   E. 1.
Salop miles.   Edgbaldenham   Heddeley.   Arms: Or, three
                 32 H. 3.   ravens, two and one,
                                                   sable.

Matilda filia ....D'ni=Robertus Corbet=Katherina fil. Joh'is D'ni   Thomas
de Tideshill [Tideshall] de Morton in co. Strange de Knokinge et   Corbet
vidua 35 E. 1.   Salop miles.   Midle vx. 1.   miles s.p.

Thomas Corbet de=Amicia.   Fulco.   Thomas Corbet ob. ante p'rem s.p.
Morton in com.   —   Arms: Or, six ravens, three, two,
Salop miles.   Johannes   and one, sable, on a canton gules
                         aº 8 E. 3.   two lions passant argent.

Robertus Corbet de Morton miles ob. 49 E. 3.=Elizabetha.

Johanna vx. Rob'ti   Thomas Corbet miles=....   Johannes Corbet de
Harley. =   de Watlesburgh.   Wylaston. =

Hamo Peshall=Alicia filia   Elizabetha filia et hæres nupta Joh'e   Thomas.
miles.   et hæres.   Ipstones militi 8 R. 2.   =

B   C   D   E   F

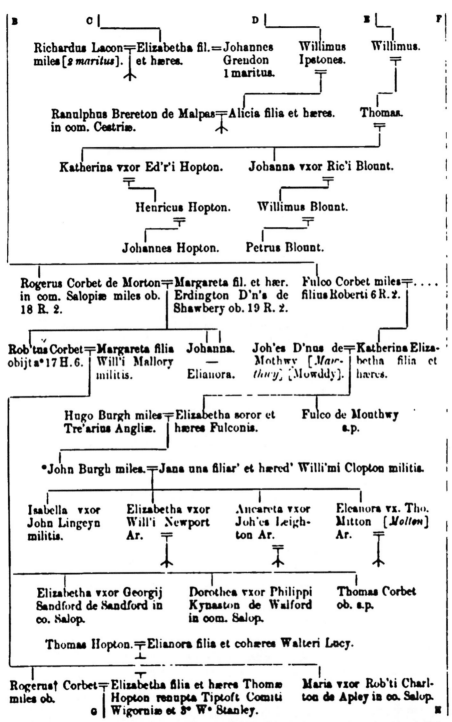

B | C | D | E | F

Richardus Lacon═Elizabetha fil.═Johannes   Willimus   Willimus.
miles [2 maritus]. | et hæres.   Grendon   Ipstones.
                                  1 maritus.

Ranulphus Brereton de Malpas═Alicia filia et hæres.   Thomas.
in com. Cestriæ.

Katherina vxor Ed'r'i Hopton.   Johanna vxor Ric'i Blount.

Henricus Hopton.   Willimus Blount.

Johannes Hopton.   Petrus Blount.

Rogerus Corbet de Morton═Margareta fil. et hær.   Fulco Corbet miles═ . . . .
in com. Salopiæ miles ob. | Erdington D'n's de   filius Roberti 6 R. 2.
18 R. 2.   Shawbery ob. 19 R. 2.

Rob'tus Corbet═Margareta filia   Johanna.   Joh'es D'nus de═Katherina Eliza-
obijt a° 17 H. 6. | Will'i Mallory   —   Mothwy [Mar- | betha filia et
                  militis.   Elianora.   thuy, [Mowddy]. hæres.

Hugo Burgh miles═Elizabetha soror et   Fulco de Mouthwy
Tre'arius Angliæ. | hæres Fulconis.   s.p.

*John Burgh miles.═Jana una filiar' et hæred' Willi'mi Clopton militis.

Isabella vxor   Elizabetha vxor   Ancareta vxor   Eleanora vx. Tho.
John Lingeyn   Will'i Newport   Joh'es Leigh-   Mitton [Molton]
militis.   Ar.   ton Ar.   Ar.

Elizabetha vxor Georgij   Dorothea vxor Philippi   Thomas Corbet
Sandford de Sandford in   Kynaston de Walford   ob. s.p.
co. Salop.   in com. Salop.

Thomas Hopton.═Elianora filia et cohæres Walteri Lacy.

Rogerus† Corbet═Elizabetha filia et hæres Thomæ   Maria vxor Rob'ti Charl-
miles ob. | Hopton renupta Tiptoft Comiti   ton de Apley in co. Salop.
          G | Wigorniæ et 3° W° Stanley.   H

* This generation is not given in Shrewsbury MS., though the next generation is included.
† A° 6 R. 4 Rex licentiam dedit Rogero Corbet de Moreton militi et Elisabethæ vxori eius
consanguineæ et vni hæredum Will'i Lacy militis quod ipsi in hereditatem suam post mortem
tam præd'c'i Will'i quam Margaretæ vxori suæ ingredi possint rot. 37. [Harl. 1396.]

G | | H |

| Anna vxor Thomæ Sturry de Rossall in co. Salop. | Maria vxor Thomæ Thornes de Sheluock [*Shelvock*] in co. Salop. | Elizabetha vx. Rich'i Cholmeley de co. Cestr' militis. | Jana vxor Tho. Cresset de Vpton in com. Salop. |

Corbet de Morton.

| Robertus Corbet obijt s.p. | Richardus Corbet de Morton Corbet in com. Salop miles ob. 8. H. 7. | Elizabetha filia Walteri D'ni Ferrers de Chartley renupta Tho. Leighton de Watlesburgh militi. |

| Maria vxor Tho. Lacon de Willey in co. Salop militis. | Anna vxor Tho. Cornwall de Burford in co. Salop militis. | Elizabetha vxor Thomæ Trentham de Shrewesbury. | Georgius Corbet s.p. |

| Robertus Corbet de Morton miles obijt aº 5 H. 8 [Sheriff 1501]. | Elizabetha filia Henrici Vernon de Haddon in co. Derby militis ob. aº 1563. | Katherina vx. Tho. Onneslow de Rodington in co. Salop. | Margareta vxor Ric'i Clyve de Walford in com. Salop. |

Rogerus* Corbet de Morton Corbet in co. Salop⹀Anna filia Andreæ obijt 1538 [Sheriff 1530]. | D'ni Windsor.

| Elianora. — Vrsula. | Walterus Corbet 3 fil. s.p. | Jeronimus Corbet 4 fil. de Bestlow vnus consiliariorum in M'chijs Walliæ. | Dorothea fil. et hæres Thomæ Poyner de Bestlow in com. Salop. |

| Rogerus 1. | Robertus 2. | Anna vxor Will'i Gatacre de Gatacre in co. Salop Ar. |

| Margareta vxor Francisci Palmer militis. | Andreas Corbet de Morton Corbet in com. Salop miles ob. 1578 [Sheriff 1551]. | Jana filia Rob'ti Nedham de Shenton [Shavington] in co. Salop militis. |

Robertus Corbet de Morton⹀Anna filia Oliueri D'ni Sᵗ John de Bletsho filius et hæres obijt aº 1583. | renupta .... Betton [*Bitton*].

| Elizabetha vxor Henrici Wallop militis. | Anna vxor Adulphi Cary militis s.p. |

| Judith fil. [Thomas] de Astin [Austin] de Oxley in com. Staff. relicta Willimi Basset de Blore. | Richardus Corbet de Morton miles balneatus 2 fil. s.p. | Maria filia Morgani Wolfe de Mereden [Meriden] in com. Warr. relicta Tho. Lee de Clatercott in com. Oxon. |

I | J | | K | L |

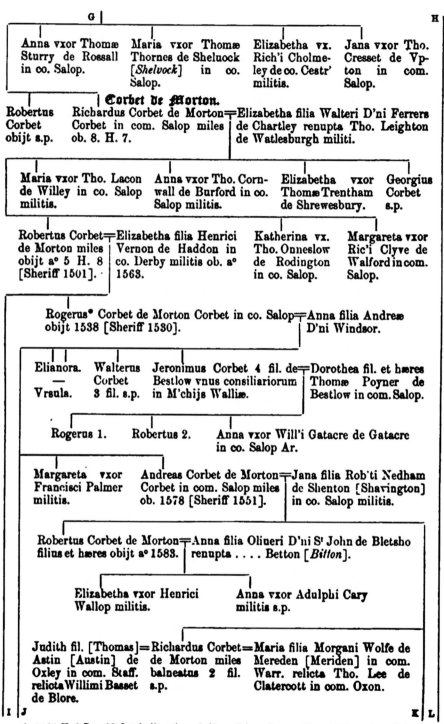

* Aº 14 H. 8 Rex 22 Octob. licentiam dedit spi'alem Rogero Corbet filio et hæredi Roberti Corbet militis ac consanguineo et hæredi Elizabethæ Leighton nuper vxoris Ricardi Corbet patris d'ci Roberti ingrediendi gr. rot. 67 et 66 et aº 23 H. 8 rot. 14. [Harl. 1396.]

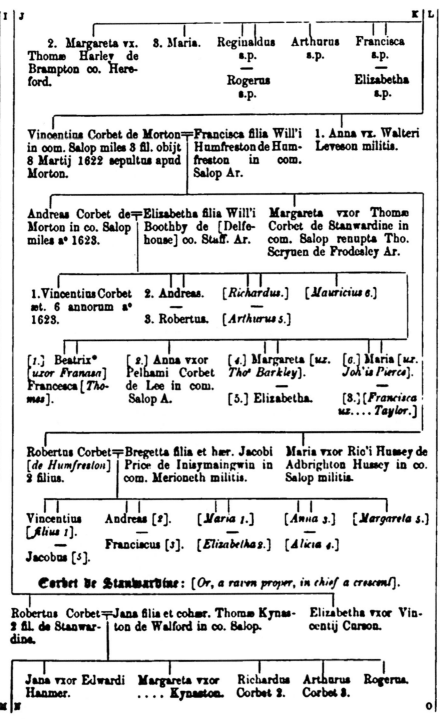

I | J   K | L

2. Margareta vx.   3. Maria.   Reginaldus   Arthurus   Francisca
Thomæ Harley de   s.p.   s.p.   s.p.
Brampton co. Here-   —   —
ford.   Rogerus   Elizabetha
                                     s.p.   s.p.

Vincentius Corbet de Morton⹀Francisca filia Will'i   1. Anna vx. Walteri
in com. Salop miles 3 fil. obijt Humfreston de Hum- Leveson militis.
8 Martij 1622 sepultus apud freston in com.
Morton.   Salop Ar.

Andreas Corbet de⹀Elizabetha filia Will'i   Margareta vxor Thomæ
Morton in co. Salop Boothby de [Delfe- Corbet de Stanwardine in
miles aᵒ 1623.   house] co. Staff. Ar. com. Salop renupta Tho.
                                         Scryuen de Frodesley Ar.

1.Vincentius Corbet   2. Andreas.   [Richardus.]   [Mauricius 6.]
æt. 6 annorum aᵒ   —
1623.   3. Robertus.   [Arthurus 5.]

[1.] Beatrix*   [2.] Anna vxor   [4.] Margareta [ux.   [6.] Maria [ux.
[uxor Franasn]   Pelhami Corbet   Thoˢ Barkley].   Joh'is Pierce].
Francesca [Tho-   de Lee in com.
mas].   Salop A.   [5.] Elizabetha.   [3.] [Francisca
                                              ux. .... Taylor.]

Robertus Corbet⹀Bregetta filia et hær. Jacobi   Maria vxor Ricᵒ'i Hussey de
[de Humfreston] Price de Inisymaingwin in Adbrighton Hussey in co.
2 filius.   com. Merioneth militis.   Salop militis.

Vincentius   Andreas [2].   [Maria 1.]   [Anna 3.]   [Margareta 5.]
[filius 1].
—   Franciscus [3].   [Elizabetha 2.]   [Alicia 4.]
Jacobus [5].

Corbet de Stanwardine: [Or, a raven proper, in chief a crescent].

Robertus Corbet⹀Jana filia et cohær. Thomæ Kynas-   Elizabetha vxor Vin-
2 fil. de Stanwar- ton de Walford in co. Salop.   centij Curson.
dine.

Jana vxor Edwardi   Margareta vxor   Richardus   Arthurus   Rogerus.
Hanmer.   .... Kynaston.   Corbet 2.   Corbet 3.

M | N   O

* In Shrewsbury MS. this appears as "Beatrix uxor Franam," and below is the same
" Thomas."

M | N

O

Susanna vx. Will'i Yonge de Kenton.

Gertrude vx. . . . . Baldwyne.

Thomas Corbet de Stanwardine in com. Salop.

Margareta filia Vincentij Corbet de Morton militis.

Thomas Scriuen de Frodesley Ar. 2 maritus.

Robertus.

Elizabetha.

Anna

Jana vxor Thomæ Lee de Langley in co. Salop.

Johanna vx. Tho. Newport.

Maria vxor Tho. Powell de Oswaldestre.

Dorothea vxor Ric'i Manwaring de Ightfeild.

[**Corbett de Edgemond**: *Or, a raven, in chief a mullet.*]

[**Corbet of Stoke.**]

Reginaldus Corbet 3 fil. vnus Justiciarior' de banco Regis de Stoke in co. Salop.

Alicia filia Johannis Grattwood [*Gratwood*] consanguinea et vna hæred' Rolandi Hill militis Maioris London.

Richardus Corbet 2 fil. [Sheriff 1561].

Margeria filia Joh'is Sauell militis.

Edwardus.

Jana.

Rolandus 2.
—
Robertus 3.

Petrus Corbet.

Elizabetha filia Thomæ Pigot de Chetwine in com. Salop.

Franciscus 4.
—
Andreas.

Reginaldus Corbet 2 filius.

Robertus Corbet.

Francesca filia et hæres Robt'i Spencer de Mansfeild in Sherwood et de Lincolns Inne.

Maria.

Francisca.
—
Alicia.

Elizabetha.

Maria.

[**Corbett de Stoke**: *Or, a raven sable.*]

Richardus Corbet de Stoke.

Anna filia Thomæ Bromeley militis Cancellarij Angliæ.

Elizabetha vx. Roberti Arden de Parkhall in com. Warr.

Maria vx. Francisci Newton de Highlee.

Anna vxor Edwardi Mitton de Halston.

Maria vx. Humfredi Lee de Langley in com. Salop Baronetti.

Elizabetha [ux. . . .].

[*Johannes Corbett de Stoke Baronettus.*

Anna fil. . . . . Manwaring de Ightfield.

Johannes fil.]

Richardus Corbet de Stoke.

Anna filia Humfr'i Weld de London militis et Aldermanni.

Jana.

Maria.

[. . . . *fil.*]

P

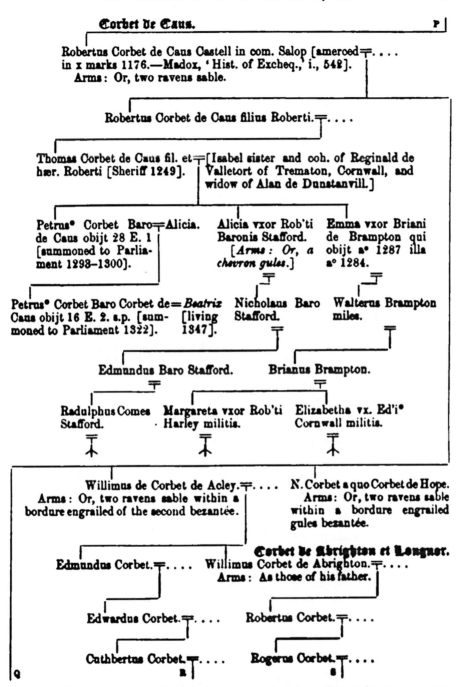

Corbet de Caus.   P

Robertus Corbet de Caus Castell in com. Salop [amerced ⊤ ....
in x marks 1176.—Madox, 'Hist. of Excheq.,' i., 542].
Arms: Or, two ravens sable.

Robertus Corbet de Caus filius Roberti. ⊤ ....

Thomas Corbet de Caus fil. et ⊤[Isabel sister and coh. of Reginald de
hær. Roberti [Sheriff 1249]. Valletort of Trematon, Cornwall, and
widow of Alan de Dunstanvill.]

Petrus* Corbet Baro ⊤ Alicia.   Alicia vxor Rob'ti   Emma vxor Briani
de Caus obijt 28 E. 1   Baronis Stafford.   de Brampton qui
[summoned to Parlia-   [Arms: Or, a   obijt a° 1287 illa
ment 1293–1300].   chevron gules.]   a° 1284.

Petrus* Corbet Baro Corbet de= Beatrix   Nicholaus Baro   Walterus Brampton
Caus obijt 16 E. 2. s.p. [sum- [living   Stafford.   miles.
moned to Parliament 1322]. 1347].

Edmundus Baro Stafford.   Brianus Brampton.

Radulphus Comes   Margareta vxor Rob'ti   Elizabetha vx. Ed'i°
Stafford.   Harley militis.   Cornwall militis.

Willimus de Corbet de Acley. ⊤ ....   N. Corbet a quo Corbet de Hope.
Arms: Or, two ravens sable within a   Arms: Or, two ravens sable
bordure engrailed of the second bezantée.   within a bordure engrailed
gules bezantée.

Corbet de Abrighton et Lengner.

Edmundus Corbet. ⊤ ....   Willimus Corbet de Abrighton. ⊤ ....
Arms: As those of his father.

Edwardus Corbet. ⊤ ....   Robertus Corbet. ⊤ ....

Cuthbertus Corbet. ⊤ ....   Rogerus Corbet. ⊤ ....
R   S

Q

* Mich. Fines n° E. 3. Salop, fol. 123. Edmundus de Cornubia et Elizabetha vxor eius tertia
sororum et hæredum Petri filij et hæredis Petri filij Thomæ Corbet dant Regi 25 marcas pro
releaio suo de proparte ipsam Elizabetham contingente de t'ris quæ fuerunt dicti Petri vis. de
quarta parte Baroniæ de Caus quam partem ydem Ed'us et Elizabetha dicunt descendisse iure
hæreddario eisdem Ed'o et Elizabethæ in propartem suam de Baroniæ præd'c'æ post mortem
p'dic' Petri filij Petri. [Harl. 1196.] (This does not agree with the pedigree above.)

Q

R | S |

Richardus Corbet.=. . . .   Willimus Corbet.=. . . .

Thomas Corbet.=. . . .   Thomas Corbet.=. . . .

Robertus Corbet.=. . . .   Ricardus Corbet de Abrighton.=. . . .

Willimus Corbet.   Johannes Corbet.=. . . .

Edwardus Corbet de Abrighton (*Albrighton*).=. . . . filia . . . . Poyner.

Thomas Corbet.=Jana filia Ed'r'i Burton de Longnorley [sic] (*Longnor*) in co. Salop.

Margeria uxor Rogeri Puleston de Emrall in com. Flint Ar.	Katherina fil. Thomæ Lee de Langley in com. Salop Ar. vxor 1.	Edwardus Corbet de Longnor in com. Salop Ar. fil. et hæres duxit Annam filiam Rogeri Browne relictam Ric'i Haughton militis et Will'i Talbot de Shifnall s.p.	Maria filia Ed'r'i Banester vxor 3.

            =⊤   =⊤

(*Elizabeth Houghton.*)   (*William Talbot.*)

Maria vxor Ric'i Brooke (*Broke*) de Blakland[s] in com. Staff.   Thomas Corbet de Longnor in com. Salop 2 fil.=Katherina relicta . . . . Browne.

Thomas Corbet de Longnor in com. Salop Ar. aº 1623.=Jana filia et cohæres Roberti Morton de Houghton in co. Salop.   Edwardus Corbet 2 fil. s.p.

EdwardusCorbet de Longnor fil. et hær. 1623 [marriage settlement 12 June 1617].	=Margareta filia Edwardi Waters [Waties] de Burway in com. Salop Ar.	Robertus Corbet de London aurifaber fil. 2, 1623.	=Etheldreda (*Elizabetha*) filia . . . . Drewry.	Thomas 3.__Richardus 4.__Georgius 5.__Rogerus 6.	Humfridus 7.__Sara s.p.__Anna.__Vrsula.

Edwardus 1 s.p.   Edwardus.   Thomas.

(*Sir William Corbet.*)=. . . .

(*Peter Corbet* of *Causes.*)=. . . .   (*Thomas.*)

T

U |

* Peter Corbett lorde of Causes did confirme to Roger Corbett my cousyn Aº quinto E. 2. Arms: Two ravens. [Harl. 615, fo. 255ᵇ.]

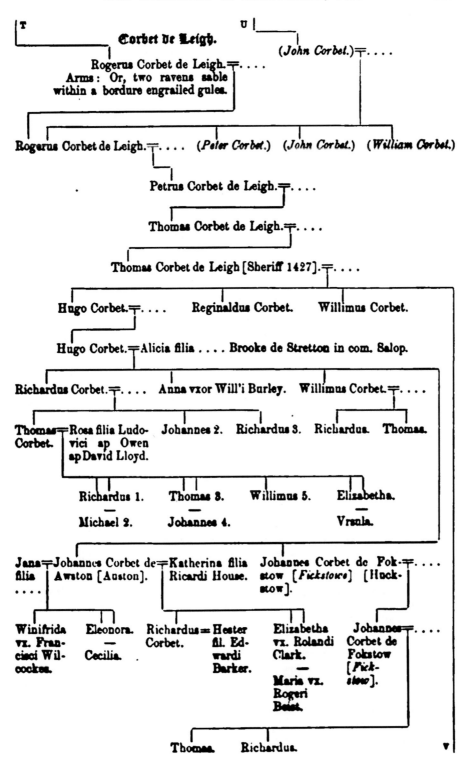

T

U

Corbet De Leigh.

Rogerus Corbet de Leigh.=....
Arms: Or, two ravens sable
within a bordure engrailed gules.

(John Corbet.)=....

Rogerus Corbet de Leigh.=.... (Peter Corbet.) (John Corbet.) (William Corbet.)

Petrus Corbet de Leigh.=....

Thomas Corbet de Leigh.=....

Thomas Corbet de Leigh [Sheriff 1427].=....

Hugo Corbet.=....   Reginaldus Corbet.   Willimus Corbet.

Hugo Corbet.=Alicia filia .... Brooke de Stretton in com. Salop.

Richardus Corbet.=....   Anna vxor Will'i Burley.   Willimus Corbet.=....

Thomas=Rosa filia Ludo-   Johannes 2.   Richardus 3.   Richardus.   Thomas.
Corbet. | vici ap Owen
        | ap David Lloyd.

Richardus 1.   Thomas 3.   Willimus 5.   Elizabetha.
—   —   —
Michael 2.   Johannes 4.   Vrsula.

Jana=Johannes Corbet de=Katherina filia   Johannes Corbet de Pok-=....
filia | Awston [Auston]. | Ricardi House.   stow [Fickstowe] [Huck-
.... | | stow].

Winifrida   Eleonora.   Richardus=Hester   Elizabetha   Johannes=....
vx. Fran-   —   Corbet.   fil. Ed- vx. Rolandi   Corbet de
cisci Wil-   Cecilia.   wardi   Clark.   Fokstow
cockes.   Barker.   —   [Fick-
                                              Maria vx.   stow].
                                              Rogeri
                                              Beist.

Thomas.   Richardus.

V

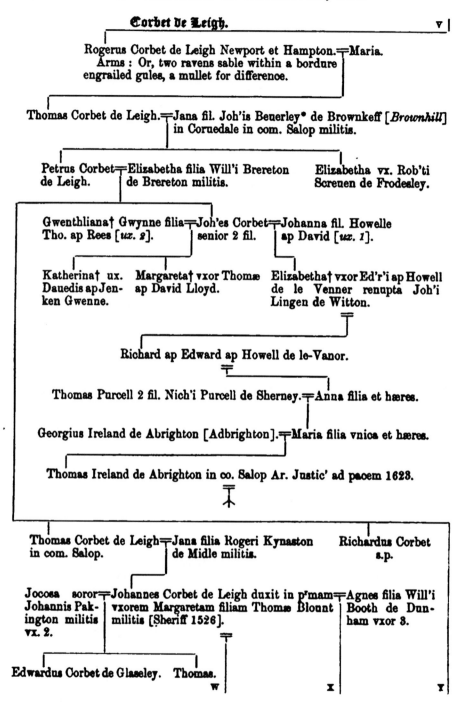

𝕮𝖔𝖗𝖇𝖊𝖙 𝖉𝖊 𝕷𝖊𝖎𝖌𝖍.　　　　　　　　　　　　　**V** |

Rogerus Corbet de Leigh Newport et Hampton.⹀Maria.
Arms : Or, two ravens sable within a bordure
engrailed gules, a mullet for difference.

Thomas Corbet de Leigh.⹀Jana fil. Joh'is Beuerley* de Brownkeff [*Brownhill*]
in Coruedale in com. Salop militis.

Petrus Corbet⹀Elizabetha filia Will'i Brereton　　　Elizabetha vx. Rob'ti
de Leigh.　　　de Brereton militis.　　　　　　　Screuen de Frodesley.

Gwenthliana† Gwynne filia⹀Joh'es Corbet⹀Johanna fil. Howelle
Tho. ap Rees [*ux. 2*].　　　senior 2 fil.　　ap David [*ux. 1*].

Katherina† ux.　　Margareta† vxor Thomæ　　Elizabetha† vxor Ed'r'i ap Howell
Dauedis ap Jen-　　ap David Lloyd.　　　　de le Venner renupta Joh'i
ken Gwenne.　　　　　　　　　　　　　　Lingen de Witton.

Richard ap Edward ap Howell de le-Vanor.

Thomas Purcell 2 fil. Nich'i Purcell de Sherney.⹀Anna filia et hæres.

Georgius Ireland de Abrighton [Adbrighton].⹀Maria filia vnica et hæres.

Thomas Ireland de Abrighton in co. Salop Ar. Justic' ad pacem 1623.

Thomas Corbet de Leigh⹀Jana filia Rogeri Kynaston　　Richardus Corbet
in com. Salop.　　　　de Midle militis.　　　　　　s.p.

Jocosa　soror⹀Johannes Corbet de Leigh duxit in p'mam⹀Agnes filia Will'i
Johannis Pak-　vxorem Margaretam filiam Thomæ Blount　Booth de Dun-
ington militis　militis [Sheriff 1526].　　　　　　ham vxor 3.
vx. 2.

Edwardus Corbet de Glaseley.　　Thomas.
　　　　　　　　　　　　　　　W |　　　　　**X** |　　　　　**Y** |

* Probably Burley of Bromcroft. John Burley of Bromcroft Castle was Sheriff 1409.
† Shrewsbury MS. makes Elizabeth the daughter of Gwenthlin, and states that Elizabeth left
issue by both of her husbands. Katherine and Margaret appear as the two daughters of Joan,
the first wife of John Corbet.

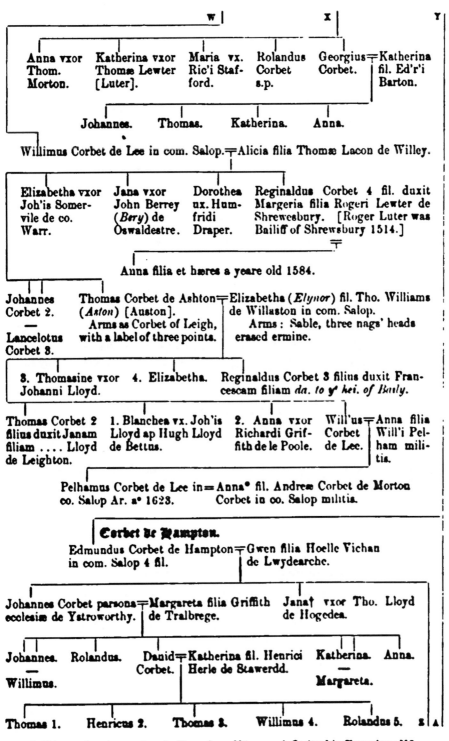

W | X | Y

Anna vxor Thom. Morton.   Katherina vxor Thomæ Lewter [Luter].   Maria vx. Ric'i Stafford.   Rolandus Corbet s.p.   Georgius⊤Katherina Corbet. | fil. Ed'r'i | Barton.

Johannes.   Thomas.   Katherina.   Anna.

Willimus Corbet de Lee in com. Salop.⊤Alicia filia Thomæ Lacon de Willey.

Elizabetha vxor Joh'is Somervile de co. Warr.   Jana vxor John Berrey (*Bery*) de Oswaldestre.   Dorothea ux. Humfridi Draper.   Reginaldus Corbet 4 fil. duxit Margeria filia Rogeri Lewter de Shrewesbury. [Roger Luter was Bailiff of Shrewsbury 1514.]
⊤

Anna filia et hæres a yeare old 1584.

Johannes Corbet 2.
—
Lancelotus Corbet 3.   Thomas Corbet de Ashton (*Aston*) [Auston]. Arms as Corbet of Leigh, with a label of three points.⊤Elizabetha (*Elynor*) fil. Tho. Williams de Willaston in com. Salop. Arms : Sable, three nags' heads erased ermine.

3. Thomasine vxor Johanni Lloyd.   4. Elizabetha.   Reginaldus Corbet 3 filius duxit Francescam filiam *da. to y* hei. of Baily.*

Thomas Corbet 2 filius duxit Janam filiam .... Lloyd de Leighton.   1. Blanchea vx. Joh'is Lloyd ap Hugh Lloyd de Bettus.   2. Anna vxor Richardi Griffith de le Poole.   Will'us⊤Anna filia Corbet | Will'i Pelde Lee. | ham militis.

Pelhamus Corbet de Lee in=Anna* fil. Andreæ Corbet de Morton co. Salop Ar. aº 1623.   Corbet in co. Salop militis.

Corbet de Hampton.

Edmundus Corbet de Hampton⊤Gwen filia Hoelle Vichan in com. Salop 4 fil. | de Lwydearche.

Johannes Corbet parsona⊤Margareta filia Griffith ecclesiæ de Ystroworthy. | de Tralbrege.   Jana† vxor Tho. Lloyd de Hogedea.

Johannes.   Rolandus.   David⊤Katherina fil. Henrici
—   Corbet. | Herle de Stawerdd.   Katherina.   Anna.
Willimus.   Margareta.

Thomas 1.   Henricus 2.   Thomas 3.   Willimus 4.   Rolandus 5.   z | A

* This marriage is not given in Shrewsbury MS.   † Omitted in Shrewsbury MS.

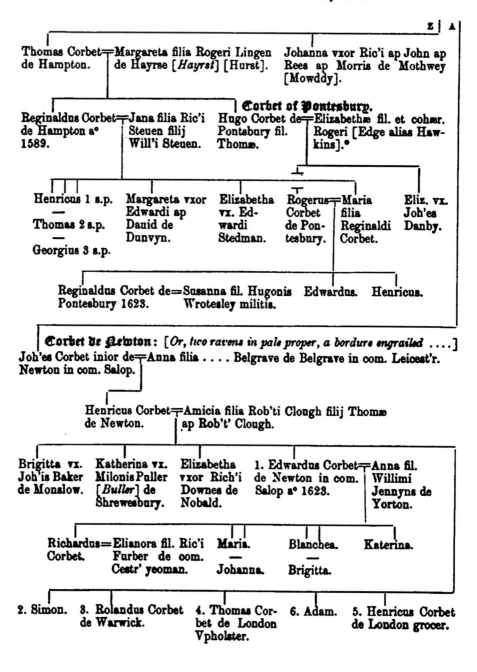

z | ▲

Thomas Corbet=Margareta filia Rogeri Lingen
de Hampton. | de Hayrse [*Hayrst*] [Hurst].

Johanna vxor Ric'i ap John ap
Rees ap Morris de Mothwey
[Mowddy].

Corbet of Pontesbury.

Reginaldus Corbet=Jana filia Ric'i
de Hampton aº | Steuen filij
1589. | Will'i Steuen.

Hugo Corbet de=Elizabethæ fil. et cohær.
Pontesbury fil. | Rogeri [Edge alias Haw-
Thomæ. | kins].*

Henricus 1 s.p.
—
Thomas 2 s.p.
—
Georgius 3 s.p.

Margareta vxor
Edwardi ap
Dauid de
Dunvyn.

Elizabetha
vx. Ed-
wardi
Stedman.

Rogerus=Maria
Corbet | filia
de Pon- | Reginaldi
tesbury. | Corbet.

Eliz. vx.
Joh'es
Danby.

Reginaldus Corbet de=Susanna fil. Hugonis
Pontesbury 1623. | Wrotesley militis.

Edwardus.   Henricus.

Corbet de Newton: [*Or, two ravens in pale proper, a bordure engrailed ....*]
Joh'es Corbet inior de=Anna filia .... Belgrave de Belgrave in com. Leicest'r.
Newton in com. Salop. |

Henricus Corbet=Amicia filia Rob'ti Clough filij Thomæ
de Newton. | ap Rob't' Clough.

Brigitta vx.
Joh'is Baker
de Monslow.

Katherina vx.
Milonis Puller
[*Buller*] de
Shrewesbury.

Elizabetha
vxor Rich'i
Downes de
Nobald.

1. Edwardus Corbet=Anna fil.
de Newton in com. | Willimi
Salop aº 1623. | Jennyns de
 | Yorton.

Richardus=Elianora fil. Ric'i
Corbet. | Furber de com.
 | Cestr' yeoman.

Maria.
—
Johanna.

Blanchea.
—
Brigitta.

Katerina.

2. Simon.   3. Rolandus Corbet
de Warwick.

4. Thomas Cor-
bet de London
Vpholster.

6. Adam.   5. Henricus Corbet
de London grocer.

* See the arms of Corbet of Pontesbury quartering Edge alias Hawkins at page 133.

Cornwall of Burford.*

Harl. 1396, fo. 91.

ARMS: Harl. 1396.—*Quarterly of eighteen:* 1, *Ermine, a lion rampant gules, within a bordure engrailed sable bezantée;* 2, *Argent, on a bend cottised sable three mullets or* [LEYNTALL of HAMPTON]; 3, *Sable, a bend lozengy argent* [LEUTON]; 4, *Barry of six argent and azure* [GREY of CODNOR]; 5, *Or, a lion rampant azure, a crescent for difference* [PERCY, EARL of WORCESTER]; 6, *Or, three pallets sable* [EARL of ARGYLE]; 7, *Gules, three garbs within a double tressure counterflory or* [LEONIN SCOTT?]; 8, *Barry of ten argent and azure, an orle of ten martlets gules* [VALENCE]; 9, *Or, three inescutcheons barry of six* [gules] *and vair* [MONTCHENSY]; 10, *Gules, a bend lozengy or* [MARSHALL, EARL of PEMBROKE]; 11, *Argent, on a chief azure three crosses formée filchée of the field* [STRONGBOW]; 12, *Sable, three garbs argent* [MACMOROUGH?]; 13, *Or, three piles in point gules, a canton vair* [BASSET]; 14, *Or, a fesse gules* [COLVILE]; 15, *Gules, three bars paly of six argent and sable* [BARRE?]; 16, *Barry of six or and azure, a bend gules* [PEMBRIDGE]; 17, *Or, on a chief gules three martlets of the field* [WOGAN of WESTON]; 18, *Argent, on a chief sable a lion passant or* [WHYTYOT].

1 CREST.—*A Cornish chough proper.*
2 CREST.—*A cockatrice argent.*

[Among the banners of those who entered France 16 June 1513 occurs: " Shropshyr Banerett—Sir Thomas Cornwell Baron of Burford bayreth Sylver a Lyon goulles powderyd wyth bessaunts and a crown apon his hed gold, and Cornish choghes. Made Banerett at this tyme." (Cotton MS. Cleop. C. v.) For a description of the Standard of the Baron of Burford, temp. Henry III., see ' Coll. Top.,' iii., 60.]

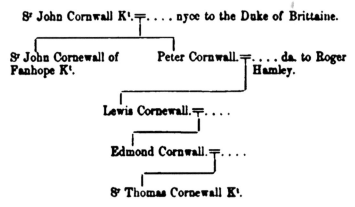

Sr John Cornwall Kt.=.... nyce to the Duke of Brittaine.

Sr John Cornewall of Panhope Kt.   Peter Cornwall.=.... da. to Roger Hamley.

Lewis Cornewall.=....

Edmond Cornwall.=....

Sr Thomas Cornewall Kt.

Sr Brian Cornwall of Kinlett Kt.=Mawde da. to the lord Strange of Blackmere.

Sr John Cornwall Kt ob. s.p.   Mabell da. & heire vx. Sr John Blount of Sodington Kt.

* The early descents of this pedigree in Harl. 1396 are very confused, parts having been cancelled, and alterations made.

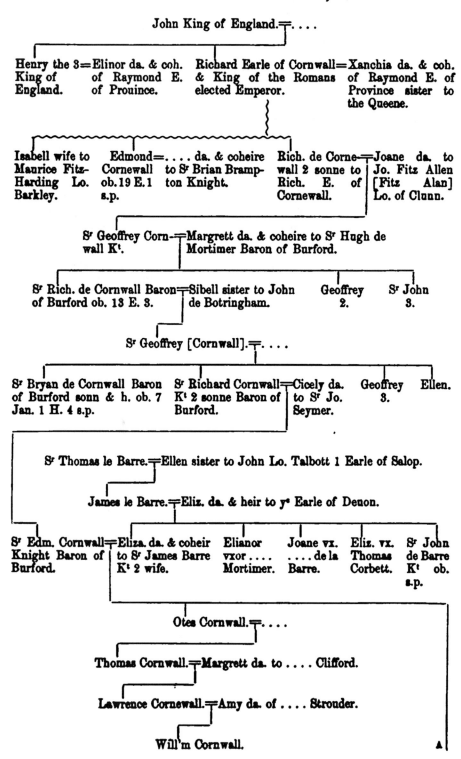

John King of England.=....

Henry the 3=Elinor da. & coh.
King of   of Raymond E.
England.   of Prouince.

Richard Earle of Cornwall=Xanchia da. & coh.
& King of the Romans   of Raymond E. of
elected Emperor.   Province sister to
                            the Queene.

Isabell wife to   Edmond=.... da. & coheire   Rich. de Corne-=Joane da. to
Maurice Fitz-   Cornewall to Sr Brian Bramp-   wall 2 sonne to | Jo. Fitz Allen
Harding Lo.   ob.19 E.1 ton Knight.   Rich. E. of | [Fitz Alan]
Barkley.   s.p.   Cornewall. | Lo. of Clunn.

Sr Geoffrey Corn-=Margrett da. & coheire to Sr Hugh de
wall Kt.   Mortimer Baron of Burford.

Sr Rich. de Cornwall Baron=Sibell sister to John   Geoffrey   Sr John
of Burford ob. 13 E. 3.   de Botringham.   2.   3.

Sr Geoffrey [Cornwall].=....

Sr Bryan de Cornwall Baron   Sr Richard Cornwall=Cicely da.   Geoffrey   Ellen.
of Burford sonn & h. ob. 7   Kt 2 sonne Baron of | to Sr Jo.   3.
Jan. 1 H. 4 s.p.   Burford. | Seymer.

Sr Thomas le Barre.=Ellen sister to John Lo. Talbott 1 Earle of Salop.

James le Barre.=Eliz. da. & heir to ye Earle of Deuon.

Sr Edm. Cornwall=Eliza. da. & coheir   Elianor   Joane vx.   Eliz. vx.   Sr John
Knight Baron of | to Sr James Barre   vxor ....de la   Thomas   de Barre
Burford. | Kt 2 wife.   Mortimer.   Barre.   Corbett.   Kt ob.
                                                                               s.p.

Otes Cornwall.=....

Thomas Cornwall.=Margrett da. to .... Clifford.

Lawrence Cornewall.=Amy da. of .... Stronder.

Will'm Cornwall.   ▲

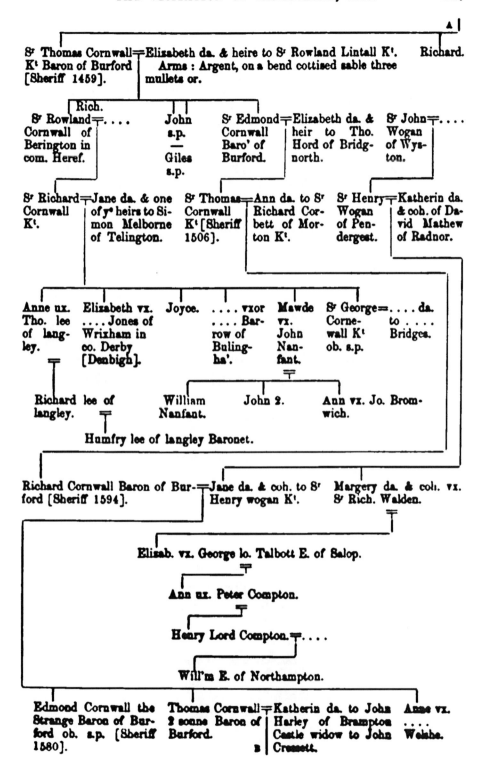

Sr Thomas Cornwall⹌Elizabeth da. & heire to Sr Rowland Lintall Kt.   Richard.
Kt Baron of Burford   Arms : Argent, on a bend cottised sable three
[Sheriff 1459].   mullets or.

Rich.
Sr Rowland⹌....   John   Sr Edmond⹌Elizabeth da. &   Sr John⹌....
Cornwall of   s.p.   Cornwall   heir to Tho.   Wogan
Berington in   —   Baro' of   Hord of Bridg-   of Wys-
com. Heref.   Giles   Burford.   north.   ton.
   s.p.

Sr Richard⹌Jane da. & one   Sr Thomas⹌Ann da. to Sr   Sr Henry⹌Katherin da.
Cornwall   of ye heirs to Si-   Cornwall   Richard Cor-   Wogan   & coh. of Da-
Kt.   mon Melborne   Kt [Sheriff   bett of Mor-   of Pen-   vid Mathew
   of Telington.   1506].   ton Kt.   dergest.   of Radnor.

Anne ux.   Elizabeth ux.   Joyce.   ....vxor   Mawde   Sr George⹌....da.
Tho. lee   .... Jones of   .... Bar-   vx.   Corne-   to ....
of lang-   Wrixham in   row of   John   wall Kt   Bridges.
ley.   co. Derby   Buling-   Nan-   ob. s.p.
⹌   [Denbigh].   ha'.   fant.
            ⹌

Richard lee of   William   John 2.   Ann vx. Jo. Brom-
langley.   Nanfant.   wich.
⹌

Humfry lee of langley Baronet.

Richard Cornwall Baron of Bur-⹌Jane da. & coh. to Sr   Margery da. & coh. vx.
ford [Sheriff 1594].   Henry wogan Kt.   Sr Rich. Walden.
                                  ⹌

Elisab. vx. George lo. Talbott E. of Salop.
              ⹌

Ann ux. Peter Compton.
             ⹌

Henry Lord Compton.⹌....

Will'm E. of Northampton.

Edmond Cornwall the   Thomas Cornwall⹌Katherin da. to John   Anne vx.
Strange Baron of Bur-   2 sonne Baron of   Harley of Brampton   ....
ford ob. s.p. [Sheriff   Burford.   Castle widow to John   Welshe.
1580].   B   Cressett.

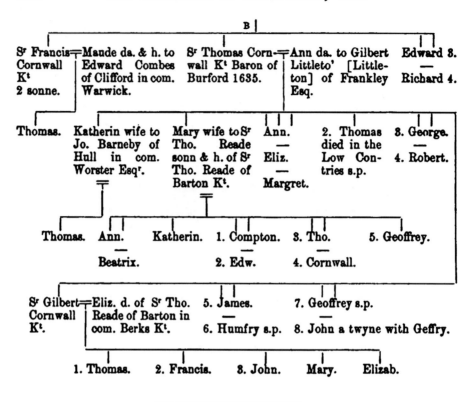

B

| Sʳ Francis Cornwall Kᵗ 2 sonne. ⊤ Maude da. & h. to Edward Combes of Clifford in com. Warwick. | Sʳ Thomas Cornwall Kᵗ Baron of Burford 1635. ⊤ Ann da. to Gilbert Littleto' [Littleton] of Frankley Esq. | Edward 3. — Richard 4. |

Thomas.

Katherin wife to Jo. Barneby of Hull in com. Worster Esqʳ. ⊤

Mary wife to Sʳ Tho. Reade sonn & h. of Sʳ Tho. Reade of Barton Kᵗ.

Ann. — Eliz. — Margret.

2. Thomas died in the Low Contries s.p.

3. George. — 4. Robert.

Thomas.   Ann.   Katherin.   1. Compton.   3. Tho.   5. Geoffrey.

Beatrix.   2. Edw.   4. Cornwall.

Sʳ Gilbert Cornwall Kᵗ. ⊤ Eliz. d. of Sʳ Tho. Reade of Barton in com. Berks Kᵗ.

5. James. — 6. Humfry s.p.

7. Geoffrey s.p. 8. John a twyne with Geffry.

1. Thomas.   2. Francis.   3. John.   Mary.   Elizab.

Coston of Coston.

Harl. 1396, fo. 71ᵇ.

ARMS: Harl. 1396.—[Argent], *a saltire* [vert], *on a chief* [gules] *a lion passant* [of the first].

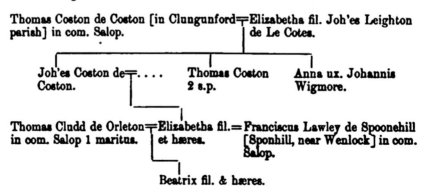

Thomas Coston de Coston [in Clungunford parish] in com. Salop. ⊤ Elizabetha fil. Joh'es Leighton de Le Cotes.

Joh'es Coston de Coston. ⊤ ....

Thomas Coston 2 s.p.

Anna ux. Johannis Wigmore.

Thomas Cludd de Orleton in com. Salop 1 maritus. ⊤ Elizabetha fil. et hæres. = Franciscus Lawley de Spoonehill [Sponhill, near Wenlock] in com. Salop.

Beatrix fil. & hæres.

Cotes of Woodcote.

Harl. 1396, fo. 82^b. S., fo. 70^b—71^b.

Ex Charti< Joh'nis Cotes de Woodcote in com. Salop Ar. 1623.

Die dominica prox' post festum S'c'i Barnabæ Ap'li A° 4 E. 2. Ita conuenit inter Robertum D'num de Knichteley ex parte vna et Rogerum le Child de eadem ex altera viz' quod d'cus Rob'tus relaxauit etc. d'co Rogero et hæredibus suis omnimodum com'u'em pasturæ quam habuit in quadam placeam bosci in Knichteley quæ vocatur Leonariewode etc. Hijs testibus Will'o de Burgo, Roberto de Knichterley et alijs a° 4 E. 2.

Sciant p'ntes et futuri quod ego Rogerus filius Rogeri de Knitchtley dedi Thomæ filio Roberti de Cotes capitale' mesuage' meum ac omnes t'ras et ten'ta mea dominium redditus et seriu' omnium tenentium meorum cum pertin' in Cotes juxta Swinulton et in Cherlton infra manerium de Eccleshall quæ et quas habui ex dona pred'c'i Thomæ fil. Rob't de Cotes etc. Habend' p'd'c'o Thomæ et hæredibus de corpore suo exe'ntibus etc. et si contingat' pred'c'm Thomam obire sine hæredibus etc. tunc integre remaneant Roberto filio Rogeri de Knyghterley fratri meo ad term'um vitæ post decessum ip'ius Roberti, integre remaneant Johanni filio Roberti pred'c'i de Knighteley et hæredibus de corpore etc. Et si contingat' pred'c'm Joh'em sine herede obire tunc Johanni filio Ric'i de Somerford integre remaneant, et si contingat' pred'c'm Joh'em sine herede obire, tunc Will'o filio Ric'i de Somerford fri eiusdem Joh'is integre remaneant, et si contingat' præd'c'm Will'm sine herede' obire, rectis hæredibus pred'c'i Roberti de Knightley integre remaneant imperpetuum. Hijs testibus Joh'e filio Rogeri de Knighteley Joh'e de Broughton Joh'e de Cogunhall Thoma de Hakedon Roberto filio Roberti de Helpeston et alijs. Dat. apud Cotes A° 49 E. 3.

[Drawing of a Seal, Plate I., Fig. 5.]

Sigillum JOH'NIS DE KNIGHTELEY.

Hæc Indentura testatur quod ego Ellena Calueley quondam vxor Joh'is Child de Emkerdon concessi ad term' viginti annorum Thomæ de Cotes juxta Swynnerton partem meam manerij de Emkerdon quæ mihi accedebat nomine dotis et aliam partem quam Agnes Knyghteley quondam vxor Roberti Fouleshurst mihi dedit per cartam etc. a° 16 R. 2.

Harl. 1396, fo. 83. Harl. 1241, fo. 70^b. S., ff. 70^b—71^b.

ARMS : Harl. 1396.—*Quarterly of nine:* 1, *Quarterly—1 and 4, Ermine—2 and 3, Paly of six or and gules,* COTES ; 2, *Argent, on a bend azure three water-bougets or,* JORCE [JOICE] ; 3, *Ermine, a cross gules,* DAVENTRE ; 4, *Argent, two organ-pipes pileways gules between nine cross-crosslets azure,* DOUNTON ; 5, *Barry of six or and gules,* ST. OWYN ; 6, *Gules, two bars argent, in chief three plates,* OTELEY [OTEBY] ; 7, *Azure, a lion rampant argent within a bordure engrailed or,* TERRELL [TIRRELL] ; 8, *Azure, a lion rampant or, crowned gules, within an orle of cross-crosslets of the second,* BREWES ; 9, *Argent, three benillets sable,* HACCOMB [HACCOMBE].

CREST.—*A cock proper, beaked, combed, and legged or.*

[Among the banners of those who entered France 16 June 1513 occurs: "Shrop.—John Cottes bayryth sylver a coke goulls his hakell and his tayll gold : and Ric. Cresset hys Pety Captayn." (Cotton MS. Cleop. C. v.))

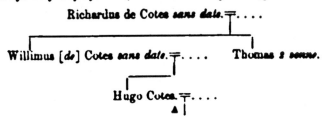

* Originally the arms of *Knightley.* Sir John Knightley, 1362, bore them, and his ancestors also, one hundred years earlier, with small variations.

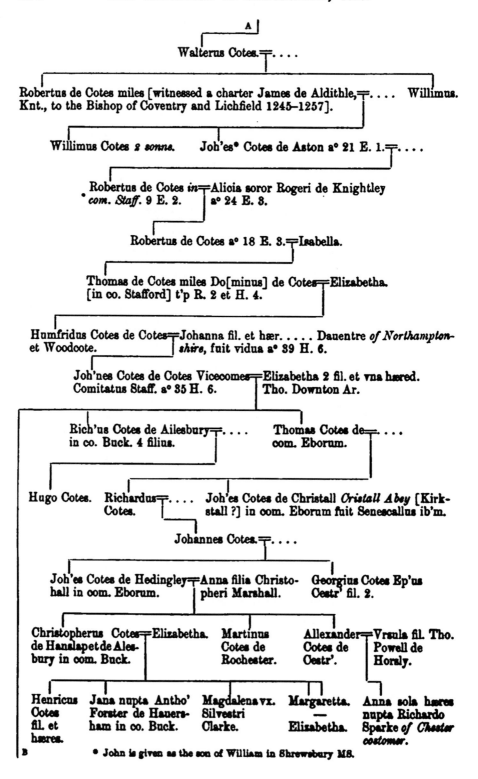

A

Walterus Cotes.=....

Robertus de Cotes miles [witnessed a charter James de Aldithle,=.... Willimus.
Knt., to the Bishop of Coventry and Lichfield 1245–1257].

Willimus Cotes *2 sonne.*   Joh'es* Cotes de Aston aº 21 E. 1.=....

Robertus de Cotes *in*=Alicia soror Rogeri de Knightley
com. Staff. 9 E. 2. | aº 24 E. 3.

Robertus de Cotes aº 18 E. 3.=Isabella.

Thomas de Cotes miles Do[minus] de Cotes=Elizabetha.
[in co. Stafford] t'p R. 2 et H. 4.

Humfridus Cotes de Cotes=Johanna fil. et hær. .... Dauentre *of Northampton-*
et Woodcote. | *shire,* fuit vidua aº 39 H. 6.

Joh'nes Cotes de Cotes Vicecomes=Elizabetha 2 fil. et vna hæred.
Comitatus Staff. aº 35 H. 6. | Tho. Downton Ar.

Rich'us Cotes de Ailesbury=....   Thomas Cotes de=....
in co. Buck. 4 filius. | com. Eborum.

Hugo Cotes. Richardus=.... Joh'es Cotes de Christall *Cristall Abey* [Kirk-
Cotes. | stall ?] in com. Eborum fuit Seneacallus ib'm.

Johannes Cotes.=....

Joh'es Cotes de Hedingley=Anna filia Christo- Georgius Cotes Ep'us
hall in com. Eborum. | pheri Marshall. Cestr' fil. 2.

Christopherus Cotes=Elizabetha. Martinus Allexander=Vrsula fil. Tho.
de Hanslapet de Ales- | Cotes de Cotes de | Powell de
bury in com. Buck. Rochester. Cestr'. Horsly.

Henricus Jana nupta Antho' Magdalena vx. Margaretta. Anna sola hæres
Cotes Forster de Hauers- Silvestri — nupta Richardo
fil. et ham in co. Buck. Clarke. Elizabetha. Sparke *of Chester*
hæres. *costomer.*

B   * John is given as the son of William in Shrewsbury MS.

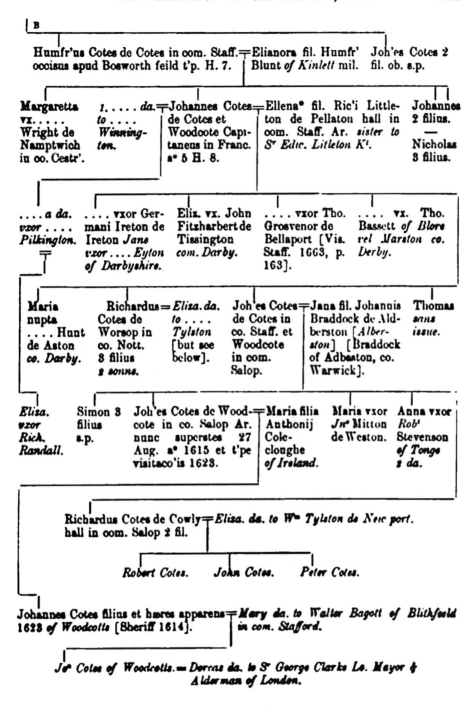

B

Humfr'us Cotes de Cotes in com. Staff.=Elianora fil. Humfr'
occisus apud Bosworth feild t'p. H. 7. | Blunt *of Kinlett* mil.

Joh'es Cotes 2
fil. ob. s.p.

Margaretta
vx....
Wright de
Namptwich
in co. Cestr'.

1..... da.=Johannes Cotes
to .... | de Cotes et
Winning- | Woodcote Capi-
ton. | taneus in Franc.
a° 5 H. 8.

=Ellena° fil. Ric'i Littleton de Pellaton hall in
com. Staff. Ar. *sister to*
S' *Edw. Litleton K'.*

Johannes
2 filius.
—
Nicholas
3 filius.

....a da.
vxor ....
Pilkington.
=

.... vxor Ger-
mani Ireton de
Ireton *Jane*
vxor .... Eyton
of Darbyshire.

Eliz. vx. John
Fitzharbert de
Tissington
com. Darby.

.... vxor Tho.
Grosvenor de
Bellaport [Vis.
Staff. 1663, p.
163].

.... vx. Tho.
Bassett *of Blore*
vel Marston co.
Derby.

Maria
nupta
.... Hunt
de Aston
co. Darby.

Richardus=*Eliza.da.*
Cotes de | *to ....*
Worsop in | *Tylston*
co. Nott. | [but see
3 filius | below].
2 sonns.

Joh'es Cotes=Jana fil. Johannis
de Cotes in | Braddock de Ald-
co. Staff. et | berston [*Alber-*
Woodcote | *ston*] [Braddock
in com. | of Adbaston, co.
Salop. | Warwick].

Thomas
sans
issue.

Eliza.
vxor
Rich.
Randall.

Simon 3
filius
s.p.

Joh'es Cotes de Wood-=Maria filia
cote in co. Salop Ar. | Anthonij
nunc superstes 27 | Cole-
Aug. a° 1615 et t'pe | cloughe
visitaco'is 1623. | *of Ireland.*

Maria vxor
Jn° Mitton
de Weston.

Anna vxor
Rob'
Stevenson
of Tonge
2 da.

Richardus Cotes de Cowly=*Eliza. da. to Wm Tylston de New* port.
hall in com. Salop 2 fil.

Robert Cotes. | *John Cotes.* | *Peter Cotes.*

Johannes Cotes filius et hæres apparens=*Mary da. to Walter Bagott of Blithfeld*
1623 of *Woodcotts* [Sheriff 1614]. | *in com. Stafford.*

Jn° Cotes of Woodcotts. == *Dorcas da. to S' George Clarke Lo. Mayor &*
Alderman of London.

° She afterwards married Sir Wm. Bassett of Blore. (Staff. Vis. 1583.)

Harl. 1241, fo. 71.

Descended of Maud sister to W^m y^e Conqueror.

Sr Raph St Owen K^t temp. Wm Conqueror.=....

Sr Robert St Owen K^t.=....   Wm Lord Bruse of Gower.

Sr Raph St Owen.=Maude da. to S^r   Piers=....   Wm Lord Bruse of Gower.
Joⁿ Oreby K^t.   Bruse.

Joⁿ St Owen.=Margarett Lady   William Bruse.=....   Wm Lord Bruse
of Whitchurch.   of Gower.

S^r Joⁿ St Owen.=....   Raph St Owen.=Julian da. of ....   Piers Bruse.=....

Raph St Owen.   Margarett.   Sr Raph S^t=Alice da. & hei.   Maud vx^r   Elizabeth
—   —   Owen K^t. to Pierre Bruse   Joⁿ de   vxor W^m
Robt St Owen.   Jane.   de Hochampe.   Vaulx.   Molineux.

2 da. the one m'ied to Richd Knightley
y^e other to Robt Coulshurst.   Phillip=Ellen da. to ....   Henry
Vaulx. Hagonett.   Molineux.

Tho. Vaulx of Hagonett.=Elinor da. to Roger Basingborne.

Elinor da. & heier vxor Tho. Lucy.

Sr Raph Tirell K^t.=....

Gilbert Tirrell.=....

Roger Tirrell.=....   Tho. Downton of Downton.=.... da. to .... Longford.

Hugh Tirrell.=....   Roger Downton of Downton=.... da. to ....
in com. Salop. Coston.

Hugh Tirell.=....   Thomas Downton.=....

Patrick S^t   John S^t=Jane da. & hei. to   Roger Tirrell.   Joⁿ Downton.=....
Owen.   Owen. Hugh Tirrell.

    A   B

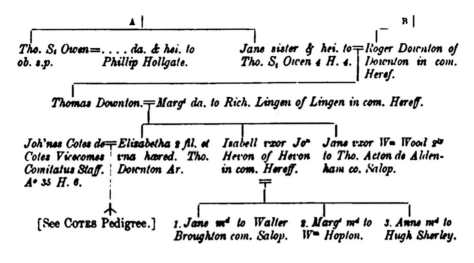

A | B |

Tho. S₁ Owen=.... da. & hei. to   Jane sister & hei. to⊤Roger Downton of
ob. s.p.   Phillip Hollgate.   Tho. S₁ Owen & H. 4.| Downton in com.
                                                              | Heref.

Thomas Downton.⊤Margᵗ da. to Rich. Lingen of Lingen in com. Heref.

Joh'nes Cotes de⊤Elizabetha 2 fil. et   Isabell vxor Joⁿ   Jane vxor Wᵐ Wood sⁿ
Cotes Vicecomes | rna hæred. Tho.   Hevon of Hevon   to Tho. Acton de Alden-
Comitatus Staff. | Downton Ar.   in com. Heref.   ham co. Salop.
A° 35 H. 6.

[See COTES Pedigree.]   1. Jane mᵈ to Walter   2. Margᵗ mᵈ to   3. Anne mᵈ to
                         Broughton com. Salop.   Wᵐ Hopton.   Hugh Sherley.

Cottingham of Wrenbury and Trebaleen.

S., fo. 17ᵇ.

[ARMS.—Sable, two hinds counter-trippant argent.

George Cottingham of Wrenburye in Cheshire.⊤....

Nich. Cottingham.⊤....

George Cottingham of Wrenbury.⊤....

Humfrey=Alice da. to William   Wᴵᴸᴸᵐ Cotting-⊤Margaret da. to   Alice vxor
Cottingham.   Saraker.   ham of Treva-| Oliver ap Ririd   ....
                                leen. | Gech of Walcott.   Masson.

William 4.   Richard 2.   Mary ux.   Edward   Amye ux.   Katherine.   Jane.
—   —   Richard   Cottingham.   Thoˢ Jones —
Henry 5.   George 3.   Morgan.   ap Hum-   Bridgett.]
                                                      frey.

x

Cotton of Coton, Alkington, and Whitchurch.

Harl. 1396, fo. 72ᵇ.   Harl. 1241, fo. 72.

ARMS OF COTTON OF COTON: Harl. 1396.—*Azure, a chevron between three cotton hanks argent.*

ARMS OF COTTON OF LONDON: Harl. 1396.—*Quarterly of six: 1 and 6, Azure, a chevron ermine between three cotton hanks argent* [COTTON]; *2, Argent, a fesse engrailed sable between three mullets gules* [COTTON]; *3, Blank; 4, Or, an eagle's leg erased at the thigh gules, on a chief indented azure a mullet argent between two plates* [TARBOCK]; *5, Argent, a chevron sable between three laurel leaves vert, a chief of the second* [SHAWBURY].

CREST: Harl. 1241.—*A falcon close argent, belled or, holding in the dexter claw a belt . . . ., buckle of the second.*

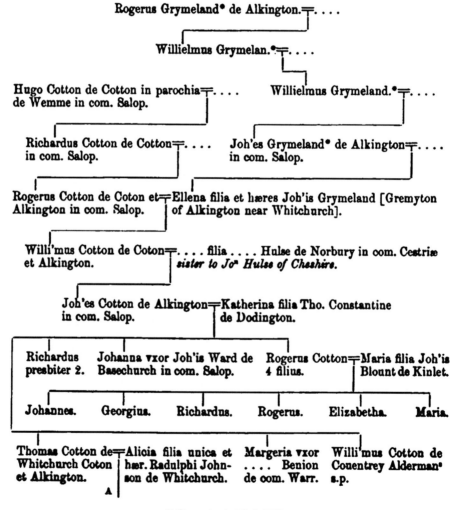

Rogerus Grymeland* de Alkington.=. . . .

Willielmus Grymelan.*=. . . .

Hugo Cotton de Cotton in parochia=. . . .
de Wemme in com. Salop.

Willielmus Grymeland.*=. . . .

Richardus Cotton de Cotton=. . . .
in com. Salop.

Joh'es Grymeland* de Alkington=. . . .
in com. Salop.

Rogerus Cotton de Coton et=Ellena filia et hæres Joh'is Grymeland [Gremyton
Alkington in com. Salop.   of Alkington near Whitchurch].

Willi'mus Cotton de Coton=. . . . filia . . . . Hulse de Norbury in com. Cestriæ
et Alkington.   *sister to Jo⁰ Hulse of Cheshire.*

Joh'es Cotton de Alkington=Katherina filia Tho. Constantine
in com. Salop.   de Dodington.

Richardus   Johanna vxor Joh'is Ward de   Rogerus Cotton=Maria filia Joh'is
presbiter 2.   Basechurch in com. Salop.   4 filius.   Blount de Kinlet.

Johannes.   Georgius.   Richardus.   Rogerus.   Elizabetha.   Maria.

Thomas Cotton de=Alicia filia unica et   Margeria vxor   Willi'mus Cotton de
Whitchurch Coton hær. Radulphi John-   . . . . Benion   Couentrey Alderman*
et Alkington.   son de Whitchurch.   de com. Warr.   s.p.
          A

* *Gremyton* in Harl. 1241.

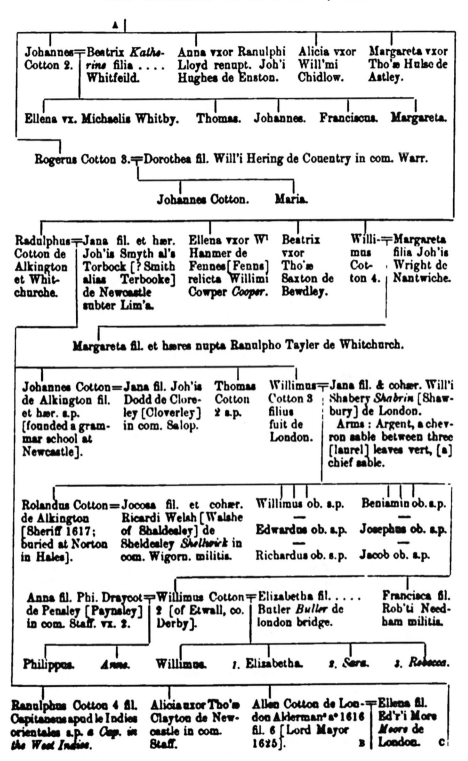

A

Johannes Cotton 2.=Beatrix *Katherine* filia .... Whitfeild.

Anna vxor Ranulphi Lloyd renupt. Joh'i Hughes de Enston.

Alicia vxor Will'mi Chidlow.

Margareta vxor Tho'æ Hulse de Astley.

Ellena vx. Michaelis Whitby. Thomas. Johannes. Franciscus. Margareta.

Rogerus Cotton 3.=Dorothea fil. Will'i Hering de Couentry in com. Warr.

Johannes Cotton. Maria.

Radulphus=Jana fil. et hær. Joh'is Smyth al's Torbock [? Smith alias Terbooke] de Newcastle subter Lim'a.
Cotton de Alkington et Whitchurche.

Ellena vxor W¹ Hanmer de Fennes[Fenns] relicta Willimi Cowper *Cooper*.

Beatrix vxor Tho'æ Saxton de Bewdley.

Willimus Cot-=Margareta filia Joh'is Wright de Nantwiche.
ton 4.

Margareta fil. et hæres nupta Ranulpho Tayler de Whitchurch.

Johannes Cotton de Alkington fil. et hær. s.p. [founded a grammar school at Newcastle].

=Jana fil. Joh'is Dodd de Clore-ley [Cloverley] in com. Salop.

Thomas Cotton 2 s.p.

Willimus=Jana fil. & cohær. Will'i Shabery *Shabrin* [Shawbury] de London.
Cotton 3 filius fuit de London.
Arms : Argent, a chevron sable between three [laurel] leaves vert, [a] chief sable.

Rolandus Cotton de Alkington [Sheriff 1617; buried at Norton in Hales].
=Jocosa fil. et cohær. Ricardi Welsh [Walshe of Shaldesley] de Sheldesley *Shelbwirk* in com. Wigorn. militis.

Willimus ob. s.p.
—
Edwardus ob. s.p.
—
Richardus ob. s.p.

Beniamin ob. s.p.
—
Josephus ob. s.p.
—
Jacob ob. s.p.

Anna fil. Phi. Draycot de Pensley [Paynsley] in com. Staff. vx. 2.
=Willimus Cotton 2 [of Etwall, co. Derby].
=Elizabetha fil. .... Butler *Buller* de london bridge.

Francisca fil. Rob'ti Needham militis.

Philippus. *Anna.* Willimus. *1.* Elizabetha. *2. Sara.* *3. Rebecca.*

Ranulphus Cotton 4 fil. Capitaneus apud le Indies orientales s.p. *a Cap. in the West Indies.*

Alicia uxor Tho'æ Clayton de Newcastle in com. Staff.

Allen Cotton de Lon-=Ellena fil. Ed'r'i More *Moore* de London.
don Alderman° a° 1616 fil. 6 [Lord Mayor 1625].
B **c**

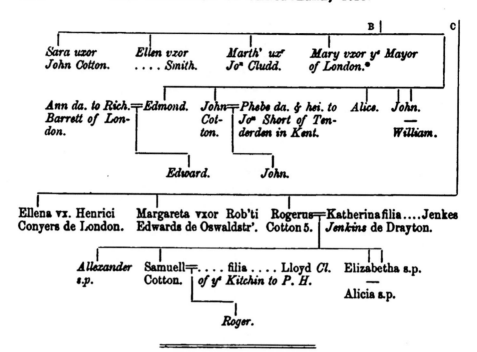

Cox of Cantlop, Harley, and Bromfield.

Harl. 1396, fo. 82. S., fo. 69.

ARMS: Harl. 1396.—*Argent, a bend azure, in sinister chief an oak-leaf of the second.*

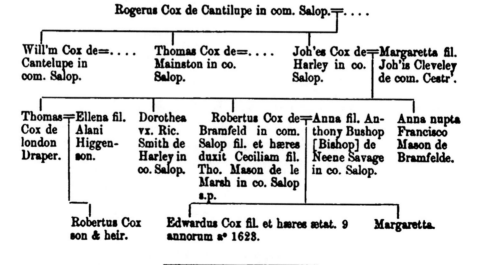

Cressett of Upton Cressett.

Harl. 1396, fo. 86ᵇ. Harl. 1241, fo. 79. S., ff. 73ᵇ, 74.

ARMS: Harl. 1396.—*Quarterly of eight: 1 and 8, Azure, a cross and bordure both engrailed or; 2, Sable, on a bend argent three trefoils of the first; 3, Argent, a lion rampant gules crowned or; 4, Argent, a fesse sable between three [six] bees volant gules; 5, Argent, a lion rampant sable [STEPLETON]; 6, Azure [argent], a buck's head cabossed gules attired or; 7, Argent, on a fesse gules a mullet pierced of the first.**

CREST.—*A demi-lion rampant guardant argent, ducally crowned or, holding in the paws a cresset or beacon of the first, fired proper.*

[Hugh Cresset of Upton Cresset, Sheriff 1435.]=....

Robertus Cressett de=Xpiana fil. et hær. Joh'es Stepleton de Stepleton
Upton Cresset in com. | mil. 2 nupta .... Eyton et 3 [*postea*] ....
Salop [Sheriff 1469]. | Byrton *Burton.*

Marya nupta Joh'is Lawley de Wenlock in co. Salop.

Elizabetha ux. .... Botterell.

Thomas Cresset=Jana fil. Rogeri Corbet de Morton militis.
de Vpton in com. Salop.

Anna vxor Laurencij Ludlow.

Cecilia ux. Tho. Leighton de Cotes.

Thomazina vx. Richardi Draper de Walton.

Elizabetha vx. Adam Lutley.

Richardus=Jana fil. Walteri Cresset de | Wrottesley de Vpton. | co. Staff.

Edmundus s.p.
—
Henricus s.p.

Jana s.p.
—
Maria s.p.

Francisca vx. *Rob't* Smith. ☦

Dorothea vx. Will'i Minde de Newton *Mynde de Myndtowne.*

Cecilia vx. Wᵐ Acton de longnor *Acton of Aldenham.*

Robert Cresset=Katherina fil. Will'us de Vpton. | Charleton de Apley.

Margaretta vx. Thomas Moore de Lawarden [Larden].

Thomas s.p.
—
Petrus s.p.

Cecillia vx. Adam Lutley.

Eliz. vx. Ed'r'i *Richᵈ* Leighton de Cotes.

Jana *Joane* nupta 1 Tho. Chetwyn 2 Roland Fewtrell.

Thomazina vx. Ric'i Draper 2 Francisco Holland.

Joh'es Cresset de Vpton=Katharina fil. Joh'is Harley de
in com. Salop. | Bramton 2 vx. Tho. Cornwall.

Richardus Cresset=Jana fil. Joh'is Hopton de Rock-
de Vpton. | hill *Jo* Hopton of Charbury.

Thomas s.p.
—
Johannes s.p.

A   B

* In Shrewsbury MS. no tinctures are given in sixth and seventh quarterings.

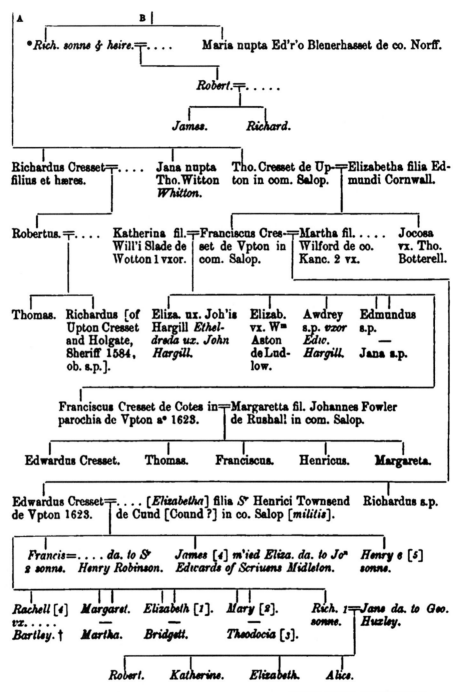

A　　　　　　　　B

*Rich. sonne & heire.=.... 　　　Maria nupta Ed'r'o Blenerhasset de co. Norff.

Robert.=.....

James.　　　Richard.

Richardus Cresset=....　　Jana nupta　　Tho. Cresset de Up-=Elizabetha filia Ed-
filius et hæres.　　　　　Tho. Witton　　ton in com. Salop.　　mundi Cornwall.
　　　　　　　　　　　　Whitton.

Robertus.=....　　Katherina fil.=Franciscus Cres-=Martha fil. ....　Jocosa
　　　　　　　　Will'i Slade de　set de Vpton in　Wilford de co.　vx. Tho.
　　　　　　　　Wotton 1 vxor.　com. Salop.　　Kanc. 2 vx.　　Botterell.

Thomas.　Richardus [of　Eliza. ux. Joh'is　Elizab.　Awdrey　Edmundus
　　　　Upton Cresset　Hargill Ethel-　vx. Wm　s.p. vxor　s.p.
　　　　and Holgate,　dreda ux. John　Aston　Edw.　　—
　　　　Sheriff 1584,　Hargill.　　de Lud-　Hargill.　Jana s.p.
　　　　ob. s.p.].　　　　　　low.

Franciscus Cresset de Cotes in=Margaretta fil. Johannes Fowler
parochia de Vpton aº 1623.　　de Rushall in com. Salop.

Edwardus Cresset.　Thomas.　Franciscus.　Henricus.　Margareta.

Edwardus Cresset=.... [Elizabetha] filia Sr Henrici Townsend　Richardus s.p.
de Vpton 1623.　　de Cund [Cound?] in co. Salop [militis].

Francis=.... da. to Sr　James [4] m'ied Eliza. da. to Joa　Henry 6 [5]
2 sonne.　Henry Robinson.　Edwards of Scriuens Midleton.　sonne.

Rachell [4]　Margaret.　Elizabeth [1].　Mary [2].　　Rich. 1=Jane da. to Geo.
vx. ....　　—　　　—　　　　—　　　　sonne.　Huxley.
Bartley. †　Martha.　Bridgett.　Theodocia [3].

Robert.　Katherine.　Elizabeth.　Alice.

FFRANCIS CRESSETT.

* Richard and his descendants are not given in Harl. 1396, nor in Shrewsbury MS.
† This marriage is not given in Shrewsbury MS.

Crompton of Acton Burnell.

S., fo. 76ᵃ.

[ARMS.—*Gules, a fesse wavy between three lions rampant or.*
CREST.—*A talbot sejant or and supporting with the paw a hank of string argent.*

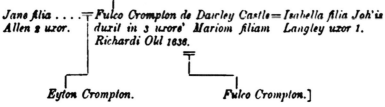

Thomas Crompton de Acton Burnell.⊤*Alicia filia Thomæ Eyton de Eyton.*

Jane filia ....⊤*Fulco Crompton de Dawley Castle*=*Isabella filia Joh'is*
Allen 2 uxor. | *duxit in 3 uxore' Mariam filiam Langley uxor 1.*
| *Richardi Old 1636.*

Eyton Crompton.   *Fulco Crompton.*]

Cupper of Stanton Lacy.

Harl. 1396, fo. 73ᵇ.

ARMS : Harl. 1396.—*Argent, on a bend engrailed between two lions rampant sable three plates, all within a bordure engrailed gules.*

Thomas Cupper de Steuenton in com. Salop gen'.⊤Isabella filia .... Cooke.

Philippus Cupper⊤....	Jobannes.	Edmundus.	Elizabetha.	Jana vxor Tho.
fil. et hær. 1598.	—	—		Carter.
	Richardus.	Walterus.		⊤

Jana vxor Thomæ   Katherina fil. 2 et cohær.   Tho. Carter de
Dios.   vx. Georgius Keistaffe.   Downton.

1. Margeria fil. & hæres⊤Ed'r'us Cupper de⊤2. Margeria fil. Ric'di
Will'i Euans de com. | Ludlow in com. | Gwytell de Ludlow.
Mongomery. | Salop 2 filius. |

Johannes	Margareta vx. Si-	Ricardus Cupper⊤Johanna fil. et vna	Margeria vx.
Cupper	monis Standish	de Stanton Lacy	hæred. Will'i Nor-	Joh'is Giggs
s.p.	de London.	in com. Salop aᵒ	ton de le Seet in	de Ludwell in
		1598.	com. Salop.	com. Oxon.

Edwardus Cupper=Johanna fil. Tho. Carter   Franciscus Cupper 2.
de Stanton Lacy et Margeriæ vxoris eius   —
in co. Sal.   filiæ Thomæ Blashfeild.   Ricardus.

Dannatt of Westhope.

S., fo. 216ᵇ.

[ARMS.—*Quarterly :* 1, *Argent, guttée de sang* [DANNATT ? a canton omitted] ; 2, *Or, two bars azure each charged with three lions rampant of the field* [DE LA HAY] ; 3, [*Azure*], *three eagles displayed in bend between two cotises* [argent], [BELKNAP] ; 4, *Checky argent and sable* [ELMERUG or ELLNBRIDGE].

CREST.—*A greyhound's head erased argent, gorged with a collar gules edged and studded or.*

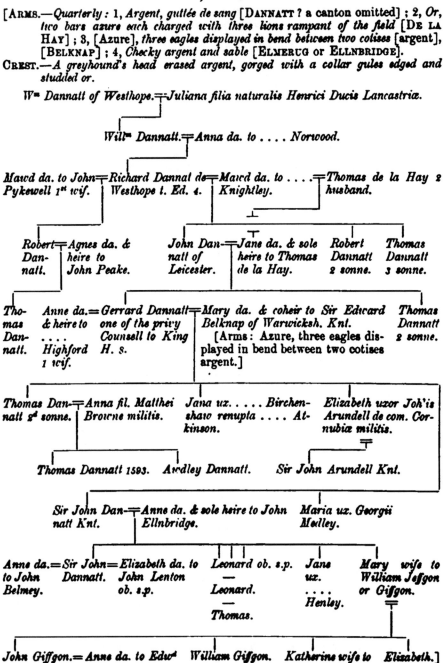

Wᵐ Dannatt of Westhope.=Juliana filia naturalis Henrici Ducis Lancastriæ.

Willᵐ Dannatt.=Anna da. to .... Norwood.

Mawd da. to John=Richard Dannal de=Mawd da. to ....=Thomas de la Hay 2
Pykewell 1ˢᵗ wif. | Westhope t. Ed. 4. | Knightley. | husband.

Robert=Agnes da. &   John Dan-=Jane da. & sole   Robert   Thomas
Dan- | heire to   natt of | heire to Thomas   Dannatt   Dannatt
natt. | John Peake. Leicester. | de la Hay.   2 sonne.   3 sonne.

Tho-   Anne da.=Gerrard Dannatt=Mary da. & coheir to Sir Edward   Thomas
mas   & heire to one of the privy Belknap of Warwicksh. Knt.   Dannatt
Dan- ....   Counsell to King   [Arms : Azure, three eagles dis-   2 sonne.
natt. Highford   H. 8.   played in bend between two cotises
1 wif.   argent.]

Thomas Dan-=Anna fil. Matthei   Jana ux. .... Birchen-   Elizabeth uxor Joh'is
natt 2ᵈ sonne. | Browne militis.   shaw renupta .... At-   Arundell de com. Cor-
   kinson.   nubiæ militis.
   =

Thomas Dannatt 1593.   Awdley Dannatt.   Sir John Arundell Knt.

Sir John Dan-=Anne da. & sole heire to John   Maria ux. Georgii
natt Knt. | Ellnbridge.   Medley.

Anne da.=Sir John=Elizabeth da. to   Leonard ob. s.p.   Jane   Mary wife to
to John   Dannatt. | John Lenton   —   ux.   William Jeffgon
Belmey.   ob. s.p.   Leonard.   ....   or Giffgon.
   —   Henley.
   Thomas.

John Giffgon.=Anne da. to Edwᵈ   William Giffgon.   Katherine wife to   Elizabeth.]
   Martin.   .... Jewell.

Davys of Marsh.*

Harl. 1896, fo. 108^b.   Harl. 1241, fo. 38.   Harl. 615, fo. 267^b.   S., fo. 86.

ARMS: Harl. 1896.—*Quarterly: 1 and 4, Sable in Harl. 1241—a goat argent—horned or in Harl. 1241—standing on a child of the same, swaddled gules, and feeding on a tree eradicated vert, a crescent for difference,* DAVYS; 2, *Argent, a lion passant sable within a bordure engrailed gules* [MEREDITH GOCH]; 3, *Azure, two chevronels or between three gryphons' heads erased argent,* MARTYN.†

CREST.—*On a mount vert a goat couchant argent under a tree proper.*

This Crest was granted to Edw. Daveys sonne & heire of Edw. Danys of Lincolns Inn Novemb. 1597.

ARMS: Harl. 615.—*Quarterly: 1 and 4,* DAVIS, *as above; 2 and 3, Or, a lion statant sable.*

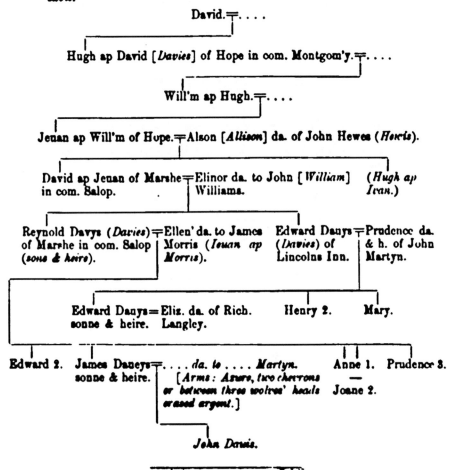

* Harl. 1241 gives the surname of *Davis* all through the pedigree.
† In Shrewsbury MS. the third and fourth quarters are blank. Harl. 1241 gives the second and third quarters as : " Or, a lion passant sable."

Day of Worfield.

S., fo. 217ª.

[ARMS.—*Per chevron or and azure, three mullets counterchanged.*

Richard Day of Worfield p'sh.=*.... da. to .... Osborne of Staffordsh.*

Alice wife to Thomas Rigeley.	*Elizabeth wife to .... Felton after to Wᵐ Barkley.*	*William Day.*=*Alice da. & sole heir of George Barker.*	*John Waverton 2ᵈ husb.*	*William Day° Deane of Windsor & Bishop of Winchester.*

Alice wife to Thomas Riley.	*Elizabeth wife to Wᵐ Buckley.*	*Richard Day.*=*Jane da. to Brian Fowler [Vis. Staff. 1583].*	*Jana wife to Sir George Bromley.*]

Dichfield alias Dycher of Shawbury and Muggleton.

S., fo. 159ᵇ.

[ARMS.—*Quarterly : 1, Azure, three pine-cones, two and one, or,* DYCHER *alias* DICHE-FIELD ; *2, Argent, a griffin segreant sable,* HERGEST ; *3, Argent, a bugle-horn stringed sable,* FORSTER ; *4, Argent, a chevron azure,* REEVE.
CREST.—*A bear statant.*

Richard Dichfield alias Dycher de Shawburie & Mugleton.=*Agnes da. of Jeffreye Yonge of Keynton.*

Thomas Dichfield.=*Margarett da. & coh. to William Reeve.*

Thoˢ ob. s.p.	*Sir Wᵐ a priest ob. s.p.*	*Robertus*=*Margarett da. to Dichfield.* | *Robᵗ Gilbert.*	*Rogerus Dich-field.*	*John 4 son Vicar of Sabri.*

Elizabeth da. to Raph Motton 2 wiffe.=*Thomas Dich-field alias Dicher.*	*Anne da. to .... Lee of Roden.*=*Robertus Dyche-field fil. 2.*	*Elizabeth da. to Robᵗ Leighton.*

Elizabeth wife to	*Maria ux. Rowl. Hill.*	*Katherina wife to John Leigh-ton.*	*Johannes Diche-field fil. 2.*	*Robertus Dychefield.*=*Maria filia Rich. Leigh-ton de Cotes.*

Richardus Dichefield.	*Maria.*	*Anna.*]

° George Day, who is omitted above, was consecrated Bishop of Chichester 1543, and died 1556. William Day, his brother, was consecrated Bishop of Winchester 1595, and died 1596 (Fuller's 'Worthies'); and there is a grant of the above arms to him by Flower, Norroy, in 1582 (Harl. MS. 1422).

Dodd of Petsey.

Harl. 1396, fo. 106[b].   Harl. 1241, fo. 140.   S., fo. 88.

ARMS: Harl. 1396.—*Argent, on a fesse gules between two barrulets wavy sable three crescents or, a fleur-de-lis for difference.*

ARMS: Harl. 1241.—*Argent, a fesse gules cottised wavy sable between three crescents of the second.*

[Both of these coats are given in Shrewsbury MS., fo. 88.]

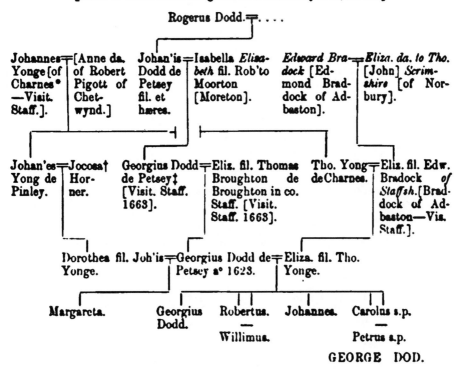

Rogerus Dodd.=. . . .

Johannes=[Anne da. | Johan'is=Isabella *Elisa-* | *Edward Bra-*=*Eliza. da. to Tho.*
Yonge [of | of Robert | Dodd de | *beth* fil. Rob'to | *dock* [Ed- | [John] *Scrim-*
Charnes* | Pigott of | Petsey | Moorton | mond Brad- | *shire* [of Nor-
—Visit. | Chet- | fil. et | [Moreton]. | dock of Ad- | bury].
Staff.]. | wynd.] | hæres. | | baston].

Johan'es=Jocosa† | Georgius Dodd=Eliz. fil. Thomas | Tho. Yong=Eliz. fil. Edw.
Yong de | Hor- | de Petsey‡ | Broughton de | deCharnes. | Bradock *of*
Pinley. | ner. | [Visit. Staff. | Broughton in co. | | *Staffsh.* [Brad-
| | 1663]. | Staff. [Visit. | | dock of Ad-
| | | Staff. 1663]. | | baston—Vis.
| | | | | Staff.].

Dorothea fil. Joh'is=Georgius Dodd de=Eliza. fil. Tho.
Yonge. | Petsey a° 1623. | Yonge.

Margareta.   Georgius   Robertus.   Johannes.   Carolus s.p.
             Dodd.   —
                        Willimus.   Petrus s.p.

GEORGE DOD.

Dodd of Cloverley.

S., fo. 215[b].

[ARMS.—*Quarterly: 1 and 4, Argent, a fesse gules between two cottises wavy sable,* DODD; *2, Checky argent and sable,* WARREN; *3, Argent, a chevron gules between three flowers azure leaved vert,* CLOVERLEY.]

[Among the banners of those who entered France 16 June 1513 occurs: "Shrop-shyr—John Dod bayryth Sylver a Blew bud or a Heydod assur. John Maynwaryng hys Pety Captayn." (Cotton MS. Cleop. C. v.)]

[*John Dodd of Knoles &*=. . . . *dt. & coh. of John Warren*
perspares (Perespares). | *of Ightfield.*

▲

* Young of Charnes bore for arms: Azure, a buck's head caboshed or, a chief sable; but Thomas was disclaimed at the Staffordshire Visitation in 1614, and John at that of 1583.

† Harl. 1241 says, "Anne da. to . . . . Pigott of Chettwyn."

‡ George Dodd, who married Eliz. Broughton, is omitted in Harl. 1241.

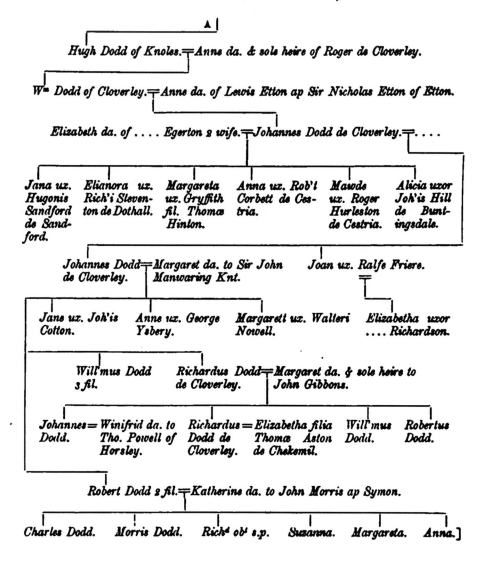

▲

Hugh Dodd of Knoles.=Anne da. & sole heire of Roger de Cloverley.

Wᵐ Dodd of Cloverley.=Anne da. of Lewis Etton ap Sir Nicholas Etton of Etton.

Elizabeth da. of . . . . Egerton 2 wife.=Johannes Dodd de Cloverley.=. . . .

Jana ux. Hugonis Sandford de Sandford.

Elianora ux. Rich'i Steventon de Dothall.

Margareta ux. Gruffith fil. Thomæ Hinton.

Anna ux. Rob't Corbett de Cestria.

Mawde ux. Roger Hurleston de Cestria.

Alicia uxor Joh'is Hill de Buntingsdale.

Johannes Dodd=Margaret da. to Sir John de Cloverley. Manwaring Knt.

Joan ux. Ralfe Friere.

Jane ux. Joh'is Cotton.

Anne ux. George Ysbery.

Margarett ux. Walteri Nowell.

Elizabetha uxor . . . . Richardson.

Will'mus Dodd 3 fil.

Richardus Dodd=Margaret da. & sole heire to de Cloverley. John Gibbons.

Johannes=Winifrid da. to Dodd. Tho. Powell of Horsley.

Richardus=Elizabetha filia Dodd de Thomæ Aston Cloverley. de Chekemil.

Will'mus Dodd.

Robertus Dodd.

Robert Dodd 2 fil.=Katherine da. to John Morris ap Symon.

Charles Dodd.   Morris Dodd.   Rich'd ob' s.p.   Suzanna.   Margareta.   Anna.]

Dodd of Broxton.

S., fo. 216.

[ARMS.—Argent, on a fesse gules cotised wavy sable three mullets or, in chief a mullet.
CREST.—A garb or, thereout issuant a serpent azure.

John Dodd of Broxton in com. Cestr'.=. . . .

Wᵐ Dodd of Broxton.=Alice da. to John Talbott.

▲

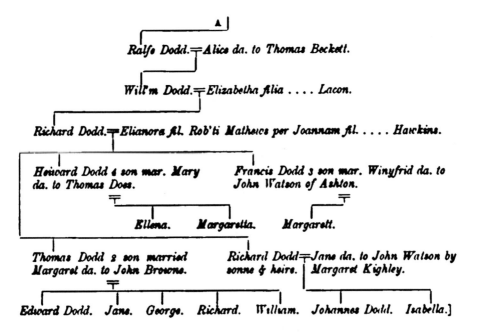

▲

Ralfe Dodd.⚯*Alice da. to Thomas Beckett.*

Will'm Dodd.⚯*Elizabetha filia .... Lacon.*

Richard Dodd.⚯*Elianora fil. Rob'ti Mathews per Joannam fil. .... Hawkins.*

Howard Dodd 4 son mar. Mary da. to Thomas Does.　　*Francis Dodd 3 son mar. Winyfrid da. to John Watson of Ashton.*

Ellena.　*Margaretta.*　　*Margarett.*

Thomas Dodd 2 son married Margaret da. to John Browne.　　*Richard Dodd*⚯*Jane da. to John Watson by sonne & heire. | Margaret Kighley.*

Edward Dodd.　*Jane.*　*George.*　*Richard.*　*William.*　　*Johannes Dodd.*　*Isabella.*]

Dodington of Dodington.

Harl. 1241, fo. 24.　Harl. 615, fo. 249.　S., fo. 297ᵃ.

ARMS: Harl. 1241.—*Quarterly:* 1, *Azure, a fesse or, in chief two mullets and in base a chevron of the second, within a bordure argent,* DODINGTON in Shrewsbury MS.; 2, *Argent, a chevron between three roses gules,* WYARD in Shrewsbury MS.; 3, *Gules, two lions passant argent—a mullet for difference,* WALTER in Shrewsbury MS.; 4, *Quarterly or and gules, in first quarter a martlet sable, within a bordure of the last bezantee.*

CREST.—*A lion's gamb couped and erect or, armed sable.*

ARMS: Harl. 615.—*Azure, a fesse or between two mullets pierced in chief and a chevron in base of the second, within a bordure engrailed argent.*

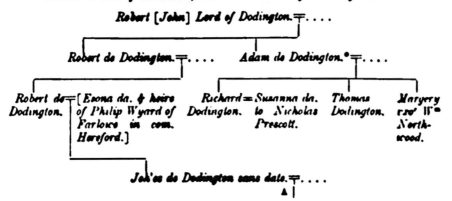

Robert [John] Lord of Dodington.⚯*....*

Robert de Dodington.⚯*....*　　*Adam de Dodington.**⚯*....*

Robert de Dodington.⚯[*Esona da. & heire of Philip Wyard of Farlowe in com. Hereford.*]　*Richard*⚯*Susanna da. Dodington. to Nicholas Prescott.*　*Thomas Dodington.*　*Margery txᵈ Wᵐ Northwood.*

Joh'es de Dodington eans date.⚯*....*

▲|

* Adam and his children are not given in Shrewsbury MS.

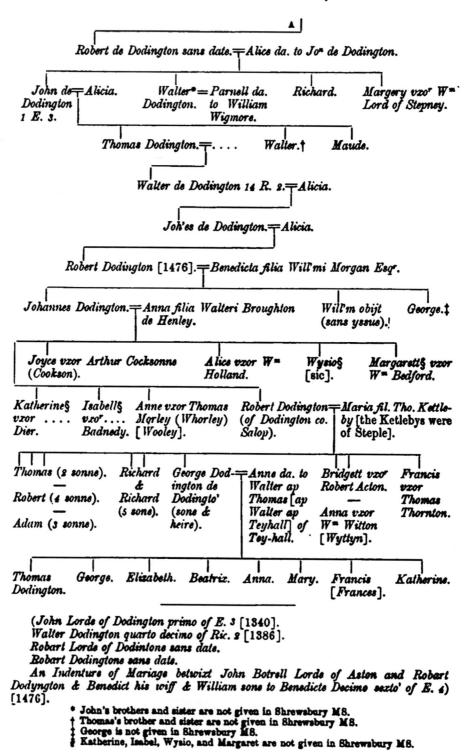

(*John Lorde of Dodington primo of E. 3* [1340].
Walter Dodington quarto decimo of Ric. 2 [1386].
Robart Lorde of Dodintons sans date.
Robart Dodingtons sans date.
An Indenture of Mariage betwixt John Botrell Lorde of Aston and Robart Dodyngton & Benedict his wiff & William sone to Benedicts Decime sexto' of E. 4) [1476].

* John's brothers and sister are not given in Shrewsbury MS.
† Thomas's brother and sister are not given in Shrewsbury MS.
‡ George is not given in Shrewsbury MS.
§ Katherine, Isabel, Wysio, and Margaret are not given in Shrewsbury MS.

Downton of Broughton and Alderton.

Harl. 1396, fo. 104ᵇ. S., fo. 87.

ARMS: Harl. 1396.—*Argent, three piles in point sable, each charged with a goat's head erased of the field armed or.*

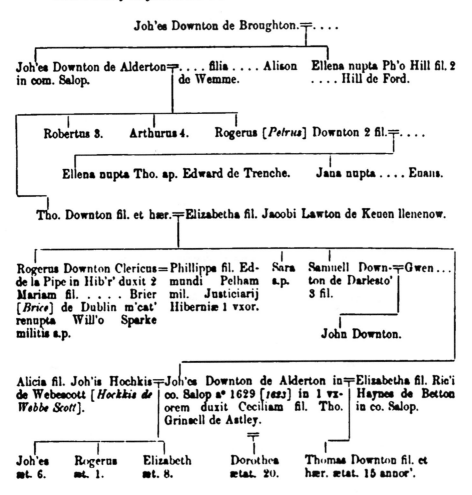

Joh'es Downton de Broughton.=. . . .

Joh'es Downton de Alderton=. . . . filia . . . . Alison   Ellena nupta Ph'o Hill fil. 2
in com. Salop.   de Wemme.   . . . . Hill de Ford.

Robertus 3.   Arthurus 4.   Rogerus [*Petrus*] Downton 2 fil.=. . . .

Ellena nupta Tho. ap. Edward de Trenche.   Jana nupta . . . . Euans.

Tho. Downton fil. et hær.=Elizabetha fil. Jacobi Lawton de Keuen llenenow.

Rogerus Downton Clericus=Phillippa fil. Ed-   Sara   Samuell Down-=Gwen . . .
de la Pipe in Hib'r' duxit 2   mundi   Pelham   s.p.   ton de Darlesto'   3 fil.
Mariam fil. . . . . Brier   mil.   Justiciarij
[*Brice*] de Dublin m'cat'   Hiberniæ 1 vxor.
renupta   Will'o   Sparke
militis s.p.   John Downton.

Alicia fil. Joh'is Hochkis=Joh'es Downton de Alderton in=Elizabetha fil. Ric'i
de Webescott [*Hochkis de*   co. Salop a° 1629 [*1623*] in 1 vx- Haynes de Betton
Webbe Scott].   orem duxit Ceciliam fil. Tho.   in co. Salop.
                               Grinsell de Astley.

Joh'es   Rogerus   Elizabeth   Dorothea   Thomas Downton fil. et
æt. 6.   æt. 1.   æt. 8.   ætat. 20.   hær. ætat. 15 annor'.

J. DOWNTON nunc Clericus Pipæ in Hiberniâ 1623.

Draper of Acton and Bromlow, from Worthen.

Harl. 1241, fo. 6ᵇ.   Harl. 615, fo. 251ᵇ.   S., fo. 298ᵃ.

ARMS: Harl. 1241.—*Quarterly : 1 and 4, Bendy of eight gules and vert, three fleurs-de-lis or, DRAPER in Shrewsbury MS. : 2 and 3, Or, three chevronels vert—on each a mullet, HAGAR in Shrewsbury MS.*

[*Per Camden Claren.*]

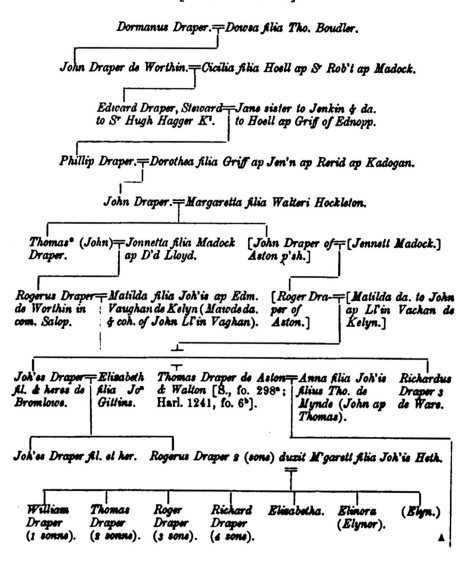

* Thomas (John) and his wife Jenetta and their descendants are not given in Shrewsbury MS.

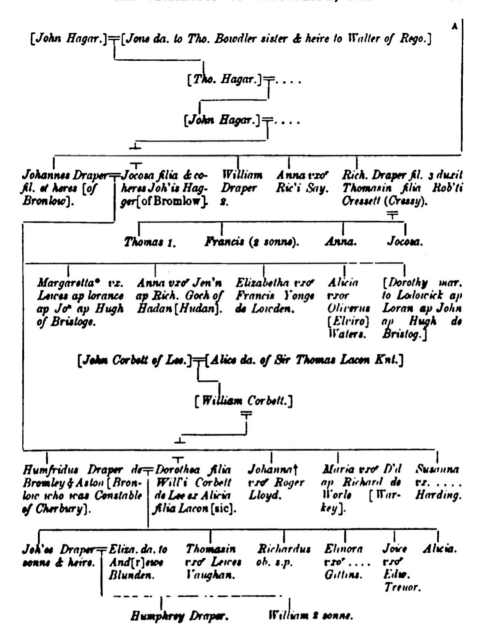

* Margaretta is omitted in Shrewsbury MS.
† Johanna is omitted in Shrewsbury MS.

z

Edge alias Hawkins.

Harl. 1241, fo. 5ᵇ.   Harl. 615, fo. 260.   S., fo. 90ᵃ.

ARMS : Harl. 1241.—*Argent*, in Harl. 615—*a hawk proper, belled or, standing on a staff couped and raguled vert.*

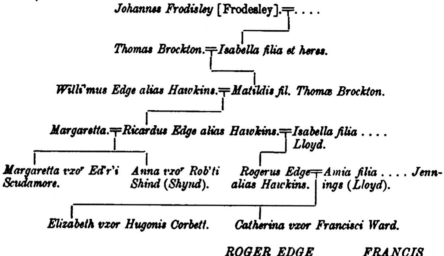

```
Johannes Frodisley [Frodesley].═ ....

    Thomas Brockton.═Isabella filia et heres.

Willi'mus Edge alias Hawkins.═Matildis fil. Thomæ Brockton.

Margaretta.═Ricardus Edge alias Hawkins.═Isabella filia ....
                                          Lloyd.

Margaretta vxoᵣ Edᵣ'i    Anna vxoᵣ Rob'ti    Rogerus Edge═Amia filia .... Jenn-
Scudamore.               Shind (Shynd).      alias Hawkins.│ ings (Lloyd).

    Elizabeth vxor Hugonis Corbett.    Catherina vxor Francisci Ward.
```

ROGER EDGE   FRANCIS
alias *HAWKINS*.   *WARD*.

Edwards of Lea, Plas Newydd, and Lydham.

Harl. 1396, fo. 109.   Harl. 1241, fo. 137.   S., ff. 90ᵃ, 91.

ARMS : Harl. 1396.—*Quarterly of twelve :* 1 *and* 12, *Per bend sinister ermine and ermines, a lion rampant or, a crescent for difference ;* 2, *Azure, a lion rampant per fesse or and argent, within a bordure of the third, pelletté* [CARADOC VREICHVRAS, EARL OF HEREFORD] ; 3, *Ermine, a lion rampant azure* [ELYDUR OF BROMFIELD] ; 4, *Gules, three chevronels argent* [JESTIN AP GWERGANT] ; 5, *Sable, three horses' heads erased argent* [BROCHWELL ISGYTHROG] ; 6, *Argent, a chevron between three birds sable, each holding in the beak an ermine spot* [LOWARCH AP BRANNE] ; 7, *Argent, a cross flory engrailed sable between four Cornish choughs proper* [EDWIN OF ENGLEFIELD] ; 8, *Gules, a chevron ermine between three men's heads side-faced in helmets proper* [EDNEVIT AP TUDOR AP GRONO] ; 9, *Ermine, a lion rampant sable* [KENRICK AP RUALLON] ; 10, *Azure, a lion passant argent* [ITHEL VYCHAM] ; 11, *Per bend sinister ermine and ermines, a lion rampant or, within a bordure gules* [JONES].

CREST.—*A man's head side-faced in a helmet proper.*

MOTTO.—A VINNO DVW DERVID.   [" A fynno Duw derfydd," that is, " God's will be done."]

```
Ednevet Gam 4 fil. Jerworth═Glwadis fil. ll'in [Llewellyn] ap Madock ap
Voel of Trevor.             ▲ │ Einion ap Edwin.
```

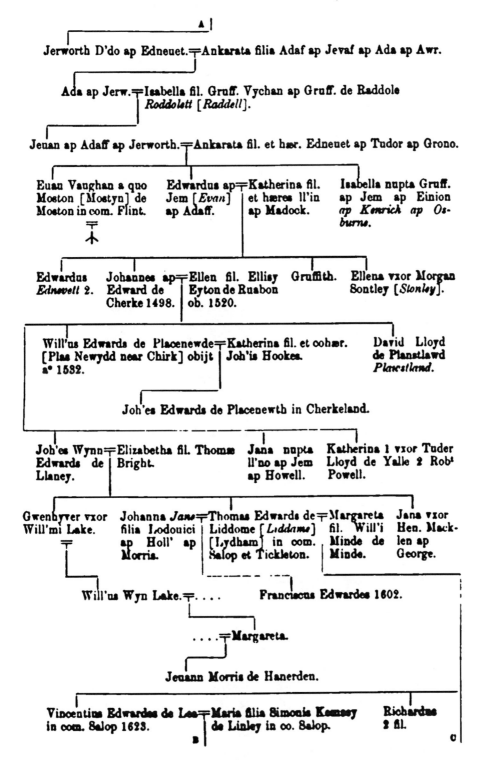

▲

Jerworth D'do ap Edneuet.⊤Ankarata filia Adaf ap Jevaf ap Ada ap Awr.

Ada ap Jerw.⊤Isabella fil. Gruff. Vychan ap Gruff. de Raddole
Roddolett [*Raddell*].

Jeuan ap Adaff ap Jerworth.⊤Ankarata fil. et hær. Edneuet ap Tudor ap Grono.

Euau Vaughan a quo Moston [Mostyn] de Moston in com. Flint.

Edwardus ap Jem [*Evan*] ap Adaff.⊤Katherina fil. et hæres ll'in ap Madock.

Isabella nupta Gruff. ap Jem ap Einion *ap Kenrich ap Osburne.*

Edwardus *Ednevett* 2.

Johannes ap Edward de Cherke 1498.⊤Ellen fil. Ellisy Eyton de Ruabon ob. 1520.

Gruffith.

Ellena vxor Morgan Sontley [*Stonley*].

Will'us Edwards de Placenewde [Plas Newydd near Chirk] obijt a° 1532.⊤Katherina fil. et cohær. Joh'is Hookes.

David Lloyd de Planstlawd *Plawstland.*

Joh'es Edwards de Placenewth in Cherkeland.

Joh'es Wynn Edwards de Llaney.⊤Elizabetha fil. Thomæ Bright.

Jana nupta ll'no ap Jem ap Howell.

Katherina 1 vxor Tuder Lloyd de Yalle 2 Rob' Powell.

Gwenhyver vxor Will'mi Lake.

Johanna *Jane* filia Lodouici ap Holl' ap Morris.⊤Thomas Edwards de Liddome [*Liddame*] [Lydham] in com. Salop et Tickleton.⊤Margareta fil. Will'i Minde de Minde.

Jana vxor Hen. Macklen ap George.

Will'us Wyn Lake.⊤. . . .

Franciscus Edwardes 1602.

. . . .⊤Margareta.

Jeuann Morris de Hanerden.

Vincentius Edwardes de Lee in com. Salop 1623.⊤Maria filia Simonis Kemsey de Linley in co. Salop.

Richardus 2 fil.

B

C

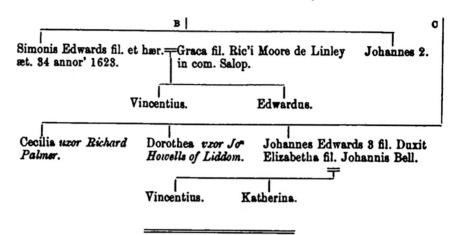

B | C

Simonis Edwards fil. et hær.⊤Graca fil. Ric'i Moore de Linley   Johannes 2.
æt. 34 annor' 1623. | in com. Salop.

        Vincentius.   Edwardus.

Cecilia *uxor Richard*   Dorothea *vxor Joᵉ*   Johannes Edwards 3 fil. Duxit
Palmer.   *Howells of Liddom.*   Elizabetha fil. Johannis Bell.

        Vincentius.   Katherina.

Edwards of Kilhendre.

Harl. 1396, fo. 110ᵇ.   Harl. 1241, fo. 33ᵇ.   S., ff. 92ᵇ, 93.

ARMS: Harl. 1241.—*Quarterly : 1 and 4, Gules, a chevron engrailed between three
    boars' heads couped close argent ; 2 and 3, Per bend sinister ermine and
    ermines, a lion rampant or* [TUDOR TREVOR].

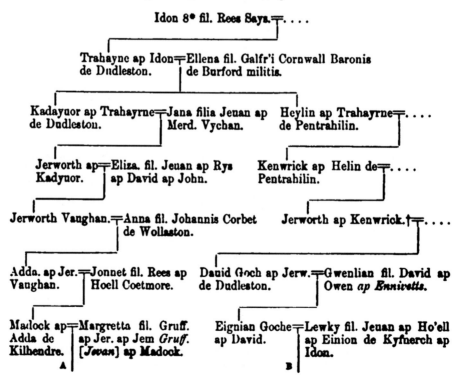

Idon 3ᵉ fil. Rees Says.⊤. . . .

Trahaync ap Idon⊤Ellena fil. Galfr'i Cornwall Baronis
de Dudleston. | de Burford militis.

Kadayuor ap Trahayrne⊤Jana filia Jeuan ap   Heylin ap Trahayrne⊤. . . .
de Dudleston. | Merd. Vychan.   de Pentrahilin.

Jerworth ap⊤Eliza. fil. Jeuan ap Rys   Kenwrick ap Helin de⊤. . . .
Kadynor. | ap David ap John.   Pentrahilin.

Jerworth Vaughan.⊤Anna fil. Johannis Corbet   Jerworth ap Kenwrick.†⊤. . . .
                | de Wollaston.

Adda. ap Jer.⊤Jonnet fil. Rees ap   Dauid Goch ap Jerw.⊤Gwenlian fil. David ap
Vaughan. | Hoell Coetmore.   de Dudleston. | Owen *ap Ennivetts.*

Madock ap⊤Margretta fil. Gruff.   Eignian Goche⊤Lewky fil. Jeuan ap Ho'ell
Adda de | ap Jer. ap Jem *Gruff.*   ap David. | ap Einion de Kyfnerch ap
Kilhendre.| [*Jevan*] ap Madock. | Idon.
    A | B |

* Harl. 1241 calls him "3 son."   † This generation is not given in Shrewsbury MS.

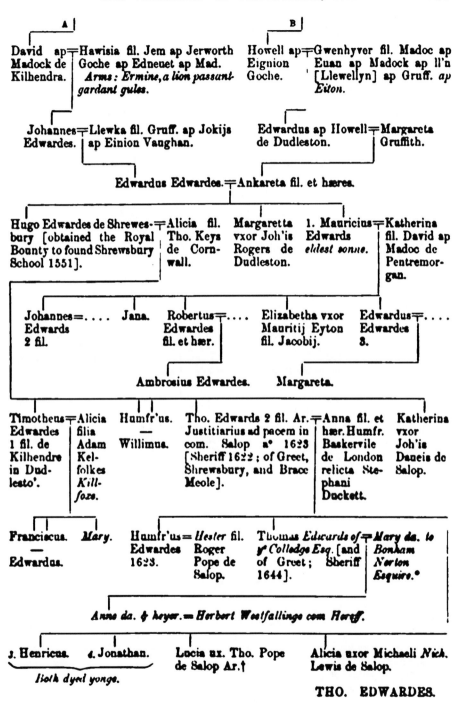

A

David ap=Hawisia fil. Jem ap Jerworth
Madock de | Goche ap Edneuet ap Mad.
Kilhendra. | *Arms: Ermine, a lion passant-
                 gardant gules.*

Johannes=Llewka fil. Gruff. ap Jokija
Edwardes. | ap Einion Vaughan.

B

Howell ap=Gwenhyver fil. Madoc ap
Eignion | Euan ap Madock ap ll'n
Goche. | [Llewellyn] ap Gruff. ap
              Eiton.

Edwardus ap Howell=Margareta
de Dudleston. | Gruffith.

Edwardus Edwardes.=Ankareta fil. et hæres.

Hugo Edwardes de Shrewes-=Alicia fil.   Margaretta   1. Mauricius=Katherina
bury [obtained the Royal | Tho. Keys   vxor Joh'is   Edwards | fil. David ap
Bounty to found Shrewsbury | de Corn- Rogers de   *eldest sonne.* | Madoc de
School 1551]. | wall.   Dudleston. | Pentremor-
                                                                  | gan.

Johannes=....   Jana.   Robertus=....   Elizabetha vxor   Edwardus=....
Edwards   Edwardes   Mauritij Eyton   Edwardes
2 fil.   fil. et hær.   fil. Jacobij.   3.

            Ambrosius Edwardes.   Margareta.

Timotheus=Alicia   Humfr'us.   Tho. Edwards 2 fil. Ar.=Anna fil. et   Katherina
Edwardes | filia   —   Justitiarius ad pacem in | hær. Humfr. vxor
1 fil. de | Adam   Willimus.   com. Salop aº 1623 | Baskervile Joh'is
Kilhendre | Kel-   [Sheriff 1622; of Greet, | de London   Daneis de
in Dud- | folkes   Shrewsbury, and Brace | relicta Ste- Salop.
lesto'. | *Kill-   Meole]. | phani
          | foxe. | Duckett.

Franciscus.   *Mary.*   Humfr'us=*Hester* fil.   *Thomas Edwards of*=*Mary da. to*
    —   Edwardes | Roger   *yᵉ Colledge Esq.* [and | *Bonham*
Edwardus.   1623. | Pope de   *of Greet; Sheriff | *Norton*
                               | Salop.   1644]. | *Esquire.*[*]

        Anne da. & heyer.==*Herbert Westfallinge com Heref.*

3. Henricus.   4. Jonathan.   Lucia ux. Tho. Pope   Alicia uxor Michaeli *Nich.*
                                 de Salop Ar.[†]   Lewis de Salop.
Both dyed yonge.

                                                THO. EDWARDES.

* Bonham Norton was the King's printer, and had arms assigned by Camden 1611.
† According to Harl. 1241 she married " Fra. Otley."

Edwards of Shrewsbury.

Harl. 1396, fo. 105[b].   Harl. 615, fo. 259.   S., fo. 87[a].

ARMS: Harl. 1396.—*Quarterly: 1 and 4, Gules, a chevron engrailed between three boars'* [heraldic tigers'] *heads erased at the neck argent, a crescent for difference; 2 and 3, Per bend sinister ermine and ermines, a lion rampant or* [TUDOR TREVOR]; *over all an escutcheon of pretence, Argent, a chevron gules between three hurts*—BASKERVILLE in Shrewsbury MS.

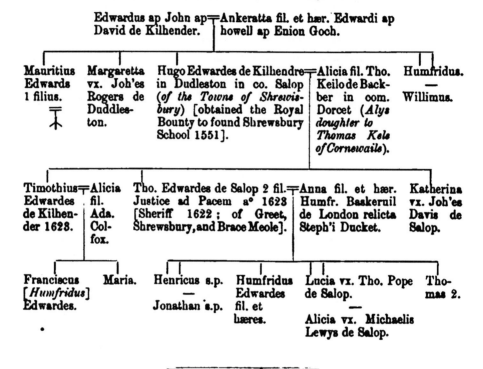

Edwardus ap John ap ⊤ Ankeratta fil. et hær. Edwardi ap
David de Kilhender. │ howell ap Enion Goch.

| Mauritius Edwards 1 filius. | Margaretta vx. Joh'es Rogers de Duddleston. | Hugo Edwardes de Kilhendre in Dudleston in co. Salop (*of the Towne of Shrewsbury*) [obtained the Royal Bounty to found Shrewsbury School 1551]. | Alicia fil. Tho. Keilo de Backber in com. Dorcet (*Alys doughter to Thomas Kele of Cornewaile*). | Humfridus. — Willimus. |

Timothius ⊤ Alicia
Edwardes │ fil.
de Kilhen- │ Ada.
der 1623. │ Col-
         │ fox.

Tho. Edwardes de Salop 2 fil. ⊤ Anna fil. et hær.
Justice ad Pacem a° 1623 │ Humfr. Baskeruil
[Sheriff 1622; of Greet, │ de London relicta
Shrewsbury, and Brace Meole]. │ Steph'i Ducket.

Katherina
vx. Joh'es
Davis de
Salop.

Franciscus
[*Humfridus*]
Edwardes.

Maria.

Henricus s.p.
—
Jonathan s.p.

Humfridus
Edwardes
fil. et
hæres.

Lucia vx. Tho. Pope
de Salop.
—
Alicia vx. Michaelis
Lewys de Salop.

Tho-
mas 2.

Egerton.

S., fo. 59.

[ARMS.—*Quarterly: 1 and 4, [Argent], a lion rampant [gules] between three pheons* [sable]; *2 and 3, [Or], three piles in point [gules], on a canton [argent] a griffin segreant [sable] [BASSETT]; all within a bordure engrailed.*
CREST.—*A lion rampant gules supporting an arrow point downwards feathered or.*
SUPPORTERS.—*Dexter: A horse argent ducally gorged or. Sinister: A griffin argent ducally gorged or.*
MOTTO.—SIC DONEC.

Sir Ralph Egerton of Ridley ⊤ Margarett da. & heire of Ralph Bassett
in com. Chester Kni. │ of Blower in co. Staff.

▲

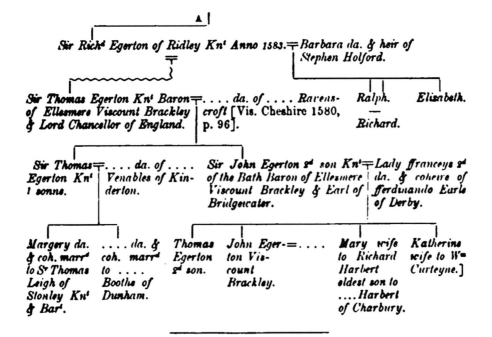

A

Sir Richd Egerton of Ridley Kn^t Anno 1583.⊤*Barbara da. & heir of Stephen Holford.*

Sir Thomas Egerton Kn^t Baron of Ellesmere Viscount Brackley & Lord Chancellor of England.⊤*.... da. of .... Ravenscroft [Vis. Cheshire 1580, p. 96].*

Ralph. — *Richard.*   *Elizabeth.*

Sir Thomas Egerton Kn^t 1 sonne.⊤*.... da. of .... Venables of Kinderton.*

Sir John Egerton 2^d son Kn^t of the Bath Baron of Ellesmere Viscount Brackley & Earl of Bridgewater.⊤*Lady ffranceys 2^d da. & coheire of fferdinando Earle of Derby.*

Margery da. & coh. marr^d to Sr Thomas Leigh of Stonley Kn^t & Bar^t.   *.... da. & coh. marr^d to .... Booths of Dunham.*   *Thomas Egerton 2^d son.*   *John Egerton Viscount Brackley.*⊤*....*   *Mary wife to Richard Harbert eldest son to ....Harbert of Charbury.*   *Katherine wife to Wm Curteyne.]*

Evans of Shrewsbury.

Harl. 1396, fo. 107.   Harl. 1241, fo. 142^b.   S., fo. 88^b.

ARMS: *Harl. 1396.—Quarterly : 1 and 4, Or, a cross moline between four lozenges azure ; 2 and 3, Argent, a cross engrailed couped the ends fleury sable between four Cornish choughs proper, on a chief azure a boar's head couped close of the first, IDNERTH BEN-VRAS.*

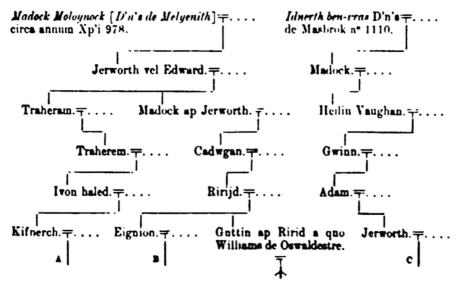

Madock Moloynock [D'n's de Melyenith]⊤*....*
circa annum Xp'i 978.

Idnerth ben-vras D'n's⊤*....*
de Maxbrok n° 1110.

Jerworth vel Edward.⊤*....*

Madock.⊤*....*

Traheran.⊤*....*   *Madock ap Jerworth.*⊤*....*

Heilin Vaughan.⊤*....*

Traherem.⊤*....*   *Cadwgan.*⊤*....*

Gwinn.⊤*....*

Ivon baled.⊤*....*   *Ririjd.*⊤*....*

Adam.⊤*....*

Kifnerch.⊤*....*   *Eignion.*⊤*....*   *Guttin ap Ririd a quo Williams de Oswaldestre.*

Jerworth.⊤*....*

A   B   C

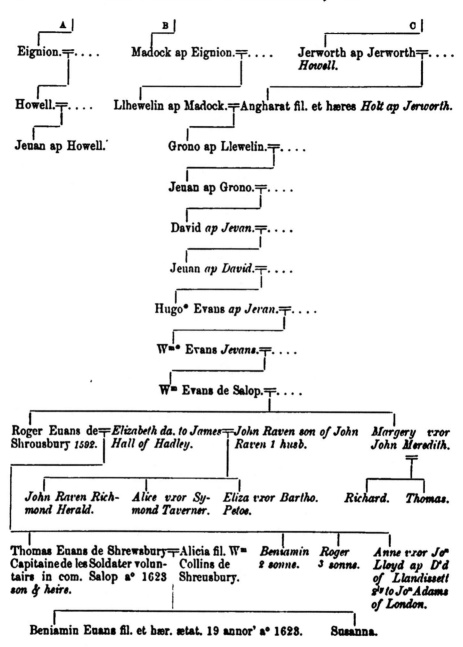

A |
Eignion.=....

Howell.=....

Jeuan ap Howell.

B |
Madock ap Eignion.=....

Llhewelin ap Madock.=Angharat fil. et hæres *Holt ap Jerworth.*

Grono ap Llewelin.=....

Jeuan ap Grono.=....

David *ap Jevan.*=....

Jeuan *ap David.*=....

Hugo[*] Evans *ap Jevan.*=....

W[m.] Evans *Jevans.*=....

Wm Evans de Salop.=....

C |
Jerworth ap Jerworth=....
Howell.

Roger Euans de=*Elizabeth da. to James*=John Raven son of John   *Margery* vxor
Shrousbury *1592.* | *Hall of Hadley.* | *Raven 1 husb.*   *John Meredith.*

John Raven Rich-   *Alice vxor Sy-*   *Eliza vxor Bartho.*   *Richard.*   *Thomas.*
mond Herald.   *mond Taverner.*   *Petoe.*

Thomas Euans de Shrewsbury=Alicia fil. W[m]   *Beniamin*   *Roger*   *Anne vxor Jo[n]*
Capitaine de les Soldater volun- | Collins de   *2 sonne.*   *3 sonne.*   *Lloyd ap D'd*
tairs in com. Salop a° 1623   Shreusbury.   *of Llandissett*
son & heire.   *s'v to Jo[n] Adams*
of London.

Beniamin Euans fil. et hær. ætat. 19 annor' a° 1623.   Susanna.

---

[*] Harl. 1241 has a *Jevan ap Hugh* between these two.

Evans of Oswestry and Treflach.

Harl. 1396, fo. 108.   S., fo. 89ᵇ.

ARMS: Harl. 1896.—*Quarterly: 1 and 4, Argent—sable* in Shrewsbury MS.—
a fesse between three fleurs-de-lis sable—or in Shrewsbury MS.; *2 and 3, Or,
a cross moline between four lozenges azure* [EVANS OF SHREWSBURY].

CREST.—*An arm embowed vested azure, cuffed or, holding in the hand a pink stalked
and leaved proper.*

Thomas Euance of Oswaldestre, exemplified by Sʳ Will'm Dethick Garter
vnder his hand and seale.

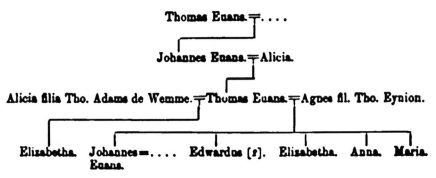

Tho. Euans de Oswaldestre in co. Salop.=Elianora fil. Ed'r'i Lloyd Ar.

Rich'us Euans de Treueleth *Trevelith* [or Tre-=Katherina fil. et cohær. Rich.
flach in the parish of Oswestry] in co. Salop Ar. | Lloyd de Swyn'ey.

Thomas=Anna fil. Dauid   Johannes   Edwardus Evans=Anna fil. Rogeri
Euans de Powell Theologia   8 fil.   de Treueleth in | Kynaston de Hor-
Ruebone | Doctoris.   com. Salop aᵒ | ley [Hordley] in
Ar.   1623.   co. Salop.

Eyton Euans   Richardus Euans fil.   Rogerus 2 [bapt. at Oswestry   Katherina.
fil. et hæres.   et hæres æt. 5 annor'   26 July 1621; Sheriff 1677].   —
           aᵒ 1623.   Margaretta.

ED. EVANCE.

Evans.

Harl. 1396, fo. 109.   S., fo. 91ᵇ.

Thomas Euans.=....

Johannes Euans.=Alicia.

Alicia filia Tho. Adams de Wemme.=Thomas Euans.=Agnes fil. Tho. Eynion.

Elizabetha.   Johannes=....   Edwardus [?].   Elizabetha.   Anna.   Maria.
           Euans.

A A

𝕰𝖛𝖆𝖓𝖘 𝖔𝖋 𝕹𝖔𝖗𝖙𝖍𝖔𝖕, 𝖈𝖔. 𝕱𝖑𝖎𝖓𝖙.

Harl. 1241, fo. 41.   Harl. 615, fo. 270^b.

ARMS: Harl. 1241.—*Quarterly: 1 and 4, Argent, a chevron between three boars' heads couped close sable;* 2 and 3, Vert, three eagles displayed in fesse or* [OWEN GWYNEDD].

CREST.—*On a ducal coronet or a boar's head couped close sable.*

ANOTHER COAT: Harl. 1241.—*Quarterly of twelve: 1, Argent, a chevron between three boars' heads couped close sable*, EDNEVED BENDE; *2, Vert, a lion rampant gules* [*Or, a lion rampant-regardant sable*], GWAITHVOED; *3, Gules, three lions passant in pale argent*, GRUFF AP CONAN; *4, Vert, three eagles displayed in fesse or*, OWEN GWYNEDD; *5, Argent, a chevron sable between three human heads affronté couped at the neck proper*, EDNEVED VYCHAN; *6, Vert, a buck trippant argent attired or*, LLOWARCH HOLBACH [LLOWARCH HOLBWRCH]; *7, Argent, three battle-axes sable, a crescent for difference*, HACKLUIT [OF YETTON, CO. HEREFORD]; *8, Gules, a chevron between three escallops argent*, MILBORNE [OF TILLINGTON, CO. GLOUC.]; *9, [Gules], fretty [ermine]*, EYNFORD [EYNESFORD]; *10, Sable, three roaches naiant in pale argent*, ROCH [ROCHE]; *11, Argent, a saltire engrailed azure within a bordure engrailed or*, DRECTES [DREET]; *12, Argent, a fesse counter-embattled sable fretty or between three lions passant gules*, CARDINGTON.

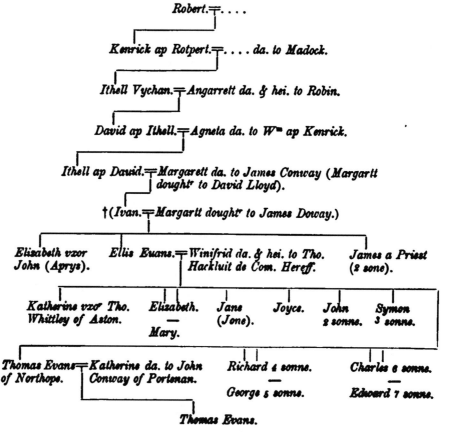

* In Harl. 615 the boars' heads are " sable, couped gules."
† This generation is omitted in Harl. 1241.

Eyton of Eyton and Dudleston, near Ellesmere.

Harl. 1396, fo. 111ᵇ.   Harl. 1241, fo. 54ᵇ.   S., ff. 95ᵇ, 96.

ARMS: Harl. 1396.—*Quarterly of twelve*: 1, *Ermine, a lion rampant azure*, ELYDER ; 2, *Argent, a chevron between three crows sable, each holding in the beak an ermine spot*, LLOWARCH AP BRANNE ; 3, *Paly of eight argent and gules, a lion rampant sable*, GRUFFITH MAYLOR ; 4, *Vert, a lion rampant or*, SANDIFF HARDD ; 5, *Azure, a lion rampant or*, KADOWEN ; 6, *Vert, three eagles displayed in fesse or*, OWYN GWYNEDD ; 7, *Vert, a chevron ermine between three wolves' heads erased argent*, RERED VLAITH ; 8, *Argent, a lion rampant sable, debruised by a bendlet sinister gules*, OWEN BROGINTYN ; 9, *Or [gules], a lion rampant gules [or] within a bordure of the second*, GWINWINN [GWENWYNWYN] ; 10, *Argent, on a chevron gules three fleurs-de-lis or*, MADOC DDU ; 11, *Ermine, a lion rampant sable*, KENDRIK RUALLON ; 12, *Vert, a boar statant or*, ROGER POWIS.

Elydor ap Rees Says.=[*Adda*] fil. Ednerth Bonfras [Adda dau. of Idnerth Benvras married Elydur ap Rees Says].

Melidor ap Elider.=. . . .

Kadwgan ap Melier.=Mynanwy fil. et hær. Edmund *Edneved* [*Ednevett*] ap Lowarch ap Branne.

Gruffith ap Kadwgan.=. . . . fil. *Fowke* Fitzwarrin de Whittington mil.

Lluellinus ap Gruff.=Ankaretta fil. et hær. Mredd. ap
de Eyton. | Madoc ap Gruffith Maylor.

Madoc ap Ll'n=Ankareta fil. David ap Grono ap Jer.
de Eyton. | ap Howell ap Mordigg ap Sandiff.

Jenan ap Madoc de Eyton.=Annesta filia Rogeri Puleston militis.

Madoc ap=Margareta filia Ed-   Ithel ap Gwrgen=. . . . fil. et hær. Madoc ap Elizaw
Euan de | nevet Gam ap Jer-   Vychan ap Gwr- | *Eliu* ap Owen Brogintinn [*Alia
Eyton. | worth Voell *ap Sᵗ*   gen ap Madoc de | et hær. ap Elisaeo ap Ivan ap
        | *Treuor.*   Pentlyn. | Owen Brogintin*].

Jacobus Eyton=Gwenllian fil. Kenwrick   Eynion ap Ithell.=. . . .
de Eyton. | ap Rotye *Rotpert.*

Johannes Eyton aᵒ 1477.=Gwenhiuer fil. et hær.

▲|

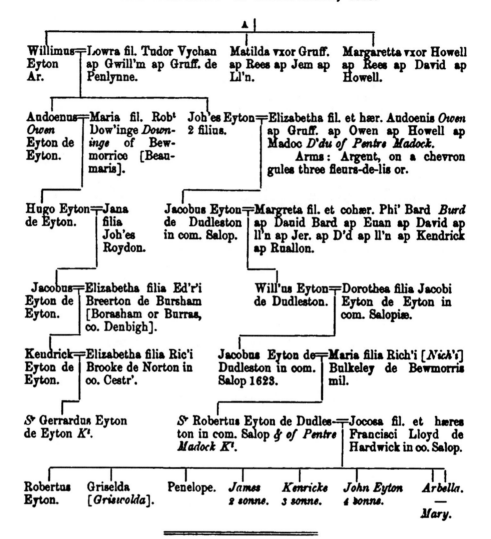

▲|

Willimus⊤Lowra fil. Tudor Vychan   Matilda vxor Gruff.   Margaretta vxor Howell
Eyton | ap Gwill'm ap Gruff. de   ap Rees ap Jem ap   ap Rees ap David ap
Ar. | Penlynne.   Ll'n.   Howell.

Audoenus⊤Maria fil. Robt   Joh'es Eyton⊤Elizabetha fil. et hær. Audoenis *Owen*
Owen | Dow'inge *Down-*   2 filius. | ap Gruff. ap Owen ap Howell ap
Eyton de| *inge* of Bew- | Madoc *D'du of Pentre Madock.*
Eyton. | morrice [Beau- | Arms: Argent, on a chevron
        | maris]. | gules three fleurs-de-lis or.

Hugo Eyton⊤Jana   Jacobus Eyton⊤Margreta fil. et cohær. Phi' Bard *Burd*
de Eyton. | filia de Dudleston| ap Dauid Bard ap Euan ap David ap
           | Joh'es in com. Salop.| ll'n ap Jer. ap D'd ap ll'n ap Kendrick
           | Roydon. | ap Ruallon.

Jacobus⊤Elizabetha filia Ed'r'i   Will'us Eyton⊤Dorothea filia Jacobi
Eyton de| Breerton de Bursham   de Dudleston.| Eyton de Eyton in
Eyton. | [Borasham or Burras, | com. Salopiæ.
        | co. Denbigh].

Keudrick⊤Elizabetha filia Ric'i   Jacobus Eyton de⊤Maria filia Rich'i [*Nich's*]
Eyton de| Brooke de Norton in   Dudleston in com.| Bulkeley de Bewmorris
Eyton. | co. Cestr'.   Salop 1623. | mil.

Sr Gerrardus Eyton   Sr Robertus Eyton de Dudles-⊤Jocosa fil. et hæres
de Eyton K^t.   ton in com. Salop *& of Pentre*| Francisci Lloyd de
                       Madock K^t. | Hardwick in co. Salop.

Robertus   Griselda   Penelope.   *James*   *Kenricke*   *John Eyton*   *Arbella.*
Eyton.   [*Griswolda*].   *2 sonne.* *3 sonne.*   *4 sonne.*   —
                                                                              Mary.

𝕰yton of 𝕰yton super 𝖂eald 𝕸ores.

Harl. 1396, fo. 112^b. Harl. 1241, fo. 74^b. S., ff. 96^b, 97.

ARMS: Harl. 1396.—*Quarterly: 1 and 4, Or, a fret azure* [EYTON]; *2 and 3,
     Gules, two bars ermine* [PANTULF].
CREST.—*A bird's head erased sable, holding in the beak a laurel branch vert.*
ANOTHER COAT: Harl. 1396.—*Quarterly: 1 and 4, Gules, two bars ermine;
     2 and 3, Or, a fret azure.*
CREST.—*A reindeer's head or, holding in the mouth an acorn gold, slipped and leaved
     vert.*
ANOTHER CREST: Shrewsbury MS.—*A lion's head or, holding in the mouth a barrel or.*

William Lord of Eyton sans date.⊤. . . .
▲|

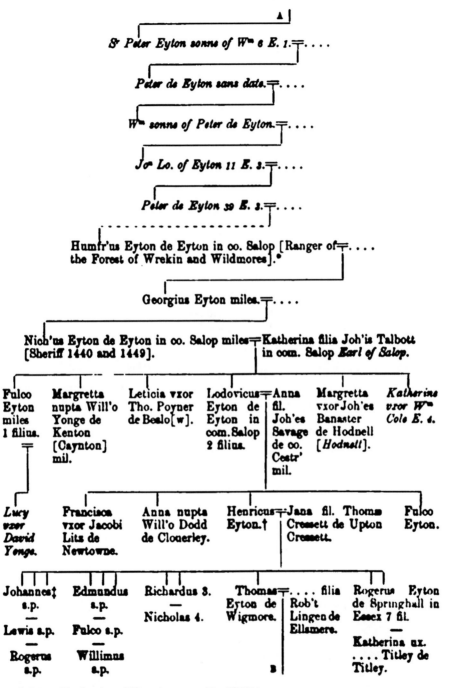

Sr Peter Eyton sonne of Wm 6 E. 1. = ...

Peter de Eyton sans date. = ...

Wm sonne of Peter de Eyton. = ...

Joᵣ Lo. of Eyton 11 E. 3. = ...

Peter de Eyton 39 E. 3. = ...

Humfr'us Eyton de Eyton in co. Salop [Ranger of = ...
the Forest of Wrekin and Wildmores].*

Georgius Eyton miles. = ...

Nich'us Eyton de Eyton in co. Salop miles = Katherina filia Joh'is Talbott
[Sheriff 1440 and 1449].   in com. Salop *Earl of Salop.*

| Fulco Eyton miles 1 filius. = | Margretta nupta Will'o Yonge de Kenton [Caynton] mil. | Leticia vxor Tho. Poyner de Bealo[w]. | Lodovicus = Anna fil. Joh'es Savage de co. Cestr' mil. Eyton de Eyton in com. Salop 2 filius. | Margretta vxor Joh'es Banaster de Hodnell [Hodnell]. | Katherine vxor Wm Cole E. 4. |

Lucy vxor David Yonge. | Francisca vxor Jacobi Litz de Newtowne. | Anna nupta Will'o Dodd de Clouerley. | Henricus = Jana fil. Thoms Cressett de Upton Cressett. Eyton.† | Fulco Eyton.

| Johannes‡ s.p. — Lewis s.p. — Rogerus s.p. | Edmundus s.p. — Fulco s.p. — Willimus s.p. | Richardus 3. — Nicholas 4. | Thomas = ... filia Rob't Lingen de Ellsmere. Eyton de Wigmore. | Rogerus Eyton de Springhall in Essex 7 fil. — Katherina ux. .... Titley de Titley. |

B

* John, elder brother of Humphrey, was Sheriff 1394.
† Harl. 1396 differs from this pedigree, but is evidently incorrect, and Shrewsbury MS. has been followed above.
‡ John, Lewis, Roger, Edmund, Fulke, William, Richard, and Nicholas are all omitted in Shrewsbury MS.

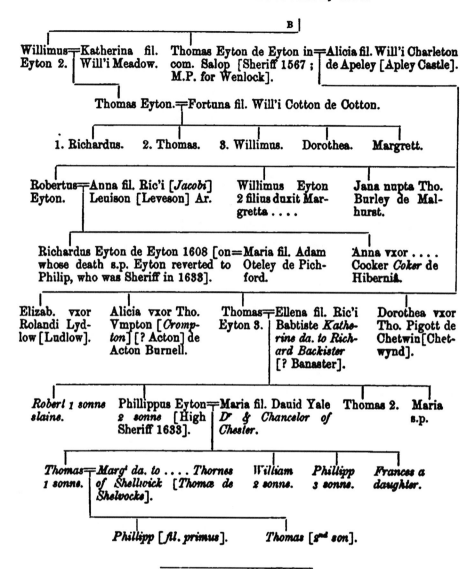

B

Willimus=Katherina fil.   Thomas Eyton de Eyton in=Alicia fil. Will'i Charleton
Eyton 2. | Will'i Meadow.   com. Salop [Sheriff 1567 ;   de Apeley [Apley Castle].
                             M.P. for Wenlock].

Thomas Eyton.=Fortuna fil. Will'i Cotton de Cotton.

1. Richardus.   2. Thomas.   3. Willimus.   Dorothea.   Margrett.

Robertus=Anna fil. Ric'i [Jacobi]   Willimus Eyton   Jana nupta Tho.
Eyton. | Leuison [Leveson] Ar.   2 filius duxit Mar-   Burley de Mal-
                                       gretta . . . .   hurst.

Richardus Eyton de Eyton 1608 [on=Maria fil. Adam   Anna vxor . . . .
whose death s.p. Eyton reverted to   Oteley de Pich-   Cooker Coker de
Philip, who was Sheriff in 1633].   ford.   Hiberniâ.

Elizab.   vxor   Alicia vxor Tho.   Thomas=Ellena fil. Ric'i   Dorothea vxor
Rolandi Lyd-   Vmpton [Cromp-   Eyton 3.| Babtiste Kathe-   Tho. Pigott de
low [Ludlow].   ton] [? Acton] de   rine da. to Rich- Chetwin[Chet-
                    Acton Burnell.   ard Backister   wynd].
                                                  [? Banaster].

Robert 1 sonne   Phillippus Eyton=Maria fil. Dauid Yale   Thomas 2.   Maria
slaine.   2 sonne [High   Dr & Chancelor of   s.p.
                    Sheriff 1633].   Chester.

Thomas=Marg⁴ da. to . . . . Thornes   William   Phillipp   Frances a
1 sonne.| of Shellwick [Thomæ de   2 sonne.   3 sonne.   daughter.
        | Shelvocks].

Phillipp [fil. primus].   Thomas [2ⁿᵈ son].

Fermor or Farmer of Hay Park.

Harl. 615, ff. 239ᵇ, 240.

(Henry Hanbury.=Alys doughter to Robert Salveyn Knyght.

William Boweles mar.=Agnes doughter to Henry Hanbury.

William Boweles mar.=Elizabethe doughter to John Gifforde Knight.

▲

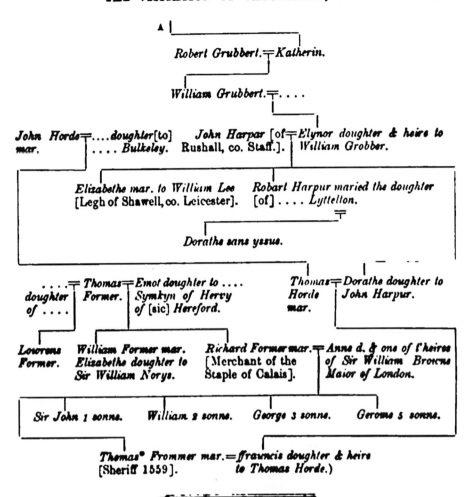

▲

Robert Grubbert.=Katherin.

William Grubbert.=....

John Horde=....doughter [to]   John Harpar [of=E'lynor doughter & heire to
mar.   .... Bulkeley.   Rushall, co. Staff.]. William Grobber.

Elizabethe mar. to William Lee   Robart Harpur maried the doughter
[Legh of Shawell, co. Leicester]. [of] .... Lyttelton.
=

Dorathe sans yssue.

....=Thomas=Emot doughter to ....   Thomas=Dorathe doughter to
doughter | Former. | Symkyn of Hervy   Horde | John Harpur.
of .... | | of [sic] Hereford.   mar. |

Lowrens | William Former mar.   Richard Former mar.=Anne d. & one of t'heires
Former. | Elizabethe doughter to   [Merchant of the | of Sir William Browne
 | Sir William Norys.   Staple of Calais]. Maior of London.

Sir John 1 sonne.   William 2 sonne.   George 3 sonne.   Gerome 5 sonne.

Thomas* Frommer mar.=ffrauncis doughter & heire
[Sheriff 1559].   to Thomas Horde.)

Fewtrell of Downe.

Harl. 1396, fo. 118ᵇ. S., fo. 106ᵇ.

ARMS: Shrewsbury MS.—*Per chevron argent and sable, three mullets counter-changed, on a chief sable three leopards' faces argent.*
CREST.—*A tiger's head argent, collared sable, thereon three mullets argent.*

Joh'is Fewterell de Downe=.... fil .... Wilcoks [Wilcocks alias Wil-
in com. Salop.   kinson] de Broseley in co. Salop.

Thomas | Leonardus Fewterell=.... fil .... Bechcote de   Johannes=....
s.p. | de Downe 3 fil. | Bechcote in com. Salop.
 | ▲   B

* Thomas Fermour, or Farmer, the Sheriff of Salop in 1559, was seated at Somerton, co. Oxford, but resided occasionally in Salop on his wife's property. She was the only child and heiress of Thomas Hord of Hord's Park, and relict of Edward Rawlegh of Farmingho in Norfolk.

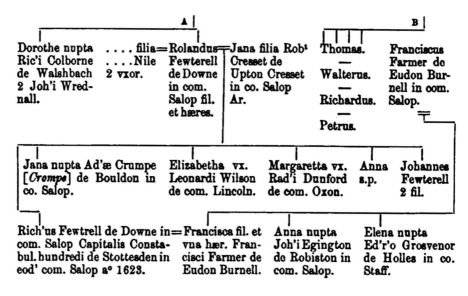

Dorothe nupta Ric'i Colborne de Walshbach 2 Joh'i Wrednall.	.... filia ....Nile 2 vxor.	Rolandus Fewterell de Downe in com. Salop fil. et hæres.	Jana filia Rob'ᵗ Cresset de Upton Cresset in co. Salop Ar.	Thomas. — Walterus. — Richardus. — Petrus.	Franciscus Farmer de Eudon Burnell in com. Salop.

Jana nupta Ad'æ Crumpe [Crompe] de Bouldon in co. Salop.	Elizabetha vx. Leonardi Wilson de com. Lincoln.	Margaretta vx. Rad'i Dunford de com. Oxon.	Anna s.p.	Johannes Fewterell 2 fil.

Rich'us Fewtrell de Downe in com. Salop Capitalis Constabul. hundredi de Stottesden in eod' com. Salop aᵒ 1623.	Francisca fil. et vna hær. Francisci Farmer de Eudon Burnell.	Anna nupta Joh'i Egington de Robiston in com. Salop.	Elena nupta Ed'r'o Grosvenor de Holles in co. Staff.

RICHARD FFEWTERELL.

Fisher of Ludlow.

Harl. 1396, fo. 119.   S., fo. 107.

ARMS: Harl. 1396.—*Per bend or and gules, a gryphon segreant counterchanged within a bordure vair.*

CREST.—*On a branch lying fessways trunked ragulé, and sprouting from the dexter end a honeysuckle proper, a kingfisher of the same holding in the beak a fish or.*

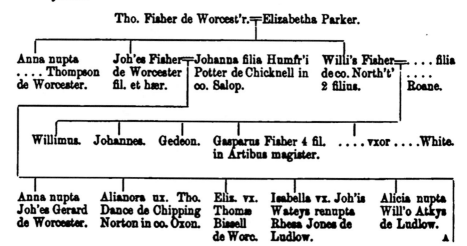

Tho. Fisher de Worcest'r.=Elizabetha Parker.

Anna nupta .... Thompson de Worcester.	Joh'es Fisher de Worcester fil. et hær.=Johanna filia Humfr'i Potter de Chicknell in co. Salop.	Willi's Fisher de co. North't' 2 filius.	= .... filia .... Roane.

Willimus.	Johannes.	Gedeon.	Gasparus Fisher 4 fil. in Artibus magister.	.... vxor .... White.

Anna nupta Joh'es Gerard de Worcester.	Alianora ux. Tho. Dance de Chipping Norton in co. Oxon.	Eliz. vx. Thomæ Bissell de Worc.	Isabella vx. Joh'is Wateys renupta Rhesa Jones de Ludlow.	Alicia nupta Will'o Atkys de Ludlow.

A

| Phil-lippus. | Rich'us Fisher de Ludlow in co. Salop Alderma' villæ Salop fil. et hær. 1623.=Maria filia Tho. Churchny de Tewesbury in co. Salop. | | Tho. Fisher de Zirickseas in Holland 3 fil. a° 1623. |

✦

| Johannes 2. | Tho. Fisher fil. et hær. apparens ætat. 21 a° 1623 in Artibus magister. | Edwardus. | Johanna. —— Maria. | Anna. —— Juditha. | Martha. |

RICHARD FFISHER.   THOMAS FFISHER.

———

Fletcher of Chester and Condover.

Harl. 1396, fo. 119[b].   Harl. 1241, fo. 132[b].   S., fo. 100[b].

ARMS: Harl. 1396.—*Sable, two battle-axes in saltire argent, each ducally crowned or.*

John Fletcher of Denbighe.=....

| W⁰ Fletcher Alderman.=Ellin da. to James Bracy of Teirton [Tiverton]. | Tho. Fletcher Alderman of Chester.=Alice da. to James Bracy of Teirton in co. Chest'.* |

| | Tho. Fletcher Mayor of Chester. | William. | Raufe. |

| John Fletcher=Margrett da. to Lawr. 1598. Woodnet *Hodnett*. | Tho. Fletcher Vicar of Condoer in co. Salop 1598.=Eliz. da. to John Hall. |

| | Rob' Fletcher Sheriff of Chest'. | Joane. |

———

Forster of Evelith near Shifnall.

S., ff. 300[a], 300[b].

[ARMS.—*Quarterly: 1, Quarterly per fesse indented [argent] and [sable], in first and fourth quarters a bugle-horn stringed [of the second]; 2, Argent, three pheons, two and one, sable; impaling, Or, fretté ...., on a chief or three round buckles gules, tongues to dexter [ROWLEY ?].*

John Forster of Evelith.=Isabella da. to .... Kuffin of Abertanat.

A

* The wife's name is omitted in Shrewsbury MS.

B B

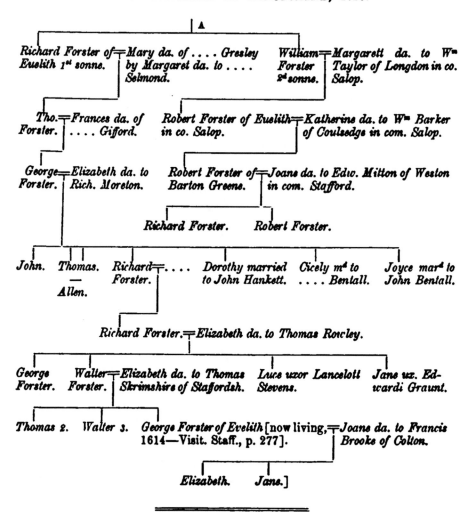

▲

Richard Forster of=Mary da. of .... Gresley   William=Margarett da. to W^m
Euelith 1st sonne. | by Margaret da. to ....   Forster | Taylor of Longdon in co.
                     | Selmond.   2^d sonne. | Salop.

Tho.=Frances da. of   Robert Forster of Euelith=Katherine da. to Wm Barker
Forster. | .... Gifford.   in co. Salop. | of Coulsedge in com. Salop.

George=Elizabeth da. to   Robert Forster of=Joane da. to Edw. Milton of Weston
Forster. | Rich. Moreton.   Barton Greene. | in com. Stafford.

          Richard Forster.   Robert Forster.

John.   Thomas.   Richard=....   Dorothy married   Cicely m^d to   Joyce mar^d to
         —   Forster.   to John Hankett. .... Bentall.   John Bentall.
        Allen.

          Richard Forster.=Elizabeth da. to Thomas Rowley.

George   Waller=Elizabeth da. to Thomas   Luce uxor Lancelott   Jane ux. Ed-
Forster.   Forster. | Skrimshire of Staffordsh. Stevens.   wardi Graunt.

Thomas 2.   Waller 3.   George Forster of Evelith [now living,=Joane da. to Francis
                        1614—Visit. Staff., p. 277]. | Brooke of Colton.

                              Elizabeth.   Jane.]

𝔉orster of 𝔚atling 𝔖treet and 𝔖utton 𝔐adoc.

Harl. 1396, fo. 117.   Harl. 1241, fo. 44.   Harl. 615, fo. 260^b.   S., fo. 105^a.

ARMS: Harl. 1396.—*Quarterly: 1, Quarterly per fesse indented argent and sable, in
the first and fourth quarters a bugle-horn stringed of the second,* FORSTER ;
2, Sable, a cross patonce argent, UPTON ; *3, Argent, on a bend azure three
oat-sheaves or,* OTELEY ; *4, Sable, a pale argent,* WEAVER.

CREST.—*A talbot statant argent, collared gules, lined or, the end tied in a knot.*

          Richard Forster.=....

          Roger Foster.=....

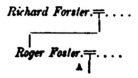

▲

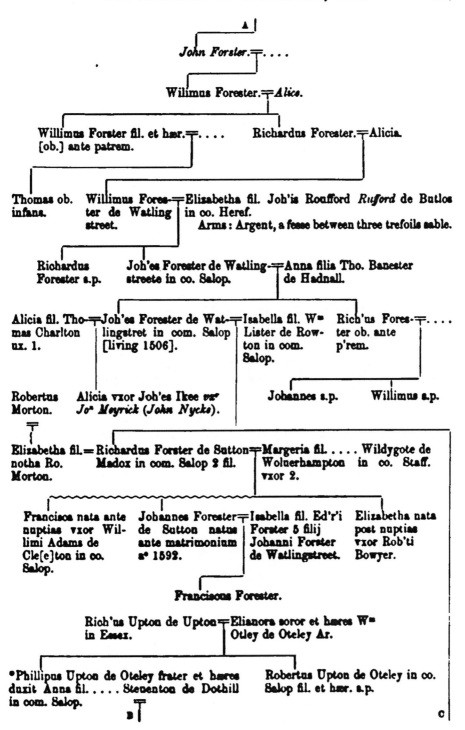

A |

John Forster.⊤....

Willimus Forester.⊤*Alice.*

Willimus Forster fil. et hær.⊤....
[ob.] ante patrem.

Richardus Forester.⊤Alicia.

Thomas ob.
infans.

Willimus Fores-⊤Elizabetha fil. Joh'is Roufford *Rufford* de Butlos
ter de Watling | in co. Heref.
street.   Arms : Argent, a fesse between three trefoils sable.

Richardus
Forester s.p.

Joh'es Forester de Watling-⊤Anna filia Tho. Banester
streete in co. Salop.   de Hadnall.

Alicia fil. Tho-⊤Joh'es Forester de Wat-⊤Isabella fil. Wm Rich'us Fores-⊤....
mas Charlton | lingstret in com. Salop | Lister de Row- ter ob. ante
ux. 1.   [living 1506].   ton in com. p'rem.
                         Salop.

Robertus   Alicia vxor Joh'es Ikee *vz*
Morton.   *Jo^n Meyrick (John Nycke).*

Johannes s.p.   Willimus s.p.

Elizabetha fil.=Richardus Forster de Sutton⊤Margeria fil .... Wildygote de
notha Ro.   Madox in com. Salop 2 fil. | Wolnerhampton in co. Staff.
Morton.   vxor 2.

Francisca nata ante   Johannes Forester⊤Isabella fil. Ed'r'i   Elizabetha nata
nuptias vxor Wil-   de Sutton natus | Forster 5 filij   post nuptias
limi Adams de   ante matrimonium | Johanni Forster   vxor Rob'ti
Cle[e]ton in co.   a° 1592.   de Watlingstreet.   Bowyer.
Salop.

Franciscus Forester.

Rich'us Upton de Upton⊤Elianora soror et hæres W^m
in Essex.   Otley de Oteley Ar.

*Phillipus Upton de Oteley frater et hæres
duxit Anna fil .... Steventon de Dothill
in com. Salop.

Robertus Upton de Oteley in co.
Salop fil. et hær. s.p.

B ⊤

C |

* Harl. 1241 makes this Philip "son of Stephen, son of Richard."

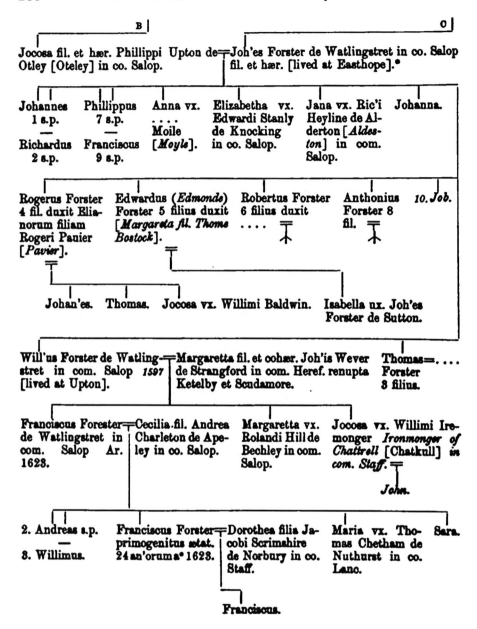

B |

C

Jocosa fil. et hær. Phillippi Upton de⊤Joh'es Forster de Watlingstret in co. Salop
Otley [Oteley] in co. Salop. | fil. et hær. [lived at Easthope].*

| Johannes 1 s.p. — Richardus 2 s.p. | Phillippus 7 s.p. — Franciscus 9 s.p. | Anna vx. .... Moile [Moyle]. | Elizabetha vx. Edwardi Stanly de Knocking in co. Salop. | Jana vx. Ric'i Heyline de Alderton [Aldeston] in com. Salop. | Johanna. |

Rogerus Forster 4 fil. duxit Elianorum filiam Rogeri Panier [Pavier].

Edwardus (Edmonde) Forster 5 filius duxit [Margareta fil. Thome Bostock].

Robertus Forster 6 filius duxit .... ⊤

Anthonius Forster 8 fil. ⊤

10. Job.

Johan'es.   Thomas.   Jocosa vx. Willimi Baldwin.

Isabella ux. Joh'es Forster de Sutton.

Will'us Forster de Watling-⊤Margaretta fil. et cohær. Joh'is Wever
stret in com. Salop *1597* | de Strangford in com. Heref. renupta
[lived at Upton]. | Ketelby et Scudamore.

Thomas=....
Forster
3 filius.

Franciscus Forester⊤Cecilia fil. Andrea
de Watlingstret in | Charleton de Ape-
com. Salop Ar. | ley in co. Salop.
1623.

Margaretta vx. Rolandi Hill de Bechley in com. Salop.

Jocosa vx. Willimi Iremonger *Ironmonger of Chattrell* [Chatkull] *in com. Staff.* ⊤

John.

2. Andreas s.p. — 3. Willimus.

Franciscus Forster⊤Dorothea filia Ja-
primogenitus ætat. | cobi Scrimshire
24 an'orum* 1623. | de Norbury in co.
| Staff.

Maria vx. Thomas Chetham de Nuthurst in co. Lanc.

Sara.

Franciscus.

                 FRAN. FORESTER.

* This John, by a grant, 1520, from Henry VIII., on account of certain diseases in his head, had leave to wear his hat at all times, " as well in our presence as elsewhere."

Fowler of Harnage Grange.

Harl. 1896, fo. 118.   Harl. 1241, fo. 128.   8., ff. 105ᵇ, 106.

ARMS: Harl. 1396.—*Quarterly of nine:* 1, *Azure, on a chevron argent—chevron engrailed or in Harl. 1241—between three lions passant-guardant or as many crosses moline sable, a mullet on a crescent for difference*—FOWLER in Shrewsbury MS.; 2, *Per pale sable and argent, an eagle displayed with two heads counterchanged, ducally gorged or*—LOVEDAY in Shrewsbury MS.; 3, *Ermine, on a canton gules an owl argent—owl or in Harl.* 1241—BARTON in Shrewsbury MS. [FOWLER OF RICOTE]; 4, *Barry of six gules and argent, on a chief or a lion passant azure*—INGLEFIELD in Shrewsbury MS.; 5, *Argent, a chevron between three birds sable;* 6, *Argent, three wolves' heads erased gules, within a bordure azure charged with eight towers or—billets in Harl. 1241* [BERRY ?]; 7, *Vairy argent and gules* [GRESLEY]; 8, *Azure, two bars argent, over all a bend componée or and gules*—LEIGH in Shrewsbury MS. [LEE, BISHOP OF LICHFIELD*]; 9, *Vert, three goats salient argent*—TROLLOP in Shrewsbury MS.

CREST.—*A cubit arm erect vested azure, cuffed . . . . , the hand proper holding a hawk's lure vert, feathered argent, garnished and lined or, the line twined round the arm.*

[Visit. Oxford gives the gravestone in Hasley Church to Dame Julian Fowler of Rycote, who died 1827, which quarters above, 3 for Fowler, 4 for Inglefield, and 7 for Gresley.

In Dugdale's MS. Staff. Vis.: Crest—A cubit arm holding an open book of music.   Given also in Harl. MS. 6128.]

Sʳ Johannes Fowler de Foxley in co. Buck.=. . . . fil. et hæres . . . . Loueday.

Sʳ Hen. Fowler de Foxley.=. . . . soror et hæres Johan's Barton *Berton*.

Will's Fowler de Ricott in com.=Cecilia fil. et vna hæredem Nicholai
Oxon. miles. | Inglefeld militis.

Richardus Fowler miles=Jana fil. Joh'is Danvers   Cecilia vxor Tho. Rookes
Cancellarius Ducatus   de Cothorp in com. Oxon.   [*Brookes*] de Falley in com.
Lancastria t'pe E. 4.   Ar.   Buck. Ar.

Richardus Fowler miles.=Eliza. fil. Thomæ et soror Andreæ D'ni Windesore.

Thomas Fowler 2=Margeria filia   Will'us Lee de Morpath=Isabella *Eliza.* fil. et
filius Armiger pro | . . . . Colenile   in co. Northumbriæ   hæres Andreæ
corpore R' Ed'ri 4. | *Mary da. to*   Thessurarius Berwici.   Trollop militis.
                    | *Edward Lee.*

Edward Fowler of Twickenham=. . . .   Tho. Fowler=Mary da. to . . . . Colevill.
in com. Rutland ["Twitnam by   Esq. of the   Arms: Or, ten billets
Richmond"—Vis. Stafford].   body to E. 4.   gules.

A   B   C

* In Bedford's 'Blazon of Episcopacy,' pages 56 and 130, the arms of Rowland Lee, who was Bishop of Lichfield 1534-1543, are given as, Vert, three bulls salient argent; and the above, the well-known coat of the Leghs of Adlington, co. Chester, is attributed to the See of Chester. It will be seen by our pedigree, that the impaled coat in Lansdowne MS. 255, quoted by Mr. Bedford, merely represents Bishop Lee's father impaling the three goats, not bulls, for Trollop.

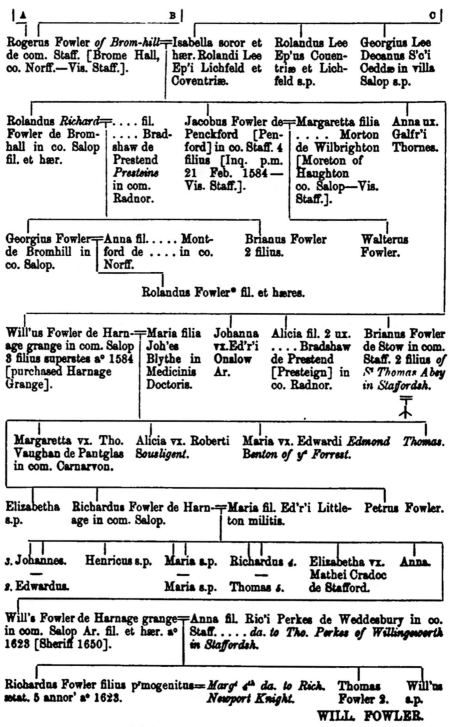

| A | B | | C |

Rogerus Fowler *of Brom-hill* de com. Staff. [Brome Hall, co. Norff.—Vis. Staff.]. =Isabella soror et hær. Rolandi Lee Ep'i Lichfeld et Coventriæ.

Rolandus Lee Ep'us Couentriæ et Lichfeld s.p.

Georgius Lee Decanus S'c'i Ceddæ in villa Salop s.p.

Rolandus *Richard* Fowler de Bromhall in co. Salop fil. et hær. =.... fil. .... Bradshaw de Prestend *Presteine* in com. Radnor.

Jacobus Fowler de Penckford [Penford] in co. Staff. 4 filius [Inq. p.m. 21 Feb. 1584—Vis. Staff.]. =Margaretta filia .... Morton de Wilbrighton [Moreton of Haughton co. Salop—Vis. Staff.].

Anna ux. Galfr'i Thornes.

Georgius Fowler de Bromhill in co. Salop. =Anna fil. .... Montford de .... in co. Norff.

Brianus Fowler 2 filius.

Walterus Fowler.

Rolandus Fowler* fil. et hæres.

Will'us Fowler de Harnage grange in com. Salop 3 filius superstes a° 1584 [purchased Harnage Grange]. =Maria filia Joh'es Blythe in Medicinis Doctoris.

Johanna vx.Ed'r'i Onslow Ar.

Alicia fil. 2 ux. .... Bradshaw de Prestend [Presteign] in co. Radnor.

Brianus Fowler de Stow in com. Staff. 2 filius *of S' Thomas Abey in Staffordsh.*

Margaretta vx. Tho. Vaughan de Pantglas in com. Carnarvon.

Alicia vx. Roberti *Sousligent.*

Maria vx. Edwardi *Edmond Benton of y' Forrest.*

Thomas.

Elizabetha s.p.

Richardus Fowler de Harnage in com. Salop. =Maria fil. Ed'r'i Littleton militis.

Petrus Fowler.

s. Johannes.

s. Edwardus.

Henricus s.p.

Maria s.p.

Maria s.p.

Richardus *4.*

Thomas *s.*

Elizabetha vx. Mathei Cradoc de Stafford.

Anna.

Will's Fowler de Harnage grange in com. Salop Ar. fil. et hær. a° 1623 [Sheriff 1650]. =Anna fil. Ric'i Perkes de Weddesbury in co. Staff. .... *da. to Tho. Perkes of Willingsworth in Staffordsh.*

Richardus Fowler filius p'mogenitus ætat. 5 annor' a° 1623. =*Marg' 4th da. to Rich. Newport Knight.*

Thomas Fowler 2.

Will'us s.p.

WILL. FOWLER.

* This son is omitted in Shrewsbury MS.

Fox of Caynham, Bromfield, Greet, etc.

Harl. 1396, fo. 115. Harl. 1241, fo. 4. Harl. 615, fo. 264ᵇ. S., ff. 102ᵃ—105ᵇ.

ARMS: Harl. 1396.—*Quarterly of eight: 1, Argent, a chevron between three foxes' heads erased gules,* FOX; *2, Argent, on a bend sable three dolphins embowed or,* STOKE; *3, Per pale indented sable and argent, on the sinister side a billet urdé at the foot of the first,* STEVINTON; *4, Gules, two lions couchant—passant in pale tails coward in* Shrewsbury MS.—*or,* PEDWARDYN; *5, Azure, a lion rampant holding a battle-axe, within a bordure engrailed, all or,* PIKENHAM; *6, Argent, three chevronels gules, a label of as many points azure [throughout],* BARRINGTON; *7, Azure, a buck lodged argent,* DOWNE; *8, Or, a fesse quarterly azure and gules, in the first and fourth quarters three fleurs-de-lis of the first, and in the second and third a lion passant-guardant gold, all within a bordure gobonée argent and of the second,* SOMERSETT.

ARMS: Harl. 1396: FOX OF BROMFELD AND WHICHOOT.—*Quarterly of ten:* 1, FOX; 2, STOKE; 3, STEVINTON; 4, PEDWARDYN; 5, *Argent, a pale fusilly sable,* DANIEL *in* Shrewsbury MS.; 6, *Azure, a chevron between three spears' heads argent imbrued gules;* 7, PIKENHAM; 8, BARRINGTON; 9, *Ermine, two boars passant gules,* WHICHCOTE *in* Shrewsbury MS.; 10, DOWNE.

CREST.—*A fox statant gules.*

MOTTO.—FIDELIS ESTO.

ARMS: Harl. 1396: FOX OF GREET.—*Quarterly of six:* 1 and 6, FOX; 2, STOKE; 3, STEVINTON; 4, PEDWARDYN; 5, DOWNE; *over all a martlet charged with an annulet for difference.*

Wilimus Stoke.⊤Johanna fil. et hær. Gregorij Stebinton [*Stevinton*] *Jane da. & heire to George Otley of Steventon com. Sal.*

Joh'es Fox de Knighton⊤Johanna *Jane* in Wales occisus in bello│fil. et hæres contra Owen Glendowr.│Will'm' Stoke.

Willimus Ped⊤Johanna fil. Will'i wardin de co.│Harley *sister to Wᵐ* Heref.│*de Harley.*

Thomas Fox de Pedwardin in Wigmore⊤Anna fil. et hæres land in com. Heref.│Will'i Pedwardyn.

Rogerus Fox de Ped⊤Elizabetha fil. wardyn et Stoke in│Ric'i Cludd de co. Hereford.│Orleton in co. Salop.

Johan'es Picken⊤Johan'a fil. et hær. .... ham *Pickenham*│Barrington de Barrington de Essex.│hall [Essex] *Jane sister & heire to .... Bassington.*

Edmundus Fox de⊤Katherina fil. et cohæres Stoke in co. Salop.│Joh'is Pickenham *sister & coh. to Jo͞r Peckenham.*

Ric'us Downe de⊤Alisona fil. et Ludlow in com.│hær. Joh's .... Salop.

Willimus Fox de S͡t Johns⊤Johanna *Jane* fil. et hær. Richardi in Ludlow.│Downe (*Downs*).

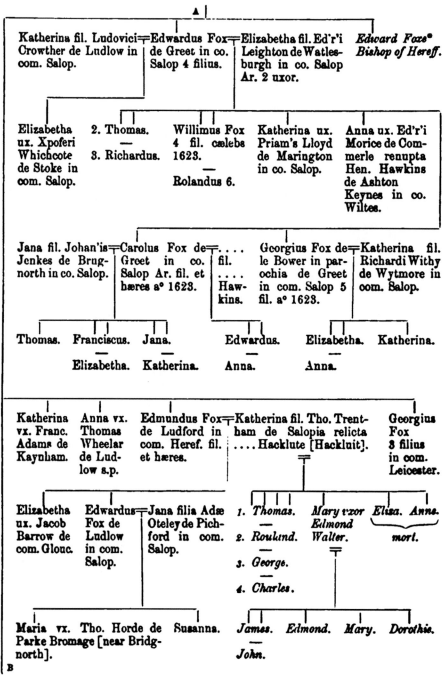

▲

Katherina fil. Ludovici ═ Edwardus Fox ┬ Elizabetha fil. Ed'r'i   *Edward Foxe*
Crowther de Ludlow in │ de Greet in co. │ Leighton de Watles-   *Bishop of Hereff.*
com. Salop. │ Salop 4 filius. │ burgh in co. Salop
│ Ar. 2 uxor.

Elizabetha   2. Thomas.   Willimus Fox   Katherina ux.   Anna ux. Ed'r'i
ux. Xpoferi   3. Richardus.   4 fil. cælebs   Priam's Lloyd   Morice de Com-
Whichcote   1623.   de Marington   merle renupta
de Stoke in   Rolandus 6.   in co. Salop.   Hen. Hawkins
com. Salop.   de Ashton
                                                                    Keynes in co.
                                                                    Wiltes.

Jana fil. Johan'is ═ Carolus Fox de ┬ . . . .   Georgius Fox de ═ Katherina fil.
Jenkes de Brug-   │ Greet in co.   │ fil.   le Bower in par- Richardi Withy
north in co. Salop. │ Salop Ar. fil. et │ . . . . ochia de Greet   de Wytmore in
                    │ hæres aº 1623. │ Haw-   in com. Salop 5   com. Salop.
                    │   │ kins.   fil. aº 1623.

Thomas.   Franciscus.   Jana.   Edwardus.   Elizabetha.   Katherina.

           Elizabetha.   Katherina.   Anna.   Anna.

Katherina   Anna vx.   Edmundus Fox ┬ Katherina fil. Tho. Trent-   Georgius
vx. Franc.   Thomas   de Ludford in │ ham de Salopia relicta   Fox
Adams de   Wheelar   com. Heref. fil. │ . . . . Hacklute [Hackluit]. 3 filius
Kaynham.   de Lud-   et hæres.   in com.
             low s.p.   Leicester.

Elizabetha   Edwardus ═ Jana filia Adæ   1. *Thomas.*   *Mary vxor*   *Eliza. Anne.*
ux. Jacob   Fox de   Oteley de Pich-   *Edmond*
Barrow de   Ludlow   ford in com.   2. *Roulund.*   *Walter.*   *mort.*
com. Glouc.   in com.   Salop.
              Salop.   3. *George.*

                                           4. *Charles.*

Maria vx. Tho. Horde de   Susanna.   *James.   Edmond.   Mary.   Dorothie.*
Parke Bromage [near Bridg-
north].   *John.*

B

* Not given in Shrewsbury MS. Edmund Foxe, Bishop of Hereford, obtained a lease of the property of the suppressed Priory of St. John the Baptist at Ludlow 20 Dec. 1537, and settled them to the use of Charles Fox, brother of said Edmund.—Duke's 'Hist. of Shropshire,' xliv. This proves the brother, but *Edward* Fox was translated to the Bishopric of Hereford in 1535.

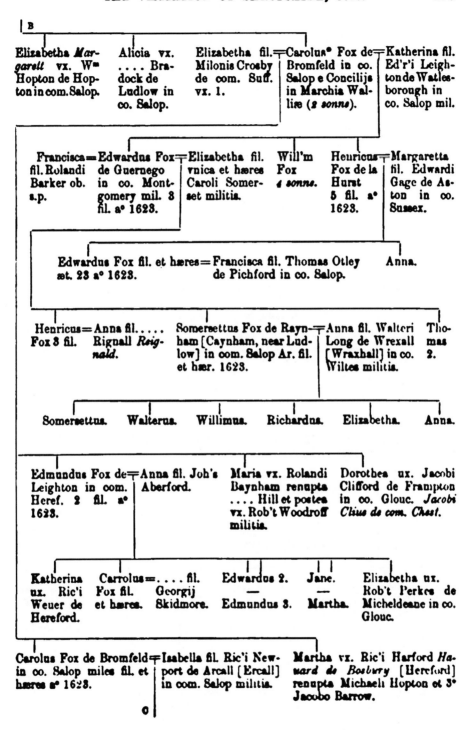

B

Elizabetha *Margarett* vx. Wm Hopton de Hopton in com. Salop.	Alicia vx. .... Bradock de Ludlow in co. Salop.	Elizabetha fil. Milonis Crosby de com. Suff. vx. 1.	Carolus* Fox de Bromfeld in co. Salop e Concilijs in Marchia Walliæ (*2 sonne*).	Katherina fil. Ed'r'i Leighton de Watlesborough in co. Salop mil.

Francisca fil. Rolandi Barker ob. s.p.═Edwardus Fox de Guernego in co. Montgomery mil. 3 fil. aº 1623.═Elizabetha fil. vnica et hæres Caroli Somerset militis.   Will'm Fox *1 sonne.*   Henricus Fox de la Hurst 5 fil. aº 1623.═Margaretta fil. Edwardi Gage de Aston in co. Sussex.

Edwardus Fox fil. et hæres═Francisca fil. Thomas Otley   Anna.
æt. 23 aº 1623.   de Pichford in co. Salop.

Henricus═Anna fil. .... Fox 3 fil. Rignall *Reignald*.	Somersettus Fox de Raynham [Caynham, near Ludlow] in com. Salop Ar. fil. et hær. 1623.═Anna fil. Walteri Long de Wrexall [Wraxhall] in co. Wiltes militis.		Thomas 2.

Somersettus.   Walterus.   Willimus.   Richardus.   Elizabetha.   Anna.

Edmundus Fox de Leighton in com. Heref. 2 fil. aº 1623.═Anna fil. Joh's Aberford.	Maria vx. Rolandi Baynham renupta .... Hill et postea vx. Rob't Woodroff militis.	Dorothea ux. Jacobi Clifford de Frampton in co. Glouc. *Jacobi Clius de com. Chest.*

Katherina ux. Ric'i Weuer de Hereford.	Carrolus═.... fil. Fox fil. Georgij et hæres. Skidmore.	Edwardus 2. — Edmundus 3.	Jane. — Martha.	Elizabetha ux. Rob't Perkes de Micheldeane in co. Glouc.

Carolus Fox de Bromfeld═Isabella fil. Ric'i Newport de Arcall [Ercall] in com. Salop militis.   Martha vx. Ric'i Harford *Haward de Bosbury* [Hereford] renupta Michaeli Hopton et 3º Jacobo Barrow.
in co. Salop miles fil. et hæres aº 1623.

C

* A Charles Fox was Sheriff in 1542.

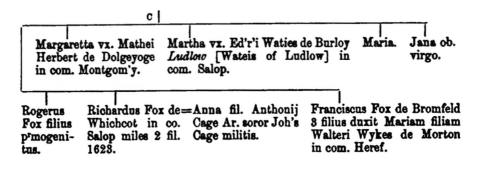

c |

| Margaretta vx. Mathei Herbert de Dolgeyoge in com. Montgom'y. | Martha vx. Ed'r'i Waties de Burloy *Ludlow* [Wateis of Ludlow] in com. Salop. | Maria. | Jana ob. virgo. |

| Rogerus Fox filius p'mogenitus. | Richardus Fox de Whichcot in co. Salop miles 2 fil. 1623.=Anna fil. Anthonij Cage Ar. soror Joh's Cage militis. | Franciscus Fox de Bromfeld 3 filius duxit Mariam filiam Walteri Wykes de Morton in com. Heref. |

RIC. FFOXE.   SOM. FOXE.   HEN. FOXE.

𝕱reere of 𝕮harlton, co. 𝖂orcester.

Harl. 1396, fo. 120. S., fo. 101ª.

ARMS: Harl. 1396.—*Quarterly: 1 and 4, Sable, a chevron between three dolphins naiant embowed argent,* FREERE; *2 and 3, Argent, a chevron between three escallops sable, a crescent for difference,* WEISSAM.

Sʳ Wᵐ Weissam of Charleton Castle in co. Worcestʳ [Wysham of Charlton].=[Margaret da. of Sir Adam Clifton, Knt.]

Jeffry Freere of Worcestersh.=[Elizabeth da. of John Lyttelton of Frankley.]   John Weissam.=. . . .

Thomas Freere.=Margrett da. & sole he. to John Weissam.

*Humfrie Freere of Charlton [co. Worcester, and of the Blankets].=Ann da. to Rich. Welle of Wellesley in co. Wor. [Richard Walsh of Shelsley].

| Thomas. | Richard Freere [of the Blankets co. Worcester].=Margrett da. to . . . . Henshaw. | Joane. | Joyce vx. Chr. Hodges of Kings Norton. | Margrett ux. John Nais of Codington in Heref. | Thomas Freere of . . . . mar. Eliz. da. to John Lewes. |

Richard Freere.=Ann da. to Tho. Sal[w]ey of Hyntip in co. Worc.   ▲

Robert Freere of Feuersham in Kent.=Margrett da. to Rich. Noble of Feuersham.   Eliz.

* This generation is omitted in Shrewsbury MS.

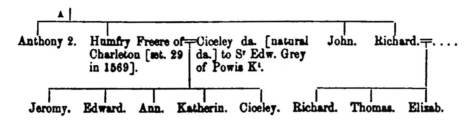

Anthony 2. Humfry Freere of ⊤ Ciceley da. [natural John. Richard. ⊤ ....
            Charleton [æt. 29 │ da.] to Sᵣ Edw. Grey
            in 1569].   │ of Powis Kᵗ.

Jeromy. Edward. Ann. Katherin. Ciceley. Richard. Thomas. Elizab.

Garbed alias Gabbitt of Condover.

8., fo. 299ᵇ.

[ARMS.—*Gules, a dragon segreant or supporting a flag-staff argent and sable with a pennon argent with two tails, thereon an eagle double-headed displayed sable.*[*]

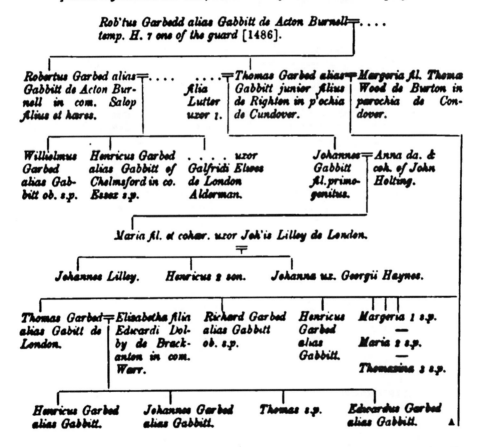

Rob'tus Garbedd alias Gabbitt de Acton Burnell ⊤ ....
temp. H. 7 one of the guard [1486].

Robertus Garbed alias ⊤ .... ⊤ Thomas Garbed alias ⊤ Margeria fil. Thoma
Gabbitt de Acton Bur-   │ Lutter │ Gabbitt junior filius │ Wood de Burton in
nell in com. Salop   filia │ de Righton in p'ochia │ parochia de Con-
filius et hæres.   Lutter │ de Cundover.   │ dover.
                       uxor 1.

Willielmus   Henricus Garbed   .... uxor   Johannes ⊤ Anna da. &
Garbed   alias Gabbitt of   Galfridi Elvos Gabbitt │ coh. of John
alias Gab-   Chelmsford in co. de London   fil. primo- │ Holting.
bitt ob. s.p. Essex s.p.   Alderman.   genitus.

Maria fil. et cohær. uxor Joh'is Lilley de London.
⊤
Johannes Lilley.   Henricus 2 son.   Johanna ux. Georgii Haynes.

Thomas Garbed ⊤ Elizabetha filia Richard Garbed Henricus Margeria 1 s.p.
alias Gabitt de │ Edwardi Dol-   alias Gabbitt   Garbed   —
London.   │ by de Brack-   ob. s.p.   alias   Maria 2 s.p.
                │ anton in com.   Gabbitt. —
                │ Warr.   Thomasina 3 s.p.

Henricus Garbed   Johannes Garbed   Thomas s.p.   Edwardus Garbed
alias Gabbitt.   alias Gabbitt.   alias Gabbitt.   ▲

[*] The 'Vis. of London, 1633,' vol. ii., p. 28, mentions that Robert Gabot of Acton Burnell had this banner given him by the Emperor Maximilian, for his services.

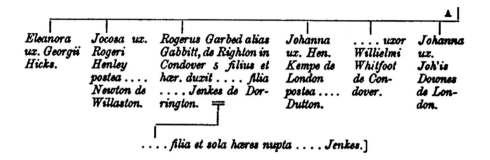

| Eleanora ux. Georgii Hicks. | Jocosa ux. Rogeri Henley postea .... Newton de Willaston. | Rogerus Garbed alias Gabbitt, de Righton in Condover 5 filius et hær. duxit .... filia .... Jenkes de Dorrington. | Johanna ux. Hen. Kempe de London postea .... Dutton. | .... uxor Willielmi Whitfoot de Condover. | Johanna ux. Joh'is Downes de London. |

.... filia et sola hæres nupta .... Jenkes.]

Gardiner of Shrewsbury.

Harl. 1396, fo. 123ᵇ. Harl. 1241, fo. 147. S., ff. 116ᵇ, 117ᵃ.

ARMS: Harl. 1396.—*Quarterly*: 1 and 4, *Per fesse argent and sable, a pale counterchanged and three gryphons' heads erased of the second*; 2, *Quarterly azure and gules, a cross engrailed or between four roses argent*—BURTON in Shrewsbury MS.; 3, *Sable, on a bend between six cross-crosslets fitchée argent three bugle-horns stringed of the first*—HORNER in Shrewsbury MS.
[CREST.—A griffin's head erased sable.]

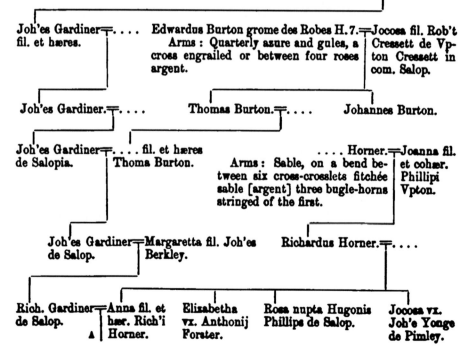

Joh'es Gardiner a Joh'e Gardiner de com. Lancastr' oriundus.=....
Arms: Per fesse argent and sable, a pale counterchanged
and three gryphons' heads erased of the second.

Joh'es Gardiner=.... fil. et hæres.

Edwardus Burton grome des Robes H.7.=Jocosa fil. Rob't Cressett de Vpton Cressett in com. Salop.
Arms: Quarterly azure and gules, a cross engrailed or between four roses argent.

Joh'es Gardiner.=....

Thomas Burton.=....

Johannes Burton.

Joh'es Gardiner=.... de Salopia.

.... fil. et hæres Thoma Burton.

.... Horner.=Joanna fil. et cohær. Phillipi Vpton.
Arms: Sable, on a bend between six cross-crosslets fitchée sable [argent] three bugle-horns stringed of the first.

Joh'es Gardiner=Margaretta fil. Joh'es de Salop. Berkley.

Richardus Horner.=....

Rich. Gardiner= de Salop.

Anna fil. et hær. Rich'i Horner.

Elizabetha vx. Anthonij Forster.

Rosa nupta Hugonis Phillips de Salop.

Jocosa vx. Joh'e Yonge de Pimley.

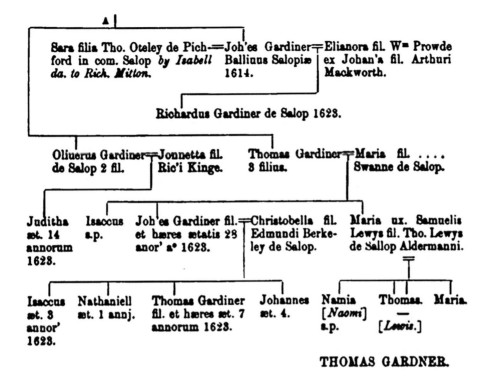

▲ |

Sara filia Tho. Oteley de Pich-═Joh'es Gardiner═Elianora fil. W⁼ Prowde
ford in com. Salop *by Isabell* Ballinus Salopiæ | ex Johan'a fil. Arthuri
da. to Rich. Mitton. 1614. Mackworth.

Richardus Gardiner de Salop 1623.

Oliuerus Gardiner═Jonnetta fil.   Thomas Gardiner═Maria fil. . . . .
de Salop 2 fil. Ric'i Kinge.   3 filius. Swanne de Salop.

Juditha Isaccus Joh'es Gardiner fil.═Christobella fil. Maria ux. Samuelis
æt. 14 s.p. et hæres ætatis 28 Edmundi Berke- Lewys fil. Tho. Lewys
annorum   anor' aᵒ 1623. ley de Salop. de Sallop Aldermanni.
1623.

Isaccus Nathaniell Thomas Gardiner Johannes Namia Thomas. Maria.
æt. 3 æt. 1 annj. fil. et hæres æt. 7 æt. 4. [*Naomi*] —
annor'   annorum 1623.   s.p. [*Lewis.*]
1623.

THOMAS GARDNER.

Gattacre of Gatacre.

Harl. 1396, fo. 124ᵇ.   Harl. 1241, fo. 77ᵇ.   S., fo. 118.

ARMS: Harl. 1396.—*Quarterly: 1 and 4, Quarterly gules and ermine, in the second
and third quarters three piles of the first, over all on a fesse azure five besants;
2, Argent, a lion rampant per fesse sable and gules [? LORTOT or LOVETT];
3, Argent, a cross formée fleurée sable [SWINNERTON].*

Joh'es Gattacre de Gattacre in com. Salop.═Jocosa fil. Jo. Burley militia.

Joh'es Gattacre de Gattacre═Jana filia Nicho. Yonge *of Kenton*
in com. Salop. [Caynton].

Joh'es Gatt-═Maria Bostock [Elizab. Humfridus Gatt-═Elianora fil. et hær.
acre de Gatt- da. of Sir Adam Bostock, acre 2 fil. Armiger Ric'i Blike de Ayles-
acre duxit slain at Bloreheath 1459, Corporis H. 6 ley in com. Salop
Eleanora mar. John Gataker — [1422-61]. [Blyke of Astley,
filia Joh'is Visit. Cheshire].   near Bridgnorth].
Acton. ▲   **B**

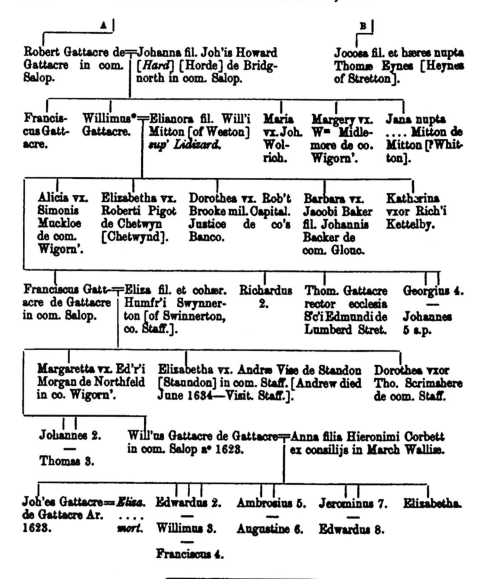

A |

Robert Gattacre de⊤Johanna fil. Joh'is Howard
Gattacre in com. | [*Hard*] [Horde] de Bridg-
Salop. | north in com. Salop.

B |

Jocosa fil. et hæres nupta
Thomæ Eynes [Heynes
of Stretton].

| Francis-cus Gatt-acre. | Willimus*⊤Elianora fil. Will'i Gattacre. | Mitton [of Weston] *sup' Lidizard.* | Maria vx. Joh. Wol-rich. | Margery vx. Wm Midle-more de co. Wigorn'. | Jana nupta .... Mitton de Mitton [?Whit-ton]. |

| Alicia vx. Simonis Muckloe de com. Wigorn'. | Elizabetha vx. Roberti Pigot de Chetwyn [Chetwynd]. | Dorothea vx. Rob't Brooke mil. Capital. Justice de co's Banco. | Barbara vx. Jacobi Baker fil. Johannis Backer de com. Glouc. | Kathærina vxor Rich'i Kettelby. |

| Franciscus Gatt-⊤Eliza fil. et cohær. acre de Gattacre | Humfr'i Swynner-in com. Salop. | ton [of Swinnerton, co. Staff.]. | Richardus 2. | Thom. Gattacre rector ecclesiæ Sc'i Edmundi de Lumberd Stret. | Georgius 4. — Johannes 5 s.p. |

| Margaretta vx. Ed'r'i Morgan de Northfeld in co. Wigorn'. | Elizabetha vx. Andreæ Vise de Standon [Staundon] in com. Staff. [Andrew died June 1634—Visit. Staff.]. | Dorothea vxor Tho. Scrimshere de com. Staff. |

Johannes 2.
—
Thomas 3.

Will'us Gattacre de Gattacre⊤Anna filia Hieronimi Corbett
in com. Salop aº 1623. | ex consilijs in March Walliæ.

| Joh'es Gattacre═*Elisa.* de Gattacre Ar. .... 1623. | *mort.* | Edwardus 2. — Willimus 3. — Franciscus 4. | Ambrosius 5. — Augustine 6. | Jerominus 7. — Edwardus 8. | Elizabetha. |

Gibbons of Shrewsbury.

Harl. 1396, fo. 121.   Harl. 1241, fo. 144.   S, fo. 114ª.

ARMS: Harl. 1396.—*Paly of six argent and gules, on a bend sable three escallops of the first.*

Robertus Gibbons oriundus e familia eiusdem⊤....
nominis in partibus Borealibus. | A |

* Harl. 1241 makes this William *son* instead of *brother* of Francis.

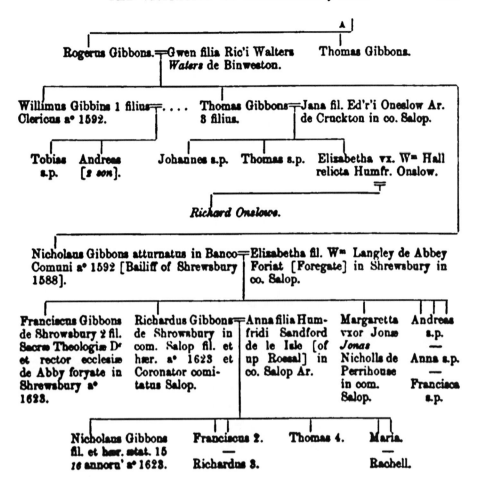

Rogerus Gibbons.=Gwen filia Ric'i Walters *Walters* de Binweston. — Thomas Gibbons.

Willimus Gibbins 1 filius=.... Clericus aº 1592.

Thomas Gibbons=Jana fil. Ed'r'i Oneslow Ar. 3 filius. de Cruckton in co. Salop.

Tobias s.p.

Andreas [2 *son*].

Johannes s.p.

Thomas s.p.

Elizabetha vx. Wm Hall relicta Humfr. Onslow.

Richard Onslowe.

Nicholaus Gibbons atturnatus in Banco=Elizabetha fil. Wm Langley de Abbey Comuni aº 1592 [Bailiff of Shrewsbury 1588]. — Foriat [Foregate] in Shrewsbury in co. Salop.

Franciscus Gibbons de Shrowsbury 2 fil. Sacræ Theologiæ Dr et rector ecclesiæ de Abby foryate in Shrewsbury aº 1623.

Richardus Gibbons=Anna filia Humde Shrowsbury in com. Salop fil. et hær. aº 1623 et Coronator comitatus Salop.

fridi Sandford de le Isle [of up Rossal] in co. Salop Ar.

Margaretta vxor Jonæ *Jonas* Nicholls de Perrihouse in com. Salop.

Andreas s.p.

Anna s.p.

Francisca s.p.

Nicholaus Gibbons fil. et hær. ætat. 15 *16* annoru' aº 1623.

Franciscus 2. — Richardus 3.

Thomas 4.

Maria. — Rachell.

FRA. GIBBONS. RICHARD GIBBONS.

Gittins.

S., ff. 214b, 215.

[ARMS.—*Gules, on a fesse between three goats' heads erased argent three pellets.*

Eignion ap Gollwin.=....

Mared'd ap Eignion.=....

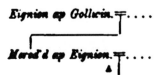

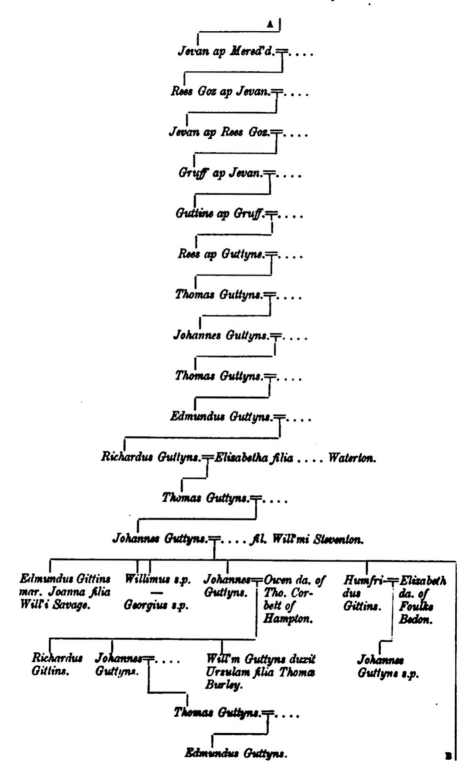

▲

Jevan ap Mered'd.=....

Rees Goz ap Jevan.=....

Jevan ap Rees Goz.=....

Gruff ap Jevan.=....

Guttine ap Gruff.=....

Rees ap Guttyne.=....

Thomas Guttyns.=....

Johannes Guttyns.=....

Thomas Guttyns.=....

Edmundus Guttyns.=....

Richardus Guttyns.=*Elizabetha filia* .... *Waterton.*

Thomas Guttyns.=....

Johannes Guttyns.=.... *fil. Will'mi Steventon.*

Edmundus Gittins mar. Joanna filia Will'i Savage.	*Willimus s.p.* — *Georgius s.p.*	*Johannes Guttyns.*=*Owen da. of Tho. Corbett of Hampton.*	*Humfri-dus Gittins.*=*Elizabeth da. of Foulke Bedon.*

Richardus Gittins.	*Johannes Guttyns.*=....	*Will'm Guttyns duxit Ursulam filia Thomæ Burley.*

Johannes Guttyns s.p.

Thomas Guttyns.=....

Edmundus Guttyns.

B

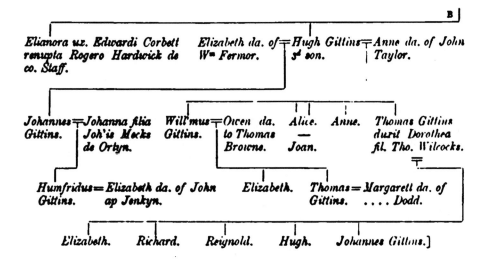

B

Elianora ux. Edwardi Corbett renupta Rogero Hardwick de co. Staff.

Elizabeth da. of Wm Fermor. = Hugh Gillins 3d son. = Anne da. of John Taylor.

Johannes Gittins. = Johanna filia Joh'is Mecks de Ortyn.

Will'mus Gittins. = Owen da. to Thomas Browne.

Alice. — Joan.

Anne.

Thomas Gittins durit Dorothea fil. Tho. Wilcocks.

Humfridus Gittins. = Elizabeth da. of John ap Jenkyn.

Elizabeth.

Thomas Gittins. = Margarett da. of .... Dodd.

Elizabeth.   Richard.   Reignold.   Hugh.   Johannes Gittins.]

Gough of the Marsh.

Harl. 1396, fo. 121b.   Harl. 1241, fo. 157.   S., ff. 114b, 115.

ARMS: Harl. 1396.—*Quarterly of six*: 1 and 6, *Sable, three horses' heads erased argent*; 2, *Or, three lions' heads erased gules within a bordure engrailed azure* [GRUFFYDD AP ALLO]; 3, ... *an eagle displayed* ....; 4, [*Azure*], *three bugle-horns* [or, EYTON]; 5, *Quarterly per fesse indented ermine and gules, a label of three points or* [FULKE FITZ WARINE].

ANOTHER SHIELD: Harl. 1396.—*Quarterly of eight*: 1, *Sable, three horses' heads erased argent* [GOUGH]; 2, *Or, three lions' heads erased gules within a bordure engrailed azure* [GRUFFYDD AP ALLO]; 3, *Gules, three chevronels argent* [JESTYN AP GWRGANT]; 4, *Sable, a buck trippant argent attired or* [HEDD MOLWYNOC]; 5, *Ermine, three fusils in fesse sable* [PIGOTT]; 6, *Azure, three bugle-horns unstringed or* [EIGHTON OF MARSH]; 7, *Quarterly per fesse indented ermine and azure, a label of three points or* [FITZWARINE]; 8, *Ermine, on a bend gules three escallops or* [MARSHE].

ARMS: Harl. 1241.—*Quarterly*: 1, *Sable, three horses' heads erased argent* [GOUGH]; 2, *Or, three lions' heads erased gules within a bordure engrailed azure* [GRUFFYDD AP ALLO]; 3, ... *an eagle displayed* ....; 4, [*Argent*], *a fret* [azure, EYTON].

Gwenwys ap Gruffith ap Beley de le Garth. = Jonetta fil. et hær. Joh'es Bewpre [Beaupre ?] de la Poole.

Kadwgan ap Gwenwys. = Agnes fil. Kynaelin ap Dolfin.

Madock ap Kadwgan. = Margaretta fil. Eigniani ap Howell ap Tudor.

▲

D D

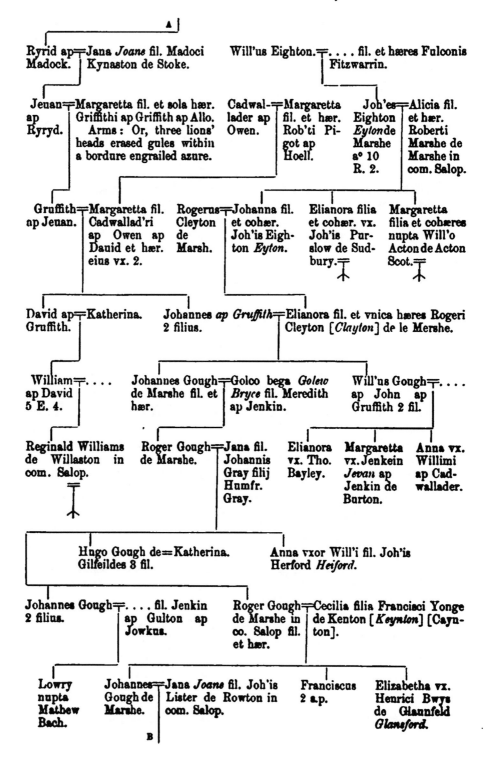

Ryrid ap⊤Jana *Joane* fil. Madoci
Madock. │ Kynaston de Stoke.

Will'us Eighton.⊤.... fil. et hæres Fulconis
│ Fitzwarrin.

Jeuan⊤Margaretta fil. et sola hær.
ap │ Griffithi ap Griffith ap Allo.
Ryryd.   Arms : Or, three lions'
    heads erased gules within
    a bordure engrailed azure.

Cadwal-⊤Margaretta
lader ap │ fil. et hær.
Owen.   Rob'ti Pi-
    got ap
    Hoell.

Joh'es⊤Alicia fil.
Eighton │ et hær.
Eylon de   Roberti
Marshe   Marshe de
aº 10   Marshe in
R. 2.   com. Salop.

Gruffith⊤Margaretta fil.
ap Jeuan. │ Cadwallad'ri
    ap Owen ap
    Dauid et hær.
    eius vx. 2.

Rogerus⊤Johanna fil.
Cleyton │ et cohær.
de   Joh'is Eigh-
Marsh.   ton *Eyton*.

Elianora filia
et cohær. vx.
Joh'is Pur-
slow de Sud-
bury.⊤

Margaretta
filia et cohæres
nupta Will'o
Acton de Acton
Scot.⊤

David ap⊤Katherina.
Gruffith.

Johannes *ap Gruffith*⊤Elianora fil. et vnica hæres Rogeri
2 filius. │ Cleyton [*Clayton*] de le Mershe.

William⊤....
ap David
5 E. 4.

Johannes Gough⊤Golco bega *Goleo*
de Marshe fil. et │ *Bryce* fil. Meredith
hær.   ap Jenkin.

Will'us Gough⊤....
ap John ap
Gruffith 2 fil.

Reginald Williams
de Willaston in
com. Salop.
⊤

Roger Gough⊤Jana fil.
de Marshe. │ Johannis
    Gray filij
    Humfr.
    Gray.

Elianora
vx. Tho.
Bayley.

Margaretta
vx. Jenkein
Jevan ap
Jenkin de
Burton.

Anna vx.
Willimi
ap Cad-
wallader.

Hugo Gough de═Katherina.
Gilfeildes 3 fil.

Anna vxor Will'i fil. Joh'is
Herford *Heiford*.

Johannes Gough⊤.... fil. Jenkin
2 filius. │ ap Gulton ap
    Jowkus.

Roger Gough⊤Cecilia filia Francisci Yonge
de Marshe in │ de Kenton [*Keynton*] [Cayn-
co. Salop fil.   ton].
et hær.

Lowry
nupta
Mathew
Bach.

Johannes⊤Jana *Joane* fil. Joh'is
Gough de │ Lister de Rowton in
Marshe.   com. Salop.

Franciscus
2 s.p.

Elizabetha vx.
Henrici Bwys
de Glaunfeld
Glansford.

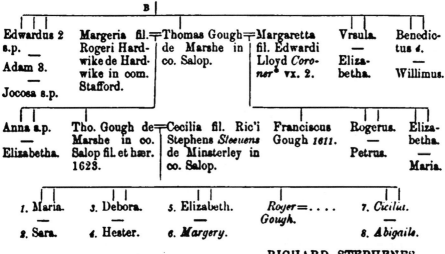

B

Edwardus 2 s.p. — Adam 8. — Jocosa s.p.

Margeria fil. Rogeri Hard-wike de Hard-wike in com. Stafford. = Thomas Gough de Marshe in co. Salop. = Margaretta fil. Edwardi Lloyd *Coro-ner*[*] vx. 2.

Vrsula. — Eliza-betha.

Benedic-tus *d*. — Willimus.

Anna s.p. — Elizabetha.

Tho. Gough de Marshe in co. Salop fil. et hær. 1623. = Cecilia fil. Ric'i Stephens *Steeuens* de Minsterley in co. Salop.

Franciscus Gough *1611*.

Rogerus. — Petrus.

Eliza-betha. — Maria.

1. Maria.
2. Sara.

3. Debora.
4. Hester.

5. Elizabeth.
6. Margery.

Royer = ... *Gough.*

7. Cicilia.
8. Abigaile.

RICHARD STEPHENES.

Gouldston.

S., fo. 301ᵃ.

[ARMS.—*Gules, on a fesse between three saltires couped argent an annulet sable.*

Francis Goulston of Goulston. = ...

Philipp Gouldston. = *Dorothy da. to Hughe Adams of Warwicksh.*

Francis Goulston of Astley s.p.

Hugh Gouldston. = ...

Humfrey Gouldston. = ...

Thomas Gould-ston. = *Dorothy da. to Richard Stamford.*

John Gould-ston. = *Anne da. of Thomas Broughton of Henley neere Lud-low.*

Elizabeth mar. to Thomas Hunt.

Dorothy mar. to . . . . Brag-don.

Jane mar. to . . . . Clark in com. War.

John Gouldston. = *Dorothy da. of Ada. Oteley of Oteley Hall.*

Lancelott Gouldston.

Francis Gouldston. ▲ = *Susanna da. to . . . . Whitton of Whitton.*

Elizabeth 1. — *Jane 2.*

Bridgett 3. — *Mary 4.*

* Probably " Coroner " is a misreading for " Crosemere," near Ellesmere, a seat of the Lloyd family.

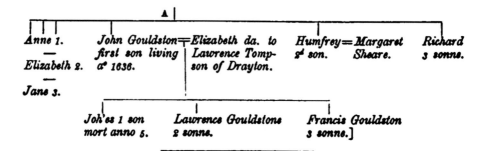

Gregory of Rodington.

Harl. 1896, fo. 123. S., ff. 115ᵇ, 116.

ARMS: Harl. 1896.—*Quarterly*: 1 *and* 4, *Per pale argent and azure, two lions rampant addorsed counterchanged*; 2, *Sable, a chevron between three spears' heads argent within a bordure of the last*—URMSTON in Shrewsbury MS.; 3, *Argent, a fesse between six birds* [? Cornish choughs] *sable*—ONDESLOWE in Shrewsbury MS. [ONSLOW OF RODINGTON].

CREST.—*Two lions' heads addorsed and erased argent and azure, collared or.*

Ex Chartis Joh'is Gregory de Rodington in com. Salop generosi 4 Octobr. 1623.

Joh'es Onslowe de Rodington & Emota vxoris concescerunt Thomæ Onslowe filio et hæred. suo mess. virgatam et nocatam* t'ræ quæ quondam fuerunt Rogeri Onslowe et Katherinæ vx. eius in Onslowe etc. Dat. apud Onslowe aᵒ 32 H. 6.

Joh'es Gregory de Pagham in com. Sussex generosus et Johannes Gregory de Grayes Inne in com. Midd. fil. et hær. d'ci Joh'is dederunt Ric'o Corbett de Paynton in com. Salop Ar. o'ia mess. terres et ten'ta in le Old Bayly London ad vsum Annæ Gregory vnius filiarum et hæredum Gregorij Onslowe nuper de Rodington in d'co com. Salop Ar. defuncti et nunc vxori p'd'c'i Johannis Gregorij filij pro termino vitæ d'cæ Annæ reman' ad vsum p'd'c'i Joh'is Gregory patris et Joh'is filij et hæredes suis masculos. Dat. aᵒ 3 E. 6.

Couenants of Mariage that George Oneslow gentleman shall marry Katherin one of the sisters of Sᵣ Robert Corbett Knight. Dated 19 Junij aᵒ 23 H. 7.

Anna Oneslow de Rodington vna fil. et hæredem Georgij Onneslowe Ar. defuncti dedit Thomæ Newport et Ad'æ Oteley Armigeris Manerium de Rodington ad opus et vsum mei p'fatæ Annæ et hær. meorum et pro defectu talis exitus remanere ad vsum Rogeri Kinaston nepotis meæ ac filij et heredis apparentis Thomæ Kynaston Ar. remanere Dorotheæ et Johannæ neptarum d'cæ Annæ Onneslow etc. Dat. 10 Maij aᵒ 3 E. 6.

An Indenture betweene John Gregory of Manchester in com. Lanc. gent. and Gilbert Gregory son & heire appar' of the said John and Anne late wife of the said John whereby it appeares that the said Gilbert Gregory maried Katherin Hulton one of the daughters of John Hulton late of Farneworth in com. Lanc. Datu' 15 July aᵒ 26 Eliz.

Adam Gregory de Highurst ⊤ . . . . filia et hæres Adami Vrmeston
in com. Lanc. | de Vrmeston in com. Lancastr'.

Joh'es Gregory de Pag- ⊤ Dorothea fil. . . . .   Georgius Onnes- ⊤ Katherina soror
ham in Sussex gen. et | Parre de Kempen-   low de Roding- | Roberti Cor-
de Highurst. | haugh [Kempnough]   ton. | bett militis 23
                     | in com. Lanc. | H. 7.

Hugo   Joh'es Gregory de Grayes Inne ⊤ Anna fil. et cohær.   Susanna cohæres vx.
2.   in co. Midd. aᵒ 3 E. 6 et de | Gregory [sic] Onne-   Tho. Kynaston de
     Highurst. | slow de Rodington.   Walford in co. Salop.

* Nocatam, a "nook" of land, *i.e.* half a virgate.

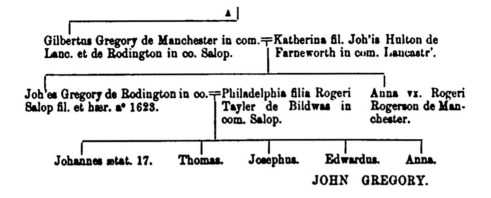

Gilbertus Gregory de Manchester in com.⊤Katherina fil. Joh'is Hulton de
Lanc. et de Rodington in co. Salop. | Farneworth in com. Lancastr'.

Joh'es Gregory de Rodington in co.⊤Philadelphia filia Rogeri   Anna vx. Rogeri
Salop fil. et hær. aº 1623. | Tayler de Bildwas in   Rogerson de Man-
com. Salop. | chester.

Johannes ætat. 17.   Thomas.   Josephus.   Edwardus.   Anna.

JOHN GREGORY.

Hall of Northall, near Kynnersley.

Harl. 1896, fo. 143ᵇ.

[Drawing of Quartered Arms, Crest, and Supporters, Plate II., Fig. 7.]

[Other copies of this 1623 Visitation give: 1 and 4, Gules, a wyvern or crowned
argent, on his breast an escutcheon or, charged with a double-headed eagle sable,
within a bordure azure charged with an enurny of eight lions and a verdoy of eight
fleurs-de-lys or, HALL; 2, Argent, a pile gules charged with a crescent or, CHANDOS;
3, Gules, a chevron argent between three wolves' heads erased or, GEDDING.

CREST.—On a castle with four towers argent, a wyvern with wings endorsed
gules, ducally gorged and lined reflexed over the back or, holding in the dexter claw
a sword erect argent hilt and pommel or.]

Leopoldus Princeps de Habspurg Comes de Kyburg et Lantgravius⊤....
Alsatiæ Imperator Augustus 1273 aº 57 H. 3; ob. 9 E. 1, 1281.

Radulphus de Habspurg   Henricus   Albertus Rex Romanor'⊤Eliz. Menhardi
Dux Sueniæ occidit   princeps   Archidux Austriæ occisus | Ducis Carinthiæ et
Regem Bohemiæ duxit   Austriæ   a Johanne nepote filie | Comitis Tyrolis
Agnetam. ⊤   sine p'le.   Radulphi fratris 1808. | filia et hæres.

Johannes Dux Sueniæ   Albertus Sapiens Secundus⊤Joanna fil. Vdalriche
occidit patruum 1808.   Archidux Austriæ. | Comitis Farratatem
sine Phirretensia.

Leopoldus Archidux Austriæ⊤Virida fil. Barnabæ dicti
occisus ab Helvetija. | vicecomitis Mediolani.

Ernestus Archidux Austriæ.⊤Zimburga filia Alexij Masaniæ Ducis.

Fredericus Archidux Austriæ⊤Leonora Edwardi Regis Portugalliæ filia.
et Imperator.

Maximilianus Romanorum Rex. = Maria filia et hæres Caroli D. Burgundi.

A}

Fredericus de Halle natus in vrbe de Halle in Comitatu Tyrolis, filius naturalis Alberti, et gubernatur Comitatus Tirolis, propter audaciam et ferocitatem appellatus Draco de Halle, vindicator necis patris occiso Johanne patrudi, tandem ab Alberto fratre vna cum vxore et sex liberis in inferiorem Germaniam relegatus vbi cum Joh'e Duce Brabantino gratiam inijt, et ab eo adiutus: postea plenus annorum a Leopoldo nepote revocatus in Austriam cum ipso ab Helvecijs trucidatur, a° ætatis 99, duxit Ingelburgam filiam Comitis de Nassaw.

Hercules. — Adulphus.

Johannes. — Ernestus.

Fran'cus Halle oriundus Garterij miles 8 filius.* = Blanchea filia Roberti de Artois Com. Richmond.

Albertus. Jacy. — Judacus.

Phillippa vx. Thomæ Do. Camoys.

Isabella vxor Caroli D'no Chabbot a vasconi.

Robertus Halle miles occisus in ec'l'ia de Westminster a° 10 R. 2. = Maria sola hæres Rob't Anketfeld de Orleton in com. Heref. militis.

Hellena vx. Henrici Bastardi Clarencia militi.

Franciscus Decanus de Wallingford.

Johannes. — Guido.

Alexander Hall duxit filia D'ni Audley.

Henricus Halle Eques auratus magister equorum cum Ric'o secundo obijt apud Rosse in Hiberniæ. = Margaritta fil. Johannis d'Eureux fr'is Caroli Regis Nauarræ.

Ludouicus Halle Ep'us Hereford.

Willimus Hall miles Capitanius Falaciæ.

Dorothea D'na Basset.

Phillippus Hall miles. = Constantia fil. Joh'e Grey de Ruthin et Constantiæ vxoris suæ filiæ Joh'e Holland Ducis Exoniæ.

Maria Sec' Monialis apud Sion.

Anna vxor Roberti Longvile.

Carolus Baro' de Aubemond in Normannia. = ...

Phillippus Awbemond factus Eques per Regem Henricum quintum Capitanus S'c'i Salvatoris Perche et Bongvile factus etiam indignea et duxit filiam D'ni Courtney.

Ludouicus de Awbemond. — Gertrudis hæres nupta Comiti de Dampmartin.

Henricus Mortimer miles. = D'na Lucia 2 fil. et vna hær. Barnabæ fratris Galencij de Millayne. = Edmundus Holland Comes Kancij p'mo maritus s.p.

B   C   D

* Sir Frank Van Halen, K.G., did not marry the wife here assigned to him, and had not the children here named. He was a Brabanter, and lies buried in St. Rombaut's Malines, having died in 1375. The arms used by his immediate descendants were: Gules, a lion rampant or crowned azure. Sir Frank owned estates near Malines, and his descendants have been recorded clearly in the Rev. A. W. Cornelius Hallen's 'Account of the Family of Hallen' (Edinburgh, 1885). It is only necessary further to say that the Garter plate attached to his stall, which bears the arms here passed by Vincent, is clearly of the time of Henry VIII., perhaps a few years before 1547. See Beltz's 'Memorial of the Order of the Garter,' pp. 122, 123, 127.

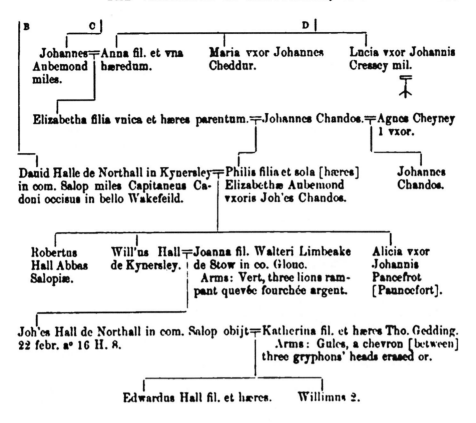

B | C | D

Johannes ⊤ Anna fil. et vna
Aubemond | hæredum.
miles.

Maria vxor Johannes
Cheddur.

Lucia vxor Johannis
Cressey mil.

Elizabetha filia vnica et hæres parentum. ⊤ Johannes Chandos. ⊤ Agnes Cheyney
1 vxor.

Dauid Halle de Northall in Kynersley ⊤ Philis filia et sola [hæres]
in com. Salop miles Capitaneus Ca- | Elizabethæ Aubemond
doni occisus in bello Wakefeild. | vxoris Joh'es Chandos.

Johannes
Chandos.

Robertus
Hall Abbas
Salopiæ.

Will'us Hall ⊤ Joanna fil. Walteri Limbeake
de Kynersley. | de Stow in co. Glouc.
⎯ Arms: Vert, three lions rampant quevée fourchée argent.

Alicia vxor
Johannis
Pancefrot
[Paunccfort].

Joh'es Hall de Northall in com. Salop obijt ⊤ Katherina fil. et hæres Tho. Gedding.
22 febr. aº 16 H. 8. | Arms: Gules, a chevron [between]
three gryphons' heads erased or.

Edwardus Hall fil. et hæres.   Willimus 2.

⎯⎯⎯⎯⎯⎯⎯

Hall of Northall.*

Harl. 1241, fo. 158ᵇ. S., fo. 149ᵇ.

ARMS: Harl. 1241.—*Quarterly: 1 and 4, Gules, a wyvern with wings expanded or,
within a bordure azure, thereon eight lions passant and as many fleurs-de-lis
alternately of the second; 2 and 3, Argent, on a pile gules a crescent or*
[CHANDOS].

CREST.—*Upon a* [castle with four towers argent],† *a wyvern sable, guttée gules,
collared and lined .... holding in the dexter claw a sword argent, hilt and
pomel* [or].

Dauid Hall of Northall in ⊤ Plotice [felicea] da. & cohei. to Robᵗ Chandows
Kinersley in com. Salop. | of Stanton in com. Cambridg.
▲

* We learn from Wood's 'Athenæ Oxon.' that Edward Hall the Chronicler, who died 1547,
was a son of John Hall of Northall. He is supposed to have been the inventor of the earlier
portion of the pedigree given on pp. 205 and 206, and probably of the coat armour. The above
pedigree of four generations seems to be authentic, and it is the only portion recorded in the
Shrewsbury School Copy of this Visitation.
† In Shrewsbury MS. the wyvern stands only upon a cushion lying on the torse.

▲

William Hall=Jeane dr. to Walter Lymbanks of Stow com. Glouc.
of Kynersley.   Arms: Vert, three iions passant argent.

Jo⁰ Hall of Northall in Kynersley=Katherine da. & hei. to Tho. Gethin [or Gedding].
ob. 22 feb. 19 H. 8 [1527-8].   Arms: Gules, a chevron argent between
[three] gryphons' or weires' heads erased or.

Edward Hall of Northall son & heire.   William Hall 2 son.

Hanmer of Porkington.

Harl. 1396, fo. 129ᵇ.   Harl. 1241, fo. 158.   S., fo. 147ᵃ.

ARMS: Harl. 1396: HANMER IMPALING LLOYD.—*Quarterly:* 1 and 4, *Azure, a lion passant-guardant coward or; 2 and 3, Ermine, a lion rampant azure* [ELIDOR AP RYS SAYS]; *impaling* LLOYD: *Quarterly,* 1 *and* 4, *Per bend sinister ermine and ermines, a lion rampant or* [TUDOR TREVOR]; 2 *and* 3, *Gules, a chevron between three esquires' helmets argent* [OWEN AP MEREDITH AP TUDOR].

CREST.—*Out of a mural crown vert* [or] *a cubit arm erect, habited quarterly or and azure, cuffed ermine, on the hand a hawk close of the second, beaked, winged, and legged of the third, belled gold.*

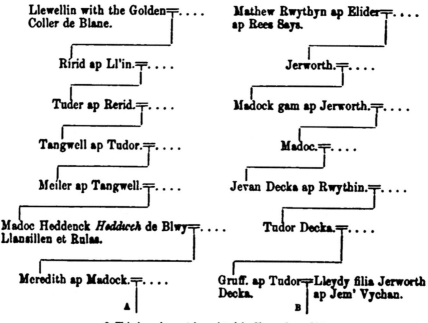

Llewellin with the Golden=....
Coller de Blane.

Ririd ap Ll'in.=....

Tuder ap Rerid.=....

Tangwell ap Tudor.=....

Meiler ap Tangwell.=....

Madoc Heddenck *Hedduch de Blwy*=....
Llansillen et Rulas.

Meredith ap Madock.=....

▲

Mathew Rwythyn ap Elider=....
ap Rees Says.

Jerworth.=....

Madock gam ap Jerworth.=....

Madoc.=....

Jevan Decka ap Rwythin.=....

Tudor Decka.=....

Gruff. ap Tudor=Lleydy filia Jerworth
Decka.   ap Jem' Vychan.

B

* This impalement is omitted in Shrewsbury MS.

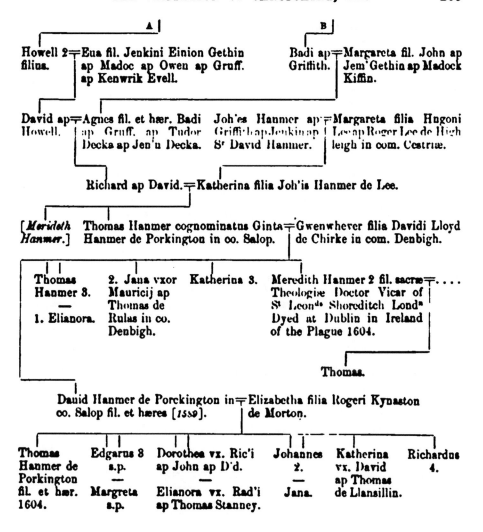

A

Howell 2⹋=Eua fil. Jenkini Einion Gethin
filius.   ap Madoc ap Owen ap Gruff.
                 ap Kenwrik Evell.

B

Badi ap⹋=Margareta fil. John ap
Griffith.   Jem' Gethin ap Madock
           Kiffin.

David ap⹋=Agnes fil. et hær. Badi
Howell.   ap Gruff. ap Tudor
           Decka ap Jen'n Decka.

Joh'es Hanmer ap⹋=Margareta filia Hugoni
Griffi' h ap Jenkin ap   Lee ap Roger Lee de High
S' David Hanmer.   leigh in com. Cestriæ.

Richard ap David.⹋=Katherina filia Joh'is Hanmer de Lee.

[*Merideth
Hanmer.*]

Thomas Hanmer cognominatus Ginta⹋=Gwenwhever filia Davidi Lloyd
Hanmer de Porkington in co. Salop.   de Chirke in com. Denbigh.

Thomas   2. Jana vxor   Katherina 3.   Meredith Hanmer 2 fil. sacræ⹋=....
Hanmer 3.   Mauricij ap   Theologiæ Doctor Vicar of
—   Thomas de   S' Leon'do Shoreditch Lond'
1. Elianora.   Rulas in co.   Dyed at Dublin in Ireland
                  Denbigh.   of the Plague 1604.

                                                          Thomas.

Dauid Hanmer de Porckington in⹋=Elizabetha filia Rogeri Kynaston
co. Salop fil. et hæres [*1589*].   de Morton.

Thomas   Edgarus 8   Dorothea vx. Ric'i   Johannes   Katherina   Richardus
Hanmer de   s.p.   ap John ap D'd.   2.   vx. David   4.
Porkington   —   —   —   ap Thomas
fil. et hær.   Margreta   Elianora vx. Rad'i   Jana.   de Llansillin.
1604.   s.p.   ap Thomas Stanney.

𝕳anmer of 𝕳anmer, 𝕰benall, and 𝕶enwick.

Harl. 1896, fo. 160ᵇ.   R, fo. 147ᵇ.

ARMS: Harl. 1396.—*Quarterly of eight:* 1 and 8, *Argent, two lions passant-guardant
azure,* HANMER; 2, *Gules, a lion rampant within a bordure engrailed or,* RICE
AP THEODER; 3, *Or, a lion's gamb in bend erased gules,* OWEN KAUELIOCK
[GWENWYNWYN]; 4, *Vert, two boars passant or,* S' ROGER POWIS; 5, *Azure,
three boars passant in pale argent,* YONAS [JONAN AP GRONO]; 6, *Argent, a
cross fleury engrailed between four choughs all sable,* EDWYN [EDWYN OF
TEGAINGLE]; 7, *Gules, three human legs flexed in triangle argent,* OWEN AP
EDWYN.

CREST.—*Upon a chapeau* (gules) *turned up ermine a lion sejant-guardant argent,
charged with a crescent for difference.*

B B

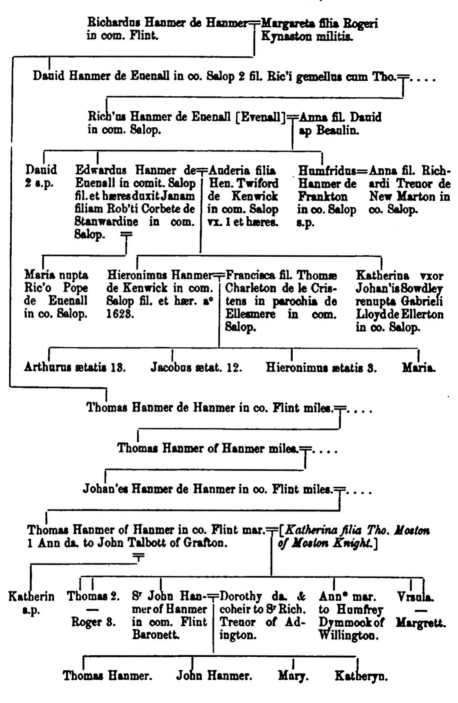

Richardus Hanmer de Hanmer=Margareta filia Rogeri
in com. Flint.   Kynaston militis.

Dauid Hanmer de Euenall in co. Salop 2 fil. Ric'i gemellus cum Tho.=....

Rich'us Hanmer de Euenall [Evenall]=Anna fil. Dauid
in com. Salop.   ap Beaulin.

Dauid | Edwardus Hanmer de=Auderia filia | Humfridus=Anna fil. Rich-
2 s.p. | Euenall in comit. Salop | Hen. Twiford | Hanmer de | ardi Treuor de
       | fil. et hæres duxit Janam | de Kenwick | Frankton | New Marton in
       | filiam Rob'ti Corbete de | in com. Salop | in co. Salop | co. Salop.
       | Stanwardine in com. | vx. 1 et hæres. | s.p. |
       | Salop. =

Maria nupta | Hieronimus Hanmer=Francisca fil. Thomæ | Katherina vxor
Ric'o Pope | de Kenwick in com. | Charleton de le Cris- | Johan'is Sowdley
de Euenall | Salop fil. et hær. a° | tens in parochia de | renupta Gabrieli
in co. Salop. | 1623. | Ellesmere in com. | Lloyd de Ellerton
              | | Salop. | in co. Salop.

Arthurus ætatis 18.   Jacobus sætat. 12.   Hieronimus ætatis 3.   Maria.

Thomas Hanmer de Hanmer in co. Flint miles.=....

Thomas Hanmer of Hanmer miles.=....

Johan'es Hanmer de Hanmer in co. Flint miles.=....

Thomas Hanmer of Hanmer in co. Flint mar.=[*Katherina filia Tho. Moston
1 Ann da. to John Talbott of Grafton.   of Moston Knight.*]
                                =

Katherin | Thomas 2. | S'r John Han-=Dorothy da. & | Ann* mar. | Vrsula.
s.p. | — | mer of Hanmer | coheir to S'r Rich. | to Humfrey | —
          | Roger 3. | in com. Flint | Treuor of Ad- | Dymmock of | Margrett.
          | | Baronett. | ington. | Willington.

Thomas Hanmer.   John Hanmer.   Mary.   Katheryn.

* Omitted in Shrewsbury MS.

Hanmer of Lwynymapsis.

Harl. 1396, fo. 161ᵇ.

ARMS.—*Quarterly: 1 and 4, Sable, three goats passant argent; 2 and 3, Vert, a lion rampant or within a bordure of the second pellettée* [WYTHE or WYCHE].

CREST.—*A cubit arm erect, vested azure, cuffed ermine, the arm encircled by an annulet vert, the hand grasping a billet or.*

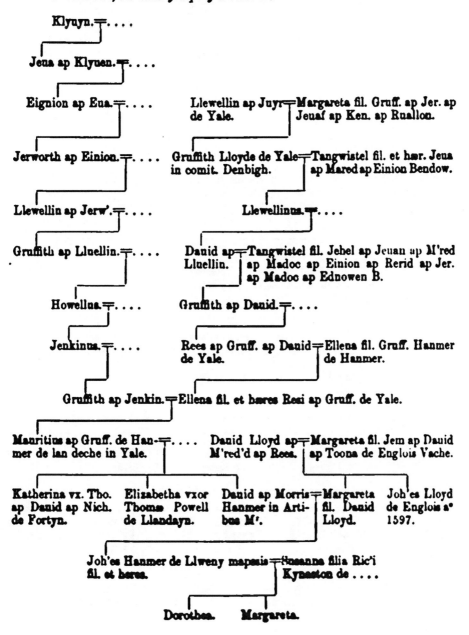

Klynyn.=....

Jena ap Klynen.=....

Eignion ap Ena.=....

Jerworth ap Einion.=....

Llewellin ap Jerw'.=....

Graffith ap Lluellin.=....

Howellns.=....

Jenkinns.=....

Llewellin ap Juyr=Margareta fil. Gruff. ap Jer. ap
de Yale.   Jeuaf ap Ken. ap Ruallon.

Gruffith Lloyde de Yale=Tangwistel fil. et hær. Jena
in comit. Denbigh.   ap Mared ap Einion Bendow.

Llewellinna.=....

Danid ap=Tangwistel fil. Jebel ap Jeuan ap M'red
Lluellin. | ap Madoc ap Einion ap Rerid ap Jer.
          ap Madoc ap Ednowen B.

Gruffith ap Danid.=....

Rees ap Gruff. ap Danid=Ellena fil. Gruff. Hanmer
de Yale.   de Hanmer.

Graffith ap Jenkin.=Ellena fil. et hæres Resi ap Gruff. de Yale.

Mauritius ap Gruff. de Han-=....   Danid Lloyd ap=Margareta fil. Jem ap Danid
mer de lan deche in Yale.   M'red'd ap Rees. | ap Toona de Englois Vache.

Katherina vx. Tho.   Elizabetha vxor   Danid ap Morris=Margareta   Joh'es Lloyd
ap Danid ap Nich.   Thomæ Powell   Hanmer in Arti- fil. Danid   de Englois aᵒ
de Fortyn.   de Llandayn.   bns M'.   Lloyd.   1597.

Joh'es Hanmer de Llweny mapsis=Susanna filia Ric'i
fil. et hæres.   Kynaston de .....

Dorothea.   Margareta.

Hanmer of Bechfield [Bettisfield], near Whitchurch.

Harl. 1396, fo. 159ᵇ.

ARMS.—*Quarterly of six:* 1, *Argent, two lions passant-guardant azure;* 2, *Gules, a lion rampant within a bordure engrailed or* [RHYS AP TUDOR]; 3, *Vert, two boars passant or* [POWIS]; 4, *Azure, three boars passant in pale argent* [JONAS AP GRONO]; 5, *Argent, a cross engrailed, the ends fleury, between four ravens* [Cornish choughs] *sable* [EDWIN OF TEGAINGLE]; 6, *Gules, three legs flexed in triangle argent* [OWEN AP EDWYN].

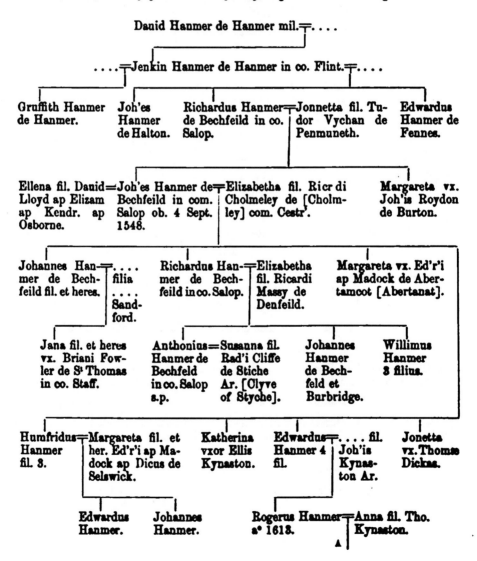

Dauid Hanmer de Hanmer mil.=. . . .

. . . .=Jenkin Hanmer de Hanmer in co. Flint.=. . . .

Gruffith Hanmer de Hanmer.

Joh'es Hanmer de Halton.

Richardus Hanmer de Bechfeild in co. Salop.=Jonnetta fil. Tudor Vychan de Penmuneth.

Edwardus Hanmer de Fennes.

Ellena fil. Dauid Lloyd ap Elizam ap Kendr. ap Osborne.=Joh'es Hanmer de Bechfeild in com. Salop ob. 4 Sept. 1548.=Elizabetha fil. Ricr di Cholmeley de [Cholmley] com. Cestr'.

Margareta vx. Joh'is Roydon de Burton.

Johannes Hanmer de Bechfeild fil. et heres.=. . . . filia . . . . Sandford.

Richardus Hanmer de Bechfeild in co. Salop.=Elizabetha fil. Ricardi Massy de Denfeild.

Margareta vx. Ed'r'i ap Madock de Abertamcot [Abertanat].

Jana fil. et heres vx. Briani Fowler de St Thomas in co. Staff.

Anthonius Hanmer de Bechfeld in co. Salop s.p.=Susanna fil. Rad'i Cliffe de Stiche Ar. [Clyve of Styche].

Johannes Hanmer de Bechfeld et Burbridge.

Willimus Hanmer 3 filius.

Humfridus Hanmer fil. 3.=Margareta fil. et her. Ed'r'i ap Madock ap Dicus de Selswick.

Katherina vxor Ellis Kynaston.

Edwardus Hanmer 4 fil.=. . . . fil. Joh'is Kynaston Ar.

Jonetta vx. Thomas Dickas.

Edwardus Hanmer.

Johannes Hanmer.

Rogerus Hanmer. aº 1613.=Anna fil. Tho. Kynaston.

▲

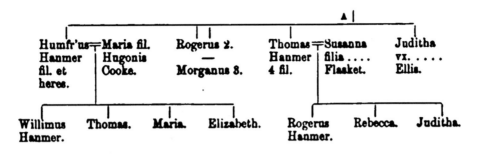

| Humfr'us Hanmer fil. et heres. | = Maria fil. Hugonis Cooke. | Rogerus 2. — Morganus 3. | Thomas Hanmer 4 fil. | = Susanna filia .... Flasket. | Juditha vx. .... Ellis. |

| Willimus Hanmer. | Thomas. | Maria. | Elizabeth. | | Rogerus Hanmer. | Rebecca. | Juditha. |

Harley of Harley, Brampton, Willey, etc.

Harl. 1396, fo. 166.   Harl. 1241, fo. 99.

ARMS: Harl. 1241.—*Or, a bend cotised sable.*

[Another copy of this Visitation gives—Quarterly: 1, as above; 2, ..., a lion rampant within a bordure ...., PRESTHOPE; 3, Azure, a fret or, WILILEYE; 4, ... on a chief .... two mullets ...., KENLEY; 5, Argent, on a bend sable three escallops argent, KENLEY; 6, Azure, a lion rampant or, STEPLETON; 7, Or, two lions passant in pale gules, BROMPTON; 8, Or, two lions passant-guardant in pale gules, VALENCE; 9, Or, a raven proper, CORBETT; 10, Sable, on a fesse dancettée or between three besants each charged with an escallop sable, three demi-lions rampant sable, WHARNCOMBE.

CREST.—A castle triple-towered proper, issuing therefrom a demi-lion rampant gules, armed and langued azure.

MOTTO.—VIRTUTE ET FIDE.   For THOMAS HARLEY A.D. 1600.]

Sᵣ Wᵐ Harley Kᵗ lo. of Harley in com. Salop went to=Catherine da. to Jerusalem in the company of Godfrey of Bullen, | Jasper Crofte Rob't Curteis Duke of Normandy, Rob't Steward of | Knight of the Scotland, where they were made Kᵗ of the Sepulchre. | Sepulchre.

Nicholas Harley lo. of=Margrett da. to Warren Bostock of Bostock in co. Cestr'. Harley in co. Salop. | *Arms: Sable, a fesse humettée argent.*

Will'm Harley=Joane da. to Sᵣ Jo. De la Bere Kᵗ. of Harley. | *Arms: Azure, a bend argent cotised or, between six martlets of the last.*

Nicho. Harley=Alice da. to Rob't Randulph al's Prescott of Westhay of Harley. | *Westhope in com. Salop.* | *Arms: Or, on a chief sable three tuns of the first.*

Robert Harley.=Alice da. & hei. to Sᵣ Roger Pulleston Kᵗ. | *Arms: Sable, three mullets argent.*

▲

Sʳ Rich. Harley Kᵗ=Burga da. & h. to Sʳ Andrew Willeigh Kᵗ *Lo. of Willeleigh.*
[Sheriff 1301].   *Arms: Azure, fretty or, a canton argent.*

Sʳ Malcolme* de Harley Kᵗ.=....

Sʳ Rob't Harley of=Margrett da. & coh. to Sʳ Bryan Brampton of Brampton [of
Harley, Willey, & | Brampton Bryan] Kᵗ.
Kinleighe Kᵗ.   [Arms: Or, two lions passant in pale gules—ancient seal.]

Sʳ Rob't Harley of Harley=Joane da. to Roger Corbett=John Daras
and Willeigh.   of Morton Kᵗ.   2 husband.

Alice da. & h. vx. Sʳ Hamon Pashley Kᵗ.   Roger ob. s.p.

Eliza. da. & hei. m'ied Sʳ Rich. Lacon of Willey Kᵗ.

Walter de Harley   Sʳ Bryan Harley of Brampton, Bugtun,=Eleanor da. to Sʳ Roger
ob. s.p.   and Bedwarden [co. Hereford].   Corbett of Moorton Kᵗ.

Bryan Harley=Isold 2 da. to Sʳ Raufe   Margrett vx. Rees Moythey 2 to
of Brampton. | Lingham *Lingen* Kᵗ.   Wᵐ Walwyn of Longward.

Richard Harley   Geoffrey Harley=Joyce *Joane* da. & h. to
ob. s.p.   brother & heire. | Sʳ John Burleigh Kᵗ.

Sʳ John Harley of Brampton Kᵗ=Jane da. to John Hacklett of Yeton Kᵗ
[Sheriff 1481; Knighted on the | *Hackluit of Eyton com. Heref.*
field at Tewkesbury 1471].

Rich. Harley of Branton.=Katherine da. to Sʳ Tho. Vaughan of Trertur Kᵗ.

Ann da. to Sʳ Edw. Rous=John Harley of Brianton.=Ann da. to Sʳ Edw.
of Worc. Kᵗ.   Croftes Kᵗ.

Alice vx. Symon Mackl'w   John Harley=Mawde da. & h. to James
Mucklowe.   of Brianton. | Warncone *Warncombe.*

B

* Harl. 1241 makes this Sʳ Malcolm *brother,* not father, of Sʳ Robert who marries Margrett
Brampton.

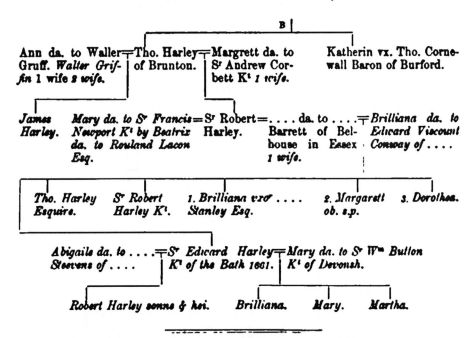

B

Ann da. to Waller=Tho. Harley=Margrett da. to   Katherin vx. Tho. Corne-
Gruff. *Walter Grif-* | of Brunton. | Sʳ Andrew Cor-   wall Baron of Burford.
fin 1 wife 2 wife. | | bett Kᵗ *1 wife.*

James   Mary da. to Sʳ Francis=Sʳ Robert=.... da. to ....=*Brilliana da. to*
Harley. Newport Kᵗ by Beatrix Harley.   Barrett of Bel- *Edward Viscount*
        da. to Rouland Lacon   house in Essex *Conway of ....*
        Esq.   *1 wife.*

Tho. Harley   Sʳ Robert   1. Brilliana vxᵒ ....   *2. Margarett   3. Dorothea.*
Esquire.   Harley Kᵗ.   Stanley Esq.   *ob. s.p.*

Abigaile da. to ....=Sʳ Edward Harley=Mary da. to Sʳ Wᵐ Button
Steevens of .... | Kᵗ of the Bath 1661. | Kᵗ of Devonsh.

Robert Harley sonne & hei.   *Brilliana.   Mary.   Martha.*

Harnage of Belswardine and Shenton.

Harl. 1396, fo. 183ᵇ. Harl. 1241, ff. 20, 48. Harl. 615, fo. 256ᵇ. S., ff. 125ᵇ, 126.

ARMS: Harl. 1396.—*Quarterly:* 1 and 4, *Argent, six torteaux, three, two, and
one, a crescent for difference;* 2, *Argent, a lion rampant gules, in chief three
torteaux* [PIARD]; 3, *Or, two bars sable, the upper charged with four and
the lower with three escallops of the first* [each charged with three escallops].*

Will'us Harnage de Belleswardin=.... fil. et hær..... Peiart
in com. Salop. | *Periart* of Norbury.

Will'us Harnage†=Jocosa filia Roberti Screuen or Scryven
de Belleswardin. | de Frodesley in com. Salop.

Hugo *Giles* Harnage de Belleswardin in com. Salop [and=Margeria filia Richardi
of Sheinton; Bailiff of Bridgnorth 1403, and Burgess of | Lacon militis.
Parliament 1402 and 1419].

Tho. Harnage=Dorothea fil.   Christo-   Elizabetha   Rich'us=.... filia ....
de Belliswar- | Tho. Smith   pherus   vx. Joh'es   Harnage | Oteley de Ote-
din in com. | de Renen-   Harnage   Meston.   de Shen- | ley in com.
Salop. | hall in com.   2 fil. s.p.   ton in | Salop.
             | Essex.   com. S.

A   B

* In Harl. 615 the arms are quarterly of the second and third quarterings only, the first
being omitted.
† Omitted in Harl. 1241.

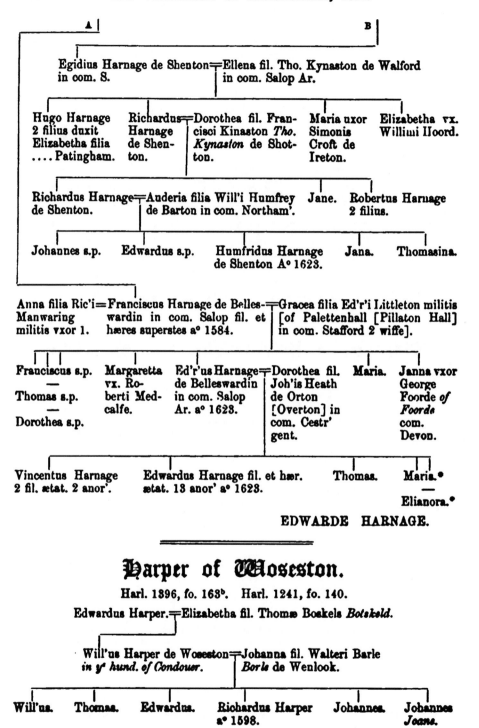

A | B |

Egidius Harnage de Shenton=Ellena fil. Tho. Kynaston de Walford
in com. S.   in com. Salop Ar.

Hugo Harnage 2 filius duxit Elizabetha filia .... Patingham. | Richardus Harnage de Shenton. =Dorothea fil. Francisci Kinaston *Tho. Kynaston* de Shotton. | Maria uxor Simonis Croft de Ireton. | Elizabetha vx. Willimi Hoord.

Richardus Harnage de Shenton.=Auderia filia Will'i Humfrey de Barton in com. Northam'. | Jane. | Robertus Harnage 2 filius.

Johannes s.p.   Edwardus s.p.   Humfridus Harnage de Shenton Aᵒ 1623.   Jana.   Thomasina.

Anna filia Ric'i Manwaring militis vxor 1.=Franciscus Harnage de Belleswardin in com. Salop fil. et hæres superstes aᵒ 1584.=Gracea filia Ed'r'i Littleton militis [of Palettenhall [Pillaton Hall] in com. Stafford 2 wiffe].

Franciscus s.p. — Thomas s.p. — Dorothea s.p. | Margaretta vx. Roberti Medcalfe. | Ed'r'us Harnage de Belleswardin in com. Salop Ar. aᵒ 1623.=Dorothea fil. Joh'is Heath de Orton [Overton] in com. Cestr' gent. | Maria. | Janna vxor George Foorde *of Foorde* com. Devon.

Vincentus Harnage 2 fil. ætat. 2 anor'.   Edwardus Harnage fil. et hær. ætat. 13 anor' aᵒ 1623.   Thomas.   Maria.* — Elianora.*

EDWARDE HARNAGE.

𝕳arper of 𝕎oseston.

Harl. 1396, fo. 163ᵇ.   Harl. 1241, fo. 140.

Edwardus Harper.=Elizabetha fil. Thomæ Boskels *Botskeld*.

Will'us Harper de Woseston *in yᵉ hund. of Condouer*.=Johanna fil. Walteri Barle *Borle* de Wenlook.

Will'us.   Thomas.   Edwardus.   Richardus Harper aᵒ 1598.   Johannes.   Johannes *Joans*.

* In Shrewsbury MS. Maria and Eleanor appear as daughters of Francis and Grace.

Harper of Amerley, co. Hereford, from Wellington, Salop.

Harl. 1396, fo. 164.   Harl. 1241, fo. 152ᵇ.

ARMS: Harl. 1396.—*Quarterly:* 1 *and* 4, *Sable* in Harl. 1241, *a chevron and canton both ermine* [HARPER]; 2 *and* 3, *Azure, on a cross engrailed argent five escallops sable* [gules, CRITOFT].

Joh'es Harper de Willington.⊤.... fil. et her.....Criktoftes.

Will'us⊤.... filia Eustacij Harper. | Witney *Whitbney*.

Johannes Bewpty⊤.... fil. et her. Dauid Lloy *Bewpey*. | ap Sʳ Gruff. Vychan.

Joh'es Harper de Willington.⊤Anna fil. Joh'is Bewpti.

Johannes Harper de Amerley in co. Hertf. *Hereffsh.* 1 fil.   Thomas.   Alicia **vx.** Johannis Wilton.   Margeria **vx.** Tho. Shipham.

Elizabetha fil. Hugonis═Anthonius Harper de⊤Johanna fil. Joh'is Gelton ex Begge *Bigge* de Salop.   Welington 2 fil. | Maria Ponsbury *Ponlesbury*.

Elizabetha.   Dorothea.   Elianora.

Harpur of Rushall.

S., ff. 111ᵇ, 112ᵃ.

[*Nigellus de Rushall D'n's de Rushall ('po Conq. et antea.*⊤.... *Arms: Argent, a lion rampant and bordure engrailed sable.*

Osbertus de Rushall filius et hær. Nigelli.⊤....

Ricardus de Rushall de familiâ Reg. H. 2 cuidam⊤.... *Rex dedit manerᵐ de Rowley juxta Dudley.*

Ric'us de Rushall junior de familiâ Rs. Johannis cuidam Rex 2 regni⊤.... *confirmavit m. de Rowley obiit in Gwen temp. H. 3.*

* Harl. 1241 gives another generation here, viz., William (son of John) Harper, who, by Jane, da. of John Whittington, had John, Anthony, and others, as above.

Y Y

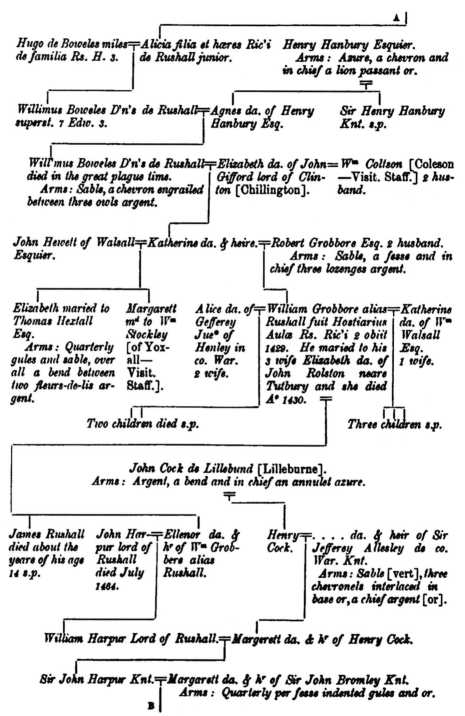

Hugo de Boweles miles=*Alicia filia et hæres Ric'i*   *Henry Hanbury Esquier.*
de familia Rs. H. 3.   *de Rushall junior.*   *Arms : Azure, a chevron and*
    in chief a lion passant or.

Willimus Boweles D'n's de Rushall=*Agnes da. of Henry*   *Sir Henry Hanbury*
superst. 7 Edw. 3.   *Hanbury Esq.*   *Knt. s.p.*

Will'mus Boweles D'n's de Rushall=*Elizabeth da. of John*=*Wm Collson* [Coleson
died in the great plague time.   *Gifford lord of Clin-*   —Visit. Staff.] *2 hus-*
    Arms: Sable, a chevron engrailed   *ton* [Chillington].   *band.*
between three owls argent.

John Hewett of Walsall=*Katherine da. & heire.*=*Robert Grobbore Esq. 2 husband.*
Esquier.   *Arms : Sable, a fesse and in*
    chief three lozenges argent.

Elizabeth maried to   *Margarett*   *Alice da. of*=*William Grobbore alias*=*Katherine*
Thomas Hextall   *m^d to W^m*   *Gefferey*   *Rushall fuit Hostiarius*   *da. of W^m*
Esq.   *Stockley*   *Jue° of*   *Aulæ Rs. Ric'i 2 obiit*   *Walsall*
    Arms : Quarterly   [of Yox-   *Henley in*   *1429. He maried to his*   *Esq.*
gules and sable, over   all—   *co. War.*   *3 wife Elizabeth da. of*   *1 wife.*
all a bend between   Visit.   *2 wife.*   *John Rolston neare*
two fleurs-de-lis ar-   Staff.].   *Tutbury and she died*
gent.   *A° 1430.* =

Two children died s.p.   *Three children s.p.*

John Cock de Lillebund [Lilleburne].
Arms : Argent, a bend and in chief an annulet azure.
=

James Rushall   *John Har-*=*Ellenor da. &*   *Henry*=*. . . . da. & heir of Sir*
died about the   *pur lord of*   *h^r of Wm Grob-*   *Cock.*   *Jefferey Allesley de co.*
yeare of his age   *Rushall*   *bere alias*   *War. Knt.*
14 s.p.   *died July*   *Rushall.*   *Arms : Sable* [vert], *three*
    1484.   *chevronels interlaced in*
    base or, a chief argent [or].

William Harpur Lord of Rushall.=*Margarett da. & h^r of Henry Cock.*

Sir John Harpur Knt.=*Margarett da. & h^r of Sir John Bromley Knt.*
    Arms : Quarterly per fesse indented gules and or.

B

* This name is spelt Ive in the Staffordshire Visitation, 1583 ; there were families named
both Jewe and Ive in Warwickshire, Staffordshire, etc.

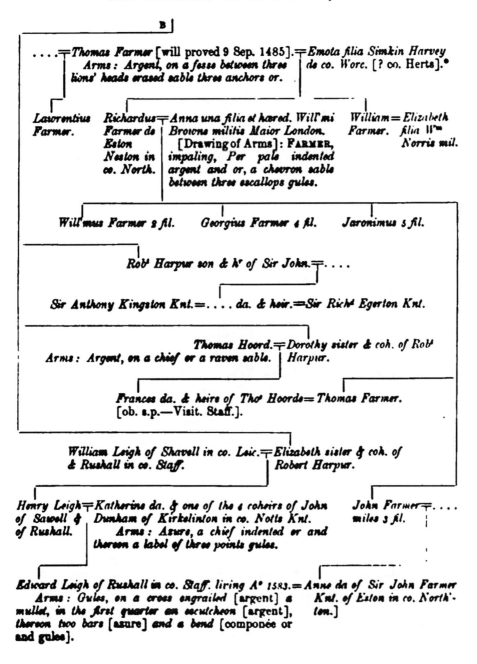

B

.... = *Thomas Farmer* [will proved 9 Sep. 1485]. = *Emota filia Simkin Harvey*
    Arms : *Argent, on a fesse between three*   *de co. Worc.* [? co. Herts].[*]
    lions' heads erased sable three anchors or.

Laurentius   *Richardus* = *Anna una filia et hared. Will'mi*   *William* = *Elizabeth*
Farmer.   *Farmer de* | *Browne militis Maior London.*   *Farmer.*   *filia W'm*
        Eston   [Drawing of Arms]: FARMER,   *Norris mil.*
        Neston in   *impaling, Per pale indented*
        co. North.   *argent and or, a chevron sable*
            between three escallops gules.

Will'mus Farmer 2 fil.   *Georgius Farmer 4 fil.*   *Jaronimus 5 fil.*

Rob' Harpur son & h' of Sir John. = ...

Sir Anthony Kingston Knt. = ... *da. & heir.* = *Sir Rich' Egerton Knt.*

                Thomas Hoord. = *Dorothy sister & coh. of Rob'*
Arms : *Argent, on a chief or a raven sable.* | *Harpur.*

    Frances da. & heire of Tho' Hoorde = *Thomas Farmer.*
    [ob. s.p.—Visit. Staff.].

William Leigh of Shavell in co. Leic. = *Elizabeth sister & coh. of*
& Rushall in co. Staff.   *Robert Harpur.*

Henry Leigh = *Katherine da. & one of the 4 coheirs of John*   *John Farmer* = ...
of Sawell &   *Dunham of Kirkelinton in co. Notts Knt.*   *miles 3 fil.*
of Rushall.   Arms : *Azure, a chief indented or and*
       thereon a label of three points gules.

Edward Leigh of Rushall in co. Staff. living A° 1583. = *Anne da of Sir John Farmer*
    Arms : *Gules, on a cross engrailed* [argent] *a*   *Knt. of Eston in co. North'-*
mullet, in the first quarter an escutcheon [argent],   *ton.*]
thereon two bars [azure] *and a bend* [componée or
and gules].

---

[*] Emmota, da. of Simkin Harvy of co. Herts, and relict of Henry Wenman of Blewbery,
co. Oxford, Arm.

Harington of Bishton.

Harl. 1396, fo. 131.

ARMS.—*Sable, a fret argent, on a chief of the second three trefoils vert.*
CREST.—*A lion's head erased or, charged with two trefoils slipped in pale vert, collared gules, the collar studded and lined argent.*

Omnibus X'pi fidelibus ad quos hoc præsens Scriptum pervenerit Georgius Comes Salop' salutem. Sciatis me pro bono consilio michi per Simonem Harington de Bysheton me pens's et imposterum michi et hæredibus meis impendend: dedisse terras in villa de Stonton infra domum meam de Idsole al's Shuffenall in com. Salop dat. 22 die mensis Decembr' anno 9 H. 7.

[Drawing of a Seal.—Plate I., Fig. 6.]

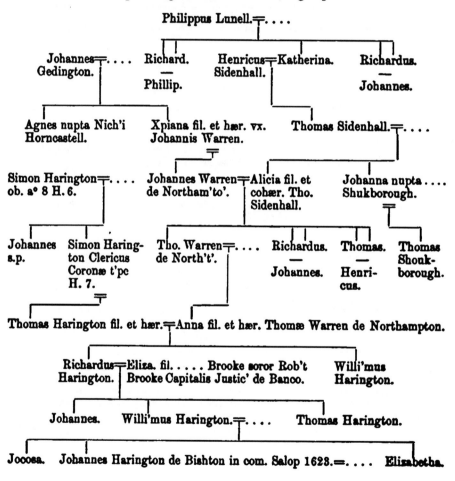

Philippus Lunell.⊤. . . .

Johannes⊤. . . .   Richard.   Henricus⊤Katherina.   Richardus.
Gedington.   —   Sidenhall.   —
     Phillip.   Johannes.

Agnes nupta Nich'i   Xpiana fil. et hær. vx.   Thomas Sidenhall.⊤. . . .
Horncastell.   Johannis Warren.

Simon Harington⊤. . . .   Johannes Warren⊤Alicia fil. et   Johanna nupta . . . .
ob. aᵒ 8 H. 6.   de Northam'to'.   cohær. Tho.   Shukborough.
                           Sidenhall.

Johannes   Simon Haring-   Tho. Warren⊤. . . .   Richardus.   Thomas.   Thomas
s.p.   ton Clericus   de North't'.   —   —   Shouk-
   Coronæ t'pc   Johannes.   Henri-   borough.
   H. 7.   cus.

Thomas Harington fil. et hær.⊤Anna fil. et hær. Thomæ Warren de Northampton.

Richardus⊤Eliza. fil. . . . . Brooke soror Rob't   Willi'mus
Harington. │ Brooke Capitalis Justic' de Banco.   Harington.

Johannes.   Willi'mus Harington.⊤. . . .   Thomas Harington.

Jocosa.   Johannes Harington de Bishton in com. Salop 1623.⹀. . . .   Elizabetha.

Harrington of Bishton.

S., fo. 124ª.

[ARMS: *Sable, a fret argent, on a chief of the second three trefoils slipped vert.*
CREST.—*A lion's head erased or, charged with two trefoils slipped in pale vert,
collared gules, lined argent, upon the collar three plates.*

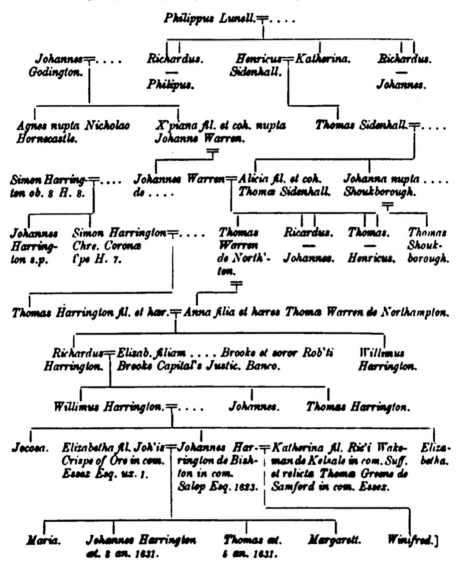

Philippus Lunell.⊤. . . .

Johannes⊤. . . .
Godington.

Richardus.
—
Philipus.

Henricus⊤*Katherina.*
Sidenhall.

Richardus.
—
Johannes.

Agnes nupta Nicholao
Hornecastle.

X'piana fil. et coh. nupta
Johanne Warren.

Thomas Sidenhall.⊤. . . .

Simon Harring-⊤. . . .
ton ob. 8 H. 8.

Johannes Warren⊤*Alicia fil. et coh.*
de . . . .   *Thomas Sidenhall.*

Johanna nupta . . . .
Shoukborough.

Johannes
Harring-
ton s.p.

Simon Harrington⊤. . . .
Chr. Coronæ
t'pe H. 7.

Thomas
Warren
de North'-
ton.

Ricardus.
—
Johannes.

Thomas.
—
Henricus.

Thomas
Shouk-
borough.

Thomas Harrington fil. et har.⊤*Anna filia et hares Thomas Warren de Northampton.*

Richardus⊤*Elizab. filiam* . . . . *Brooke et soror Rob'ti*
Harrington. | *Brooke Capital's Justic. Banco.*

Willimus
Harrington.

Willimus Harrington.⊤. . . .   *Johannes.*   *Thomas Harrington.*

Jocosa.

Elizabetha fil. Joh'is
Crispe of Ore in com.
Essex Esq. ux. 1.

Johannes Har-⊤*Katherina fil. Ric'i Wake-*
rington de Bish- | *man de Kelsale in com. Suff.*
ton in com. | *et relicta Thomas Greene de*
Salop Esq. 1623. | *Samford in com. Essex.*

Eliza-
betha.

Maria.

Johannes Harrington
æt. 3 an. 1631.

Thomas æt.
5 an. 1631.

Margarett.

Winifred.]

Harris of Abcott.

Harl. 1396, fo. 180ᵇ. S., fo. 123ᵇ.

ARMS: Harl. 1396.—*Azure, on a chevron argent between three hedgehogs or a crescent for difference.*

Thomas Harris de Abcotte in co. Salop.=Jana fil. Joh'is Sonnybanke de Ludlow in com. Salop.

Galfr'us Harris de Abcott in com. Salop.=Katherina fil. Joh'is Eastope de Eastope in com. Wigorn'.

| Alicia vx. Joh'is Cooke. | Johanna vx. Tho. Metton [*Mitton*]. | Anna nupta Ed'r'o Langford. | Maria nupta Roger Collimor de London. |

Henricus Harris 2.=Johanna fil. Joh'is Danies.

Rich'us Harris de Abcott in com. Salop.=Brigitta fil. Thomæ Barkley [Berkeley] de Ewdnes in com. Salop.

Samuell Harris* æt. 7 anor' a° 1623.

Will'us Harris de Abcott in co. Salop a° 1623.=Alicia fil. Will'i Lane de Ludlow in com. Salop Clerici Signeti.

Franciscus 2.*
—
Richardus 3.*

Maria.*
—
Brigitta.*

WILL. HARRIES.

Harris of Stockton.

Harl. 1396, fo. 148.   Harl. 1241, fo. 124.   S., ff. 141ᵇ, 142.

ARMS: Harl. 1396.—*Azure, a chevron argent between three hedgehogs or.*†

Henricus Hull al's Harris.=Sion'et [*Sionett*] filia M'red'd ap howell de Geri.

Joh'es Hill al's Harris de com. Staff.=Jocosa filia Ric'i Acton.

Johannes Harris de Stocton in com. Salop.=Jonetta filia Simonis Henalt Ar.

Johan's Harris de Stockton in co. Salop.=Katherinæ fil. Jenkin ap Jem Vychan.

* Samuel, Francis, Richard, Mary, and Bridget appear as sons and daughters of Geoffrey and Katherine in Shrewsbury MS.

† Harl. 1241 gives the same arms as Harris of Crockton.

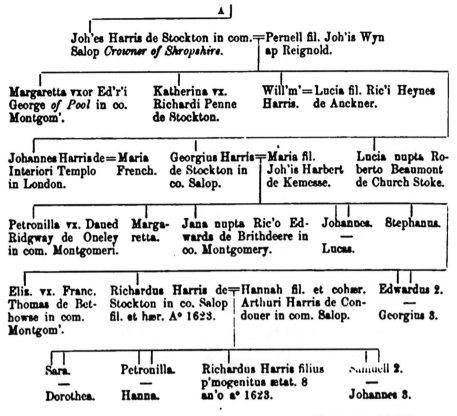

▲

Joh'es Harris de Stockton in com.=Pernell fil. Joh'is Wyn
Salop *Crowner of Shropshire.* | ap Reignold.

Margaretta vxor Ed'r'i
George *of Pool* in co.
Montgom'.

Katherina vx.
Richardi Penne
de Stockton.

Will'm'=Lucia fil. Ric'i Heynes
Harris. | de Anckner.

Johannes Harris de=Maria
Interiori Templo | French.
in London.

Georgius Harris=Maria fil.
de Stockton in | Joh'is Harbert
co. Salop. | de Kemesse.

Lucia nupta Ro-
berto Beaumont
de Church Stoke.

Petronilla vx. Daued
Ridgway de Oneley
in com. Montgomeri.

Marga-
retta.

Jana nupta Ric'o Ed-
wards de Brithdeere in
co. Montgomery.

Johannes.
—
Lucas.

Stephanus.

Eliz. vx. Franc.
Thomas de Bet-
howse in com.
Montgom'.

Richardus Harris de=Hannah fil. et cohær.
Stockton in co. Salop | Arthuri Harris de Con-
fil. et hær. A° 1623. | douer in com. Salop.

Edwardus 2.
—
Georgius 3.

Sara.
—
Dorothea.

Petronilla.
—
Hanna.

Richardus Harris filius
p'mogenitus ætat. 8
an'o a° 1623.

Samuell 2.
—
Johannes 3.

RICHARD HARRYES.

Harris of Cruckton and Tong Castle.

Harl. 1396, fo. 135. S., ff. 126ᵇ, 127.

ARMS: Harl. 1396.—*Barry of eight ermine and azure, over all three annulets or.*
CREST.—*A hawk argent, beaked and belled or, preying on a pheasant of the first.*

ARMS :* Shrewsbury MS.—*Argent, a lion rampant gules [sable] within an orle of
cinquefoils gules.*
1 CREST.—*A wolf statant gules.*
2 CREST.—*A lion rampant sable between two wings argent.*
MOTTO.—PIE REPONE TE.

Joh'es Harris de Cruckton in co. Salop.=. . . .

Richardus Harris de Cruktoo.=Elianora fil. Will'i Jennyns de Wallyborne
▲ | in co. Salop.

* These are the arms, crests, and motto of Pierpoint.

Joh'es Harris de══Elianora fil. Tho. Prowde
Cruckton in com. │ de Sutton in com. Salop.
Salop.

Katherina ux. Joh'is Corbett de
Alston renupta Jacobo Morris
de Aston.

Thomas Harris de Tonge══Elianora filia Rogeri
Castell in com. Salop Baro-│Gifforde de London
nettus Serviens ad legem │in Medicinus Doc-
et Justiciarius pacis in │toris R'næ Eliz.
eodem comitatu 1623.

Rolandus Harris══Jana fil.
de Ludlow in │Thomæ
com. Salop 2 fil. │Langford
│de Ludlow.

Franciscus
Harris fil.
p'mogenitus
ætat. 24 an'
aº 1623.

Elizabetha [*da. & coh. to whom
her father gave Tonge Castle and
had Croxden by y° death of her
sister Margaret without issue*].

Margareta
[*ob. virgo*].

Thomas. Anna.

Johannis
2.

[*Sir Henry Perpoint of Holme Perpoint*══*Frances da. to Sir Wm Cavendish
in com. Nottingham K^t 1614.* │*of Hardwick Kn^t.*

Robert Perpoint de Holme Perpoint Esq. was created══*Gertrude da. & coheir to
Baron of Holme Perpoint and Viscount Newarke │Henry Talbott brother to
20 Junii 1627 and Earl of Kingston upon Hull 25 July │Gilbert Earle of Shrews-
1628. │bury.*]

Anna* vxor Joh'is Wilde══[*William Perpoint
de Wiche [? Droitwich] │of Tong Castle s^d
in com. Wigorn'. │son.*

Henry Perpoint══*Cecilia da. of
Viscount New- │Paul Viscount
arke. │Baininge.*]

Arthurus Harris══Jana filia ....
de Prestock in │Newton de
com. Salop 3 fil. │Prestock.

Richardus Harris de══Anna filia Thomæ
Cruckton in com. │Smalman de Wider-
Salop 4 fil. 1623. │top [Wildertop].

Johannes Harris fil.
et hæres ætat. 15
annor' aº 1623.

Thomas 2.
——
Stephanus 3.

Franciscus 4.
——
Jacobus 5.

Isaack 6.
——
Walterus 7.

Maria.

RICHARD HARRIES.

* Her monument in Tong Church says she died in childbed, 6 May 1624, in the sixteenth
year of her age.

Hatton.

Harl. 1396, fo. 138ᵇ.   Harl. 1241, fo. 89ᵇ.   S., ff. 130ᵇ—135ᵃ.

ARMS: Harl. 1396.—*Quarterly of ten : 1, Azure, a chevron between three garbs or,* HATTON ; *2, Barry of four and lozengy counterchanged argent and sable,* CRISPIN ; *3, Argent, a cross patonce between four martlets gules,* GOLBORN ; *4, Argent, an eagle displayed sable,* BRUYN ; *5, Argent, on a bend sable three covered cups of the first,* RIXTON ; *6, Sable, a cross engrailed ermine,* HALOM ; *7, Or, a saltire sable,* HELLESBY ; *8, Sable, a fesse humettée argent, a crescent for difference,* BOSTOCK ; *9, Azure, two bars argent,* VENABLES ; *10, Argent, a cross sable, the ends terminating in fleurs-de-lis or,* NEWTON.

[CREST.—A hind trippant or.]

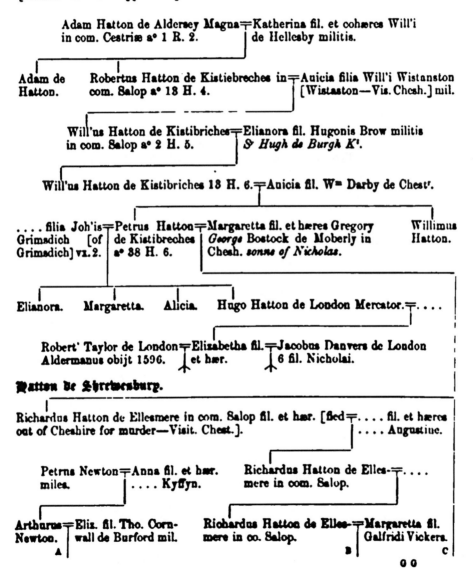

Adam Hatton de Aldersey Magna⊤Katherina fil. et cohæres Will'i
in com. Cestriæ aᵒ 1 R. 2. │ de Hellesby militis.

Adam de Hatton. │ Robertus Hatton de Kistiebreches in⊤Auicia filia Will'i Wistanston com. Salop aᵒ 18 H. 4. │ [Wistaston—Vis. Chesh.] mil.

Will'us Hatton de Kistibriches⊤Elianora fil. Hugonis Brow militis
in com. Salop aᵒ 2 H. 5. │ *& Hugh de Burgh Kᵗ.*

Will'us Hatton de Kistibriches 18 H. 6.⊤Auicia fil. Wᵐ Darby de Chestʳ.

.... filia Joh'is⊤Petrus Hatton⊤Margaretta fil. et hæres Gregory   Willimus
Grimsdich [of │ de Kistibreches │ *George* Bostock de Moberly in   Hatton.
Grimsdich] vx. 2. │ aᵒ 38 H. 6. │ Chesh. *sonne of Nicholas.*

Elianora.   Margaretta.   Alicia.   Hugo Hatton de London Mercator.⊤ ....

Robertᵗ Taylor de London⊤Elizabetha fil.⊤Jacobus Danvers de London
Aldermanus obijt 1596. │ et hær. │ 6 fil. Nicholai.

Hatton de Shrewsbury.

Richardus Hatton de Ellesmere in com. Salop fil. et hær. [fled⊤.... fil. et hæres
out of Cheshire for murder—Visit. Chest.]. │ .... Augustine.

Petrus Newton⊤Anna fil. et hær.   Richardus Hatton de Elles-⊤....
miles. │ .... Kyffyn.   mere in com. Salop.

Arthurus⊤Eliz. fil. Tho. Corn-   Richardus Hatton de Elles-⊤Margaretta fil.
Newton. │ wall de Burford mil.   mere in co. Salop. │ Galfridi Vickers.

A   B   C

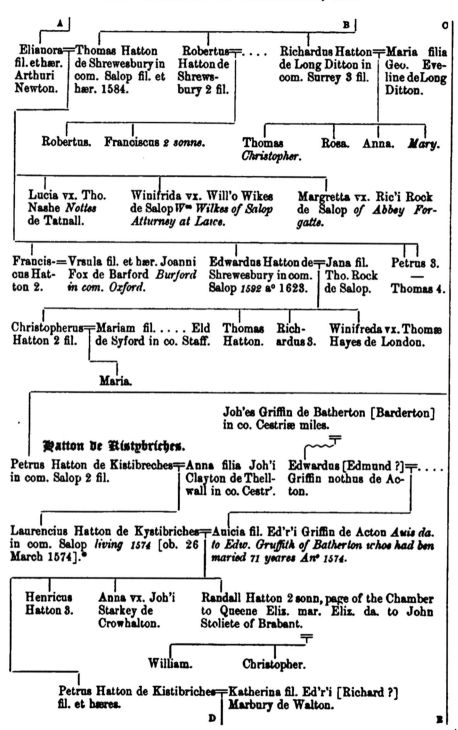

A | **B** | **C**

Elianora=Thomas Hatton de Shrewesbury in com. Salop fil. et hær. 1584. | Robertus=. . . . Hatton de Shrewsbury 2 fil. | Richardus Hatton=Maria filia de Long Ditton in com. Surrey 3 fil. | Geo. Eveline de Long Ditton.

fil. et hær. Arthuri Newton.

Robertus.   Franciscus *2 sonne.*

Thomas Christopher.   Rosa.   Anna.   *Mary.*

Lucia vx. Tho. Nashe *Nottes* de Tatnall.

Winifrida vx. Will'o Wikes de Salop *Wm Wilkes of Salop Atturney at Lawe.*

Margretta vx. Ric'i Rock de Salop *of Abbey Forgatte.*

Francis-=Vrsula fil. et hær. Joanni cus Hat- | Fox de Barford *Burford* ton 2. | *in com. Oxford.*

Edwardus Hatton de=Jana fil. Shrewesbury in com. | Tho. Rock Salop *1592 a° 1623.* | de Salop.

Petrus 3. ——— Thomas 4.

Christopherus=Mariam fil. . . . . Eld Hatton 2 fil. | de Syford in co. Staff.

Thomas Hatton.

Richardus 3.

Winifreda vx. Thomæ Hayes de London.

Maria.

Joh'es Griffin de Batherton [Barderton] in co. Cestriæ miles.
⊤

Hatton de Kistybriches.

Petrus Hatton de Kistibreches=Anna filia Joh'i in com. Salop 2 fil. | Clayton de Thellwall in co. Cestr'.

Edwardus [Edmund ?]=. . . . Griffin nothus de Acton.

Laurencius Hatton de Kystibriches=Auicia fil. Ed'r'i Griffin de Acton *Auis da.* in com. Salop *living 1574* [ob. 26 | *to Edw. Gruffith of Batherton whoe had ben* March 1574].* | *maried 71 yeares An° 1574.*

Henricus Hatton 3.

Anna vx. Joh'i Starkey de Crowhalton.

Randall Hatton 2 sonn, page of the Chamber to Queene Eliz. mar. Eliz. da. to John Stoliete of Brabant.
⊤

William.   Christopher.

Petrus Hatton de Kistibriches=Katherina fil. Ed'r'i [Richard ?] fil. et hæres. | Marbury de Walton.

D | **E**

* " Was married 71 yeares."—Visit. Chesh. 1580.

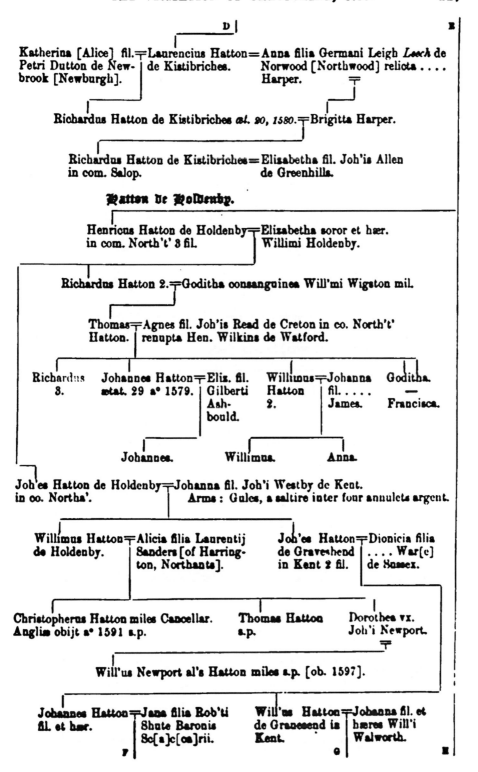

D |

Katherina [Alice] fil.⹀Laurencius Hatton=Anna filia Germani Leigh *Leech* de
Petri Dutton de New- | de Kistibriches. Norwood [Northwood] relicta . . . .
brook [Newburgh]. Harper.
⹀

Richardus Hatton de Kistibriches *æt. 20, 1580.*⹀Brigitta Harper.

Richardus Hatton de Kistibriches=Elizabetha fil. Joh'is Allen
in com. Salop. de Greenhills.

𝕳𝖆𝖙𝖙𝖔𝖓 𝖉𝖊 𝕳𝖔𝖑𝖉𝖊𝖓𝖇𝖞.

Henricus Hatton de Holdenby⹀Elizabetha soror et hær.
in com. North't' 3 fil. Willimi Holdenby.

Richardus Hatton 2.⹀Goditha consanguinea Will'mi Wigston mil.

Thomas⹀Agnes fil. Joh'is Read de Creton in co. North't'
Hatton. | renupta Hen. Wilkins de Watford.

| Richardus 3. | Johannes Hatton *ætat.* 29 a° 1579.⹀Eliz. fil. Gilberti Ashbould. | Willimus Hatton 2.⹀Johanna fil. . . . . James. | Goditha. — Francisca. |

Johannes. Willimus. Anna.

Joh'es Hatton de Holdenby⹀Johanna fil. Joh'i Westby de Kent.
in co. Northa'. Arms : Gules, a saltire inter four annulets argent.

Willimus Hatton⹀Alicia filia Laurentij Joh'es Hatton⹀Dionicia filia
de Holdenby. Sanders [of Harring- de Graveshend . . . . War[e]
ton, Northants]. in Kent 2 fil. de Sussex.

Christopherus Hatton miles Cancellar. Thomas Hatton Dorothea vx.
Angliæ obijt a° 1591 s.p. s.p. Joh'i Newport.
⹀

Will'us Newport al's Hatton miles s.p. [ob. 1597].

Johannes Hatton⹀Jana filia Rob'ti Will'us Hatton⹀Johanna fil. et
fil. et hær. | Shute Baronis de Graveshend in | hæres Will'i
Sc[a]c[ca]rii. Kent. Walworth.

F | G | H |

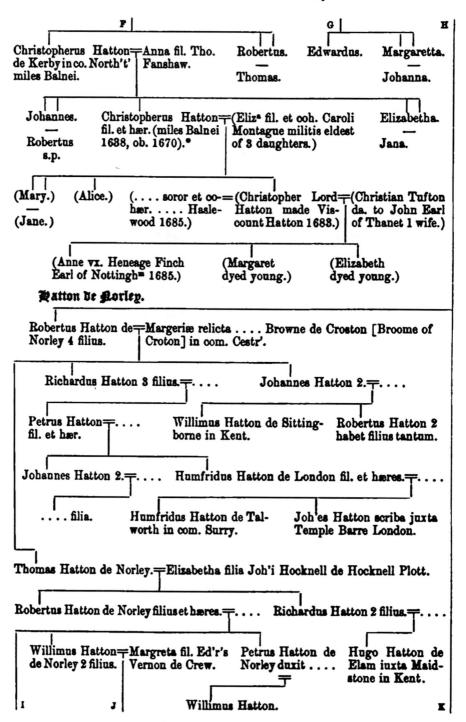

F | **G** | **H**

Christopherus Hatton=Anna fil. Tho.
de Kerby in co. North't' | Fanshaw.
miles Balnei.

Robertus.
—
Thomas.

Edwardus.

Margaretta.
—
Johanna.

Johannes.
—
Robertus
s.p.

Christopherus Hatton=(Eliz⁸ fil. et ooh. Caroli
fil. et hær. (miles Balnei | Montague militis eldest
1638, ob. 1670).* | of 3 daughters.)

Elizabetha.
—
Jana.

(Mary.)
—
(Jane.)

(Alice.)

(.... soror et co-=(Christopher Lord=(Christian Tufton
hær. .... Hasle- | Hatton made Vis- | da. to John Earl
wood 1685.) | count Hatton 1683.) | of Thanet 1 wife.)

(Anne vx. Heneage Finch
Earl of Nottingh⁻ 1685.)

(Margaret
dyed young.)

(Elizabeth
dyed young.)

𝕳𝖆𝖙𝖙𝖔𝖓 𝖉𝖊 𝕹𝖔𝖗𝖑𝖊𝖞.

Robertus Hatton de=Margeriæ relicta .... Browne de Croston [Broome of
Norley 4 filius. | Croton] in com. Cestr'.

Richardus Hatton 3 filius.=....

Johannes Hatton 2.=....

Petrus Hatton=....
fil. et hær.

Willimus Hatton de Sitting-
borne in Kent.

Robertus Hatton 2
habet filius tantum.

Johannes Hatton 2.=....

Humfridus Hatton de London fil. et hæres.=....

.... filia.

Humfridus Hatton de Tal-
worth in com. Surry.

Joh'es Hatton scriba juxta
Temple Barre London.

Thomas Hatton de Norley.=Elizabetha filia Joh'i Hocknell de Hocknell Plott.

Robertus Hatton de Norley filius et hæres.=....

Richardus Hatton 2 filius.=....

Willimus Hatton=Margreta fil. Ed'r's
de Norley 2 filius. | Vernon de Crew.

Petrus Hatton de
Norley duxit ....
=

Hugo Hatton de
Elam iuxta Maid-
stone in Kent.

Willimus Hatton.

I | **J** | **K**

* The parts within parentheses, at the end of this pedigree, have been added in a later hand,
and do not occur in Shrewsbury MS.

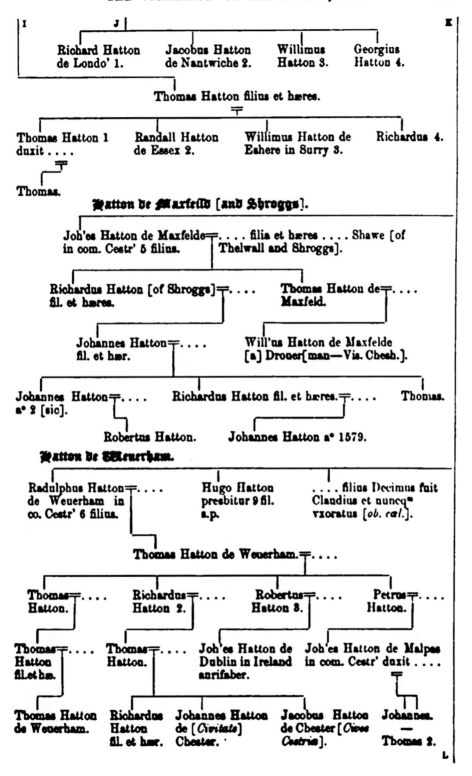

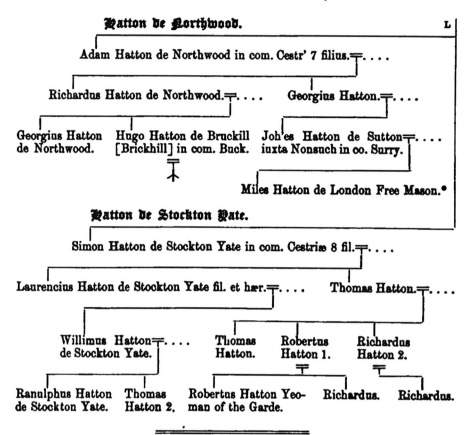

Hatton de Northwood.

L

Adam Hatton de Northwood in com. Cestr' 7 filius.=....

Richardus Hatton de Northwood.=....   Georgius Hatton.=....

Georgius Hatton de Northwood.   Hugo Hatton de Bruckill [Brickhill] in com. Buck.   Joh'es Hatton de Sutton iuxta Nonsuch in co. Surry.=....

Miles Hatton de London Free Mason.*

Hatton de Stockton Yate.

Simon Hatton de Stockton Yate in com. Cestriæ 8 fil.=....

Laurencius Hatton de Stockton Yate fil. et hær.=....   Thomas Hatton.=....

Willimus Hatton de Stockton Yate.=....   Thomas Hatton.   Robertus Hatton 1.   Richardus Hatton 2.

Ranulphus Hatton de Stockton Yate.   Thomas Hatton 2.   Robertus Hatton Yeoman of the Garde.   Richardus.   Richardus.

Haughton of Beckbury.

Harl. 1396, fo. 157.   Harl. 1241, fo. 154ᵇ.   S., fo. 146ᵃ.

ARMS: Harl. 1396.—*Argent, a cross sable, in dexter chief and sinister base an owl proper.*

Rogerus Houghton de Swynney in com. Salop.=....

Rogerus Houghton.=....

Rogerus Haughton de Beckbury in com. Salop.=Margareta fil..... Wolriche de Dudmaston.   Anna vxor .... Oteley de Oteley renupta Humfr'o Onneslow.

Rogerus Haughton de Beckbury in com. Salop fil. et heres.=Maria fil. Ed'r'i Gray de Whittington militis.   Anna nupta Ed'r'o Cole de Shrewesbury.   Alicia nupta Thomæ Eyton de Eyton.

* " A Mason in London."—Vis. Chesh. 1580.

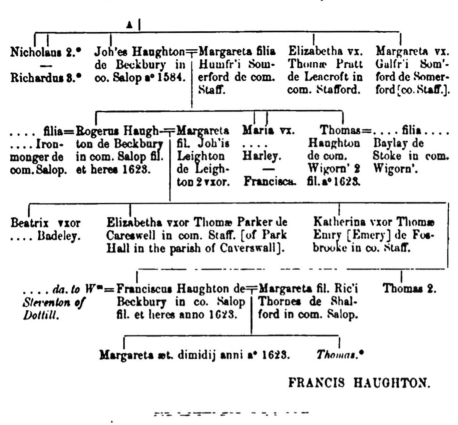

FRANCIS HAUGHTON.

Heale of Stretton.

Harl. 1396, fo. 125ᵇ.   Harl. 1241, fo. 129ᵇ.

Walterus Heale⚭ .... fil. et cohær. *sole hei.* .....
de Stretton. │ Salter de Carcyn *Cardington.*

Thomas Heale de Stretton.⚭ ....

Ed'r'us Heale⚭Margretta fil. Petri Higons *Higgs* renupta
de Stretton. │ Will'o Harris parsona de Stretton.

| Elizabetha vxor Joh'is Jenkins. | Joh'es Heale⚭Maria fil. Ed'r'i de Stretton in │ Jenkins de Dod-com. Salop. │ ington. | Alicia vxor Will'i Cowper *Cooper.* | Maria vxor Ed'r'i Gitton *Gittons.* |

William Heale.   Edward 2 sonne.   Joyce.

* Nicholas, Richard, and Thomas are omitted in Shrewsbury MS.

𝔥𝔢𝔡𝔩𝔢𝔶.

Harl. 1396, fo. 159.   S., fo. 137ᵇ.

ARMS : Harl. 1396.—*Argent, on a bend azure* [sable ?] *three leopards' faces or.*

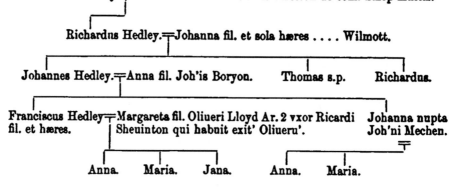

Richardus Hedley.⊤Anna fil. et coheres Joh'is Stretton de com. Salop militis.

Richardus Hedley.⊤Johanna fil. et sola hæres .... Wilmott.

Johannes Hedley.⊤Anna fil. Joh'is Boryon.   Thomas s.p.   Richardus.

Franciscus Hedley⊤Margareta fil. Oliueri Lloyd Ar. 2 vxor Ricardi   Johanna nupta
fil. et hæres.   Sheuinton qui habuit exit' Oliueru'.   Joh'ni Mechen.
                                                                          ⊤

Anna.   Maria.   Jana.   Anna.   Maria.

𝔥𝔢𝔯𝔦𝔫𝔤𝔢 𝔬𝔣 𝔖𝔥𝔯𝔢𝔴𝔰𝔟𝔲𝔯𝔶 𝔞𝔫𝔡 𝔒𝔰𝔴𝔢𝔰𝔱𝔯𝔶.

Harl. 1396, fo. 164ᵇ.   Harl. 1241, fo. 143.

ARMS : Harl. 1396.—*Azure, crusily fitchée* [semée of cross-crosslets fitchée] *or, six herrings hauriant, three, two, and one, of the second* [argent ?].

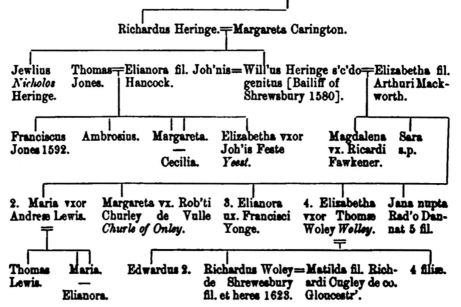

Will'us Heringe de Owsley minor *maior*⊤Alicia Pickering.
iuxta Couentrey in com. Warr.

Richardus Heringe.⊤Margareta Carington.

Jewlius   Thomas⊤Elianora fil. Joh'nis⸺Will'us Heringe s'c'do⊤Elizabetha fil.
Nicholos   Jones. Hancock.   genitus [Bailiff of   Arthuri Mack-
Heringe.   Shrewsbury 1580].   worth.

Franciscus   Ambrosius.   Margareta.   Elizabetha vxor   Magdalena   Sara
Jones 1592.   —   Joh'is Feste   vx. Ricardi   s.p.
                         Cecilia.   *Yesst.*   Fawkener.

2. Maria vxor   Margareta vx. Rob'ti   3. Elianora   4. Elizabetha   Jana nupta
Andreæ Lewis.   Churley de Vulle   ux. Francisci   vxor Thomæ   Rad'o Dan-
    ⊤   *Churle of Onley.*   Yonge.   Woley *Wolley.*   nat 5 fil.
                                                              ⊤

Thomas   Maria.   Edwardus 2.   Richardus Woley⸺Matilda fil. Rich-   4 filiæ.
Lewis.   —   de Shrewesbury   ardi Ougley de co.
    Elianora.   fil. et heres 1623.   Gloucestr'.

Heylyn of Alderton.

Harl. 1396, fo. 153. S., fo. 145ᵃ.

ARMS: Harl. 1396.—*Quarterly of six*: 1, *Sable, three horses' heads erased argent*;
2, *Per pale or and gules, two lions rampant addorsed counterchanged*—BUTLER
in Shrewsbury MS.; 3, *Azure, a bend between six covered cups or*—BUTLER
in Shrewsbury MS.; 4, *Argent, a lion rampant sable* [KYNASTON]; 5, *Argent,
a chevron engrailed between three mullets pierced sable*—KYNASTON in Shrewsbury MS.; 6, *Ermine, a chevron gules* [AUDLEY for KYNASTON].
CREST.—*A bear passant sable gorged with a collar and bell or.*
ANOTHER CREST.—*A bear passant sable feeding on a vine fructed proper.*

Rowland Heylin in the old Jury London altered the Creast.

["The pious and munificent Rowland Heylyn, Alderman of London, promoter
of the Welsh translation of the Bible, and of every other laudable undertaking in
his day."—Blakeway's 'Sheriffs,' p. 120.]

Gwyn ap Heylin ap Jeua ap Adam.═ . . . .

Jerworth ap Gwyn.═Juliana fil. et hær. Haneon Butler Do[minus] de Felton.

Rogerus ap Jerworth.═ . . . .   Gruffith Kynaston.═ . . . .

Dauid Heilyn ap Roger.═ . . . .   Jenkynus Kynaston.═ . . . .

Rogerus Heilyn ap Dauid.═ . . . .   Willimus Kynaston.═ . . . .

Rich'us Heilyn apud Roger.═ . . . .   Dauid Kynaston.═ . . . .

Gruffith Heilyn de Alderton in co. Salop.═Beatrix fil. et hæres Dauid K.

Joh'es Heilyn de Alderton═Galewbrid fil. Joh'is Tannat
in com. Salop.   de Abertannett.

Thomas Heilyn 4.═Margareta filia . . . . Kynaston de Ryton.	6. Johanna innupta.	Willim's Heilyn 3.═Margareta filia Goghe de Oswaldstree.	7. Eleanora vx. Will'i Genow de London.

Richardus Heilyn.	Thomas Heilyn.	Maria nupta Joh'i Prichard [*Pichard*].	Anna.	Jana.

Emma vxor Rog. Thomas de Kynton.	Jana nupta Rob'to Lloyd de Daywell.	Margareta vxor Joh'nis Hilley de Hilley.	5. Elizabetha vx. Georgij Gruffith de Shewerdon. ▲

H H

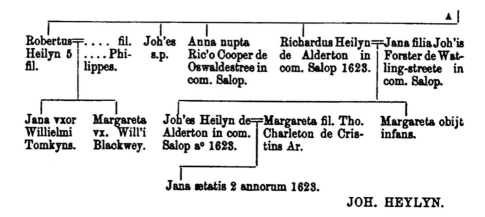

Robertus =.... fil.   Joh'es   Anna nupta   Richardus Heilyn =Jana filia Joh'is
Heilyn 5 | ....Phi-   s.p.   Ric'o Cooper de de Alderton in   Forster de Wat-
fil. | lippes.   Oswaldestree in com. Salop 1623. ling-streete in
         | com. Salop.   com. Salop.

Jana vxor   Margareta   Joh'es Heilyn de =Margareta fil. Tho.   Margareta obijt
Willielmi   vx. Will'i   Alderton in com. Charleton de Cris-   infans.
Tomkyns.   Blackwey.   Salop aº 1623.   tins Ar.

                  Jana ætatis 2 annorum 1623.

                                              JOH. HEYLYN.

Heynes or Eynnes of Stretton.

Harl. 1396, fo. 156.   Harl. 1241, fo. 32.   Harl. 615, fo. 238.   S., ff. 185ᵇ, 136.

ARMS: Harl. 1396.—*Quarterly of six:* 1 and 6, *Or, on a fesse gules three bezants,
in chief a greyhound courant sable, collared of the second;* 2, *Quarterly gules
and ermine, in the second and third three piles of the first, over all on a fesse
azure five bezants*—GATTACRE in Shrewsbury MS.; 3, *Sable, a chevron
between three leopards' faces argent*—BLIKE in Shrewsbury MS.; 4, *Argent,
three leopards' faces sable, in chief a lion passant-guardant gules*—FILILODE
in Shrewsbury MS.; 5, *Azure, a cinquefoil pierced ermine, within a bordure
engrailed of the second*—ASTLEY in Shrewsbury MS.

1 CREST.—*An eagle displayed standing on a tortoise.*
2 CREST.—*An eagle displayed azure, semée of estoiles or.*

Trehayrne Val Gwyr de Glynn in com. Montgomer'. =....

                  Howell. =....

                  Rerydd. =....

                  Eignion. =....

            Einnes ap Einion.* =....

Johannes Einnes =Gwenhwyuer filia Gruff ap Gwilliam ap M'red'd
de Boseley. | ap Holl' ap Trahayrne ap Pasgen.

Thomas Einnes =Elizabetha fil. Rogeri ap Rys   Joh'es Gattacre de Gattacre =....
alias Heynes. | Owen ap Gruff ap Jeuan ap   in com. Salop.
  ▲ | Rerydd Vlayth.   B

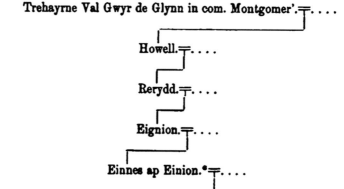

* This generation is omitted in Shrewsbury MS.

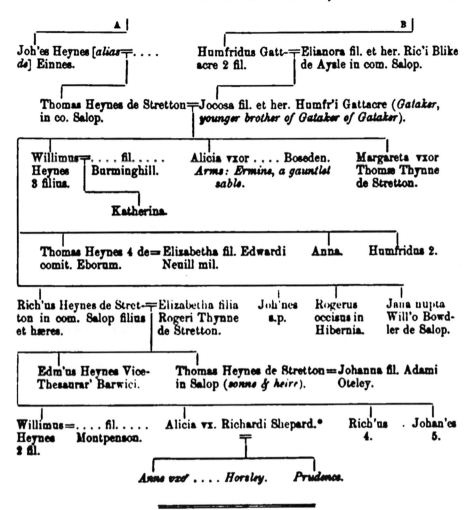

A |
B |

Joh'es Heynes [*alias* ⊤ ....
de] Einnes.

Humfridus Gatt- ⊤ Elianora fil. et her. Ric'i Blike
acre 2 fil. | de Ayale in com. Salop.

Thomas Heynes de Stretton ⊤ Jocosa fil. et her. Humfr'i Gattacre (*Gataker,*
in co. Salop.   *younger brother of Gataker of Gataker*).

Willimus ⊤ .... fil. ....
Heynes | Burminghill.
3 filius.

Alicia vxor .... Boseden.
*Arms: Ermine, a gauntlet
sable.*

Margareta vxor
Thomæ Thynne
de Stretton.

Katherina.

Thomas Heynes 4 de= Elizabetha fil. Edwardi
comit. Eborum.   Neuill mil.

Anna.

Humfridus 2.

Rich'us Heynes de Stret- ⊤ Elizabetha filia
ton in com. Salop filius | Rogeri Thynne
et hæres.   de Stretton.

Joh'nes
s.p.

Rogerus
occisus in
Hibernia.

Jana nupta
Will'o Bowd-
ler de Salop.

Edm'us Heynes Vice-
Thesaurar' Barwici.

Thomas Heynes de Stretton = Johanna fil. Adami
in Salop (*sonne & heire*).   Oteley.

Willimus = ... fil. ....
Heynes   Montpenson.
2 fil.

Alicia vx. Richardi Shepard.*
⊤

Rich'us
4.

Johan'es
5.

Anne vxor .... Horsley.

Prudence.

Heyward of Bridgnorth.

S., fo. 95ᵃ.

[ARMS.—*Quarterly of five:* 1, [Gules], *a lion rampant* [or], *crowned* [argent];
2, ..., *two palets engrailed* ....: 3, ..., *on a saltire* .... *five fleurs-de-
lis* ....; 4, ..., *a lion rampant* .... *and in chief two mullets;* 5, Or
[argent?], *an eagle displayed sable.*

George Heyward de Bridgenorth. ⊤ ....

Sir Rowland Heyward Kn' Lord Maior of London 1570. ⊤ ....

Sir George Heyward Kn' obiit s.p.

Sir John Heyward Kn' obiit s.p.]

* The children of Richard Shepard are omitted in Shrewsbery MS.

Hibbins of Weo and Rowton.

Harl. 1396, fo. 130.   S., fo. 123ᵃ.

ARMS: Harl. 1396.—*Or, on a chevron embattled* [counter-embattled] *between three towers triple-towered gules as many guttées d'or.*

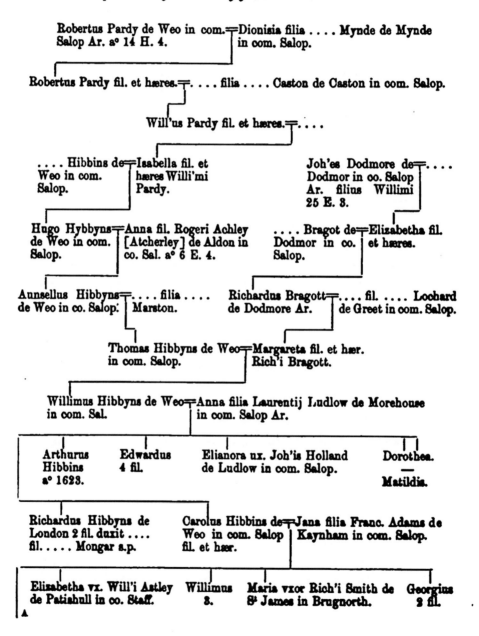

Robertus Pardy de Weo in com.=Dionisia filia .... Mynde de Mynde
Salop Ar. aᵒ 14 H. 4.   in com. Salop.

Robertus Pardy fil. et hæres.=.... filia .... Caston de Caston in com. Salop.

Will'us Pardy fil. et hæres.=....

.... Hibbins de=Isabella fil. et   Joh'es Dodmore de=....
Weo in com.   hæres Willi'mi   Dodmor in co. Salop
Salop.   Pardy.   Ar. filius Willimi
    25 E. 3.

Hugo Hybbyns=Anna fil. Rogeri Achley   .... Bragot de=Elizabetha fil.
de Weo in com.   [Atcherley] de Aldon in   Dodmor in co.   et hæres.
Salop.   co. Sal. aᵒ 6 E. 4.   Salop.

Aunsellus Hibbyns=.... filia ....   Richardus Bragott=.... fil. .... Lochard
de Weo in co. Salop.   Marston.   de Dodmore Ar.   de Greet in com. Salop.

Thomas Hibbyns de Weo=Margareta fil. et hær.
in com. Salop.   Rich'i Bragott.

Willimus Hibbyns de Weo=Anna filia Laurentij Ludlow de Morehouse
in com. Sal.   in com. Salop Ar.

Arthurus   Edwardus   Elianora ux. Joh'is Holland   Dorothea.
Hibbins   4 fil.   de Ludlow in com. Salop.   —
aᵒ 1623.   Matildis.

Richardus Hibbyns de   Carolus Hibbins de=Jana filia Franc. Adams de
London 2 fil. duxit ....   Weo in com. Salop   Kaynham in com. Salop.
fil. .... Mongar s.p.   fil. et hær.

Elizabetha vx. Will'i Astley   Willimus   Maria vxor Rich'i Smith de   Georgius
de Patishull in co. Staff.   3.   St James in Brugnorth.   2 fil.

A

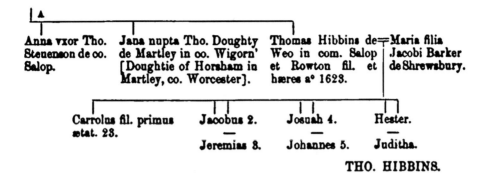

Anna vxor Tho. Stevenson de co. Salop.

Jana nupta Tho. Doughty de Martley in co. Wigorn' [Doughtie of Horsham in Martley, co. Worcester].

Thomas Hibbins de Weo in com. Salop et Rowton fil. et hæres aº 1623.═Maria filia Jacobi Barker de Shrewsbury.

Carrolus fil. primus ætat. 23.

Jacobus 2.
—
Jeremias 3.

Josuah 4.
—
Johannes 5.

Hester.

Juditha.

THO. HIBBINS.

Hide of Hopton Wafers.

Harl. 1396, fo. 185ᵇ.   Harl. 1241, fo. 92ᵇ.   S., ff. 127ᵇ, 128.

ARMS: Harl. 1396.—*Quarterly:* 1, *Azure, a chevron between three lozenges or, an annulet for difference—sable* in Harl. 1241—HIDE; 2, *Per pale .... and ...., on a fesse* .... *three fleurs-de-lis,* PLEYLEY; 3, *Argent, three bars-gemelles sable,* CARISWELL [CARSWELL]; 4, *Gules, a fesse wavy argent between three plates,* WAFRE.

CREST.—*A hawk with wings endorsed proper, beaked and legged or.*

Rogerus Wafre *Wafers* miles D'nus de Hopton Wafres.═....

Petrus Careswell miles D'nus de Hopton Wafres.═Alicia filia et hær. Rogeri Wafre militis.

Thomas Hide de Norbury in com. Cestriæ.═.... filia .... Kniveton [Kinaston ?] de com. Derby.

Gregorius *George* Pleyley D'nus de Hopton Wafres in com. Salop.═Katherina filia et hæres Petri Careswell.

Robertus Hide de Norbury in com. Cestriæ.═Margaretta fil. .... Holland de Denton in com. Lancastriæ.

Egidius Hide de Hopton Wafres in co. Salop Junior filius [called Giles in Vis. Chesh. 1580].═Alicia filia et hæres Gregorij Pleyley *Plelley.*

Hamo Hyde de Norbury in com. Cestriæ.†═Margaretta filia Laurentij Warren de Poynton.

Robert Hyde of Norbury.═Jane da. of Wᵐ Davenport of Bromhall.

▲   B

* A chevron according to Harl. 1241.
† The descendants of Hamon and Margaret are omitted in Shrewsbury MS.

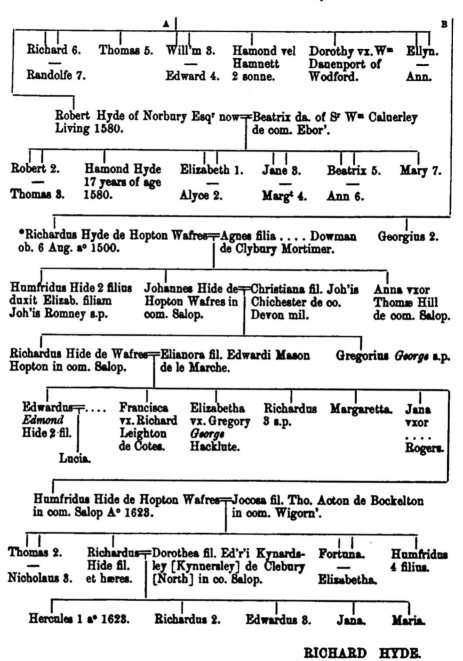

A | B |

Richard 6.	Thomas 5.	Will'm 3.	Hamond vel	Dorothy vx. W^m	Ellyn.
—		—	Hamnett	Danenport of	—
Randolfe 7.		Edward 4.	2 sonne.	Wodford.	Ann.

Robert Hyde of Norbury Esqr now=Beatrix da. of Sr Wm Caluerley
Living 1580.   de com. Ebor'.

Robert 2.	Hamond Hyde	Elizabeth 1.	Jane 3.	Beatrix 5.	Mary 7.
—	17 years of age	—	—	—	
Thomas 3.	1580.	Alyce 2.	Marg^t 4.	Ann 6.	

*Richardus Hyde de Hopton Wafres=Agnes filia .... Dowman   Georgius 2.
ob. 6 Aug. a° 1500.   de Clybury Mortimer.

Humfridus Hide 2 filius	Johannes Hide de=Christiana fil. Joh'is	Anna vxor
duxit Elizab. filiam	Hopton Wafres in	Chichester de co.	Thomæ Hill
Joh'is Romney s.p.	com. Salop.	Devon mil.	de com. Salop.

Richardus Hide de Wafres=Elianora fil. Edwardi Mason   Gregorius George s.p.
Hopton in com. Salop.   de le Marche.

Edwardus=....	Francisca	Elizabetha	Richardus	Margaretta.	Jana
Edmond	vx. Richard	vx. Gregory	3 s.p.		vxor
Hide 2 fil.	Leighton	George			....
	de Cotes.	Hacklute.			Rogers.
Lucia.					

Humfridus Hide de Hopton Wafres=Jocosa fil. Tho. Acton de Bockelton
in com. Salop A° 1623.   in com. Wigorn'.

Thomas 2.	Richardus=Dorothea fil. Ed'r'i Kynards-	Fortuna.	Humfridus
—	Hide fil.	ley [Kynnersley] de Clebury	—	4 filius.
Nicholaus 3.	et hæres.	[North] in co. Salop.	Elizabetha.	

Hercules 1 a° 1623.	Richardus 2.	Edwardus 3.	Jana.	Maria.

RICHARD HYDE.

* This generation is omitted in Harl. 1241.

Higgens of Boycott and Newnham.

Harl. 1896, fo. 165ᵇ. S., fo. 148ᵇ.

ARMS: Harl. 1396.—*Quarterly*: 1 *and* 4, *Vert, three cranes'* [?] *heads erased argent, a mullet for difference; 2 and 3, Argent, a chevron between three lobsters' claws erased sable* [HUGONS].

Hugo Higgins de Boycoote.=Elizabetha fil. Hugonis Corbet de Alaston.

Richardus=Elizabetha filia Rob'ti Jeninges.
Higgens.

Ric'us Higgens de=Jocosa filia Joh'is Newenham. Palmer.

Hugo.

Hugo Higgeus de Stretton.=Elianora fil. Rogeri Collat de Stapleton.

Willimus=Katherina fil. Will'i Norgrane.
Higgons 1.

Richardus=Elizabetha fil. Johannis Ap . . . .
Higgens.

Anna nupta Wᵒ Nomly [Noneley of Noneley ?].

Maria.

Hugo Higgens.

Georgius [*Higgins*].   Richardus [*Higgins*].

The marke of HUGH ∧ HIGGENS of Stretton.

Higges.

Harl. 1896, fo. 125ᵇ. Harl. 1241, fo. 132ᵇ.

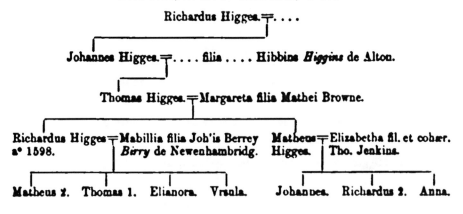

Richardus Higges.=. . . .

Johannes Higges.=. . . . filia . . . . Hibbins *Higgins* de Alton.

Thomas Higges.=Margareta filia Mathei Browne.

Richardus Higges=Mabillia filia Joh'is Berrey
aᵒ 1598.   *Berry* de Newenhambridg.

Matheus=Elizabetha fil. et cohær.
Higges.   Tho. Jenkins.

Matheus 2. Thomas 1. Elianora. Vrsula.

Johannes. Richardus 2. Anna.

Higgins of Stretton.

Harl. 1241, fo. 151.

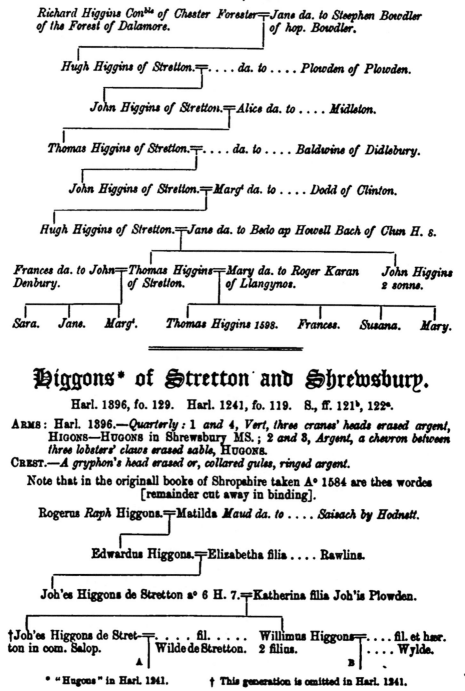

Richard Higgins Con^ble of Chester Forester=Jane da. to Steephen Bowdler
of the Forest of Dalamore. | of hop. Bowdler.

Hugh Higgins of Stretton.=. . . . da. to . . . . Plowden of Plowden.

John Higgins of Stretton.=Alice da. to . . . . Midleton.

Thomas Higgins of Stretton.=. . . . da. to . . . . Baldwine of Didlebury.

John Higgins of Stretton.=Marg^t da. to . . . . Dodd of Clinton.

Hugh Higgins of Stretton.=Jane da. to Bedo ap Howell Bach of Clun H. s.

Frances da. to John=Thomas Higgins=Mary da. to Roger Karan   John Higgins
Denbury. | of Stretton. | of Llangynos.   2 sonns.

Sara.   Jane.   Marg^t.   Thomas Higgins 1598.   Frances.   Susana.   Mary.

Higgons* of Stretton and Shrewsbury.

Harl. 1896, fo. 129.   Harl. 1241, fo. 119.   S., ff. 121^b, 122^a.

ARMS: Harl. 1896.—*Quarterly:* 1 *and* 4, *Vert, three cranes' heads erased argent,*
HIGONS—HUGONS in Shrewsbury MS.; 2 *and* 3, *Argent, a chevron between*
three lobsters' claws erased sable, HUGONS.

CREST.—*A gryphon's head erased or, collared gules, ringed argent.*

Note that in the originall booke of Shropshire taken A° 1584 are thes wordes
[remainder cut away in binding].

Rogerus *Raph* Higgons.=Matilda *Maud* da. to . . . . Saisach by Hodnett.

Edwardus Higgons.=Elizabetha filia . . . . Rawlins.

Joh'es Higgons de Stretton a° 6 H. 7.=Katherina filia Joh'is Plowden.

†Joh'es Higgons de Stret-=. . . . fil. . . . .   Willimus Higgons=. . . . fil. et hær.
ton in com. Salop. | Wilde de Stretton.   2 filius. | . . . . Wylde.
      A   **B**

* "Hugons" in Harl. 1241.   † This generation is omitted in Harl. 1241.

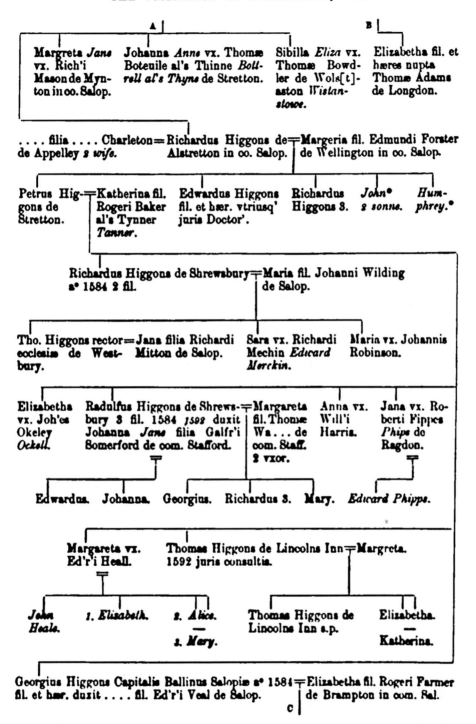

A   **B**

Margreta *Jane* vx. Rich'i Mason de Mynton in co. Salop.

Johanna *Anne* vx. Thomæ Boteuile al's Thinne *Bottrell al's Thyne* de Stretton.

Sibilla *Eliza* vx. Thomæ Bowdler de Wols[t]aston *Wistanstowe.*

Elizabetha fil. et hæres nupta Thomæ Adams de Longdon.

.... filia .... Charleton de Appelley *s wife.* = Richardus Higgons de Alstretton in co. Salop. = Margeria fil. Edmundi Forster de Wellington in co. Salop.

Petrus Higgons de Stretton. = Katherina fil. Rogeri Baker al's Tynner *Tanner.*

Edwardus Higgons fil. et hær. vtriusq' juris Doctor'.

Richardus Higgons 3.

John s sonne.[*]

Humphrey.[*]

Richardus Higgons de Shrewsbury a° 1584 2 fil. = Maria fil. Johanni Wilding de Salop.

Tho. Higgons rector ecclesiæ de Westbury. = Jana filia Richardi Mitton de Salop.

Sara vx. Richardi Mechin *Edward Merckin.*

Maria vx. Johannis Robinson.

Elizabetha vx. Joh'es Okeley *Ockell.*

Radulfus Higgons de Shrewsbury 3 fil. 1584 *1592* duxit Johanna *Jane* filia Galfr'i Somerford de com. Stafford. = Margareta fil. Thomæ Wa... de com. Staff. 2 vxor.

Anna vx. Will'i Harris.

Jana vx. Roberti Fippes *Phips* de Ragdon.

Edwardus.   Johanna.   Georgius.   Richardus 3.   Mary.   *Edward Phipps.*

Margareta vx. Ed'r'i Heall.

Thomas Higgons de Lincolns Inn 1592 juris consultis. = Margreta.

John Heale.   1. *Elizabeth.*   2. *Alice.*   —   3. *Mary.*

Thomas Higgons de Lincolns Inn s.p.

Elizabetha. — Katherina.

Georgius Higgons Capitalis Ballinus Salopiæ a° 1584 fil. et hær. duxit .... fil. Ed'r'i Veal de Salop. = Elizabetha fil. Rogeri Farmer de Brampton in com. Sal.

C

* John and Humphrey appear in Harl. 1241 in place of Edward and Richard, but they are not given in Shrewsbury MS.

11

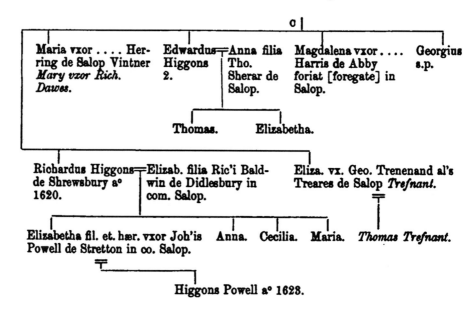

Richardus Higgons=Elizab. filia Ric'i Bald-
de Shrewsbury a°   win de Didlesbury in
1620.   com. Salop.

Eliza. vx. Geo. Trenenand al's
Treares de Salop *Trefnant.*

Thomas Trefnant.

Elizabetha fil. et. hær. vxor Joh'is   Anna.   Cecilia.   Maria.
Powell de Stretton in co. Salop.

Higgons Powell a° 1623.

Hill of Court of Hill.

Harl. 1396, fo. 186ᵇ.   Harl. 1241, fo. 107.   S., ff. 128ᵃ—180ᵃ.

ARMS: Harl. 1396.—*Quarterly: 1 and 4, Ermine, on a fesse sable a castle triple-
towered argent* [HILL]; *2, Sable, a lion rampant argent, crowned or, between
three crosses formée fitchée of the second* [LONGSLOW]; *3, Per pale or and
argent, an eagle displayed sable* [BIRD].

ARMS OF ROWLAND HILL, Lord Mayor of London, *vide* p. 245: Harl. 1396.—*Azure,
two bars argent, a quarter sable, thereon, upon a chevron between three
pheons of the second, a wolf's head erased between two mullets of the third
—gules* in Shrewsbury MS.

CREST.—*A wolf's head erased azure charged with two bars argent and holding in the
mouth a trefoil vert.*

[These are the arms of Wilbraham of Woodhey (the mother of Thomas Hill)
with a canton based upon the coat of Malpas, from which family he was descended.]

ARMS:* Harl. 1241.—*Quarterly: 1, Ermine, on a fesse sable a castle triple-towered
argent; 2, Sable, a lion rampant argent, crowned or, between three crosses formée
fitchée of the second* [LONGSLOW]; *3, Per pale or and argent, an eagle displayed
sable* [BIRD]; *4, Gules, a chevron between three pheons argent* [HILL OF
BUNTINGSDALE].

Hugo de Wlonkeslow *Hawkeslowe* [now Longslow].=. . . .

Hugo Hull† de Hull in com. Salop.=Elianora filia   Isabella fil. et cohæres
Arms: Ermine, on a fesse sable   et cohær.   uxor Thomæ Stuich
a castle triple-towered argent.   [Stuche or Styche].

* Not given in Shrewsbury MS.   † "Hill" throughout in Harl. 1241.

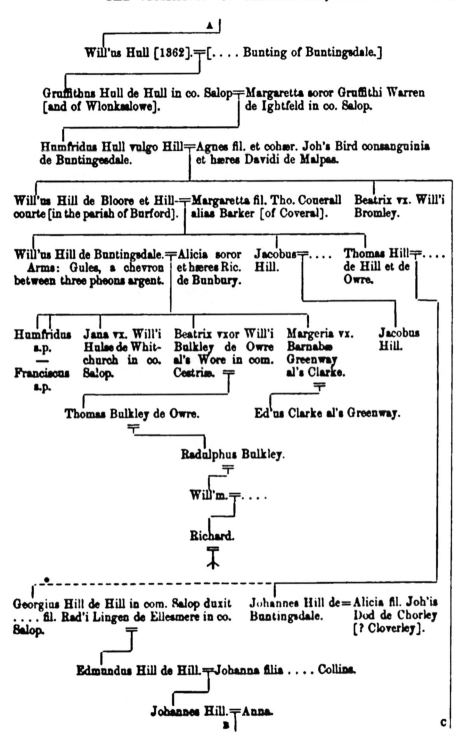

▲

Will'us Hull [1362].=[.... Bunting of Buntingsdale.]

Gruffithus Hull de Hull in co. Salop=Margaretta soror Gruffithi Warren
[and of Wlonksalowe]. de Ightfeld in co. Salop.

Humfridus Hull vulgo Hill=Agnes fil. et cohær. Joh's Bird consanguinia
de Buntingesdale. et hæres Davidi de Malpas.

Will'us Hill de Bloore et Hill-=Margaretta fil. Tho. Couerall Beatrix vx. Will'i
courte [in the parish of Burford]. alias Barker [of Coverall]. Bromley.

Will'us Hill de Buntingsdale.=Alicia soror Jacobus=.... Thomas Hill=....
Arms: Gules, a chevron et hæres Ric. Hill. de Hill et de
between three pheons argent. de Bunbury. Owre.

Humfridus Jana vx. Will'i Beatrix vxor Will'i Margeria vx. Jacobus
s.p. Hulse de Whit- Bulkley de Owre Barnabæ Hill.
— church in co. al's Wore in com. Greenway
Franciscus Salop. Cestriæ. al's Clarke.
s.p.

Thomas Bulkley de Owre. Ed'us Clarke al's Greenway.

Radulphus Bulkley.

Will'm.=....

Richard.

Georgius Hill de Hill in com. Salop duxit Johannes Hill de=Alicia fil. Joh'is
.... fil. Rad'i Lingen de Ellesmere in co. Buntingsdale. Dod de Chorley
Salop. [? Cloverley].

Edmundus Hill de Hill.=Johanna filia .... Collins.

Johannes Hill.=Anna.

B

C

* In the Shrewsbury MS. this line is not dotted, but is an ordinary line.

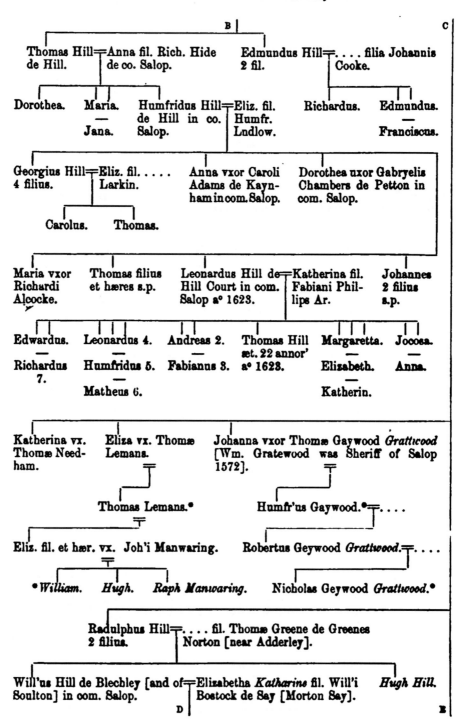

B | C

Thomas Hill=Anna fil. Rich. Hide de Hill. de co. Salop.

Edmundus Hill=.... filia Johannis Cooke. 2 fil.

Dorothea. Maria. — Jana.

Humfridus Hill=Eliz. fil. de Hill in co. Humfr. Salop. Lndlow.

Richardus.

Edmundus. — Franciscus.

Georgius Hill=Eliz. fil. .... 4 filius. Larkin.

Anna vxor Caroli Adams de Kaynham in com. Salop.

Dorothea uxor Gabryelis Chambers de Petton in com. Salop.

Carolus. Thomas.

Maria vxor Richardi Alcocke.

Thomas filius et hæres s.p.

Leonardus Hill de=Katherina fil. Hill Court in com. Fabiani Phil- Salop aº 1623. lips Ar.

Johannes 2 filius s.p.

Edwardus. — Richardus 7.

Leonardus 4. — Humfridus 5. — Matheus 6.

Andreas 2. — Fabianus 3.

Thomas Hill æt. 22 annor' aº 1623.

Margaretta. Elizabeth. Katherin.

Joccsa. Anna.

Katherina vx. Thomæ Need- ham.

Eliza vx. Thomæ Lemans. =

Johanna vxor Thomæ Gaywood *Gratticood* [Wm. Gratewood was Sheriff of Salop 1572].

Thomas Lemans.* =

Humfr'us Gaywood.*=....

Eliz. fil. et hær. vx. Joh'i Manwaring. =

Robertus Geywood *Gratticood.*=....

*William. *Hugh.* *Raph Manwaring.*

Nicholas Geywood *Gratticood.**

Radulphus Hill=.... fil. Thomæ Greene de Greenes 2 filius. Norton [near Adderley].

Will'us Hill de Blechley [and of=Elizabetha *Katharine* fil. Will'i Soulton] in com. Salop. Bostock de Say [Morton Say].

Hugh Hill.

D   E

* These generations are omitted in Shrewsbury MS., and Thomas Lemans and Humphrey Gaywood are omitted in Harl. 1241.

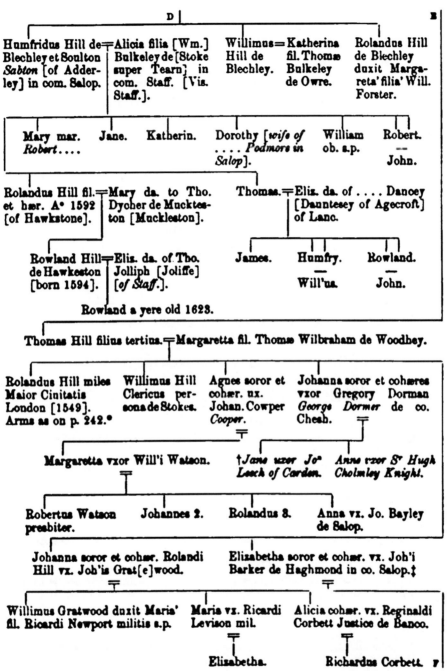

D | E

Humfridus Hill de=Alicia filia [Wm.]   Willimus=Katherina   Rolandus Hill
Blechley et Soulton | Bulkeley de [Stoke Hill de | fil. Thomæ de Blechley
Sabton [of Adder- | super Tearn] in Blechley. | Bulkeley   duxit Marga-
ley] in com. Salop. | com. Staff. [Vis. | de Owre.   reta' filia' Will.
                     | Staff.].   Forster.

Mary mar.   Jane.   Katherin.   Dorothy [*wife of*   William   Robert.
Robert....   .... *Podmore in*   ob. s.p.   —
                                             Salop].   John.

Rolandus Hill fil.=Mary da. to Tho.   Thomas.=Eliz. da. of .... Dancey
et hær. A° 1592 | Dycher de Mucktes- | [Dauntesey of Agecroft]
[of Hawkstone]. | ton [Muckleston]. | of Lanc.

                                              James.   Humfry.   Rowland.
                                                        —   —
Rowland Hill=Eliz. da. of Tho.   Will'ns.   John.
de Hawkeston | Jolliph [Joliffe]
[born 1594]. | [*of Staff.*].

          Rowland a yere old 1623.

Thomas Hill filius tertius.=Margaretta fil. Thomæ Wilbraham de Woodhey.

Rolandus Hill miles   Willimus Hill   Agnes soror et   Johanna soror et cohæres
Maior Ciuitatis   Clericus per-   cohær. ux.   vxor Gregory Dorman
London [1549].   sona de Stokes. Johan. Cowper   *George Dormer* de co.
Arms as on p. 242.*   *Cooper.*   Chesh.
                                           ⊤   ⊤

     Margaretta vxor Will'i Watson.   †*Jane uxor Jo°*   *Anne vxor S' Hugh*
                ⊤   *Leech of Carden.* *Cholmley Knight.*

Robertus Watson   Johannes 2.   Rolandus 3.   Anna vx. Jo. Bayley
presbiter.   de Salop.

Johanna soror et cohær. Rolandi   Elizabetha soror et cohær. vx. Joh'i
Hill vx. Job'is Grat[e]wood.   Barker de Haghmond in co. Salop.‡
            ⊤   ⊤

Willimus Gratwood duxit Maria'   Maria vx. Ricardi   Alicia cohær. vx. Reginaldi
fil. Ricardi Newport militis s.p. Levison mil.   Corbett Justice de Banco.
                                       ⊤   ⊤

                                   Elizabetha.   Richardus Corbett. F

* The old emblasoned family pedigree contains a copy of a grant by Wm. Hervy, Claren-
cieux, dated 3 Nov. 1562, authorizing Alice Corbet, daughter of John Gratewood by Jane Hill,
then married to Reginald Corbet, and William Gratewood, son of the same John, and James
Barker, son of John Barker by Elizabeth, sister of the said Sir Rowland Hill, Knt., late Lord
Mayor, and Rowland Barker, son and heir of James Barker, son and heir of the said John Barker
by the said Elizabeth Hill, to join the said Arms with their own.
  † This generation is not given in Shrewsbury MS.
  ‡ The descendants of John Barker are omitted in Shrewsbury MS.

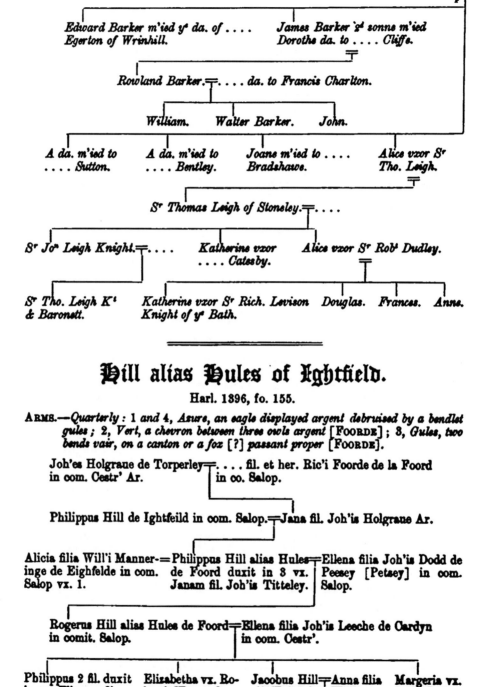

F

Edward Barker m'ied y* da. of . . . .
Egerton of Wrinhill.

James Barker *2d* sonne m'ied
Dorothe da. to . . . . Cliffe.

Rowland Barker.=. . . . da. to Francis Charlton.

William.   Walter Barker.   John.

A da. m'ied to
. . . . Sutton.

A da. m'ied to
. . . . Bentley.

Joane m'ied to . . . .
Bradshawe.

Alice vxor S*r*
Tho. Leigh.

S*r* Thomas Leigh of Stoneley.=. . . .

S*r* Jo*n* Leigh Knight.=. . . .

Katherine vxor
. . . . Catesby.

Alice vxor S*r* Rob*t* Dudley.

S*r* Tho. Leigh K*t*
& Baronett.

Katherine vxor S*r* Rich. Levison
Knight of y* Bath.

Douglas.   Frances.   Anne.

Hill alias Hules of Ightfield.

Harl. 1396, fo. 155.

ARMS.—*Quarterly: 1 and 4, Azure, an eagle displayed argent debruised by a bendlet gules; 2, Vert, a chevron between three owls argent [FOORDE]; 3, Gules, two bends vair, on a canton or a fox [?] passant proper [FOORDE].*

Joh'es Holgraue de Torperley=. . . . fil. et her. Ric'i Foorde de la Foord
in com. Cestr' Ar.   in co. Salop.

Philippus Hill de Ightfeild in com. Salop.=Jana fil. Joh'is Holgraue Ar.

Alicia filia Will'i Manner-=Philippus Hill alias Hules=Ellena filia Joh'is Dodd de
inge de Eighfelde in com.   de Foord duxit in 3 vx.   Peesey [Petsey] in com.
Salop vx. 1.   Janam fil. Joh'is Titteley. Salop.

Rogerus Hill alias Hules de Foord=Ellena filia Joh'is Leeche de Cardyn
in comit. Salop.   in com. Cestr'.

Philippus 2 fil. duxit
in vx. Ellenam fil.
Johannis Downton
de Broughton.

Elizabetha vx. Ro-
berti Weuer de
[Aston Mondram]
com. Cestr'.

Jacobus Hill=Anna filia
al's Hules de Will'i
Foord fil. et Lewter de
her.   Salop.

▲

Margeria vx.
Rad'i Parkes
de Harles-
court in com.
Salop.

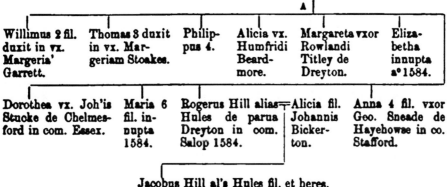

A

| Willimus 2 fil. duxit in vx. Margeria' Garrett. | Thomas 3 duxit in vx. Margeriam Stoakes. | Philippus 4. | Alicia vx. Humfridi Beardmore. | Margareta vxor Rowlandi Titley de Dreyton. | Elizabetha innupta aº 1584. |

| Dorothea vx. Joh'is Stuoke de Chelmesford in com. Essex. | Maria 6 fil. innupta 1584. | Rogerus Hill alias Hules de parua Dreyton in com. Salop 1584. | Alicia fil. Johannis Bickerton. | Anna 4 fil. vxor Geo. Sneade de Hayehowse in co. Stafford. |

Jacobus Hill al's Hules fil. et heres.

Hill of Bewdley.

Harl. 1396, fo. 149ᵇ. Harl. 1241, fo. 18. S., fo. 143ᵇ.

ARMS: Harl. 1396.—*Or, on a chief vert three bulls' heads couped [erased] of the first.*

CREST.—*A bull's head erased or between the horns of a crescent vairé of the first and azure.*

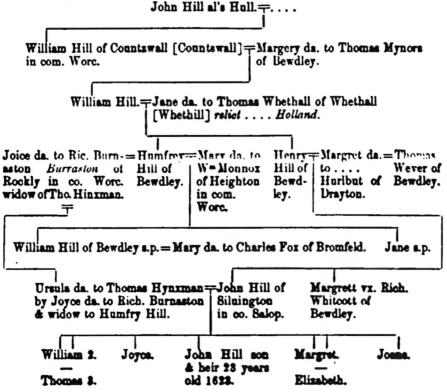

John Hill al's Hull. ⊤ . . . .

William Hill of Countzwall [Countswall] ⊤ Margery da. to Thomas Mynors in com. Worc. | of Bewdley.

William Hill. ⊤ Jane da. to Thomas Whethall of Whethall [Whethill] *relict* . . . . *Holland.*

| Joice da. to Ric. Burnaston *Burraston* of Rockly in co. Worc. widow of Tho. Hinxman. ⊤ | Humfrey Hill of Bewdley. ⊤ Mary da. to Wm Monnox of Heighton in com. Worc. | Henry Hill of Bewdley. ⊤ Margret da. to . . . . Hurlbut of Drayton. | Thomas Wever of Bewdley. |

William Hill of Bewdley s.p. ⊤ Mary da. to Charles Fox of Bromfeld.   Jane s.p.

| Ursula da. to Thomas Hynxman by Joyce da. to Rich. Burnaston & widow to Humfry Hill. ⊤ John Hill of Siluington in co. Salop. | Margrett vx. Rich. Whitcott of Bewdley. |

| William 2. — Thomas 3. | Joyce. | John Hill son & heir 23 years old 1623. | Margret. — Elizabeth. | Joane. |

JOHN HILL.

𝕳inton of 𝕳inton.

Harl. 1396, fo. 163.   Harl. 1241, fo. 67ᵇ.

ARMS: Harl. 1396.—*Quarterly: 1 and 4, Argent, on a bend sable three martlets of the first* [HINTON] ; *2 and 3, Per fesse dancettée argent and sable, six fleurs-de-lis counterchanged* [HINTON].

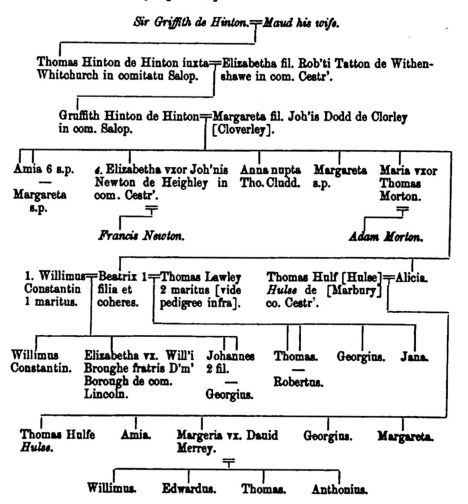

Sir Griffith de Hinton.=Maud his wife.

Thomas Hinton de Hinton iuxta=Elizabetha fil. Rob'ti Tatton de Withen-
Whitchurch in comitatu Salop.   shawe in com. Cestr'.

Gruffith Hinton de Hinton=Margareta fil. Joh'is Dodd de Clorley
in com. Salop.   [Cloverley].

Amia 6 s.p.   4. Elizabetha vxor Joh'nis   Anna nupta   Margareta   Maria vxor
—   Newton de Heighley in   Tho. Cludd.   s.p.   Thomas
Margareta   com. Cestr'.   Morton.
s.p.

Francis Newton.   Adam Morton.

1. Willimus=Beatrix 1=Thomas Lawley   Thomas Hulf [Hulse]=Alicia.
Constantin   filia et   2 maritus [vide   *Hulse* de [Marbury]
1 maritus.   coheres.   pedigree infra].   co. Cestr'.

Willimus   Elizabetha vx. Will'i   Johannes   Thomas.   Georgius.   Jana.
Constantin.   Broughe fratris D'm'   2 fil.   —
Boroughe de com.   —   Robertus.
Lincoln.   Georgius.

Thomas Hulfe   Amia.   Margeria vx. Dauid   Georgius.   Margareta.
Hulse.   Merrey.

Willimus.   Edwardus.   Thomas.   Anthonius.

Hockleton.

Harl. 1396, fo. 162.   Harl. 1241, fo. 186.   S., fo. 138ª.

ARMS: Harl. 1396.—*Vert, a lion rampant argent.*

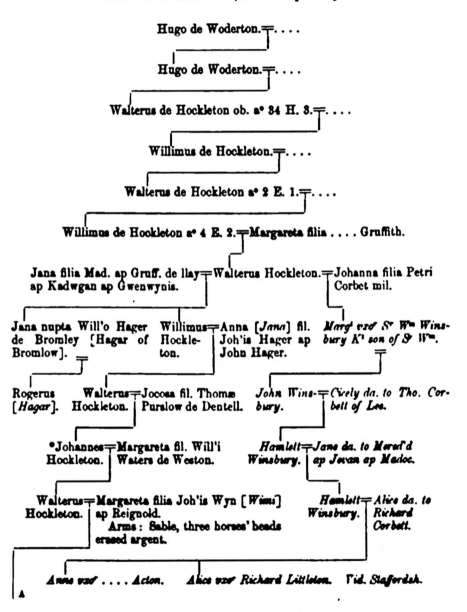

Hugo de Woderton.=. . . .

Hugo de Woderton.=. . . .

Walterus de Hockleton ob. aº 34 H. 3.=. . . .

Willimus de Hockleton.=. . . .

Walterus de Hockleton aº 2 E. 1.=. . . .

Willimus de Hockleton aº 4 E. 2.=Margareta filia . . . . Gruffith.

Jana filia Mad. ap Gruff. de Ilay=Walterus Hockleton.=Johanna filia Petri
ap Kadwgan ap Gwenwynis.   Corbet mil.

Jana nupta Will'o Hager   Willimus=Anna [*Jana*] fil.   *Margᵗ vxᵈ Sʳ Wᵐ Wins-*
de Bromley [Hagar of   Hockle- Joh'is Hager ap   *bury Kᵗ son of Sʳ Wᵐ.*
Bromlow].   ton.   John Hager.

Rogerus   Walterus=Jocosa fil. Thomæ   *John Wins-=Cicely da. to Tho. Cor-*
[*Hagar*]. Hockleton. | Purslow de Dentell.   *bury. | bett of Lee.*

*Johannes=Margareta fil. Will'i   *Hamlett=Jane da. to Morel'd*
Hockleton. | Waters de Weston.   *Winsbury. | ap Jevan ap Madoc.*

Walterus=Margareta filia Joh'is Wyn [*Winn*]   *Hamlett=Alice da. to*
Hockleton. | ap Reignold.   *Winsbury. | Richard*
           Arms: Sable, three horses' heads   *Corbett.*
        erased argent.

Anne vxᵈ . . . . Acton.   Alice vxᵈ Richard Littleton.   Vid. Staffordsh.

▲

* This generation is omitted in Shrewsbury MS.

K K

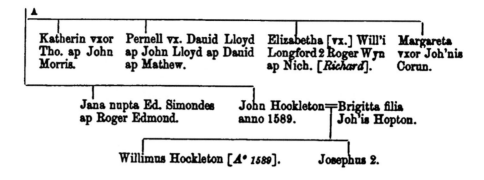

▲

| Katherin vxor Tho. ap John Morris. | Pernell vx. Dauid Lloyd ap John Lloyd ap Dauid ap Mathew. | Elizabetha [vx.] Will'i Longford 2 Roger Wyn ap Nich. [*Richard*]. | Margareta vxor Joh'nis Corun. |

Jana nupta Ed. Simondes ap Roger Edmond.

John Hookleton⹀Brigitta filia
anno 1589. Joh'is Hopton.

Willimus Hockleton [*A° 1589*]. Josephus 2.

ℌolland of ℬurwarton, ℙickthorne, and ℭharlecott.

Harl. 1396, fo. 148ᵇ.   Harl 1241, fo. 116ᵇ.   S., ff. 142ᵇ, 143.

ARMS: Harl. 1396.—*Azure, semée of plates and a lion rampant-guardant within a bordure argent.*

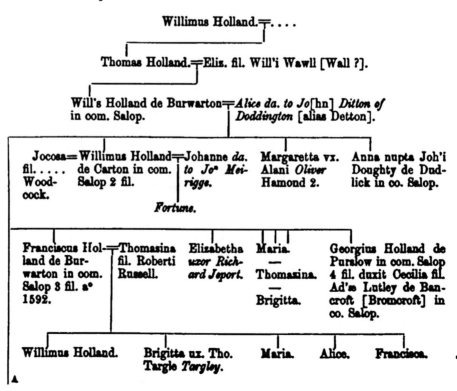

Willimus Holland.⹀ . . . .

Thomas Holland.⹀Eliz. fil. Will'i Wawll [Wall ?].

Will's Holland de Burwarton⹀*Alice da. to Jo*[hn] *Ditton of*
in com. Salop. *Doddington* [alias Detton].

| Jocosa fil. . . . . Wood-cock. | ⹀ | Willimus Holland de Carton in com. Salop 2 fil. | ⹀ | Johanne *da. to Jo° Mei-rigge.* | Margaretta vx. Alani *Oliver* Hamond 2. | Anna nupta Joh'i Doughty de Dud-lick in co. Salop. |

Fortune.

| Franciscus Hol-land de Bur-warton in com. Salop 3 fil. a° 1592. | ⹀ | Thomasina fil. Roberti Russell. | Elizabetha *uxor Rich-ard Jeport.* | Maria. — Thomasina. — Brigitta. | Georgius Holland de Purslow in com. Salop 4 fil. duxit Cecilia fil. Ad'æ Lutley de Ban-croft [Bromcroft] in co. Salop. |

| Willimus Holland. | Brigitta ux. Tho. Targle *Targley.* | Maria. | Alice. | Francisca. |

▲

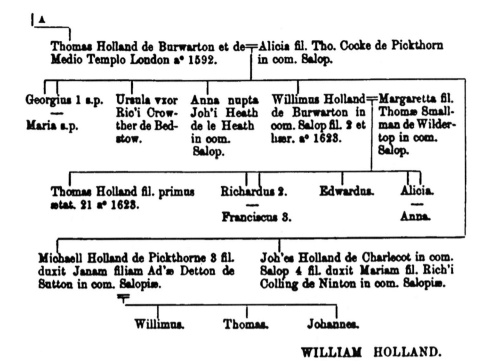

Thomas Holland de Burwarton et de Medio Templo London a° 1592. = Alicia fil. Tho. Cooke de Pickthorn in com. Salop.

Georgius 1 s.p. — Maria s.p.

Ursula vxor Ric'i Crowther de Bedstow.

Anna nupta Joh'i Heath de le Heath in com. Salop.

Willimus Holland de Burwarton in com. Salop fil. 2 et hær. a° 1623. = Margaretta fil. Thomæ Smallman de Wildertop in com. Salop.

Thomas Holland fil. primus ætat. 21 a° 1623.

Richardus 2. — Franciscus 3.

Edwardus.

Alicia. — Anna.

Michaell Holland de Pickthorne 3 fil. duxit Janam filiam Ad'æ Detton de Sutton in com. Salopiæ.

Joh'es Holland de Charlecot in com. Salop 4 fil. duxit Mariam fil. Rich'i Colling de Ninton in com. Salopiæ.

Willimus. Thomas. Johannes.

WILLIAM HOLLAND.

Hoorde* of Bridgnorth and Parkbromage.

Harl. 1396, fo. 126. Harl. 1241, fo. 26ᵇ. Harl. 615, fo. 236. 8., fo. 119ᵃ.

ARMS: Harl. 1396.—*Quarterly of nine*: 1, *Argent, on a chief or a bird sable,* HOORD; 2, *Azure—gules* in Harl. 1241—*an orle between eight cross-crosslets or,* PALMER; 3, *Gules—sable* in Harl. 1241—*on a chevron between three leopards' faces or as many mullets sable,* PERELL—PERRELL in Harl. 1241; 4, *Azure—or* in Harl. 1241—*a lion rampant queue fourchée or—azure* in Harl. 1241—STAPLETON; 5, *Argent, a Cornish chough proper*—MATHEWE in Harl. 1241; 6, *Argent—vert* in Harl. 1241—*on a bend sable three calves passant or,* VEEL—VEALE in Harl. 1241; 7, *Quarterly or and gules, in first quarter a lion passant-guardant azure,* SAYE—SAY in Harl. 1241 [MASSY OF MASEY OF CHERFIELD, co. Glouc.]; 8, *Sable, a lion rampant queue fourchée or,* KINGSTON—KINASTON in Harl. 1241; 9, *Gules, two bars or, in chief a lion passant of the second, an annulet for difference—or* in Harl. 1241 [VYELL].
CREST.—*A horse's head—erased* in Harl. 1241—*argent, maned or.*

Richardus Hoorde. = Jocosa fil. Nich'i Yonge militis.

Joh'es Hoord de Wallrode *called* y' *Black.* = ... fil. et cohær. .... Mortimer de Blorord.

A

Edwardus Palmer. = ...

B

* " Hoorde " in Harl. 615.

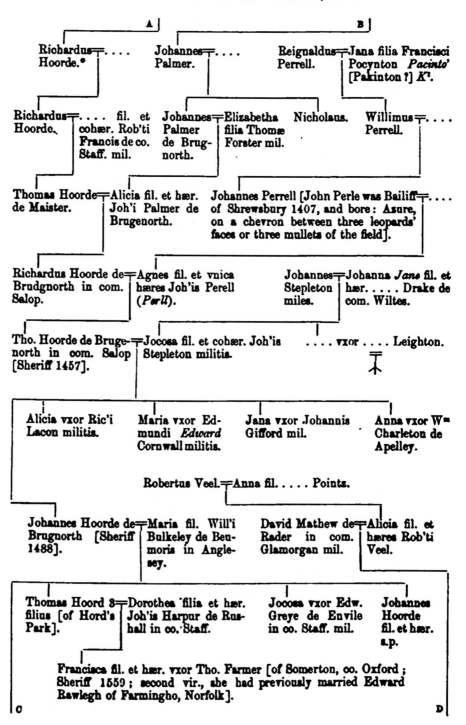

A |

B |

Richardus⹀....   Johannes⹀....   Reignaldus⹀Jana filia Francisci
Hoorde.*   Palmer.   Perrell. | Pocynton *Pacinto'*
                                                      [Pakinton ?] *K*[r].

Richardus⹀.... fil. et   Johannes⹀Elizabetha   Nicholaus.   Willimus⹀....
Hoorde. | cohær. Rob'ti   Palmer | filia Thomæ   Perrell.
        | Francis de co.   de Brug- | Forster mil.
        | Staff. mil.   north.

Thomas Hoorde⹀Alicia fil. et hær.   Johannes Perrell [John Perle was Bailiff⹀....
de Maister. | Joh'i Palmer de   of Shrewsbury 1407, and bore: Azure,
             | Brugenorth.   on a chevron between three leopards'
                               faces or three mullets of the field].

Richardus Hoorde de⹀Agnes fil. et vnica   Johannes⹀Johanna *Jane* fil. et
Brudgnorth in com. | hæres Joh'is Perell   Stepleton | hær..... Drake de
Salop. | (*Perll*).   miles. | com. Wiltes.

Tho. Hoorde de Bruge-⹀Jocosa fil. et cohær. Joh'is   .... vxor .... Leighton.
north in com. Salop | Stepleton militia.
[Sheriff 1457].

Alicia vxor Ric'i   Maria vxor Ed-   Jana vxor Johannis   Anna vxor W[m]
Lacon militia.   mundi *Edward*   Gifford mil.   Charleton de
                Cornwall militia.   Apelley.

Robertus Veel.⹀Anna fil..... Points.

Johannes Hoorde de⹀Maria fil. Will'i   David Mathew de⹀Alicia fil. et
Brugnorth [Sheriff | Bulkeley de Beu-   Rader in com. | hæres Rob'ti
1488]. | moris in Angle-   Glamorgan mil. | Veel.
            | sey.

Thomas Hoord 3⹀Dorothea filia et hær.   Jocosa vxor Edw.   Johannes
filius [of Hord's | Joh'is Harpur de Rus-   Greye de Envile   Hoorde
Park]. | hall in co. Staff.   in co. Staff. mil.   fil. et hær.
                                                    s.p.

Francisca fil. et hær. vxor Tho. Farmer [of Somerton, co. Oxford;
Sheriff 1559; second vir., she had previously married Edward
Rawlegh of Farmingho, Norfolk].

C | D |

* Blakeway calls this person *Roger* Hoorde, and states that he was Sheriff in 1381.

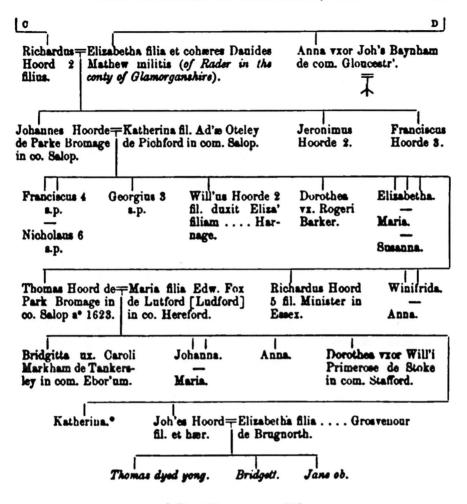

C / D /

Richardus ⊤ Elizabetha filia et cohæres Danides   Anna vxor Joh's Baynham
Hoord 2 | Mathew militis (*of Rader in the*   de com. Gloucestr'.
filius. | *conty of Glamorganshire*).

Johannes Hoorde ⊤ Katherina fil. Ad'æ Oteley   Jeronimus   Franciscus
de Parke Bromage | de Pichford in com. Salop.   Hoorde 2.   Hoorde 8.
in co. Salop.

Franciscus 4   Georgius 3   Will'us Hoorde 2   Dorothea   Elizabetha.
s.p.   s.p.   fil. duxit Eliza'   vx. Rogeri   —
—   filiam .... Har-   Barker.   Maria.
Nicholaus 6   nage.   —
s.p.   Susanna.

Thomas Hoord de ⊤ Maria filia Edw. Fox   Richardus Hoord   Winifrida.
Park Bromage in | de Lutford [Ludford]   5 fil. Minister in   —
co. Salop a° 1623. | in co. Hereford.   Essex.   Anna.

Bridgitta ux. Caroli   Johanna.   Anna.   Dorothea vxor Will'i
Markham de Tankers-   —   Primerose de Stoke
ley in com. Ebor'um.   Maria.   in com. Stafford.

Katherina.*   Joh'es Hoord ⊤ Elizabetha filia .... Grosvenour
fil. et hær. | de Brugnorth.

Thomas dyed yong.   *Bridgett.*   *Jane ob.*

𝕳𝖔𝖕𝖙𝖔𝖓 𝖔𝖋 𝕾𝖙𝖆𝖓𝖙𝖔𝖓.

S., ff. 112ᵃ—113ᵇ.

[ARMS.—(Gules), *semée of cross-crosslets fitchée, a lion rampant* [or].

Sir Walter Hopton Knt. ⊤ ....

Sir Henry Hopton Knt. ⊤ ....

Sir Walter Hopton Knt. ⊤ *Joane da. & heire to Rob' de Cures.*
Arms : Azure, a mermaid argent.

▲

* Omitted in Shrewsbury MS.

▲|

Sir Walter Hopton Knt.=Isabel da. to Henry Staunton sister & heir to Henry.
　　　　　　　　　　　Arms: Vairé sable and argent, a canton gules.

Sir Peeter Hopton Knt. of Stanton.=....

Sir Walter Hopton Knt.=Jone da. & heire to Robert Longbrughe.
　　　　　　　　　　　Arms: Gules, a bend between two crescents or.

Sir Walter Hopton Knt.=....

Sir Walter Hopton Knt.=....

Sir John Hopton Knt.=Alice da. to yͤ Lord Strange.

Sir John Burley Kᵗ of the Garter Ric. 2.=....
Arms: Barry of six sable and or, on a chief or two pallets
sable, over all an inescutcheon barry of six gules and ermine.

Sͬ Roger=Lucy da. to Wᵐ Gilford relicta　　Symon Burley Knt. of yͤ Garter Con-
Burley　.... Browne.　　　　　　　　　stable of the Castle of Dover s.p.
Knt.　　Arms: Or, a saltire between　　　Arms: Argent, a lion rampant
　　　　four martlets sable.　　　　　　　sable debruised by a fesse counter-
　　　　　　　　　　　　　　　　　　　componée azure and or.

Richard Burley Knt.　　Sir John=Alice da. to Richard Pembridge Knt. of yͤ
of the Garter ob. s.p.　Burley　Garter & sister & heire to Walter Pembridge.
　　　　　　　　　　　Knt.　　Arms: Barry of six or and azure, a
　　　　　　　　　　　　　　bend gules.

Jocosa uxor　　Elizabeth ux.　　Katherine ux.　　Maud ux.　　Ellianora ux.
Johannis　　Reginaldi　　　Godfridi Har-　　....　　John Corbett
Gattacre a　　Corbett of　　ley of Bromp-　　Playdon of　　de Lee.
quo Haynes.　Lee Kᵗ.　　　ton.　　　　　Playdon.

Anna uxor Rolandi Wynesbury.　　Margaretta　　William Burley 2 sonn.=....
　　Arms: Or, a fesse counter-　　uxor ....　　　Arms: Argent, a lion
componée gules and or, in chief　Mitton de　　rampant sable debruised
three piles azure.　　　　　　　Weston.　　　by a fesse counter-com-
　　　　　　　　　　　　　　　　　　　ponée azure and or.

Richard Burley.=....

B　　　　　　　　　　　　　　　C|　　　　　　　　　　　　D|

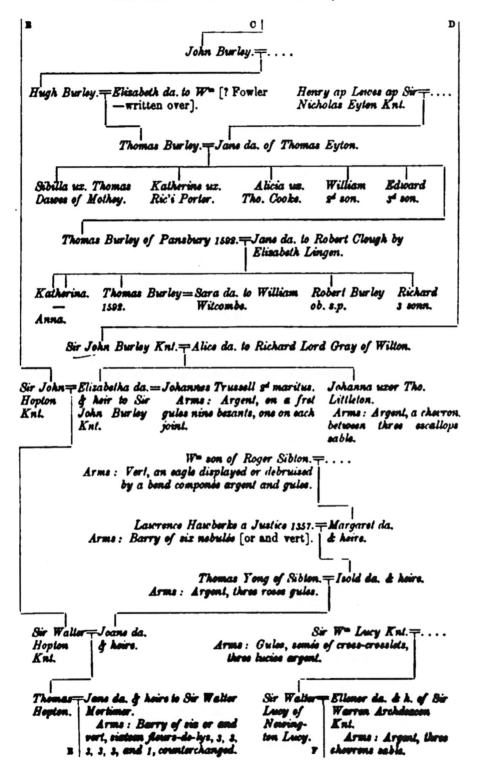

B   C   D

John Burley.=....

Hugh Burley.=Elizabeth da. to W^m [? Fowler —written over].

Henry ap Lewes ap Sir=....
Nicholas Eyton Knt.

Thomas Burley.=Jane da. of Thomas Eyton.

Sibilla ux. Thomas Dawes of Mothey.   Katherine ux. Ric's Porter.   Alicia ux. Tho. Cooke.   William 2^d son.   Edward 3^d son.

Thomas Burley of Pansbury 1592.=Jane da. to Robert Clough by Elizabeth Lingen.

Katherina. — Anna.   Thomas Burley 1592.=Sara da. to William Witcombe.   Robert Burley ob. s.p.   Richard 3 sonn.

Sir John Burley Knt.=Alice da. to Richard Lord Gray of Wilton.

Sir John Hopton Knt.=Elizabetha da. & heir to Sir John Burley Knt. =Johannes Trussell 2^d maritus. Arms: Argent, on a fret gules nine bezants, one on each joint.   Johanna uxor Tho. Littleton. Arms: Argent, a chevron between three escallops sable.

W^m son of Roger Siblon.=....
Arms: Vert, an eagle displayed or debruised by a bend componée argent and gules.

Lawrence Hawberks a Justice 1357.=Margaret da. & heire.
Arms: Barry of six nebulée [or and vert].

Thomas Yong of Siblon.=Isold da. & heire.
Arms: Argent, three roses gules.

Sir Walter Hopton Knt.=Joane da. & heire.   Sir Wm Lucy Knt.=....
Arms: Gules, semée of cross-crosslets, three lucies argent.

Thomas Hopton.=Jane da. & heire to Sir Walter Mortimer.
Arms: Barry of six or and vert, sixteen fleurs-de-lys, 3, 3, 3, 3, 3, and 1, counterchanged.
E

Sir Walter Lucy of Newington Lucy.=Ellinor da. & h. of Sir Warren Archdeacon Knt.
Arms: Argent, three chevrons sable.
F

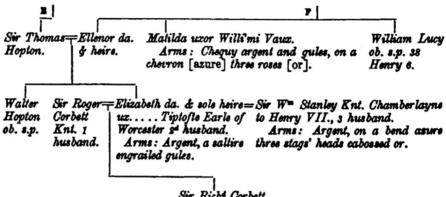

B |

F

Sir Thomas=Ellenor da.
Hopton. & heire.

Matilda uxor Willi'mi Vaux.
Arms : Chequy argent and gules, on a
chevron [azure] three roses [or].

William Lucy
ob. s.p. 38
Henry 6.

Walter   Sir Roger=Elizabeth da. & sole heire=Sir Wm Stanley Knt. Chamberlayne
Hopton   Corbett   ux..... Tiptofte Earle of   to Henry VII., 3 husband.
ob. s.p.   Knt. 1   Worcester 2^d husband.   Arms : Argent, on a bend azure
              husband.   Arms : Argent, a saltire   three stags' heads cabossed or.
                          engrailed gules.

Sir Richd Corbett.
Arms : Or, a raven proper.]

Hopton of Hopton, and of Canon Frome, co. Hereford.

Harl. 1396, fo. 127.   Harl. 1241, ff. 2, 43^b.   S., ff. 119^b, 120.

ARMS : Harl. 1396.—*Quarterly of eight* : 1, *Gules, semée of cross-crosslets fitchée
and a lion rampant or* [HOPTON] ; 2, *Azure, a bend argent cottised or between
six cross-crosslets or, within a bordure gules charged with ten plates* [HOPTON] ;
3, *Bendy of six or and gules* [EYTON OF EYTON, near Bishop's Castle] ;
4, *Azure, three boars' heads couped close or between nine cross-crosslets fitchée
argent* [or—HEVYN OF CLEOBURY] ; 5, *Argent, semée of cross-crosslets and
two organ-pipes pileways gules* [DOWNTON] ; 6, *Barry of six gules and or*
[ST. OWEN] ; 7, *Azure, a lion rampant within a bordure engrailed argent*
[TIRRELL] ; 8, *Argent, a lion rampant gules charged on the shoulder with a
trefoil or* [? WALKER alias LEIGH OF STRETTON].
[1 CREST.—Out of a ducal coronet or, a griffin's head argent holding in the beak a
hand proper.
2 CREST.—A lion's head erased or charged on the neck with a bend gules,
thereon three cross-crosslets fitchée or.]

Richardus Hopton de Hopton=.... fil. et hær..... Kensingford
in com. Salop.   de com. Salop.

Will'us Hopton de Hopton=.... fil. et hæres .... Eyton de
in co. Salop Ar.   Eyton in com. Salop.

Nicholaus Hopton de Hopton in co. Salop.=....

Will'us Hopton de Hopton=Margareta* fil. et cohær. Joh'is Heuyn de
in com. Salop Ar.   Clybery [Cleobury] in com. Salop.

▲

* Harl. 1241 makes Margaret wife of Nicholas the father of William.

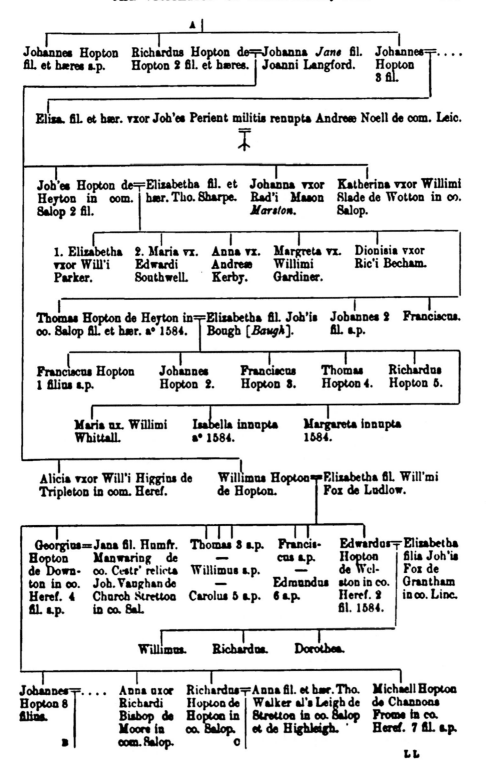

A

Johannes Hopton fil. et hæres s.p.

Richardus Hopton de Hopton 2 fil. et hæres. ═ Johanna *Jane* fil. Joanni Langford.

Johannes Hopton 3 fil. ═ ....

Eliza. fil. et hær. vxor Joh'es Perient militis renupta Andreæ Noell de com. Leic.

Joh'es Hopton de Heyton in com. Salop 2 fil. ═ Elizabetha fil. et hær. Tho. Sharpe.

Johanna vxor Rad'i Mason *Marston*.

Katherina vxor Willimi Slade de Wotton in co. Salop.

1. Elizabetha vxor Will'i Parker.

2. Maria vx. Edwardi Southwell.

Anna vx. Andreæ Kerby.

Margreta vx. Willimi Gardiner.

Dionisia vxor Ric'i Becham.

Thomas Hopton de Heyton in co. Salop fil. et hær. aº 1584. ═ Elizabetha fil. Joh'is Bough [*Baugh*].

Johannes 2 fil. s.p.

Franciscus.

Franciscus Hopton 1 filius s.p.

Johannes Hopton 2.

Franciscus Hopton 3.

Thomas Hopton 4.

Richardus Hopton 5.

Maria ux. Willimi Whittall.

Isabella innupta aº 1584.

Margareta innupta 1584.

Alicia vxor Will'i Higgins de Tripleton in com. Heref.

Willimus Hopton de Hopton. ═ Elizabetha fil. Will'mi Fox de Ludlow.

Georgius ═ Jana fil. Humfr. Hopton de Down- Manwaring de ton in co. co. Cestr' relicta Heref. 4 Joh. Vaughan de fil. s.p. Church Stretton in co. Sal.

Thomas 3 s.p.
—
Willimus s.p.
—
Carolus 5 s.p.

Franciscus s.p.
—
Edmundus 6 s.p.

Edwardus ═ Elizabetha Hopton filia Joh'is de Wel- Fox de ston in co. Grantham Heref. 2 in co. Linc. fil. 1584.

Willimus.

Richardus.

Dorothea.

Johannes Hopton 8 filius. ═ ....

Anna uxor Richardi Bishop de Moore in com. Salop.

Richardus Hopton de Hopton in co. Salop. ═ Anna fil. et hær. Tho. Walker al's Leigh de Stretton in co. Salop et de Highleigh.

Michaell Hopton de Channons Frome in co. Heref. 7 fil. s.p.

B

C

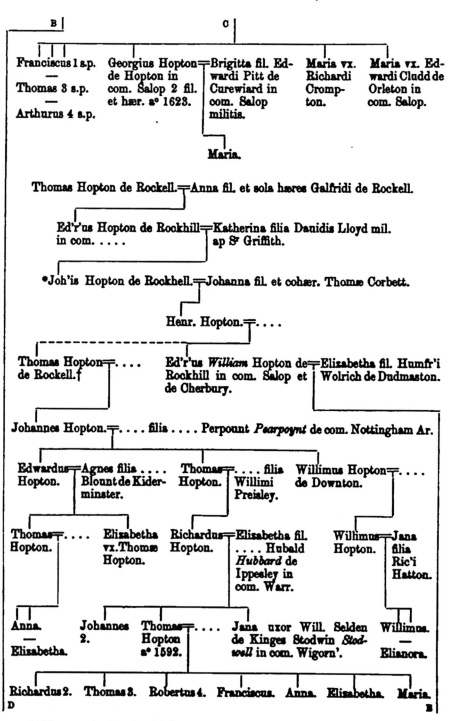

B | C |

Franciscus 1 s.p.
—
Thomas 3 s.p.
—
Arthurus 4 s.p.

Georgius Hopton=Brigitta fil. Ed-
de Hopton in | wardi Pitt de
com. Salop 2 fil. | Curewiard in
et hær. aº 1623. | com. Salop
  | militis.

Maria vx.
Richardi
Cromp-
ton.

Maria vx. Ed-
wardi Cludd de
Orleton in
com. Salop.

Maria.

Thomas Hopton de Rockell.=Anna fil. et sola hæres Galfridi de Rockell.

Ed'r'us Hopton de Rockhill=Katherina filia Dauidis Lloyd mil.
in com. . . . .   ap Sr Griffith.

*Joh'is Hopton de Rockhell.=Johanna fil. et cohær. Thomæ Corbett.

Henr. Hopton.=. . . .

Thomas Hopton=. . . .
de Rockell.†

Ed'r'us *William* Hopton de=Elizabetha fil. Humfr'i
Rockhill in com. Salop et | Wolrich de Dudmaston.
de Cherbury.

Johannes Hopton.=. . . . filia . . . . Perpount *Pearpoynt* de com. Nottingham Ar.

Edwardus=Agnes filia . . . .
Hopton. | Blount de Kider-
  | minster.

Thomas=. . . . filia
Hopton. | Willimi
  | Preisley.

Willimus Hopton=. . . .
de Downton.

Thomas=. . . .
Hopton.

Elizabetha
vx.Thomæ
Hopton.

Richardus=Elizabetha fil.
Hopton. | . . . . Hubald
  | *Hubbard* de
  | Ippesley in
  | com. Warr.

Willimus=Jana
Hopton. | filia
  | Ric'i
  | Hatton.

Anna.
—
Elizabetha.

Johannes
2.

Thomas=. . . .
Hopton
aº 1592.

Jana uxor Will. Selden
de Kinges Stodwin *Stod-
well* in com. *well*
Wigorn'.

Willimus.
—
Elianora.

Richardus 2.   Thomas 3.   Robertus 4.   Franciscus.   Anna.   Elizabetha.   Maria.

D | E

* This generation is omitted in Harl. 1241.
† Harl. 1241, fo. 96, makes Thomas Hopton son of Thomas Hopton by Anne Rockell.

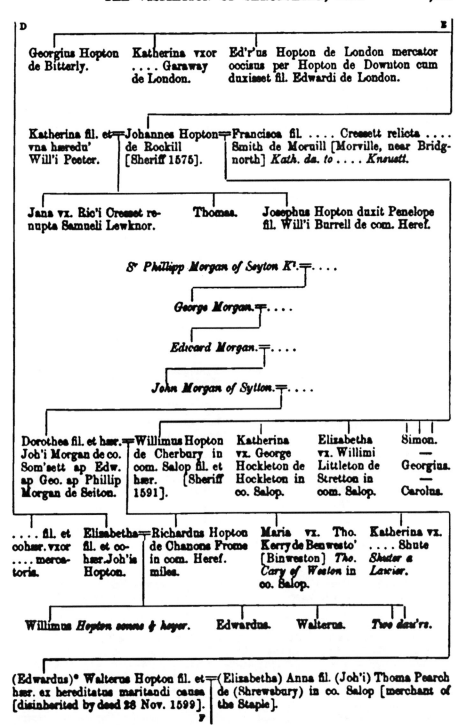

D

E

Georgius Hopton de Bitterly.

Katherina vxor .... Garaway de London.

Ed'r'us Hopton de London mercator oocisus per Hopton de Downton cum duxisset fil. Edwardi de London.

Katherina fil. et vna hæredu' Will'i Peeter. = Johannes Hopton de Rockill [Sheriff 1575]. = Francisca fil. .... Cressett relicta .... Smith de Moruill [Morville, near Bridgnorth] Kath. da. to .... Knsuett.

Jana vx. Ric'i Cresset renupta Samueli Lewknor.

Thomas.

Josephus Hopton duxit Penelope fil. Will'i Burrell de com. Heref.

Sr Phillipp Morgan of Seyton Kt. = ...

George Morgan. = ...

Edward Morgan. = ...

John Morgan of Sytton. = ...

Dorothea fil. et hær. Job'i Morgan de co. Som'sett ap Edw. ap Geo. ap Phillip Morgan de Seiton. = Willimus Hopton de Cherbury in com. Salop fil. et hær. [Sheriff 1591].

Katherina vx. George Hockleton de Hockleton in co. Salop.

Elizabetha vx. Willimi Littleton de Stretton in com. Salop.

Simon.
—
Georgius.
—
Carolus.

.... fil. et cohær. vxor .... mercatoris. = Elizabetha fil. et cohær. Joh'is Hopton. = Richardus Hopton de Chanons Frome in com. Heref. miles.

Maria vx. Tho. Kerry de Benwesto' [Binweston] Tho. Cary of Weston in co. Salop.

Katherina vx. .... Shute Shuter a Lawier.

Willimus Hopton sonne & heyer.

Edwardus.

Walterus.

Two dau'rs.

(Edwardus)* Walterus Hopton fil. et hær. ex hereditatus maritandi causa [disinherited by deed 26 Nov. 1599]. = (Elizabetha) Anna fil. (Joh'i) Thoma Pearch de (Shrewsbury) in co. Salop [merchant of the Staple].

F

* The words at the end of the pedigree within parentheses are additions in a later hand.

F |

(Morgan Hopton Rector of St Andrew Holborne⊤(Ann da. of Ant. Swetenham of
London only sonne æt. 58 an' 1659.) | Som'ford in com. Cestr'.)

(Jane.) (Hellin vx. Joh'i (Radul- (Edw. Hopton sone⊤(Sara da. of Peter
— Burch de New- phus 2 & heire æt. 25 an' | Newton of Heigley
(Sara.) bery in com. æt. 18 1659 now of Grays | [Heightley] in com.
— Berks.) an'1659.) Inn 1661.) | Salop Esq. ob. 23
(Ann.) | Sept. 1661.)

Horne of Pikesley and Little Ercall.

Harl. 1396, fo. 162^b. Harl. 1241, fo. 16^b. Harl. 615, fo. 265^b. S., ff. 107^b—108.

ARMS : Harl. 1396.—*Quarterly of six* : 1 and 6, *Gules, a fesse vair*—HORNE in
Shrewsbury MS. ; 2, *Sable, a bend between six martlets or*—WILLASCOTT in
Shrewsbury MS. ; 3, *Argent, a chevron gules between three square buckles sable*
[MOORTOWN] ; 4, *Azure, a chevron between three water-bougets or*—WOODOOT
in Shrewsbury MS. ; 5, *Sable, three mullets argent*—PULLESTON in
Shrewsbury MS.

Michael Morton.⊤....

.... Wilascot⊤.... fil. .... Lee de   Edmundus⊤Ellena fil. et her. Rob.
de co. Salop. | Langley (*co. Salope*).   Morton. | de Wodcote.

Willimus Horne.⊤Jana (*Jone*) fil.   Johannes⊤Elizab. fil. et heres Jordani
| et heres.   Morton. | Puleston ex filia Adami de
| | Chetwyn[d].

Willimus⊤Jana fil. .... Adoney   Thomas⊤Juliana fil. Rad'i Butler 2 fr'is
Horne. | (*Jane doughtr of* ....   Morton. | .... Butler de Norbury.
| *Adonaye*).

Johannes Hornes.⊤Margeria fil. et heres.

Will'us 1   Reginaldus Horne de Pikesby⊤Margeria filia .... Lee de
s.p.   in co. Salop. | Whichurch *Whittchurch*.

Matilda   Winifrida vx.   Joh'es Horne de parua⊤Jana filia Tho.   Ellena vxor
vx. Will'i   Mathei Dor-   Arcole alias Childes | Morton de   Rob. Cooke
Shewell.   ington (*Dar-*   Arnold (*Arcole*) in com. | Ingleton in co.   (*Ooke*).
| *ington*).   Salop.[*] | Salop(*Stafford*).

Johannes 2.   Thomas 3.   Reginaldus Horne⊤....   Anna   Margareta.   Maria.
| filius et heres. | (*Alys*).

[*] The Visitation of Stafford, 1583, styles John Horne "of Stoke, co. Warwick," and gives his wife.

𝕳osier of 𝕴oodcote, Cruckton, and Shrewsbury.

Harl. 1396, fo. 152.   S., fo. 144ª.

ARMS: Harl. 1396.—*Quarterly of six:* 1 and 6, *Per bend sinister ermine and ermines, a lion rampant or,* TUDER TREUOR [HOSIER]; 2, *Azure, a lion rampant per fesse or and argent within a bordure of the last* [and ducally crowned argent], KARADOC VRICHFAS; 3, *Ermine, a lion rampant gules* [azure], ELIDER AP REES SAIS; 4, *Gules, three chevrons argent,* JESTIN AP GWRGANT; 5, *Sable, three horses' heads erased argent,* BROCHWELL ISCEDROCK [ISGITHROCK].

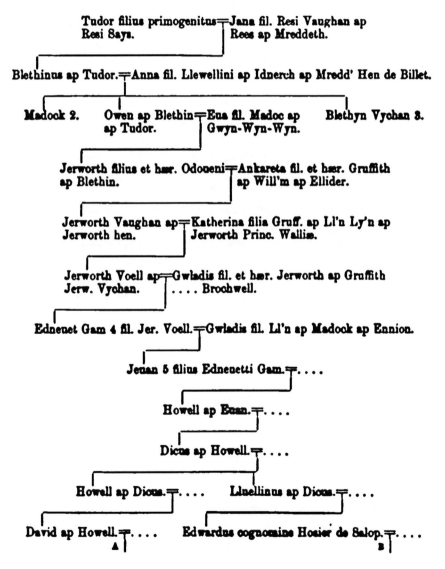

Tudor filius primogenitus=Jana fil. Resi Vaughan ap Resi Says. | Rees ap Mreddeth.

Blethinus ap Tudor.=Anna fil. Llewellini ap Idnerch ap Mredd' Hen de Billet.

Madock 2. | Owen ap Blethin ap Tudor.=Eua fil. Madoc ap Gwyn-Wyn-Wyn. | Blethyn Vychan 3.

Jerworth filius et hær. Odoueni ap Blethin.=Ankareta fil. et hær. Gruffith ap Will'm ap Ellider.

Jerworth Vaughan ap Jerworth hen.=Katherina filia Gruff. ap Ll'n Ly'n ap Jerworth Princ. Wallis.

Jerworth Voell ap Jerw. Vychan.=Gwladis fil. et hær. Jerworth ap Gruffith . . . . Brochwell.

Edneuet Gam 4 fil. Jer. Voell.=Gwladis fil. Ll'n ap Madock ap Ennion.

Jeuan 5 filius Edneuetti Gam.=. . . .

Howell ap Euan.=. . . .

Dicus ap Howell.=. . . .

Howell ap Dicus.=. . . . | Llnellinus ap Dicus.=. . . .

David ap Howell.=. . . . | Edwardus cognomine Hosier de Salop.=. . . .

▲ | B |

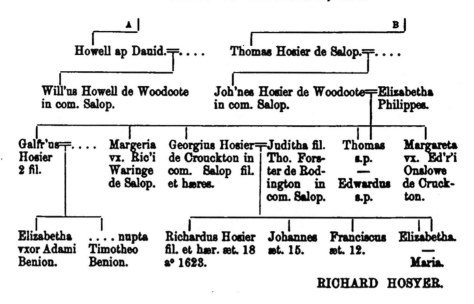

A | Howell ap Dauid.=....

B | Thomas Hosier de Salop.=....

Will'us Howell de Woodcote in com. Salop.

Joh'nes Hosier de Woodcote=Elizabetha Philippes.

Galfr'us Hosier 2 fil.=....

Margeria vx. Ric'i Waringe de Salop.

Georgius Hosier de Crouckton in com. Salop. fil. et hæres.=Juditha fil. Tho. Forster de Rodington in com. Salop.

Thomas s.p. — Edwardus s.p.

Margareta vx. Ed'r'i Onslowe de Crouckton.

Elizabetha vxor Adami Benion.

.... nupta Timotheo Benion.

Richardus Hosier fil. et hær. æt. 18 aᵒ 1623.

Johannes æt. 15.

Franciscus æt. 12.

Elizabetha. — Maria.

RICHARD HOSYER.

Hughes alias Higgins of Stretton.

Harl. 1396, fo. 128ᵇ.

Ex libro Joh'is Taylor pictoris in Fleet Street penultimo Januar' 1623.

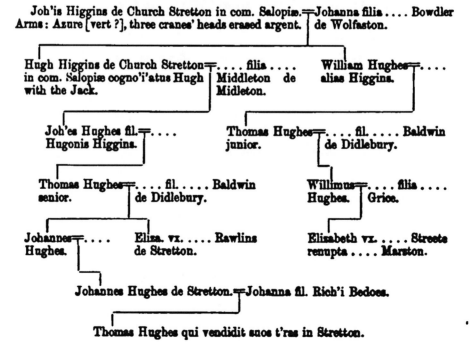

Joh'is Higgins de Church Stretton in com. Salopiæ.=Johanna filia .... Bowdler de Wolfaston.

Arms: Azure [vert ?], three cranes' heads erased argent.

Hugh Higgins de Church Stretton in com. Salopiæ cogno'i'atus Hugh with the Jack.=.... filia .... Middleton de Midleton.

William Hughes alias Higgins.=....

Joh'es Hughes fil. Hugonis Higgins.=....

Thomas Hughes junior.=.... fil. .... Baldwin de Didlebury.

Thomas Hughes senior.=.... fil. .... Baldwin de Didlebury.

Willimus Hughes.=.... filia .... Grice.

Johannes Hughes.=....

Eliza. vx. .... Rawlins de Stretton.

Elizabeth vx. .... Streete renupta .... Marston.

Johannes Hughes de Stretton.=Johanna fil. Rich'i Bedoes.

Thomas Hughes qui vendidit suos t'ras in Stretton.

Humfreston* of Humfreston.

Harl. 1396, fo. 132.   Harl. 1241, fo. 141.   S., fo. 125.

ARMS: Harl. 1896.—*Argent, an eagle displayed vert—sable* in Harl. 1241—*over all a chevron gules charged with three roses of the first.*

[There was a monumental brass in St. Alkmond's, Shrewsbury, to the memory of John Humfreston of Shrewsbury, ob. 1497, which displayed these arms.]

Will'us Humfreston de Humfreston in com. Salop.⁑Alicia.

Will'us Humfreston de Humfreston in com. Salop.⁑Katherina fil. Roberti Pigot.

Will'us Humfreston⁑Margaretta fil. Willimi Trobrige.	Francisca vx. S'
de Humfreston in	*Arms: Or, a bridge embattled of five*	Vincentij Corbet
com. Salop fil. et	*arches . . . . with as many streams trans-*	de Moorton in
hæres a° 1623.	*fluent azure over the base argent, over the*	com. Salop.
	centre arch a fane argent. [The arms of	
	Trowbridge of Modbury, Devon.]	

. . . . *da. to* . . . .=Willi'm' Humfreston fil. et hæres apparens=Prudencia filia
Scrimsher.   ætatis 2 a° 1623 *1613.*   . . . . Porter.

WILL'M HVMFRESTON.

Hunt of Longnor.

Harl. 1396, fo. 158ᵇ.   S., fo. 146ᵇ.

ARMS: Harl. 1396.—*Quarterly: 1 and 4, Per pale argent and sable, a saltire counterchanged, a crescent for difference* [HUNT]; *2, Gules, a hind trippant argent between three bugle-horns stringed or* [HUNT]; *3, Argent, on a pale sable a conger's head couped or* (GASCOIGNE).

1 CREST.—*A lion's head erased per pale argent and sable, collared gules, lined or.*
2 CREST.—*A hind's head couped argent, vulned in the neck with a pheon sable, and bleeding proper.*
3 CREST.—*A conger's head erect couped or.*

. . . . Hunt⁑ . . . .

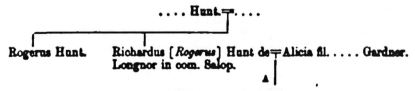

Rogerus Hunt.   Richardus [*Rogerus*] Hunt de⁑Alicia fil. . . . . Gardner.
                     Longnor in com. Salop.

* "Humphreyston" in Harl. 1241.

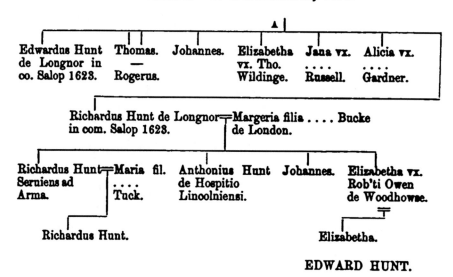

Edwardus Hunt de Longnor in co. Salop 1623. Thomas. — Rogerus. Johannes. Elizabetha vx. Tho. Wildinge. Jana vx. .... Russell. Alicia vx. .... Gardner.

Richardus Hunt de Longnor in com. Salop 1623.=Margeria filia .... Bucke de London.

Richardus Hunt Seruiens ad Arma.=Maria fil. .... Tuck. Anthonius Hunt de Hospitio Lincolniensi. Johannes. Elizabetha vx. Rob'ti Owen de Woodhowse.

Richardus Hunt.

Elizabetha.

EDWARD HUNT.

Hunt of Milson.

Harl. 1896, fo. 158 [a pedigree inserted].

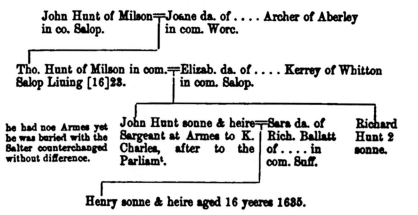

John Hunt of Milson in co. Salop.=Joane da. of .... Archer of Aberley in com. Worc.

Tho. Hunt of Milson in com. Salop Liuing [16]23.=Elizab. da. of .... Kerrey of Whitton in com. Salop.

he had noe Armes yet he was buried with the Salter counterchanged without difference. John Hunt sonne & heire Sergeant at Armes to K. Charles, after to the Parliam't.=Sara da. of Rich. Ballatt of .... in com. Suff. Richard Hunt 2 sonne.

Henry sonne & heire aged 16 yeeres 1635.

This Discent taken by the relation of Sergeant Hunt p' me Jo. Withy but could proue noe Armes yet neuer the less when he dyed he was buried with Escocheons which was p'ty p' pale indented A. et S. a Salter counterchanged.

Hussey of Adbrighton Hussey, Leighton, Criggion, and Coton.

Harl. 1396, ff. 145, 146.

Ex Chartis Ricardi Hussey, de Adbrighton Hussey, in com. Salop, militis, 4 Octobris aᵒ 1623.

Sciant p'ntes et futuri quod Ricardus filius Will'i de Baldreton et haeredes sui terram quam haereditario tenent de Waltero Hose et haeredibus suis in villa de Balderton non debent nec dare nec ad term' Committere ad nocumentum d'ci Walteri haeredum suorum. Sans dat'.

Conuentio inter Joh'em filium Joh'is Husey Dominum de Adbritten et Hugonem Bernard Burgensem Salop' vir⁴ quod praed'ctus Joh'es dedit praed'c'o Hugoni estouarium in Bosco suo de Adbritton Husey ad domos suas et Sepes faciend'. Testibus Richardo de Letton mil., Will'o Banester, Ric'o de Letton, Will'o de Williscot et alija. Dat. apud Salop aᵒ 33 E. I.

Sciant p'ntes et futuri quod ego Ric'us Husee de Adbrighton Hesse dedi Joh'i Hesee fratri meo et Ceciliae vxori eius placea vasti in Adbrighton iuxta cimiterium quam placeam habuit ex dono meo etc. Testibus Will'o Banester, Rogero Banest'r, Johanne de Smethcot et alija. Dat. aᵒ 3 E. 3.

Rich'us Dominus de Adbrighton Husee concessit et confirmauit Joh'i Husee fratri suo et Ceciliae vxori eius et Isabella filia eorundem septem acras regales vasti sui iacentes iuxta Boscum suum de Adbrighton etc. Testibus Will'o Banest'r de Smethcote, Johanni de Lea, Rogero Banester de Hadenhall, Thome Husee et alija. Dat. apud Adbrighton Husee aᵒ 3 E. 3.

Henricus dei gra⁴ etc. Salutem Omnibus ad quos etc. Sciatis quod concessimus et licenciam dedimus dil'co nobis Ricardo Huse Ar. quod ip'e duas t'ras in Adbrighton Huse in com. Salop iacentes in quodam campo vocato Hayteleyfaild in quo Bellum inter nos et Henricum Percy nuper aduersarium n'r'm defunctum et sibi adhaerentes exeitit, dare possit Rogero Yse capellano et Joh'i Gilbert capellano in puram elemosinam diuina singulis diebus in quadam Capella per ip'm ib'm de nouo faciend' et edificand' pro salubri statu n'ro et pro a'i'abus qui in eodem bello interfecti fuerunt et ib'm humati existant, necnon pro animabus omnium fidelium defunctorum ordinac'o'em ip'ius Rogeri in hac parte faciend' celebratur etc. Teste meip'o aped Westm' 28 Octobre aᵒ regni n'ri octauo. Sub Magno Angliae Sigillo.

Henricus dei gra⁴ etc. Omnibus etc. Sciatis quod inspeximus quoddam scriptum finalis concordiae inter Ric'um Campden vtriusq' iuris baccalaurium et decanum liberae capellae cm'e beatae Mariae Salop et Adam Huijes Ar. nuper Domini' de Adbrighton Husee tanquam Matrici Eccli'e suae liberae capellae regiae praed'c'm pro decimis etc. eidem Capellae accedentibus de capella Adbrighton Husee pro 100 annis concesserit annua'm pensionem soluend' annuatim prout in originali carta specificatur praed'c'i Tamen Ric'us et canonici sui de termino perpetuitatem constituere cupientes p'dui Adam pro se et haered' suis et pr'd'c'us Will'm Concesserunt p'dictum annua'm pensionem annuatim soluend' vt praemittitur praefatis Canonicis et eorum successoribus, vt pro sua parte omnium decimorum et obuentionum depred'c'm capella regiae etc. Dat. apud Adbrighton 2 Junij aᵒ D'ni 1336. In cuius rei testimonum etc. Teste meip'o aped Westm' 20 Junij aᵒ regni n'ri etc. Sub Magno Angliae Sigillo.

Charta Ric'i Husee de Adbrighton Ar. data aᵒ 22 H. 6.

Ex Chartis Roberti Hussey de Leighton in com. Salop Ar. 4 Septembr. aᵒ 1623.

Sciant p'ntes et futuri quod Ego Roberti Lee de Rodon dedi Will'o Poyner de Wroxeter omnia t'ras et ten'ta quae Joh'is Clone tenet de me in Preston super le Were vocat Sutton Lond. Testibus Ric'o de Otteley, Ric'o de Bernwika, Roberto Lee de Uffington, Ric'o Yonge. Dat. aᵒ 31 R. 2.

Omnia x'pi fidelibus ad quos etc. Sciatis me Richardum Drayten relaxasse Will'o Poyner Totam ius meum in Manerio de Preston super le Were etc. Testibus Ph'o Willeyly, Ricardo Oteley, Ric'o Benlow, Joh'e de Rykedon, Ric'o Swetenham. Dat. apud Preston aᵒ 3 H. 4.

Endentura parentre Thomas Coant D'arundell et de Sarr. d'un part et Will'm Poynour et Will'm son fils d'autre part testmoigne que le dic Coante ad grauntes et lesses au dit Will'm et William touts le demaesnes terre et tenementes quer Thomas de Conde tenoit du dic Coante en la ville de Conede a terme de lour deux vies, redant annualment quarrant et deux souls et dis deniers. Donne a Salope le p'mer iour de Maij aᵒ 5 H. 4.

Omnibus x'pi fidelibus ad quos etc. Thomas Poyner de Benlow in com. Salop Ar. Salutem. Noueritis me praefatam Thomam attornasse et loco meo possisse dilector mihi in x'po W. Ypris et R. Berdmeos aeros attornatos ad liberandam nomine meo plenam seisinom Rogero Poyner filio et haeredi meo et Katharinae vxoris eius filim Roberti Scryven Ar. de et in omnibus t'ris meis in Choriton Aston subtus le Wrekyn, Opinton, Drayton Abbatis, et Eton Constantine in com. Salop. Dat. aᵒ 16 R. 4.

——————————

Harl. 1896, fo. 146[b].　Harl. 1241, fo. 60.　8., ff. 189[a]—141[a].

ARMS: Harl. 1896.—*Quarterly: 1 and 4, Barry of six gules and ermine,* HUSSEY;
2, Argent, three boots sable, turned up ermine, spurred or, BROWNE; *8, Argent,
on a bend azure three garbs or.*

CREST.—*A boot sable, turned up ermine, spurred or.*

[CREST, temp. H. VIII.: A hind courant argent, ducally gorged and chained or.
('Collect. Topog.,' vol. iii., p. 60.)　The seal of Richard Hussey of Adbrighton Hussey, 1415, shews a leg or boot in bend; perhaps derived from Browne
of Worfield.]

ARMS: Harl. 1896: HUSSEY OF LEIGHTON.—*Quarterly of fourteen:* 1, HUSSEY;
2, BROWNE; 8, *Argent, a chevron between three mullets sable* [BROWNE OF
MORFE]; 4, OTELEY; 5, *Argent, a chevron gules between three scorpions
sable* [COLE]; 6, *Gules, an eagle displayed with two heads or;* 7, *Azure,
three bars or, in chief as many gryphons' heads erased of the second;*[*] 8, *Gules,
three birds each standing on a stump of a tree couped and eradicated argent;*
9, *Argent, a fesse gules between six* [Cornish choughs proper, ONSLOW];
10, *Argent, a chevron gules between three talbots passant sable;* 11, *Gules,
a fleur-de-lis or;*[†] 12, *Azure, a fesse between six crosses formée fitchée or;*
18, *Argent, a fesse azure, in chief a bull's head erased sable, and in base a
gryphon passant of the third winged or* [PIPE alias WALKER]; 14, *Or, a
parrot vert legged gules* [POYNER].

Hussey D'n's Manerior' de Abrighton Hussey, Nather Carthor, Norton Themoin com. Staff.,
Bradeley, Leighton et Garmaston Apud Conquest Angles.—Harl. 1241.

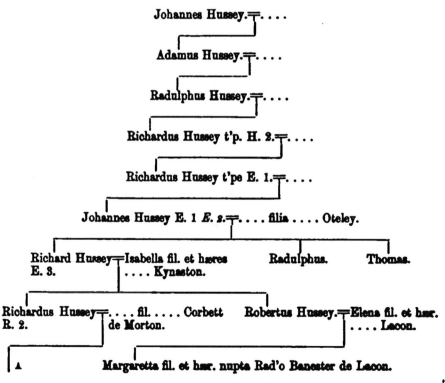

* Perhaps for Barker *alias* Coverall of co. Salop.—Visit. Warw. 1619, page 80.
† Gerband, Lord of Trefnant, bore these arms in 1278.

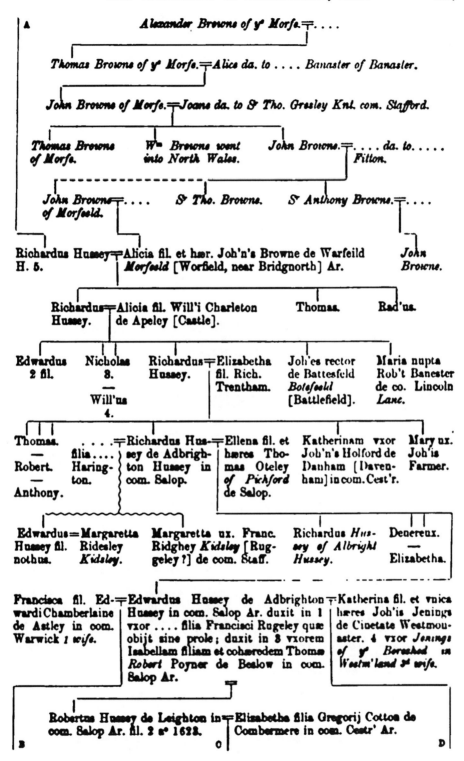

A

Alexander Browne of yᵉ Morfe.⊤....

Thomas Browne of yᵉ Morfe.⊤Alice da. to .... Banaster of Banaster.

John Browne of Morfe.⊤Joane da. to Sᵗ Tho. Gresley Knt. com. Stafford.

Thomas Browne of Morfe. | Wᵐ Browne went into North Wales. | John Browne.⊤.... da. to ..... Fitton.

John Browne⊤.... of Morfeeld. | Sᵗ Tho. Browne. | Sᵗ Anthony Browne.⊤....

Richardus Hussey H. 5.⊤Alicia fil. et hær. Joh'n's Browne de Warfeild Morfeeld [Worfield, near Bridgnorth] Ar. | John Browne.

Richardus Hussey.⊤Alicia fil. Will'i Charleton de Apeley [Castle]. | Thomas. | Rad'us.

Edwardus 2 fil. | Nicholas 8. — Will'us 4. | Richardus Hussey.⊤Elizabetha fil. Rich. Trentham. | Joh'es rector de Battesfeld Botefeeld [Battlefield]. | Maria nupta Rob't Banester de co. Lincoln Lanc.

Thomas. — Robert. — Anthony. | .... filia .... Haring-ton.⊤Richardus Hus-sey de Adbrigh-ton Hussey in com. Salop.⊤Ellena fil. et hæres Tho-mas Oteley of Pickford de Salop. | Katherinam vxor Joh'n's Holford de Danham [Daven-ham] in com. Cest'r. | Mary ux. Joh'is Farmer.

Edwardus Hussey fil. nothus.⊤Margaretta Ridesley Kidsley. | Margaretta ux. Franc. Ridghey Kidsley [Rug-geley ?] de com. Staff. | Richardus Hus-sey of Albright Hussey. | Denereux. — Elizabetha.

Francisca fil. Ed-wardi Chamberlaine de Astley in com. Warwick 1 wife.⊤Edwardus Hussey de Adbrighton Hussey in com. Salop Ar. duxit in 1 vxor .... filia Francisci Rugeley quæ obijt sine prole; duxit in 2 vxorem Isabellam filiam et cohæredem Thomæ Robert Poyner de Bealow in com. Salop Ar.⊤Katherina fil. et vnica hæres Joh'is Jenings de Cinetate Westmou-aster. 4 vxor Jenings of yᵉ Boreshed in Westm'land 3ᵈ wife.

Robertus Hussey de Leighton in com. Salop Ar. fil. 2 aᵒ 1623.⊤Elizabetha filia Gregorij Cotton de Combermere in com. Cestr' Ar.

B | C | D

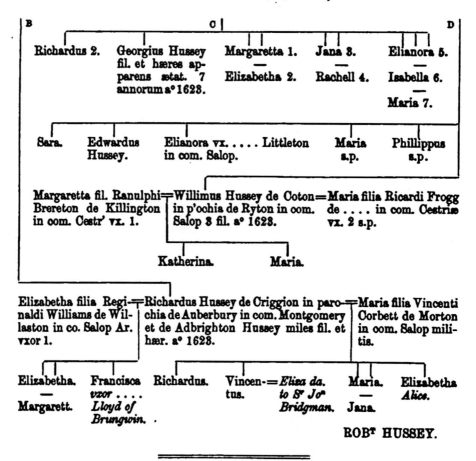

B

C

D

Richardus 2.

Georgius Hussey fil. et hæres apparens ætat. 7 annorum aº 1623.

Margaretta 1.
—
Elizabetha 2.

Jana 3.
—
Rachell 4.

Elianora 5.
—
Isabella 6.
—
Maria 7.

Sara.

Edwardus Hussey.

Elianora vx. .... Littleton in com. Salop.

Maria s.p.

Phillippus s.p.

Margaretta fil. Ranulphi⹀Willimus Hussey de Coton⹀Maria filia Ricardi Frogg Brereton de Killington in p'ochia de Ryton in com. de .... in com. Cestriæ in com. Cestr' vx. 1. Salop 3 fil. aº 1623. vx. 2 s.p.

Katherina.

Maria.

Elizabetha filia Regi⹀Richardus Hussey de Criggion in paro⹀Maria filia Vincenti naldi Williams de Wil⹀chia de Auberbury in com. Montgomery Corbett de Morton laston in co. Salop Ar. et de Adbrighton Hussey miles fil. et in com. Salop mili⹀ vxor 1. hær. aº 1623. tis.

Elizabetha.
—
Margarett.

Francisca vxor .... Lloyd of Brungwin. .

Richardus.

Vincen⹀=Eliza da. tus. to Sr Joⁿ Bridgman.

Maria.
—
Jana.

Elizabetha Alice.

ROBᵀ HUSSEY.

Hynde of Evelith.

Harl. 1396, fo. 181ᵇ. S., fo. 124ᵇ.

ARMS: Harl. 1396.—*Quarterly of eight : 1 and 8, Argent, on a chevron azure three escallops of the field, on a chief of the second a lion passant argent ; 2, Argent, on a bend vert three wolves' heads erased of the first* [MIDDLETON] ; *3, Vert, a chevron between three wolves' heads erased argent* [RERID VLAITH] ; *4, Argent, three greyhounds courant in pale sable collared of the first* [ARGLWYD Y BRYH] ; *5, Azure, a wolf passant argent* [BLAIDD RHYDD] ; *6, Gules, on a bend or three lions passant sable* [WYNNESBURY] ; *7, Argent, two ravens sable* [BOWDLER].
CREST.—*A lion's head erased argent.*

Will'us Hynde de Mydleton in Ep'atu' Dunelm'.⹀.... fil .... Muckleston.

Joh'es Hinde⹀Sibilla filia unica et hær. Georgij Middleton de Cherbury de London. in com. Salop [Equerry to Queen Elizabeth].

A

A

| Thomas Hinde de london 2 filius duxit Elizabetha' filiam Willimi Sparehurst s.p. | Georgius Hinde de Euelith [juxta Shiffnall] in com. Salop fil. et hæres superstes aº 1623. | Elizabetha fil. Tho. Skrimshire de Aquilat in co. Staff. relicta Walteri Forster de Euelith Ar. | Margareta vxor Richardi Joanes de Denbigh. |

| Howardus Hinde fil. et hær. apparens ætatis 7 annorum aº 1623 [died un-married—Visit. Staff.]. | Franciscus [he was afterwards of Pershall juxta Eccleshall, co. Staff., and was aged 41 in 1663]. | Sibilla.   Georgius s.p.

[Died unmarried— Visit. Staff.] |

G. HYNDE.

Ireland of Adbrighton.

Harl. 1396, fo. 169ᵇ.   Harl. 1241, fo. 80.   S., ff. 152ᵇ—155ᵇ.

ARMS: Harl. 1396.—*Quarterly of twelve: 1, Gules, six fleurs-de-lis, three, two, and one, argent,* IRELAND; *2, Paly of six argent and gules, a bordure engrailed azure, over all a canton of the second charged with a spur leathered or,* KNIGHT; *3, Quarterly per fesse indented argent and sable, in first and fourth quarters a bugle-horn stringed of the second,* FORSTER; *4, Azure, three lapwings' heads erased argent,* WARING [called also JUELD]; *5, Gules, on a fesse or between three goldfinches argent as many fleurs-de-lis azure,* GOLDSMITH; *6, Azure, a lion rampant or within a bordure engrailed also or [gules?], over all a canton of the second,* JAYE; *7, Barry nebulee of six argent and gules, on a bend sable three boars' heads couped close of the first,* PURCELL; *8, Or, a fesse gules within a bordure sable,* HENOLTE; *9, Argent, three bendlets azure, on a canton sable a lion passant or,* SHARSHALL; *10, Gules, on a fesse engrailed or between three bucks' heads cabossed argent as many bugle-horns, unstrung, sable,* WARING; *11, Sable, three horses' heads erased argent,* BROCKWELL; *12, Or, two ravens sable within a bordure engrailed gules,* CORBETT [of Lee].

CREST.—*A dove argent holding in the beak an olive-branch vert.*

Robertus Ireland de Oswaldstre in com. Salop filius iunior = ...
Ad'm Ireland de la Hale & Hutt [co. Lancaster].

Robertus Ireland. = ...

Richardus Ireland [of Oswaldstre 1390]. = ...

Rogerus Ireland. = Cecilia.

| Thomas Ireland. | Anna filia Ranulphi Brereton. = Richardus Ireland de Oswaldstre.*
A | Tibota filia Rogeri Salter de Oswaldstre.
B |

* Appointed, 1434, Receiver for the King in Coventry and Shrewsbury in Merchia Wallie, on the death of John, Earl of Arundel (Originalia 13 Henry VI., rot. 17).

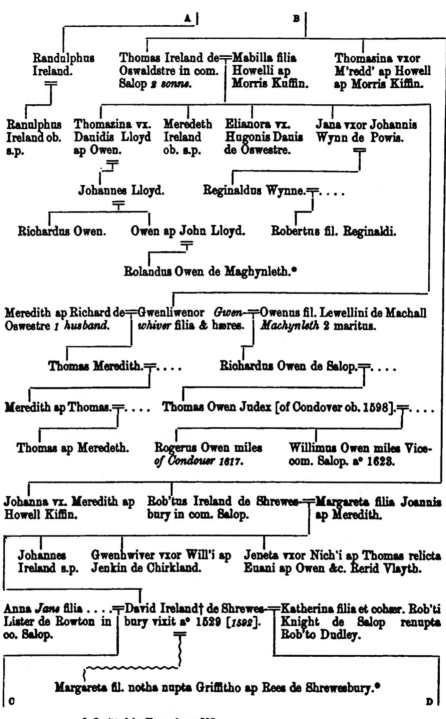

A | B

Randulphus Ireland.

Thomas Ireland de Oswaldstre in com. Salop 2 sonne. = Mabilla filia Howelli ap Morris Kuffin.

Thomasina vxor M'redd' ap Howell ap Morris Kiffin.

Ranulphus Ireland ob. s.p.

Thomazina vx. Danidis Lloyd ap Owen.

Meredeth Ireland ob. s.p.

Elianora vx. Hugonis Danis de Oswestre.

Jana vxor Johannis Wynn de Powis.

Johannes Lloyd.

Reginaldus Wynne. = ...

Richardus Owen.

Owen ap John Lloyd.

Robertus fil. Reginaldi.

Rolandus Owen de Maghynleth.*

Meredith ap Richard de Oswestre 1 husband. = Gwenliwenor whiver filia & hæres. Gwen- whiver = Owenus fil. Lewellini de Machall Machynleth 2 maritus.

Thomas Meredith. = ...

Richardus Owen de Salop. = ...

Meredith ap Thomas. = ...

Thomas Owen Judex [of Condover ob. 1598]. = ...

Thomas ap Meredeth.

Rogerus Owen miles of Condover 1617.

Willimus Owen miles Vice-com. Salop. aº 1623.

Johanna vx. Meredith ap Howell Kiffin.

Rob'tus Ireland de Shrewesbury in com. Salop. = Margareta filia Joannis ap Meredith.

Johannes Ireland s.p.

Gwenhwiver vxor Will'i ap Jenkin de Chirkland.

Jeneta vxor Nich'i ap Thomas relicta Euani ap Owen &c. Rerid Vlayth.

Anna Jane filia .... Lister de Rowton in co. Salop. = David Ireland† de Shrewesbury vixit aº 1529 [1592]. = Katherina filia et cohær. Rob'ti Knight de Salop renupta Rob'to Dudley.

Margareta fil. notha nupta Griffitho ap Rees de Shrewesbury.*

C D

* Omitted in Shrewsbury MS.
† Harl. 1241 gives all his children as by Katherine Knight.

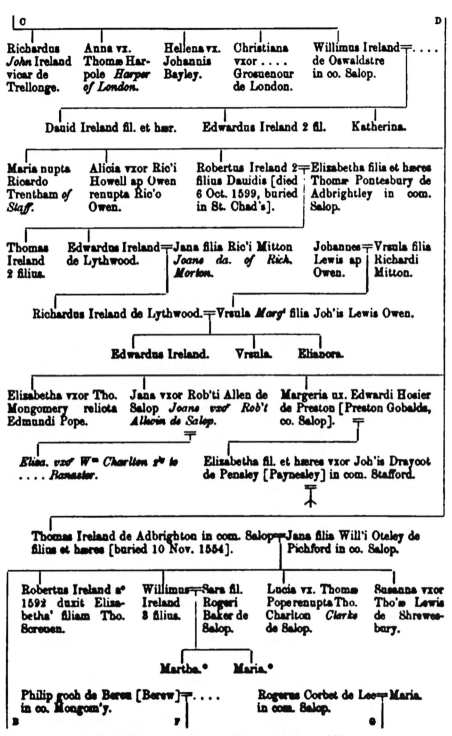

Richardus *John* Ireland vicar de Trellonge.

Anna vx. Thomæ Harpole *Harper of London.*

Hellena vx. Johannis Bayley.

Christiana vxor .... Grosuenour de London.

Willimus Ireland⹋.... de Oswaldstre in co. Salop.

Dauid Ireland fil. et hær.   Edwardus Ireland 2 fil.   Katherina.

Maria nupta Ricardo Trentham *of Staff.*

Alicia vxor Ric'i Howell ap Owen renupta Ric'o Owen.

Robertus Ireland 2⹋Elizabetha filia et hæres filius Dauidis [died 6 Oct. 1599, buried in St. Chad's].

Thomæ Pontesbury de Adbrightley in com. Salop.

Thomas Ireland 2 filius.

Edwardus Ireland⹋Jana filia Ric'i Mitton de Lythwood. *Joane da. of Rich. Morton.*

Johannes⹋Vrsula filia Lewis ap Owen.

Richardi Mitton.

Richardus Ireland de Lythwood.⹋Vrsula *Mary* filia Joh'is Lewis Owen.

Edwardus Ireland.   Vrsula.   Elianora.

Elizabetha vxor Tho. Mongomery relicta Edmundi Pope.

Jana vxor Rob'ti Allen de Salop *Joane vxo' Rob't Allevin de Salop.*

Margeria ux. Edwardi Hosier de Preston [Preston Gobalds, co. Salop].⹋

Elisa. vxo' W'm Charlton s'o to .... Ranaster.

Elizabetha fil. et hæres vxor Joh'is Drayot de Pensley [Paynesley] in com. Stafford.

Thomas Ireland de Adbrighton in com. Salop⹋Jana filia Will'i Oteley de filius et hæres [buried 10 Nov. 1554].   Pichford in co. Salop.

Robertus Ireland a° 1592 duxit Elizabetha' filiam Tho. Scrouen.

Willimus⹋Sara fil. Ireland Rogeri 3 filius. Baker de Salop.

Lucia vx. Thomæ Pope renupta Tho. Charlton *Clerke* de Salop.

Susanna vxor Tho's Lewis de Shrewesbury.

Martha.*   Maria.*

Philip gooh de Berew [Berew]⹋.... in co. Mongom'y.

Rogerus Corbet de Lee⹋Maria. in com. Salop.

* Harl. 1241 places Martha and Mary as daughters of Robert.

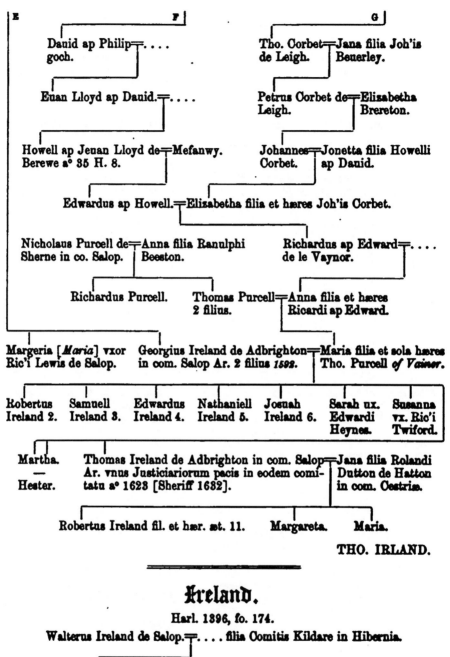

E   F   G

Dauid ap Philip=.... goch.

Tho. Corbet=Jana filia Joh'is de Leigh. Beuerley.

Euan Lloyd ap Dauid.=....

Petrus Corbet de=Elizabetha Leigh. Brereton.

Howell ap Jeuan Lloyd de=Mefanwy. Berewe aº 35 H. 8.

Johannes=Jonetta filia Howelli Corbet. ap Dauid.

Edwardus ap Howell.=Elizabetha filia et hæres Joh'is Corbet.

Nicholaus Purcell de=Anna filia Ranulphi Sherne in co. Salop. Beeston.

Richardus ap Edward=.... de le Vaynor.

Richardus Purcell.

Thomas Purcell=Anna filia et hæres 2 filius. Ricardi ap Edward.

Margeria [*Maria*] vxor Ric'i Lewis de Salop.

Georgius Ireland de Adbrighton=Maria filia et sola hæres in com. Salop Ar. 2 filius *1592*. Tho. Purcell *of Vaisor*.

Robertus Ireland 2. Samuell Ireland 3. Edwardus Ireland 4. Nathaniell Ireland 5. Josuah Ireland 6. Sarah ux. Edwardi Heynes. Susanna vx. Ric'i Twiford.

Martha.
—
Hester.

Thomas Ireland de Adbrighton in com. Salop=Jana filia Rolandi Ar. vnus Justiciariorum pacis in eodem comi- Dutton de Hatton tatu aº 1623 [Sheriff 1632]. in com. Cestriæ.

Robertus Ireland fil. et hær. æt. 11. Margareta. Maria.

THO. IRLAND.

Ireland.

Harl. 1396, fo. 174.

Walterus Ireland de Salop.=.... filia Comitis Kildare in Hibernia.

Johannes Ireland fil. et hæres.=Susanna fil. Rich'i Eyton.

Isabella vxor Joh'is Pryde. Alicia nupta Rogeri Berington. Christiana vxor Rob'ti Rodington.

Jay of Jaye.

Harl. 1396, ff. 167—169.   S., ff. 150ᵃ—151ᵇ.

Ex Chartis Thomæ Ireland de Adbrighton in com. Salop Ar. 11ᵉ Septemb. aᵒ 1623.

Sciant p'ntes et futuri quod ego Willielmus de Burlegia concessi et hac carta mea confirmavi Briano de Jaie et hæredibus suis quod si ego hæredes non habuero de Edelina sponsa mea filia iam dicti Briani, tota terra quam ipse Brianus et ipsius hæredes reuertetur. Huius rei testes sunt Radulfus abbas de Wigemora, Helias de Hugelegia, Willielmus de Weldebef, et Willielmus filius eius Philippus de Jaie.

[Drawing of a Seal, Plate III., Fig. 13.]

Sciant p'ntes et futuri quod ego Joh'es de Jay filius Briani de Jay dedi Rogero Vachan de Wygemor' totum illam pratum quod vocatur Wlrichesmedue etc. testibus Briano de Brampton' Simone de Hauberdon Waltero de Hopton Hugone Anglico militibus Rogero de Pedword' Roberto de Jay Hen. Makelin et multis alijs.

[Drawing of a Seal, Plate III., Fig. 14.]

Sciant p'ntes et futuri quod ego Joh'es de Jaia dedi et concessi in feodo et hæreditate Roberto de Jaia fratri meo et vt clameum dimitteret quod habuit in illas quatuor virgatas terræ quæ fuerunt auunculi n'ri Philippi de Jaia vnam virg' t'ræ in Bekeiaia etc.

Sigillum vt supra.

Walterus de Nouo Meinil concensu Saræ vxoris eius concessit Joh'i de Jaia tenementum de feodo suo in Wigemor' quod Brianus pater einsdem Joh'is tenuit de Ricardo Labanc antecessore d'ci Walteri etc. Sans date.

Sciant præsentes et futuri quod ego Gilb'tus de Bukehul dedi Waltero filio Joh'is de Jaye de Johanna filia mea procreato pro homagio et seruicio suo vnam acram terræ quæ vocatur le Farroc etc. testibus d'no Simone de Buri' Waltero de Hopton Hugone de Jaye et multis alija.

Ego Gilbertus de Bukenhull me obligaui similiter cum fide mea quod si Margeria soror mea aut Egidius de Seinleger sponsus eius vexant Joh'em de Jaya aut heredes suos de t'ra quæ d'ca Margeria habuit in dotem de Elia de Jaya in villa de Bedeston et in villa de Bekeiaya quod tunc ego dabo Joh'i de Jaya aut hæredibus suis quatuor marcas et dimidium et illud totum quod Joh'es de Jaya aut hæredes sui ponunt aut dispendant propter placitum præd'c'm t'ram.

[Drawing of a Seal, Plate III., Fig. 15.]

Omnibus ad quos præsens scriptum peruenerit D'nus Brianus de Brompton miles salutem. Noueritis me reddidisse et remisisse pro me et hær. meis Waltero de Jaye militi totum pratum illud quod vocatur Gunnyldemede etc. Hijs testibus d'no Waltero de Hopton d'no Waltero de Brompton d'no Waltero de Bokenhull d'no Waltero de Pedwardin Ric'o de Lecton et a'ijs.

[Drawing of a Seal, Plate III., Fig. 17.]

Atouts iceaus qe ceste lettre verrunt ou orrunt Edmund Counte de Arundell saluts. Sache v're vaiuersite nous auoir grantze que le maner de Jaye od les apurtenances le quel Nichol de Reygate rendi a Thomas le fiz Wauter de Jaye et a Johanne sa femme et a Johan le fiz les auant ditz Thomas et Johanne, remeyne a les auant ditz Johanne et Johan apres la mort le dit Thomas sauns challenge cleym ou destarbaance de nous ou nous heires. Done a Oznebold le vendredy prochein apres la feste de Seint Nicholas en ian 10 E. 2.

[Drawing of a Seal, Plate III., Fig. 18.]

Patent vaiuersis me Constanciam de Hauberdeya relictam Joh'is le Saltar' in pura vidaitate mea remisisse Johanne D'no de Jaye et Thomæ filio suo et hæredibus ipsius Thomæ totam ius meum in omnibus t'ris etc. in Beokaye et Bedeston etc. Dat. aᵒ 17 E. 2.

Omnibus x'pi fidelibus etc. Thomas de Jay d'nus de eadem salutem. Noueritis me concessisse tenentibus meis totam illam communiam quam solebant habere ex antiq' tempore in loco vocato le Oldtowne pro pecoribus suis ibidem pastorandis etc. Dat. apud Lodelowe aᵒ 7 H. 5.

[Drawing of a Seal, Plate III., Fig. 16.].

Sigillum HENRICI GRAY.

N N

Sciant p'ntes et futuri quod ego Thomas Jay dedi Joh'i Hory et Ric'o Ewyas manerium meum de Jay cum suis pertinen' necnon o'ia alia t'ras et ten'ta in villa de Bekkey et Bodeston etc. Dat. apud Jay die Lunæ prox' post festum in Ramis palmarum a° 8 H. 5.

[Drawing of a Seal, Plate III., Fig. 16.]

Sciant præsentes et futuri quod ego Joh'es filius Thomæ Jay et hæres eiusdem Thomæ dedi Ric'o Hord de Brugemorth manerium meum de Jay vna cum omnibus alijs t'ris tenementi redditibus et seruicijs meis quæ habeo infra comitatum Herefordiæ et d'n'cum de Wyggemore. Habend' etc. Datum apud manerium de Jay a° 4 H. 6.

[Drawing of a Seal, Plate III., Fig. 16.]

Ex chartis Thomæ Ireland de Adbrighton in com. Salop Ar. 12 Septembris a° 1623.

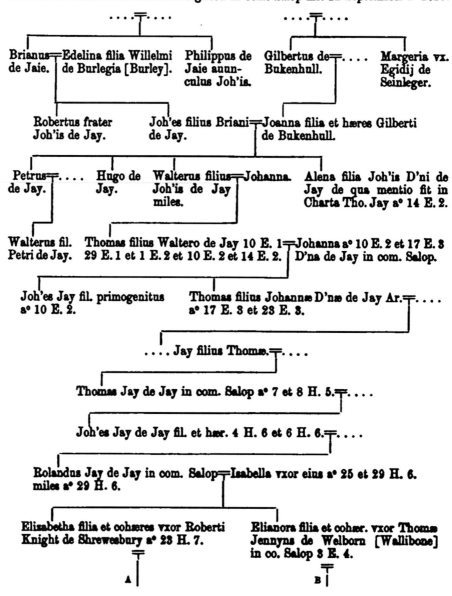

Brianus de Jaie. = Edelina filia Willelmi de Burlegia [Burley].

Philippus de Jaie auunculus Joh'is.

Gilbertus de Bukenhull. = ...

Margeria vx. Egidij de Seinleger.

Robertus frater Joh'is de Jay.

Joh'es filius Briani de Jay. = Joanna filia et hæres Gilberti de Bukenhull.

Petrus = ... de Jay.

Hugo de Jay.

Walterus filius = Johanna. Joh'is de Jay miles.

Alena filia Joh'is D'ni de Jay de qua mentio fit in Charta Tho. Jay a° 14 E. 2.

Walterus fil. Petri de Jay.

Thomas filius Waltero de Jay 10 E. 1 = Johanna a° 10 E. 2 et 17 E. 3 29 E. 1 et 1 E. 2 et 10 E. 2 et 14 E. 2. D'na de Jay in com. Salop.

Joh'es Jay fil. primogenitus a° 10 E. 2.

Thomas filius Johannæ D'næ de Jay Ar. = ... a° 17 E. 3 et 23 E. 3.

.... Jay filius Thomæ. = ...

Thomas Jay de Jay in com. Salop a° 7 et 8 H. 5. = ...

Joh'es Jay de Jay fil. et hær. 4 H. 6 et 6 H. 6. = ...

Rolandus Jay de Jay in com. Salop = Isabella vxor eius a° 25 et 29 H. 6. miles a° 29 H. 6.

Elizabetha filia et cohæres vxor Roberti Knight de Shrewesbury a° 23 H. 7.

Elianora filia et cohær. vxor Thomæ Jennyns de Welborn [Wallibone] in co. Salop 3 E. 4.

A

B

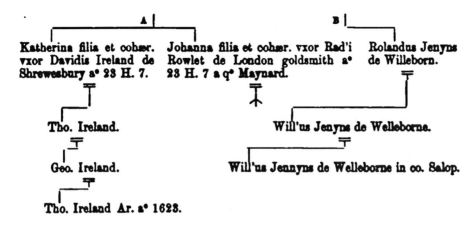

A | B |

Katherina filia et cohær.   Johanna filia et cohær. vxor Rad'i   Rolandus Jenyns
vxor Davidis Ireland de   Rowlet de London goldsmith aᵒ   de Willeborn.
Shrewesbury aᵒ 23 H. 7.   23 H. 7 a qᵒ Maynard.

Tho. Ireland.   Will'us Jenyns de Welleborne.

Geo. Ireland.   Will'us Jennyns de Welleborne in co. Salop.

Tho. Ireland Ar. aᵒ 1623.

Jenkes of Wolverton.

Harl. 1396, fo. 150ᵇ.   Harl. 1241, ff. 72ᵇ, 164.   S., ff. 157ᵇ, 158.

ARMS: Harl. 1396.—*Argent, three boars' heads couped close sable, a chief indented of the second.*

CREST.—*A dexter arm embowed habited sable, cuffed argent, enfiled with a ducal coronet or, the hand proper holding a sword proper.*

The Armes confirmed & the Creast giuen to George Jenkes of the Countie of Salop, Gent. by Robert Cooke, Clarenceux, 1 May Aᵒ 1582, 25 Q. Eliz.

ARMS: Harl. 1241, fo. 164.—*Quarterly: 1 and 4, Gules, a lion rampant-reguardant or* [ELYSTAN YLODRYTH]; *2 and 3, Argent, three boars' heads couped close sable.*

Elistan Glodred lord of Ferlexland [Ferlix] betwene Wy and Seuerne.=....

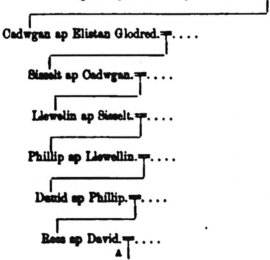

Cadwgan ap Elistan Glodred.=....

Sisselt ap Cadwgan.=....

Llewelin ap Sisselt.=....

Phillip ap Llewellin.=....

Dauid ap Phillip.=....

Ress ap David.=....

A |

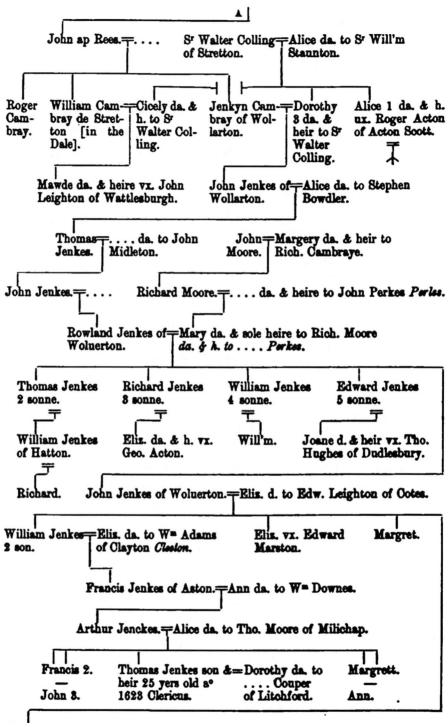

A

John ap Rees.=....   Sᵣ Walter Colling=Alice da. to Sᵣ Will'm
                       of Stretton.   Staunton.

Roger   William Cam-=Cicely da. &   Jenkyn Cam-=Dorothy   Alice 1 da. & h.
Cam-   bray de Stret- h. to Sᵣ   bray of Wol- 3 da. &   ux. Roger Acton
bray.   ton [in the   Walter Col- larton.   heir to Sᵣ of Acton Scott.
           Dale].   ling.   Walter
                                                      Colling.

           Mawde da. & heire vx. John   John Jenkes of=Alice da. to Stephen
           Leighton of Wattlesburgh.   Wollarton.   Bowdler.

           Thomas=.... da. to John   John=Margery da. & heir to
           Jenkes. Midleton.   Moore. Rich. Cambraye.

John Jenkes.=....   Richard Moore.=.... da. & heire to John Perkes *Perles*.

       Rowland Jenkes of=Mary da. & sole heire to Rich. Moore
       Woluerton.   *da. & h. to .... Perkes.*

Thomas Jenkes   Richard Jenkes   William Jenkes   Edward Jenkes
2 sonne.   3 sonne.   4 sonne.   5 sonne.
   =   =   =   =
William Jenkes   Eliz. da. & h. vx.   Will'm.   Joane d. & heir vx. Tho.
of Hatton.   Geo. Acton.   Hughes of Dudlesbury.
   =
Richard.   John Jenkes of Woluerton.=Eliz. d. to Edw. Leighton of Cotes.

William Jenkes=Eliz. da. to Wᵐ Adams   Eliz. vx. Edward   Margret.
2 son.   of Clayton *Cleeton*.   Marston.

       Francis Jenkes of Aston.=Ann da. to Wᵐ Downes.

       Arthur Jenckes.=Alice da. to Tho. Moore of Milichap.

Francis 2.   Thomas Jenkes son &=Dorothy da. to   Margrett.
—   heir 25 yers old aᵒ   .... Couper   —
John 3.   1623 Clericus.   of Litchford.   Ann.

Thomas Jenkes of Wolnerton.=Joyce da. & h. to Jo. Baldwyn of Vnder Heyton.
                           B

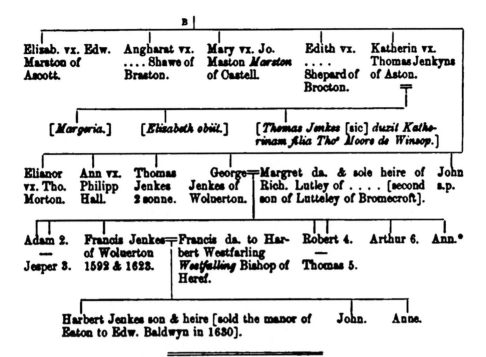

B |

Elizab. vx. Edw. Marston of Ascott. Angharat vx. .... Shawe of Braston. Mary vx. Jo. Maston *Marston* of Castell. Edith vx. .... Shepard of Brocton. Katherin vx. Thomas Jenkyns of Aston.

[*Margeria.*] [*Elizabeth obiit.*] [*Thomas Jenkes* [sic] *duxit Katherinam filia Tho° Moore de Winsop.*]

Elianor vx. Tho. Morton. Ann vx. Philipp Hall. Thomas Jenkes 2 sonne. George=Margret da. & sole heire of Jenkes of Wolverton. Rich. Lutley of .... [second son of Lutteley of Bromecroft]. John s.p.

Adam 2. — Jesper 3. Francis Jenkes of Wolverton 1592 & 1623. =Francis da. to Harbert Westfarling *Westfalling* Bishop of Heref. Robert 4. — Thomas 5. Arthur 6. Ann.*

Harbert Jenkes son & heire [sold the manor of Eaton to Edw. Baldwyn in 1630]. John. Anne.

Jenkes of Downton.

Harl. 1396, fo. 178b.

Rogerus Jenkes de Tally-pont.=....

Rogerus Jenkes de Downton in com. Salop.=Johanna fil. Rogeri Blakway de Egiams parish.

Rogerus Jenkes.=Ermyn fil. Will'i Spencer de Winton. Alicia nupta Olivero Lloyd.

Jennins of Wallibone.

Harl. 1396, fo. 175b. Harl. 1241, fo. 41b. Harl. 615, fo. 269. S., fo. 152.

ARMS: Harl. 1396.—*Quarterly: 1 and 4, Ermine, a lion rampant gules; 2 and 3, Azure, a lion rampant within a bordure engrailed or—gules* in Harl. 615—*a canton of the second*—JAY in Shrewsbury MS.

Sr *Rowland Jay of Jay* Kt.=....

Thomas Jennings.=Elianora fil. et her. Rolandi Jay de Jay in co. Salop mil. ....vxor *Robert Knight*.

A | B |

* Harl. 1241 gives a daughter as wife of Richard Jones, Serjeant at Arms.

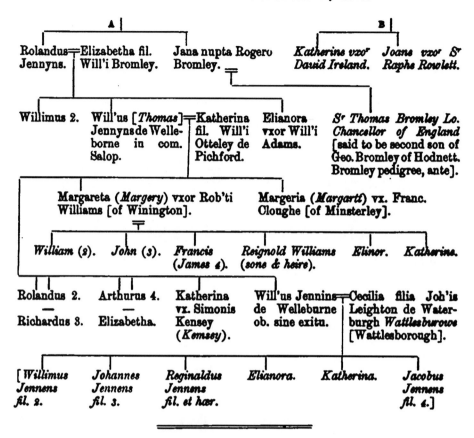

A   **B**

Rolandus=Elizabetha fil.   Jana nupta Rogero   *Katherine vxo^r*   *Joane vxo^r S^r*
Jennyns. | Will'i Bromley.   Bromley.   *Dauid Ireland.*   *Raphe Rowlett.*

Willimus 2.   Will'us [*Thomas*]=Katherina   Elianora   *Sr Thomas Bromley Lo.*
         Jennyns de Welle-| fil. Will'i   vxor Will'i   *Chancellor of England*
         borne in com. | Otteley de   Adams.   [said to be second son of
         Salop.   Pichford.   Geo. Bromley of Hodnett.
                                               Bromley pedigree, ante].

Margareta (*Margery*) vxor Rob'ti   Margeria (*Margartt*) vx. Franc.
Williams [of Winington].   Clonghe [of Minsterley].

William (*2*).   *John* (*3*).   *Francis*   *Reignold Williams*   *Elinor.*   *Katherine.*
                       (*James 4*).   (*sone & heire*).

Rolandus 2.   Arthurus 4.   Katherina   Will'us Jennins=Cecilia filia Joh'is
     —   —   vx. Simonis   de Welleburne | Leighton de Water-
Richardus 3.   Elizabetha.   Kensey   ob. sine exitu. | burgh *Wattlesburowe*
                        (*Kemsey*).   [Wattlesborough].

[*Willimus*   *Johannes*   *Reginaldus*   *Elianora.*   *Katherina.*   *Jacobus*
Jennens   *Jennens*   *Jennens*   *Jennens*
fil. 2.   *fil. 3.*   *fil. et har.*   *fil. 4.*]

𝕵𝖊𝖛𝖆𝖓𝖘 𝖔𝖋 𝕾𝖍𝖗𝖊𝖜𝖘𝖇𝖚𝖗𝖞.

Harl. 1396, fo. 174^b.

Eynion de Ewyn tudmon.=. . . .

Yollyn ap Eynion.=. . . .

Lluellyn goch t'pe H. 7.=Myuanwy filia . . . . M'redd.

Jem ap Ll'n de Ewyn todman.=. . . .

Hugo ap Jem de Frankweth.=Beatrix filia Will'i Braen de Salop.

Willimus Jenans de   Matheus   Isabella vxor Ric'i Harris de Salop.
Salop a° 1602.   Jenans.

                                                 Thomas Harris.

𝔍obber of 𝔞ston.

Harl. 1396, fo. 175.   Harl. 1241, fo. 151ᵇ.   S., fo. 159ᵃ.

ARMS: Harl. 1396.—*Vert, a fesse ermine.*

[These arms, quartering Littleton, are upon a monument in Shiffnal Church.]

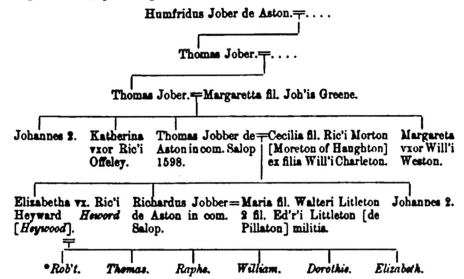

Humfridus Jober de Aston.═ . . . .

Thomas Jober.═ . . . .

Thomas Jober.═Margaretta fil. Joh'is Greene.

Johannes 2. Katherina vxor Ric'i Offeley. Thomas Jobber de Aston in com. Salop. 1598.═Cecilia fil. Ric'i Morton [Moreton of Haughton] ex filia Will'i Charleton. Margareta vxor Will'i Weston.

Elizabetha vx. Ric'i Heyward [*Heywood*]. *Heword*═ Richardus Jobber de Aston in com. Salop.═Maria fil. Walteri Litleton 2 fil. Ed'r'i Littleton [de Pillaton] militis. Johannes 2.

*Rob't. *Thomas. *Raphe. *William. *Dorothie. *Elizabeth.*

𝔍ones of 𝔅rocton, 𝔏ublow, 𝔚enlock, 𝔏eebotwood, etc.

Harl. 1396, fo. 173ᵇ.   Harl. 1241, fo. 127ᵇ.   S., fo. 156ᵇ.

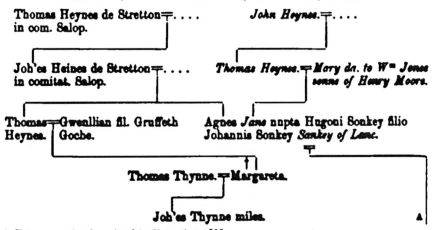

Thomas Heynes de Stretton═ . . . . in com. Salop.   *John Heynes.*═ . . . .

Joh'es Heines de Stretton═ . . . . in comitat. Salop.   *Thomas Heynes.*═*Mary da. to Wᵐ Jones sonne of Henry Moore.*

Thomas Heynes.═Gwenllian fil. Gruffeth Gocbe.   Agnes *Jane* nupta Hugoni Sonkey filio Johannis Sonkey *Sonkey of Lanc.*

Thomas Thynne.═Margareta.

Joh'es Thynne miles.   ▲

* This generation is omitted in Shrewsbury MS.
† In Shrewsbury MS. the line of descent from Thomas Heynes and Gwenllian is carried on to Thomas Thynne instead of only to Margareta.

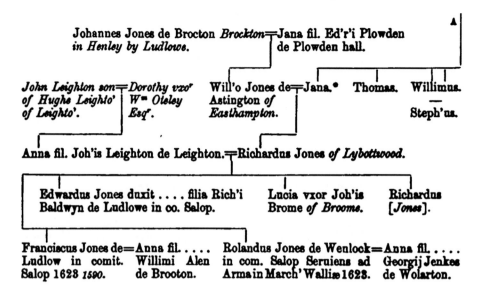

Johannes Jones de Brocton *Brockton*—Jana fil. Ed'r'i Plowden
in Henley by Ludlowe.   de Plowden hall.

John Leighton son—*Dorothy vxo*   Will'o Jones de—Jana.*   Thomas.   Willimus.
of Hughe Leighto' | *W*^m *Oteley* Astington *of*   ——
of Leighto'. | *Esq*^r. *Easthampton.*   Steph'us.

Anna fil. Joh'is Leighton de Leighton.—Richardus Jones *of Lybottwood.*

Edwardus Jones duxit .... filia Rich'i   Lucia vxor Joh'is   Richardus
Baldwyn de Ludlowe in co. Salop.   Brome *of Broome.*   [*Jones*].

Franciscus Jones de—Anna fil ....   Rolandus Jones de Wenlock—Anna fil ....
Ludlow in comit.   Willimi Alen   in com. Salop Seruiens ad   Georgij Jenkes
Salop 1628 *1590.* de Brooton.   Arma in March' Wallise 1628. de Wolarton.

Jones of Claberley.

S., fo. 157ª.

[ARMS.—*Azure, a lion stalant between three crosses pattée fitchée or, a chief or.*
CREST.—*A lion rampant or supporting an anchor azure.*

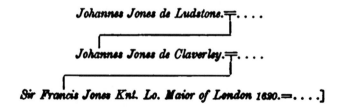

Per Wm *Camden Clarenc*^s *10 die Novemb.* 1610.

Johannes Jones de Ludstone.—....

Johannes Jones de Claverley.—....

Sir Francis Jones Knt. Lo. Maior of London 1620.=....]

* In Shrewsbury MS. Jones is given below, but the marriage with Jane Sonksy is omitted.

Jones of Chilton, Uckington, and Shrewsbury.

Harl. 1396, fo. 173.   S., ff. 155ᵇ, 156ᵃ.

ARMS: Harl. 1396.—*Argent, a lion rampant vert vulned in the mouth [breast] gules.*
CREST.—*The sun in splendour or, each ray terminating in a flame of fire proper.*

The Crest giuen to Will'm Jones sonne of Tho. Jones sonne of Will'm Jones
sonne of Richard Jones of Holt in com. Denbigh in North Wales esq' vnder the
hand oneley of Sʳ Wᵐ Segar Garter and the hand and Seale of Richard Sᵗ george
Norroy 16° Jan'y 1607 aᵒ 5 Jacobi R'.

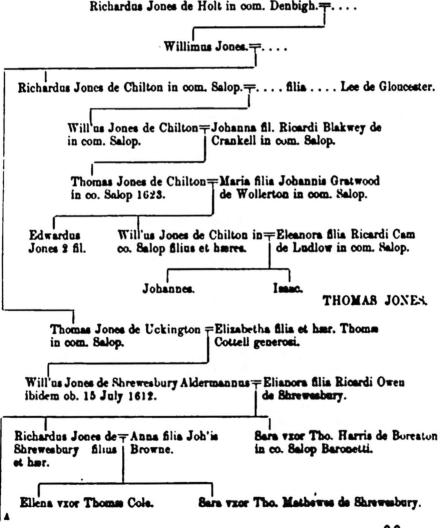

Richardus Jones de Holt in com. Denbigh.=....

Willimus Jones.=....

Richardus Jones de Chilton in com. Salop.=.... filia .... Lee de Gloucester.

Will'us Jones de Chilton=Johanna fil. Ricardi Blakwey de
in com. Salop.   Crankell in com. Salop.

Thomas Jones de Chilton=Maria filia Johannis Gratwood
in co. Salop 1623.   de Wollerton in com. Salop.

Edwardus   Will'us Jones de Chilton in=Eleanora filia Ricardi Cam
Jones 2 fil.   co. Salop filius et hæres.   de Ludlow in com. Salop.

Johannes.   Isaac.

THOMAS JONES.

Thomas Jones de Uckington=Elizabetha filia et hær. Thomæ
in com. Salop.   Cottell generosi.

Will'us Jones de Shrewesbury Aldermannus=Elianora filia Ricardi Owen
ibidem ob. 15 July 1612.   de Shrewesbury.

Richardus Jones de=Anna filia Joh'is   Sara vxor Tho. Harris de Boreaton
Shrewesbury filius | Browne.   in co. Salop Baronetti.
et hær.

Ellena vxor Thomæ Cole.   Sara vxor Tho. Mathewes de Shrewesbury.

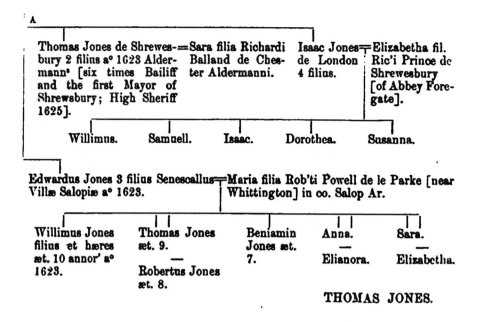

A

Thomas Jones de Shrewes-=Sara filia Richardi   Isaac Jones=Elizabetha fil.
bury 2 filius aᵒ 1623 Alder- Balland de Ches-   de London   Ric'i Prince de
mannˢ [six times Bailiff ter Aldermanni.   4 filius.   Shrewesbury
and the first Mayor of   [of Abbey Fore-
Shrewsbury; High Sheriff   gate].
1625].

Willimus.   Samuell.   Isaac.   Dorothea.   Susanna.

Edwardus Jones 3 filius Senescallus=Maria filia Rob'ti Powell de le Parke [near
Villæ Salopiæ aᵒ 1623.   Whittington] in co. Salop Ar.

Willimus Jones   Thomas Jones   Beniamin   Anna.   Sara.
filius et hæres   æt. 9.   Jones æt.   —   —
æt. 10 annor' aᵒ   —   7.   Elianora.   Elizabetha.
1623.   Robertus Jones
               æt. 8.

THOMAS JONES.

𝔍𝔬𝔯𝔡𝔢𝔫 𝔬𝔣 𝔚𝔢𝔩𝔶𝔫𝔱𝔬𝔫.

Harl. 1396, fo. 176.   S., fo. 160ᵃ.

ARMS: Harl. 1396.—*Argent, a chevron between three greyhounds courant gules.*

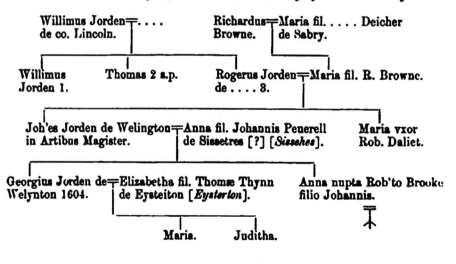

Willimus Jorden=....   Richardus=Maria fil. .... Deicher
de co. Lincoln.   Browne.   de Sabry.

Willimus   Thomas 2 s.p.   Rogerus Jorden=Maria fil. R. Browne.
Jorden 1.   de .... 3.

Joh'es Jorden de Welington=Anna fil. Johannis Penerell   Maria vxor
in Artibus Magister.   de Sissetres [?] [*Sissehes*].   Rob. Daliet.

Georgius Jorden de=Elizabetha fil. Thomæ Thynn   Anna nupta Rob'to Brooke
Welynton 1604.   de Eysteiton [*Eysterton*].   filio Johannis.

Maria.   Juditha.

CPSIA information can be obtained at www.ICGtesting.com
Printed in the USA
BVOW031138040113

309832BV00016B/542/P